A TREASURY OF PHILOSOPHY

A Treasury of Philosophy

Edited by

DAGOBERT D.
RUNES

Volume II

Grolier
INCORPORATED
NEW YORK

A TREASURY OF PHILOSOPHY

JONSON, BEN

JONSON, BEN (1573-1637). Starting as a bricklayer, Ben Jonson made his way to become a dramatic poet who held a dominant place in English literary life during the last years of Queen Elizabeth and the reign of James I. In his progress to this position, Jonson was a soldier who distinguished himself on the battlefield. He fought many duels, and attacked many of his fellow-writers with the weapon of sarcasm, though he respected the gentle Shakespeare. Because he killed an actor, Jonson narrowly escaped capital punishment. While in prison he became a convert to the Catholic Church, but twelve years thereafter, he returned to Protestantism.

Ben Jonson's best known works are his plays *Every Man in His Humour* (1598) and *Volpone* (1605). In his essays *Timber* or *Discoveries Made Upon Men and Matters,* he dealt mostly with the dignity and value of literature, while he also cast sidelights on the daily life of his time. Algernon Charles Swinburne praised these essays, and put them above those of Francis Bacon. Recent scholars have discovered that Jonson was much indebted to Latin authors, but they do not deny that he also relied on personal observation and expressed original views.

THE DIGNITY OF SPEECH

CUSTOM is the most certain mistress of language, as the public stamp makes the current money. But we must not be too frequent with the mint, every day coming. Nor fetch words from the extreme and utmost ages; since the chief virtue of a style is perspicuity, and nothing so vicious in it, as to need an interpreter. Words borrowed of antiquity do lend a kind of majesty to style, and are not without their delight sometimes. For they have the authority of years, and out of their intermission do win to themselves a kind of grace-like newness. But the eldest of the present, and newness of the past language, is the best. For what was the ancient language, which some men so dote upon, but the ancient custom? Yet when I name custom, I understand not the vulgar custom: For that were a precept no less dangerous to language, than life, if we should speak or live after the manners of the vulgar: But that I call custom of speech, which is the consent of the learned; as custom of life, which is the consent of the good. Virgil was most loving of antiquity; yet how rarely doth he insert *aquai* and *pictai!* Lucretius is scabrous and rough in these; he seeks them: As some do Chaucerisms with us, which were better expunged and banished. Some words are to be culled out for ornament and color, as we gather flowers to strew houses, or make garlands; but they are better when they grow to our style; as in a meadow, where through the mere grass and greenness delights; yet the variety of flowers doth heighten and beautify. Marry, we must not play, or riot too much with them, as in *Paranomasies*: Nor use too swelling or ill-sounding words; *Quae per salebras, altaque saxa cadunt.* It is true, there is no sound but shall find some lovers, as the bitterest confections are grateful to some palates. Our composition must be more accurate in the beginning and end than in the midst; and in the end more than in the beginning; for through the midst the stream bears us. And this is attained by custom more than care or diligence. We must express readily, and fully, not profusely. There is difference between a liberal and a prodigal hand. As it is a great point of art, when our matter requires it, to enlarge, and veer out all sail; so to take it in and contract it is of no less praise when the argument doth ask it. Either of them hath their fitness in the place. A good man always profits by his endeavour, by his help; yea, when he is absent; nay, when he is dead by his example and memory. that, where you can take away nothing without loss, and that loss to be manifest.

[196]

JOUBERT, JOSEPH

JOUBERT, JOSEPH (1754-1824). With regard to psychological refinement and literary skill, Joubert belongs to that line of French moralists whose outstanding representatives are Montaigne and La Rochefoucauld. However, Joubert differs from them in that he is more interested in psychological curiosities than in truth and morals and he prefers aesthetical enjoyment to knowledge of the facts. In his youth, Joubert was a lay-brother but he left the cloister because he was fond of worldly life and could not renounce his associations with women. He was always sincere when he professed his predilection for the Catholic Church and his hatred of the philosophy, and even more so of the philosophers, of the Enlightenment. He did not conceal that his judgment relied on taste, not on faith. He disliked Diderot and D'Alembert because he considered them "vulgar," and for the same reason, he was horrified by the French Revolution. Under Napoleon, he was appointed inspector-general of the University. But the Emperor's favor entailed the disgrace of the restored Bourbons, and Joubert had always sympathized with royalism.

To Joubert, Plato did not Platonize enough. In fact, Joubert was more akin to Epicureanism, though he felt uneasy while enjoying life. Enjoyment of perfumes, flowers, refined cuisine, precious silk was a vital point to him. But enjoyment could not overcome his feelings of tediousness. Joubert was of very delicate health, but he enjoyed suffering because he believed that sickness made his soul more subtle. As a psychologist of morbidity, Joubert anticipated many psychological discoveries of recent times.

PLATO

PLATO shows us nothing; but he brings us brightness with him; he puts light into our eyes, and fills us with a clearness by which all objects afterward become illuminated. He teaches us nothing; but he prepares us, fashions us, and makes us ready to know all. Somehow or other, the habit of reading him augments in us the capacity for discerning and entertaining whatever fine truths may afterward present themselves. Like mountain air, it sharpens our organs, and gives us an appetite for wholesome food. . . . Plato loses himself in the void; but one sees the play of his wings, one hears their rustle. . . . It is good to breathe the air of Plato; but not to live upon him.

WHICH is best, if one wants to be useful and to be really understood, to get one's words in the world, or to get them in the schools? I maintain that the good plan is to employ words in their popular sense rather than in their philosophical sense; and the better plan still to employ them in their natural sense rather than in their popular sense. By their natural sense, I mean the popular and universal acceptation of them brought to that which in this is essential and invariable. To prove a thing by definition proves nothing if the definition is purely philosophical; for such definition only binds him who makes it. But to prove a thing by definition when the definition expresses the necessary, inevitable, and clear idea which the world at large attaches to the object, is, on the contrary, all in all; because then what one does is simply to show people what they do really think, in spite of themselves and without knowing it. The rule that one is free to give to words what sense one will, and that the only thing needful is to be agreed upon the sense one gives them, is very well for the mere purposes of argumentation; but in the true-born and noble science of metaphysics, and in the genuine world of literature, it is good for nothing.

[197]

JUNG, CARL GUSTAV

JUNG, CARL GUSTAV (1875-   ). From 1906 to 1913, Jung was one of the most enthusiastic adherents and disciples of Sigmund Freud. He was the editor of the *Annual for Psychoanalytic Research*, and, at Freud's suggestion, was appointed the first president of the International Psychoanalytical Association. His separation from Freud hurt the latter a great deal, and Freud subsequently criticized Jung's own theories with animosity, which was paid back in kind by Jung.

Jung started as a clinical psychiatrist but, at the same time he showed great sympathy for spiritism, and has retained in his late years a special interest in occult forces and mystical experiences. In addition to his temporary devotion to Freud's psycho-analysis, Jung has also been a student of the philosopher Heinrich Rickert, whose distinction between the methods of natural and social sciences he adopted.

Jung called his own doctrine "analytical psychology," at first and then "complex psychology." To him psychical is the true reality, and all conflicts between mind and nature are of no fundamental importance but are derived from the difference of origin of psychic contents. He conceives the psychic as of both individual and general character. The conscious personality is the focus of psychic processes. Without such a focus, no organized ego, no continuity of experience is possible. But the contents of psychic experience, Jung insists, reach beyond the range of individual consciousness. The individual is in a state of fusion with his environment, with the social group to which he belongs, with his nation and race. This fusion is taking place in the realm of the unconscious which completes and compensates the conscious in man. Any psychical structure of the human individual is shaped by the tension between the conscious and the unconscious, and the extension of the unconscious to the psychic life of the group, nation and race is of fundamental importance for the psychology of the individual. Its attitude toward the objects is determined by the tendency to either introversion or extraversion, one which is predominant and forms the humane type. This classification of men has aroused general interest and is the most frequently mentioned part of Jung's doctrine. However, according to Jung, the aim of mature man must be totality of the psychic, harmony between the cultivation of the self and the devotion to the outer world. He regards progress of culture as conditioned by the enlargement of the realm of consciousness. Both the progress of culture and the development of the individual are placed and kept in motion by what Jung calls energy, but which he tries to differentiate from physical energy.

Despite secession and mutual polemics, Jung has retained many of Freud's conceptions. However, Jung has substituted a general principle of energy for Freud's sexual drive as the moving cause of human life and destiny, and his interpretation of dreams and their symbols is different from the methods used by the founder of psychoanalysis. While Freud, notwithstanding his interest in instinctual drives, is essentially a rationalist, Jung, although proclaiming the increase of consciousness as the cultural goal, is, by nature, a romanticist.

THE HUMAN PSYCHE

IT is, to my mind, a fatal mistake to consider the human

psyche as a merely personal affair and to explain it exclusively from a personal point of view. Such a mode of explanation is only applicable to the individual in his ordinary everyday occupations and relationships, If, however, some slight trouble occurs, perhaps in the form of an unforeseen and somewhat extraordinary event, instantly instinctive forces are called up, forces which appear to be wholly unexpected, new, and even strange. They can no longer be explained by personal motives, being comparable rather to certain primitive occurrences like panics at solar eclipses and such things. To explain the murderous outburst of Bolshevistic ideas by a personal father complex appears to me as singularly inadequate.

The change of character that is brought about by the uprush of collective forces is amazing. A gentle and reasonable being can be transformed into a maniac or a savage beast. One is always inclined to lay the blame on external circumstances, but nothing could explode in us if it had not been there. As a matter of fact, we are always living upon a volcano and there is, as far as we know, no human means of protection against a possible outburst which will destroy everybody within its reach. It is certainly a good thing to preach reason and common sense, but what if your audience is a lunatic asylum or a crowd in a collective seizure? There is not much difference either, because the madman as well as the mob is moved by nonpersonal, overwhelming forces.

As a matter of fact, it needs as little as a neurosis to conjure up a force that cannot be dealt with by reasonable means. Our cancer case shows clearly how impotent human reason and intellect are against the most palpable nonsense. I always advise my patients to take such obvious but invincible nonsense as the manifestation of a power and a meaning not yet understood. Experience has taught me that it is a much more effective method of procedure to take such a fact seriously and to seek for a suitable explanation. But an explanation is suitable only when it produces a hypothesis equal to the morbid effect. Our case is confronted with a will power and a suggestion more than equal to anything his consciousness can put against it. In this precarious situation it would be bad strategy to convince the patient that he is somehow, though in a highly incomprehensible way, at the back of his own symptom, secretly inventing and supporting it. Such a suggestion would instantly paralyze his fighting spirit, and he would get demoralized. It is much better if he understands that his complex is an autonomous power directed against his conscious personality. Moreover, such an explanation fits the actual facts much better than a reduction to personal motives. An apparent personal motivation does exist, but it is not made by intention, it just happens to the patient.

[198]

JUSTIN MARTYR

JUSTIN MARTYR (About 110-165). The earliest defense of Christianity against paganism using philosophical arguments was written by Justin, who later suffered a martyr's death in Rome. Justin's *Apologies* is also of interest because it describes Christian worship as it was performed in early times, refutes accusations against members of the Christian community and tries to convince pagan philosophers by using their own terms. Justin, who was born in the Samaritan town of Flavia Neapolis, the old Shechem which had been destroyed by Vespasian in 67 A.D. and which is called Nablus today, probably was not of Samaritan but of pagan descent. Evidently he had studied pagan philosophy before his conversion, and acquired, if not profound knowledge, a fluency of style and ability in using philosophical terms. Justin also had a controversy with a Jewish scholar on which he reported in his *Dialogue with Tryphon*. Tryphon probably was a real person, known as Tarfon the Tanna, who was opposed to Christianity but who died before Justin was grown up.

THE EUCHARIST

AFTER the believer is baptized, and so incorporated or made one with us, we lead him to the congregation of the brethren, as we call them, and then with great fervency pour out our souls in common prayers both for ourselves, for the person baptized, and for all others all the world over; that having embraced the truth, our conversation might be as becometh the gospel, and that we may be found doers of the world, and so at length be favored with an everlasting salvation. Prayers being over we salute each other with a kiss; After this, bread and a cup of wine and water are brought to the president or bishop, which he takes, and offers up praise and glory to the Father of all things, through the name of His Son and the Holy Spirit; and this thanksgiving to God for vouchsafing us worthy of these His creatures, is a prayer of more than ordinary length. When the bishop has finished the prayers, and the thanksgiving service, all the people present conclude with an audible voice, saying, Amen; now Amen in the Hebrew tongue, is, so be it. The eucharistical office being thus performed by the bishop, and concluded with the acclamation of all the people, those we call deacons distribute to everyone present to partake of this eucharistical bread and wine, and water, and then they carry it to the absent.

This food we call the eucharist, of which none are allowed to be partakers, but such only as are true believers, and have been baptized in the Laver of Regeneration for the remission of sins, and live according to Christ's precepts; for we do not take this as common bread, and common wine. But as Jesus Christ our Saviour was made flesh by the *logos* of God, and had real flesh and blood for our salvation, so are we taught that this food, which the very same *logos* blessed by prayer and thanksgiving, is turned into the nourishment and substance of our flesh and blood; and is in some sense the flesh and blood of the incarnate Jesus. For the Apostles, in their commentaries called the Gospels, have left this command upon record, "That Jesus took bread, and when He had given thanks, He said, Do this in commemoration of Me, for this is My body; And in like manner He took the cup, and when He had given thanks, He said, This is My blood," and delivered it to them only. And this very solemnity too the evil spirits have introduced in the mysteries of *Mithra;* for you do, or may know, that when any one is initiated into this religion, bread and a cup of water, with a certain form of words are made use of in the sacrifice. After this sacrament is over, we remind each other of the obligations to his duty, and the rich relieve the poor; and upon such charitable accounts we visit some or other every day.

[199]

K

KALLEN, HORACE MAYER

KALLEN, HORACE MAYER (1882-   ). A unique position in American philosophy is occupied by Kallen who resolved not to devote himself to philosophy exclusively, although he feels it as his very vocation, although he enjoys teaching it and has been a highly successful teacher, as he is a successful author of a large number of important books. Of all philosophical branches, it is aesthetics that attracts Kallen's highest and most enduring interest. But he has overcome this inclination because he held that active participation in political and economic movements is of greater importance and more urgent. Kallen has taken a leading part in the defense of civil rights, of freedom of thought and conscience, in advocating the demands of American labor, in the foundation of consumers' cooperatives, and in Jewish affairs, not least in Zionism. In doing so, he sometimes refrained from philosophizing although he did not abandon philosophy. For he always maintained that ideas are events in man's life; whatever else they may be, they certainly form human attitudes, determine the decisions of the individual and give experience its meaning. It is the belief in the power of ideas that supports Kallen's pluralistic views on life and culture. Philosophy should not rely on an exclusive system, but it must confront diverse passions, thoughts, experiences and find their point of junction. This pluralistic view is the basis for Kallen's conception of freedom, the "right to be different," and it has enabled him to clarify the extent and variety of experiencing freedom. In *The Liberal Spirit*, (1948) Kallen not only discussed the content and value of the idea of freedom but also the possibilities of its realization in a human community. In *The Education of Free Men* (1950) he developed his philosophy of education, refuting totalitarian despotism of any origin.

Pluralism has prevented Kallen from any over-simplification of philosophical and vital problems. According to Kallen, to deny difficulties and complications is to multiply them, just as to deny reality to evil is to aggravate evil. He holds that the world has not been created for the use and pleasure of mankind, but that Man is capable and, therefore, obliged to improve the world he lives in. Conscious of the fact that vital problems are and remain tough and complicated, and that ideals demand hard work and courageous fighting, Kallen need not be afraid that his seriousness may be questioned when he undertakes to harmonize modern science and religion, particularly Judaism, his own faith.

THE CHOICE OF FREEDOM

WHAT may be said of the impulsions of this freedom, which takes determinism for its instrument? What does it lead to? Where and how may it go?

Our time resounds with the warnings of Cassandras who prophesy that to these questions science can give no answer. All men, they chant, all values, are indifferent to science, for whose detached and impersonal view abundance signifies no more than scarcity, freedom than bondage, the tyrant than the slave. All are events in an indifferent sequence of cause and effect, and in the scientist's task of searching out measurable specific causes for measurable specific effects, a man is worth only as much as a thing. When psychologists, educators, college administrators equally with personnel managers and employment agents endeavor to define the qualities of men by means of machines that test and measure, do they not use the scientific understanding of nature in order to dissolve personal character into mechanical clockworks? Do they not dissolve the human being into the non-human event? Science can free men or enslave them, enrich men or impoverish them, but *which* is not itself a decision within the power of science to make.

The decision is not within the power of science because science, we are told, being the embodiment of modern man's insight into nature, takes determinism for its ground and postulates only uniformity, regularity, repetition in all things. The decision is not within the power of science because technics, being modern man's system of the applications of his embodied insight, postulates mechanism as the ground of works, so that engineers and architects are but machinists *in excelsis.* And our modern psychologists and social scientists, are they, it is asked, anything different? Do they not start from these same postulates in their study of man? Do they not seek for their disciplines the same certainty of belief, the same precision of prediction and control which are the envied excellences of the sciences of nature? To merit the praise which the word *science* and its derivatives carry, the study of man must meet the determinist criteria of the study of the stars and the stuffs and articulations of earth. Until psychology and sociology and economics and politics become as physics and chemistry and biology and mechanics and astronomy, they will not merit the eulogium *science.*

But if they become like unto these, must they not also postulate that what the Declaration of Independence has written down about freedom as a self-evident truth is a self-evident error? Then what becomes of the problems of freedom which so vex our time? Are they not in truth abolished? If determinism is true, must not freedom be false, or else, with all the values men set their hearts upon, outside the realm of science altogether? And if they are outside, what good are the methods and results of science in solving the modern man's problem of freedom? Yet scientific determinist as he is, modern man's care for freedom is far more urgent than that of his unmodern forebears. He does believe with a fighting faith, that freedom *is* an inalienable right of every man, and he bled and died to vindicate this right throughout modern times. Only, uniquely, in modern times, have free men fought not alone for their own liberties but also to set slaves free as in the American Civil War. Daily modern man experiences freedom, seeks freedom, and uses freedom. So far as living his life goes, scientific determinism has been among his best means to freedom. Can science then make no deliverances about freedom's nature and intent?

So formulated, the question reinstates the dilemma of determinism with which William James challenged philosophers half a hundred years ago, and which he himself learned from the revolutionary French libertarian Charles Renouvier, a generation before. In a world all of whose events are automatic and predetermined—the argument runs —the urge and idea of freedom and its conflict with the idea of determinism must also be automatic and predetermined. The foreordained choice between them cannot fail to lead to momentous consequences for the chooser. Whichever he decides upon, he could not have decided otherwise. Yet the choice of one means necessity, repetition, everlastingly recurring cycles of old thoughts and old things moving in old directions upon old ways. It means there can be no contingencies and no disjunctions nor any true alternatives. It means that control must be error and the very choice which affirms it, illusion. It means that freedom is but the synonym for ignorance. Since events must be the necessary repetition of identicals, a passage from ignorance to knowledge is ruled out. Yet in fact such passages do occur, and in both directions. In fact, illusion is changed over into reality and error is confronted and overruled by truth, and vice versa. Such events strict determinism can neither explain nor explain away. It can only establish the believer as a resigned and submissive do-nothing or as a bullying fanatic. His world is inalterably either the best possible or the worst possible, and no thing in it can be otherwise than it is. Or, its compulsions—which he calls his Fate or Destiny and which he can neither confront nor escape—drive him against all men, and he cannot do otherwise than he does. World and man both, if they move at all, move inalterably to an inalterable end.

The choice of freedom, on the other hand, does not abolish determinism. The choice of freedom only limits and checks determinism. It simply adds to repetition and recurrence spontaneity and originality. It accepts our experiences of chance and contingency as experiences of the real. It takes at its face value the experience of new events confluent with old but not compelled by them; new events initiating new turns upon new ways in new directions toward new alternatives of thoughts or things. The choice of freedom grounds the fact that knowledge does replace ignorance, truth, error, and power helplessness. Choosing freedom, a man can stand up. A man can believe at his own risk and fight for his faith in his own power. Determinism, to this believer, is changed by his belief from a totalitarian metaphysics of existence into a method of understanding and managing an untotalizable existence. It becomes a consequence and vindication of freedom. In the daily life we experience existence now as free, now as determined, and again as both and neither. Carried down from the abstractions of the philosopher to the enterprises of the workaday world, in the daily life the sciences become transvalued from an effort to uncover an inert and immutable order into a succession of determinations, with which by trying out theories, experiments, and verifications and again and again revising them we slowly and assiduously shape new truths and transform old ones into new error. When freedom is the choice, science is realized as an open, imaginative, self-correcting adventure in perception, understanding and management —a free enterprise which works its way through a boundless world on hypotheses that aim at unguaranteed consequences, not at foregone conclusions.

[200]

KANT, IMMANUEL

KANT, IMMANUEL (1724-1804). The ancestors of Immanuel Kant on his father's side were Scotch. Had he kept the original spelling of Cant, the citizens of Königsberg would have pronounced his name "Zand." His entire well-ordered life, with the exception of a negligible period, was spent in that East Prussian city whose burghers used to set their watches when he passed under their windows on his daily walks. After mature reflection, Kant decided to stay single. From theological student he rose to Privatdozent and full professor of philosophy, and with his epoch-making answer to the problems posed by David Hume, he became not only Germany's greatest philosopher, but one of the greatest philosophers of all times.

In his famous *Critique of Pure Reason* he showed that knowledge *a priori* is possible, which means that by virtue of the forms and categories of the mind, like space, time and causality, man possesses the presuppositions for coherent and intelligible experience. To be sure, we know only appearances, colors, sounds and the like, never the thing-in-itself. Kant maintained that true knowledge cannot transcend or go beyond experience. Still, for the sake of religion and morality, we need such concepts as God, soul, freedom and immortality. To satisfy these demands of human nature, Kant wrote the *Critique of Practical Reason*, in which he acknowledged the necessity and validity of these values.

In the categorical imperative Kant laid a solid foundation for morality by enjoining man to act in such a way that the maxim of his will may at the same time be raised into a principle of universal law. Religionists called him the all-devourer, but they failed to recognize his deep piety expressed in these lines: "Two things fill the soul with ever new and increasing wonder and reverence the oftener and the more fervently reflection ponders on it: The starry heavens above and the moral law within." Scientists know him as the co-author of the Kant-Laplace theory of the heavens. And lovers of freedom are inspired by his treatise on eternal peace. All modern philosophy must orient itself to Kant.

JUDGMENTS

THIS may well be called the age of criticism, a criticism from which nothing need hope to escape. When religion seeks to shelter itself behind its sanctity, and law behind its majesty, they justly awaken suspicion against themselves, and lose all claim to the sincere respect which reason yields only to that which has been able to bear the test of its free and open scrutiny.

Metaphysics has been the battlefield of endless conflicts. Dogmatism at first held despotic sway; but . . . from time to time scepticism destroyed all settled order of society; . . . and now a widespread indifferentism prevails. Never has metaphysics been so fortunate as to strike into the sure path of science, but has kept groping about, and groping, too, among mere ideas. What can be the reason of this failure? Is a science of metaphysics impossible? Then, why should nature disquiet us with a restless longing after it, as if it were one of our most important concerns? Nay more, how can we put any faith in human reason, if in one of the very things that we most desire to know, it not merely forsakes us, but lures us on by false hopes only to cheat us in the end? Or are there any indications that the true path has hitherto been missed, and that by starting afresh we may yet succeed where others have failed?

It seems to me that the intellectual revolution, by which at a bound mathematics and physics became what they now are, is so remarkable, that we are called upon to ask what was the essential feature of the change that proved so advantageous to them, and to try at least to apply to metaphysics as far as possible a method that has been successful in other sciences of reason. In mathematics I believe that, after a long period of groping, the true path was disclosed in the happy inspiration of a single man. If that man was Thales, things must suddenly have appeared to him in a new light, the moment he saw how the properties of the isosceles triangle could be demonstrated. The true method, as he found, was not to inspect the visible figure of the triangle, or to analyze the bare conception of it, and from this, as it were, to read off its properties, but to bring out what was necessarily implied in the conception that he had himself formed *a priori*, and put into the figure, in the construction by which he presented it to himself.

Physics took much longer time than mathematics to enter on the highway of science, but here, too, a sudden revolution in the way of looking at things took place. When Galileo caused balls which he had carefully weighed to roll down an inclined plane, or Torricelli made the air bear up a weight which he knew beforehand to be equal to a standard column of water, a new light broke on the mind of the scientific discoverer. It was seen that reason has insight only into that which it produces after a plan of its own, and that it must itself lead the way with principles of judgment based upon fixed laws, and force nature to answer its questions. Even experimental physics, therefore, owes the beneficial revolution in its point of view entirely to the idea, that, while reason can know nothing purely of itself, yet that which it has itself put into nature must be its guide to the discovery of all that it can learn from nature.

In metaphysical speculations it has always been assumed that all our knowledge must conform to objects; but every attempt from this point of view to extend our knowledge of objects *a priori* by means of conceptions has ended in failure. The time has now come to ask, whether better progress may not be made by supposing that objects must conform to our knowledge. Plainly this would better agree with the avowed aim of metaphysics, to determine the nature of objects *a priori*, or before they are actually presented. Our suggestion is similar to that of Copernicus in astronomy, who, finding it impossible to explain the movements of the heavenly bodies on the supposition that they turned round the spectator, tried whether he might succeed better by supposing the spectator to revolve and the stars to remain at rest. Let us make a similar experiment in metaphysics with *perception.* If it were really necessary for our perception to conform to the nature of objects, I do not see how we could know anything of it *a priori;* but if the sensible object must conform to the constitution of our faculty of perception, I see no difficulty in the matter. Perception, however, can become knowledge only if it is related in some way to the object which it determines. Now here again I may suppose, either that the *conceptions* through which I effect that determination conform to the objects, or that the objects, in other words the experience in which alone the objects are known, conform to conceptions. In the former case, I fall into the same perplexity as before, and fail to explain how such conceptions can be known *a priori.* In the latter case, the outlook is more hopeful. For, experience is itself a mode of knowledge which implies intelligence, and intelligence has a rule of its own, which must be an *a priori* condition of all knowledge of objects presented to it. To this rule, as expressed in *a priori* conceptions, all objects of experience must necessarily conform, and with it they must agree.

Our experiment succeeds as well as we could wish, and gives promise that metaphysics may enter upon the sure course of a science, at least in its first part, where it is occupied with those *a priori* conceptions to which the corresponding objects can be given. The new point of view enables us to explain how there can be *a priori* knowledge, and what is more, to furnish satisfactory proofs of the laws that lie at the basis of nature as a totality of objects of experience. But the consequences that flow from this deduction of our faculty of *a priori* knowledge, which constitutes the first part of our inquiry, are unexpected, and at first sight seem to be fatal to the aims of metaphysics, with which we have to deal in the second part of it. For we are brought to the conclusion that we never can transcend the limits of possible experience, and therefore never can realize the object with which metaphysics is primarily concerned. In truth, however, no better indirect proof could be given that we were correct in holding, as the result of our first estimate of the *a priori* knowledge of reason, that such knowledge relates not at all to the thing as it exists in itself, but only to phenomena. For that which necessarily forces us to go beyond the limits of experience and of all phenomena is the *unconditioned*, which reason demands of things in themselves, and by right and necessity seeks in the complete series of conditions for everything conditioned. If, then, we find that we cannot think the unconditioned without contradiction, on the supposition of our experience conforming to objects as things in themselves; while, on the contrary, the contradiction disappears, on the supposition that our knowledge does not conform to things in themselves, but that objects as they are given to us as phenomena conform to our knowledge; we are entitled to conclude that what we at first assumed as an hypothesis is now established as a truth.

[200]

KIERKEGAARD, SÖREN

KIERKEGAARD, SÖREN AABY (1813-1855). A little boy of twelve, cold and hungry, tending the sheep on a lonely pasture, suddenly went in despair to the next hillock and there cursed God. This was not our philosopher, it was his father; but this deed hung heavily over the Kierkegaard family, denying the young Sören a happy youth and making him the prophet of anxiety. Only the comfortable income inherited from his father, who after that experience on the heath, had gone into the wool business and thrived, his native humor mixed with asceticism and an interest in the sorrows of his fellow men, preserved him from insanity. In excessive measure he shared the melancholy so typical of many a Dane; but, artist and poet that he was at heart and in language, he concealed much of it in his virile and colorful style which he devoted to showing that life ever leads to crossroads and demands decisions that need be made abruptly, by fits or jumps in attitude to tide us between the rational and the irrational. The title of one of his most important works *Either—Or* ironically became his nickname among the "common men" to whom he fled in his daily wanderings through Copenhagen. In a sense, he was the Danish counterpart of Schopenhauer with whom he shared his view of women.

Only recently influential, Kierkegaard, having admired Hegel and Schelling and discarded them, had the avowed intention of creating difficulties instead of solving them. The relation between the knowing mind and eternal truth he considered the great paradox. Truth is attainable only subjectively and subjectivity is truth.

Of Christianity he thought so much that he dissuaded people from joining the church. Having used up his inheritance, spent himself at last in argumentation and written all he wanted to write, he was picked up in the streets and died in a hospital, not yet 43 years of age.

NATURAL SCIENCES

IF the natural sciences had been developed in Socrates' day as they are now, all the sophists would have been scientists. One would have hung a microscope outside his shop in order to attract customers, and then would have had a sign painted saying: 'Learn and see through a giant microscope how a man thinks' (and on reading the advertisement Socrates would have said: 'that is how men who do not think behave'). An excellent subject for an Aristophanes, particularly if he let Socrates look through a microscope.

There is no use at all in going in for natural science. One stands there defenseless and without any control. The scientist begins at once to distract one with all his details, at one moment one is in Australia, at another in the moon, in the bowels of the earth, and the devil knows where—chasing a tape worm; at one moment one has to use a telescope and at the next a microscope, and who the devil can stand that kind of thing.

But joking apart; the confusion lies in the fact that it is never dialectically clear what is what, how philosophy is to make use of natural science. Is the whole thing a brilliant metaphor (so that one might just as well be ignorant of it)? is it an example and analogy? or is it of such importance that theory should be formed accordingly?

There is no more terrible torture for a thinker than to have to continue living under the strain of having details constantly uncovered, so that it always looks as though the thought is about to appear, the conclusion. If the natural scientist does not feel that torture he cannot be a thinker. Intellectually that is the most terrible tantalization! A thinker is, as it were, in hell until he has found spiritual certainty: *hic Rhodus, hic salta,* the sphere of faith where, even if the world broke to pieces and the elements melted, thou shalt nevertheless believe. There one cannot wait for the latest news, or till one's ship comes home. That spiritual certainty, the most humbling of all, the most painful to a vain spirit (for it is so superior to look through a microscope), is the only certainty.

The main objection, the whole objection to natural science may simply and formally be expressed thus, absolutely: it is incredible that a man who has thought infinitely about himself as a spirit could think of choosing natural science (with empirical material) as his life's work and aim. An observant scientist must *either* be a man of talent and instinct, for the characteristic of talent and instinct is not to be fundamentally dialectical, but only to dig up things and be brilliant—not to understand himself (and to be able to live on happily in that way, without feeling that anything is wrong because the deceptive variety of observations and discoveries continuously conceals the confusion of everything); *or* he must be a man who, from his earliest youth, half consciously, has become a scientist and continues out of habit to live in that way—the most frightful way of living: to fascinate and astonish the world by one's discoveries and brilliance, and not to understand oneself. It is self-evident that such a scientist is conscious, he is conscious within the limits of his talents, perhaps an astonishingly penetrating mind, the gift of combining things and an almost magical power of associating ideas, etc. But at the very most the relationship will be this: an eminent mind, unique in its gifts, explains the whole of nature—but does not understand itself. Spiritually he does not become transparent to himself in the moral appropriation of his gifts. But that relationship is scepticism, as may easily be seen (for scepticism means that an unknown, an X, explains everything. When everything is explained by an X which is not explained, then in the end nothing is explained at all). If that is not scepticism then it is superstition.

[202]

KLAGES, LUDWIG

KLAGES, LUDWIG (1872-   ). Between the two world wars, Klages was one of the most influential harbingers of German anti-intellectualism, and his latest utterances seem to indicate that, even after Germany's catastrophe, he is not prepared to recant. He has remained a rabid sympathizer with Nazism, although he preferred to live in democratic Switzerland and to admire the house Hitler built without moving in. But even after the end of World War II, Klages continued to express hostility toward democracy, Western civilization, reason and logic, while enjoying the indulgence of a democratic government.

649

In his youth, Klages was associated with the German poet Stefan George who, inspired by Baudelaire and Mallarmé, adhered to the theory of art for art's sake but declared that the cult of artistic form realized the highest ideals of human beings. Devoted to Roman Catholic traditionalism George and his circle detested the principal tendencies of 19th century civilization, especially positivism, naturalism, materialism and rationalism. From this position, Klages, after a period of graphological and character-ological studies, proceeded to extreme anti-intellectualism, denouncing thinking consciousness as a destroying force. In his principal work *Spirit, the Adversary of Soul*, Klages holds that body and soul form the natural unity of human existence in which spirit has invaded from outside in order to split this unity and in this way to kill the foundation of life. While the soul, directed by instincts, feelings and traditions, forms a sensually colorful world, spirit analyzes this world into abstract atoms, in order to subject nature to human will. This is condemned by Klages as sacrilege. While combating natural science as the main representative of the destructive spirit, Klages denies the value and right of any conscious and voluntary knowledge. Return to unconscious life is regarded by him as the way to salvation.

THE HYSTERICAL PERSON

THE typical hysterical person is incapable of not following his longing to represent; but that does not mean at all that he cannot control himself. If, for example, it is necessary to represent self-control, then he can endure with remarkable equanimity insults, mockery, degradations, and bodily torments of the severest kind. One thing only he can never repress—his desire to represent. For he has not a single substantial interest of real importance to oppose to this desire, and the rich store of energy at his disposal pours undivided and not to be dammed into this one craving. If one wanted to call him a mere actor, it would be necessary to add that he suffers from a passion to simulate passions, and that no genuine passion could be more irresistible, overpowering, and consistent (that is, like an impulse) than this. And if one wanted to call him thoroughly sophisticated, then it would have to be considered again that a permanent spice of intentionality does in fact flavor his every attitude, but in a different manner, and in one much harder to recognize than in a man who has ceased to be naive merely because he has inhibitions; for here the mask itself has become sovereign. He is not an actor so much as a man wearing a mask which has grown into his flesh; or rather, he carries behind the mask no living being but a clockwork, ready to follow the suggestions of the mask. In *Klein Zaches oder Zinnober*, Amadeus Hoffmann has prophetically dealt with the reflective nature which assimilates everything, and, by excelling makes it valueless; and, in the *Sandmann*, has given a fantastic treatment to the life-mimicking automaton.

The definite characteristic of the hysterical attitude is, that there is a relationship to the spectator. Those who must represent something, represent it for the benefit of a spectator; by choice a real stranger, if not an imaginary one, or as a last resource the spectator within himself. Accordingly no hysterical person is ever attentive to the matter in hand, and whatever he does or leaves undone is not done or left undone with a view to the effect, but is itself the effect by anticipation which itself suggests the idea of the goal from moment to moment; hence a change of surroundings may be accompanied by a change in behaviour of a kind which shows some points of similarity with that of a medium.

Here the type of hysterical exaltation is sharply distinguished from the vain man and from those who require to please or to win approval. The latter wish to appear superior in some respect, or to evoke affection or gain esteem; but the hysterical type wishes to excite attention either by creating amazement or admiration, or by challenging those other feelings, which are even more suitable for the purpose, of aversion, loathing, disgust, horror, indignation, contempt, and fury. It happens quite commonly that faults are invented, that a hysterical woman claims to have been raped, and a man to have raped, and even fictitious confessions of alleged murder have been known. The typically hysterical crime of Herostratus may here be recalled.

[203]

KOMENSKY, AMOS. See COMENIUS, JOHANN AMOS.

KREBS, NICHOLAS. See CUSA, NICHOLAS OF.

KROPOTKIN, PRINCE PETER

KROPOTKIN, PRINCE PETER (1842-1921). Administrative experience and Utopian vision became confused in the mind of Prince Kropotkin, the founder of communist, or, more precisely, communalist anarchism. For free communities are the political form which he thought social revolution should assume.

At the age of 19, Kropotkin, who had attended the Imperial Military School for Pages, became an officer of the Cossacks, and went with his regiment to Transbaikalia and Manchuria. In this capacity, he undertook numerous exploring expeditions and was also entrusted with administrative tasks. It was in this latter activity that he became imbued with animosity toward centralized government. Although he was decorated by the Tsar for his exploration and governmental services, Kropotkin became an ardent revolutionary. He professed socialist views, but was as opposed to the centralist systems of Saint-Simon and Marx as he was to centralist Tsarism. In 1874, Kropotkin was arrested by the Russian police because of his revolutionary activities. However, in 1876, he escaped to England. After a stay in Switzerland, he was expelled from that country at the request of the Tsarist police. In 1883 he was imprisoned in France, also at the instigation of the Russian police, but was released in 1886 at the personal order of President Jules Grévy. Thereafter he lived in England. Kropotkin made valuable contributions to geology, geography, chemistry, economics, sociology and history. Without systematic erudition, he proved to have vision in all fields of his scientific activities. He especially succeeded in elucidating important stages of the French Revolution in his book *The Great Revolution* (1909). His social system is explained in his book *Mutual Aid—A Factor in Evolution* (1902). The First World War isolated Kropotkin, who sided with the Western Allies against Germany and his anarchist followers. In 1917, he supported Kerensky against the Bolshevists.

ANARCHISM

ANARCHISM, the no-government system of socialism, has a double origin. It is an outgrowth of the two great movements of thought in the economic and the political fields which characterize the nineteenth century, and especially its second part. In common with all socialists, the anarchists hold that the private ownership of land, capital, and machinery has had its time; that it is condemned to disappear; and that all requisites for production must, and will, become the common property of society, and be managed in common by the producers of wealth. And in common with the most advanced representatives of political radicalism, they maintain that the ideal of the political organization of society is a condition of things where the functions of government are reduced to a minimum, and the individual recovers his full liberty of initiative and action for satisfying, by means of free groups and federations—freely constituted—all the infinitely varied needs of the human being.

As regards socialism, most of the anarchists arrive at its ultimate conclusion, that is, at a complete negation of the wage-system and at communism. And with reference to political organization, by giving a further development to the above-mentioned part of the radical program, they arrive at the conclusion that the ultimate aim of society is the reduction of the functions of government to *nil*—that is, to a society without government, to an-archy. The anarchists maintain, moreover, that such being the ideal of social and political organization, they must not remit it to future centuries, but that only those changes in our social organization which are in accordance with the above double ideal, and constitute an approach to it, will have a chance of life and be beneficial for the commonwealth.

As to the method followed by the anarchist thinker, it entirely differs from that followed by the utopists. The anarchist thinker does not resort to metaphysical conceptions (like "natural rights," the "duties of the State," and so on) to establish what are, in his opinion, the best conditions for realizing the greatest happiness of humanity. He follows, on the contrary, the course traced by the modern philosophy of evolution. He studies human society as it is now and was in the past; and without either endowing humanity as a whole, or separate individuals, with superior qualities which they do not possess, he merely considers society as an aggregation of organisms trying to find out the best ways of combining the wants of the individual with those of cooperation for the welfare of the species. He studies society and tries to discover its *tendencies*, past and present, its growing needs, intellectual and economic, and in his ideal he merely points out in which direction evolution goes. He distinguishes between the real wants and tendencies of human aggregations and the accidents (want of knowledge, migrations, wars, conquests) which have prevented these tendencies from being satisfied. And he concludes that the two most prominent, although often unconscious, tendencies throughout our history have been: first, a tendency towards integrating labor for the production of all riches in common, so as finally to render it impossible to discriminate the part of the common production due to the separate individual; and second, a tendency towards the fullest freedom of the individual in the prosecution of all aims, beneficial both for himself and for society at large. The ideal of the anarchist is thus a mere summing-up of what he considers to be the next phase of evolution. It is no longer a matter of faith; it is a matter for scientific discussion.

[204]

KUNG FU TSE. See CONFUCIUS.

L

LAIRD, JOHN

LAIRD, JOHN (1887-1946). Although in his early days, Laird was attached to the British movement of New Realism, he has since proceeded to metaphysical views. At first the problem of sensory perception was the center of his interests, and he rejected the subjective and phenomenalist theories of knowledge. In his books, *The Idea of Value* (1929) and *Knowledge, Belief, and Opinion* (1930), he dealt with the forms and motives of assent and valuation. Of special significance became his criticism of the subjectivist theory of value. Laird demonstrated that this theory is concerned with only one of several aspects of the value phenomenon, namely appreciation, which, however, has significance only through reference to objective values and even presupposes for its existence a class of valuing—namely, choosing within the cosmos. Laird holds, in agreement with Alfred Whitehead and Samuel Alexander, that value is to be read in the constituents of the universe. Turning to the philosophy of religion, Laird published, in 1942, *Theism and Cosmology.*

DEISM AND THEISM

CERTAINLY it may be argued that a creative God, in the more usual sense of creation, is volitional as well as intelligent, that mere intelligence may be as much of an abstraction and as little of a concrete reality in heaven as it is on earth, and that there would be a shocking lack of intelligence if an orderly world were created for any other purpose than the bringing of beauty or of moral excellence or of some other great value into existence. If so, it might very justly be inferred that the philosophy of a bolder and more opulent theism is more readily defensible than the precarious because over-cautious doctrines of a spare, unadventurous deism.

From this point of view the appearance of anthropomorphism may be simply another way of saying that man, in the finer part of him, is made in God's image and a little lower than the angels, or, more modestly, that God is less inadequately portrayed when he is represented as akin to man's nobler attributes than when all such resemblance is denied. Anthropomorphism itself, some would say, is defensible, and theism is the stronger for employing such conceptions.

However that may be, it is preposterous to assert either that mere deism is the sum of "natural" theology, or that there can be no philosophical grounds for a theism that exceeds mere deism. My plea for the recognition of deism in natural theology is not conceived in any such spirit, and I am anxious to say that it is not. On the other hand, the deist's caution, even if it is mistaken, should not be summarily condemned. His reluctance to wander blithely and almost carelessly on the resilient turf of familiar Christian apologetics is reasoned and may not be unreasonable. Deists may be illiberal and short-sighted in their views, and their opponents may be better cosmologists than they are; but even a narrow cosmology may be better than a perfunctory cosmology. If cosmology is an embarrassment to theism, such a theism is self-condemned.

Deism, to be brief, is a species of philosophical theism. It is a cosmological theory of the origin and stability of the universe, conceived upon principles that philosophical theism may rightly decide to incorporate. It is bad policy on the part of a theist to neglect what deists assert through distaste for what more deists deny. If deists draw their boundaries in the wrong places, their mistake, as regards the philosophy of it, has to be shown by philosophical argument to be a mistake. It has also to be shown that there are no similar boundaries in any other place for example, regarding God's "personality"; and the notion that there are such boundaries, to certain apologists, is an idea almost as distasteful as mere deism itself. Frontiers are obscured but not removed by raising a dust in their neighborhood.

[205]

LALANDE, ANDRÉ

LALANDE, ANDRÉ (1867-   ). One of the most comforting auguries of the spiritual recovery of France from the collapse of 1940
is the appearance of the fifth edition of Lalande's *Vocabulaire
Technique et Critique de la Philosophie* in 1947, a work of immense knowledge and acuteness, and universally hailed by historians of philosophy of all nations to whom it renders invaluable
services. Aided by an imposing array of French philosophers,
in this book, Lalande has given not the definitions of terms which
he himself considers adequate, but those which are used by various
philosophers from ancient times to the present day, and to these
semantics he has added a restrained critique of the philosophical
use of language.

Lalande's own philosophy, of course, is more disputable. He
revolts against favorite ideas, especially against monistic evolutionism. According to Lalande, two laws rule over the world.
The one, evolution, is dominant in biology, the other, involution,
a term nearly identical with entropy, in the physico-chemical world.
Life, as it can be observed, results from a compromise between two
antagonistic tendencies of which the one is directed toward increasing individual differences, and the other toward eliminating
them. Man's will must choose between these two tendencies. He is
bound to decide because Lalande denies that the vital impetus is
a reliable guide for the organization of human life. Opposed to
Spencer and critical of Bergson, Lalande adheres to a moral rationalism.

Lalande's principal work *Les Illusions Évolutionistes* was published, in its definitive form, in 1931.

INVOLUTION

SCIENCE is not "a development of the Homogeneous toward
the Heterogeneous," like the increase of species, but it is
a free assimilation of one mind to another, of one thing to
another, of the things to the minds. That is rather easily
recognized. But social progress, if observed without prejudice, becomes manifest not so much as an equilibrium organized by individual ambitions as rather as an *involution*.
That, above all, must penetrate to-day into common sense.
It must be inculcated as deeply as the contrary prejudice

has been inculcated. Practically, an improvement has taken place and continues to proceed through the lowering and even the extinction of the organic structures whereto social life at first had evolved spontaneously. The dissolution of the rule of caste and slavery, whose meticulous social differentiation was by heredity, has given room to aristocratic societies which were already less biomorphical but still neighboring, by virtue of their "states," to the organic structure of the living bodies and the societies of the animals; then these aristocratic societies have been dissolved almost everywhere into egalitarian states which appeal to an ideal of assimilation among their citizens. At the same time it has become evident that these egalitarian states are less warlike than the monarchies, dictatorships and oligarchies.

It might be objected that this great *involution* does not exclude inverse movements. Industrial, commercial, financial struggles are too clear examples of that fact. But when vast transformations of the entire status are at stake, there is no progress that is not accompanied by return-currents and reactionary turns. Who is the philosophical mind that would consider mercantilism a progress of civilization, or be happy that an oligarchy of money was established upon the ruins of an aristocracy of birth?

At the same time, the progress of civilization has universalized the principles and formulas of the law. There will be noticed also an assimilation of singular rapidity between the social functions of men and those of women, and a retrogression of the old forms of the family which had been organically differentiated. . . .

The essential task of science in our epoch is to make human masses understand that the *imago mundi* that led the first years of the 19th century back in the direction of barbary, has not been confirmed by an impartial and scientific reflection. . . . Without any doubt, the individual cannot live without conceding a minimum of satisfaction to its egoistical needs, and it is the same with the nations and social groups. But that is a concession and not an ideal.
[206]

LAMARCK, JEAN

LAMARCK, JEAN (1744-1829). The modern theory, called Lamarckism, according to which acquired properties of an organism can become hereditary, has little connection with the thoughts of Jean Lamarck who disregarded the phenomenon of heredity. But he was one of the first scientists to transform the static conception of the universe into an evolutionist one, and was a precursor of modern theories of environment. In doing so, he experienced the truth of Voltaire's saying that it is dangerous to be right while all contemporary authorities are wrong. Cuvier's opposition to and Comte's severe criticism of Lamarck's statements diverted the attention of the scientists from his work for more than one generation. Even Charles Darwin, generally reserved in the expression of his opinion, found in Lamarck's works nothing but "nonsense," "rubbish" or, at best, "uselessness."

During his whole life, Lamarck, the descendant of an impoverished noble family, was a poor man, and in his last years he lost the modest sum he had saved for his children. His temper revolted against the ecclesiastical life to which he was dedicated in his boyhood. At the age of seventeen he entered the French Army. Discharged, after five years of service he became a clerk in a banking house, in order to earn the money he needed to study medicine. Having attained this end, he concentrated upon observing insects and worms, and then proceeded to the investigation of the laws which govern organic and inorganic bodies. In 1776, he wrote *Recherches sur les Causes des Principaux Faits Physiques*, which he could publish only in 1794, and then, as a sincere adherent of the Jacobins, dedicated to the French people while the government of terror was at its height. In 1795, his *Système de la Nature* appeared and, in 1809, his *Philosophie Zoologique*. Lamarck remained a republican under Napoleon and the restored Bourbons.

Lamarck took great care to distinguish between nature and the Supreme Being, and between nature and the physical universe which he regarded as an inactive and powerless mass of substances. To him, the study of nature is the study of motion, and nature a system of laws which rule over life. The motions which are peculiar to beings endowed with life are clearly distinguished from the physical motions. Life is marked by irritability and the faculty to react to the challenge of influences from without. It is this faculty which develops the nervous system. Changes of circumstances cause changes of both needs and faculties. The lower forms of life are

659

moulded by environment. Higher forms, by virtue of their nervous system, tend to modify their environment by active urge or desire. The interaction of urge and environment produces new characters which either become permanent or perish, according to their respective capability of subsisting.

Lamarck combined sober observation with vivid imagination, which enabled him to behold ideal structures and the real characteristics of organic life.

UNDEVELOPED KNOWLEDGE

ONLY a vast and inconceivable man of genius could brace himself to the contemplation of the principal facts of the universe, and comprehend the extents, densities, distances and motions of the stars which seem to be its large and principal parts. Only a man of genius could embrace at one stretch the vast totality of all existing things. It seems to me, however, that man has to meet with no lesser difficulties when he tries to reduce the particular facts, witnessed daily by him, to their real causes. This is especially the case when he observes his immediate environment.

Our knowledge of the qualities of matter, of the nature of elements and their real properties, of their mutual relations, of the modifications of which several of them are susceptible, and of the real state of the compounds we observe in nature, is still, I think, mostly uncertain.

But of all the knowledge man tries to acquire, the possession of physical and chemical knowledge is most important because of the necessary connection of man's physical existence with all things that surround him or are needed by him. Now it seems that the great discoveries which are apparently outside the range of human mind, are just those by which human science distinguishes itself most, since we have made inconceivable progress in celestial physics, while there are still confused and poorly systematized ideas on the nature and properties of fire, air, etc., prevalent. Most of these ideas are incompatible with the facts which are to be explained. Just as man has surpassed himself by obtaining knowledge of sublime things, just so he seems to be inferior to himself in as far as mostly obscure and disparate hypotheses have been advanced to explain the particular phenomena which Man's environment constantly presents to his eyes.

[207]

LAMB, CHARLES

LAMB, CHARLES (1775-1834). The *Essays of Elia* (1823), one of the most popular books in English literature, is a kind of auto-biography of its author, Charles Lamb, who was a clerk in the East India House, a very sociable man, loved by his friends, and a master of conversation. According to Hazlitt, Lamb "always made the best pun and the best remark in the course of the evening." He was capable of imparting the charm of his conversation to written words. But he never mentioned the misfortune of his life. Lamb never married because he had been insane for six weeks, and, until his death, he guarded with loving care his sister Mary who, in a fit of insanity, had killed her own mother.

MORALITY

NOT childhood alone, but the young man till thirty, never feels practically that he is mortal. He knows it indeed, and, if need were, he could preach a homily on the fragility of life; but he brings it not home to himself, any more than in a hot June we can appropriate to our imagination the freezing days of December. But now, shall I confess a truth?—I feel these audits but too powerfully. I begin to count the probabilities of my duration, and to grudge at the expenditure of moments and shortest periods, like misers' farthings. In proportion as the years both lessen and shorten, I set more count upon their periods, and would fain lay my ineffectual finger upon the spoke of the great wheel. I am not not content to pass away "like a weaver's shuttle." Those metaphors solace me not, nor sweeten the unpalatable draught of mortality. I care not to be carried with the tide, that smoothly bears human life to eternity; and reluct at the inevitable course of destiny. I am in love with this green

earth; the face of town and country, the unspeakable rural
solitudes, and the sweet security of streets.

[208]

LAMENNAIS, ROBERT FÉLICITÉ DE

LAMENNAIS, ROBERT FÉLICITÉ DE (1782-1854). Although
Lamennais radically changed his religious and political standpoint
at least three times and cursed what he had adored in the preceding period of his life, his mind preserved, despite all shifts, traits
of imposing constancy. Lamennais was a keen metaphysician and,
at the same time, a passionate sociologist, a thinker whom Schelling, after a long discussion with him, called "the greatest dialectician of the epoch," and an enthusiast whose imagination evidenced
dramatic tension and power.

In his early youth, Lamennais, like his father who was a
corsair and a descendant of corsairs, was an ardent supporter of
the left wing of the French Revolution. In 1804 he abjured all
revolutionary ideas and subsequently became a Catholic priest.
His *Essai sur l'indifférence en matière de religion* (1817), translated into English, German, Italian and Spanish, maintains that
religion is the fundamental principle of human action. Society, therefore, cannot be indifferent to religious doctrines, and must crush
atheists, deists and heretics. In 1824, Lamennais reached the zenith
of his ultramontanism, displaying more papal-mindedness than the
Pope himself, as well as extreme royalism. But, in 1829, he advocated separation of Church and State, admonished the Church
to sever its cause from that of the kings, and advocated the alliance between the Catholic Church and democracy, while maintaining the principle of the spiritual leadership of the Pope. Severely rebuked by the Pope, Lamennais, in 1834, published his *Paroles
d'un Croyant* (Words of a Believer) of which more than 100,000
copies were sold within a few weeks. He returned to the deism of his
youth, and became the herald of "spiritual democracy" and radical
republicanism, yet always protesting that without faith in God,
human rights and duties must collapse and no civil loyalty can
persist.

Lamennais was one of the founders of the Second French Republic, the initiator of Catholic liberalism and Christian socialism.

JUSTICE AND LIBERTY

HE who asketh himself how much justice is worth profaneth

justice in his heart; and he who stops to calculate what liberty will cost hath renounced liberty in his heart. Liberty and justice will weigh you in the same balance in which you have weighed them. Learn, then, to know their value.

There have been nations who have not known that value, and never misery equalled theirs.

If there be upon earth anything truly great, it is the resolute firmness of a people who march on, under the eye of God, to the conquest of those rights which they hold from Him, without flagging for a moment; who think not of their wounds, their days of toil and sleepness nights, and say, "What are all these? Justice and liberty are well worthy of severer labors." Such a people may be tried by misfortunes, by reverses, by treachery; nay, may even be sold by some Judas: but let nothing discourage them. For in truth I say unto you that when, like the Saviour of the world, they shall go down into the tomb, like Him they shall come forth again, conquerors over death, and over the prince of this world and his servants.

The laborer beareth the burden of the day, exposed to the rain and sun and winds, that he may by his labor prepare that harvest which shall enrich his granaries in autumn.

Justice is the harvest of nations.

The workman rises before the dawn, he lights his little lamp, and endures ceaseless fatigue, that he may gain a little bread with which to feed himself and his children.

Justice is the bread of nations.

The merchant shrinks from no labor, complains of no trouble, exhausts his body, and forgets repose, that he may amass wealth.

Liberty is the wealth of nations.

The mariner traverses seas, trusts himself to wave and tempest, risks his body amid the rocks, and endures heat and cold, that he may secure repose in his old age.

Liberty is the repose of nations.

The soldier submits to many hard privations, he watches, fights, and sheds his blood, for what he calls glory.

Liberty is the glory of nations.

If there be on earth a people who think less of justice and liberty than the laborer does of his harvest, or the workman of his daily bread, or the merchant of his wealth, or the mariner of his repose, or the soldier of his glory:— build around that people a high wall, that their breath may not infect the rest of the world.

When the great day of judgment for nations shall come, it will be said to that people, "What hast thou done with thy soul? There is neither sign nor trace of it to be seen. The enjoyments of the brute have been everything to thee. Thou hast loved the mire—go, wallow in the mire."

And that people who, rising above mere material good, have placed their affections on the true good; who, to obtain that true good, have spared no labor, no fatigue, no sacrifice, shall hear this word: "For those who have a soul, there is the recompense of souls. Because thou hast loved justice and liberty before all things, come and possess forever liberty and justice."

[209]

LAMETTRIE, JULIEN OFFRAY DE

LAMETTRIE, JULIEN OFFRAY DE (1709-1751). This "scapegoat of 18th century materialism," as Friedrich Albert Lange rightly called him, has been blamed and despised by many who had not read a single page of his books. Lamettrie was a physician in the French army. In this capacity he entered into conflict first with medical routine, then with his superiors, and, finally, the government. He was dismissed, and emigrated to Holland. In his books *L' homme machine* and *L'homme plante* (1748), Lamettrie demonstrated by comparative methods the relationship between man and other living beings, and proceeded to a theory of the evolution of organisms. He stated that psychical life is observable already on the lowest level of the evolution. Investigating the functions of the brain, Lamettrie tried to discern various stages of its formation which are of primary importance in the development of mental life. Also, he protested against an evaluation of the moral character of men which depends on the acceptance of religious doctrines. Although Lamettrie was decried as a crude materialist, he also influenced idealist philosophers. To him Goethe owes the inspiration for his botanical ideas.

FOOD AND TEMPER

THE human body is a machine that winds up its own springs: it is a living image of the perpetual motion. Food nourishes what a fever heats and excites. Without proper food the soul languishes, raves, and dies with faintness. It is like a taper, which revives in the moment it is going to be extinguished. Give but good nourishment to the body, pour into its tubes vigorous juices and strong liquors; then the soul, generous as these, arms itself with courage; and a soldier, whom water would have made run away, becoming undaunted, meets death with alacrity amidst the rattle of drums. Thus it is that hot water agitates the blood, which cold had calmed.

What a vast power there is in a repast! Joy revives in a disconsolate heart; it is transfused into the souls of all the guests, who express it by amiable conversation, or music. The hypochondriac mortal is overpowered with it; and the lumpish pedant is unfit for the entertainment.

Raw meat gives a fierceness to animals; and man would also become fierce by the same nourishment. This is so true that the English, who eat not their meat so well roasted or boiled as we, but red and bloody, seem to partake of this fierceness more or less, which arises in part from such food, and from other causes, which nothing but education can render ineffectual. This fierceness produces in the soul pride, hatred, contempt of other nations, indocility, and other bad qualities that deprave man's character, just as gross phlegmatic meat causes a heavy, cloudy spirit, whose favorite attributes are idleness and indolence.

*　　*　　*

There was, in Switzerland, a magistrate called Monsieur Steiguer, of Wittighofen: this gentleman was, when fasting, the most upright and merciful judge; but woe to the wretch who came before him when he had made a hearty dinner! He was then disposed to hang everybody, the inno- cent as well as the guilty.

We think not, nay, we are not honest men, but as we are cheerful, or brave; all depends on the manner of wind- ing up our machine. A person would be tempted to think, at certain times that the soul is lodged in the stomach, and that Van Helmont in placing it in the pylorus is not deceived but by taking a part for the whole.

To what rage and extravagance cannot hunger drive us? No longer is there any respect shown to the bowels, to which we owe, or to which we have given, life. They are torn and devoured in a detestable feast; and in the madness that seizeth us, the weakest are always sure to fall a prey to the strongest.

[210]

LANGE, FRIEDRICH ALBERT

LANGE, FRIEDRICH ALBERT (1828-1875). Germany has pro- duced very few philosophers who are as lucid, judicious and sin- cere as Lange, whose *History of Materialism* (1866) has maintained its value as a standard work and an example of philosophical historiography despite the change of time and the increase of knowledge. Lange, a leader of Neo-Kantianism, demonstrated ma- terialism but, on the other hand, he taught us to appreciate the materialistic philosophers whose independence of idealistic tradi- tions has often obtained sound results and has been directed by true critical insight. Above all, Lange destroyed the not uncommon prej- udice that the adoption of idealistic views on metaphysics would guarantee higher moral standards than could be achieved by the conduct of life of those who professed materialism in metaphysics.

Before Lange published his history of materialism, his book *Die Arbeiterfrage* (The Workers' Question, 1865) created quite a stir in German social politics. Lange, a professor at the University of Marburg, energetically defended the interests of the workers and their political and economic demands, and he was eager to improve their educational and cultural conditions. He often debated with the earliest leaders of German socialism, and quite as often supported them, speaking at meetings arranged by them. Lange honestly tried to ally German democrats and socialists. His premature death was mourned by intellectuals and workers alike.

REALITY AND THE IDEAL WORLD

ONE thing is certain, that man needs to supplement reality by an ideal world of his own creation, and that the highest and noblest functions of his mind cooperate in such creations. But must this act of intellectual freedom always keep on assuming the deceptive form of a demonstrative science? In that case materialism, too, will always reappear, and will destroy the bolder speculations with an attempt to satisfy the instinct of the reason towards unity by a minimum of exaltation above the real and demonstrable.

We may not doubt of another solution of the problem, especially in Germany, since we have in the philosophical poems of Schiller a performance which unites with the noblest vigor of thought the highest elevation above reality, and which lends to the ideal an overpowering force by removing it openly and unhesitatingly into the realm of fantasy. This must not be taken to mean that all speculation must also assume the form of poetry. Schiller's philosophical poems are more than mere products of the speculative instinct. They are emanations of a truly religious elevation of the soul to the pure and troubled sources of all that man has ever worshipped as divine and supermundane. May metaphysics ever continue its efforts towards the solution of its insoluble problem! The more it continues theoretical, and tries to compete in certainty with sciences of reality, all the less will it succeed in obtaining general importance. The more, on the other hand, it brings the world of existence into connection with the world of values, and tries to raise itself by its apprehension of phenomena to an ethical influence, the more will it make form predominate over matter, and, without doing violence to the facts, will erect in the architecture of its ideas a temple of worship to the eternal and divine. Free poetry, however, may entirely leave the ground of reality and make use of myth in order to lend words to the unutterable.

Here then we stand too before an entirely satisfactory solution of the question as to the immediate and more distant future of religion. There are only two ways which can permanently call for serious consideration, after it has been shown that mere rationalism loses itself in the sands of superficiality, without ever freeing itself from untenable dogmas. The one way is the complete suppression and abolition of all religions, and the transference of their functions to the state, science, and art; the other is to penetrate to the core of religion, and to overcome all fanaticism and superstition by conscious elevation above reality and definitive renunciation of the falsification of reality by myths, which, of course, can render no service to knowledge.

The first of these ways involves the danger of spiritual impoverishment; the second has to deal with the great question whether, at this very time, the core of religion is not undergoing a change which makes it difficult to apprehend it with certainty. But the second difficulty is the lesser one, because the very principle of the spiritualization of religion must facilitate and lend a more harmonious form to every transition rendered necessary by the intellectual requirements of a progressive age.   [211]

LAOTSE (Lao Tsu)

LAOTSE (LAO TSU) (About the 4th Century B.C.). The traditional assumption that Laotse was a contemporary of Confucius, and, as the author of the book *Tao Te Ching* (Teaching on the Power of the Way), the founder of Taoism, has been disproved by recent scholars. In all probability, the spiritual movement, later called Taoism, started long before the book *Tao* was written, and that book must be considered not so much the creation, as rather a condensation of already current Taoist ideas. It has been said that Lao was a custodian of documents and a priest-teacher. He has been worshipped since the third century A. D.

Tao, the Way, means the cosmic order of Nature that cannot be grasped by human intellects or expressed in words, according to Taoism and contrary to the Confucian meaning of Tao that concerns guidance of moral conduct of life. Taoism is a doctrine of a reality which is different from the world perceptible by the senses. In many regards it is similar to the reality assumed by Plato, and even more so to the Hindu distinction between the world of appearances and true existence. In its later development, Taoism became mixed with ideas of various origin, but it has remained a mystical faith in the unity of Pure Being.

TAO TE CHING

IF the Tao could be comprised in words, it would not be the unchangeable Tao:

(For) if a name may be named, it is not an unchangeable name.

When the Tao had no name, that was the starting-point of heaven and earth:

Then when it had a name, this was 'mother of all creation.'

Because all this is so, to be constantly without desire is the way to have a vision of the mystery (of heaven and earth):

For constantly to have desire is the means by which their limitations are seen.

These two entities although they have different names emerged together;

And (emerging) together means 'in the very beginning.'

But the very beginning has also a beginning before it began—

This door into all mystery!

*   *   *

The whole world knows that beauty is beauty: and this is (to know) ugliness.

Every one knows that goodness is goodness; and this is (to know) what is not good.

Thus it is: existence and nonexistence give birth to each other:

The hard and the easy complete each other:

The long and the short are comparatively so:

The high and the less high are so by testing:

The orchestra and the choir make a harmony:

And the earlier and the later follow on each other.

669

And puts into practice wordless teaching.
Since all things have been made, he does not turn his back.
This is why the sage abides by actionless activity,
   on them:
Since they have life, he does not own them:
Since they act, he does not entrust himself to them.
When he has achieved any success, he does not stay by it.
In this not saying by his success he is unique;
And this is why he is not deprived of it.

*   *   *

Let there be no putting of the best people into office: this will stop vicious rivalry among the people. Let there be no prizing of rare merchandise; this will stop robbing among the people. Let nothing desirable be visible; this will save the people's minds from (moral) confusion.
This is why the sage's form of government
Empties the people's minds and fills their stomachs,
Weakens their ambitions and strengthens their bones,
Unfailingly makes the ordinary man ignorant and passionless,
The wise man afraid to take action.
(For,) if action is actionless, there is nothing not under control.

*   *   *

The Tao is hollow: use it and there is no overflowing.
How fathomless it is! It makes one think of a common ancestor to all creatures,
One who blunts their cutting edges, unties their knots,
Makes a harmony of the lights (in the heavens) and lays the dust (of this grimy world).
How limpid it is, as if it would stay so for ever!
And yet we do not know whose son (this common ancestor could be),
This image of something before the High God!

*   *   *

Heaven and earth are not human-hearted: for them all
  creatures are but straw dogs.
A sage also is not human-hearted: for him also the hundred
  clans are but straw dogs.
Here is this space between heaven and earth, a bellows as
  it were,
Which is empty but does not buckle up, which the more it
  is worked the more it gives forth.
But, however many words are used, the number comes to an
  end.
It is better (to say nothing and) to hold fast to the mean
  (between too much and too little confidence in heaven and
  earth).

*   *   *

The spirit [divine significance?] of a valley is to be undying.
It is what is called 'the Original Female,'
And the Doorway of the Original Female is called 'the root
  from which heaven and earth sprang.'
On, on goes this spirit for ever, functioning without any
  special effort.

*   *   *

The heavens continue, and the earth endures;
And that in them which makes them so permanent
Is that they do not live for themselves.
Thus it is that they can live so long.
This is why a sage puts himself second and then (finds)
  himself in the forefront;
Puts himself outside (of things and events) and survives in
  them.
Surely it is because he has no personal desires that he is
  able to fulfil his desires.

*   *   *

The higher form of goodness is like water;
For water has the skill of profiting all creatures
Without striving with them.

671

It puts itself in the (lowly) place which everybody hates.
So near the Tao is it.
The goodness of houses consists in their being on the ground:
The goodness of men's minds consists in their being profound:
The goodness of companionship consists in human-heartedness:
The goodness of speech consists in its being reliable:
The goodness of government consists in bringing good order:
The goodness of any business consists in its being efficiently done:
The goodness of any movement consists in its being timely.
Only in all this there must be no striving,
For thus only can nothing go wrong.

*　　　*　　　*

To set out deliberately to be full to the brim [i.e. satisfy every desire] is not so good as (to know when) to stop.
If you are thorough in sharpening (a sword), you cannot preserve its edge for long.
If you fill your hall with gold and jade, there is no way by which you can guard it.
If you are rich and of exalted station, you become proud, and thus abandon yourself to unavoidable ruin.
When everything goes well, put yourself in the background:
That is the way Heaven acts.
Are you able, as you carry on with the restless physical soul, to embrace the oneness (of the universe) without ever losing hold?
Are you able as you control your breathing and make it more and more gentle, to become an (unself-conscious) babe?
Are you able, as you cleanse the Mysterious Mirror, to leave no traces of self-consciousness?
Are you able to love the people and rule a state, without being known to men?
Are you able, whether Heaven's Door is open or closed, to be the (passive, receptive) Female?

Are you able to have a right understanding of all creatures and never interfere?
Give life to them and nourish them;
(For) to give life but not to own, to make but not depend on,
To be chief amongst but not to order about,
This is what is meant by 'the Dark Power' (of unconscious influence).

*   *   *

Thirty spokes together make one wheel;
And they fit into 'nothing' (at the centre):
Herein lies the usefulness of a carriage.
The clay is moulded to make a pot;
And the clay fits round 'nothing':
Herein lies the usefulness of the pot.
Doors and windows are pierced in the walls of a house,
And they fit round 'nothing':
Herein lies the usefulness of the house.
Thus it is that, while it must be taken to be advantageous to have something there,
It must also be taken as useful to have 'nothing' there.

*   *   *

The men who set out to capture all under heaven and make it their own, according to my observation do not succeed.
What is under heaven is a sacred vessel,
Not to be treated in such fashion,
And those who do so bring it to ruin.
Those who hold on to it, lose it.
The truth is that some creatures go before and others follow behind,
Some breathe one way, and others breathe another,
Some feel strong, and others feel weak,
Some like constructing and others like destroying.
This is why the sage has nothing to do with the excessive, the extravagant, or with being exalted.

*   *   *

The man who uses the Tao in the service of an autocrat
Does not war down the states by force of arms.
His business is to long for the return (to peace and inaction):
For where soldiers are, there thorns and brambles grow:
After the passing of a great army,
The harvest is sure to be bad.
A really able commander stops when he has some success:
He dare not exploit his command of force.
Having some success he must not be elated:
Yes, having some success, he must not boast:
Yes, having some success, he must not become ungovernably
    proud.
That success may have been an unavoidable step,
But the (real) success must not be one of force;
For the weakness of old age accompanies the vigor of youth.
The explanation is this: force is not of the Tao;
And what is not of the Tao quickly perishes.

*　　*　　*

Tao is eternal, but has no fame (name);
The Uncarved Block, though seemingly of small account,
Is greater than anything that is under heaven.
If kings and barons would but possess themselves of it,
The ten thousand creatures would flock to do them homage.
Heaven-and-earth would conspire.
To send Sweet Dew,
Without law or compulsion, men would dwell in harmony.
Once the block is carved, there will be names,
And so soon as there are names
Know that it is time to stop.
Only by knowing when it is time to stop can danger be
    avoided.
To Tao all under heaven will come
As streams and torrents flow into a great river or sea.

*　　*　　*

To know men is to be wise:

To know one's self is to be illumined.
To conquer men is to have strength:
To conquer one's self is to be stronger still,
And to know when you have enough is to be rich:
For vigorous action may bring a man what he is determined to have,
But to keep one's place (in the order of the universe) is to endure;
And to die and not be lost, this is the real blessing of long life.

*   *   *

The Supreme Tao, how it floods in every direction!
This way and that, there is no place where it may not go.
All things look to it for life, and it refuses none of them:
(Yet) when it has done its work, it has no fame to be its distinctive clothing.
(For) while it nourishes all things, it does not lord it over them.
Since unfailingly it has no wants toward them,
It may be classed among things of low estate:
Since all things belong to it, but it does not lord it over them,
It may be named the Supreme:
But—to say the last word—it does not arrogate supremacy to itself,
And thus it is that it fulfils its supremacy.

*   *   *

If you grasp the Supreme Symbol (of nothingness) and go all over the country,
There will be no harm (to any one) in your going.
Indeed, the peace and quiet will be beyond bounds:
Music and cake and ale,
And the passing stranger (made to) stop.
(Yet) the words from the mouth of the Tao, how insipid they are!

675

There is no taste to them at all.
Look for the Tao, and it is not enough to be seen,
Listen for the Tao, and it is not enough to be heard.
(Ah, but) use the Tao and it is not enough to come to a stop.

*　　*　　*

The high exponent of power in personality is without power
[i.e. power personal to him]; and this is why he has
(real) power in personality.
The inferior exponent is (set on) not losing his power; and
this is why he has no (real) power in personality.
The high exponent taking no action has no ulterior ends,
Whilst the inferior exponent has ulterior ends to his activity.
(Thus) the high exponent of human-heartedness has no
ulterior ends to his activity,
Whilst the high exponent of justice has.
(Thus) the high exponent of ritual [i.e. social and religious
conventions], when he acts and fails to get the due
response,
Bares his arm and uses force.
Thus it is that when the Tao is lost, there is personal power,
When that is lost, there is human-heartedness;
And when that is lost, there is justice;
And when that is lost, there are the conventions of ritual.
In relation to sincerity of heart and speech, ritual only goes
skin-deep, and is thus the starting-point of moral anarchy;
And foreknowledge of events to come is but a pretentious
display of the Tao, and is thus the door to benightedness.
This is why the really grown man concentrates on the core
of things and not the husk,
And thus it is that he rejects 'the That' and lays hold of 'the
This.'

*　　*　　*

The most yielding thing [the Tao?] in our world of experience can master the most immovable:
Since it is 'nothing' [i.e. immaterial], it can penetrate 'no
space' [i.e. the material].

676

Hence we know that inaction is the profitable course.
(Yet) the truths which cannot be compassed in words,
And the profit which comes from inaction,
These men rarely grasp.

*   *   *

Not to go out of the house is to know the world of men,
Not to look out of the window is to know the ways of the
heavens;
For the further a man travels,
The less he knows.
This is how the sage knows without going anywhere,
Can name things without seeing them,
Can bring them to completion without doing anything (to
them).

[212]

LA ROCHEFOUCAULD, FRANÇOIS VI DUC DE

(Prince De Marsillac)

LA ROCHEFOUCAULD, FRANÇOIS VI DUC DE (PRINCE DE MARSILLAC) (1613-1680). The almighty Cardinal Richelieu and his successor, the no less powerful Cardinal Mazarin, were defied by the Duke of La Rochefoucauld who, descending from a family as noble and as old as the Plantagenets, treated the statesmen—virtually absolute rulers over France—as snobs. Fearless on the military and political battlefield, La Rochefoucauld lacked and detested brutality. He was a brilliant soldier, but no warrior. Twice exiled because of his frankness, La Rochefoucauld was more inclined to observation and meditation, and thinking gave him solace for his experiences without mellowing his impressions. His sentiments were benevolent but his eyes and ears were inexorable. He called himself an Epicurean and a sceptic. In fact, La Rochefoucauld, a *grand-seigneur* of the highest rank in the French kingdom, was melancholic. What he had experienced and observed he condensed with admirable artistic skill in his Maxims (1665). He had seen the triumph of intrigues, the victory of meanness over generosity, and he had penetrated into the secrets of statesmen and kings, of court-cabals and political plotters. He had participated in foreign and

677

civil wars, and felt himself defeated and disappointed. From all these occurrences he drew the conclusion that egoism is the rule of human actions. His feelings were in constant revolt against this knowledge of his comprehensive mind. The *Maxims* scandalized the society of his time but were eagerly read and translated into many languages, and their resigned wisdom continues to attract philosophers and laymen in France and elsewhere, despite all cultural changes.

REFLECTIONS

WHAT we term virtue is often but a mass of various actions and divers interests, which fortune, or our own industry, manage to arrange; and it is not always from valor or from chastity that men are brave, and women chaste.

Self-love is the greatest of flatterers.

Passion often renders the most clever man a fool, and even sometimes renders the most foolish man clever.

Great and striking actions which dazzle the eyes are represented by politicians as the effect of great designs, instead of which they are commonly caused by the temper and the passions. Thus the war between Augustus and Antony, which is set down to the ambition they entertained of making themselves masters of the world, was probably but an effect of jealousy.

Passions often produce their contraries: avarice sometimes leads to prodigality, and prodigality to avarice; we are often obstinate through weakness and daring through timidity.

Whatever care we take to conceal our passions under the appearances of piety and honor, they are always to be seen through these veils.

The clemency of princes is often but policy to win the affections of the people.

This clemency, of which they make a merit, arises oftentimes from vanity, sometimes from idleness, oftentimes from fear, and almost always from all three combined.

We have all sufficient strength to support the misfortunes of others.

The constancy of the wise is only the talent of concealing the agitation of their hearts.

Those who are condemned to death affect sometimes a constancy and contempt for death which is only the fear of facing it; so that one may say that this constancy and contempt are to their mind what the bandage is to their eyes.

Few people know death, we only endure it, usually from determination, and even from stupidity and custom; and most men only die because they know not how to prevent dying.

We need greater virtues to sustain good than evil fortune.

Neither the sun nor death can be looked at without winking.

People are often vain of their passions, even of the worst, but envy is a passion so timid and shame-faced that no one ever dare avow her.

The evil that we do does not attract to us so much persecution and hatred as our good qualities.

Jealousy lives upon doubt; and comes to an end or becomes a fury as soon as it passes from doubt to certainty.

It would seem that nature, which has so wisely ordered the organs of our body for our happiness, has also given us pride to spare us the mortification of knowing our imperfections.

Those who apply themselves too closely to little things often become incapable of great things.

A man often believes himself leader when he is led; as his mind endeavors to reach one goal, his heart insensibly drags him towards another.

Whatever difference there appears in our fortunes, there is nevertheless a certain comprehension of good and evil which renders them equal.

The contempt of riches in philosophers was only a hidden desire to avenge their merit upon the injustice of fortune, by despising the very goods of which fortune had deprived them; it was a secret to guard themselves against the degradation of poverty, it was a back way by which to arrive at that distinction which they could not gain by riches.

To establish ourselves in the world we do everything to appear as if we were established.

Although men flatter themselves with their great actions, they are not so often the result of a great design as of chance.

Happiness is in the taste, and not in the things themselves; we are happy from possessing what we like, not from possessing what others like.

We are never so happy or so unhappy as we suppose.
[213]

LASSALLE, FERDINAND

LASSALLE, FERDINAND (1825-1864). It was one of the many paradoxes in Ferdinand Lassalle's life that he was mortally wounded in a duel, although he constantly struggled against obsolete institutions and conventions. He often perplexed both his admirers and his adversaries by the contradictory traits in his character. But it was just his inner contrasts that were the main constituents of the brilliancy and fascinating power of his personality.

August Boeckh, one of the most famous philologists and historians of that time, worded the epitaph of Lassalle's tombstone in the Breslau Jewish cemetery: "Here rests what was mortal of Ferdinand Lassalle, the thinker and fighter." Lassalle, when engaged in a conflict, fought recklessly and with relentless audacity. As a thinker he destroyed illusions but not ideals. While vindicating the rights of the working people, he appealed to the brutal facts of economic and political power as well as to humanitarian ideas. He was a profound scholar, whose work on Heraclitus is still consulted by students ninety years after its appearance, and whose *System der Erworbenen Rechte* (1861) contains remarks of great consequence for the philosophy of law. He was also a great organizer who created the first political party of workers in Germany, and a popular leader whose oratorical campaigns enraptured the masses. Adolf Hitler, despite his rabid anti-Semitism, studied Lassalle's public speeches, and tried to imitate some of their effects. But Hitler could grasp only the passionate, hypnotizing power of Lassalle's behavior. He was incapable of understanding Lassalle's clarity and mental culture, and his steady endeavor to raise the intellectual level of his audiences.

680

THE LAW OF WAGES

UNDER free competition the relation of an employer to the employed is the same as to any other merchandise. The worker is work, and work is the cost of its production. This is the leading feature of the present age. In former times the relations were those of man to man: after all, the relations of the slaveowner to the slave, and of the feudal lord to the serf, were human. The relations in former times were human, for they were those of rulers to the ruled; they were relations between one man and another man. Even the ill-treatment of the slaves and serfs proves this; for anger and love are human passions; and those ill-treated in anger were still treated as men. The cold, impersonal relation of the employer to the employed, as to a thing which is produced like any other ware on the market, is the specific and thoroughly inhuman feature of the Middle Class Age.

The Middle Class hate the idea of a State; they would replace the State by a Middle Class society permeated with free competition; for in a State, workers are still treated as men, while under the Middle Class regime the workers are like any other merchandise, and are only taken into consideration according to the cost of production.

Ancient civilization is shown by what Plutarch wrote of Marcus Crassus and his slaves: "He (Crassus) used to attend to their education and often gave them lessons himself; esteeming it the principal part of the business of a master to inspect and take care of his servants, whom he considered as the living instruments of economy. In this he was certainly right if he thought, as he frequently said, that other matters should be managed by servants, but the servants by the master." Contrast this with the words of a Liberal professor: "Swiss manufacturers boast that they can manufacture at less cost than the Germans because the Swiss have no compulsory education."

Wages, on the average, are reduced to the necessary

means of subsistence. But if this be the reward of labor, what becomes of the excess of the prices paid for the articles produced over the cost of subsistence of the workers whilst the articles are being made? This excess is divided between the employer and other capitalists, pure and simple, such as the holders of land, bankers, etc.

. . . There is not a single drop of the sweat of the workers that is not paid back to capital in the price of produce. Every pound in the hands of the employers produces another pound. With this increase the power of capital increases, so that every effort of the workers enables the capitalist to compel the workers to further toil. And when it is possible to reduce the prices of the products and thus cheapen the means of subsistence, then the increase of the workers does not increase with the increased produce of labor, but the power of capital does.

Take all those who have worked together in the production of some article—those who have worked with their brains as well as those who have worked with their hands; add together what they have received for their work, and they will not be able to recover the product of their labor! And when machinery is employed, thus causing a greater production with the same amount of labor, then it becomes more and more impossible for the workers to buy back with their wages the product of their work, and they become poorer and poorer.

[214]

LAVATER, JOHANN KASPAR

LAVATER, JOHANN KASPAR (1741-1801). Protestant orthodoxy and pietism, formerly opposed to each other, became allied in the mind of Lavater, whose complicated character made him sometimes obstinate, sometimes humble. He always tried to realize, by his thinking and conduct of life, the ideal of Christian humanity. He also tried to combine belief in miracles with the modern cult of poetic genius. Trained in psychological self-analysis, he was, nevertheless a helpless illusionist, whose extreme gullibility exposed him to the suspicion of being insincere. A staunch adversary of rationalism, Lavater was often the victim of fanatics, charlatans and crooks who exploited his longing for miracles and the manifestation of supernatural forces. Notwithstanding his attempts to reach simple faith, an unsophisticated belief in the Word of the Bible, he was never satisfied with plain truth, and was always ready to take divination for knowledge and phantoms for reality because they stirred his imagination more than did reason. But when he was not occupied with the propaganda for his ideas, Lavater always proved to be a noble-minded and charitable man. However, it was not his theological writings that made him famous but his *Physiognomics* (1774-78), which was translated into several languages. This work contains a wealth of material and has inspired psychologists and poets, but it lacks scientific method. Lavater, who collected and interpreted a great number of historical or artistic portraits, was convinced that his physiognomical studies would promote not only a knowledge of man but also a mutual love of men.

MAXIMS

MAXIMS are as necessary for the weak as rules for a beginner: the master wants neither rule nor principle— he possesses both without thinking of them.

Who pursues means of enjoyment contradictory, irreconcilable, and self-destructive, is a fool, or what is called a sinner—sin and destruction of order are the same.

He knows not how to speak who cannot be silent; still less how to act with vigor and decision. Who hastens to the end is silent: loudness is impotence.

Wishes run over in loquacious impotence. *Will* presses on with laconic energy.

All affectation is the vain and ridiculous attempt of poverty to appear rich.

There are offenses against individuals, to all appearance trifling, which are capital offenses against the human race:—flay him who can commit them.

Who will sacrifice nothing, and enjoys all, is a fool.

Call him wise whose actions, words, and steps, are all a clear *because* to a clear *why*.

Say not you know another entirely till you have divided an inheritance with him.

Who without call or office, industriously recalls the remembrance of past errors to confound him who has repented of them is a villain.

Too much gravity argues a shallow mind.

Who makes too much or too little of himself has a false measure for everything.

The more honesty a man has, the less he affects the air of a saint—the affectation of sanctity is a blotch on the face of piety.

Kiss the hand of him who can renounce what he has publicly taught, when convicted of his error, and who with heartfelt joy embraces truth, though with the sacrifice of favorite opinions.

The friend of order has made half his way to virtue.

Whom mediocrity attracts, taste has abandoned.

The art to love your enemy consists in never losing sight of *man* in him. Humanity has power over all that is human: the most inhuman still remains man, and never can throw off all taste for what becomes a man—but you must learn to wait.

The merely just can generally bear great virtues as little as great vices.

He has not a little of the devil in him who prays and bites.

Be not the fourth friend of him who had three before, and lost them.

She neglects her heart who always studies her glass.

Who comes from the kitchen smells of its smoke; who adheres to a sect has something of its cant; the college air pursues the student, and dry inhumanity him who herds with literary pedants.

He knows little of the epicurism of reason and religion who examines the dinner in the kitchen.

Let none turn over books or scan the stars in quest of God who sees Him not in man.

He knows nothing of men who expects to convince a

determined party man; and he nothing of the world who despairs of the final impartiality of the public.

He who stands on a height sees farther than those beneath; but let him not fancy that he shall make them believe all he sees.

Pretend not to self-knowledge if you find nothing worse within you than what enmity or calumny dares loudly lay to your charge. Yet you are not very good if you are not better than your best friends imagine you to be.

He who wants witnesses in order to be good has neither virtue nor religion.

He submits to be seen through a microscope who suffers himself to be caught in a fit of passion.

Receive no satisfaction for premeditated impertinence. Forget it, forgive it—but keep him inexorably at a distance who offered it.

The public seldom forgives twice.

He surely is most in want of another's patience who has none of his own.

[215]

LEIBNIZ, GOTTFRIED WILHELM

LEIBNIZ, GOTTFRIED WILHELM (1646-1716). Born at the end of the Thirty Years' War, Leibniz constantly longed for peace and the reconciliation of warring parties. He was by nature one of the greatest mediators in the history of mankind. As a diplomat, he endeavored to unite the nations of Europe. As a theologian, he devoted much of his energy to a plan for the revision of the Christian Churches. As a philosopher, he tried, according to his own words, to connect Plato with Democritus, Aristotle with Descartes, the Scholastics with modern physicists, theology with reason. His philosophical conception of the Universe united aesthetical and mathematical, historical and logical, psychological and biological points of views with metaphysical feelings which were inspired by his confidence in God, the creator of the best of possible worlds. The elements of this world are called *monads* by Leibniz. They are characterized by him as the "true atoms," as metaphysical beings. They are not agglomerations of qualitatively undistinguishable

685

particles but individual centers of force, endowed with the faculty of perception and appetition. Insisting upon their immaterial, metaphysical essence, Leibniz denied the possibility of any physical interaction between them. Their coexistence and intercourse are regulated by the "pre-established harmony" which is the work of God.

Before Leibniz began to construct his philosophical system, he had, in 1684, discovered the differential calculus which, as he expected, would make the analytical method of mathematics applicable to all objects of science.

The belief in the intrinsic value of an infinite variety of individual beings, which he refused to regard as modifications of but one substance, made Leibniz the first modern pluralist. At the end of the 19th century, pluralism seemed to be definitely defeated. But it has been restored, particularly in America, by thinkers like William James, F. J. E. Woodbridge and John Dewey.

CONCERNING DIVINE PERFECTION

THE conception of God which is the most common and the most full of meaning is expressed well enough in the words: God is an absolutely perfect being. The implications, however, of these words fail to receive sufficient consideration. For instance, there are many different kinds of perfection, all of which God possesses, and each one of them pertains to him in the highest degree.

We must also know what perfection is. One thing which can surely be affirmed about it is that those forms or natures which are not susceptible of it to the highest degree, say the nature of numbers or of figures, do not permit of perfection. This is because the number which is the greatest of all (that is, the sum of all the numbers), and likewise the greatest of all figures, imply contradictions. The greatest knowl edge, however, and omnipotence contain no impossibility. Consequently power and knowledge do admit of perfection, and in so far as they pertain to God they have no limits.

Whence it follows that God who possesses supreme and infinite wisdom acts in the most perfect manner not only metaphysically, but also from the moral standpoint. And with respect to our selves it can be said that the more we are enlightened and informed in regard to the works of God the more will we be disposed to find them excellent and conforming entirely to that which we might desire.

*　　*　　*

Therefore I am far removed from the opinion of those who maintain that there are no principles of goodness or perfection in the nature of things, or in the ideas which God has about them, and who say that the works of God are good only through the formal reason that God has made them. If this position were true, God, knowing that he is the author of things, would not have to regard them afterwards and find them good, as the Holy Scripture witnesses. Such anthropological expressions are used only to let us know that excellence is recognized in regarding the works themselves, even if we do not consider their evident dependence on their author. This is confirmed by the fact that it is in reflecting upon the works that we are able to discover the one who wrought. They must therefore bear in themselves his character. I confess that the contrary opinion seems to me extremely dangerous and closely approaches that of recent innovators who hold that the beauty of the universe and the goodness which we attribute to the works of God are chimeras of human beings who think of God in human terms. In saying, therefore, that things are not good according to any standard of goodness, but simply by the will of God, it seems to me that one destroys, without realizing it, all the love of God and all his glory; for why praise him for what he has done, if he would be equally praiseworthy in doing the contrary? Where will be his justice and his wisdom if he has only a certain despotic power, if arbitrary will takes the place of reasonableness, and if in accord with the definition of tyrants, justice consists in that which is pleasing to the most powerful? Besides it seems that every act of willing supposes some reason for the willing and this reason, of course, must precede the act. This is why, accordingly, I find so strange those expressions of certain philosophers who say that the eternal truths of metaphysics and Geometry, and consequently the principles of goodness, of justice, and of perfection, are effects only of the will of God. To me it seems that all these follow from his understanding, which does not depend upon his will any more than does his essence.

* * *

No more am I able to approve of the opinion of certain modern writers who boldly maintain that that which God has made is not perfect in the highest degree, and that he might have done better. It seems to me that the consequences of such an opinion are wholly inconsistent with the glory of God. *Uti minus malum habet rationem boni, ita minus bonum habet rationem mali.* I think that one acts imperfectly if he acts with less perfection than he is capable of. To show that an architect could have done better is to find fault with his work. Furthermore this opinion is contrary to the Holy Scriptures when they assure us of the goodness of God's work. For if comparative perfection were sufficient, then in whatever way God had accomplished his work, since there is an infinitude of possible imperfections, it would always have been good in comparison with the less perfect; but a thing is little praiseworthy when it can be praised only in this way.

I believe that a great many passages from the divine writings and from the holy fathers will be found favoring my position, while hardly any will be found in favor of that of these modern thinkers. Their opinion is, in my judgment, unknown to the writers of antiquity and is a deduction based upon the too slight acquaintance which we have with the general harmony of the universe and with the hidden reasons for God's conduct. In our ignorance, therefore, we are tempted to decide audaciously that many things might have been done better.

These modern thinkers insist upon certain hardly tenable subtleties, for they imagine that nothing is so perfect,

This is an error. They think, indeed, that they are thus safe-guarding the liberty of God. As if it were not the highest liberty to act in perfection according to the sovereign reason. For to think that God acts in anything without having any reason for his willing, even if we overlook the fact that such action seems impossible, is an opinion which conforms little to God's glory. For example, let us suppose that God chooses between A and B, and that he takes A without any reason for preferring it to B. I say that this action on the part of God is at least not praiseworthy, for all praise ought to be founded upon reason which *ex hypothesi* is not present here. My opinion is that God does nothing for which he does not deserve to be glorified.

The general knowledge of this great truth that God acts always in the most perfect and most desirable manner possible, is in my opinion the basis of the love which we owe to God in all things; for he who loves seeks his satis-faction in the felicity or perfection of the object loved and in the perfection of his actions. *Idem velle et idem nolle vera amicitia est.* I believe that it is difficult to love God truly when one, having the power to change his disposition, is not disposed to wish for that which God desires. In fact those who are not satisfied with what God does seem to me like dissatisfied subjects whose attitude is not very different from that of rebels. I hold therefore, that on these principles, to act conformably to the love of God it is not sufficient to force oneself to be patient, we must be really satisfied with all that comes to us according to his will. I mean this acquiescence in regard to the past; for as regards the future one should not be a quietist with the arms folded, open to ridicule, awaiting that which God will do; according to the sophism which the ancients called the lazy reason. It is necessary to act conformably to the presumptive will of God as far as we are able to judge of it, trying with all our might to contribute to the general welfare and particularly to the ornamentation and the perfection of that which touches us, or of that which is nigh and so to speak at our hand. For if the future shall perhaps show that God has not wished our good intention to have its way, it does not follow that he has not wished us to act as we have; on the contrary, since he is the best of all masters, he ever demands only the right intentions, and it is for him to know the hour and the proper place to let good designs succeed.

*　　*　　*

It is sufficient therefore to have this confidence in God, that he has done everything for the best and that nothing will be able to injure those who love him. To know in particular, however, the reasons which have moved him to choose this order of the universe, to permit sin, to dispense his salutary grace in a certain manner,—this passes the capacity of a finite mind, above all when such a mind has not come into the joy of the vision of God. Yet it is possible to make some general remarks touching the course of providence in the government of things. One is able to say, therefore, that he who acts perfectly is like an excellent Geometer who knows how to find the best construction for a problem; like a good architect who utilizes his location and the funds destined for the building in the most advantageous manner, leaving nothing which shocks or which does not display that beauty of which it is capable; like a good householder who employs his property in such a way that there shall be nothing uncultivated or sterile; like a clever machinist who makes his production in the least difficult way possible; and like an intelligent author who encloses the most of reality in the least possible compass.

Of all beings those which are the most perfect and occupy the least possible space, that is to say those which interfere with one another the least, are the spirits whose perfections are the virtues. That is why we may not doubt that the felicity of the spirits is the principal aim of God and that he puts this purpose into execution, as far as the general harmony will permit. We will recur to this subject again.

690

When the simplicity of God's way is spoken of, reference is specially made to the means which he employs, and on the other hand when the variety, richness and abundance are referred to, the ends or effects are had in mind. Thus one ought to be proportioned to the other, just as the cost of a building should balance the beauty and grandeur which is expected. It is true that nothing costs God anything, just as there is no cost for a philosopher who makes hypotheses in constructing his imaginary world, because God has only to make decrees in order that a real world come into being; but in matters of wisdom the decrees or hypotheses meet the expenditure in proportion as they are more independent of one another. The reason wishes to avoid multiplicity in hypotheses or principles very much as the simplest system is preferred in astronomy.

*　　　*　　　*

The activities or the acts of will of God are commonly divided into ordinary and extraordinary. But it is well to bear in mind that God does nothing out of order. Therefore, that which passes for extraordinary is so only with regard to a particular order established among the created things, for as regards the universal order, everything conforms to it. This is so true that not only does nothing occur in this world which is absolutely irregular, but it is even impossible to conceive of such an occurrence. Because, let us suppose for example that some one jots down a quantity of points upon a sheet of paper helter skelter, as do those who exercise the ridiculous art of Geomancy; now I say that it is possible to find a geometrical line whose concept shall be uniform and constant, that is, in accordance with a certain formula, and which line at the same time shall pass through all of those points, and in the same order in which the hand jotted them down; also if a continuous line be traced, which is now straight, now circular, and now of any other description, it is possible to find a mental equivalent, a formula or an equation common to all the points of this line by virtue of which formula the changes in the direction of the line must occur. There is no instance of a face whose contour does not form part of a geometric line and which can not be traced entire by a certain mathematical motion. But when the formula is very complex, that which conforms to it passes for irregular. Thus we may say that in whatever manner God might have created the world, it would always have been regular and in a certain order. God, however, has chosen the most perfect, that is to say the one which is at the same time the simplest in hypotheses and the richest in phenomena, as might be the case with a geometric line, whose construction was easy, but whose properties and effects were extremely remarkable and of great significance. I use these comparisons to picture a certain imperfect resemblance to the divine wisdom, and to point out that which may at least raise our minds to conceive in some sort what cannot otherwise be expressed. I do not pretend at all to explain thus the great mystery upon which depends the whole universe.

[216]

L E N I N , V . I .

LENIN, V. I. (1870-1924). When, under the leadership of Lenin, the Bolshevik party seized political power in Russia on November 7, 1917, a new chapter was opened in the history not only of Russia but of the whole world. The character and effects of the Bolshevist revolution and of that party's regime are a matter of endless dispute. There is, furthermore, no agreement concerning Lenin's personality and the part played by him in the Russian revolution. But there is one fact that seems to be certain—that without Lenin, Marxian socialism in its rigid shape would not have been established and maintained as the exclusively ruling creed in Russia. Whether or not the governmental practice of the Bolshevist State has remained in accordance with the official creed is another question. However, it was Lenin, and he alone, who was responsible for the inauguration and continuance of a governmental course which, although in practice is sometimes ready to accept compromises or deviations, insists on the exclusive authority of socialism of the Marxian stamp and suppresses any attempt to express, let alone to practice, heterodox views. For this reason, Lenin is frequently considered, even by non-Bolshevists, as the greatest thinker of the Russian revolution. But his undisputed authority as leader of his party and as ruler over his country does not mean that he was equally superior in the realm of thought.

It is true that Lenin had spent about twenty years in preparing a theoretical and organizational basis for the Bolshevist revolution, and, undisturbed by delays and reverses, he had elaborated the main features of his governmental program when the moment came for seizing power. Lenin, whose original name was Vladimir Ilyich Ulianov, had studied the strategy of civil war, the tactics of sabotage, the weak points of dissenting groups, and the malleability of the mass of the Russian people. But, in his general ideas, he depended upon Marx. According to Lenin, Marx had sufficiently explained the world, and left to him the task of changing this world. He was not even interested in the philosophical foundation of Marxism. Lacking intellectual curiosity, Lenin was unwilling to indulge in thinking activity for its own sake. *Materialism and Empirio-Criticism*, (1909), Lenin's only work on philosophical principles, abounds in misunderstandings. Its aim is to deter socialists from reading Avenarius or Mach rather than to refute their arguments. Lenin's book on *Imperialism* (1916) is not an original analysis of political, economic or sociological facts, but it is, instead, a collection of comments on quotations from the German socialist Rudolph Hilferding's *Finanzkapital*. In his numerous disputes with dissenting socialists, Lenin contented himself with producing a text from Marx or Engels in order to crush his adversaries. This confidence in his masters was a source of strength for Lenin, the party leader and statesman. Apart from his Marxian orthodoxy, Lenin remained versatile and resourceful, not in the least because of his lack of philosophical interest. On the other hand, he was far from considering any of his collaborators as efficient if the latter was only an orthodox Marxian. Noncommunist foreigners were often impressed by Lenin's sarcastic remarks on incapable communist zealots, and took his frankness as a proof of his freedom from prejudice. But, although he judged men and their faculties with acuteness and almost without any bias, he remained fanatically devoted to his creed, and he was aware that he owed his leadership not to his theoretical thinking or his practical ability but to his fervor, his energy, his commanding glance, his educational talents and his skill in maintaining discipline.

THE THREE SOURCES OF MARXISM

THE teaching of Marx evokes throughout the civilized world

the greatest hostility and hatred on the part of all bourgeois science (both official and liberal) which regards Marxism as something in the nature of a "pernicious sect." No other attitude is to be expected, since there can be no "impartial" social science in a society which is built up on the class struggle. *All* official and liberal science *defends* wage slavery in one way or another, whereas Marxism has declared relentless war on that slavery. To expect science to be impartial in a society of wage slavery is as silly and naive as to expect impartiality from employers on the question as to whether the workers' wages should be increased by decreasing the profits of capital.

However, this is not all. The history of philosophy and that of social science shows with perfect clearness that there is nothing in Marxism resembling "sectarianism" in the sense of a secluded, fossilised doctrine originating somewhere away from the high road of development of world civilization. On the contrary, the genius of Marx manifested itself in that he provided the answers to questions which had already been put by the advanced brains of humanity. His teaching came as a direct and immediate *continuation* of the teaching of the greatest representatives of philosophy, political economy, and socialism.

The teaching of Marx is all-powerful because it is true. It is complete and harmonious, providing men with a consistent view of the universe, which cannot be reconciled with any superstition, any reaction, any defense of bourgeois oppression. It is the lawful successor of the best that has been created by humanity in the nineteenth century—German philosophy, English political economy and French socialism.

It is these three sources, which are also the three component parts of Marxism, that we will briefly dwell upon.

The philosophy of Marxism is *materialism*. Throughout the recent history of Europe, and particularly at the end of the eighteenth century in France, which was the scene of the decisive battle against every kind of medieval rubbish, against serfdom in institutions and ideas, materialism proved to be the only consistent philosophy, true to all the teachings of natural science, hostile to superstitions, cant, etc. The enemies of democracy tried, therefore, with all their energy, to "overthrow," undermine and defame materialism and defended various forms of philosophic idealism, which always leads, in one way or another, to the defense and support of religion.

Marx and Engels always defended philosophic materialism in the most determined manner, and repeatedly explained the profound error of every deviation from this basis. Their views are more clearly and fully expounded in the works of Engels, *Ludwig Feuerbach* and *Anti-Dühring*, which, like *The Communist Manifesto*, are household books for every conscious worker.

However, Marx did not stop at the materialism of the eighteenth century but moved philosophy forward. He enriched it by the achievements of German classical philosophy especially by Hegel's system, which in its turn had led to the materialism of Feuerbach. Of these the main achievement is *dialectics*, *i.e.*, the doctrine of development in its fuller, deeper form, free from one-sidedness—the doctrine, also, of the relativity of human knowledge that provides us with a reflection of eternally developing matter. The latest discoveries of natural science—radium, electrons, the transmutation of elements—are a remarkable confirmation of the dialectical materialism of Marx, despite the doctrines of bourgeois philosophers with their "new" returns to old and rotten idealism.

While deepening and developing philosophic materialism, Marx carried it to its conclusion; he extended its perception of nature to the perception of *human society*. The *historical materialism* of Marx represented the greatest conquest of scientific thought. Chaos and arbitrariness, which reigned until then in the views on history and politics, were replaced by a strikingly consistent and harmonious scientific theory, which shows how out of one order of social life another and higher order develops, in consequence of the growth of the productive forces—how capitalism, for instance, grows out of serfdom.

Just as the cognition of man reflects nature (*i.e.* developing matter) which exists independently of him, so also the *social cognition* of man (*i.e.* the various views and doctrines —philosophic, religious, political, etc.) reflects the *economic order* of society. Political institutions are a superstructure on the economic foundation. We see, for example, that the various political forms of modern European states serve the purpose of strengthening the domination of the bourgeoisie over the proletariat.

The philosophy of Marx is a perfected philosophic materialism which has provided humanity, and especially the working class, with a powerful instrument of knowledge.

Having recognized that the economic order is the foundation upon which the political superstructure is erected, Marx devoted all the greater attention to the study of that economic order. The principal work of Marx, *Capital,* is devoted to a study of the economic order of modern, *i.e.,* capitalist society.

Classical political economy, before Marx, was built up in England, the most developed capitalist country. Adam Smith and David Ricardo, in their investigations of the economic order, laid the foundations of the *labor theory of value.* Marx continued their work. He strictly proved and consistently developed this theory. He showed that the value of every commodity is determined by the quantity of socially-necessary labor time spent in its production.

Where the bourgeois economists saw a relation of things (the exchange of one commodity for another) Marx revealed a *relation between men.* The exchange of commodities expresses the connection between individual producers by means of the market. *Money* signifies that this connection is becoming closer and closer, inseparably combining the enure economic life of the individual producers into one whole. *Capital* signifies a further development of this connection: the labor power of man becomes a commodity. The wage laborer sells his labor power to the owner of land, of factories and instruments of labor. The worker uses one part of the labor day to cover the expenditure for the maintenance of himself and his family (wages), and the other part of the day he toils without remuneration and creates *surplus value* for the capitalist, which is the source of profit, the source of wealth of the capitalist class.

The doctrine of surplus value is the corner-stone of the economic theory of Marx.

Capital, created by the labor of the worker, presses upon the workers, ruins the petty owners and creates an army of unemployed. In industry the victory of large-scale production may be seen at once, but we also see the same phenomenon in agriculture: the superiority of big capitalist agriculture becomes greater, the application of machinery grows, peasant economy is caught in the noose of money-capital, it declines and becomes ruined under the burden of a backward technique. In agriculture, the forms of decline of petty production are different, but the decline itself is an indisputable fact.

By beating petty production, capital leads to the increase of the productivity of labor and to the establishment of a monopoly position for associations of the biggest capitalists. Production itself becomes more and more social; hundreds of thousands and millions of workers are linked up in a systematic economic organism, but the product of the collective labor is appropriated by a handful of capitalists. Anarchy of production, crises, a furious hunt after markets, and the insecurity of existence for the masses of the population, are on the increase.

While increasing the dependence of the workers upon capital the capitalist system creates the great power of combined labor.

Marx traced the development of capitalism from the first germs of commodity economy and simple exchange, to its highest forms, to large-scale production.

And the experience of all countries, whether old or new, clearly shows year after year, to an ever greater number of workers, the truth of Marx's teaching.

Capitalism has been victorious all over the world, but this victory is only the eve of the victory of labor over capital.

After the overthrow of serfdom, when a *"free"* capitalist society appeared, it was at once discovered that this freedom signified a new system of oppression and exploitation of the toilers. Various socialist doctrines immediately began to arise as a reflection of this oppression and protest against it. But socialism in its first origin was *utopian*. It criticised the capitalist society, it condemned it and damned it, it dreamed of its destruction, it drew phantastic pictures of a better order and endeavored to convince the rich of the wickedness of exploitation.

But utopian socialism was unable to show a real way out. It could not explain either the essence of wage slavery under capitalism, or discover the laws of its development, or find the *social force* which was capable of becoming the creator of a new society.

In the meantime, the stormy revolutions which accompanied the fall of feudalism and serfdom everywhere in Europe, and especially in France, revealed ever more clearly the *struggle of classes* as the basis of the whole development and its motive force.

Not a single victory of political freedom over the class of feudal lords was won without desperate resistance. Not a single capitalist country was established on a more or less free and democratic basis without a life and death struggle between the different classes of capitalist society.

Marx was a genius because he was able before anyone else to draw from these facts and consistently elaborate the conclusion which world history teaches. This conclusion is the doctrine of the *class struggle.*

People always were and always will be the stupid victims of deceit and self-deceit in politics, as long as they have not learned to discover the *interests* of one or another of the classes behind any moral, religious, political and social phrases, declarations and promises. The supporters of reforms and improvements will always be fooled by the defenders of the old, as long as they will not realize that every institution, however absurd and rotten it may appear, is kept in being by the forces of one or the other of the ruling classes. And there is *only one* way of breaking the resistance of these classes, and that is to find, in the very society which surrounds us, and to enlighten and organize for the struggle, the forces which can and, by their social position, *must* form the power capable of sweeping away the old and of establishing the new.

Only the philosophic materialism of Marx showed the proletariat the way out of the spiritual slavery in which all oppressed classes have languished up to the present. Only the economic theory of Marx explained the real position of the proletariat in the general system of capitalism.

The independent organizations of the proletariat are multiplying throughout the world from America to Japan and from Sweden to South Africa. The proletariat is being enlightened and educated in waging the class struggle, it is ridding itself of the prejudices of bourgeois society, consolidating itself ever more closely and learning to take the measure of its successes; it is hardening its forces and growing irresistibly.

[217]

LESSING, GOTTHOLD EPHRAIM

LESSING, GOTTHOLD EPHRAIM (1729-1781). The idea of religious tolerance has been given its noblest poetic symbolization in Lessing's drama *Nathan the Wise* (1779), which also became the model for Goethe's and Schiller's classical dramas. For admonishing the German people to love their fellow men without prejudice, Lessing was hated by German zealots of religious, political and racial orthodoxy, and considered to be not a genuine German but of Slavic origin.

Poet, dramatist, critic of art and literature, archeologist, historian and theologian, Lessing was the first man of letters in Germany who dared to earn his living as a free-lance writer. Living among people who recoiled from activities involving personal responsibility, Lessing valued independent thinking and feeling, criticism and knowledge as the highest energies of life and mind, and endeavored to awaken the spirit of responsibility among the German people. He rehabilitated wrongly depreciated or condemned thinkers of the past, he struggled against wrong authorities of his time, he tried to secure liberty of expression for a German literature that did not yet exist when he wrote his principal works. But he was not satisfied with his success in combating prejudices and narrowing rules. He also tried to establish standards of judgment and principles of poetic and artistic creation. This he did in his *Hamburgische Dramaturgie* and *Laokoon* (1766-67). Open revolt against the absolutist regime, in particular that of Frederick II of Prussia, was considered hopeless by Lessing, who limited his political criticism to some sporadic bitter remarks in his printed works but branded the political and social conditions of Germany with mordant sarcasm in his correspondence. At the end of his life, Lessing concentrated upon the theological disquisitions and defending himself against attacks on the part of orthodox clergymen. In this struggle that threatened his civil existence, Lessing proclaimed that he put striving for truth above possession of truth.

MAN'S FUTURE PERFECTION

WHAT education is for the individual, revelation is for the whole human race. Education is revelation that affects the individual; revelation is education which has affected and still affects the race. . . . In the early days of Christianity, the word "mystery" connoted something quite different from what we now understand by it. And the development of revealed truths into truths of reason is absolutely necessary if the human race is to be helped by them. When they were revealed, they were not, indeed, truths of reason; but they were revealed in order to become so.

700

Why should we not also be able to be conducted by a religion (notwithstanding that its historical truth, if you will, appears so doubtful), to more exact and better conceptions of the divine Being, of our nature, of our relation to God—conceptions to which the human reason would, of itself, never have strived.

Moreover, in this selfish state of the human heart, to incline to the exercise of the understanding only on those things which concern corporeal needs, would blunt it rather than whet it. It positively will be exercised on spiritual concerns if it is to attach to complete clarification and bring out this purity of heart which qualifies us to love virtue for its own sake.

Human education aims at that, and shall divine education not stretch so far? What art succeeds in doing for the individual, shall nature not succeed in doing for the whole? Blasphemy! Blasphemy!

No! it will come, it will surely come, the time of perfection when man—the more convinced his understanding feels of an ever better future—will not, however, have to borrow from this future motives for his actions, when he will do the good because it is the good, and not because there were imposed upon it arbitrary rewards which were earlier intended merely to steady his inconstant vision and strengthen it to recognize the inner, better rewards.

The time of a new, eternal gospel which is promised in the primers of the New Covenant will surely come to us.

[218]

LEONE, EBREO. See ABRAVANEL, JUDAH.

LEUCIPPUS

LEUCIPPUS (About 460 B.C.). All modern physicists may be regarded as followers of Leucippus of Miletus, the founder of atomism whose way of thinking has led to immense results in science and practical life. His theory that the Universe is composed of an in-

701

finite number of elements which are characterized by quantitative differences has undergone many and important modifications, but it has maintained its validity even after the "indivisible" atoms could be split.

All of Leucippus' works, among which the book *Megas Diakosmos* (The Great Order of the Universe) and *Peri Nou* (On Mind) were most famous, are lost. In the fourth century B.C. his writings were re-edited together with those of his disciple Democritus in one and the same collection. This led Epicurus to deny the historical existence of Leucippus, and some recent scholars have professed the same opinion. But, as Aristotle and Theophrastus remarked, there are differences between the doctrines of Leucippus and Democritus. Although Leucippus created the vocabulary of Greek atomism he remained in many respects more closely connected with the Ionian cosmologists of the older schools, while Democritus proceeded to a strictly scientific view on physical and mental phenomena.

ON ATOMISM

LEUCIPPUS thought he had a theory which was in harmony with sense-perception, and did not do away with coming into being and passing away, nor motion, nor the multiplicity of things. He made this concession to experience, while he conceded, on the other hand, to those who invented the One that motion was impossible without the void, that the void was not real, and that nothing of what was real was not real. "For," said he, "that which is, strictly speaking, real is an absolute plenum: but the plenum is not one. On the contrary, there are an infinite number of them, and they are invisible owing to the smallness of their bulk. They move in the void (for there is a void); and by their coming together they effect coming into being; by their separation, passing away."

He says that the worlds arise when many bodies are collected together into the mighty void from the surrounding space and rush together. They come into collision, and those which are of similar shape and like form become entangled, and from their entanglement the heavenly bodies arise.

[219]

LÉVY-BRUHL, LUCIEN

LÉVY-BRUHL, LUCIEN (1857-1939). When Lévy-Bruhl died, the Sorbonne, the University of Paris, deplored the loss of one of its most brilliant teachers; the French people mourned a staunch defender of human rights and a convinced and active republican and democrat; tens of thousands of political refugees, of human beings persecuted for religious or racial reasons, felt themselves deprived of the moral and material support of a true humanitarian; and experts in sociology, psychology, philosophy, epistemology and many branches of linguistics began to miss the inspiring influence of a scholar whose ideas had offered them new aspects.

Lévy-Bruhl had published solid and significant works on the history of German and French philosophy before he began his important investigations of primitive society. He penetrated into the soul of prelogical man who thought mystically. The philosophical problem that was raised by the results of his inquiries can be formulated as follows: Although all physio-psychological processes of perception of the primitive man are the same as those of modern, logical man—although both have the same structure of brain, the primitive man does not perceive as modern man does. The external world which the primitive man perceives is different from that of modern man, just as the social environments of both are different. Death forced Lévy-Bruhl to commit to his successors the responsibility of drawing further conclusions from his statements.

THE MIND OF THE PRIMITIVE MAN

THE primitive mind, like our own, is anxious to find the reasons for what happens, but it does not seek these in the same direction as we do. It moves in a world where innumerable occult powers are everywhere present, and always in action or ready to act. . . . Any circumstance, however slightly unusual it may be, is at once regarded as the manifestation of one or another of them. If the rain occurs at a time when the fields are badly needing water, it is because the ancestors and spirits of the neighborhood are content, and are thus manifesting their goodwill. If a persistent drought parches the corn and causes the cattle to perish, some *tabu* must have been violated, or possibly an ancestor considers himself injured, and his wrath must be appeased. In the same way, no enterprise will succeed unless the unseen powers give it their support. No one will start out hunting or fishing, nor begin a campaign; he will not attempt to cultivate a field or build a house, unless the auguries are favorable, and the mysterious guardians of the social group have explicitly promised their aid; it is necessary that the very animals needed should have given their consent, and the tools required have been consecrated and invested with magic qualities, and so forth. In short, the visible world and the unseen world are but one, and the events occurring in the visible world depend at all times upon forces which are not seen. Hence the place held in the life of primitives by dreams, omens, divination in its various forms, sacrifices, incantations, ritual ceremonies and magic. A man succumbs to some organic disease or to snake-bite; he is crushed to death by the fall of a tree, or devoured by a tiger or crocodile: to the primitive mind, his death is due neither to disease nor to snake-venom; it is not the tree or the wild beast or reptile that has killed him. If he has perished, it is undoubtedly because a wizard had "doomed" and "delivered him over." Both tree and animal are but instruments, and in default of the one, the other would have carried out the sentence. They were, as one might say, interchangeable, at the will of the unseen power employing them.

To minds thus orientated there is no circumstance which is purely physical. No question relating to natural phenomena presents itself to primitives as it does to us. When we want to explain any such we look for the conditions which would be necessary and sufficient to bring it about, in the series of similar phenomena. If we succeed in determining them, we ask no more; knowing the general law, we are satisfied. The primitive's attitude is entirely different. He may have remarked the unvarying antecedents of the phenomenon which interests him, and in acting he relies a good deal on what he has observed. But he will always seek the true cause in the world of unseen powers, above and beyond what we call Nature, in the "metaphysical" realm, using the word in its literal sense. In short, our problems are not his, and his are foreign to us. That is why we find ourselves in a blind alley, when we seek how he would treat one of ours, and imagine it and try to draw from it inferences which would explain such-and-such a primitive institution.

[220]

LEWES, GEORGE HENRY

LEWES, GEORGE HENRY (1817-1878). Victorian morality was challenged by Lewes who, from 1854 until his death, lived with Mary Ann Evans, the novelist known by the name of George Eliot. Lewes also broke through the moral framework of British life of his time on other occasions, but he knew how to maintain his social credit. He was a versatile, enterprising and often successful man of letters, the founder of the *Fortnightly Review*, which became of primary importance in British literary and political life and still exists, the author of a popular biography of Goethe, biographer of Robespierre, a novelist and playwright, an anatomist and physiologist, and a more gifted than trained thinker. His *Biographical History of Philosophy* (1845) met with great applause. His *Problems of Life and Mind* in four volumes (1874-79) became, despite its weak points, of major significance to the history of modern thought, although not all of those who were indebted to it have admitted the fact.

Lewes was inspired by Comte, whose philosophy he dealt with in *Comte's Philosophy of the Sciences* (1853). His first aim was to disentangle from philosophy all the metaphysical elements which he considered insoluble and meaningless, and to restate its problems in a form corresponding to terms of experience. Later Lewes admitted metaphysics as a science of highest generalities. His principal interest was directed to the question of what the conscious life means and how it is connected with the body. He criticized the mechanical interpretation of organic processes and introduced the concept of emergence which became important to C. L. Morgan, Broad and other thinkers. He also stressed the social factor in the development of the mind and tried to show its way of working. These efforts led him to form a new concept of the general mind and to connect biological, sociological and spiritual terms of evolution.

THE nature of philosophy condemns its followers to wander forever in the same labyrinth, and in this circumscribed space many will necessarily fall into the track of their predecessors. In other words, coincidences of doctrine at epochs widely distant from each other are inevitable.

Positive science is further distinguished from philosophy by the incontestable *progress* it everywhere makes. Its methods are stamped with certainty, because they are daily extending our certain knowledge; because the immense experience of years and of myriads of intelligences confirm their truth, without casting a shadow of suspicion on them. Science, then, progresses, and must continue to progress. Philosophy only moves in the same endless circle. Its first principles are as much a matter of dispute as they were two thousand years ago. It has made no progress, although in constant movement. Precisely the same questions are being agitated in Germany at this moment as were being discussed in ancient Greece, and with no better means of solving them, with no better hopes of success. The united force of thousands of intellects, some of them among the greatest that have made the past illustrious, has been steadily concentrated on problems, supposed to be of vital importance, and believed to be perfectly susceptible of solution, without the least result. All this meditation and discussion has not even established a few first principles. Centuries of labor have not produced any perceptible progress.

The history of science, on the other hand, is the history of progress. So far from the same questions being discussed in the same way as they were in ancient Greece, they do not remain the same for two generations. In some sciences —chemistry for example—ten years suffice to render a book so behind the state of knowledge as to be almost useless. Everywhere we see progress, more or less rapid, according to the greater or less facility of investigation.

In this constant movement of philosophy and constant linear progress of positive science, we see the condemnation of the former. It is in vain to argue that because no progress has yet been made, we are not therefore to conclude none will be made; it is in vain to argue that the difficulty of philosophy is much greater than that of any science, and therefore greater time is needed for its perfection. The difficulty is impossibility. No progress is made because no certainty is possible. To aspire to the knowledge of more than phenomena, their resemblances and successions, is to aspire to transcend the limitations of human faculties. To *know* more we must *be* more.

This is our conviction. It is also the conviction of the majority of thinking men. Consciously or unconsciously, they condemn philosophy. They discredit or disregard it. The proof of this is in the general neglect into which philosophy has fallen, and the greater assiduity bestowed on positive science. Loud complaints of this neglect are heard. Great contempt is expressed by the philosophers. They may rail, and they may sneer, but the world will go its way. The empire of positive science is established.

We trust that no one will suppose we think slightingly of philosophy. Assuredly we do not, or else why this work? . . . But we respect it as a great power that *has been,* and no longer *is.* It was the impulse to all early speculation: it was the parent of positive science. It nourished the infant mind of humanity; gave it aliment, and directed its faculties, rescued the nobler part of man from the dominion of brutish ignorance; stirred him with insatiable thirst for knowledge, to slake which he was content to undergo amazing toil. But its office has been fulfilled; it is no longer necessary to humanity, and should be set aside. The only interest it can have is a historical interest.

[221]

LEWIS, CLARENCE IRVING

LEWIS, CLARENCE IRVING (1883-1947). Lewis, professor of philosophy at Harvard and an outstanding representative of modern philosophical naturalism, has given in *A Survey of Symbolic Logic* (1918) the most comprehensive and complete exposition of the various systems of symbolic logic, traced from Leibniz to the 20th century, and he has discussed therein the relation of a "system of strict implication" to systems of material implication and to the classical algebra of logic. In *Symbolic Logic* (1932), Lewis, in collaboration with Cooper Harold Langford, deals systematically with symbolic logic. The conception of consistency between propositions is brought into harmony with mathematical conception. The distinction between the logic of intension and the logic of extension is basic to the discussion of the whole book, in which the plurality of logical truth is maintained.

In *An Analysis of Knowledge and Valuation* (1947), Lewis exposes a naturalistic conception of values by dealing with the relations between the supreme good and justice. He holds that, for naturalistic ethics, determination of the good must precede the determination of what is right, since the justification of any action depends on the desirability of its contemplated effects. Contrary to many European theorists of values, Lewis characterizes valuation as a type of empirical cognition, not fundamentally different, in what determines their truth or falsity and what determines their validity or justification, from other kinds of empirical knowledge. According to Lewis, for contemporary empiricism, the theory of meaning has the same intimate connection with epistemology that rationalistic or idealistic conceptions previously assigned to metaphysics. Consequently, it has become useless to suppose that the *a priori* truth, known independently of sense particulars, describes something that is metaphysically relevant to reality. Ethics is the capstone of an edifice that rests upon the theory of meaning. Ethics, epistemology and the theory of meaning are essentially connected.

EVALUATION

WE cannot make even a good beginning in the consideration of evaluations in general until we untangle the question what basic good is and what goods are derivative, from the question of the subjectivity or objectivity of value-predications. And a first step here is to observe that there are three main types of value-predication, corresponding to the three main types of empirical statements in general.

First, there is expressive statement of a value-quality found in the directly experienced. One who says at the concert, "This is good," or who makes a similar remark at table, is presumably reporting a directly experienced character of the sensuously presented as such. He might, of course, have a quite different intention; he might be meaning to assert that the selection being played has a verifiably satisfactory character best attested by those endowed with musical discrimination and having long experience and training in music; or that the food verifiably meets all dietetic standards in high degree. In that case, the immediately experienced goodness would, presumably, provide the empirical cue to his judgment, but what is *judged* would be no more than partially verified in this directly apprehended quality of the given—which itself requires no judgment. Such judged and verifiable goodness of the musical selection or the viands, is an objective property, comparable to the objective roundness of a plate, or the objective frequency of vibrations in the surrounding atmosphere.

Directly experienced goodness or badness, like seen redness or felt hardness, may become, when attended, the matter of a formulation or report which intends nothing more than this apparent quality of what appears. There are any number of questions about value-quality as thus immediate, which will have to be discussed in the next chapter. But it will hardly be denied that there is what may be called 'apparent value' or 'felt goodness,' as there is seen redness or heard shrillness. And while the intent to formulate just this apparent value-quality of what is given, without implication of anything further, encounters linguistic difficulties, surely it will not be denied that there are such immediate experiences of good and bad to be formulated. We shall probably agree also that without such direct value-apprehensions, there could be no determination of values, or of what is valuable, in any *other* sense, or any significance for value-terms at all. Without the experience of felt value and disvalue, evaluations in general would have no meaning.

Any such formulation or report of apparent value, taken by itself and divested of all further implication, is an expressive statement; self-verifying (for him who makes it) in the only sense in which it could be called verifiable, and subject to no possible error, unless merely linguistic error in the words chosen to express it. Such a statement is true or false, since we could not tell lies about the quality of immediate experience; but the apprehension is not a judgment, and is not to be classed as knowledge, in the sense in which we have used that word.

Second, there are evaluations which are terminating judgments; the prediction, in the circumstances as apprehended, or in other and similarly apprehensible circumstances, of the possible accrual of value-quality in experience —for example, of enjoyment or of pain—conditional upon adoption of a particular mode of action. If I taste what is before me, I shall enjoy it: if I touch this red-glowing metal, I shall feel pain. Such judgments may be put to the test by acting on them, and are then decisively and completely verified or found false. Being predictive—verifiable but not verified—and subject to possible error, they represent a form of knowledge.

Third, there is that most important and most frequent type of evaluation which is the ascription of the objective property of being valuable to an existent or possible existent; to an object, a situation, a state of affairs, or to some *kind* of such thing. Such objective judgments of value are . . . considerably more complex than objective judgments of other characters than value. There is also much diversity amongst them: "*X* is valuable," in this objective sense, is a form of statement covering a great variety of meanings, and subject to troublesome ambiguities by reason of the difficulty of distinguishing these. But they all possess the common character of being what we have called non-terminating judgments.

[222]

710

LICHTENBERG, GEORG CHRISTOPH

LICHTENBERG, GEORG CHRISTOPH (1742-1799). Aphorism is a form of literary art that corresponds to the character of Lichtenberg, the ironic sceptic of German enlightenment. He liked to collect observations of daily life, curiosities, oddities, psychological experiences, and to shape them into short and easy sentences which mirrored his general philosophical outlook. Lichtenberg, professor of mathematics and natural sciences at the University of Göttingen, had a high idea of spiritual freedom, and he was not afraid to defend it. He particularly liked to ridicule orthodoxy and missionary zeal. Combining common sense and refinement of feeling, Lichtenberg remained lonely among German writers and thinkers.

ALL KINDS OF THOUGHTS

THE intercourse with reasonable people is advisable to everybody because, in this way, a blockhead can become wise by imitation, for the greatest blockheads can imitate, even apes and elephants can do it.

You must not allow your reading to dominate you but you should dominate your reading.

Before one blames, one should always find out whether one cannot excuse. To discover little faults has been always the particularity of such brains that are a little or not at all above the average. The superior ones keep quiet or say something against the whole and the great minds transform without blaming.

Do not have too artificial an idea of man but judge him naturally. Don't consider him too good or too bad. It is a golden rule that one should not judge people according to their opinions, but according to what these opinions make of them.

Popularizing should always be done in such a manner that one would elevate people by it. If one stoops down, one should always take care of elevating even those people to whom one descends.

The inclination of people to consider small things as important has produced many great things.

People don't think so differently about the events of life as they talk about them.

We live in a world in which one fool makes many fools but one wise man only a few wise men.

The highest point a poor brain can reach from experience is the ability to find out the weaknesses of superior people.

Concerning the body, there are at least as many, if not more, imaginary sick as really sick people. Concerning the mind, there are as many, if not more, imaginary sane people as really sane ones.

The late M. who had a Catholic maid, once told me entirely bona fide: This person is a Catholic, it is true, but she is an honest, good soul. Recently she committed a perjury on my behalf.

There are people that can believe everything they want. These are happy creatures.

People that never have time do the least of all.

How happy would many people live if they cared about other people's affairs as little as about their own.

One should never trust a person who, while assuring you of something, puts his hands on his heart.

[223]

LINCOLN, ABRAHAM

LINCOLN, ABRAHAM (1809-1865). Compared with Abraham Lincoln, many great figures in the history of the world, many really great leaders of nations, seem to be actors playing the roles of great men. There was nothing of the actor in Lincoln. His behavior was so simple that not only his adversaries but his political followers and many of his subordinates could not imagine that he was a hero. As Emerson said in his funeral discourse, Lincoln was a plain man of the people, a middle-class president, "yes, in manners and sympathies, but not in powers for his powers were superior." Lincoln never lost the characteristics of a small-town lawyer, indulging often in the jocular talk in which he relished and in which he was a past master. But through the atmosphere of jocularity flashed the brilliance of his hard thinking and tragic earnestness, the flame of his devotion to the nation. To that which Lincoln considered identical with the spirit of the nation—the cause of popular government, his name remains inseparably connected. Little by little Lincoln's sagacity, his valor and patience, his sense of justice and his generosity were recognized, at first by the people of the Union, and thereafter by the whole world. He was recognized as a good and wise man whose wisdom was the result of strenuous life, self-education and appreciation of the apparently unimportant events and accidents in the lives of small people, of enjoyment and resignation. Even his famous Gettysburg Address, from which his expression of confidence in the "government of the people, by the people and for the people" has been and will be quoted again and again, did not immediately work up his audience. It took time before the public was moved by Lincoln's words, but then the deep impression lasted. Lincoln possessed the art of making simple words meaningful and of coining sentences which have become proverbial wisdom in almost all languages. He appealed to the intelligence not to the brute instincts of the public, and he knew how to make difficult decisions and questions understandable to the untrained mind.

THE PERPETUITY OF THE UNION

IT is seventy-two years since the first inauguration of a President under our National Constitution. During that period fifteen different and greatly distinguished citizens have in succession administered the Executive branch of the Government. They have conducted it through many perils, and generally with great success. Yet with all this scope for precedent, I now enter upon the same task for the brief constitutional term of four years under great and peculiar difficulty. A disruption of the Federal Union, heretofore only menaced, is now formidably attempted.

I hold that, in contemplation of universal law, and of the Constitution, the union of these States is perpetual. Perpetuity is implied, if not expressed in the fundamental law of all national governments. It is safe to assert that no government proper ever had a provision in its organic law for its own termination. Continue to execute all the express provisions of our national government, and the Union will endure forever—it being impossible to destroy it except by some action not provided for in the instrument itself. Again, if the United States be not a government proper, but an association of States in the nature of contract merely, can it, as a contract, be peaceably unmade by less than all the parties who made it? One party to a contract may violate it—break it, so to speak—but does it not require all to lawfully rescind it?

But if destruction of the Union by one or by a part only of the States be lawfully possible, the Union is less perfect than before—the Constitution having lost the vital element of perpetuity. It follows from these views that no State, upon its own motion, can lawfully get out of the Union; that resolves and ordinances to that effect are legally void; and that acts of violence within any State or States, against the authority of the United States, are insurrectionary or revolutionary, according to circumstances.

I therefore consider that, in view of the Constitution and the laws, the Union is unbroken; and to the extent of my ability I shall take care, as the Constitution expressly enjoins upon me, that the laws of the Union be faithfully executed in all the States. Doing this I deem to be only a simple duty on my part; and I shall perform it, so far as practicable, unless my rightful masters, the American people, shall withhold the requisite means, or in some authoritative manner direct the contrary. I trust that this will not be regarded as a menace, but only as the declared purpose of the Union that it will constantly defend and maintain itself.

In your hands, my dissatisfied fellow-countrymen, and not in mine, are the momentous issues of civil war. The Government will not assail you. You can have no conflict without being yourselves the aggressors. You have no oath registered in Heaven to destroy the Government, whilst I shall have the most solemn one to "Preserve, protect, and defend" it.

I am loath to close. We are not enemies but friends.

We must not be enemies. Though passion may have strained, it must not break our bonds of affection. The mystic cords of memory, stretching from every battlefield and patriot grave to every living heart and hearthstone all over this broad land, will yet swell the chorus of the Union, when again touched, as they surely will be, by the better angels of our nature.

THE EMANCIPATION PROCLAMATION

Now, therefore I, Abraham Lincoln, President of the United States, by virtue of the power in me vested as Commander-in-Chief of the Army and Navy of the United States in time of actual armed rebellion against the authority and government of the United States, and as a fit and necessary war measure for suppressing said rebellion, do on this first day of January, in the year of our Lord one thousand eight hundred and sixty-three, order and designate as States and parts of States wherein the people thereof respectively are this day in rebellion against the United States, the following, to wit: . . .

And by virtue of the power, and for the purpose aforesaid, I do order and declare that all persons held as slaves within such designated States and parts of States are, and henceforward shall be free; and the Executive Government of the United States, including the military and naval authorities thereof, will recognize and maintain the freedom of said persons. And upon this act, sincerely believed to be an act of justice, warranted by the Constitution upon military necessity, I invoke the considerate judgment of mankind, and the gracious favor of Almighty God.

THE GETTYSBURG ADDRESS

FOURSCORE and seven years ago our fathers brought forth upon this continent a new nation conceived in liberty, and dedicated to the proposition that all men are created equal. Now we are engaged in a great civil war, testing whether that nation or any nation so conceived and so dedicated, can long endure. We are met on a great battle-field of that war. We have come to dedicate a portion of that field as a final resting-place for those who here gave their lives that that nation might live. It is altogether fitting and proper that we should do this.

But in a larger sense *we* cannot dedicate, *we* cannot consecrate, *we* cannot hallow this ground. The brave men, living and dead, who struggled here, have consecrated it far above our power to add or detract. The world will little note nor long remember what we say here; but it can never forget what *they* did here. It is for us—the living—rather, to be dedicated here to the unfinished work which they who fought here have thus far so nobly advanced. It is rather for us to be here dedicated to the great task remaining before us, that from these honored dead we take increased devotion to that cause for which they gave the last full measure of devotion; that we here highly resolve that these dead shall not have died in vain, that this nation, under God, shall have a new birth of freedom; and that government of the people, by the people, and for the people, shall not perish from the earth.

MALICE TOWARD NONE — CHARITY FOR ALL

FONDLY do we hope, fervently do we pray, that this mighty scourge of war may speedily pass away. Yet if God wills that it continue until all the wealth piled by the bondsman's two hundred and fifty years of unrequited toil shall be sunk, and until every drop of blood drawn with the lash shall be paid by another drawn with the sword, as was said three thousand years ago, so still it must be said, that the judgments of the Lord are true and righteous altogether.

With malice toward none, with charity for all, with

firmness in the right, as God gives us to see the right, let us finish the work we are in—to bind up the nation's wounds; to care for him who shall have borne the battle and for his widow and his orphans; to do all which may achieve and cherish a just and lasting peace among ourselves and with all nations.

[224]

LINNAEUS, CAROLUS

LINNAEUS, CAROLUS (1707-1778). On New Year's Day of 1730, the dean of the University of Upsala, Sweden, found on his desk a peculiar form of season's greetings. It was a manuscript, written by an unknown student and entitled *Preliminaries on the Marriage of Plants*. In his preface, the author of the manuscript confessed to his incapability of making verses, and excused himself for having, instead, written a juvenile treatise, in which he handled the analogy between plants and animals as he saw it.

This manuscript contained the germ of Linnaeus' great contribution to botany. Searching for a principle for the classification of plants, Linnaeus, dissatisfied with any division according to color, use or the season of flowering, found the key in the reproductive parts of the plants, and classified them according to their different ways of producing offshoots. In addition to this sexual system, Linnaeus also contributed to the natural sciences by originating the binominal system of naming plants and animals. The first name indicates the genus and the second, the particular species by Latin or Greek words. In this way, Linnaeus made his naming system internationally applicable. Linnaeus furthermore contributed to mineralogy and ethnology by his report on his scientific expedition to Lapland and his miscellaneous essays. He was a charming writer because he was a loving character and a unique observer. As a great scientist said, Linnaeus saw plants "just as an insect sees them." Born in a small farm cottage in a remote district of Sweden, Linnaeus as a little boy already astonished his relatives and teachers by his interest in, and knowledge of, plants. He liked to remember his native village and preserved his country-boy's outlook even after he had become internationally renowned. It is an almost general custom among botanists to make a botanical excursion on Linnaeus' birthday, although modern botany has ceased to concern itself with the flowers in the fields and has become a kind of department of physics and chemistry.

MANKIND, as well as all other creatures, being formed with such exquisite and wonderful skill that human wisdom is utterly insufficient to imitate the most simple fibre, vein, or nerve, much less a finger, it is perfectly evident, that all these things must originally have been made by an omnipotent and omniscient Being, for "He who formed the ear, shall He not hear; and He who made the eye, shall He not see?" If we consider the *generation* of animals, we find that each produces an offspring after its own kind; so that all living things, plants, animals, and even mankind themselves —form one "chain of universal being," from the beginning to the end of the world. While we turn our minds to the contemplation of the wonders and beauties which surround us, we are also permitted to employ them for our benefit. If the Maker of all things, who has done nothing without design, has furnished this earthly globe like a museum, with the most admirable proofs of His wisdom and power; if, moreover, this splendid theatre would be adorned in vain without a spectator, it follows that man is made for the purpose of studying the Creator's works, that he may be the publisher and interpreter of the wisdom of God. In order to lead us toward our duty, the Deity has so closely connected the study of His works with our general convenience and happiness that the more we examine them, the more we discover for our use and gratification. Can any work be imagined more forcibly to proclaim the majesty of its Author than a little inactive earth rendered capable of contemplating itself, as animated by the hand of God? of studying the dimensions and revolutions of the celestial bodies, rolling at an almost infinite distance, as well as the innumerable wonders dispersed by the Creator over this globe? The Author of Nature has frequently decorated even the minutest insects, and worms themselves, which inhabit the bottom of the sea, in so exquisite a manner that the most polished metal looks dull beside them. He who has given life to animals has given to them all different means of supporting it. The Silurus Callichthys, when the rivulet which it inhabits becomes dry, has a power of traveling over land till it finds more copious streams. The flying squirrel has a power of extending the skin on each side of its body in such a manner that, being enabled to descend by a precipitate flight from one branch to another, it easily avoids its enemies. Thus also has He lengthened out the fins on the breast of the flying-fish that it might seek for safety in the air, when pursued by its enemies in the water. He has likewise formed an appendage to the tail of the great cuttlefish (Sepia Loligo) by means of which it springs out of the sea, at the same time being furnished with a bladder, full of a sort of ink, with which it darkens the water and eludes the sight of its pursuers. The sucking-fish (Echeneis remora), which of itself could not, without great difficulty, swim fast enough to supply itself with food, has an instrument not unlike a saw, with which it affixes itself to ships and the larger kinds of fishes, and in this manner is transported gratis from one shore of the world to another. The same Divine Artificer has given the sluggish fishing-frog (Lophius piscatorius) a kind of rod, furnished with a bait, by which it beguiles little fishes into its jaws. The slow-paced Lemur tardigradus is supplied with double ears that he may betake himself to the trees in time to avoid danger. We cannot avoid thinking that those which we know of the Divine works are much fewer than those of which we are ignorant.

[225]

LIPPS, THEODOR

LIPPS, THEODOR (1851-1914). During the decade that preceded the outbreak of the First World War, Theodor Lipps was one of the most influential professors in the German universities. His name attracted many students from other countries. Because of his mordant sarcasm he was dreaded as a critic, but notwithstanding his fondness for irony, he was a rigorous though by no means a narrow-minded moralist. He professed political and cultural liberalism, and was not afraid of defending freedom of thought and art in public meetings. Sometimes he defied openly his government.

After experimental studies on optical illusions, Lipps adopted the notion of empathy (*Einfuehlung*), which had been formulated by Robert Vischer, a historian of art, and made it more and more the center of his thinking. At the same time, he enlarged its meaning and possibility of application. In particular, aesthetic experience was defined by Lipps as empathy, as a psychic process by means of which he who enjoys a work of art is enabled to penetrate into its form and essence, and into the soul of the creative artist. Consequently, Lipps was opposed to all theories of art according to which the artistic work produces the illusion of a reality, or the spectator becomes aware of an illusion. From the aesthetic empathy, Lipps proceeded to its conception as the basis of the feeling and recognition of other egos. Death prevented Lipps from further elaboration of these conceptions. In his last years he adopted some notions of Husserl. On the other hand, Lipps broached various questions which Max Scheler later tried to answer, though he did so a different way.

THE SCIENCE OF AESTHETICS

AESTHETICS is the science of the "beautiful"; implicitly also of the "ugly." An object is called beautiful because it arouses or is able to arouse within me a special feeling, that which we call the "sense of beauty." In any case, we call beauty the faculty of an object to provoke within me a certain effect. In whatever manner we might determine it more properly, this effect, as an effect within me, is a psychological fact. Aesthetics seeks to determine, to analyze, to describe, to delimit the nature of this effect. Moreover, aesthetics seeks to make it understandable. For the latter purpose, it must indicate the factors that combine within me to produce such an effect. Especially it has to demonstrate the conditions which have to be fulfilled in an object so that this object shall be capable of provoking such an effect within me. It must find out the laws according to which these conditions work. This is a psychological task. Aesthetics, therefore, is a psychological discipline.

At the same time the aesthetician looks necessarily at the beautiful objects existing in nature and art. Not just at any object but just at those objects he tries to make aesthetically understandable. He applies his psychological insight to them. In so far, aesthetics may be called a discipline of applied psychology.

In so far as aesthetics describes, clarifies or explains, it is a describing or explaining science. In sharp contrast to such sciences one has placed the normative sciences. This contrast seems to be entirely clear. It is something different whether I ask what a thing is and why it is the way it is, or whether I ask whether or how a thing shall be. There is a difference between the statement of a fact and the laws governing a fact and the prescription, the request, in one word—the norm.

Yet this contrast is no contrast at all. Supposing I know the conditions for the production of a feeling of beauty, I know that, and why, these particular factors are apt to produce it, while others are not likely to produce it. I know the laws according to which certain conditions in their action and combined action evoke the feeling of beauty while others interfere in a disturbing manner. Then I can also indicate without ado which conditions have to be fulfilled and which have to be avoided whenever feeling of beauty in question shall be produced. That means the insight into the real fact is at the same time a prescription. That matters not only here but in all possible fields—namely, wherever a theory is confronted with a technique. Physical insights are at the same time prescriptions for a physical technique, physiological insights prescriptions for a physiological technique (that is, the medical practice). And aesthetical insights are necessarily prescriptions for the aesthetical technique (that is, for art).

[226]

LOCKE, JOHN

LOCKE, JOHN (1632-1704). It is an incontestable fact that the germs of the American Declaration of Independence are contained in the second of John Locke's *Two Treatises on Government*, published in 1690 in order to justify the British Whig Revolution of two years before. It is also generally acknowledged that Locke, by proving, in his *Letter on Toleration* (1689), the necessity of separating Church and State, deeply influenced constitutional and cultural life in the United States. For many decades during the 18th century, Americans could rightly claim to be the true inheritors of Locke's political will, which was neglected in England, the philosopher's home. British liberalism became powerful when it returned to Locke, whose ideas, with Montesquieu and Voltaire as intermediaries, had conquered France, and subsequently imbued the spirit of Holland and Scandinavia.

Locke's political theory was based upon his conception of human nature which was formed by extensive studies and, even more, by the experiences of his life. He had suffered in political persecution, had been active as a diplomat, and engaged in physical, chemical and medical observations before and while he was writing on philosophical subjects. Locke always stressed his conviction that philosophy must be of practical use. He disliked school-dust. He never consciously forced a fact to fit his theory. He rather risked being accused of inconsistency. Modern historians, however, have stated that Locke was very often more cautious in his wording than his numerous and most famous critics had been.

The great task of an inquiry into the faculties and limits of human mind was accomplished by Locke in his *Essay on Human Understanding* (1690), the result of seventeen years of work. This is an immense topography of the realm of mental activities and, since the problem of knowledge is placed upon a psychological basis, the first comprehensive study in analytical psychology. It inaugurated the age of empiricism, and directed the thoughts of many philosophers in various periods. Still in the 20th century, Alfred North Whitehead, though diverging widely from Locke's main positions, used to extol Locke's "admirable adequacy," and thought that Locke had anticipated the principal points of the philosophy of organism.

When King William III appointed Locke minister to the court of the Hohenzollerns at Berlin, the philosopher, who in his early years had been an attaché there, declined this honor, objecting that hard drinking was indispensable for a minister at that court, and that he, "the soberest man in the kingdom," could not be of any use there. Locke was a sober man not only in the regard mentioned by him on that occasion.

IDEAS AND SENSES

It is an established opinion among some men that there are in the understanding certain *innate principles;* some primary notions, characters, as it were, stamped upon the mind of man; which the soul receives in its very first being, and brings into the world with it. It would be sufficient to convince unprejudiced readers of the falseness of this supposition, if I should only show . . . how men, barely by the use of their natural faculties, may attain to all the knowledge they have, without the help of any innate impressions; and may arrive at certainty, without any such original notions or principles. For I imagine anyone will easily grant that it would be impertinent to suppose the ideas of colors innate in a creature to whom God hath given sight, and a power to receive them by the eyes from external objects: and no less unreasonable would it be to attribute several truths to the impressions of nature, and innate characters, when we may observe in ourselves faculties fit to attain as easy and certain knowledge of them as if they were originally imprinted on the mind.

But because a man is not permitted without censure to follow his own thoughts in the search of truth, when they lead him ever so little out of the common road, I shall set down the reasons that made me doubt of the truth of that opinion, as an excuse for my mistake, if I be in one; which I leave to be considered by those who, with me, dispose themselves to embrace truth wherever they find it.

There is nothing more commonly taken for granted than that there are certain *principles* both *speculative* and *practical,* (for they speak of both), universally agreed upon by all mankind; which, therefore, they argue, must needs be the constant impressions which the souls of men receive in their first beings and which they bring into the world with them, as necessarily and really as they do any of their inherent faculties.

This argument, drawn from universal consent, has this misfortune in it, that if it were true in matter of fact, that there were certain truths wherein all mankind agreed, it would not prove them innate, if there can be any other way shown how men may come to that universal agreement, in the things they do consent in, which I presume may be done.

But, which is worse, this argument of universal consent, which is made use of to prove innate principles, seems to me a demonstration that there are none such: because there are none to which all mankind gives an universal assent. I shall begin with the speculative, and instance in those magnified principles of demonstration, "Whatever is, is," and "It is impossible for the same thing to be and not to be"; which, of all others, I think have the most allowed title to innate. These have so settled a reputation of maxims universally received, that it will no doubt be thought strange if anyone should seem to question it. But yet I take liberty to say, that these propositions are so far from having an universal assent, that there are a great part of mankind to whom they are not so much as known.

*　　*　　*

Every man being conscious to himself, that he thinks; and that which his mind is applied about while thinking being the ideas that are there, it is past doubt that men have in their minds several ideas,—such as are those expressed by the words *whiteness, hardness, sweetness, thinking, motion, man, elephant, army, drunkenness,* and others: it is in the first place, then, to be inquired, *How he comes by them?* I know it is a received doctrine, that men have native ideas, and original characters, stamped upon their minds in their very first being. This opinion I have at large examined already; and I suppose what I have said in the foregoing Book will be much more easily admitted, when I have shown whence the understanding may get all the ideas it has; and by what ways and degrees they may come into the mind;—for which I shall appeal to every one's own observation and experience.

Let us then suppose the mind to be, as we say, white paper, void of all characters, without any ideas;—how comes it to be furnished? Whence comes it by that vast store which the busy and boundless fancy of man has painted on it with an almost endless variety? Whence has it all the materials of reason and knowledge? To this I answer, in one word, from *experience*. In that all our knowledge is founded; and from that it ultimately derives itself. Our observation, employed either about external sensible objects, or about the internal operations of our minds, perceived and reflected on by ourselves, is that which supplies our understandings with all the *materials* of thinking. These two are the fountains of knowledge, from whence all the ideas we have, or can naturally have, do spring.

First our senses, conversant about particular sensible objects, do convey into the mind several distinct perceptions of things, according to those various ways wherein those objects do affect them. And thus we come by those ideas we have of *yellow, white, heat, cold, soft, hard, bitter, sweet,* and all those which we call sensible qualities; which when I say the senses convey into the mind, I mean, they from external objects convey into the mind what produces there those perceptions. This great source of most of the ideas we have, depending wholly upon our senses, and derived by them to the understanding, I call *Sensation.*

Secondly, the other fountain from which experience furnisheth the understanding with ideas is,—the perception of the operations of our own mind within us, as it is employed about the ideas it has got;—which operations, when the soul comes to reflect on and consider, do furnish the understanding with another set of ideas, which could not be had from things without. And such are *perception, thinking, doubting, believing, reasoning, knowing, willing,* and all the different actings of our own minds; which we being conscious of and observing in ourselves, do from these receive into our understandings as distinct ideas as we do from bodies affecting our senses. This source of ideas every man has wholly in himself; and though it be not sense, as having nothing to do with external objects be called *internal sense*. But as I call the other sensation, so I call this Reflection, the ideas it affords being such only as the mind gets by reflecting on its own operations within itself. By reflection then, in the following part of this discourse, I would be understood to mean that notice which the mind takes of its own operations, and the manner of them, by reason whereof there come to be ideas of these operations in the understanding. These two, I say, viz. external material things, as the objects of sensation, and the operations of our minds within, as the objects of reflection, are to me the only originals from whence all our ideas take their beginnings. The term *operations* here I use in a large sense, as comprehending not barely the actions of the mind about its ideas, but some sort of passions arising sometimes from them, such as is the satisfaction or uneasiness arising from any thought.

The understanding seems to me not to have the least glimmering of any ideas which it doth not receive from one of these two. *External objects* furnish the mind with the ideas of sensible qualities, which are all those different perceptions they produce in us; and the *mind* furnishes the understanding with ideas of its own operations.

These, when we have taken a full survey of them, and their several modes [combinations, and relations], we shall find to contain all our whole stock of ideas; and that we have nothing in our minds which did not come in one of these two ways. Let any one examine his own thoughts, and thoroughly search into his understanding; and then let him tell me, whether all the original ideas he has there, are any other than of the objects of his senses, or of the operations of his mind, considered as objects of his reflection. And how great a mass of knowledge soever he imagines to be lodged there, he will, upon taking a strict view, see that he has not any idea in his mind but what one of these two have imprinted,—though perhaps with infinite variety compounded and enlarged by the understanding, as we shall see hereafter.

*   *   *

To discover the nature of our ideas the better, and to discourse of them intelligibly, it will be convenient to distinguish them as they are *ideas or perceptions in our minds*; and as they are *modifications of matter in the bodies that cause such perceptions in us*; that so we may not think (as perhaps usually is done) that they are exactly the images and resemblances of something inherent in the subject; most of those of sensation being in the mind no more the likeness of something existing without us, than the names that stand for them are the likeness of our ideas, which yet upon hearing they are apt to excite in us.

Whatsoever the mind perceives in itself, or is the immediate object of perception, thought, or understanding, that I call *idea*; and the power to produce any idea in our mind, I call *quality* of the subject wherein that power is. Thus a snowball having the power to produce in us the ideas of white, cold, and round,— the power to produce those ideas in us, as they are in the snowball, I call qualities; and as they are sensations or perceptions in our understandings, I call them ideas; which ideas, if I speak of sometimes as in the things themselves, I would be understood to mean those qualities in the objects which produce them in us.

[Qualities thus considered in bodies are, *First*, such as are utterly inseparable from the body, in what estate soever it be]; and such as in all the alterations and changes it suffers, all the force can be used upon it, it constantly keeps; and such as sense constantly finds in every particle of matter which has bulk enough to be perceived; and the mind finds inseparable from every particle of matter, though less than to make itself singly be perceived by our senses: v.g. take a grain of wheat, divide it into two parts; each part has still solidity, extension, figure, and mobility; divide it again, and it retains still the same qualities; and so divide it on, until the parts become insensible; they must retain still each of them all those qualities. For division (which is all that a mill, or pestle, or any other body, does upon another, in reducing it to insensible parts) can never take away either solidity, extension, figure, or mobility from any body, but only makes two or more distinct separate masses of matter, of that which was but one before; all which distinct masses, reckoned as so many distinct bodies, after division, make a certain number. [These I call *original* or *primary* qualities of body, which I think we may observe to produce simple ideas in us, viz. solidity, extension, figure, motion or rest, and number.]

Secondly, such qualities, which in truth are nothing in the objects themselves but powers to produce various sensations in us by their primary qualities, i.e., by the bulk, figure, texture, and motion of their insensible parts, as colors, sounds, tastes, etc. These I call *secondary qualities.* To these might be added a *third* sort, which are allowed to be barely powers; though they are as much real qualities in the subject as those which I, to comply with the common way of speaking, call qualities, but for distinction, *secondary* qualities. [For the power in fire to produce a new color, or consistency, in wax or clay,—by its primary qualities, is as much a quality in fire, as the power it has to produce in *me* a new idea or sensation of warmth or burning, which I felt not before,—by the same primary qualities, viz. the bulk, texture, and motion of its insensible parts].

[The next thing to be considered is, how bodies produce ideas in us; and that is manifestly by impulse, the only way which we can conceive bodies to operate in].

If, then, external objects be not united to our minds when they produce ideas therein; and yet we perceive these original qualities in such of them as singly fall under our senses, it is evident that some motion must be thence continued by our nerves, or animal spirits, by some parts of our

bodies, to the brains or the seat of sensation, there to produce in our minds the particular ideas we have of them. And
since the extension, figure, number, and motion of bodies of
an observable bigness, may be perceived at a distance by
the sight, it is evident some singly imperceptible bodies must
come from them to the eyes, and thereby convey to the brain
some motion; which produces these ideas which we have of
them in us.

After the same manner that the ideas of these original
qualities are produced in us, we may conceive that the ideas
of *secondary* qualities are also produced, viz. by the operation of insensible particles on our senses. For, it being
manifest that there are bodies and good store of bodies, each
whereof are so small, that we cannot by any of our senses
discover either their bulk, figure, or motion,—as is evident
in the particles of the air and water, and others extremely
smaller than those, perhaps as much smaller than the particles of air or water, as the particles of air or water are
smaller than peas or hail stones;—let us suppose at present
that the different motions and figures, bulk and number, of
such particles, affecting the several organs of our senses,
produce in us those different sensations which we have from
the colors and smells of bodies; v.g. that a violet, by the
impulse of such insensible particles of matter, of peculiar
figures and bulks, and in different degress and modifications
of their motions, causes the ideas of the blue color, and sweet
scent of that flower to be produced in our minds. It being
no more impossible to conceive that God should annex such
ideas to such motions, with which they have no similitude,
than that he should annex the idea of pain to the motion of
a piece of steel dividing our flesh, with which that idea hath
no resemblance.

What I have said concerning colors and smells, may be
understood also of tastes and sounds, and other the like
sensible qualities; which, whatever reality we by mistake
attribute to them, are in truth nothing in the objects themselves, but powers to produce various sensations in us; and

depend on those primary qualities, viz. bulk, figure, texture, and motion of parts [as I have said].

From whence I think it is easy to draw this observation, —that the ideas of primary qualities of bodies are resemblances of them, and their patterns do really exist in the bodies themselves, but the ideas produced in us by these secondary qualities have no resemblance of them at all. There is nothing like our ideas, existing in the bodies themselves. They are, in the bodies we denominate from them, only a power to produce those sensations in us; and what is sweet, blue, or warm in idea, is but the certain bulk, figure, and motion of the insensible parts, in the bodies themselves, which we call so.

The qualities, then, that are in bodies, rightly considered, are of three sorts:—

First, The bulk, figure, number, situation, and motion or rest of their solid parts. Those are in them, whether we perceive them or not; and when they are of that size that we can discover them, we have by these an idea of the thing as it is in itself; as is plain in artificial things. These I call *primary qualities.*

Secondly, The power that is in any body, by reason of its insensible primary qualities, to operate after a peculiar manner on any of our senses, and thereby produce in *us* the different ideas of several colors, sounds, smells, tastes, etc. These are usually called *sensible qualities.*

Thirdly, The power that is in any body, by reason of the particular constitution of its primary qualities, to make such a change in the bulk, figure, texture, and motion of *another body,* as to make it operate on our senses differently from what it did before. Thus the sun has a power to make wax white, and fire to make lead fluid. [These are usually called *powers*].

The first of these, as has been said, I think may be properly called real, original, or primary qualities; because they are in the things themselves, whether they are perceived or not; and upon their different modifications it is that the secondary qualities depend.

The other two are only powers to act differently upon other things; which powers result from the different modifications of those primary qualities.

But, though the two latter sorts of qualities are powers barely, and nothing but powers, relating to several other bodies, and resulting from the different modifications of the original qualities, yet they are generally otherwise thought of. For the second sort, viz. the powers to produce several ideas in us, by our senses, are looked upon as real qualities in the things thus affecting us; but the *third* sort are called and esteemed barely powers. V.g. The idea of heat or light, which we receive by our eyes, or touch, from the sun are commonly thought real qualities existing in the sun, and something more than mere powers in it. But when we consider the sun in reference to wax, which it melts or blanches, we look on the whiteness and softness produced in the wax, not as qualities in the sun, but effects produced by powers in it. Whereas, if rightly considered, these qualities of light and warmth, which are perceptions in me when I am warmed or enlightened by the sun, are no otherwise in the sun, than the changes made in the wax, when it is blanched or melted, are in the sun. They are all of them equally *powers in the sun, depending on its primary qualities;* whereby it is able, in the one case, so to alter the bulk, figure, texture, or motion of some of the insensible parts of my eyes or hands, as thereby to produce in me the idea of light or heat; and in the other, it is able so to alter the bulk, figure, texture, or motion of the insensible parts of the wax, as to make them fit to produce in me the distinct ideas of white and fluid.

The reason why the one are ordinarily taken for real qualities and the other only for bare powers, seems to be, because the ideas we have of distinct colors, sounds, etc., containing nothing at all in them of bulk, figure, or motion, we are not apt to think them the effects of these primary qualities; which appear not, to our senses, to operate in their

731

production, and with which they have not any apparent congruity or conceivable connection. Hence it is that we are so forward to imagine, that those ideas are the resemblances of something really existing in the objects themselves; since sensation discovers nothing of bulk, figure, or motion of parts in their production; nor can reason show how bodies, *by their bulk, figure, and motion,* should produce in the mind the ideas of blue or yellow, etc. But, in the other case, in the operations of bodies changing the qualities one of another, we plainly discover that the quality produced hath commonly no resemblance with anything in the thing producing it; wherefore we look on it as a bare effect of power.

For, through receiving the idea of heat or light from the sun, we are apt to think *it* is a perception and resemblance of such a quality in the sun; yet when we see wax, or a fair face, receive change of color from the sun, we cannot imagine *that* to be the reception or resemblance of anything in the sun, because we find not those different colors in the sun itself. For, our senses being able to observe a likeness or unlikeness of sensible qualities in two different external objects, we forwardly enough conclude the production of any sensible quality in any subject to be an effect of bare power, and not the communication of any quality which was really in the efficient, when we find no such sensible quality in the thing that produced it. But our senses, not being able to discover any likeness between the idea produced in us, and the quality of the object producing it, we are apt to imagine that our ideas are resemblances of something in the objects, and not the effects of certain powers placed in the modification of their primary qualities, with which primary qualities the ideas produced in us have no resemblance.

[227]

LOMBARD, PETER

LOMBARD, PETER (About 1100-1160). For more than two centuries, Peter Lombard's *Four Books of Sentences* has been used as

732

the chief textbook by students of theology. Born in the town of Lumello in Lombardy, Peter became a professor of theology at the Cathedral School of Notre Dame, Paris, and in 1159, he was Bishop of Paris. He was associated with St. Bernard and the teacher of Abailard, his later adversary.

He thought little of logic and epistemology. According to him, human knowledge is bound to remain fragmentary, but true knowledge is higher than faith which, on its part is higher than opinion. The tenets of metaphysics are to be verified by the study of the Holy Scriptures and thereupon defended by "Catholic reason." In order to offer his pupils a reliable basis for disputations, he compiled his collection of *Sentences* from the Fathers and early teachers of the Church.

TRINITY

THE truth of God could be known in a great many ways. Although, then, God is a single, simple essence, which consists of no diversity of parts or of accidents, still the Apostle says in the plural: "the invisible things of God," because the truth of God is known in many ways through things which have been made. For the eternal author is understood from the perpetuity of creatures; the omnipotent author from the magnitude of creatures; the wise author from the order and disposition; the good author from their government. But all these relate to revealing the unity of Deity. . . .

The image of the Trinity is revealed in a certain manner of its creatures; to be sure, no sufficient knowledge of the Trinity can be had, nor could it be had by the contemplation of creatures without the revelation of doctrine or of inward inspiration, wherefore, those ancient philosophers saw truth as if through a shadow and from a distance, failing in the sight of the Trinity as did the magicians of Pharaoh in the third sign. We are aided, none the less, in the faith of invisible things by the things which have been made. . . .

Memory, understanding, will are one, one mind, one essence. . . . In those three a kind of Trinity appears. Consequently, the rational mind, considering these three and that one essence in which they are, extends itself to the contemplation of the Creator and sees unity in trinity, and trinity in unity. For it understands that there is one God, one essence, one principle. It understands also that, if there were two, either both would be insufficient or one would be superfluous; because if something were lacking to one, which the other had, there would not be supreme perfection in it; but if nothing were lacking to one which the other had, since all things would be in one, the other would be superfluous. The rational mind understood therefore, that there is one God, one author of all things.

[228]

LONGINUS, CASSIUS

LONGINUS, CASSIUS (Third century A.D.). The author of the treatise *On the Sublime* has been called "the most modern of all the ancient Greek philosophers" and "next to Aristotle, the greatest literary critic of ancient Greece." All that is known about his personality has been drawn from some passages of his essay, for no other information about him exists. Only this fact is undisputed—that Longinus, the minister of Queen Zenobia of Palmyra, is not the author of the treatise. Longinus, to whom *On the Sublime* has been attributed for centuries, lived from about 213 to 273 A.D., while the treatise must have been written about 50 A.D.

Many authorities agree with Theodor Mommsen that the author probably was a Jew, and those who do not adopt that supposition cannot refute it. For it would have been quite improbable that any gentile author at that time or during the following century and a half could quote from the Old Testament, not even if he were interested, for one reason or another, in the laws and customs of the Jews.

The author surely revered Homer and Moses alike. He speaks of himself as a Greek. But so does Philo whose loyalty to Judaism is beyond doubt. The author, evidently a disciple of Plato and the Stoics, attacks severely another Jew, named Cecilius, who had mordantly criticized Plato in a work that is lost. Cecilius was probably the first to compare Greek, Latin and Hebrew poetry, and his anonymous adversary follows this method.

From Boileau and Milton to Burke and Kant, European aesthetics and literary criticism have been inspired by this anonymous writer. Some of his concepts have been only slightly modified by Hegel and his successors, and even in the twentieth century more than one critic and poet continue to apply the principles of diction which were originally formulated by the unknown Jewish Platonist or perhaps by his fellow-Jew, Cecilius.

THE SUBLIME IN HOMER AND MOSES

I HAVE hinted in another place that the Sublime is an image reflected from the inward greatness of the soul. Hence it comes to pass that a naked thought, without words, challenges admiration, and strikes by its grandeur. Such is the silence of Ajax in the *Odyssey*, which is undoubtedly noble and far above expression. To arrive at excellence like this, we must needs suppose that which is the cause of it. I mean that an orator of true genius must have no mean and ungenerous ways of thinking. For it is impossible that those who have grovelling and servile ideas, or are engaged in the sordid pursuits of life should produce anything worthy of admiration and the perusal of all posterity. Grand and sublime expressions must flow from them—and them alone—whose conceptions are stored and big with greatness.

And hence it is that the greatest thoughts are always uttered by the greatest souls. When Parmenio cried, "I would accept these propositions if I were Alexander," Alexander made this reply, "And so would I, if I were Parmenio." His answer showed the greatness of his mind. So the space between heaven and earth marks out the vast reach and capacity of Homer's ideas when he says:

"Whilst scarce the skies her horrid head can bound, She stalks on earth."

This description may with more justice be applied to Homer's genius than to the extent of discord. But what disparity, what a fall there is in Hesiod's description of melancholy, if the poem of *The Shield* may be ascribed to him: "A filthy moisture from her nostrils flowed." He has not represented his image as terrible, but loathsome and nau-

735

seous. On the other hand, with what majesty and pomp does Homer exalt his deities:

"Far as a shepherd, from some point on high
O'er the wide main extends his boundless eye;
Through such a space of air, with thundering sound
At one long leap the immortal coursers bound."

He measures the leap of the horses by the extent of the world; and who is there that, considering the superlative magnificence of this thought, would not with good reason cry out that if the steeds of the Deity were to take another leap, the world itself would want room for it? How grand and pompous also are those descriptions of the combats of the gods:

"Heaven in loud thunder bids the trumpets sound,
And wide beneath them groans the rending ground.
Deep in the dismal regions of the dead
The Infernal Monarch reared his horrid head;
Leapt from his throne lest Neptune's arm should lay
His dark dominions open to the day,
And pour in light on Pluto's drear abodes,
Abhorred by men, and dreadful e'en to gods."

What prospect is here! The earth is laid open to its centre; Tartarus itself disclosed to view; the whole world in commotion and tottering on its basis, and what is more, Heaven and Hell—things mortal and immortal—all combating together, and, sharing in the danger of this immortal battle. But yet these bold representations—if not allegorically understood—are downright blasphemy, and extravagantly shocking. For Homer, in my opinion, when he gives us a detail of the wounds, the seditions, the punishments, imprisonments, tears of the deities, with those evils of every kind under which they languish, has to the utmost of his power exalted his heroes who fought at Troy into gods, and

736

degraded his gods into men. Nay, he makes their condition worse than human, for when man is overwhelmed in misfortune death affords a comfortable port, and rescues him from misery. But he represents the infelicity of the gods as everlasting as their nature. And how far does he excel those descriptions of the gods when he sets a deity in his true light, and paints him in all his majesty, grandeur, and perfection, as in that description of Neptune which has been already applauded by several writers:

"Fierce, as he passed, the lofty, mountains nod,
The forests shake, earth trembled as he trod,
And felt the footsteps of the immortal god.
His whirling wheels the glassy surface sweep.
The enormous monsters rolling on the deep,
Gambol around him on the watery way,
And heavy whales in awkward measure play.
The sea subsiding spreads a level plain,
Exults, and owns the monarch of the main;
The parting waves before his coursers fly;
The wondering waters leave the axles dry."

So, likewise the Jewish legislator—not an ordinary person—having conceived a just idea of the power of God, has nobly expressed it in the beginning of his law: "And God said, Let there be light, and there was light; Let the earth be, and the earth was."

[229]

LOTZE, RUDOLPH HERMANN

LOTZE, RUDOLPH HERMANN (1817-1881). Lotze dealt with the principal problems of his philosophy three times and each time somewhat differently. At the age of 24, he published his first *Metaphysics,* and two years later, in 1843, his first *Logic.* He developed his views on metaphysics, logic, ethics and other topics in his *Microcosmos* (1856-1864), and wrote a third *Logic* (1874) and a third *Metaphysics* (1879). Death prevented him from revising his

737

Ethics and other disquisitions. Although his *Microcosmos* was not meant as his last word, his name remains connected with this work which is regarded as one of the most important documents of modern German philosophy, and has influenced many great thinkers in foreign countries, not least of all America. Before the publication of *Microcosmos*, Lotze was regarded as a physiologist rather than a philosopher. He had studied and taught medicine and physiology, and had become known by his theory of "local signs," an attempt to establish relations between sensory affections and areas of the brain, and even more by his rigorous criticism of the concept of "vital force," by demonstrating that physiological processes can and must be explained by strictly mechanistic terms. In his first *Logic*, he protested against any blending of logic with metaphysics. In his first *Metaphysics* he severely criticized German idealism. Lotze's *Microcosmos* is of anthropocentric character, and in this work the effort to reconcile philosophy and religion, philosophy and science, knowledge and the needs of human nature is conspicuous. Maintaining his conviction of the mutual affection of mind and body, Lotze proceeds to a monism which he characterizes as teleological idealism, sometimes as panpsychism. The mechanistic interpretation of nature is considered unavoidable, but Lotze insists that there are ideal interests, values and duties which are not to be rejected as phantoms because they cannot be proved mechanistically, and that psychic life cannot be compared with external, natural occurrences. All concepts of the cosmic order are reduced to a consciousness of truth, facts and values. Evidently inspired by Malebranche, Lotze assumes God as the ultimate cause of all events, all becoming, and the condition of the possible.

In his third stage, Lotze tried to formulate his ideas more precisely. He abandoned panpsychism. Always devoted to modern humanism, Lotze abhorred the idea of revolution, and did not like democracy.

SOUL-LIFE

IT is a strange and yet an intelligible pride that our scientific illuminati take in requiring for the explanatory reconstruction of reality in thought no other postulates than an original store of matter and force, and the unshaken authority of a group of universal and immutable laws of Nature. Strange, because after all these are no trifling postulates, and because it might be expected to be more in accordance with the comprehensive spirit of the human reason to acknowledge the unity of a creative cause than to have imposed on it as the starting-point of all explanation the promiscuous variety of merely actually existent things and notions. And yet intelligible, for in return for this single sacrifice the finite understanding may now enjoy the satisfaction of never again being overpowered by the transcendent significance and beauty of any single phenomenon; however wondrous and profound may appear to it any work of Nature, those universal laws, which are to it perfectly transparent, give it the means of warding off a disagreeable impression, and, while proving how perfectly it understands that even this phenomenon is but an incidental result of a well-known order of Nature, it succeeds in drawing within the limits of its own finitude what to the unprejudiced mind is conceivable only as a product of infinite wisdom.

These tendencies and habits of scientific culture it will be hard to shake, especially by the arguments usually brought to bear on them by the believers in a higher, intelligent guidance of the course of Nature. For however distinctly unbiased observation may suggest this belief, so that it may seem alike foolish and tedious to attempt to understand the order of Nature without it, the supporters of the mechanical conception can always with justice reply that nevertheless in the explanation of details their road is always entered by those who on the whole believe unquestioningly in the government of an intelligent working power. They, too, are not content till, for each result ordained by this power, they have one by one traced out the efficient means through whose necessary and blind causal connection the required effect must be brought about. Even they will never seriously believe that within Nature as it lies patent to our senses, this purposive power makes new beginnings of working, such as, if traced further back, would not always prove to be the necessary results of a prior state of things. While thus even to those who hold the more religious view, the course of events is again converted into the unbroken chain of mechanical sequence, from the scientific point of view the latter alone is conspicuous, and the idea of free action on the part of an intelligent force, to which no sphere of action can be assigned, is readily dropped. Science might be able to allow that the origin of the whole, whose internal relations alone form the subject of its investigations, may be attributed to a Divine Wisdom, but it would demand facts that, within the sphere of experience, made a continuous dependence of the creation on the preserving providence of its author a necessary condition of explanation. Too ingenuous and self-confident, the believers in this living interference of reason working towards an end bring forward only the fair aspects of life, and for the time forget its shadows; in their admiration of the wondrous harmony of organized bodies, and of their careful adaptation to the ends of mental life, they do not think of the bitter persistence with which this same organized life transmits ugliness and disease from generation to generation, or of the manifold hindrances that come in the way of the attainment even of modest human aims. How little, then, can this conception of the universe—to which the presence of evil is, if not an insoluble, at least an unsolved problem—hope by its assaults to overcome a habit of mind that finds numberless special confirmations in observation, and is inaccessible to any feeling of the universal deficiency under which we suppose it to labor!

And is it compelled to make even the acknowledgment which it will perhaps make, that this world of blind necessity came forth at least primarily from the wisdom of a supreme creator? Doubtless it can reply that even the purposiveness of the present fabric, as it now is, could certainly have been evolved from the confusion of an original chaos under the sway of universal laws. For all that was brought together by a planless vortex, in unmeaning aggregation and without the internal equilibrium of constituents and forces that might have secured to it a longer existence in the struggle with the onward-sweeping course of external Nature: all this has long since perished. Along with and after numberless unsuccessful attempts at formation, which per-

740

haps filled primeval times in a rapid alternation of rise and decay, Nature gradually shrank into a narrower channel, and only those select creatures were preserved on which a happy combination of their constituent parts had bestowed the power of withstanding the pressure of surrounding stimuli, and of propagating their kind throughout an indefinite period. However little we may probably esteem this theory, we could yet hardly snatch it from those whom it satisfies, and we ourselves cannot wholly disallow the charm that scientific ingenuity will always find in the attempt to evolve from the formless chaos of whirling motions the necessity of a gradual sifting, and the spontaneous formation of permanent forms of succession of phenomena.

But all such attempts rest on the common assumption that the universal sway of unchanging laws prescribes the kind and amount of the reciprocal actions engaged in by the several substances of the original chaos, and thereby compels them to withdraw from combinations in which no equilibrium is possible, and to enter into others in which they are at rest, or can retain a constant mode of motion. This assumption it is whose trustworthiness we must now test; with it stands or falls the proud certainty of the mechanical conception of the universe. Is this veneration for an all-prevailing law of Nature, as the only bond that forces the scattered elements of the course of things into mutual active relations and determines the character of their results, itself a possible conception, and can it put the finishing touch to our view of Nature, whose perfecting in detail we ourselves have everywhere looked to it to accomplish?

Let us suppose two elements originally in existence, not produced by anything, not sprung from any common source, existing from eternity as things actual without any antecedents, but existing so that they have no other community than that of contemporaneous existence: how could the influence of the one be communicated to the other, seeing that each is as it were in a separate world, and that between them there is nothing? How is the efficacy of the one to make its way to the other through this nothing, offering no means of transmission? And if we suppose that the energy of each element constantly diffused itself like a separable atmosphere through a common space, effective like the rays of light where it met with anything on which to act, and floating idly in vacuo where nothing presented itself, what should we have gained? We would not understand our own conception, either how the action could issue from the limits of that in which it was generated; nor how, floating for some interval of time between its source and that which was to be its object, it maintained itself in vacuo; nor, lastly, how, in the end reaching the latter, it was able to exert a transforming power over its states. For while space would offer no obstacle to the mutual action of that which, though separated by it, was yet united by an inherent relation, contact in space would not involve any necessity of reciprocal action, or explain the possibility of it between beings each of which in its complete self-dependence was divided from the other by the impassable gulf of inherent indifference. The transmission of action from the one to the other seems simple only to him who, looking at the question in a superficial, commonplace way, thinks he can distinctly perceive it in the external motions by which it is accompanied; to any one examining it more deeply, it becomes more and more inexplicable how the condition of the one can contain a force compelling the other to a change of its own internal states. As, before, we were unable to follow our will in its outflow into the moveable extremities, but had to acknowledge that all volition remains confined to the willing mind, and that the execution following it is the work of an incomprehensible power: in like manner all the forces which we suppose in any form to inhere in the one element, will be inadequate to give rise to an influence on that in which they do not inhere. Now, can the conception of the universal course of Nature supplied by our previous speculations, can the idea of a realm of eternally and universally valid laws, fill this hiatus, and weld the brittle and isolated fragments into the solid whole of a reciprocally acting world?

Certainly it cannot; for how could laws exist of themselves, as a necessity prescribing particular results for particular cases? There can be nothing besides being and its inherent states; and a universal order, before that of which it is the order has come into existence, cannot spring up between beings as a self-existent background holding them together, an efficient, controlling power. If we look back on our human life, we shall find that the laws of our social relations do not exist beside and between us in independent reality, are not powers to direct and control us from without because there they are; they exist only in the consciousness of the individuals who feel bound by them; they receive sanction and reality only through the actions of living persons; they are nothing but the harmoniously and inwardly-developed direction of many individual wills, which to the later generalizing scrutiny of observation appears as a highly externally-directing power because in its common authority over many it no longer presents itself as exclusively the product of one. The laws of Nature may be superior to the ordinances of the human mind; while the latter may be gainsaid and disobeyed, the commands of the former are unlimited and resistless; nevertheless Nature cannot bring to pass what is self-contradictory, or bestow independent existence on that which can have its being only in and through what is self-existent. We are apt to be led astray in these speculations by a widely diffused usage of thought and speech that exercises no prejudicial effect on our judgment of the incidents of daily life, in reference to which it has arisen. We speak of ties uniting things, of relations into which they enter, of an order which embraces them, finally, of laws under whose sway they respectively stand; and we hardly notice the contradiction contained in these notions of relations lying ready before the things came to enter into them, of an order waiting to receive the things ordered, finally, of ties stretched like solid threads—of a material that we could not describe—across the abyss that divides one being from another. We do not consider that all relations and connections exist only in the unity of observing consciousness, which, passing from one element to another, knits all together by its comprehensive activity, and that in like manner all efficacious order, all laws, that we are fain to conceive as existing between things independently of our knowledge, can exist only in the unity of the One that binds them all together. Not the empty shadow of an order of Nature, but only the full reality of an infinite living being of whom all finite things are inwardly cherished parts, has power so to knit together the multiplicity of the universe that reciprocal actions shall make their way across the chasm that would eternally divide the several distinct elements from one another. For action, starting from one being, is not lost in an abyss of nothing lying between it and another; but as in all being the truly existent is one and the same, so in all reciprocal action the infinite acts only on itself, and its activity never quits the sure foundation of being. The energizing of one of its parts is not confined to that and isolated from the rest; the single state has not to travel along an indescribable path in order to seek another element to which it may impart itself, nor has it to exert an equally incomprehensible force in order to compel that indifferent other element to participate in it. Every excitation of the individual is an excitation of the whole Infinite, that forms the living basis even of the individual's existence, and every one can therefore act upon every other which has the same living basis; for it is this which from the unity of its own nature causes the finite event here to be followed by its echo there. It is not anything finite that out of itself as finite acts upon something else; on the contrary, every stimulation of the individual, seeing that it affects the eternal basis that in it, as in all, forms the essence of its finite appearance, can through this continuity of related being—but through this alone—act upon the apparently remote.

We are not constrained to this recognition of an Infinite

Substance, that instead of an unsubstantial and unreal law unites all things by its actual reality, merely by admiration for single spheres of phenomena, by whose special significance we are impressed; nay, every example of reciprocal action however insignificant, every instance of causality, forces us, in order to understand the possibility of a transference of influence, to substitute for a merely natural connection a substantial Infinite, containing unseparated the manifold that in phenomenal existence is separated. We could not seek such a bond between the constituents of the living body alone, or between body and soul pre-eminently, as if we did not need it everywhere; on the contrary, seeing that we look on all that happens, however it may be designated, as but the manifested internal energy of a single Infinite Being, the later course of our speculations will carry us further from the resuscitated mythology that, like the ancient sagas, allots to certain distinguished phenomena their special genii, and leaves the remaining work-day reality to take care of itself.

For this Universal Being is not a mere bond, a mere indifferent bridge, having no other office than to form a way for the passage of action from one element to another: it is at the same time the sovereign power that for every antecedent fixes the form and degree of its consequent, for each individual the sphere of its possible activity, for every single manifestation of the latter its particular mode. We deceive ourselves when we imagine we can derive the modes in which things act on one another, as self-evident results, from the particular properties that now constitute their nature, and from the joint influence of the circumstances of each occasion. Honest consideration, on the contrary, leads us to make the acknowledgment that the effects actually presented to us by experience are not to be got as necessary conclusions from these premises alone, however we may analyze and recombine their content, but that an unknown power, as it were, having respect to something that we do not meet with among these prior conditions, has annexed to their form the particular form of the result. The Infinite is this secret power, and that to which it has respect in the determination of results is its own presence in all finite elements, by which the universe receives the unity of a being, and on account of which the course of its events must receive the unity of a connected manifestation of the content of that being. Every finite thing, therefore, possesses the capability of action only in such amount and such quality as it is permitted by the Infinite to contribute to the realization of the whole.

[230]

LOVEJOY, ARTHUR ONCKEN

LOVEJOY, ARTHUR ONCKEN (1873-). Shortly before the twentieth century began, two young, and then unknown, American philosophers made a horse-car trip during which one, named William P. Montague, asked the other whose name was Arthur O. Lovejoy, what he considered the chief end of man, and Lovejoy answered: self-consciousness, just what most philosophers regard as the starting point of their thinking. This viewpoint has remained characteristic of Lovejoy's philosophy. What other thinkers are apt to take for granted, he deals with as a problem.

Lovejoy calls his position "temporalized realism." To him, the most indubitable fact of all our experience is that experience itself is temporal. This cognition has been used by him as a touchstone to be applied to all theories about the nature of reality or of knowledge. He has used it for the rejection of all dominant forms of idealism and monism. He maintains that rationality, when conceived as complete and excluding all arbitrariness, becomes itself a kind of irrationality, excluding any limiting and selective principle. The world of concrete existence is a contingent world whose laws show some inexpugnable traits of arbitrariness. Otherwise it would be a world without power of choice, without character. Man is, by the most distinctive impulse of his nature, an interpretative animal who seeks to know the causes of things through trial and error in the course of time. The history of man's reflection, and the history of philosophy especially, is, to a large extent, a history of confusion of ideas, and Lovejoy has devoted much of his energy to analyze and unravel this confusion. An outstanding example of his method is in his book *The Great Chain of*

746

Being (1936). Thus Lovejoy's interest in critical philosophy is closely interwoven with his interest in historical thought and research.

THE COMPLEXITY OF ISMS

IDEALISM, romanticism, rationalism, transcendentalism, pragmatism—all these trouble-breeding and usually thought-obscuring terms . . . are names of complexes, not of simples. They stand, as a rule, not for one doctrine, but for several distinct and often conflicting doctrines held by different individuals or groups to whose way of thinking these appellations have been applied either by themselves or in the traditional terminology of historians; and each of these doctrines, in turn, is likely to be resolvable into simpler elements, often very strangely combined and derivative from a variety of dissimilar motives and historic influences. The term "Christianity," for example, is not the name for any single unit of the type for which the historian of specific ideas looks. I mean by this not merely the notorious fact that persons who have equally professed and called themselves Christians have, in the course of history, held all manner of distinct and conflicting beliefs under the one name, but also that any of these persons and sects has, as a rule, held under that name a very mixed collection of ideas, the combination of which into a conglomerate bearing a single name and supposed to constitute a real unity was usually the result of historic processes of a highly complicated and curious sort. It is, of course, proper and necessary that ecclesiastical historians should write books on the history of Christianity; but in doing so they are writing of a series of facts which, taken as a whole, have almost nothing in common except the name; the part of the world in which they occurred; the reverence for a certain person, whose nature and teaching, however, have been most variously conceived, so that the unity here too is largely a unity of name; and the identity of a part of their historic antecedents, of certain causes or influences which, diversely combined with other causes, have made each of these systems what it is. In the whole series of creeds and movements going under the one name, and in each of them separately, it is needful to go behind the superficial appearance of singleness and identity, to crack the shell which holds the mass together, if we are to see the real units, the effective working ideas, which, in any given case, are present.

[231]

LUCRETIUS (Titus Lucretius Carus)

LUCRETIUS (TITUS LUCRETIUS CARUS) (98-55 B.C.). The system of Epicurus was converted into a striking picture of cosmic and human life by Lucretius in his poem *De Rerum Natura* (On the Nature of Things). A tense, electric atmosphere permeates this poem. Much more than a didactic work, it is the confession of a man of violent passions who is longing for equanimity, and, while cleansing his own mind of false ideas, proves to be ready to sacrifice even those illusions that apparently promise peace of mind.

The only extant report of Lucretius' life was written by Jerome, the Father of the Church, who certainly does not approve of the poet's opinions and quite possibly is not an impartial biographer. According to Jerome, Lucretius was afflicted by intermittent insanity, and committed suicide. Some sayings of Lucretius himself indicate that he was threatened by mental disease, and it is probable that he became resolved to die voluntarily when he felt that he had lost the tranquil mind which alone, in his belief, makes life tolerable.

It almost happened that Lucretius' poem was entirely lost. Emperor Augustus, who tried to restitute ancient religion, stigmatized Lucretius, whose memory vanished subsequently, and all but one manuscript of his poems was destroyed. The epoch of the Renaissance meant also the revival of Lucretius, who has since been considered one of the greatest poets of world literature. He was admired by Milton, Shelley and Walt Whitman, whose "Apostrophe to Death" may be traced to his reading of Lucretius. Alfred Tennyson, relying on Jerome, made Lucretius the object of a pathological study.

ATOMIC MATERIALISM

ALL nature, as it exists by itself, is founded on two things: there are bodies and there is void in which these bodies are placed and through which they move about. If room and space which we call void did not exist, bodies could not be placed anywhere nor move about at all to any side. Moreover, there is nothing which you can affirm to be at once separate from all body and quite distinct from void, which would, so to say, count as the discovery of a third nature. For whatever shall exist, this of itself must be something or other. Now if it shall admit of touch in however slight and small a measure, it will, be it with a large or be it with little addition, provided it does exist, increase the amount of body and join the sum. But if it shall be intangible and unable to hinder any thing from passing through it on any side, this you are to know will be that which we call empty void. Therefore, besides void and bodies no third nature taken by itself can be left in the number of things, either such as to fall at any time under the ken of our senses or such as any one can grasp by the reason of his mind.

Since there has been found to exist a twofold and widely dissimilar nature of two things, that is to say of body and of place in which things severally go on, each of the two must exist for and by itself and quite unmixed. For wherever there is empty space which we call void, there body is not; wherever again body maintains itself, there empty void nowise exists. First bodies, therefore, are solid and without void.

Again, since there is void in things begotten, solid matter must exist about this void, and no thing can be proved by true reason to conceal in its body and have within it void, unless you choose to allow that which holds it in is solid. Again that can be nothing but a union of matter which can keep in the void of things. Matter, therefore, which consists of a solid body, may be everlasting, though all things else are dissolved.

Moreover, if there were no empty void, the universe would be solid; unless, on the other hand, there were certain bodies to fill up whatever places they occupied, the existing universe would be empty and void space. Therefore, sure enough, body and void are marked off in alternate layers, since the universe is neither of a perfect fullness nor a perfect void.

Therefore, if first bodies (atoms) are, as I have shown, solid and without void, they must be everlasting. Again, unless matter had been eternal, all things before this would have utterly returned to nothing and whatever things we see would have been born anew from nothing. But since I have proved above that nothing can be produced from nothing, and that what is begotten cannot be recalled to nothing, first-beginnings must be of an imperishable body, into which all things can be dissolved at their last hour, that there may be a supply of matter for the reproduction of things. Therefore, first-beginnings (atoms) are of solid singleness, and in no other way can they have been preserved through ages during infinite time past in order to reproduce things.

The nature of the mind and soul is bodily; for when it is seen to push the limbs, rouse the body from sleep, and alter the countenance, and guide and turn about the whole man, and when we see that none of these effects can take place without touch nor touch without body, must we not admit that the mind and the soul are of a bodily matter? Therefore, the nature of the mind must be bodily, since it suffers from bodily weapons and blows.

I will now go on to explain of what kind of body the mind consists and out of what it is formed. First of all I say that it is extremely fine and formed by exceedingly minute bodies. That this is so you may perceive from what follows; nothing that is seen takes place with a velocity equal to that of the mind when it starts some suggestion and actually sets it agoing; the mind, therefore, is stirred with greater rapidity than any of the things whose nature stands out visible to sight. But that which is so passing nimble must consist of seeds exceedingly round and exceedingly minute, in order to be stirred and set in motion by a small moving power. Thus water is moved and heaves by ever so small a force, formed as it is of small particles apt to roll. But the nature of honey is more sticky, its liquid more sluggish, and its movement more dilatory; for the whole mass of matter coheres more closely, because it is made of bodies not so smooth, fine, and round. Since, then, the nature of the mind has been found to be eminently easy to move, it must consist of bodies exceedingly small, smooth, and round.

A tree cannot exist in the ether, nor clouds in the deep sea, nor fishes live in the fields, nor blood exist in woods, nor sap in stones. Where each thing can grow and abide is fixed and ordained. Thus the nature of the mind cannot come into being alone without the body nor exist far away from the sinews and blood. But since in our body even it is fixed and seen to be ordained where the soul and the mind can severally be and grow, it must still more strenuously be denied that it can abide and be born out of the body altogether. Therefore, when the body has died, we must admit that the soul has perished, wrenched away throughout the body.

Death, therefore, to us is nothing, concerns us not a jot, since the nature of the mind is proved to be mortal; and as in time long gone by we felt no distress when the Carthagian hosts came, and all things were shaken by war's troublous uproar, and mortal men were in doubt which of the two peoples it should be to whose empire all must fall by sea and land alike, thus when we shall no more, when there shall have been a separation of body and soul, out of both of which we are each formed into a single being, to us, you may be sure, who then shall be no more, nothing whatever can happen to excite sensation, not if earth shall mingle with sea and sea with heaven.

And even supposing the nature of the mind and power of the soul do feel, after they have been severed from our body, yet that is nothing to us who by the binding tie of marriage between body and soul are formed each into one single being. And if time should gather up our matter after our death and put it once more into position in which it now is, and the light of life be given to us again, this result even would concern us not at all, when the chain of our self-consciousness has once been snapped asunder.

[232]

LULLY, RAYMOND (Raymundus Lullus)

LULLY, RAYMOND (RAYMUNDUS LULLUS) (1235-1315). Because of his great learning, Lully was called "Doctor Illuminatus." He was born on the island of Majorca, where Christian civilization was in close contact with Jewish and Arabic lore. Lully was the first Christian scholar to study the Cabala, which he regarded as a divine science and a true revelation for the rational soul. He also studied Arabic philosophy but became a sworn adversary of Averröism. In 1275 he published his *Ars Generalis,* intended to serve as a basis for all sciences and as a key to invention and discovery. This work was much admired, even several hundred years later by Giordano Bruno and Leibniz. Lully was a great linguist and in 1311 he obtained the consent of the Council of Vienna for teachers of Hebrew and Arabic to be admitted to the papal schools and the great universities. His great ambition was to convert Moslems to Christianity. He agitated for crusades and travelled alone through Islamic North Africa. Probably he suffered a martyr's death. Lully was also a prolific poet, and is considered to have been a great master of the Catalan language.

ON LOVE

LONG and perilous are the paths by where the Lover seeks the Beloved. They are peopled by cares, sighs and tears. They are lit up by love.

Between Hope and Fear, Love made her home. She lives on thought, and when she is forgotten, dies. So unlike the pleasures of this world are their foundations.

There was a contention between the eyes and the memory of the Lover. For the eyes said that it was better to see the Beloved than to remember Him. But Memory said that remembering brings tears to the eyes, and makes the heart to burn with love.

The Lover asked the Understanding and the Will which of them was the nearer to his Beloved. And the two ran, and the Understanding came nearer to the Beloved than did the Will.

The keys of the gate of love are gilded with cares and desires, sighs and tears; the cord which binds them is woven of conscience, devotion, contrition and atonement; the door is kept by justice and mercy.

The path of love is both long and short. For love is clear, pure, and bright, subtle, yet simple, strong, diligent, brilliant, and abounding both in fresh thoughts and old memories.

"What meanest thou by love?" said the Beloved. And the Lover answered "It is to bear on one's heart the sacred marks and the sweet words of the Beloved. It is to long for Him with desire and with tears. It is boldness. It is fervor. It is fear. It is the desire for the Beloved above all things. It is that which causes the Lover to grow faint when he hears the Beloved's praises. It is that in which I die and in which is all my will."

[233]

LU WANG (Lu Hsiang-Shan)

LU WANG (LU HSIANG-SHAN) (1139-1192). Confucianism has become most scholastic in the philosophy of Lu Wang, whose thinking was imbued with the spirit of Buddhism although his terminology remained Confucian. He considered mind as the embodiment of reason, and taught training of the mind by "tranquil repose," in which state the essences of truth and goodness will be perceived by intuition, and the individual will be united with the universe. Neo-Confucianism revolted against Lu Wang's metaphysics which regards moral conduct as a mere consequence of intuitive insight into the essences of reality. In recent times, Lu Wang's philosophy was revived by Liang Sou-ming whose book *The Civilization and Philosophy of the East and the West* (1921) was a great sensation in China.

753

HUMAN Nature is originally good. Any evil in it results from the changes made upon it by [external] things. He who knows the injury caused by [those external] things and who can revert to himself [i.e. can return to his original condition], can then know that goodness is the innate possession of our Nature.

*　　　*　　　*

Mind should not be contaminated with anything; it should stand alone and independent. In its original state, the Mind of Man contains no disorder, [but gradually and] confusedly it is led astray by [external] things. If one has the proper spirit, he will immediately rise [above things], and will [attain the original] good. But if one continuously moves away [from the Original Mind], he will then become corrupted.

*　　　*　　　*

Where there is good there must be evil. [The transition from one to the other] is truly [like] the turning over of one's hand. Goodness, however, is so from the very beginning, whereas evil comes into existence only as a result of such a 'turning over.'

What is it that will injure your Mind? It is Desire. When Desires are many, what we can preserve of our [Original] Mind is inevitably little; and [conversely], when the Desires are few, what we can preserve of our [Original] Mind is inevitably much. Therefore, the Superior Man does not worry that his Mind is not preserved, but rather worries that his Desires are not made few. For if the Desires were eliminated, the Mind would automatically be preserved. Thus, then, does not the preserving of what is good in our Mind depend upon the elimination of what does it injury?

*　　　*　　　*

Common men and vulgarians are submerged [either] by poverty or wealth, or by high or low position, or by benefit or injury, or by profit or loss, or by sounds and colors, or by sensuality and Desire. They [thus] destroy their 'virtuous Mind,' and have no regard for Righteousness and Law. How very lamentable it is!

If scholars of today could only concentrate their attention on Truth and Law—in every affair being observant of the right, and refusing to follow the Passions and Desires—then, even though their understanding were not wholly complete and clear, and their conduct were not entirely according to the mean and moderate, yet they would not fail to be the successors of good men and correct scholars [i.e., of the sages and worthies of ancient times].

*   *   *

There is not one who does not love his parents and respect his elder brother. But when one is blinded by profit and Desire, then it is otherwise.

*   *   *

Those who follow Material Desires gallop [after them] without knowing [where] to stop. Those who follow [superficial] opinions also gallop [after them] without knowing [where] to stop. Therefore, 'although the Way is near, yet they seek for it afar; although a thing is easy [to deal with], yet they seek for it in its difficult [aspects].' But is the Truth [really] remote or the things [really] difficult? [It is because] their opinions are unsound, that they make difficulties for themselves. If one fully realizes one's error, then one's becloudings and doubts will be dissipated and one will reach the place in which to stop.

[234]

LUZZATTO, MOSES HAYIM

LUZZATTO, MOSES HAYIM (1707-1747). Some occurrences in Luzzatto's life show a parallel to that of Spinoza. Just as Spinoza earned his living by grinding optical lenses, Luzzatto did the same by lenses. Like Spinoza, he was ex-communicated from his coreligionists. But Luzzatto remained a faithful Jew, ardently devoted to the cause of Judaism. He even felt himself, like the Messiah, bound to rescue the Jewish people from danger and misery, and he believed that the study of the Cabala would enable him to perform that mission. Notwithstanding pressure on the part of orthodox rabbis, Luzzatto did not turn his thoughts from the mysticism that not only incited his loftiest aspirations but also inspired him to the conception of high ethical principles. Luzzatto was a versatile and gifted writer whose Hebrew style is much admired. He composed a drama, many liturgical poems and philosophical treatises in Hebrew, while his mystical works were written in Aramaic. His best-known book is *Mesillat Yesharim* (Path of the Upright, 1740) which has been compared with Bunyan's *Pilgrim's Progress* though it was not influenced by the latter. In 1746, Luzzatto emigrated to the Holy Land where he died shortly after his arrival.

UNDERSTANDING AND UPRIGHTNESS

UNDERSTANDING: O Uprightness, beloved of my soul, let thy heart take courage; like a girdle gird on strength! For when assistance seems very far away, relief comes suddenly to us. When in the blazing heat, in summer drought, the sky is covered with thick darkness of the clouds, whose thunder's roaring makes the earth beneath to quake; when lightning flashes like an arrow; when the wind rends the mounts, as though they were earthen pitchers; when at the sound of the abundance of rain, all ears grow deaf; then the beasts of the forest all together take refuge, and all the young doves flee unto the clefts of rocks. But in a moment, with the radiance of its light, the sun shines forth, and breaks through, and dispels all clouds and darkness, so that the storm is then as though it had not been. Thus likewise He, who rules the world with might, causes relief from trouble to spring forth within a moment unto the contrite.

Uprightness: O Understanding, O joy of my heart, thy comforting has surely enlarged my heart. For now it seems as though from the words of thy mouth I behold an opening for my hope. But be so kind, if thou hast good tidings, withhold it not from me.

Understanding: Would that I had good tidings! I would not hide it. Howbeit, I hope to bring it to thee, though not now. For the worker of righteousness shall not forever fail, nor shall the hope of the perfect perish forever. Though Arrogance now rises high, reaches to the clouds, and rides prosperously on the high places of the earth; he is strong and firmly rooted, waxes mighty in his strength; he abstains not from all his lusts, and sees no trouble, neither does he know affliction's cords; but he will be brought down unto the nether-world, and there shall his pride of heart be humbled; instead of haughtiness he will clothe himself with disgrace like a garment; instead of glory, he shall take shame for ever. But thou, the fruit of thy faithfulness shalt thou find in due time; the end of all the troubles of thy soul shalt thou behold, and be for ever satisfied. And when relief comes, thou wilt be thankful for thy affliction; for sorrows which are past and gone are even as great joys esteemed on the day of bliss; for the recollection of them increases our gladness.

Uprightness: Fain would I (if I could muster strength) endure bravely by bitter lot, according to my wish, O Understanding; but it is hard for me, whenever mine eyes see the two stones of stumbling, Deceit and Folly, who take counsel together to be as pricks to me and cause me grief of soul. For noisily Folly shouts on the street; she treads on all the highest places of the town with impudent countenance; she knows no fear, and knows no shame; she breaks all covenants, annuls all laws; there is no faithfulness in her; falsehood is her right hand; her merchandise is violence, perjury, and treachery. She is a sister to all evil and a mother to all sin; but all the sons of prudence she oppresses unto death; she sits and speaks against them, and slanders them amidst bowls of wine; her inner thoughts are for evil against them; if she were able, she would devour them as a fish, or would bite them like an ass, and break their bones. And likewise is Deceit; for with the flattering of his mouth he hunts for souls as for a bird, and he feeds the dolt and fool with poison and death covered with honey; he bites when he kisses, and when his hands pretend to cure he bruises; he does according to all his desire, and yet succeeds.

Understanding: Indeed, it is but the illusion of our eyes, for they are eyes of flesh, and, therefore, they confound truth with falsehood. They change darkness into light, and light into darkness. Now, if in matters that they can perceive, they err at every occasion and chance, how greatly must they err in matters hidden and concealed from them! Look at the end of an oar put in the water: Lo, it appears to thee twisted and crooked, although thou knowest in thy heart that in reality it is straight. Sheshai and Talmai appear like ants, when reflected in a concave mirror; but in a convex mirror the effect is reversed. Consider now our spirit, which is like the sea ceaselessly agitated by the conflicts with the wind: its billows surge wildly, and are tossed about from place to place; even so our spirit is never free from grief. And as our sorrows change the moods of our spirit, so are our senses changed from time to time: We only see what we desire; our ears only hear what we long for, or that which our imagination conceives. If we would have seen this world with clear eyes but once, then could we have beheld these our enemies together so afflicted, stricken, and distressed, that we would have said: 'Enough! we have had our fill of vengeance!' Lo, as thine eyes see them all filled with bliss, and satisfied with ease, so truly are their feet entangled in the net, where they are held since long, and whence they will not escape; their steps take hold on the depth of the nether-world; as soon as their feet slip, they will have no power to rise there again. Now take thou courage, gird on strength! I shall go now and look about; if there is aught I hear, I shall return, and tell thee; for the present rest thou still, and direct the meditations of thy heart and all thy thoughts according to thy wisdom. Lo, there is no bravery like the bravery of a man who conquers his strong passions and rules over his spirit; only the heart that keeps vexation far away rests and reposes.

[235]

$\mathcal{M}$

MACH, ERNST

MACH, ERNST (1838-1916). Mach made important discoveries and wrote a number of standard works in the fields of mechanics, theory of heat, optics and acoustics. He was also an academic teacher to whom his audience was enthusiastically devoted. While he refused to be called a philosopher, he did accept acknowledgment as a methodologist of science and a psychologist of knowledge. In fact, he formulated positivism anew, differing from Comte in attributing an equal importance to psychic as to physical facts. His aim was to attain a standpoint entirely free from metaphysics, and to eliminate all hypotheses which cannot be controlled by experience, to create an epistemology which preserves all advantages of empiricism without any ontological implication, be it idealistic or materialistic. Trying to avoid all anthropomorphical conceptions in science, he even regarded causality as a remainder of primitive religion, and would only admit functional dependence, as it is used in mathematical terminology. To him, laws of nature were only more and more improved propositions of experience. The ordinary conception of things was criticized by Mach's statement that language signifies them by the same proper names even when they change. Instead, things were characterized by Mach as symbols for a complex of sensations, such as sounds, colors, smells, pressures, temperature, spatial and temporal impressions. Consequently, the ego, as far as it is scientifically cognizable, is reduced to a bundle of changing sensations, and no fundamental difference between the psychic and physical world is admitted. However, Mach insisted that there are no isolated acts of sensing, feeling, willing and thinking, and that psychic life is not only receptive but also active, although his investigation concentrated upon its receptive side. Mach explained his theories in *Analysis of Sensations* (1886) and *Knowledge and Error* (1905).

To a person accustomed to looking at things from the point of view of the theory of evolution, the high development of modern music as well as the spontaneous and sudden appearance of great musical talent seem, at first glance, a most singular and problematic phenomenon. What could this remarkable development of the power of hearing have had to do with the preservation of the species? Does it not far exceed the measure of the necessary or the useful? What can possibly be the significance of a fine discriminative sense of pitch? Of what use to us is a perceptive sense of pitch? Of what use to us is a perceptive sense of intervals, or of the acoustic colorings of orchestral music?

As a matter of fact, the same question may be proposed with reference to every art, no matter from what province of sense its material is derived. The question is pertinent, also, with regard to the intelligence of a Newton, an Euler, or their like, which apparently far transcends the necessary measure. But the question is most obvious with reference to music, which satisfies no practical need and for the most part depicts nothing. Music, however, is closely allied to the decorative arts. In order to be able to see, a person must have the power of distinguishing the *directions* of lines. Having a *fine* power of distinction, such a person may acquire, as a sort of collateral product of his education, a feeling for *agreeable* combinations of lines. The case is the same with the sense of *color-harmony* following upon the development of the power of distinguishing colors, and so, too, it undoubtedly is with respect to music.

We must bear in mind that talent and genius, however gigantic their achievements may appear to us, constitute but a slight departure from normal endowment. Talent may be resolved into the possession of psychical power slightly above the average in a certain province. And as for genius, it is talent supplemented by a capacity of adaptation extending beyond the youthful period, and by the retention of freedom to overstep routine barriers. The naiveté of the child delights us, and produces almost always the impression of genius. But this impression as a rule quickly disappears, and we perceive that the very same utterances which, as adults, we are wont to ascribe to freedom, have their source, in the child, in a lack of fixed character.

[236]

MACHIAVELLI, NICCOLO

MACHIAVELLI, NICCOLO (1469-1527). In private life it is never a compliment to anyone of whom it is said that he thinks or acts as a Machiavellian. Statesmen, philosophers of history and historians, on the other hand, have often discussed whether or not Machiavelli's principles are sound and of basic importance for political success, or even for public welfare at all.

Machiavelli's disciples have rarely been frank. King Frederick II of Prussia wrote a book opposing Machiavelli, but he practically adopted his views and acted in accordance with them. Mussolini was a great admirer of Machiavelli, but he would not allow his subjects to read his idol's work, *The Prince*, which was written in 1514 and dedicated to Lorenzo de' Medici, whose daughter, Queen Catherine of France, and one of the earliest disciples of the author, was responsible for the notorious Massacre of St. Bartholomew (1572) where the leaders of French Protestantism were murdered.

The Prince contains advice to sovereigns about how to become successful, how to obtain and maintain power, and, especially, how to render political adversaries harmless and to check a dissatisfied people. This advice was founded upon the author's knowledge of, or ideas on, the possibilities and limitations of human nature. Any moral standard is consciously eliminated. Reality, as Machiavelli saw it, is put above ideals. Success, as the end, has to justify the means. Man, especially the man of genius, was regarded by Machiavelli as an aesthetic phenomenon, and his struggle for existence and power seemed to him like a drama on the stage.

Since Machiavelli professed republicanism in other writings, and since he served the republican government of Florence, his native city, for fourteen years it has often been doubted whether he meant what he said in *The Prince*. Probably he was a republican in principle, but, in the actual situation of Italy at that time, Machiavelli, an ardent Italian patriot, built all his hopes upon a tyrant.

As a statesman, Machiavelli was a failure. As a philosopher, he was to say the least, disputable. But he was a magnificent writer, and his work is, apart from its great influence, valuable as a document of the spirit, or, at least of a tendency, of the Renaissance.

PROMISES AND PRINCES

How honorable it is for a prince to keep his word, and act rather with integrity than collusion, I suppose everybody understands: nevertheless, experience has shown in our times that those princes who have not pinned themselves up to that punctuality and preciseness have done great things, and by their cunning and subtility have not only circumvented those with whom they had to deal, but have overcome and been too hard for those who have been so superstitiously exact. For further explanation you must understand there are two ways of contending—by law and by force: the first is proper to men; the second to beasts; but because many times the first is insufficient, recourse must be had to the second. It belongs, therefore, to a prince to understand both—when to make use of the rational and when of the brutal way; and this is recommended to princes, though abstrusely, by ancient writers, who tell them how Achilles and several other princes were committed for education to Chiron the Centaur, who was half man and half beast—thus showing how necessary it is for a prince to be acquainted with both natures, for one without the other will be of little duration. Seeing, therefore, it is of such importance to a prince to take upon him the nature and disposition of a beast, of all the whole flock he ought to imitate the lion and the fox; for the lion is in danger of toils and snares, and the fox of the wolf; so that he must be a fox to find out the snares, and a lion to fight away the wolves, but they who keep wholly to the lion have no true notion of themselves. A prince, therefore, who is wise and prudent, cannot or ought not to keep his word, when the keeping of it is to his prejudice, and the causes for which he promised removed. Were men all good this doctrine would not be taught, but because they are wicked and not likely to be punctual with you, you are not obliged to any such strict-ness with them; nor was there ever any prince that lacked lawful pretence to justify his breach of promise. I might give many modern examples, and show how many confed-erations, and peaces, and promises have been broken by the infidelity of princes, and how he that best personated the fox had the better success. Nevertheless, it is of great consequence to disguise your inclination, and to play the hypocrite well; and men are so simple in their temper and so submissive to their present necessities that he that is neat and cleanly in his collusions shall never want people to practice them upon. I cannot forbear one example which is still fresh in our memory. Alexander VI never did, nor thought of, anything but cheating, and never wanted matter to work upon; and though no man promised a thing with greater asseveration, nor confirmed it with more oaths and imprecations, and observed them less, yet understanding the world well he never miscarried.

A prince, therefore, is not obliged to have all the fore-mentioned good qualities in reality, but it is necessary he have them in appearance; nay, I will be bold to affirm that, having them actually, and employing them upon all occa-sions, they are extremely prejudicial, whereas, having them only in appearance, they turn to better account; it is honor-able to seem mild, and merciful, and courteous, and reli-gious, and sincere and indeed to be so, provided your mind be so rectified and prepared that you can act quite contrary upon occasion. And this must be premised, that a prince, especially if come but lately to the throne, cannot observe all those things exactly which cause men to be esteemed vir-tuous, being oftentimes necessitated, for the preservation of his state, to do things inhuman, uncharitable, and irreli-gious; and, therefore, it is convenient for his mind to be at his command, and flexible to all the puffs and variations of fortune; not forbearing to be good while it is in his choice, but knowing how to be evil when there is a necessity. A prince, then, is to have particular care that nothing falls

from his mouth but what is full of the five qualities aforesaid, and that to see and hear him he appears all goodness,
integrity, humanity, and religion, which last he ought to pretend to more than ordinarily, because more men do judge by
the eye than by the touch; for everybody sees but few understand; everybody sees how you appear, but few know what
in reality you are, and those few dare not oppose the opinion of the multitude, who have the majesty of their prince
to defend them; and in the actions of all men, especially
princes, where no man has power to judge, everyone looks
to the end. Let a prince, therefore, do what he can to preserve his life, and continue his supremacy, the means which
he uses shall be thought honorable, and be commended by
everybody; because the people are always taken with the
appearance and event of things, and the greatest part of the
world consists of the people; those few who are wise taking
place when the multitude has nothing else to rely upon.
There is a prince at this time in being (but his name I shall
conceal) who has nothing in his mouth but fidelity and peace;
and yet had he exercised either the one or the other, they
had robbed him before this both of his power and reputation.

[237]

MAETERLINCK, MAURICE

MAETERLINCK, MAURICE (1862-1949). Motoring, canoeing,
skating, bicycling, and, in his earlier years, even boxing, were
Count Maeterlinck's recreations, even in his advanced age. Perhaps
he was the greatest sportsman among poets and thinkers, since the
end of the ancient Greek civilization. But, as a poet and thinker,
Maeterlinck has conceived of life mostly as a fragile, human existence troubled by indefinite fright or as the presentiment of an
inevitable catastrophe. His principal experience is the awareness
that the sentiments, instincts and ideas of humanity are incapable
of remaining consistent as soon as what he called the Unknown
appears in life. He was convinced that no human concept of reality
corresponds to the metaphysically Real, and that, when the Unknown and the metaphysically Real interfere with human life,
man's habitual connection between his ideas and senses is dis-

765

rupted. All this drove Maeterlinck to a mysticism, though it did not prevent him from remaining fond of science. He proved to be an excellent empirical scientist, observing the life of bees, ants and spiders with unsurpassed accuracy. Maeterlinck's mysticism was founded upon pantheism and a sympathy with whatever exists. He felt himself in intimate touch with whatever suffers and desires, and his moral teachings pronounced universal love.

Maeterlinck studied the mystical authors of the Christian Middle Ages, but it was two American authors who influenced him decisively in his formative years. Edgar Allan Poe impressed him by his poetry of horror, and Ralph Waldo Emerson revealed to him the sense of spiritual life, and gave his thinking the direction toward the contemplation of eternity. Maeterlinck also strongly sympathized with Walt Whitman with whom he shared the conviction that nothing can perish definitely. Maeterlinck was no traditionalist. He did not regret any abandonment of a creed, or even the collapse of a civilization that has lost its vitality. In his later years, Maeterlinck turned more and more from mysticism to modern science.

LOOK OVER YOUR SHOULDER

WE are all searching for happiness, yet can anyone define it? A friend of mine was recently trying to tell her small daughter what it is. After a long dissertation she asked the child: "Now do you understand?" Whereupon the little girl replied disarmingly: "Yes, Mother, except when you explain." Definitions abound, but I know perfectly as long as I am not asked!

How charming is the old Persian legend about the king who was very powerful but also very unhappy. He consulted his seers to find out what he must do to be happy. After diligent research they found a clue to the dilemma. "Your Majesty," they said, "you must wear the shirt of a happy man." There followed a long search and finally a poor peasant was found who was perfectly happy. He was a ragged fellow who wore no shirt.

The more we reflect on this phantom called happiness which we all seek so eagerly, the more we perceive its dependence upon the happiness of other people.

I once knew a man who died, leaving a vast fortune

which he himself said in an obituary letter was more than any one man should possess. He went on to say how he had spent futile years trying to find happiness. Doubtless he had everything that money could offer, yet the answer to his problem was actually unbuyable. It was probably over his shoulder, to be had free of charge.

Another man I knew was a helpless cripple, and utterly incurable. I could not help asking him whether his affliction colored his views. "Yes," he answered, "but I make the colors!"

Indeed, the strenuous soul would seem to be built up of disillusions. Every deception and disappointment, every hope that has crumbled to dust, is possessed of a hidden strength of its own that adds strength to all truths. The more disillusions that fall at our feet, the more surely and nobly will great reality shine on us.

Many a happiness in life, as many a disaster, can be due to chance, but the peace within us can never be governed by chance. Call it what you may, heart, will, soul or conscience, these words mean more or less the same thing: the spiritual riches of man. Without peace in our hearts how can we expect peace in the world?

I would not go so far as to say that it is given to all men to be happy in exterior things. External circumstances can do a lot; but it lies within the power of the least favored amongst us to find a happy inner life by being gentle and just and generous. He should learn to look on his fellows without envy or malice or futile regret, the things which most militate against true happiness.

Remember that happiness is as contagious as gloom. It should be the first duty of those who are happy to let others know of their gladness.

The French word for happiness is *bonheur*, meaning "good hour." Let us gather hours of gladness. So many are lost because we are not conscious of them at the time.

We are now living in a rare epoch of history when, in the space of a few raging years, the character and destiny of the world is being determined for an unknown length of time. The hope of earthly salvation should fill all of our hearts and should rest mainly on solidarity and her companion goodness.

With this anticipation for the benefit of collective mankind, let us start individually by making life less difficult for each other in every way possible.

Never forget that those who bring happiness to the lives of others cannot keep it from themselves. And more often than not the opportunity lies over your shoulder!

[238]

MAIMON, SALOMON

MAIMON, SALOMON (1753-1800). Immanuel Kant recognized Maimon as the most acute of all his critics. The famous author of the *Critique of Pure Reason* probably knew what hardships Maimon had endured before he could publish his *Versuch ueber die Transcendentalphilosophie,* in which he successfully dealt with problems not understandable to the great majority of German thinkers of that time. When Maimon, in 1778, left his native village of Nieszwicz, Lithuania, he had been trained in the Heder and Yeshiva, had studied the Talmud, the Cabala and Maimonides, but had had no opportunity to be taught a modern language. Without any teacher he had deciphered the German alphabet by means of adventurous combinations and immense labor; but he could not pronounce a German word correctly when he crossed the borders of Prussia. It took him a long time to learn German thoroughly. It took him even more time to adapt himself to the moderate mentality of his German contemporaries. For many years, his violent temper prevented him from concentrating upon the studies he had longed for. He provoked the indignation of his protector Moses Mendelssohn by his radical views and his licentiousness. He perplexed a Protestant minister who was to baptize him by his declaration that he regarded Judaism a religion superior to Christianity. After twelve years of wandering, Maimon anticipated many important views of post-Kantian philosophy, and influenced Fichte particularly. More than a century after Maimon's death, his thoughts became even more influential than during his lifetime. But great as his philosophical thinking has been, his most interesting work is his autobiography which, in 1792, the German psychologist Karl

768

Philipp Moritz edited under the title *Salomon Maimons Eigene Lebensgeschichte*. This book contains a charming description of Jewish life in Lithuania and a courageous vindication of rabbinic Judaism.

ON JEWISH RELIGION

POSITIVE religion is distinguished from *natural* in the very same way as the positive laws of a state from natural laws. The latter are those which rest on a self-acquired, indistinct knowledge, and are not duly defined in regard to their application, while the former rest on a distinct knowledge received from others, and are completely defined in regard to their application.

A *positive* religion however must be carefully distinguished from a *political* religion. The former has for its end merely the correction and accurate definition of knowledge, that is, *instruction* regarding the first cause: and the knowledge is communicated to another, according to the measure of his capacity, just as it has been received. But the latter has for its end mainly the welfare of the state. Knowledge is therefore communicated, not just as it has been received, but only in so far as it is found serviceable to this end. Politics, merely as politics, requires to concern itself about *true religion* as little as about *true morality*. The injury, that might arise from this, can be prevented by other means which influence men at the same time, and thus all can be kept in equilibrium. Every political religion is therefore at the same time positive, but every positive religion is not also political.

Natural religion has no *mysteries* any more than merely positive religion. For there is no mystery implied in one man being unable to communicate his knowledge to another of defective capacity with the same degree of completeness which he himself has attained; otherwise mysteries might be attributed to all the sciences, and there would then be *mysteries of mathematics* as well as *mysteries of religion*. Only *political religion* can have mysteries, in order to lead men in an indirect way to the attainment of the *political end*, inasmuch as they are made to believe that thereby they can best attain their *private ends,* though this is not always in reality the case. There are *lesser* and *greater* mysteries in the political religions. The former consist in the *material* knowledge of all particular operations and their connection with one another. The latter, on the contrary, consist in the knowledge of the *form,* that is, of the end by which the former are determined. The former constitute the totality of the *laws of religion,* but the latter contains the *spirit of the laws.*

The *Jewish religion,* even at its earliest origin among the nomadic patriarchs, is already distinguished from the *heathen* as *natural religion,* inasmuch as, instead of the *many incomprehensible* gods of heathenism, the *unity of an incomprehensible* God lies at its foundation. For as the particular causes of the effects, which in general give rise to a religion, are in themselves unknown, and we do not feel justified in transferring to the causes the attributes of the particular effects, in order thereby to characterize them, there remains nothing but the idea of cause in general, which must be related to all effects without distinction. This cause cannot even be *analogically* determined by the effects. For the effects are opposed to one another, and neutralize each other even in the same object. If therefore we ascribed them all to one and the same cause, the cause could not be analogically determined by any.

The *heathen* religion, on the other hand, refers every kind of effect to a special cause, which can of course be characterized by its effect. As a *positive* religion the Jewish is distinguished from the heathen by the fact, that it is not a merely political religion, that is, a religion which has for its end the social interest (in opposition to true knowledge and private interest); but in accordance with the spirit of its founder, it is adapted to the theocratic form of the national Government, which rests on the principle, that only the true religion, based on rational knowledge, can harmonize with the interest of the state as well as of the individual. Considered in its *purity*, therefore, it has no mysteries in the proper sense of the word; that is to say, it has no doctrines which, in order to reach their end, men *will* not disclose, but merely such as *can* not be disclosed to all.

[239]

MAIMONIDES (Moses Ben Maimon)

MAIMONIDES (MOSES BEN MAIMON) (1135-1204). Among the rabbis of the later Middle Ages and centuries thereafter, an adage was current, saying, "From Moses to Moses there is none like unto Moses." It means simply that Maimonides is to be regarded as the greatest figure in Jewish history since the man who delivered the Ten Commandments to the Jewish people. In fact, the spiritual development of Judaism up to the present age is incomprehensible without taking account of Maimonides' activities as a codifier, judge and commentator of the Bible and the Talmud. His *Mishneh Torah* (Copy of the Law) was the first systematic exposition of Jewish religion. His "articles of faith" are either quoted or poetically paraphrased in modern Jewish prayer books.

The philosophical thoughts of Maimonides strongly influenced not only Jewish but also Islamic and Christian philosophers. The intention of his main work *Moreh Nebuchim* (Guide of the Perplexed, in Arabic *Dalalat al Hairin*) was to prove that the teachings of Judaism are in harmony with the results of philosophical thinking, and that beyond that, they offer insight which reason alone cannot obtain. For this purpose, Maimonides prevalently used the works of Aristotle, and, to a lesser extent, those of Plato. Christian philosophers were eager to apply Maimonides' doctrine to the defense of their own religion or to the explanation of general principles. Thus did William of Auvergne, Alexander of Hales, Albertus Magnus, Meister Eckhart, Thomas Aquinas and, through him, all medieval and modern Thomists. The great jurist, Hugo Grotius, was inspired by Maimonides' views on the history of religion.

Born in Cordova, Spain, Maimonides was forced to emigrate, at first to Morocco, then to Egypt where he earned his living by practicing medicine. In his medical treatises he anticipated modern discoveries concerning the affliction of the body by psychic factors, allergies, epilepsy, the nervous system and individual constitution. Almost all of his books were written in Arabic and shortly thereafter translated into Hebrew and Latin.

A MAN MUST CHOOSE THE GOLDEN MEAN

MEN have various dispositions, which are different from, and diametrically opposed to, one another. There is one man who is irascible, and is continually angry; while there is another who is of a calm disposition and does not get angry at all; and even if he gets angry, his wrath is mild, and this only happens once in several years. There is one man who is exceedingly haughty, while there is another who is exceedingly meek. There is one man who is voluptuous, whose soul can never be satisfied with indulging in pleasures; while there is another whose heart is so pure, that he desires not even the bare necessities which the body requires. There is one man who is exceedingly avaricious, whose soul cannot be satisfied with all the riches of the world, as it is written: 'He that loveth silver shall not be satisfied with silver;' while there is another who is so unambitious, that he is content with a small thing which is hardly sufficient for him, and does not strive to obtain all that he needs. There is one man who emaciates himself by starvation, and saves all his money, and is very grieved when he has to spend a Perutah for his food; while there is another who wilfully squanders all his possessions. And in the same manner are all other dispositions, as for instance, one man is hilarious, while another is melancholy; one is niggardly, while another is generous; one is cruel, while another is merciful; one is faint-hearted, while another is courageous, and so forth.

Between two contrary dispositions which are at the two extremes there are intermediate dispositions which are likewise different from one another. There are some dispositions which are inherent in a man from his very birth, in accordance with the nature of his body; while there are others to which a man's nature is so predisposed, that they are readily adopted by him sooner than any other; and there are still others which are not inherent in a man from his very birth, but are acquired by him through imitating other men, or are adopted by him of his own accord because of an idea that occurred to him, or because, having heard that this disposition was good for him and worthy of being cultivated, he regulated his conduct accordingly, until it has become fixed in his heart.

The two diametrically opposed extremes of all dispositions are not the good way, and it behooves no man to walk therein, nor to adopt them. If a man finds that his nature inclines toward one of them, or is predisposed to adopt it, or that he has already acquired it, and regulated his conduct accordingly, he should return to that which is good, and walk in the way of the good ones, which is the right way.

The right way is the intermediate quality of every disposition of man, and that is the disposition which is equidistant from both extremes, being neither nearer to the one nor to the other. The ancient sages have therefore commanded that a man should always put, arrange, and direct his dispositions in the middle course, so that he may be sound in his body. In what manner? He should not be irascible, easily provoked to anger, nor as a dead man that is insensible, but should take the middle course: he should only get angry on account of an important matter, when it behooves to show anger in order that a similar offense should not be again committed. Similarly, a man should only desire those things which are necessary and indispensable for his body, as it is written: 'The righteous eateth to the satisfying of his desire.' In like manner, he should not exert himself in his business more than to obtain the necessities of life, as it is written: 'A little is good for the righteous.' He should not be too niggardly, nor squander his money, but should give charity according to his means, and in a fitting manner lend to him who is in need. He should not be hilarious and mirthful, nor gloomy and melancholy, but always happy and contented and of cheerful countenance. In the same manner should all his dispositions be. This way is the way of the wise; every man whose dispositions are intermediate, that is to say, in the middle course, is called wise.

A man who is very strict with himself, and removes himself from the middle course slightly toward one side or another, is called pious. In what manner? He who removes himself from haughtiness toward the other extreme, and is very humble, is called pious; and this is the quality of piety. If, however, he moves only as far as the middle, and is modest, he is called wise; and this is the quality of wisdom. In the same manner are all other dispositions. The pious men of ancient times used to turn their dispositions from the middle course toward the extremes; some dispositions were made to incline toward the one extreme, while others toward the other extreme; this is beyond the line required by the law. We, however, are commanded to walk in middle courses, which are the good and upright ways, as it is written: 'And thou shalt walk in His ways.' In interpreting this commandment, the sages say: 'As He is called gracious, so shalt thou be gracious; as He is called merciful, so shalt thou be merciful; as He is called holy, so shalt thou be holy.' And for this reason did the prophets call God by all these attributes: slow to anger, abundant in lovingkindness, righteous, upright, perfect, mighty, strong, and so forth, in order to let us know that these are good and upright ways, according to which a man is obliged to regulate his conduct, so that he may be like unto Him, as far as lies in his power.

In what manner should a man accustom himself to these dispositions, so that they should become part of his nature? He should do once, and twice, and three times the deeds which he is to do according to the intermediate dispositions, and should always keep on repeating them until they have become so easy for him that he can do them without the slightest effort; the dispositions will then become fixed in his soul. Because the Creator is called by these names, they are according to the middle course wherein we are obliged to walk, and this way is called the way of God; it is the one which Abraham taught his children, as it is written: 'For I have known him, to the end that he may command. . . .' And he who walks in this way brings welfare and blessing to himself, as it is written: 'To the end that the Lord may bring upon Abraham that which He hath spoken of Him.'

[240]

MAINE DE BIRAN
(Pierre Francois Gonthier De Biran)

MAINE DE BIRAN (PIERRE FRANÇOIS GONTHIER DE BIRAN) (1766-1824). Maine de Biran was a man of strong moral and metaphysical feelings, but his psychological curiosity was always stronger and sometimes diverted his thoughts from their initial aims. For years his military and political activities prevented him from concentrating upon philosophy. He was strictly opposed to Condillac and Cabanis whom he regarded as the representatives of the spirit of the eighteenth century and whom he accused of evaporating human feelings by their analysis; but, in fact, as a psychologist, Maine de Biran was closer to them than he supposed himself to be. Nevertheless, many of his ideas seem to be anticipations of those of Whitehead, Santayana, Hocking, Bergson, Scheler and recent existentialism.

Serving in King Louis XVI's bodyguard, Maine de Biran was wounded in the fight against the people of Paris during the early revolutionary days of July 1789. After his regiment had been disbanded, he turned to mathematics and philosophy. Despite his ardent royalism and hatred of the Revolution, he served under the Directory from 1795 on, and was elected a member of the Council of the Five Hundred in 1797. The coup d'état of Fructidor induced him to retire into private life until Napoleon, in 1805, appointed him sub-prefect and member of the Corps Législatif. In 1811, Maine de Biran abandoned the Emperor in favor of the Bourbons whose return to power he openly demanded. King Louis XVIII awarded him many honors but the ultra-reactionary faction accused him of being too moderate.

From the time of his childhood, Maine de Biran was, as he said, "astonished while feeling that I exist," and he was led by an instinct to analyze his consciousness in order "to know how I can live and be myself." Contrary to Descartes, he conceived man as a willing creature. *Volo, ergo sum* is his device. Will signifies the constant tension in man that urges him to act. Will is the primary fact of consciousness that gives man the feeling of being united with a body and brings him into contact with the outer world and its resistance to his actions. The knowledge of substance is derived

775

from observation of the will. In his *New Essays on Anthropology* which were not finished when he died, Maine de Biran describes three stages of life. The first is that of animal life which is dominated by blind passions which are independent of the will. The second experience is will, intelligence, the meaning of ideas and words, and the conflict of wills. The third stage is that of spirit in which man identifies himself with the eternal source of power and insight. At its height, man is happy to lose his ego. At any stage, man needs the support of God.

Maine de Biran claimed to have overcome all difficulties which are the result of an erroneous tendency to comprehend in abstract or separate terms what is given in relatives or to divide into sections what really is a running stream.

THE IMPRESSIONS MOST WEAKENED BY REPETITION

OUR sensations certainly fade and vanish sooner and more completely in proportion to the *passivity* of their respective organs. This condition is bound up with the forced continuance of impressions, since then the will cannot directly react to distract or to stop them.

And first, inner impressions, however little they persist in the same degree, tend to be converted into habits of *temperament* and, although in this state they continue to influence the feeling of existence, which they make sad or painful, easy or agreeable, they cease nevertheless to be felt in themselves, but are lost and merged in this multitude of vague impressions, which cooperate to form the habitual inner feeling of our passive existence. Such an effect indeed seems to be connected with the equilibrium or the equal reaction of sensory forces which are coordinated with each other in course of time in such a way that one impression does not continue to dominate too much over the others. But we shall consider them soon in another connection.

Passive touch, spread over the whole surface of the body, is exposed at all points to the equal, continued or varied excitation of surrounding fluids or objects in motion, which stimulate it, titillate it, prick it, etc., without its being able to react in order to change or suspend their effects. But sensitivity is incessantly on the watch and puts itself on an equality with impressions by moderating and annulling them (always excepting cases of serious and sudden lesions).

The equilibrium of which we have spoken and the action of the sensory principle to re-establish it, are manifest in no other kind of impressions more clearly than in those which correspond to tactile sensations and particularly to those of heat or cold. It is well known how easily our bodies are adapted to changes of climate and temperature, provided that the transition is not too sudden; how a uniform temperature long continued becomes insensible to us; how the sensation is always proportional to the actual condition of the organ (so that such and such a degree alternately freezes or burns us); how from this organ it is extended from point to point and affects us the more intensely the more concentrated it is. In short, it is well known that the sensitive principle always tends to maintain in us an almost even heat, which it can do only by successively raising or lowering our temperature and restoring the inner equilibrium, which without this activity would be disturbed every instant.

Odors also gradually become fainter and end by becoming insensible. "My sachet scented with flowers," said Montaigne, "is first of service to my nose; but, after I have used it a week, it is no longer of any use except to the noses of bystanders." Odors are necessarily continuous since their organ is passive and breathing cannot be interrupted. First they stimulate the whole system, which attunes itself to them and soon ceases to experience any change from them. In relation to appetite they have other effects which we shall presently indicate.

Tastes become deadened more through repetition than through their continuance and always in proportion as the organ is more passive in experiencing them. Many an agreeable or disagreeable taste, which has affected us in the beginning, particularly in a drink, soon becomes through custom absolutely insensible—nauseous flavors excepted. Taste, like odor, becomes accustomed to the strongest artificial irritants and it is almost paralyzed by their repeated activity and, nevertheless, these same irritants become imperious needs.

Sounds, considered as passive impressions of an organ devoid of mobility, can undergo all the gradual fading which results from the repetition and continuance to which they are particularly susceptible. We experience daily how easy it is to become accustomed to every kind of noise to the point of becoming absolutely unconscious of it. This body, this *material* of sound, moreover, which in the beginning affects us so poignantly by itself and independently of any perceived relation, of any effect of melody, loses also through its frequency all power to stimulate. But though the impression in this case weakens like sensation, it is not obedient to the same law, to the same mode of diminishing, as perception. The motor activity, combined with the sensory, changes the simple results and gives rise to other habits. The auditory impression may lose its power of attraction, but the vocal impression will keep its distinctness.

Light stimulates the fibres of the retina with a certain force. Sensitivity—put into play—contracts or dilates the pupil through an activity quite independent of the will. It raises the tone of the organ, adjusts it, accommodates it to the degree of the external stimulus, in such a way that it is no longer affected, that it no longer feels the continued or repeated impression in the same degree.

[241]

MALEBRANCHE, NICOLAS

MALEBRANCHE, NICOLAS (1638-1715). Malebranche came to philosophy in a way that differs from that of many other philosophers. He began to study it, and, disappointed by its methods and results, turned to theology. He became a member of the Congregation of the Oratory, displayed religious ardor, accepted the doctrines of the Church as unchanging truth, though he was never quite satisfied with the arguments used by traditional theology. In

1664, by chance, he picked up in a bookstore Descartes' treatise *On Man*, and after perusing some pages fugitively, became fascinated by the author's ideas. For the following three years, Malebranche studied Descartes' works, doing nothing else. In 1674, ten years after his haphazard acquaintance with Descartes, he published the first volume of his *Recherche de la Vérité* (Investigation of Truth).

Following Descartes' example, Malebranche looked upon philosophical doubt as his indispensable starting point. But he deviated from his master by conceiving doubt as an act of will, of freedom.

Contrary to Descartes as well as to Bacon, Spinoza and many others, knowledge was not to him of causal determination or explanation. For, according to Malebranche there is no cause in the world but God. All creatures are united with God in an immediate manner. They depend essentially and directly on Him. There is no dependence of one creature or thing on another, since all things are powerless without God's will. All being, all knowing, all acting are produced by God. Man has only the faculties of desire and choice which are constituents of his liberty. As far as he has love of God, he has a will. As far he has a vision of God, he has reason. What he regards as causal connection of things is not conditional but only apparent, or as Malebranche says, occasional causes.

Since Malebranche reserved all causal acting to God alone, causality was completely abandoned by him as a principle of knowledge. Knowledge was to Malebranche evidence of intuition. He went so far as to declare evidence superior to faith. For faith may change but evidence shall subsist.

By emphasizing evidence, Malebranche influenced Leibniz, Locke, Berkeley and Hume. In modern times, Santayana, Husserl and Scheler adopted similar views.

ON GOD'S INTERVENTION

You cannot of yourself move your arm or alter your position, situation, posture, do to other men good or evil, or effect the least change in the world. You find yourself in the world, without any power, immovable as a rock, stupid, so to speak, as a log of wood. Let your soul be united to your body as closely as you please, let there come about a union between it and all the bodies of your environment. What advantage would you derive from this imaginary union? What would you do in order merely to move the tip of your finger, or to utter even a monosyllable? Alas! unless God came to your aid, your efforts would be vain, the desires which you formed impotent; for just think, do you know what is necessary for the pronunciation of your best friend's name, or for bending or holding up that particular finger which you use most? But let us suppose that you know quite well what no one knows, about which even some scientists are not agreed, namely, that the arm can be moved only by means of the animal spirits, which flowing along the nerves to the muscles make them contract and draw towards themselves the bones to which they are attached. Let us suppose that you are acquainted with the anatomy and the action of your mechanism as well as a clockmaker is acquainted with his handiwork. But, at any rate, remember the principle that no one but the Creator of bodies can be their mover. This principle is sufficient to bind, indeed to annihilate, all your boasted faculties; for, after all, the animal spirits are bodies, however small they may be. They are, indeed, nothing but the subtlest parts of the blood and the humors. God alone, then, is able to move these small bodies. He alone knows how to make them flow from the brain along the nerves, from the nerves through the muscles, from one muscle to its antagonist—all of which is necessary for the movement of our limbs. It follows that, notwithstanding the conjunction of soul and body in whatever way it may please you to imagine it, you would be dead and inert if it were not for the fact that God wills to adapt his volitions to yours—His volitions, which are always effective, to your desires, which are always impotent. This then is the solution of the mystery. All creatures are united to God alone in an immediate union. They depend essentially and directly upon Him. Being all alike equally impotent, they cannot be in reciprocal dependence upon one another. One may, indeed, say that they are united to one another and that they depend upon one another. I grant this, provided it is not understood in the ordinary and vulgar sense of the term, provided that one agrees that they are so only in consequence of the immutable and ever effective will of the Creator, only in consequence of the general laws which He has established, and by means of which He regulates the ordinary course of His providence. God has willed that my arm shall be set in motion at the instant that I will it myself (given the necessary conditions). His will is efficacious, His will is immutable, it alone is the source of my power and faculties. He has willed that I should experience certain feelings, certain emotions, whenever there are present in my brain certain traces, or whenever a certain disturbance takes place therein. In a word, He has willed— He wills incessantly—that the modifications of the mind and those of the body shall be reciprocal. This is the conjunction and the natural dependence of the two parts of which we are constituted. It is but the mutual and reciprocal dependence of our modifications based on the unshakable foundation of the divine decrees—decrees which through their efficacy endow me with the power which I have over my body, and through it over certain other bodies—decrees which through their immutability unite me with my body, and through it to my friends, my possessions, my whole environment. I derive nothing whatever from my own nature, nothing from the nature imagined by the philosophers—all comes from God and His decrees. God has linked together all His works, though He has not on that account produced in them entities charged with the function of union. He has subordinated them to one another without endowing them with active qualities. The latter are but the vain pretensions of human pride, the chimerical productions of the philosophers' ignorance. Men's senses being affected by the presence of objects, their minds being moved by the inner feeling which they have of their own movements, they have not recognized the invisible operations of the Creator, the uniformity of His mode of action, the fruitfulness of His laws, the ever-present efficacy of His volitions, the infinite wisdom of His providence. Do not say any more that your soul is united to your body more intimately than to anything else; since its immediate union is with God alone, since the divine decrees are the indissoluble bonds of union between the various parts of the universe and of the marvellous network of all the subordinate causes.

ON METAPHYSICS

THEOTIMUS. But let us return to metaphysics. Our soul is not united to our body in the ordinary sense of these terms. It is immediately and directly united to God alone. It is through the efficacy of His action alone that the three of us are here together; nay, more, that we all share the same opinion, are penetrated by the same truth, animated, it seems to me, by the same spirit, kindled with the same enthusiasm. God joins us together by means of the body, in consequence of the laws of the communication of movements. He affects us with the same feelings in consequence of the laws of the conjunction of body and soul. But, Aristes, how comes it about that we are so strongly united in mind? Theodore utters some words unto your ears. These are but the air struck by the organs of the voice. God transforms, so to speak, this air into words, into various sounds. He makes you understand these various sounds through the modifications by which you are affected. But where do you get the sense of the words from? Who is it that discloses to you and to myself the same truth as Theodore is contemplating? If the air which He forces back when speaking does not contain the sounds you hear, assuredly it will not contain the truths which you understand.

ARISTES. I follow you, Theotimus. We are united in mind because all of us are united to the universal Reason which illumines all intelligences. I am wiser than you think. Theodore has already led me to the point to which you wish to conduct me. He has convinced me that there is nothing visible, nothing which can act upon the mind and reveal itself thereto, but the substance of Reason, which is not only efficacious but also intelligent. Yes, nothing that is created can be the immediate object of our knowledge. We see things in this material world, wherein our bodies dwell, only because our mind through its attention lives in another world, only because it contemplates the beauties of the archetypal and intelligible world which Reason contains. As our bodies live upon the earth and find sustenance in the fruits which it produces, so our minds feed on the same truths as the intelligible and immutable substance of the divine Word contains. The words which Theodore utters into my ears urge me, in consequence of the law of the conjunction of soul and body, to be attentive to the truths which he is discovering in the supreme Reason. This turns my mind in the same direction as his. I see what he sees because I look where he looks, and by means of the words whereby I reply to his words, though both alike are, in themselves, devoid of sense, I discuss with him and enjoy with him a good which is common to all, for we are all essentially united to Reason, so united that without it we could enter into no social bond with anyone.

THEOTIMUS. Your reply, Aristes, surprises me extremely. How, knowing all that you are now telling me, could you reply to Theodore that we are united to our body more intimately than to anything else?

ARISTES. I did so because one is inclined to say only what is present to the memory, and because abstract truths do not present themselves to the mind so naturally as those that one has heard all one's life. When I have meditated as much as Theotimus I shall speak no more in mechanical fashion, but regulate my words in accordance with the deliverances of inner truth. I understand then now, and I shall not forget it all my life, that we are united immediately and directly to God. It is in the light of His wisdom that He makes us see the magnificence of His works, the model upon which He forms them, the immutable art which regulates their mechanism and movements, and it is through the efficacy of His will that He unites us to our body, and through our body to all those in our environment.

THEODORE. You might add that it is through the love

which He bears to Himself that He communicates to us that invincible enthusiasm which we have for the Good. But of this we shall speak on another occasion. It is sufficient for the present that you are quite convinced that the mind can be united immediately and directly to God alone, that we can have no intercourse with created beings except by the power of the Creator, which is communicated to us only in consequence of His laws, and that we can enter into no social union amongst ourselves and with Him except through the Reason with which He is consubstantial. This once granted, you will see that it is of the highest importance for us to try to acquire some knowledge of the attributes of this supreme Being, since we are so much dependent upon Him; for, after all, He acts upon us necessarily according to His nature. His mode of activity must bear the character of His attributes. Not only must our duties tend towards His perfections, but our whole course of action ought to be so regulated in accordance with His that we may take the proper measures for the realization of our purposes, and that we may find a combination of causes which is favorable to these designs. In this connection, faith and experience teach us many truths by means of the short-cut of authority and by the proofs of very pleasant and agreeable feelings. But all this intelligence does not give us forthwith; it ought to be the fruit and the recompense of our work and application. For the rest, being made to know and love God, it is clear that there is no occupation which is preferable to the meditation upon the divine perfections which should animate us with charity and regulate all the duties of a rational creature.

ARISTES. I understand quite well, Theodore, that the worship which God demands from minds is a spiritual worship. It consists in being full of the knowledge of Him, full of love of Him, in forming judgments of Him which are worthy of His attributes, and in regulating in accordance with His will all the movements of our heart. For God is spirit, and He wishes to be worshipped in spirit and in truth. But I must confess that I am extremely afraid lest I should form judgments on the divine perfections which would dishonor them. Is it not better to honor them by silence and admiration, and to devote ourselves solely to investigation of the less sublime truths and those which are more in proportion to the capacity of our minds?

THEODORE. How do you mean, Aristes? You are not thinking of what you are saying. We are made to know and love God. Do you mean, then, to say that you do not want us to think of Him, speak of Him, I might even add worship Him? We ought, you say, to worship Him by silence and admiration. Yes by a respectful silence which the contemplation of His greatness imposes upon us, by a religious silence to which the glory of His majesty reduces us, by a silence forced upon us, so to speak, due to our impotence, and not having as its source a criminal negligence or a misguided curiosity to know, instead of Him, objects less worthy of our application. What do you admire in the Divine if you know nothing of Him? How could you love Him if you did not contemplate Him? How can we instruct one another in charity if we banish from our discussion Him whom you have just recognized as the soul of all the intercourse which we have with one another, as the bond of our little society? Assuredly, Aristes, the more you know the supreme Being, the more you will admire His infinite perfections. Do not fear lest you should meditate too much upon Him and speak of Him in an unworthy way, providing you are led by faith. Do not fear lest you should entertain false opinions of Him so long as they are in conformity with the notion of the infinitely perfect Being. You will not dishonor the divine perfections by judgments unworthy of them, provided you never judge of Him by yourself, provided you do not ascribe to the Creator the imperfections and limitations of created beings. Think of this, therefore. I, too, shall think of it, and I hope Theotimus will do so likewise. That is necessary for the development of the principle which I think I ought to put before you. We shall meet to-morrow then, at the usual hour, for it is time for me to leave.

ARISTES. Adieu, Theodore. I beg of you, Theotimus, that the three of us should meet at the hour arranged.

THEOTIMUS. I am going with Theodore but I shall come back with him, as you desire it. Ah, Theodore, how changed Aristes is! He is attentive, he scoffs no more, he is no longer a stickler for forms—in a word, he listens to reason and submits to it in good faith.

THEODORE. That is true, but his prejudices still come in the way and somewhat confuse his ideas. Reason and prejudice both have their turn in what he says. Now truth makes him speak, now memory plays tricks upon him. But his imagination dares no longer to revolt. This indicates that he is sound at heart and encourages me a good deal.

THEOTIMUS. What do you expect, Theodore? Prejudices are not easily got rid of as an old coat which is no longer thought of. It seems to me that we have been like Aristes, for we were not born but became philosophers. It will be necessary to repeat to him the great principles ceaselessly, in order that he should think of them so often that his mind will obtain mastery over them, and that in the moment of need they may occur to him quite naturally.

THEODORE. That is what I have been trying to do hitherto. But this makes it difficult for him, for he loves detail and variety of thoughts. I beg of you always to dwell upon the necessity of a thorough understanding of principles, in order to stop the vivacity of his mind, and please do not forget to meditate upon the subject of our discussion.

[243]

MARITAIN, JACQUES

MARITAIN, JACQUES (1882-   ). Jacques Maritain, one of the most influential contemporary Neo-Thomists, is the descendant of a family of free-thinkers. His mother's father was Jules Favre, one of the founders of the Third French Republic and an ardent adversary of clericalism. Maritain kept himself outside the Catholic Church until he was converted by the mystic and eccentric poet, Léon Bloy, who lived in a world of supranatural symbols but was not at all interested in philosophy. After his conversion, which, in some respects, was prepared by his devotion to Henri Bergson, Maritain went to Heidelberg to study biology with Hans Driesch. Until 1926, Maritain was associated with the *Action Française*, the French royalist shock troop, and, in accordance with its program, he professed strong opposition to republicanism, democracy and liberal ideas. After the *Action Française* was condemned by Pope Pius XI in 1926, Maritain began to profess confidence in a democracy inspired by Christian faith. At the same time, he turned from speculative metaphysics to history and sociology.

Although Maritain has remained a staunch defender of the Catholic Church and Scholasticism, he does not regard the Christian Middle Ages as the obligatory model of human civilization. Rather, he is inclined to acknowledge the rights of a plurality of civilizations, all of which are guided by Divine providence, and proves his ability to expound historical and contemporary, human and social problems in Thomist terms, which, in his opinion, enable him to discover the relations between historical phenomena and the supratemporal order. Proceeding from these views, Maritain maintains that the value of the human person is rooted in an order which is created by God and strives toward God. The Catholic Church is acknowledged by Maritain as universal, supranational, supraracial and supratemporal, but he is eager to avoid any romanticizing of what he demands to be respected. He insists that the Church is not the home of the elect but the refuge of sinners. On the other hand, he is, on the ground of his conception of the Church, as strongly opposed to Nazism as he is to Bolshevism.

Any contradiction between the Christian faith and modern science is, according to Maritain, due to ontological ambitions on the part of Descartes and Newton, and will vanish after science will have elaborated a thoroughly nonmetaphysical approach. But he does not believe that, even in a distant future, science and faith will cooperate without friction.

THE DIVINE PLAN

THE divine plan is not a scenario prepared in advance, in which free subjects would play parts and act as performers. We must purge our thought of any idea of a play written in advance, at a time prior to time—a play in which time unfolds, and the characters of time read, the parts. On the contrary, everything is improvised, under the eternal and immutable direction of the almighty Stage Manager. The divine plan is the ordination of the infinite multiplicity of things, and of their becoming, by the absolutely simple gaze of the creative knowledge and the will of God. It is eternal and immutable, but it could have been otherwise (since it could not have been had there not been things). *Once fixed* from all eternity, once *assumed* as fixed in such and such a way from all eternity, it is immutable. And it is by virtue of the eternal presence of time in eternity (even before time was), by virtue of the embrace, by the eternal instant, of history in the making (perpetually fresh in its newness and indeed— as regards free acts—in its unforeseeability) that the divine plan is immutably fixed in heaven from all eternity, directing history towards the ends willed by God and disposing towards those ends all the actors in the drama and all the good God causes in them, while taking advantage, on behalf of those ends, of the evil itself of which they are the nihilating first cause and which God permits without having caused it.

By reason of this free nihilating, the creature has a portion of first initiative in the drama. Unless the free existent has received at one stroke an unshatterable impetus to good, it depends solely upon him whether he will or will not take the initiative of nihilating or of non-consideration of the rule, under the motions and activations which bear him towards good. Will he or will he not nihilate under the hand of the potter? As concerns his good or evil act, and the repercussions it may have upon what follows in the drama, it is at that instant in time, known from all eternity, that the immutable plan is simultaneously established from all eternity. Let us suppose that the free creature has not, in that instant, the initiative of the thing that is nothing. The initiative of nihilating not being seen (from all eternity) in the free existent by the 'science of vision,' from all eternity, the primordial will of God (which willed the good act of this creature in the direction of the particular end towards which it ordained him) is confirmed by the definitive or circumstanced will. Thus from all eternity the accomplishment of this good act by this creature is immutably fixed in the eternal plan.

[244]

MARX, KARL

MARX, KARL (1818-1883). To the impact of Marx's doctrine on political and social ideas and the subsequent changes of social structure there is no parallel in the whole history of philosophy. Only religious reformers have produced similar changes. What distinguishes Marx from other philosophers who more or less deeply influenced political and social ideas is the simple fact that his teachings directly affected the mind of the masses of working people in various nations, not only by appealing to their material interests but even more so by imbuing them with an apparently imperturbable confidence in the absolute truth of his statements and predictions. In his *Theses on Feuerbach* (1845), Marx, who had turned from the political radicalism of the Left Hegelians to what he then called communism and later scientific socialism, declared that the question of absolute truth is not one of theory but a practical one, and that the reality and power of thought must be demonstrated in practice by both interpreting and changing the world. But he always insisted that a vigorous theory is as indispensable to the destruction of a corrupted society and the construction of a new one as is drastically disciplined action. When, in his *Critique of Political Economics,* (1859), Marx called his method empirical, he did so in order to mark his opposition to abstract spiritualism. But he continued to sneer at pure empiricists. He turned Hegel's dialectic upside down because he thought that Hegel's way of proceeding from the abstract to the concrete, from the ideal to the real could reach reality, and that Hegel's conception of the dialectical motion as the development of consciousness was bound to miss human totality. But when Marx declared in opposition to Hegel that it is not consciousness that determines the existence of man but that the social existence of man determines his consciousness, he nevertheless, was regarding dialectic as the only infallible method of scientific thinking to which all empirical knowledge of facts is subordinated. He reproached Feuerbach for having abandoned not only idealism, of which he approved, but also dialectics of history which, to Marx, meant renouncing scientific exactness. In the same way, although he applied his theory mainly to economic and social life, and devoted much of his energy to the direction of political movements, Marx remained the philosopher of the dialectical movement who retained both Hegel's conviction that the real is rational and Hegel's dialectical concept of becoming. He continued to agree with Hegel that reality is a process, that life means itself and its contradiction, and that as soon as contradiction ceases to act, life will come to an end.

The fundamental characteristic of Marx's doctrine is not his theory of the concentration of wealth in the hands of a few powerful capitalists, or the condemnation of the "exploitation of man by his fellow-man." These views are borrowed from Saint-Simon, Sismondi and Constantin Pecqueur. Nor is it his theory of class struggle, borrowed from French historians of his time, or his theory of surplus value, owed to English economists. What really dominates the unity of his thinking is his conception of history, according to which the forms of economic production determine the formation of human society and the consciousness of its members so that ideas, moral values, aesthetic standards, political and social concepts, educational and religious systems are to be conceived as produced by the economic situation. As long as the "ideological superstructure" remains in accordance with the conditions of economic production, civilization is healthy. But, since these conditions are changing more rapidly than the superstructure, cultural crises are unavoidable, and, when people, incapable of understanding the laws of history, resist the changes dictated by it, revolution becomes necessary. In his principal work *Das Kapital* (1867 and later) Marx developed his philosophy by applying it to modern economic life, demonstrating by a historico-sociological analysis of economics that that which he calls the *bourgeoisie* has accomplished its historical task by great performances but that it is not capable any longer of adapting itself to the changed conditions of production and must give room to the proletariat.

Marx tried to regard phenomena as incessantly changing, life as continual movement of growth and destruction, so that nothing immutable remains except movement itself. For that reason, said his intimate friend and collaborator Friedrich Engels, Marx refrained from offering in his principal work any fixed and universally applicable definition. Marx even criticized the German Social Democratic Party which, in its program of 1875, mentioned the "present-day State." Marx maintained the "present-day State" to be a fiction since it differed from one country to another.

Although, in his later years, Marx became more and more reluctant to define concepts, because he was afraid lest he should admit in this way any fixed existence, he maintained his belief in the dynamics of economic change as the prime mover of historic life. He presented this conviction as an eternally valid law of nature, as the highest tribunal from which no appeal to another court is possible. He did it by an inexorable diction, fond of disillusioning and with dry irony, sneering at moralists, utopians, reformers who, as he said, tried in vain to escape the compulsion dictated by historical laws, such as are revealed by the right use of dialectics. He, on his part, claimed to teach how to cooperate with the due course of historical evolution. When each science will have become perfect, philosophy will be useless except formal logic and dialectic. Of these two disciplines, dialectic is declared superior, as a method of advancing from the known to the unknown. According to Marx, dialectic forces the way beyond the narrow horizon of formal logic, because it contains the germ of a more developed view of the world. He was fond of dialectic because he conceived of it as of constant fermentation. Marx's search for the causation and end of the historical process, which assumes that men, while producing the means of material existence, enter human relations independently of their will and change these human relations independently of their will when the way of production changes, has been much disputed. But many philosophers, historians and sociologists who contradict him, are ready to admit that he has created a working hypothesis.

THE HISTORICAL TENDENCY
OF CAPITALIST ACCUMULATION

WHAT does the *primitive accumulation of capital, i.e.,* its historical genesis, resolve itself into? In so far as it is not immediate transformation of slaves and serfs into wage laborers, and therefore a *mere change of form,* it only means the *expropriation of the immediate producers, i.e., the dissolution of private property based on the labor of its owner.* Private property, as the antithesis to social, collective property, exists only where the instruments of labor and the external conditions of labor belong to private individuals. But according as these private individuals are laborers or not laborers, private property has a different character. The numberless shades that it at first sight presents reflect only the intermediate stages lying between these two extremes. The private property of the laborer in his means of production is the foundation of petty industry whether agricultural, manufacturing, or both; petty industry, again, is an essential condition for the development of social production and of the free individuality of the laborer himself. Of course this petty mode of production exists also under slavery, serfdom, and other states of dependence. But it flourishes, it lets loose its whole energy, it attains its adequate classical form, only where the laborer is the free private owner of his own conditions of labor manipulated by himself: the peasant of the land which he cultivates, the artisan of the tool which he handles as a virtuoso. This model of production presupposes parcelling of the soil, and scattering of the other means of production. As it excludes the *concentration* of the means of production, so also its excludes cooperation, division of labor within each separate process of production, the social mastery and control over nature, and the free development of the *social* productive forces. It is compatible only with a system of production, and a society, moving within narrow and more or less primitive bounds. To perpetuate it would be, as Pecqueur rightly says, "to decree universal mediocrity." At a certain level of development it brings into being the material agencies for its own dissolution. From that moment new forces and new passions spring up in the bosom of society; but the old social organization fetters them and keeps them down. It must be annihilated; it is annihilated. Its annihilation, *the transformation of the individualized and scattered means of production into socially concentrated ones*, of the pigmy property of the many into the huge property of the few, *the expropriation of the great mass of the people from the soil, from the means of subsistence, and from the instruments of labor*, this fearful and painful *expropriation of the mass of the people*, forms the prelude to the history of capital. It comprises a series of forcible methods, of which we have passed in review only those that have been epoch-making as methods of the primitive accumulation of capital. The expropriation of the immediate producers was accomplished with merciless vandalism, and under the stimulus of passions the most infamous, the most sordid, the pettiest, the most meanly odious. Self-earned private property that is based so to say, on the fusing together of the isolated, independent laboring individual with the conditions of his labor, is supplanted by capitalist private property, which rests on exploitation of the nominally free labor of others, *i.e.*, on wage labor.

As soon as this process of transformation has sufficiently decomposed the old society from top to bottom, as soon as the laborers are turned into proletarians, their means of labor into capital, as soon as the capitalist mode of production stands on its own feet, then the further socialization of labor and further transformation of the land and other means of production into socially exploited and, therefore, common means of production, as well as the further expropriation of private proprietors, takes a new form. That which is now to be expropriated is no longer the laborer working for himself, but the capitalist exploiting many laborers. This expropriation is accomplished by the action of the immanent laws of capitalist production itself, by the centralization of capital. One capitalist always kills many. Hand in hand with this centralization, or this expropriation of many capitalists by few, develop, on an ever extending scale, the co-operative form of the labor process, the conscious technical application of science, the methodical cultivation of the soil, the transformation of the instruments of labor into instruments of labor only usable in common, the economizing of all means of production by their use as the means of production of combined, socialized labor, the entanglement of all peoples in the net of the world market, and with this, the international character of the capitalist regime. Along with the constantly diminishing number of the magnates of capital who usurp and monopolize all advantages of this process of transformation, grows the mass of misery, oppression, slavery, degradation, exploitation; but with this, too, grows the revolt of the working class, a class always increasing in numbers, and disciplined, united, organized by the very mechanism of the process of capitalist production itself. The monopoly of capital becomes a fetter upon the mode of production, which has sprung up and flourished along with, and under it. Centralization of the means of production and socialization of labor reach a point where they become incompatible with their capitalist integument. This integument is burst asunder. The knell of capitalist private property sounds. The expropriators are expropriated.

The capitalist mode of appropriation, the result of the capitalist mode of production, produces capitalist private property. This is the first negation of individual private property, as founded on the labor of the proprietor. But capitalist production begets, with the inexorability of a law of nature, its own negation. It is the negation of negation. This does not reestablish property for the producer, but gives him individual property based on the acquisitions of the capitalist era: *i.e.*, on cooperation and the possession in common of the land and of the means of production produced by labor itself.

The transformation of scattered private property, arising from individual labor, into capitalist private property is, naturally, a process incomparably more protracted, violent, and difficult than the transformation of capitalist private property already in fact resting on socialized production, into socialized property. In the former case, we had the expropriation of the mass of the people by a few usurpers; in the latter, we have the expropriation of a few usurpers by the mass of the people.

[245]

MASARYK, THOMAS GARRIGUE

MASARYK, THOMAS GARRIGUE (1850-1937). The son of a blacksmith, Masaryk became the father of a democratic people. After achieving fame as a scholar, a political economist and a historian, he became a legendary figure, the founder of a modern state. In all situations of his life, as a teacher, a member of parliament, an exile and a ruler, he proved to be a critical and constructive thinker.

"Truth conquers" was Masaryk's motto. He fought for truth when he discovered the forgery of an allegedly old document, without any regard to the fact that his discovery hurt Czech national pride. He fought for truth while denouncing the manner in which the "ritual murder" trial at Polna had been conducted in 1899, and he exposed the forgeries fabricated by members of the Austro-Hungarian Legation in Belgrade in 1910. He risked his popularity, his security and his life in order to prove the tenets of his philosophy, according to which Man is bound to collaborate with God, to follow the command of his conscience and to act as an individual responsible to humanity. Equally opposed to despotism and anarchy, Masaryk was a champion of democracy, convinced that the philosophy of history is identical with the philosophy of democracy. Dissatisfied with intellectualism and mysticism, Masaryk, as a thinker, endeavored to establish an equilibrium between emotional and intellectual tendencies. As a Czech, he professed solidarity with all Slavic nations, but he was a severe critic of Russian thought. His fundamental ideas were rooted in the philosophy of enlightenment and positivism, but he was very cautious concerning Locke and Comte, notwithstanding his personal sympathies with these thinkers. He regarded the leading trends of European history as the development of the ideas of the French Revolution of 1789 but, critical as he remained of religious, social and political traditions, he always tried to awake the sense of responsibility to the maintenance and promotion of the common good and to establish new norms of human conduct in accordance with the new forms of human life, to vivify religious feelings and to justify a sober criticism, to harmonize reason and living faith. Among Masaryk's philosophical works are *The Scientific and Philosophical Crisis of Contemporary Marxism* (1898), *The Ideals of Humanity* (1902) and *The Spirit of Russia* (1917).

MORALITY

I CLASS myself among those who base morality on emotion, but I do not think that emotion ought to be in opposition to reason. Among feelings there are: good and bad, noble and ignoble, exalted and brutal. Ethics based on sentiment should not lose itself in emotion. I think that the harmony of feeling with reason (and, to some extent, the supremacy of feeling over reason) is the foundation of morality. . . . The foremost principle of modern ethics . . . is not anything new but the old and universally acknowledged law: 'Love thy neighbor as thyself.' Who, however, is my neighbor? We speak of the ideal of humanity. I accept this ideal. It has for me a double meaning. It is, first of all, the ideal of proper manhood; to be a man. Secondly, it involves consid-eration for our fellow humans in the widest sense.

Love of humanity tends readily, however, to become abstract, to exist in fancy rather than in reality. Love needs to be concentrated on specific objects. One cannot love all men equally. We choose, and we ought to choose the objects of our love. We need to have some particular objective . . . Love, humanity, must be positive. People often take the hatred of another nation to be love of one's own. It is far higher to feel no hatred, but to love positively . . . Love is no sentimentality. We are too sentimental, and sentimental-ity is egoism. Morality is founded on emotion, but not every emotion is just and good. . . . Emotion is blind and needs illumination by reason.

True love rests on hope, the hope of eternal life. Such love alone is true, because the eternal cannot be indifferent to the eternal. Eternity does not just commence with death. Eternity is here now, at this moment, at every moment. . . . In fixing your gaze upon eternity do not despise matter, the body, because of the superiority of mind. There is no matter, there is no body which is worthless. It is not matter or the body which is the source of evil; it is mind. . . .

The hope in eternal life is, then, the basis of our faith in life. Our faith, I say, for life and work depend on faith.
[246]

MAZZINI, GIUSEPPE

MAZZINI, GIUSEPPE (1805-1872). When the Prince of Metter-nich was still considered the most powerful man in Europe, he said that "no one gave me more trouble than a devil of an Italian, emaciated, pale, poor, but eloquent as a tempest, inspired as an apostle, sly as a thief, and tireless as a lover—his name is Giuseppe Mazzini." In his private life, simple, kindly, affectionate, some-times even playful, Mazzini, during the twenty years preceding 1850, was regarded by the revolutionaries of all the countries of Europe as their master, by the Italian people as the prophet of their future greatness, and, when he took refuge in England, Mazzini, a defeated man roused the enthusiasm of philosophers like Henry Sidgwick and John Morley, and of poets like Wordsworth, Swin-burne and Meredith, and was, notwithstanding their dissension in fundamental political questions, a highly respected and dear friend of Thomas Carlyle.

It is characteristic of Mazzini that he embraced the cause of European revolution and the unification of Italy only when he saw proscripts who, after the collapse of their uprising of 1821, asked his mother for charity. His vision of the future was colored by pity for the poor and the suffering. He did not neglect the social aspect of the revolution, but he condemned the theory of class struggle and did not recognize chosen classes or chosen nations. He always put humanity above nations, his own included, and God above humanity. Equally opposed to Marx as to the Pope and the kings, Mazzini believed in the ultimate victory of disinterested mo-tives over egoism, of idealism over materialism and utilitarianism, and in a religion of humanity freed from prejudices, aware of the cultural values of the Biblical tradition, and able to enhance the dignity of the human individual. He proclaimed the rights as well as the duties of Man. Although he did not conceive new ideas, he was a moral power of considerable influence.

INTERESTS AND PRINCIPLES

PRINCIPLES alone are constructive. Ideals are never trans-lated into facts without the general recognition of some strong belief. Great things are never done except by the re-jection of individualism and a constant sacrifice of self to the common progress. Now, self-sacrifice is the sense of Duty in action. And the sense of Duty cannot spring from individual interests, but postulates the knowledge of a su-perior, inviolable Law. Every law rests on a principle: other-wise it is arbitrary and its violation is *permissible*. This prin-ciple must be freely accepted by everybody: otherwise the law is despotic and its violation is a *duty*. The application of principle lies in a life in conformity with law. To discover, to study, to preach the *principle* which shall be the basis of the social law of the country and of the times in which he lives, should be the aim of every man who directs his thought to any political organization. *Faith* in that principle is the parent of effective and lasting work. The isolated and barren knowledge of *individual interests* can only lead to the isolated and barren knowledge of *individual right*. And the knowledge of individual right will, where that right is denied, lead in its turn to discontent, opposition, strife, sometimes insurrection, but insurrection which, like that of Lyons, results only in a bitterer hostility between the classes which compose society. Whenever, therefore, we desire to do one of those great deeds called Revolutions, we must always return to the knowledge and preaching of principles. The true instrument of the progress of the peoples is to be sought in the *moral* factor.

But do we, therefore, neglect the *economic* factors, material interests; the importance of industrial victories, and the labors that won them? Do we preach principles for principles' sake, faith for faith's sake, as the romantic school of literature to-day preaches *art for art's sake.*

God forbid! We do not suppress the *economic* factor: we believe, on the contrary, that it is destined in the society of the future to admit an ever-increasing extension of the principle of *equality*, and to incorporate the fruitful principle of *association*. But we subordinate the economic to the *moral* factor, because if withdrawn from its controlling influence, dissociated from principles, and abandoned to the theories of individualism which govern it to-day, it would result in brutish egotism; in perpetual strife between men who should be brothers; in the expression of the *appetites* of the human species, whilst it ought rather to represent on the ascending curve of progress the material translation of man's activity, the expression of man's industrial mission.

No, we do not neglect material interests: on the contrary, we reject as imperfect and irreconcilable with the needs of the age every doctrine which does not include them,

or regards them as less important than they really are. We believe that to every stage of progress there should be a corresponding positive improvement in the material condition of
the people; and this successive improvement, in a certain
manner, verifies for us the progress made. But we maintain
that material interests cannot be developed alone, that they
are dependent on principles, that they are not the *end and
aim* of society; because we know that such a theory is destructive of human dignity; because we remember that when
the *material* factor began to hold the field in Rome, and duty
to the people was reduced to giving them *bread* and *public
shows*, Rome and its people were hastening to destruction;
because we see to-day in France, in Spain, in every country,
liberty trodden under foot or betrayed precisely in the name
of commercial interests and that servile doctrine which parts
material well-being from principles.

[247]

McDOUGALL, WILLIAM

McDOUGALL, WILLIAM (1871-1938). McDougall has called himself "arrogant," and the behaviorists, psychoanalysts, Gestalt psychologists, pragmatists and a host of men of other philosophical
and psychological schools attacked by him are far from denying
him that quality. Honored as McDougall was as a professor at
Oxford and Harvard, he always felt himself living in an adverse
intellectual atmosphere. Indeed, he had reason for becoming embittered, for he was aware that his theories were often misrepre-
sented. His work has been discussed from the viewpoint of instinct
theory. But, in fact, McDougall regarded the instinctive nature
of man only as a foundation, and maintained that the theory of
sentiments furnishes the key to his system according to which in
the man of developed character very few actions proceed directly
from his instinctive foundation.

In addition to extensive travels through India, Indonesia and
China in order to "hear the East," McDougall prepared his approach to the problems of the human mind by neurological and
psychological studies. However, after his *Physiological Psychology*
(1905), he concentrated upon psychological introspection and retro-
spection. His *Introduction to Social Psychology* (1908) challenged

799

all previous conceptions and provoked animated controversies. He held that neither instinct, regarded as a working hypothesis, nor the human individual, characterized as an abstraction, can provide the basic data for social psychology but rather molding influences of social environment. The basic fact of human behavior is *purposive striving*. Consequently, McDougall calls psychology *hormic,* from the Greek *horme*—vital impulse, urge to action, which is to him a property of the mind, while he regarded intellect not as a source of energy but as the integrated system of man's beliefs (later as the sum total of man's innate and acquired cognitive abilities). In *Body and Mind* (1911) McDougall stated that mind must be considered a potent cause of evolution. McDougall also wrote *The Group Mind* (1920), *The Frontiers of Psychology* (1936) and *The Riddle of Life* (1938).

INDIVIDUAL AND GROUPS

IT is a notorious fact that, when a number of men think and feel and act together, the mental operations and the actions of each member of the group are apt to be very different from those he would achieve if he faced the situation as an isolated individual. Hence, though we may know each member of a group so intimately that we can, with some confidence, foretell his actions under given circumstances, we cannot foretell the behavior of the group from our knowledge of the individuals alone. If we would understand and be able to predict the behavior of the group, we must study the way in which the mental processes of its members are modified in virtue of their membership. That is to say, we must study the interactions between the members of the group and also those between the group as a whole and each member. We must examine also the forms of group organization and their influence upon the life of the group.

Groups differ greatly from one another in respect of the kind and degree of organization they possess. In the simplest case the group has no organization. In some cases the relations of the constituent individuals to one another and to the whole group are not in any way determined or fixed by previous events; such a group constitutes merely a mob. In other groups the individuals have certain determinate relations to one another which have arisen in one or more of three ways:

(1) Certain relations may have been established between the individuals, before they came together to form a group; for example, a parish council or a political meeting may be formed by persons belonging to various definitely recognized classes, and their previously recognized relations will continue to play a part in determining the collective deliberations and actions of the group; they will constitute an incipient organization.

(2) If any group enjoys continuity of existence, certain more or less constant relations, of subordination, deference, leadership and so forth, will inevitably become established between the individuals of which it is composed; and, of course, such relations will usually be deliberately established and maintained by any group that is united by a common purpose, in order that its efficiency may be promoted.

(3) The group may have a continued existence and a more or less elaborate and definite organization independent of the individuals of which it is composed; in such a case the individuals may change while the formal organization of the group persists; each person who enters it being received into some more or less well-defined and generally recognized position within the group, which formal position determines in great measure the nature of his relations to other members of the group and to the group as a whole.

We can hardly imagine any concourse of human beings, however fortuitous it may be, utterly devoid of the rudiments of organization of one or other of these three kinds; nevertheless, in many a fortuitous concourse the influence of such rudimentary organization is so slight as to be negligible. Such a group is an unorganized crowd or mob. The unorganized crowd presents many of the fundamental phenomena of collective psychology in relative simplicity; whereas the higher the degree of organization of a group, the more complicated is its psychology.

[248]

MEAD, GEORGE HERBERT

MEAD, GEORGE HERBERT (1863-1931). After Mead's death, one of his graduate students declared that for many years to come articles and even books would continue to be published of which the first author was George Mead. John Dewey, his intimate friend, has said that Mead had "a seminal mind of the first order," and Alfred Whitehead, after reading some of Mead's posthumously published books, publicly endorsed this view. Dewey also recognized that Mead, whose scholarship in the natural sciences was superior to his own, had influenced him by conversations which were continued over a period of years.

Mead published little during his lifetime, and wrote no systematic work, but he was a consistent thinker. He constantly expressed his antipathy for metaphysics and was equally opposed to idealism and materialism. His principal interests were devoted to the investigation of the consequence of biological theories to scientific psychology. He held that psychological phenomena, including those of thinking and knowing, must be described as actions or reactions of the organism that lives in an environment and regulates its relations to objective conditions of life by means of the nervous system of which the brain is a part. To Mead, the psychical is the state which occurs when previously formed relations of the organism to its environment break down and new ones are not yet built up. Acts are the unity of existence of the individual that is proclaimed as a concrete, inimitable, nonrationalizable unit, but modifiable through its relation to society. Mead tried to maintain a balance between the determination by the individual of the whole, be it society or the world, and the determination by the whole of the individual.

SOCIAL PSYCHOLOGY

SOCIAL Psychology studies the activity or behavior of the individual as it lies within the social process; the behavior of an individual can be understood only in terms of the behavior of the whole social group of which he is a member, since his individual acts are involved in larger, social acts which go beyond himself and which implicate the other members of that group.

We are not, in social psychology, building up the behavior of the social group in terms of the behavior of the separate individuals composing it; rather, we are starting out with a given social whole of complex group activity, into which we analyze (as elements) the behavior of each of the separate individuals composing it. We attempt, that is, to explain the conduct of the individual in terms of the organized conduct of the social group rather than to account for the organized conduct of the social group in terms of the conduct of the separate individuals belonging to it. For social psychology, the whole (society) is prior to the part (the individual), not the part to the whole; and the part is explained in terms of the whole, not the whole in terms of the part or parts. The social act is not explained by building it up out of stimulus plus response; it must be taken as a dynamic whole—as something going on—no part of which can be considered or understood by itself—a complex organic process implied by each individual stimulus and response involved in it.

In social psychology we get at the social process from the inside as well as from the outside. Social psychology is behavioristic in the sense of starting off with an observable activity—the dynamic, on-going social process, and the social acts which are its component elements—to be studied and analyzed scientifically. But it is not behavioristic in the sense of ignoring the inner experience of the individual—the inner phase of that process or activity. On the contrary, it is particularly concerned with the rise of such experience within the process as a whole. It simply works from the outside to the inside instead of from the inside to the outside, so to speak, in its endeavor to determine how such experience does arise within the process. The act, then, and not the tract, is the fundamental datum in both social and individual psychology when behavioristically conceived and it has both an inner and an outer phase, an internal and an external aspect.

These general remarks have had to do with our point of approach. It is behavioristic, but unlike Watsonian behaviorism it recognizes the parts of the act which do not come to external observation, and it emphasizes the act of the human individual in its natural social situation.

[249]

MEINONG, ALEXIUS VON

MEINONG, ALEXIUS VON (1853-1920). When Meinong expressed opinions about political facts, he was convinced of being just and right. As a philosopher, however, he remained conscious that to err means to be a human being. He thought that scientists could not obtain definite results, save some fortunate exceptions that prove the rule, and that one might be satisfied with exploring more favorable starting points to broach old questions.

It is true that Meinong did not claim to have found definite truth. But he claimed to have established a new science, namely—the *Theory of Objects*, which, as he said, was bound to fill a gap which had been left by epistemology, metaphysics and psychology. His theory of objects differs from psychology because it does not envisage the psychic acts but the objects. It differs from metaphysics since it also comprises the non-real. It differs from ontology by stressing the experience of resistance to the experiencing subject on the part of the object. It was developed by its founder to a new doctrine of perception and of value and valuing. Ethics is regarded as a part of the theory of values, and ethical values comprise moral as well as nonmoral values.

Meinong, who first studied history and philology, came to philosophy, as he said, by chance and as an autodidact. He was encouraged by Franz Brentano, who later rejected many of Meinong's statements. Meinong was rather surprised when he was appointed a professor by the Austrian government. He had numerous disciples, some of whom modified Meinong's theory and brought it close to phenomenology.

THE PROBLEM OF CAUSALITY

HABENT *sua fata cogitationes*—and the idea of causality is without any doubt one of those whose fate has been eventful. Its fates have been recorded in the teachings of leading minds of both former and present days. But the manner in which public opinion of those who are more or less led has reacted to it should have been recorded, for history has to deal not only with kings but also with peoples. Especially at those times can you recognize it when its characteristic features lie above all in the specific manner of such reactions. A glance at the last few decades of our immediate past shows that the history of the idea of causality especially does not lack such times. When Hume, in spite of all sagacity, had played once with the sceptical fire not much more seriously than his predecessors—when Kant had hoped to forestall the threatening danger for good, one might consider these deeds as royal deeds. However, when the positivistic and empiriocritical wind blew the spark not into beaming but into singeing flames, then very little could be discovered of the characteristics of royal builders. In our days, wherever one deals with science in a philosophical manner, and even more so where one deals with it in an unphilosophical manner, there appears all the more clearly the tendency to defy the authority of the principle, if not examined afresh. In spite of some isolated attacks, this principle had been considered the pillar of science. Now it became fashionable to avoid, if possible, any reference to it if one was not downright resolved to deny the validity of the general law of causality. Needless to say how well that suits that agnosticism which otherwise promises satisfaction to many metaphysical and ethical needs. It goes without saying that there is no lack of those who, not because of their needs but because of their absence of needs, show great ease in considering everyone as backward who speaks of causal and not of functional relationships. One cannot therefore say that the destructive trend, proper to the more recent theories of causality, has begun to become a practice in our time. The general law of causality, claimed so often and with such emphasis as an indispensable requirement of scientific working, has lost its validity in the eyes of more than one who is resolved to think scientifically to the best of his capacity.

The question whether there is such a law has never been less academic than today.

[250]

MEISTER ECKHART. See ECKHART, JOHANNES.

MELISSOS

MELISSOS (Fifth Century, B.C.). We know practically nothing of the life of Melissos save the one great fact that he was the general of Samos that defeated the Athenian fleet in 440 B.C.

FRAGMENTS

IF nothing is, what can be said of it as of something real?

* * *

What was was ever, and ever shall be. For, if it had come into being, there must needs have been nothing before it came into being. Now, if nothing were to exist, in no wise could anything have arisen out of nothing.

* * *

Since, then, it has not come into being and since it is, it was ever and ever shall be, and has no beginning or end, but is infinite. For, if it had come into being, it would have had a beginning (or it would have begun to come into being at some time or other) and an end (for it would have ceased to come into being at some time or other); but, if it neither began nor ended, it ever was and ever shall be, and has no beginning or end; for it is not possible for anything to be ever without being all.

* * *

Further, just as it ever is, so it must ever be infinite in magnitude (for if it had bounds, it would be bounded by empty space).

But nothing which has a beginning or end is either eternal or infinite.

For if it is (infinite), it must be one; for if it were two, it could not be infinite; for then it would be bounded by another.

806

(And, since it is one, it is alike throughout; for if it were unlike, it would be many and not one).

So then it is eternal and infinite and one and all alike. And it cannot perish nor become greater, nor does it suffer pain or grief. For, if any of these happened to it, it would no longer be one. For, if it is altered, then the real must needs not be all alike, but what was before must pass away, and what was not must come into being. Now, if the all had changed by so much as a single hair, in thirty thousand years, it would all perish in the whole of time.

Further, it is not possible either that its order should be changed; for the order which it had before does not perish, nor does that which was not come into being. But, since nothing is either added to it or passes away or is altered, how can any real thing have had its order changed? For if anything became different, that would amount to a change in its order.

Nor does it suffer pain; for the All cannot be in pain. For a thing in pain could not be ever, nor could it have the same power as what is whole. It is only from the addition or subtraction of something that it could feel pain, and then it would no longer be like itself. Nor could what is whole possibly begin to feel pain; for then what was whole and what was real would pass away, and what was not would come into being. And the same argument applies to grief as to pain.

Nor is anything empty. For what is empty is nothing. . . . What is nothing, then, cannot be.

Nor does it move; for it has nowhere to betake itself to, but is full. For if there were empty space, it would betake itself to empty space. But, since there is no empty space, it has no place to betake itself to.

And it cannot be dense and rare; for it is not possible for what is rarefied to be as full as what is dense, but what is rare is ipso facto emptier than what is dense.

This is the way in which we must distinguish between what is full and what is not full. If a thing has room for anything else, and takes it in, it is not full; but if it has no room for anything and does not take it in, it is full.

Now, it must needs be full if there is no empty space, and if it is full, it does not move.

If what is real is divided, it moves; but if it moves, it cannot have body; for, if it had body it would have parts, and would no longer be one.

*   *   *

This argument, then, is the greatest proof that it is one alone; but the following are proofs of it also. If it were a many, these would have to be of the same kind as I say that the one is. For if there is earth and water, and air and iron, and gold and fire, and if one thing is living and another dead, and if things are black and white and all that men say they really are,—if that is so, and if we see and hear aright, each one of these must be such as we at first concluded that reality was, and they cannot be changed or altered. Whereas we say that we see and hear and understand aright, and yet we believe that what is warm becomes cold, and what is cold warm; that what is hard turns soft, and what is soft hard; that what is living dies, and that things are born from what lives not; and that all those things are changed. We think that iron, which is hard, is rubbed away with the finger, pass-ing away in rust; and so with gold and stone and everything which we fancy to be strong, so that it turns out that we neither see nor know realities. Earth, too, and stone are formed out of water. Now these things do not agree with one another. We said that there were many things that were eternal and had forms and strength of their own, and yet we fancy that they all suffer alteration, and that they change with each perception. It is clear, then, that we did not see aright after all, nor are we right in believing that all these things are many. They would not change if they were real, but each thing would be just what we believed it to be; for nothing is stronger than true reality. But if it has changed, what was has passed away, and what was not is come into

being. So then, if there were many things they would have
to be just of the same nature as the one.

[251]

MENASSEH BEN ISRAEL

MENASSEH BEN ISRAEL (1604-1657). It was an apocalyptic mystic, expecting the fulfilment of the Messianic promises, who, in
1655, accomplished with extraordinary worldly ability the political
and diplomatic task of securing permission for the Jews to settle
again in England, from which they had been expelled in 1290.
Menasseh ben Israel, who was able to put Oliver Cromwell in a
mood favorable to his demands for readmission of the Jews to
England, was also highly respected by Queen Christina of Sweden,
had studied philosophy with Descartes, and his scholarship was
exalted by men like Hugo Grotius and the learned theologian Johannes Buxtorff. Until the end of the 18th century, Menasseh ben
Israel was considered a high authority in history, linguistics and
theology by great scholars in Holland, England, France and Germany. Even greater was his influence with Christian mystics. He
had studied the Cabala but was also well acquainted with orthodox
rabbinic literature. His own writings, devoted to the vindication of
Judaism, to its defense against accusations or to its reconciliation
with philosophical and mystical doctrines, show him to be a versatile rather than a profound thinker. Among them, *Hope of Israel*
(1650), dedicated to the Parliament of England, and *Vindication
of the Jews* (1656) were written for political purposes, while *The
Statue of Nebuchadnèzzar* (1656), a commentary on Daniel's interpretation of the Babylonian king's dream, outlines a mystical philosophy of history. This book, when first printed, was decorated
with four etchings by Rembrandt who, from 1645 on, was his intimate friend.

ON HUMAN LIFE

THE life of man has a determined and fixed period.

It may be considered in three modes; either according to the constitution and temperament of the body, the
strength communicated it to the natal hour or time of
conception by the planets, or the general period of existence
of the age.

This period considered in either way is not immutable but variable. Life may be shortened by providence, nature or accident.

The observance of the Divine precepts, both in theory and practice, and meditation in the Holy Law, lead to prolongation.

It is not only lawful but imperative that recourse should be had to physicians and medicines when requisite.

Although from eternity God knows the period of existence allotted to everyone yet it is in the power of man, by upright conduct, to ameliorate his condition.

The knowledge of how God's prescience and regulation of the future is consistent with existence of contingencies in nature, requires much longer detail and many arguments; but it may be briefly observed that . . . all contingencies are infallibly known to God, as they are subject to the Divine sight, from His omnipotence; and, withal, are only future contingencies when compared with their causes. Thus the First Cause not only sees the actions of man as future, but as present and already performed: in the same way as one person, seeing another do an act, would not say, because he was looking on, it was obliged to be done, so God, because he sees the action as present, does not oblige him who performs it, to do it, but leaves him to his liberty and the operating contingency.

God does not grant His grace to individuals, but He gives the same disposition to all mankind, by which every one may alike become meritorious, and by their own actions secure their felicity. Therefore, it being necessary that merit should precede grace, the Lord by His prophet said: "Turn unto Me, and I will turn unto you," for then grace and help infallibly follow.

The advantage a wise man has over a fool is the same as the humble has over the rich. For the humble knows how to walk to everlasting life, and the wealthy miser to death with eyes constantly fixed on the earth and its productions, gold and silver. But the wise man, with eyes raised to the heaven, satisfied with a moderate maintenance and clothing, walks to everlasting life.

[252]

MENCIUS (Meng Tzu)

MENCIUS (MENG TZU) (372-289 B.C.). In his efforts to educate kings, Meng Tzu (Master Meng) seems to have been no more successful than his Greek contemporary Aristotle. But to a greater extent than Aristotle, Meng used his personal experiences for the development of his philosophical teachings.

Meng was a disciple of Tzu, who was the grandson of Confucius and himself an influential philosopher, though of lesser importance to the history of Confucianism than his pupil Meng. It was Meng who restored the authority of Confucius by successfully combating deviating opinions such as were advanced by Mo-Ti and Yang Chou, both of whom had become extremely popular and had tried to discredit the cult and doctrine of Confucianism. At the end of his life, Meng composed the book that bears his name and, in the Sung era, was canonized. Extracts from the book became favorite reading in Europe early in the eighteenth century and have continued in their popularity. The book is the fruit of experiences collected during long, extensive travels, and of keen observations of people of all classes from kings down to beggars. Meng declared that man is good by nature but that he has to develop his own nature to the greatest possible perfection. The government, said Meng, must serve the people and promote their welfare. Revolt against bad rulers is permitted. War is branded as a crime. Meng has been quoted more than once by Voltaire and Rousseau. In this way he influenced, at least indirectly, many leaders of the French Revolution.

ON BENEVOLENCE

BENEVOLENCE brings glory to an individual and its opposite brings disgrace. For people of the present day to hate disgrace and yet live complacently doing what is not benevolent, is like hating moisture and yet living in low country.

If a man hates disgrace, the best course for him to pursue is to esteem virtue and honor virtuous scholars, giving the worthiest among them places of dignity, and the able offices of trust.

People take advantage of the time, when throughout the land there are leisure and rest, to abandon themselves to pleasure and indolent indifference; they, in fact, seek for calamities for themselves.

Calamity and happiness in all cases are men's own seeking. This is illustrated by what is said in The Book of Poetry:

> Be always studious to be in harmony with the ordi-
>   nances of God,
> So you will certainly get for yourself much hap-
>   piness;

and by the passages of the Tai Chia: "When Heaven sends down calamities, it is still possible to escape from them; when we occasion the calamities ourselves, it is not possible any longer to live."

*　　　*　　　*

If a ruler give honor to men of talents and virtue and employ the able, so that the offices shall all be filled by the individuals of distinction and mark—then all the scholars of the land will be pleased. . . .

All men have a mind which cannot bear to see the suffering of others. The ancient kings had this commiserating mind, and they, as a matter of course, had likewise a commiserating government. When with a commiserating mind was practiced a commiserating government, the government of the land was as easy a matter as the making anything go round in the palm.

When I say that all men have a mind which cannot bear to see the suffering of others, my meaning may be illustrated thus: even nowadays, if men suddenly see a child about to fall into a well, they will without exception experience a feeling of alarm and distress. They will feel so, not as a ground on which they may gain the favor of the child's parents, nor as a ground on which they may seek the praise of their neighbors and friends, nor from a dislike to the reputation of having been unmoved by such a thing.

From this case we may perceive that the feeling of commiseration is essential to man, that the feeling of shame and dislike is essential to man, that the feeling of modesty and complacence is essential to man.

*   *   *

The feeling of commiseration is the principle of benevolence. The feeling of shame and dislike is the principle of righteousness. The feeling of modesty and complacence is the principle of propriety. The feeling of approving and disapproving is the principle of knowledge.

Men have these four principles just as they have their four limbs. When men, having these four principles, yet say of themselves that they cannot develop them, they play the thief with themselves and he who says of his neighbor that he cannot develop them, plays the thief with his neighbor.

Since all men have these four principles in themselves, let them know to give them all their development and completion, and the issue will be like that of fire which has begun to burn, or that of a spring which has begun to find vent. Let them have their complete development and they will suffice to love and protect all within the four seas.

The choice of a profession, therefore, is a thing in which great caution is required. Confucius said, "It is virtuous manners which constitute the excellence of a neighborhood. If a man in selecting a residence, does not fix on one where such prevail, how can he be wise?"

Now, benevolence is the most honorable dignity conferred by heaven, and the quiet home in which man should dwell. Since no one can hinder us from being so, if yet we are not benevolent, we are unwise.

From the want of benevolence and the want of wisdom will ensue the entire absence of propriety and righteousness.

[253]

MENDELSSOHN, MOSES

MENDELSSOHN, MOSES (1729-1786). In the late seventeenth century, Father Pierre Bonhours, a Jesuit and a refined art critic, published a pamphlet in which he held that a German could never be a poet or an artist, nor could he understand aesthetical problems and phenomena. Of course, the booklet aroused indignation in Germany, and provoked violent counter-attacks. At that time, however, Frenchmen and Germans agreed that a Jew could never become integrated into modern culture, let alone contribute to its development. This opinion remained constant until, by 1755, the surprising news was spread in literary circles that there was in Berlin a Jew called Moses Mendelssohn who could not only speak and write German flawlessly but who could discuss philosophical and literary problems and was even esteemed by Lessing, the most feared German critic of his time, as an authority in aesthetics and psychology. Many otherwise independent thinkers would simply not believe that the news was true. Some of them went to Berlin in order to gaze in astonishment at such a curiosity. Then, for some years, even Mendelssohn's sincere admirers, such as Kant and Lessing, expressed doubts that he could continue to be devoted to German culture and at the same time remain loyal to Judaism. Later they recognized that he could do both.

Mendelssohn enriched descriptive psychology by his treatise on mixed sentiments. His essay on evidence in metaphysical sciences was awarded the prize by the Prussian Academy against his competitor, Immanuel Kant. His *Phaedon* (1767), defending the idea of the immortality of the soul, was a favorite book of German Jews and Christians alike for more than two generations. With his *Jerusalem* (1783), he deeply impressed Kant, who became convinced that Judaism was a true world religion. Mendelssohn also translated the Hebrew Bible into German and demanded civil rights for the Jews as well as the separation of Church and State. With him came the beginning of a new epoch in the history of the Jews, not only those of Germany. Still four decades after his death, hymns to his praise were sung by Christians and Jews united in their adherence to Mendelssohn's ideas. Lessing raised a poetic monument to his friend by using him as model for the hero of his drama *Nathan The Wise*.

ON PROGRESS

PROGRESS is for individual man, who is destined by Providence to pass a portion of his eternity here on earth. Every one goes his own way through life. One's route leads him over flowers and meadows; another's across desert plains, over steep mountains or by the side of dangerous precipices. Yet they all get on in the journey, pursuing the road to happiness, to which they are destined. But that the bulk, or the whole human race here on earth, should be constantly moving forth in progress of time, and perfecting itself, seems to me not to have been the design of Providence.

Do you want to divine the design of Providence with man? Then forge no hypotheses; look only around you at what actually does pass—and if you can take a general view of the history of all ages—at what has passed from the beginning. That is fact: that must have belonged to the design; that must have been approved of in the plan of Wisdom, or at least have been admitted in it. Providence never misses its aim. That which actually happens must have been its design from the beginning, or have belonged to it. Now, in respect to the human race at large, you do not perceive a constant progress of improvement that looks as if approaching nearer and nearer to perfection. On the contrary, we see the human race as a whole subject to slight swings; and it never yet made some steps forward but what it did, soon after, slide back again into its previous station, with double the celerity. Most nations of the earth pass many ages in the same degree of civilization in the same crepusculous light, which appears much too dim for our spoiled eyes. Now and then a particle of the grand mass will kindle, become a bright star, and run through an orbit, which, now after a longer, now after a shorter period, brings it back again, to its standstill, or sets it down at no great distance from it. Man goes on; but mankind is constantly swinging to and fro, within fixed boundaries; but, considered as a whole, retains, at all periods of time, about the same degree of morality, the same quality of religion and irreligion, of virtue and vice, of happiness and misery; the same result, when the same is taken into account against the same; of all the good

815

and evil as much as was required for the transit of individual men, in order that they might be trained here on earth, and approach as near to perfection as was allotted and appointed to every one of them.

[254]

MILL, JOHN STUART

MILL, JOHN STUART (1806-1873). Modern progressive pedagogists must be horrified by the methods which were employed for the education of John Stuart Mill by his father, the stern utilitarian James Mill. The latter was not only his son's sole teacher. He was even his sole intercourse, instructing him on walks as well as at home. At the age of three, John Stuart Mill learned Greek. At seven he studied Plato's dialogues. At eight he had to teach his sister Latin. When he was fifteen years old, he was initiated into Bentham's doctrine of the greatest happiness of the greatest number, which struck him as a revelation and made him a convert to utilitarianism for his lifetime.

But far from being an uncritical and orthodox adept of the philosophy which was cherished by his father, John Stuart, recognizing its flaws, became interested in romantic poetry, and, though opposed to Coleridge's political and religious standpoint, praised him as "the awakener of the philosophical spirit in England." Of greater importance, however, was the influence of Comte, Guizot and Tocqueville, to whom Mill owed the enlargement of his historical views and, above all, his awareness of the great social change and its consequences. Mill remained a staunch defender of individual liberty because he was convinced of its social usefulness. But he was ready to sacrifice individual property rights when they endangered the common good. He remained the advocate of representative government, but he considered the social question of increasing importance and became more and more devoted to the cause of the working class, without, however, any intention of idealizing the workers. When he campaigned for a seat in Parliament, he warned his constituents that he would do nothing for their special interests but only what he thought to be right. He also fought for women's suffrage and for the rights of colored people.

Mill's philosophy combined British utilitarianism and French positivism, but, as his last essays prove, would have developed farther if he had lived longer. The main task of his *System of Logic* (1843) is the analysis of inductive proof. His canons of inductive methods for comprehending the causal relations between phenomena are valid under the assumption of the validity of the law of causality; Mill, however, admitted that this law cannot be accepted except on the basis of induction, which, on its part, is fundamentally a matter of enumeration.

Mill was a courageous and considerate fighter for human rights, always trying to understand the fair side of his adversary. During the second half of the 19th century, his ascendancy over the spirit of European philosophy was immense. Since then it has withered. But many of those who used to belittle Mill are, in fact, obligated to him. What he has said of Bentham may be also true of Mill himself: "He was not a great philosopher but a great reformer in philosophy."

LIBERTY OF THE INDIVIDUAL

THERE is a sphere of action in which society, as distinguished from the individual, has, if any only an indirect interest; comprehending all that portion of a person's life and conduct which affects only himself or if it also affects others, only with their free, voluntary, and undeceived consent and participation. When I say only himself, I mean directly, and in the first instance: for whatever affects himself may affect others through himself; and the objection which may be grounded in this contingency, will receive consideration in the sequel. This, then, is the appropriate region of human liberty. It comprises, first, the inward domain of consciousness; demanding liberty of conscience, in the most comprehensive sense; liberty of thought and feeling; absolute freedom of opinion and sentiment on all subjects, practical or speculative, scientific, moral, or theological. The liberty of expressing and publishing opinions may seem to fall under a different principle, since it belongs to that part of the conduct of an individual which concerns other people; but, being almost of as much importance as the liberty of thought itself, and resting in great part on the same reasons, is practically inseparable from it. Secondly, the principle requires liberty of tastes and pursuits; of framing the plan of our life to suit our own character; of doing as we like, subject to such consequences as may follow: without impediment from our fellow creatures, so long as what we do does not harm them, even though they should think our conduct foolish, perverse, or wrong. Thirdly, from this liberty of each individual, follows the liberty, within the same limits, of combination among individuals; freedom to unite, for any purpose not involving harm to others: the persons combining being supposed to be of full age, and not forced or deceived.

No society in which these liberties are not, on the whole, respected, is free, whatever may be its form of government; and never is completely free in which they do not exist absolute and unqualified.

THE TRIUMPH OF TRUTH

THE dictum that truth always triumphs over persecution, is one of those pleasant falsehoods which men repeat after one another till they pass into commonplaces, but which all experience refutes. History teems with instances of truth put down by persecution. If not suppressed forever, it may be thrown back for centuries. To speak only of religious opinions: the Reformation broke out at least twenty times before Luther, and was put down. . . . Even after the era of Luther, wherever persecution was persisted in, it was successful. In Spain, Italy, Flanders, the Austrian Empire, Protestantism was rooted out; and most likely, would have been so in England, had Queen Mary lived, or Queen Elizabeth died. Persecution has always succeeded, save where the heretics were too strong a party to be effectually persecuted. No reasonable person can doubt that Christianity might have been extirpated in the Roman Empire. It spread, and became predominant, because the persecutions were only occasional, lasting but a short time, and separated by long intervals of almost undisturbed propagandism. It is a piece of idle sentimentality that truth, merely as truth, has any inherent power denied to error, of prevailing against the dungeon and the stake. Men are not more zealous for truth than they often are for error, and a sufficient application of legal or even of social penalties will generally succeed in stopping the propagation of either. The real advantage which truth has, consists in this, that when an opinion is true, it may be extinguished once, twice, or many times, but in the course of ages there will generally be found persons to rediscover it, until some one of its reappearances falls on a time when from favorable circumstances it escapes persecution until it has made such head as to withstand all subsequent attempts to suppress it.

INDIVIDUAL AND STATE

THE worth of a State, in the long run, is the worth of the individuals composing it; and a State which postpones the interests of *their* mental expansion and elevation, to a little more of administrative skill, or that semblance of it which practice gives, in the details of business; a State which dwarfs its men, in order that they may be more docile instruments in its hands even for beneficial purposes, will find that with small men no great thing can really be accomplished; and that the perfection of machinery to which it has sacrificed everything, will in the end avail it nothing, for want of the vital power which, in order that the machine might work more smoothly it has preferred to banish.

THE PUREST OF WISDOM

WHEN we consider either the history of opinion, or the ordinary conduct of human life, to what is to be ascribed that the one and the others are no worse than they are? Not certainly to the inherent force of the human understanding; for, on any matter not self-evident, there are ninety-nine persons totally incapable of judging it, for one who is capable; and the capacity of the hundredth person is only comparative; for the majority of the eminent men of every past generation held many opinions now known to be erroneous, and did or approved numerous things which no one will now justify. Why is it, then, that there is on the whole a preponderance among mankind of rational opinions and rational conduct? If there really is this preponderance—which there must be, unless human affairs are, and have always been, in an almost desperate state—it is owing to a quality of the human mind, the source of everything respectable in man either as an intellectual or as a moral being, namely, that his errors are corrigible. He is capable of rectifying his mistakes, by discussion and experience. Not by experience alone. There must be discussion, to show how experience is to be interpreted. Wrong opinions and practices gradually yield to fact and argument: but facts and arguments, to produce any effect on the mind, must be brought before it. Very few facts are able to tell their own story, without comments to bring out their meaning. The whole strength and value, then, of human judgment, depending on the one property, that it can be set right when it is wrong, reliance can be placed on it only when the means of setting it right are kept constantly at hand. In the case of any person whose judgment is really deserving of confidence how has it become so? Because he has kept his mind open to criticism of his opinions and conduct. Because it has been his practice to listen to all that could be said against him; to profit by as much of it as was just, and expound to himself, and upon occasion to others, the fallacy of what was fallacious. Because he has felt, that the only way in which a human being can make some approach to knowing the whole of a subject, is by hearing what can be said about it by persons of every variety of opinion, and studying all modes in which it can be looked at by every character of mind. No wise man ever acquired his wisdom in any other manner.

MAN THE INDIVIDUAL

HE who lets the world, or his own portion of it, choose his plan of life for him, has no need of any other faculty than the ape-like one of imitation. He who chooses his plan for himself employs all his faculties. He must use observation to see, reasoning and judgment to foresee, activity to gather materials for decision, discrimination to decide, and when he has decided, firmness and self-control to hold to his deliberate decision. And these qualities he requires and exercises exactly in proportion as the part of his conduct which he determines according to his own judgment and feelings is a large one. It is possible that he might be guided in some good path, and kept out of harm's way, without any of these things. But what will be his comparative worth as a human being? It really is of importance, not only what men do, but what manner of men they are that do it. Among the works of man, which human life is rightly employed in perfecting and beautifying, the first in importance is surely man himself. Supposing it were possible to get houses built, corn grown, battles fought, causes tried, and even churches erected and prayers said, by machinery—by automatons in human form—it would be a considerable loss to exchange for these automatons even the men and women who at present inhabit the more civilized parts of the world, and who assuredly are but starved specimens of what nature can and will produce. Human nature is not a machine to be built after a model, and set to do exactly the work prescribed for it, but a tree, which requires to grow and develop itself on all sides, according to the tendency of the inward forces which make it a living thing.

[255]

MOHAMMED

MOHAMMED (570-632). As with every founder of a religion, the life and personality of Mohammed, the founder of Islam, have been transformed by legends which picture him as the only perfect man, the greatest of all saints, the only one worthy of becoming the instrument of divine revelation. Mohammed himself, however, thought otherwise. He said that he was sent by God as a "witness, as a hopeful and warning messenger, as a torch," but he refused to be regarded as an example of virtue. He did not feel that he was a saint, and consciously refrained from performing miracles. He certainly was a fanatic but occasionally he showed a sense of humor, and several of his jokes have been transmitted to posterity.

The original name of Mohammed (The Praised One) was Ubu'l Kassim. He was a merchant in Mecca where plutocracy offended his social feelings, as the idolatry of the whole population offended his reason and piety. Broodings, dreams and visions led him to the belief that he was chosen by God to save the Arabian people from spiritual and moral corruption by announcing the coming judgment of humanity and teaching faith in Allah, the one and omnipotent God.

At the age of 40, Mohammed began his religious mission. The citizens of Mecca sneered at him and forced him to flee. In 622, he came to the city of Jathrib where he was well received and actively supported. Jathrib, therefore, was subsequently renamed Medina (City of the Prophet), and became the base of his power and his religious and military expeditions. The flight of 622 (Hejira) became an event of greatest importance to the history of the world. In Medina, Mohammed, once a lonesome missionary, became a spiritual and military ruler and conqueror, and his religious doctrine was shaped to the religion of Islam, an institution, and, at the same time, a warlike organization. Mohammed subdued Mecca, his native town that had expelled him. But when he died he could not foresee the future expansion of Islam.

The basis of Islamic religion is the *Koran* (Recitations), written by Mohammed who claimed to be inspired by Gabriel, the archangel. It consists of 114 sections (Suras), the first third of which was conceived in Mecca and deals with the creation and future fate of the world, the proofs of the omnipotence of Allah and the teachings of a moral conduct of life as a preparation for standing the test on the Day of Judgment. The remainder of the *Koran*, accomplished in Medina, contains polemics against other religious and civil legislation.

Mohammed claimed that he restored the religion of Abraham which, according to him, had been distorted by Judaism and Christianity. Mohammed adopted many of the Judaic and Christian, gnostic, and Babylonian traditions but, the older he grew, the more he stressed the importance of the sword as a means of propagating the right faith. Without Mohammed's *Koran*, the world religion of Islam cannot be understood. However, Islam cannot be understood only by the study of the *Koran*. The moral and dogmatic evolution of Mohammedanism did not stop by any means after Mohammed's death.

THE EXORDIUM

In the name of God, the compassionate, Compassioner: Praise be to God, the Lord of the worlds, the compassionate Compassioner, the Sovereign of the day of judgment. Thee do we worship, and of Thee do we beg assistance. Direct us in the right way; in the way of those to whom Thou hast been gracious, on whom there is no wrath, and who go not astray.

CONCERNING ALMSGIVING

If ye make your alms to appear, it is well; but if ye conceal them, and give to the poor, this will be better for you, and will atone for your sins; and God is well informed of that which ye do. The direction of them belongeth not unto thee; but God directeth whom He pleaseth. The good that ye shall give in alms shall redound unto yourselves; and ye shall not give unless out of desire of seeing the face of God. And what good things ye shall give in alms, it shall be repaid you. They who distribute alms of their substance night and day, in private and in public, shall have their reward with their Lord; on them shall no fear come, neither shall they be grieved.

CONCERNING USURY

They who devour usury shall not arise from the dead, but as he ariseth whom Satan hath infected by a touch. This shall happen to them because they say, "Truly selling is but as usury;" and yet God hath permitted selling and forbidden usury. He therefore who, when there cometh unto him an admonition from his Lord, abstaineth from usury for the future, shall have what is past forgiven him; and his affair belongeth unto God. But whoever returneth to usury, they shall be the companions of hell-fire; they shall continue therein forever.

CONCERNING CONTRACTS

Deal not unjustly with others, and ye shall not be dealt

with unjustly. If there be any debtor under a difficulty of paying his debt, let his creditor wait till it be easy for him to do it; but if he remit it as alms, it will be better for you, if ye knew it. And fear the day when ye shall return unto God; then shall every soul be paid what it hath gained, and they shall not be treated unjustly.

O true believers, when ye bind yourselves one to the other in a debt for a certain time, write it down; and let a writer write between you according to justice; and let not a writer refuse writing according to what God hath taught him; but let him write, and let him who oweth the debt dictate, and let him fear God his Lord, and not diminish aught thereof. But if he who oweth the debt be foolish or weak, or be not able to dictate himself, let his agent dictate according to equity; and call to witness two witnesses of your neighboring men; but if there be not two men, let there be a man and two women of those whom ye shall choose for witnesses; if one of these women should mistake, the other of them shall cause her to recollect. And the witnesses shall not refuse, whensoever they shall be called. And disdain not to write it down, be it a large debt, or be it a small one, until its time of payment. This will be more just in the sight of God, and more right for bearing witness, and more easy, that ye may not doubt. And take witnesses when ye shall sell one to the other, and let no harm be done to the writer nor to the witness, which if ye do it will surely be injustice to you; and fear God, and God will instruct you, for God knoweth all things.

[256]

MONTAGUE, WILLIAM PEPPERELL

MONTAGUE, WILLIAM PEPPERELL (1873-1953). During his childhood, Montague used to bother his parents by questioning them about his soul, the relations between mind and body, and the soul of the universe. He was neither satisfied with his mother's evasive answers, nor terrified by his father's impatience. In his advanced age, Montague declared that he has continued ever since to ask the same questions and that he has not been satisfied by the solutions of the Church or of his teachers, among whom Royce, James, Santayana and Palmer were outstanding, or of his colleagues and critics. However, reared in a New England congregation, he developed "a poignant sense of the beauty of the Christian doctrine." He devoted his life to the reconciliation of his inquiring spirit with his faith, seeking to establish God as the solid basis of natural knowledge. He found out that the problem of God is insoluble in terms of traditional theism and traditional atheism but that Man craves infinity, and that higher religion has the best chances of being proved to be true. To him it does not matter whether his philosophy is called a cosmological spiritualism that, in a sense, can be expressed in physical terms, or as spiritualistic, or even animistic, materialism.

Montague's metaphysics is founded upon an epistemological realism which he had to defend on more than one front. Against idealism Montague maintains the independence of reality from consciousness. Against pragmatism he adheres to the idealist conception of truth as independent of its working in practice. In 1910 he was associated with the group of "New Realists," but subsequently had to stress the difference of his views from those of the other members of the group and from "objective" and "critical" realism. None of these controversies could weaken his conviction that theism is "an exciting and momentous hypothesis" rather than either a dialectical truism or a dogma to be adopted uncritically. But he declares that religion must claim a knowledge of nature to go beyond what any reasonable person considers a matter of course. To him, religion is concerned with the values in the realm of existence, while philosophy is concerned with the values in the life of the spirit. Philosophy is a vision as religion is a faith.

PROMETHEAN CHALLENGE TO RELIGION

THE moral ideal of Christian love is like a pillar of flaming light extending from earth to heaven, but the supernatural religion of freedom, solace, and joy that should have evolved from it was choked and poisoned. The successors of Christ, from St. Paul down to the censors, obscurantists, and tyrants of today have done their conscientious worst to hide the light from men. The long series of authoritarians and ascetics have changed the clear into the obscure, the beautiful into the ugly, and with what was most gentle and generous they have associated what was most cruel and mean. They have debauched a religion of liberty, service, tolerance, and progress to their own base ends of persecution, reaction, and gloom.

Through all the world today there is an ominous muttering. Not only the small though growing army of scientists who view the efforts of religious fanatics to check the teachings of science with a contempt so deep and cold that they can hardly be brought to express it, and not only the men of letters and liberal authors who show a more voluble contempt for the spirit of censorious puritanism which is growing beyond the stage of an ugly American joke are significant; but far more meaningful than these is the sullen rage of the multitude of workers throughout the world who for the first time are really coming to hate the Christian scheme.

If religion is to be saved from destruction from without, it must be revolutionized from within. And it is a Promethean revolution that is needed: no new prophet as substitute for Christ, but a great purging and cleansing of Christianity and of all religion as it exists today.

What would a Prometheanized religion be like? Would there be left of Christianity, for example, anything more than a vague and worldly humanitarianism, a platitudinous philanthropy touched with inarticulate emotion? Many liberal and well-meaning people so believe, and, though aware of the anomalies of orthodoxy and of the growing dangers to the whole structure of religion, they fear that any breach in the ranks of authority would be more dangerous still. I think such fears are completely ungrounded, and by way of conclusion I will attempt to outline some of the principal characteristics of a religion transfigured by a Promethean revolution.

First of all, there would be the welcome and luminous absence of sacrosanct authority. Such dogmas as remained, and they would be many, would be transformed into hypothesis. The most fantastic theory of the supernatural, if held as a hypothesis, is honorable, and belief in it is honest and to be respected. There would be no lack of propaganda and missionary zeal. Those who had faith in a theory would be proud to have it vindicated by criticism. For the irreligious free-thinking would be optional, but for religionists it would be compulsory. A church member who refused to allow his belief to be tested in the light of reason would be expelled as one of little faith. The various schools and sects would not persecute one another, for why should one seeker for truth hate another? Why should he not rather co-operate with him the better to realize their common end? If a theory is not true, no one would wish it to survive; if it is true, it will survive. How senseless and perverse not to test it!

Not only would theists cease to hate another—they would cease to hate atheists. They would love and respect them. For if you are walking comfortably in the light of a supernatural faith that the universe is on your side, why should you not love and respect the man who walks in darkness, crippled by the fear that the things we care for most are at the mercy of blind force—deprived of your hope of God and another world, yet fighting bravely by your side for the same ideals for which you fight? A strange inversion of Christian charity to hate such a one.

And in this Promethean religion, heaven would be no less free than earth of that hateful spirit of monarchical authority. We should not love goodness because it is commanded by God, but should love God because He is good. We should base our religion on our ethics; not as now, our ethics on a supernatural physics. And there would be no longer that curious double standard, according to which the same God who commands us to forgive our enemies no matter how many times they offend, reserves for Himself the right to wreak infinite vengeance on His enemies after one trial life on earth. That nightmare monster of authoritarian religion, veritable anti-Christ, would have been consigned to his own hell, the single one of all imagined beings who would really deserve it.

As in our religion, so in our ethics. The principle of authority would be gone, and with it the great clutter of prohibitions and taboos—rules taken as ends in themselves rather than as means to happiness. The one supreme and single purpose of morality would be the making of life more abundant, which means the developing to a maximum the potentialities of every creature. Love and work by all for the maximum well-being of all. All moral rules— the oldest and most revered, like those established for marriage and property, no less than the newest and queerest proposals— would be appraised without prejudice and in the cold light of intelligence, to be accepted or rejected only according to their efficiency in promoting the ideal of freer and more abundant living.

The banishment of asceticism and authoritarianism would for the first time in history bring human ethics into active partnership with human science. Once clear away the morality of taboos, and all the forces of intelligence could be mobilized in the service of progress, and the vast energies of thought and will that have been wasted in religious wars could be utilized for moral and religious work.

[257]

MONTAIGNE, MICHEL D'EYQUEM DE

MONTAIGNE, MICHEL D'EYQUEM DE (1533-1592). While noblemen used to adorn their coats-of-arms with grandiloquent devices, Montaigne wrote under his own: "Que sais-je?" (What do I know?). His lifetime was a period of constant quarreling between theologians, philosophers and scientists, and a time of bloody religious wars. Montaigne fought for peace and tolerance, using, for that purpose, the weapons of irony and scepticism. Against fanaticism he appealed to clear thinking and considerate reason, and, due to his literary skill, he succeeded in inspiring confidence in the value of reason at least in small circles of men everywhere in Europe, though most of the rulers, politicians and theologians continued to incite the fanaticism of the masses.

Montaigne, born in the castle of Montaigne near Bordeaux, France, was the son of a father who probably was of Jewish descent, and a mother, whose family was certainly Jewish. Some of Montaigne's relatives were Marranos, baptized Jews who secretly continued to profess Judaism, and Montaigne knew that. He admired the tenacity with which the Jews held to their faith in the face of persecution, and doubted that any one of them became a true convert to another religion.

Montaigne tried to undermine the position of any orthodoxy and fanaticism by showing the common weaknesses of men in order to make them aware of the possibility that other people might be right and they themselves could be wrong. He declared that arrogance is the natural and characteristic disease of man who, in fact, is the most fragile of all creatures. But his manner of exhorting to humility had nothing in common with that of ecclesiastical sermons. Montaigne completely changed the tone of religious and philosophical discussions. He did not express indignation. He emphasized the personal character of his views and experiences, and did not exclude other people's opinions on the same items. He understood men of genius as well as plain people. He studied Athens' civilization and was interested in the life of American Indians. At those who think that the entire universe is established and moving only for the commodity and the service of human beings he smiled. But while rejecting anthropocentric teleology and opposing any belief in absolute knowledge, Montaigne far from denied the values of human life and character, of nature, beauty, the arts and sciences. The relativity of values was to him no proof that there are no values or duties at all. Kindness toward fellow men was presented as an almost absolute value by Montaigne.

For his confessions, Montaigne created a new literary form— namely, the essay. It was used by Bacon, Descartes, Locke, Rousseau, and Voltaire, among others, and has remained popular to the present day. One of Montaigne's most interested readers was William Shakespeare and he was followed by Molière, Laurence Sterne, Anatole France and a host of others.

HAPPINESS CAN ONLY BE JUDGED AFTER DEATH

Scilicet ultima semper
Expectanda dies homini est, dicique beatus
Ante obitum nemo, supremaque funera debet.

Till man's last day is come we should not dare
Of happiness to say what was his share;

829

Since of no man can it be truly said
That he is happy till he first be dead.

CHILDREN know the story of King Croesus to this effect, that, having been taken prisoner by Cyrus and condemned to die, as he was on the point of execution he cried out, "O Solon, Solon!" This being reported to Cyrus, and he inquiring what it meant, Croesus gave him to understand that he now found the warning Solon had once given to him true to his cost, which was, that men, however fortune may smile upon them, cannot be called happy till they have been seen to pass through the last day of their lives, because of the uncertainty and mutability of human things, which at a very slight impulse change from one state to another, wholly different. And it was therefore that Agesilaus, to one who was saying that the King of Persia was happy to come so young to so mighty a kingdom, made answer: "'Tis true, but neither was Priam unhappy at his years." Sometime kings of Macedon, successors to that mighty Alexander, become joiners and scriveners at Rome; the tyrants of Sicily become school-masters at Corinth. A conqueror of one-half of the world and ruler of so many armies is turned into a miserable suppliant to the rascally officers of a king of Egypt: so much did the prolongation of five or six months of life cost the great Pompey. And, in our fathers' days, Ludovico Sforza, the tenth Duke of Milan, under whom all Italy had so long trembled, was seen to die a prisoner at Loches, but not till he had lived in that state ten years, which was the worst part of his fortune. *The fairest of queens, widow of the greatest king in Christendom, has she not just died by the hand of an executioner?* And a thousand such examples. For it seems that as storms and tempests are provoked against the pride and loftiness of our buildings, there are also spirits above that are envious of the grandeurs here below,

Usque adeo res humanas vis abdita quædam
Obterit, et pulchros fasces sævasque secures

Proculcare, ac ludibrio sibi habere videtur.

So greatly does some hidden power contemn
Our human fortunes, and is often seen
To trample down and make a laughing-stock
Of all the symbols of imperial power.

And it would seem that Fortune sometimes lies in wait
for precisely the last day of our lives, to show her power
to overthrow in a moment what she was so many years in
building, making us cry out with Laberius, "Nimirum hac
die una plus vixi, mihi quam vivendum fuit." "Truly I have
this day lived one day longer than I should."

In this sense may the good advice of Solon reasonably
be taken. But, inasmuch as he is a philosopher (with whom
the favors and disgraces of Fortune rank neither as happiness nor unhappiness, and grandeurs and power are accidents of a quality almost indifferent), I think it probable
that he had some further aim, and that his meaning was, that
this same felicity of our life, which depends upon the tran-
quillity and contentment of a well-born spirit, and the resolution and assurance of a well-ordered mind, ought never
to be attributed to any man till he has been seen to play the
last, and doubtless the hardest, act of his comedy. There
may be disguise in all the rest: either these fine philosophical
arguments are only by way of appearance, or circumstances,
not testing us to the quick, give us leisure still to preserve
the composure of our features. But in this last scene between
death and ourselves, there is no more counterfeiting: we must
speak out plain, and display what there is that is good and
clean at the bottom of the pot.

Nam veræ voces tum demum pectore ab imo
Ejiciuntur, et eripitur persona, manet res.

> Truth then is forced
> From his inmost heart: the mask is torn aside,
> The real man remains.

That is why all the other actions of our life ought to be tried and tested by this final act. It is the master-day, it is the day that is judge of all the rest; "it is the day," says one of the ancients, "that must be judge of all my past years." To death do I refer the proof of the fruit of all my studies; we shall then see whether my reasonings come only from my mouth or from my heart.

I have seen many by their death give a reputation for good or ill to their whole life. Scipio, the father-in-law of Pompey, by a worthy death wiped away the ill opinion that till then everyone had conceived of him. Epaminondas, being asked which of the three he had in greatest esteem, Chabrias, Iphicrates, or himself, replied: "You must first see us die, before the question can be decided." In truth, Epaminondas himself would be deprived of much of his lustre if we should weigh him without regard to the honor and grandeur of his end.

God has ordered things as it has pleased Him; but in my time three of the most execrable persons that ever I knew in all manner of abominable living, and the most infamous, have had a death that was decorous and perfectly attuned in every circumstance.

There are brave and fortunate deaths. I have seen death cut the thread of the progress of a marvellous advancement, and that in the flower of its growth; and with an ending so magnificent that, in my opinion, the man's ambitious and courageous designs had nothing in them so high as their interruption. He reached, without moving, the place he was aiming at, more grandly and gloriously than he could either have hoped or desired. By his fall he carried his power and name beyond the point to which he aspired in his career. In the judgment I make of another man's life, I always observe how its last scene is passed; and among the principal concerns of my own life is that its last scene shall be passed well, that is to say, calmly and insensibly.

[258]

MONTESQUIEU, CHARLES DE SECONDAT

MONTESQUIEU, CHARLES DE SECONDAT (1689-1755). The principle of separation of powers, or of checks and balances, which is characteristic of the Constitution of the United States was formulated in such a striking manner by Montesquieu that Jefferson, Hamilton, Adams and Madison and other founders of the United States were deeply impressed by it, and held it more or less clearly in their minds when they gave the Constitution its shape.

Montesquieu was a high judge in France but he was very critical of the regime which he served. In his youth he had been a member of the "First Floor Club" in Paris, a secret society strongly opposed to absolutism and clerical orthodoxy. He remained faithful to the club's principles but became rather moderate in his judgment on the advantages of other political systems. His *Persian Letters* (1721) a thinly veiled satirical criticism of French life, made a great sensation. His *Reflections on the Causes of the Greatness and the Decadence of the Romans* (1734) is considered one of the most important monuments of modern historical literature. The very spirit of Roman civilization is grasped and brilliantly illustrated by Montesquieu, however much scholars of later times may object to his treatment of details. Montesquieu's principal work *The Spirit of the Laws* (1748) was the result of fourteen years of strenuous study into political history and comparative legislation, of reading sources and observing life by traveling through many countries of Europe, and above all, of a stay in England where he arrived on Lord Chesterfield's yacht. Montesquieu admired England, though not uncritically. Its institutions, in his opinion, guaranteed and realized the highest possible degree of freedom, and he derived this view from the application of the principle of checks and balances. This view is not shared by modern constitutional historians or jurists, least of all concerning the England of Montesquieu's days. But his work has been of lasting value to the development of methods of analyzing political, social and legal conditions and their connection. Next to Locke, Montesquieu was the most influential champion of liberalism in the 18th century.

LAWS, in their most general signification, are the necessary relations arising from the nature of things. In this sense all beings have their laws: the Deity His laws, the material world its laws, the intelligences superior to man their laws, the beasts their laws, man his laws.

They who assert that a blind fatality produced the various effects we behold in this world talk very absurdly; for can anything be more unreasonable than to pretend that a blind fatality could be productive of intelligent beings?

There is, then, a prime reason; and laws are the relations subsisting between it and different beings, and the relations of these to one another.

God is related to the universe, as Creator and Preserver; the laws by which He created all things are those by which He preserves them. He acts according to these rules, because He knows them; He knows them, because He made them; and He made them, because they are in relation to His wisdom and power.

Since we observe that the world, though formed by the motion of matter, and void of understanding, subsists through so long a succession of ages, its motions must certainly be directed by invariable laws, and could we imagine another world, it must also have constant rules, or it would inevitably perish.

Thus the creation, which seems an arbitrary act, supposes laws as invariable as those of the fatality of the Atheists. It would be absurd to say that the Creator might govern the world without those rules, since without them it could not subsist.

These rules are a fixed and invariable relation. In bodies moved, the motion is received, increased, diminished, or lost, according to the relations of the quantity of matter and velocity; each diversity is *uniformity*, each change is *constancy*.

Particular intelligent beings may have laws of their

own making, but they have some likewise which they never made. Before there were intelligent beings, they were possible; they had therefore possible relations, and consequently possible laws. Before laws were made, there were relations of possible justice. To say that there is nothing just or unjust but what is commanded or forbidden by positive laws, is the same as saying that before the describing of a circle all the radii were not equal.

We must therefore acknowledge relations of justice antecedent to the positive law by which they are established: as, for instance, if human societies existed, it would be right to conform to their laws; if there were intelligent beings that had received a benefit of another being, they ought to show their gratitude; if one intelligent being had created another intelligent being, the latter ought to continue in its original state of dependence; if one intelligent being injures another, it deserves a retaliation; and so on.

But the intelligent world is far from being so well governed as the physical. For though the former has also its laws, which of their own nature are invariable, it does not conform to them so exactly as the physical world. This is because, on the one hand, particular intelligent beings are of a finite nature, and consequently liable to error; and on the other, their nature requires them to be free agents. Hence they do not steadily conform to their primitive laws; and even those of their own instituting they frequently infringe.

Whether brutes be governed by the general laws of motion, or by particular movement, we cannot determine. Be that as it may, they have not a more intimate relation to God than the rest of the material world; and sensation is of no other use to them than in the relation they have either to other particular beings or to themselves.

By the allurement of pleasure they preserve the individual, and by the same allurement they preserve their species. They have natural laws, because they are united by sensation; positive laws they have none, because they are not connected by knowledge. And yet they do not invariably conform to their natural laws; these are better observed by vegetables, that have neither understanding nor sense.

Brutes are deprived of the high advantages which we have; but they have some which we have not. They have not our hopes, but they are without our fears; they are subject like us to death, but without knowing it; even most of them are more attentive than we to self-preservation, and do not make so bad a use of their passions.

Man, as a physical being, is like other bodies governed by invariable laws. As an intelligent being, he incessantly transgresses the laws established by God, and changes those of his own instituting. He is left to his private direction, though a limited being, and subject, like all finite intelligences, to ignorance and error: even his imperfect knowledge he loses; and as a sensible creature, he is hurried away by a thousand impetuous passions. Such a being might every instant forget his Creator; God has therefore reminded him of his duty by the laws of religion. Such a being is liable every moment to forget himself; philosophy has provided against this by the laws of morality. Formed to live in society, he might forget his fellow-creatures; legislators have therefore by political and civil laws confined him to his duty.

*   *   *

Antecedent to the above-mentioned laws are those of nature, so called, because they derive their force entirely from our frame and existence. In order to have a perfect knowledge of these laws, we must consider man before the establishment of society: the laws received in such a state would be those of nature.

The law which, impressing on our minds the idea of a Creator, inclines us towards Him, is the first in importance, though not in order, of natural laws. Man in a state of nature would have the faculty of knowing, before he had acquired any knowledge. Plain it is that his first ideas would not be of a speculative nature; he would think of the preservation of his being, before he would investigate its origin. Such a man would feel nothing in himself at first but impotency and weakness; his fears and apprehensions would be excessive; as appears from instances (were there any necessity of proving it) of savages found in forests, trembling at the motion of a leaf, and flying from every shadow.

In this state every man, instead of being sensible of his equality, would fancy himself inferior. There would therefore be no danger of their attacking one another; peace would be the first law of nature.

The natural impulse or desire which Hobbes attributes to mankind of subduing one another is far from being well founded. The idea of empire and dominion is so complex, and depends on so many other notions, that it could never be the first which occurred to the human understanding.

Hobbes inquires, *For what reason go men armed, and have locks and keys to fasten their doors, if they be not naturally in a state of war?* But is it not obvious that he attributes to mankind before the establishment of society what can happen but in consequence of this establishment, which furnishes them with motives for hostile attacks and self-defense?

Next to a sense of his weakness man would soon find that of his wants. Hence another law of nature would prompt him to seek for nourishment.

Fear, I have observed, would induce men to shun one another; but the marks of this fear being reciprocal, would soon engage them to associate. Besides, this association would quickly follow from the very pleasure one animal feels at the approach of another of the same species. Again, the attraction arising from the difference of sexes would enhance this pleasure, and the natural inclination they have for each other would form a third law.

Besides the sense or instinct which man possesses in common with brutes, he has the advantage of acquired knowledge; and thence arises a second tie, which brutes have not. Mankind have therefore a new motive of uniting; and a fourth law of nature results from the desire of living in society.

As soon as man enters into a state of society he loses the sense of his weakness; equality ceases, and then commences the state of war.

Each particular society begins to feel its strength, whence arises a state of war between different nations. The individuals likewise of each society become sensible of their force; hence the principal advantages of this society they endeavor to convert to their own emolument, which constitutes a state of war between individuals.

These two different kinds of states give rise to human laws. Considered as inhabitants of so great a planet, which necessarily contains a variety of nations, they have laws relating to their mutual intercourse, which is what we call the *law of nations*. As members of a society that must be properly supported, they have laws relating to the governors and the governed, and this we distinguish by the name of *political law*. They have also another sort of laws, as they stand in relation to each other; by which is understood the *civil law*.

The law of nations is naturally founded on this principle, that different nations ought in time of peace to do one another all the good they can, and in time of war as little injury as possible, without prejudicing their real interests.

The object of war is victory; that of victory is conquest; and that of conquest preservation. From this and the preceding principle all those rules are derived which constitute the *law of nations*.

All countries have a law of nations, not excepting the Iroquois themselves, though they devour their prisoners: for they send and receive ambassadors, and understand the rights of war and peace. The mischief is that their law of nations is not founded on true principles.

Besides the law of nations relating to all societies, there is a polity or civil constitution for each particularly considered. No society can subsist without a form of government. *The united strength of individuals,* as Gravina well observes, *constitutes what we call the body politic.*

The general strength may be found in the hands of a

single person, or of many. Some think that nature having established paternal authority, the most natural government was that of a single person. But the example of paternal authority proves nothing. For if the power of a father relates to a single government, that of brothers after the death of a father, and that of cousin-germans after the decease of brothers, refer to a government of many. The political power necessarily comprehends the union of several families.

Better is it to say, that the government most conformable to nature is that which best agrees with the humor and disposition of the people in whose favor it is established.

The strength of individuals cannot be united without a conjunction of all their wills. *The conjunction of those wills,* as Gravina again very justly observes, *is what we call the civil state.*

Law in general is human reason, inasmuch as it governs all the inhabitants of the earth: the political and civil laws of each nation ought to be only the particular cases in which human reason is applied.

They should be adapted in such a manner to the people for whom they are framed that it should be a great chance if those of one nation suit another.

They should be in relation to the nature and principle of each government; whether they form it, as may be said of political laws; or whether they support it, as in the case of civil institutions.

They should be in relation to the climate of each country, to the quality of its soil, to its situation and extent, to the principal occupation of the natives, whether husbandmen, huntsmen, or shepherds: they should have relation to the degree of liberty which the constitution will bear; to the religion of the inhabitants, to their inclinations, riches, numbers, commerce, manners, and customs.

[259]

MOORE, GEORGE EDWARD

MOORE, GEORGE EDWARD (1873-   ). There has been a debate between G. E. Moore and Bertrand Russell which is quite different from the usual disputes recorded in the history of philosophy. Russell declared in the preface to *Principia Mathematica*, "On fundamental questions of philosophy my position in all of its chief features is derived from G. E. Moore." But Moore, on his part, protested that if there were a question concerning who had learned from whom, then Russell was the teacher and himself the disciple. Literally, Moore was right but in reality Russell was right. It was Moore who started the movement of British New Realism by publishing his essay *Refutation of Idealism in Mind* in 1903. He holds that knowing means apprehension of the objectively real because in the mental act the object becomes transparent. A sense datum, therefore, is not the subjective image of the mind of something corresponding to it in the outer world but it is the object itself which immediately enters into the mind which looks through it. This view has been, with more or less modification, accepted by a great number of British philosophers of recent time. It has led to a partial rehabilitation of common sense.

Moore has also, especially in his *Principia Ethica* (1903) made a considerable contribution to axiology. Moore principally fought what he called the "naturalistic fallacy." He demonstrated the failure of any attempt to derive value from existent things or to define value in terms of relations between existing things. But together with evolutionary naturalism and utilitarianism he also refutes all metaphysical foundations of value, accusing all of them of trying in vain to derive the "ought" from the "is." He is also opposed to any subjectivist theory of value. According to Moore, value is not subjective but depends on intrinsic properties which, however, cannot be defined. "Good is good, and that is the end of the matter," says Moore. Good is not identical with being willed. Right and wrong are not names of the characteristic of values. They are emotive, not cognitive expressions, meaning only approval or disapproval, and do not mean any metaphysical or natural property.

Moore's method is called "microscopic." It concentrates on isolating and questioning, and most of its results lead to new questions.

WHAT IS GOOD?

WHAT . . . is good? How is good to be defined? Now, it may be thought that this is a verbal question. A definition does indeed often mean the expressing of one word's meaning in other words. But this is not the sort of definition I am asking for. Such a definition can never be of ultimate importance in any study except lexicography. If I wanted that kind of definition I should have to consider in the first place how people generally used the word 'good'; but my business is not with its proper usage, as established by custom. I should, indeed, be foolish, if I tried to use it for something which it did not usually denote: if, for instance, I were to announce that, whenever I used the word 'good,' I must be understood to be thinking of that object which is usually denoted by the word 'table.' I shall, therefore, use the word in the sense in which I think it is ordinarily used; but at the same time I am not anxious to discuss whether I am right in thinking that it is so used. My business is solely with that object or idea, which I hold, rightly or wrongly, that the word is generally used to stand for. What I want to discover is the nature of that object or idea, and about this I am extremely anxious to arrive at an agreement.

But, if we understand the question in this sense, my answer to it may seem a very disappointing one. If I am asked 'What is good?' my answer is that good is good, and that is the end of the matter. Or if I am asked 'How is good to be defined?' my answer is that it cannot be defined, and that is all I have to say about it. But disappointing as these answers may appear, they are of the very last importance. To readers who are familiar with philosophic terminology, I can express their importance by saying that they amount to this: That propositions about the good are all of them synthetic and never analytic; and that is plainly no trivial matter. And the same thing may be expressed more popularly, by saying that, if I am right, then nobody can foist upon us such an axiom as that 'Pleasure is the only good' or that 'The good is the desired' on the pretence that this is 'the very meaning of the word.'

Let us, then, consider this position. My point is that 'good' is a simple notion, just as 'yellow' is a simple notion; that, just as you cannot, by any manner of means, explain to any one who does not already know it, what yellow is, so you cannot explain what good is. Definitions of the kind that I was asking for, definitions which describe the real nature of the object or notion denoted by a word, and which do not merely tell us what the word is used to mean, are only possible when the object or notion in question is something complex. You can give a definition of a horse, because a horse has many different properties and qualities, all of which you can enumerate. But when you have enumerated them all, when you have reduced a horse to his simplest terms then you can no longer define those terms. They are simply something which you think of or perceive, and to any one who cannot think of or perceive them, you can never, by any definition, make their nature known. It may perhaps be objected to this that we are able to describe to others, objects which they have never seen or thought of. We can, for instance, make a man understand what a chimaera is, although he has never heard of one or seen one. You can tell him that it is an animal with a lioness's head and body, with a goat's head growing from the middle of its back, and with a snake in place of a tail. But here the object which you are describing is a complex object; it is entirely composed of parts, with which we are all perfectly familiar—a snake, a goat, a lioness; and we know, too, the manner in which those parts are to be put together, because we know what is meant by the middle of a lioness's back, and where her tail is wont to grow. And so it is with all objects, not previously known, which we are able to define: they are all complex; all composed of parts, which may themselves, in the first instance, be capable of similar definition, but which must in the end be reducible to simplest parts, which can no longer be defined. But yellow and good, we say, are not complex: they are notions of that simple kind, out of which definitions are composed and with which the power of further defining ceases.

When we say, as Webster says, 'The definition of horse is "A hoofed quadruped of the genus Equus," ' we may, in fact, mean three different things. (1) We may mean merely: 'When I say "horse," you are to understand that I am talking about a hoofed quadruped of the genus Equus.' This might be called the arbitrary verbal definition: and I do not mean that good is indefinable in that sense. (2) We may mean, as Webster ought to mean: 'When most English people say "horse," they mean a hoofed quadruped of the genus Equus.' This may be called the verbal definition proper, and I do not say that good is indefinable in this sense either; for it is certainly possible to discover how people use a word: otherwise, we could never have known that 'good' may be translated by 'gut' in German and by 'bon' in French. But (3) we may, when we define horse, mean something much more important. We may mean that a certain object, which we all of us know, is composed in a certain manner: that it has four legs, a head, a heart, a liver, etc., etc., all of them arranged in definite relations to one another. It is in this sense that I deny good to be definable. I say that it is not composed of any parts, which we can substitute for it in our minds when we are thinking of it. We might think just as clearly and correctly about a horse, if we thought of all its parts and their arrangement instead of thinking of the whole: we could, I say, think how a horse differed from a donkey just as well, just as truly, in this way, as now we do, only not so easily; but there is nothing whatsoever which we could so substitute for good; and that is what I mean, when I say that good is indefinable.

But I am afraid I have still not removed the chief difficulty which may prevent acceptance of the proposition that good is indefinable. I do not mean to say that *the* good, that which is good, is thus indefinable; if I did think so, I should not be writing on Ethics, for my main object is to

843

help towards discovering that definition. It is just because I think there will be less risk of error in our search for a definition of 'the good,' that I am now insisting that *good* is indefinable. I must try to explain the difference between these two. I suppose it may be granted that 'good' is an adjective. Well 'the good,' 'that which is good,' must therefore be the substantive to which the adjective 'good' will apply: it must be the whole of that to which the adjective will apply, and the adjective must *always* truly apply to it. But if it is that to which the adjective will apply, it must be something different from that adjective itself; and the whole of that something different, whatever it is, will be our definition of *the* good. Now it may be that this something will have other adjectives, beside 'good,' that will apply to it. It may be full of pleasure, for example; it may be intelligent: and if these two adjectives are really part of its definition, then it will certainly be true, that pleasure and intelligence are good. And many people appear to think that, if we say 'Pleasure and intelligence are good,' or if we say 'Only pleasure and intelligence are good,' we are defining 'good.' Well, I cannot deny that propositions of this nature may sometimes be called definitions; I do not know well enough how the word is generally used to decide upon this point. I only wish it to be understood that that is not what I mean when I say there is no possible definition of good, and that I shall not mean this if I use the word again. I do most fully believe that some true proposition of the form 'Intelligence is good and intelligence alone is good' can be found; if none could be found, our definition of *the* good would be impossible. As it is, I believe *the* good to be definable; and yet I still say that good itself is indefinable.

'Good,' then, if we mean by it that quality which we assert to belong to a thing, when we say that the thing is good, is incapable of any definition, in the most important sense of that word. The most important sense of 'definition' is that in which a definition states what are the parts which invariably compose a certain whole; and in this sense 'good' has no definition because it is simple and has no parts. It is one of those innumerable objects of thought which are themselves incapable of definition, because they are the ultimate terms by reference to which whatever *is* capable of definition must be defined. That there must be an indefinite number of such terms is obvious, on reflection; since we cannot define anything except by an analysis, which, when carried as far as it will go, refers us to something, which is simply different from anything else, and which by that ultimate difference explains the peculiarity of the whole which we are defining: for every whole contains some parts which are common to other wholes also. There is, therefore, no intrinsic difficulty in the contention that 'good' denotes a simple and indefinable quality.

[260]

MORE, THOMAS

MORE, THOMAS (1478-1535). Although Thomas More did not live in accordance with the ideas developed in his *Utopia* (1516), he was a man of principles and became a martyr to his convictions.

In the book *Utopia*, after which numerous utopias have been named, More described an imaginary island where a perfectly wise and happy people had established the best imaginable commonwealth by means of ideal institutions, living in peace and abhorring war and oppression of any kind.

More, however, had to live in Tudor England, and, although his spiritual horizon was larger and his moral consciousness was scrupulous, he had to adapt his thoughts and actions to the customs of his contemporary fellow Englishmen and, above all, to the desires of the king. For a time he seemed to be a conformist but when he had to choose between his loyalty to the king and the demands of his conscience, he decided against the royal arbitrary power and faced execution with equanimity.

Having intended to become a priest, More spent four years, from 1499 to 1503, in religious contemplation. Then he suddenly abandoned the idea of ecclesiastical life. Nevertheless, he remained a pious Catholic, although devoted to the "new learning" of humanism. He was an intimate friend of John Colet and Erasmus and participated in their efforts to reform the Catholic Church, to purify religious life and to reconcile religious traditions with the new science of humanism. He wrote poetry, books about English history, a biography of Pico della Mirandola, and protected the painter Hans Holbein and other artists.

After being elected member of Parliament in 1504, he had a brilliant career, was knighted in 1521, and succeeded Cardinal Wolsey as Lord Chancellor of England in 1529. But he was opposed to King Henry VIII's *Act of Supremacy* and *Act of Succession* because the former meant the secession from the Roman Catholic Church, and the latter the nullification of the king's first marriage. The whole of Catholic Europe was startled when it learned that More was executed for his decision to disobey the King. As a prisoner in the Tower, More wrote his *Dialogue of Comfort Against Tribulation* and died as an upright and courageous man.

MILITARY PRACTICE IN UTOPIA

WHEN they draw out troops of their own people, they take such out of every city as freely offer themselves, for none are forced to go against their wills, since they think that if any man is pressed that wants courage, he will not only act faintly, but by his cowardice dishearten others. But if an invasion is made on their country they make use of such men, if they have good bodies, though they are not brave; and either put them aboard their ships or place them on the walls of their towns, that being so posted they may find no opportunity of flying away; and thus either shame, the heat of action, or the impossibility of flying, bears down their cowardice; they often make a virtue of necessity and behave themselves well, because nothing else is left them. But as they force no man to go into any foreign war against his will, so they do not hinder those women who are willing to go along with their husbands; on the contrary, they encourage and praise them, and they stand often next their husbands in the front of the army. They also place together those who are related, parents and children, kindred, and those that are mutually allied, near one another; that those whom nature has inspired with the greatest zeal for assisting one another, may be the nearest and readiest to do it; and it is matter of great reproach if husband or wife survive one another, or if a child survives his parents, and therefore when they come to be engaged in action they continue to fight to the last man, if their enemies stand before them.

And as they use all prudent methods to avoid the en-dangering of their own men, and if it is possible let all the action and danger fall upon the troops that they hire, so if it becomes necessary for themselves to engage, they then charge with as much courage as they avoided it before with prudence; nor is it a fierce charge at first, but it increases by degrees; and as they continue in action, they grow more obstinate and press harder upon the enemy, insomuch that they will much sooner die than give ground; for the cer-tainty that their children will be well looked after when they are dead, frees them from all that anxiety concerning them which often masters men of great courage; and thus they are animated by a noble and invincible resolution. Their skill in military affairs increases their courage; and the wise sentiments which, according to the laws of their country, are instilled into them in their education, give additional vigor to their minds: for as they do not undervalue life so as prodigally to throw it away, they are not so indecently fond of it as to preserve it by base and unbecoming methods. In the greatest heat of action, the bravest of their youth, who have devoted themselves to that service, single out the gen-eral of their enemies, set on him either openly or by ambus-cade, pursue him everywhere, and when spent and wearied out, are relieved by others, who never give over the pursuit; either attacking him with close weapons when they can get near him, or with those which wound at a distance, when others get in between them; so that unless he secures himself by flight, they seldom fail at last to kill or to take him prisoner.

[261]

MORGAN, C. LLOYD

MORGAN, C. LLOYD (1852-1936). As a boy, Morgan had an almost exclusively literary education. He was devoted to Byron,

Keats, Shelley, Moore and Scott. Then, while in college, the philosophy of Spinoza, Berkeley and Hume had a strong appeal for him.
He had intended to become an engineer but, as a student, was
drawn by T. H. Huxley to the interpretation of nature by biological
studies. His principal interest remained fixed on the borderline of
life and mind, and he became more and more convinced that a
synthesis of philosophy and science was possible and necessary.

Such a synthesis was, in Morgan's opinion, "bound to take a
risk." The risk he took was to acknowledge things, to accept realism.
Things were defined by him as "clusters of events," quite in accordance with modern physics. With his principal books *Animal Life
and Intelligence* (1891), *Habit and Instinct* (1896) and *Emergent
Evolution* (1923), Morgan has inspired biologists, psychologists
and philosophers both in England, his homeland, and America. His
ideas have also been accepted by outstanding French thinkers. Morgan defined evolution as a constructive scheme which shall provide
for a physical realism but also for "something of at least in the
same genre as Platonic realism." Emergent evolution was conceived
as selective synthesis at certain critical turning points in the course
of evolutionary advance. Darwin's conception of evolution as a
steady, gradual process was abandoned by Morgan. On a broader
basis, he developed T. H. Huxley's and G. H. Lewes's criticism of
Darwin's theory and that which is called the theory of mutation. In
this way he inspired Henri Bergson and Samuel Alexander, among
others, at least by offering them rich material of concrete facts.

MAN'S THREE-FOLD NATURE

If all art is constructive the comprehensive aim of philosophy as an art is to express in a representative 'vision' the
whole nature of reality which shall include the whole nature
of man.

Of any man I should say: He is body as a center which
is recipient of physical influence from a material world of
which he is part, and influences some of the physical events
therein. He is mind as a center of experience from which
there is reference to the physical world and to other minds.
He is also a center of active causality.

Here I start with the frankly hypothetical assumption
that such is man's three-fold nature. But what I reach is a
considered assurance that this probably (I dare not say
more) represents his real nature.

To this tripartite nature there are, as I think, three distinguishable avenues of approach which I label B inquiry (physical), C inquiry (psychological), and A inquiry (metaphysical). Philosophy includes all three.

Since on these terms the physical universe is not the subject-matter of C inquiry, the empirical psychologist, as such, has nothing to tell us about it. He leaves that to his colleague the physicist. Still in broader philosophical regard he may (or perhaps may not) acknowledge its continuant existence. So too since Activity is not the subject-matter of his empirical inquiry he has nothing to tell us about it, though, in his philosophical capacity, he may (or may not) acknowledge its abiding subsistence.

On these terms a physical world on the one hand and, on the other hand, activity as final cause, lie outside his specialized province of inquiry. None the less it *does* fall within that province to deal with the process and products of human thought. Since, then, an outcome of that thought is a distinction of body, mind, and active causality, the genetic origin of this distinction in thought falls within the subject-matter of psychological inquiry.

However it came about in the natural course of mental development, this distinction has taken definite form in some minds. I, for one, have been led to accept its representative validity. I may then be asked: How have these three—body, mind, and active causality—so come together in man as to constitute this tripartite nature? To this question I reply that I have no assurance that they have done so. I started long ago with this widespread animistic assumption. I cannot now endorse it with later assurance. My considered belief goes no further than the tenet that they *are* inseparably together in the three-fold nature of man.

Similarly when I pass to the whole nature of the cosmos of which man is a part. If in philosophical regard there be a directive Source of all processes current in things and in minds, such a Source there abidingly *is*, not apart from them, but always one with them.

[262]

MO-TI

MO-TI (About 470-396 B.C.). After Mencius had been successful in discrediting the doctrine of Mo-Ti, it was ignored by Chinese thinkers and the public for twelve centuries. Only Chinese Buddhism retained some of Mo-Ti's tenets. Recently Mohism, as the school of Mo-Ti is called, has been adopted anew by many young Chinese, who regard it as a way to China's salvation from the troubles of the present time. Mo-Ti was a victorious general and an efficient civil servant.

His philosophy combines religious spirituality and utilitarian rationalism. He was also a refined logician and experienced in dialectic. After having adhered to Confucianism he accused Confucius' successors of exaggerated ritualism and rejected his former Master's belief in fate. He set purity of the heart higher than formal correctness in fulfilling ceremonial laws. He pronounced universal love without regard to legal status, and therefore was called "an apostle of human brotherhood." While justifying his doctrine, he declared that universal love was demanded by Heaven, the Supreme Being, as well as by the innermost strivings of the human individual for happiness, and that it would always pay to love his fellow men. His aim was promotion of general welfare by both moral elevation and economic improvement. Devoted to the cause of peace, Mo-Ti allowed defensive war only, and he is credited with having averted several wars.

ON STANDARD PATTERNS

OUR Master Mo said: Any one in the Great Society who takes any business in hand, cannot dispense with a standard pattern. For there to be no standard and the business to succeed, this just does not happen. Even the best experts who act as generals and councillors-of-state, all have standards (of action); and so also even with the best craftsmen. They use a carpenter's square for making squares and compasses for making circles: a piece of string for making straight lines and a plumb line for getting the perpendicular. It makes no difference whether a craftsman is skilled or not: all alike use these five (devices) as standards, only the skilled are accurate. But, although the unskilled fail to be

850

accurate, they nevertheless get much better results if they follow these standards in the work which they do. Thus it is that craftsmen in their work have the measurements which these standards give.

Now take the great ones who rule our Great Society, and the less great ones who rule the different states, but who have no standards of measurement (for their actions). In this they are less critically minded than the craftsman. That being so, what standard may be taken as suitable for ruling? Will it do if everybody imitates his father and mother? The number of fathers and mothers in the Great Society is large, but the number of human-hearted ones is small. If everybody were to imitate his father and mother, this standard would not be a human-hearted one. For a standard, however, to be not human-hearted makes it impossible for it to be a standard. Will it do then if everybody imitates his teacher? The number of teachers is large, but the number of human-hearted ones is small. If everybody were to imitate his teacher . . . this standard would not be a human-hearted one. Will it do then if everybody imitates his sovereign? The number of princes is large, but the number of human-hearted ones is small. If everybody imitated his sovereign, this standard would not be a human-hearted one. Hence, fathers and mothers, teachers and sovereigns cannot be taken as standards for ruling.

That being so, what standard may be taken as suitable for ruling? The answer is that nothing is equal to imitating Heaven. Heaven's actions are all-inclusive and not private-minded, its blessings substantial and unceasing, its revelations abiding and incorruptible. Thus it was that the Sage-kings imitated it. Having taken Heaven as their standard, their every movement and every action was bound to be measured in relation to Heaven. What Heaven wanted, that they did: what Heaven did not want, that they stopped doing.

The question now is, what does Heaven want and what does it hate? Heaven wants men to love and be profitable to each other, and does not want men to hate and maltreat each other. How do we know that Heaven wants men to love and be profitable to each other? Because it embraces all in its love of them, embraces all in its benefits to them. How do we know that Heaven embraces all . . .? Because it embraces all in its possession of them and in its gifts of food.

Take then the Great Society. There are no large or small states: all are Heaven's townships. Take men. There are no young men or old, no patricians or plebeians: all are Heaven's subjects. This is so, for there is no one who does not fatten oxen and sheep and dogs and pigs and make pure wine and sacrificial cakes with which to do reverence and service to Heaven. Can this be anything else than Heaven owning all and giving food to all? Assuming then that Heaven embraces all and gives food to all, how could it be said that it does not want men to love and benefit each other?

Hence I say that Heaven is sure to give happiness to those who love and benefit other men, and is sure to bring calamities on those who hate and maltreat other men. I maintain that the man who murders an innocent person will meet with misfortune. What other explanation is there of the fact that when men murder each other, Heaven brings calamity on them? This is the way in which we know that Heaven wants men to love and benefit each other and does not want them to hate and maltreat each other.

[263]

MUNK, KAJ

MUNK, KAJ (1898-1944). Kaj Munk, pastor of a village in Denmark, had inherited a bent posture from his father who had been a tanner, but he was one of the most upright men who ever defied Nazi tyranny. His moral power was rooted in the orthodox Lutheran faith that accepted the possibility of miracles as the basis of prayer. Munk regarded it as "God's way of telling me that my difficulty in keeping a straight back in a physical sense would help me keep a straight back in a spiritual sense."

When the Germans occupied Denmark in 1940, Munk was unrelenting in preaching resistance against the invaders. Standing by as a passive spectator would have meant to him to "feel myself a traitor to my Christian faith, my Danish outlook and my ordination vow."

In his sermons, Munk compared the people of Denmark to the people of Israel, exiled in Babylon and longing to become free from bondage. These sermons, delivered in the church of a small village, spread over the whole Danish country. The Gestapo took the preacher from his home on January 4, 1944, shot him through the head, and threw his body into a ditch by the roadside where it was found the following day.

MOSES AND CHRIST

MOSES and Jesus are two figures of the most tragic types, the one more tragic than the other.

It is almost laughable to think of them.

And yet they are the only two whose names today shine as stars over mankind. By them the name of man is, all things to the contrary, a noble name. It happens to the beasts of the jungle that one night a song sounds through the jungle forest. Some of them lift their heads and listen. This is the distant morning song of the stars.

And there are beasts among us whose hearts tremble in longing, a longing so great that the sneer dies on our lips, the sneer at the content of the song of the stars.

We know this is impossible. But the song is so powerful that we do not believe that it is impossible anyway.

Because there are some, and there always have been and always will be some in the jungle world in whom the song of the stars, the song of fight and hope, lives, we may believe that it will happen.

The great "thou shalt not" will change us into human beings, and the powerful "thou shalt" will perfect the work of the law.

[264]

853

MÜNSTERBERG, HUGO

MÜNSTERBERG, HUGO (1863-1916). The current of Münster-berg's life, which had seemed to take a slow course along German university lines, was suddenly turned to new tasks, experiences and ideas by a letter written to him by William James on February 21, 1892. James, who had met Münsterberg at an international congress three years before, had been impressed by his psychological methods and philosophical views, and now invited him to direct the Psychological Laboratory of Harvard University, claiming that in the whole world no better man could be found for that post than Münsterberg. The latter accepted and, apart from the years 1895 to 1897 and 1910 to 1911, taught at Harvard until his death.

Throughout his life in America, Münsterberg scientific interests were intertwined with cultural and political interests. Fascinated by American life, he tried to interpret it to Germany, his native country, and to acquaint Americans with German cultural performances and scientific methods. His position became precarious after the outbreak of the First World War, when Münsterberg did not conceal his sympathy with Germany, without, however, approving all the measures taken by the German government.

Münsterberg's scientific creed was that psychology must fit into a system of causally connected elements. The function of psychology is to analyze life into elements parallel to the elements of matter that physics reconstructs; but he emphatically warned against confusing that existence, postulated by psychological analysis, with the immediate reality of life, such as becomes manifest in moral and practical activities, in the arts and religion. Causal psychology must be completed by purposive psychology, and the latter must be founded upon a theory of values.

Münsterberg also took great care in applying psychology to education, psychotherapy, the courtroom, vocational training and increase of industrial efficiency. He was the first psychologist to recognize the artistic importance and possibilities of the motion picture.

RELATIVE AND ABSOLUTE VALUES

IN the realm of nature, the bodily and the mental nature, we could not find any values because nature as such has no relation to will. Now we enter the realm of immediate life-experience. Here we are subjects of will. Here our decision is no longer the effect of foregoing causes, but comes in question with reference to our purposes and to our aims. Have we now a firm anchorage for the values of the world? Can we understand the value in its pure validity from the will of individuals? But this question evidently has no meaning so long as we simply identify value with that which is the goal of our will. In that case we could not desire anything which would not by this mere fact of our desire be raised to the dignity of a value. For certain human interests we are accustomed to such terms. The political economist, for instance, is in the habit of calling the things which are desired, values. If the philosopher follows in this path, he needs of course, every time, qualifying additions, if his inquiry into values is to have any meaning. If he studies the character of values he does not intend to discuss the value of butter and eggs. The philosopher in his sphere of thought might even hesitate to call food valuable at all, in spite of the fact that the hungry man longs for it, that the consumer enjoys it, and that the grocer in buying and selling measures it by the standard of other desired things. If the philosopher is ready to use the word "value" in such a colorless way, and to concede to the economist that everything is valuable which is object of desire, he has simply to divide the values at once into two large groups. He must make from the start a sharp demarcation line between relative values and absolute values. Whether in reality two such kinds of values exist has to be examined. It would be thinkable that only the relative values have existence, that is, that everything would be valuable only for this or that individual, in this or that position, under this or that condition. But even if the reality of absolute values is denied, this separation remains necessary. In the spirit of critical philosophy, value always means an absolute value. But if we use the word in its wider sense, our question is now clear. That there exist relative values in the world of immediate life is then a matter of course to us. As it is a world in which the personalities are subjects of will, everything which is object of their will

855

must have such conditional value. Our real question remains. It is the question whether, in this sphere of individual
desires, there exist also unconditional absolute values, values
which are valuable in themselves without reference to this
or that individual and his wishes. So long as we were speaking of nature, the separation into relative and absolute values
was superfluous, as a world in which there is no will can
have no values whatever.

If all values in the world are based on the fact that
individuals as individuals desire and prefer for themselves
certain things, evidently we have only the one class of values,
the relative ones. Every one who wants to acknowledge only
the absolute values as true values would have to claim in
this case that the world has merely pseudo-values. Indeed,
it is impossible ever to deduce an absolute value from the
world of individual personal desires. There exists no bridge
from the individual pleasure and displeasure to the absolute
value. So long as we start from the selfish desire of individuals,—and there may be unlimited millions of them,—we
shall always come only to social and economic values which
have relative validity. A value which without reference to
individual pleasures and displeasures belongs to the world
of reality itself, and which thus stands above all individual
desires, remains out of the question there. Nature did not
know any unconditional values, because nature had no relation at all to will; but the world of personal desires has no
unconditional values, because in it every relation to will
lacks the general necessary unconditional character. Whoever is convinced that all values in the world can be, and
ultimately must be, based on the desire for pleasure in individuals, is certainly more consistent if he denies every
absolute value than if, as frequently happens, he bolsters
up the conditional values into eternal ones.

[265]

N

NATORP, PAUL

NATORP, PAUL (1854-1924). Until his late years, Natorp was a faithful follower of Hermann Cohen. It was due to the excitement of the war years, 1914-1918, that he deviated slightly from his master's tenets and became more inclined to exalt the German national character and civilization in his book *Deutscher Weltberuf* (*Germany's Vocation in the World*, 1918). Natorp's interpretation of Plato's doctrine of ideas was much discussed. So was his *General Psychology* (1912). More successful was his *Socialpaedagogik* (1899) which was re-edited several times. According to Natorp, education must influence all social and economic activities as well as schools and universities in order to realize national solidarity and social peace.

ON COGNITION

THE objects are inexhaustible; cognition however which, tending toward the object, believes to draw closer and closer to it and still never reaches it, is following its inherent fundamental law always one and the same. The objects seem to stand outside of us at a certain distance. With the progress of cognition we believe we diminish this distance between them and us. To our amazement we discover that they remain always equally distant from us, nay that they draw farther and farther away from us. Only cognition remains ours, for it is consciousness and consciousness is, if anything, our own.

One well known example suffices to clarify this relationship. For the thinking of antiquity and the Middle Ages the outer universe ended with the ninth or eleventh etc. of these celestial spheres which, inserted one into the other like onion skins, one thought eternally revolving in changeless circular motions around their center the earth. Copernicus destroyed this artistically constructed edifice. The earth had to cede its central position to the sun and had to remain satisfied with a modest place among the planets. The sphere of the fixed stars withdrew to hitherto unexpected distances. This system too was superseded. The sun as little as the earth forms the center of the universe. The immovable sphere to which the fixed stars were attached has become a myth. Their name only (fixed stars) keeps, like a fossil remnant, the memory of their former importance. In reality they are only slowly moving planets of a superior order. The formerly assumed distances and periods of revolution have been surpassed by myriads. The aided eye finds only in its own imperfection and the imperfection of its instruments not in the object its barrier. Infinity has room for worlds and worlds of worlds without end. We call that progress of knowledge and count them among the greatest ones humanity has to record. Unfortunately, what we were looking forward to, the closed unity of the universe, the unity of the cosmos, has not been brought nearer to us, it has only been pushed farther and farther away from us. More than ever are we remote from a system of the universe. The Ancients had a system, Copernicus and still Kepler had theirs. We have none. But cognition has won immensely. And what is most amazing, the principle of cognition has remained the same. It is the same law of cognition to which Eudoxus and Ptolemy, Copernicus and Kepler, Newton, Kant and Laplace obeyed. Only its application to more remote fields of given phenomena, to the more thoroughly understood problems, had to lead to other results.

[266]

858

NICHOLAS OF CUSA. See CUSA, NICHOLAS OF.

NICOLAI, FRIEDRICH

NICOLAI, FRIEDRICH (1733-1811). The world record in being vilified by the greatest number of his most illustrious contemporaries can hardly be disputed to be held by Nicolai, who was a bookseller, publisher, editor of reviews, novelist, and theological and philosophical writer. For about a decade (1755-1765), Nicolai's good reputation was not attacked. He was the friend of Gotthold Ephraim Lessing and Moses Mendelssohn, and was considered a man of sound ideas, a fighter for the Enlightenment that flourished in Germany during that period. But then, for more than forty-five years, Nicolai was the object of satires, polemical pamphlets, literary assaults and expressions of indignation and contempt. Among Nicolai's most violent enemies were Immanuel Kant and Fichte, Goethe and Schiller, the poets of the movement of Storm and Stress and the leaders of German romanticism.

After Lessing's and Mendelssohn's deaths, Nicolai, almost alone, answered the attacks directed against him, sometimes with humor, sometimes with serious arguments, always with equanimity, though not always adequately. It cannot be denied that he was inferior to Kant, and that most of his debates with Kant resulted in his defeat. It cannot be denied that his devotion to the ideas of the Enlightenment was stiffened by a sort of orthodoxy. Nicolai was a fanatic adversary of sentimentalism, superstition, of obscurantism of any kind. He was a champion of common sense, and therefore became suspicious of Kant's criticism and Fichte's idealism. The poetry of Goethe, especially his *Werther*, was accused by him of favoring exaggeration of sentiments, and romanticism was, to him, identical with a return to the Middle Ages in politics, thought and religion. In all these struggles, the German public acclaimed Nicolai's adversaries. He was not discouraged nor afraid of replying to the romanticist Friedrich Schlegel, who exalted Fichte's doctrine of science, concerning which he, Nicolai, thought the introduction of planting potatoes was of greater importance to humanity. Nicolai's novels contain some interesting descriptions. His *Sebaldus Nothanker* (1773) gives a clear picture of Berlin under Frederick II.

German historians and philosophers still continue to sneer at Nicolai who defended common sense and felt that the German spirit took a dangerous route.

ON JEWISH PHILOSOPHY

WHICH philosophical writings I read and what influence they had on me during the 32 years which I spent and philosophized with Moses Mendelssohn—for I always found time for studies and the development of my spirit, though not for writing—all that would lead me into unnecessary and prolix details. Two very different philosophers, whose acquaintance I had made through Moses Mendelssohn, have given to my philosophical thinking an even more varified turn. Shaftesbury taught us both a more human manner of philosophizing which, with all the profoundness of this philosopher, gives an insight into the real world and unites again what the dry abstraction, for its commodity, has isolated although in nature it is coherent. And then I heard Moses Mendelssohn's excellent ideas on the cabalistic philosophy of the Hebrews. He explained in a very comprehensive manner that the strange aspect of the sentences of these oriental philosophers and their obscurity stems from the poverty of the Hebrew language in expressions of philosophical concepts, combined with the images customary in the Orient, so typical for uncultivated languages. In addition he showed that, given freedom from both cloaks, they have a very consistent sense, and that if one interprets the allegorical images literally and weaves them into new flowery commentaries the crudest nonsense and eccentricity is born, under which the religion of the Jews is still sighing and by which many Christian mystagogues have become complete fools. And then my friend showed very clearly how Spinoza, as a Jew, by combining the cabalistic philosophy, which he had inherited from his youth, with the sentences of Cartesius had to come quite naturally to the point where he imagined God as the only and general substance of which the world is only a modification. Through these lucid ideas I clarified my knowledge of ecclesiastical history commencing with Jewish and Christian gnostics, who played such an important

860

part in the formation of Christianity and whose opinions, which originated in the cabalistic philosophy, modified the Christian theology until the Middle Ages, as the study of the Manicheans and Albigenses shows.

[267]

NIETZSCHE, FRIEDRICH

NIETZSCHE, FRIEDRICH (1844-1900). The fact that Nietzsche was insane for the last twelve years of his life has often been exploited by unfair adversaries who embarrassed serious critics of his doctrines.

Before Nietzsche took his Ph.D. degree, he had already been appointed a full professor of classical philology at the University of Basel in 1869. But scholarship, which promised him a brilliant career, did not satisfy him. The aim of his life was a philosophy that would comprise both cool analysis and enthusiastic vision, a synthesis of a new religious creed and merciless criticism. Apollo, the god of lucid wisdom, and Dionysos, the god of orgiastic mysticism, were taken for its symbols.

Nietzsche is acknowledged, even by most of his opponents, as a great psychologist who, particularly by using the concept of "resentment," succeeded in unmasking hypocrisy, in exposing delusions, perversion of feeling and judgment or intellectual timidity, and opened new ways by his much-disputed inquiry into the formation of morality.

But the view of the philosopher, as Nietzsche conceived it, is not confined to things past and present. His task is not so much to take care of the well-being of his contemporary fellow men as rather to pave the way for the future development which will change man into a higher type, the superman. For the sake of the future, Nietzsche violently fought against Christianity, whose ethics were depreciated by him as "slave morality," and he pronounced the necessity of a general "trans-valuation of values." Nietzsche's ideal of human personality meant the union of physical strength and mental energy. It combined the virtues of the warrior and the independent thinker. It was founded upon his conviction that the "will to power" is the ruling principle of all life, and that life on earth has an absolute value. Nietzsche's ethics, however, does not preach self-indulgence or regard suffering as an evil. It demands fearlessness, not love of pleasure. It prefers the dangerous life to the comfortable one.

861

While endeavoring to grasp the essential features of cosmic life or to predict a far future, Nietzsche constantly kept his eye upon the cultural situation of his own time, foreboding a terrible catastrophe. Nihilism and decadence seemed to him the greatest dangers that threaten European civilization. He was equally opposed to democracy, socialism and nationalism, and most of all, to the national aspirations and pride of the Germans. He proclaimed the ideal of a "good European."

No philosopher has raged as vehemently against his own soul as Nietzsche did by glorifying physical strength and the will to power. In reality, he was gentle, always in poor health, hating noise and trying to avoid quarrels.

ZARATHUSTRA

WHEN Zarathustra arrived at the nearest town which adjoineth the forest, he found many people assembled in the market-place; for it had been announced that a rope-dancer would give a performance. And Zarathustra spake thus unto the people:

I teach you the Superman. Man is something that is to be surpassed. What have ye done to surpass man?

All beings hitherto have created something beyond themselves: and ye want to be the ebb of that great tide, and would rather go back to the beast than surpass man?

What is the ape to man? A laughing-stock, a thing of shame. And just the same shall man be to the Superman: a laughing-stock, a thing of shame.

Ye have made your way from the worm to man, and much within you is still worm. Once were ye apes, and even yet man is more of an ape than any of the apes.

Even the wisest among you is only a disharmony and hybrid of plant and phantom. But do I bid you become phantoms or plants?

Lo, I teach you the Superman!

The Superman is the meaning of the earth. Let your will say: The Superman *shall be* the meaning of the earth!

I conjure you, my brethren, *remain true to the earth,*

and believe not those who speak unto you of superearthly hopes! Poisoners are they, whether they know it or not.

Despisers of life are they, decaying ones and poisoned ones themselves, of whom the earth is weary: so away with them!

Once blasphemy against God was the greatest blasphemy; but God died, and therewith also those blasphemers. To blaspheme the earth is now the dreadfulest sin, and to rate the heart of the unknowable higher than the meaning of the earth!

Once the soul looked contemptuously on the body, and then that contempt was the supreme thing:—the soul wished the body meagre, ghastly, and famished. Thus it thought to escape from the body and the earth.

Oh, that soul was itself meagre, ghastly, and famished; and cruelty was the delight of that soul!

But ye, also, my brethren tell me: What doth your body say about your soul? Is your soul not poverty and pollution and wretched self-complacency?

Verily, a polluted stream is man. One must be a sea, to receive a polluted stream without becoming impure.

Lo, I teach you the Superman: he is that sea; in him can your great contempt be submerged.

What is the greatest thing ye can experience? It is the hour of great contempt. The hour in which even your happiness becometh loathsome unto you, and so also your reason and virtue.

The hour when ye say: "What good is my happiness! It is poverty and pollution and wretched self-complacency. But my happiness should justify existence itself!"

The hour when ye say: "What good is my reason! Doth it long for knowledge as the lion for his food? It is poverty and pollution and wretched self-complacency!"

The hour when ye say: "What good is my virtue! As yet it hath not made me passionate. How weary I am of my good and my bad! It is all poverty and pollution and wretched self-complacency!"

The hour when ye say: "What good is my justice! I do not see that I am fervour and fuel. The just, however, are fervour and fuel!"

The hour when we say: "What good is my pity! Is not pity the cross on which he is nailed who loveth man? But my pity is not a crucifixion."

Have ye ever spoken thus? Have ye ever cried thus? Ah! would that I have heard you crying thus!

It is not your sin—it is your self-satisfaction that crieth unto heaven; your very sparingness in sin crieth unto heaven!

Where is the lightning to lick you with its tongue? Where is the frenzy with which ye should be inoculated?

Lo, I teach you the Superman: he is that lightning, he is that frenzy!—

When Zarathustra had thus spoken, one of the people called out: "We have now heard enough of the rope-dancer; it is time now for us to see him!" And all the people laughed at Zarathustra. But the rope-dancer, who thought the words applied to him, began his performance.

*   *   *

Zarathustra, however, looked at the people and wondered. Then he spake thus:

Man is a rope stretched between the animal and the Superman—a rope over an abyss.

A dangerous crossing, a dangerous wayfaring, a dangerous looking-back, a dangerous trembling and halting.

What is great in man is that he is a bridge and not a goal: what is lovable in man is that he is an *over-going* and a *down-going*.

I love those that know not how to live except as downgoers, for they are the over-goers.

I love the great despisers, because they are the great adorers, and arrows of longing for the other shore.

I love those who do not first seek a reason beyond the stars for going down and being sacrifices, but sacrifice themselves to the earth, that the earth of the Superman may hereafter arrive.

I love him who liveth in order to know, and seeketh to know in order that the Superman may hereafter live. Thus seeketh he his own down-going.

I love him who laboreth and inventeth, that he may build the house for the Superman, and prepare for him earth, animal, and plant: for thus seeketh he his own down-going.

I love him who loveth his virtue: for virtue is the will to down-going, and an arrow of longing.

I love him who reserveth no share of spirit for himself, but wanteth to be wholly the spirit of his virtue: thus walketh he as spirit over the bridge.

I love him who maketh his virtue his inclination and destiny: thus, for the sake of his virtue, he is willing to live on, or live no more.

I love him who desireth not too many virtues. One virtue is more of a virtue than two, because it is more of a knot for one's destiny to cling to.

I love him whose soul is lavish, who wanteth no thanks and doth not give back: for he always bestoweth, and desireth not to keep for himself.

I love him who is ashamed when the dice fall in his favor, and who then asketh: "Am I a dishonest player?" —for he is willing to succumb.

I love him who scattereth golden words in advance of his deeds, and always doeth more than he promiseth: for he seeketh his own down-going.

I love him who justifieth the future ones, and redeemeth the past ones: for he is willing to succumb through the present ones.

I love him who chasteneth his God, because he loveth his God: for he must succumb through the wrath of his God.

I love him whose soul is deep even in the wounding, and may succumb through a small matter: thus goeth he willingly over the bridge.

I love him whose soul is so overfull that he forgetteth himself, and all things are in him: thus all things become his down-going.

I love him who is of a free spirit and a free heart: thus is his head only the bowels of his heart; his heart, however, causeth his down-going.

I love all who are like heavy drops falling one by one out of the dark cloud that lowereth over man: they herald the coming of the lightning, and succumb as heralds.

Lo, I am a herald of the lightning, and a heavy drop out of the cloud: the lightning, however, is the *Superman*.

[268]

NOÜY, PIERRE LECOMTE DU

NOÜY, PIERRE LECOMTE DU (1883-1947). A descendant of the great French dramatist Pierre Corneille, and of many generations of important artists, the son of an authoress of numerous novels, one of which *Amitié Amoureuse* ran into six hundred editions in France and was translated into sixteen languages, Pierre du Noüy has been the first member of that family to turn to science. It was in 1915, when he, then an officer in the French Army, met Dr. Alexis Carrell, that he became interested in problems of science and philosophy. Shortly thereafter du Noüy won international fame by his pioneering efforts in applying mathematics to biology. Apart from his sensational method of expressing mathematically the process of healing of wounds by representing the process of cicatrization through an equation, he introduced the concept of "physiological age" as different from that measured by the calendar, and of "biological time" different from physical time, which led him to the conclusion that time has different values for children and for adults.

In *Human Destiny* (1947) du Noüy emphasizes that we must have confidence in science but that we must be aware that we know less about the material world than is usually believed. What we know is subjective and conditioned by the structure of our brain. He admits that the laws established by science express an order of sequence and quantitative variations. But, he continues, that is true only when life is inert. Du Noüy's principal tenet is that the concept of evolution cannot be thought of without that of finality, that finality dominates evolution. His doctrine of "telefinalism" declares that the laws of inorganic evolution contradict those of the evolution of life, and that the destiny of mankind is incomparable to that of any other existent. In the evolution of mankind he finds a striking parallel between biological, psychic and moral evolution,

866

but biological evolution is progressing far more· slowly than the other two.

On this ground, Du Noüy confirms Christian religion and ethics, saying that man has to choose whether he will be a "co-worker with God" or a "dreg of evolution." Man has to use reason but he must also listen to heart. He must learn to think universally and to develop collective conscience for the sake of universal peace and solidarity.

ON EVOLUTION

IF we accept the idea of evolution, we must recognize the fact that, *on an average,* since the beginning of the world it has followed an ascending path, always oriented in the same direction. The objection has been made that many transformations of animals did not constitute a progress; the exaggerated development of the antlers of certain Cervidae, for instance. This is true, and that is the reason why we suggest the hypothesis of a finality comparable to gravitation in the above analogy, that is to say, a "telefinality" direct-ing evolution as a whole. There is no doubt that there have been trials of all sorts, sometimes successful and sometimes unsuccessful. If we imagine a goal to be attained, acting like gravitation, once the start was given, all possible com-binations had to be tried and their interest or their value proved by their reaction to the environment. If the new forms were badly adapted, incapable of serving as a starting point for a new stage of evolution, if they were surpassed by other strains, they disappeared progressively, or vegetated, cut off from the principal effort. The fate of the species itself thus becomes a secondary issue. What matters is the fate of the species *considered as a link in evolution as a whole.* Prodigies of adaptation were hardly more important than extraordinary performances in the circus. Adaptation and natural selection are no longer identified with evolution. The latter is differentiated from the former by its distant goal, which dominates all the species.

In this hypothesis, and in opposition to what Darwin thought, the survival of the fittest can no longer be considered as the *origin* of the evolving strain, and the fittest of a certain line can eventually give birth to a species destined to disappear or vegetate if the external conditions (climate, etc.), are modified or if other individuals, more apt from the final teleologic point of view, displace them.

Let us make this point quite clear: the properties or qualities of living organisms are *not* attributed to special principles as was done by the old vitalist doctrines, but it is simply assumed that a goal must be attained, by means of the most varied methods, *in conformity with the physico-chemical laws and the ordinary biological laws*. Nature often has recourse to chance, to probabilities, in living beings. Fish lay hundreds of thousands of eggs, as if they knew that, owing to the conditions under which these eggs will hatch, ninety per cent of them are destined to be destroyed.

We can no more consider evolutive transformations separately than we can consider physiological functions separately, if we aim to understand the evolution of living beings or the psychology of man.

In brief, evolution should be considered as a global phenomenon, irreversibly progressive, resulting from the combined activity of elementary mechanisms such as adaptation (Lamarck), natural selection (Darwin), and sudden mutations (Naudin—de Vries). Evolution begins with amorphous living matter or beings such as the Coenocytes, still without cell structure, and ends in thinking Man, endowed with a conscience. It is concerned *only* with the principal line thus defined. It represents *only* those living beings which constitute this unique line zigzagging intelligently through the colossal number of living forms.

Evolution, we repeat, is comprehensible only if we admit that it is dominated by a finality, a precise and distant goal. If we do not accept the reality of this orienting pole, not only are we forced to recognize that evolution is rigorously incompatible with our laws of matter, as we demonstrated above, but—and this is serious—that the appearance of moral and spiritual ideas remains an absolute mystery. Mystery for mystery, it seems wiser, more logical and more intelligent to choose the one which explains, thus satisfying our need to comprehend; the one which opens the doors to hope, rather than the one which closes those doors and explains nothing.

Adaptation, natural selection, mutations are, on the contrary, mechanisms which have contributed to the slow edification of evolution *without being themselves always progressive.* Strictly speaking these mechanisms are not determining factors in general evolution, any more than the mason is a determining factor in the cathedral on which he works. The mason represents, in himself, a very complex element obeying physico-chemical, biological, human, social laws. His sole contact with the cathedral is his trowel, and from the point of view of the architect, he is only a trowel. His private life, his intimate tragedies, his illnesses are immaterial. For the bishop, who willed the cathedral, the architect himself is but a means. The same is true of the processes lumped together under the generic name of "Mechanisms of Evolution." Each one contributes materially, statistically, to evolution, but the laws which they obey are not really identical with those of evolution which dominate and correlate them. In a similar way, the laws which govern the movements of particles in an atom are special and differ from those which govern the chemical properties of the atoms themselves. The latter are, as far as our actual science is concerned, without qualitative or quantitative relation to our psychological activity. To extrapolate and predict that such a relation will be discovered some day is not substantiated by facts, and entirely hypothetical.

Indeed, man must beware more of scientific extrapolations than of moral ones, because his scientific experience has been much shorter than his psychological experience. New facts are frequently found in science which compel him to revise completely his former concepts. The history of science is made up of such revolutions: the atomic theory, the kinetic theory, the granular theories of electricity, energy, and light, radioactivity, relativity have successively transformed our point of view from top to bottom. The future of science is always at the mercy of new discoveries and new theories. The science of matter is not two hundred years old, while the science of man is over five thousand years old. Empirical psychology was highly advanced at the time of the third Egyptian dynasty, and great philosophers twenty-six hundred years ago displayed a knowledge of man which has not been surpassed, but only confirmed today. Therefore, it can be reasonably assumed that moral extrapolations are much safer than scientific ones, even though they cannot be expressed mathematically.

[269]

O

OCKHAM, WILLIAM OF

OCKHAM, WILLIAM OF (1280-1348). No other Christian thinker of the Middle Ages rejected so many or such important assumptions which were prevalent in his times as did Ockham. His great aim was to teach men to think, and the result of his teachings was the elaboration of laic consciousness in the State, the reduction of the influence of the Church in human society, and the preparation for a new interpretation of the physical world. Although these results were counteracted by men and circumstances, Ockham must be considered as one of the principal agents of the dissolution of the Medieval synthesis of philosophy and theology. In the struggle between Pope John XXII and Emperor Louis of Bavaria, Ockham, collaborating with Marsilius of Padua, defended the rights of secular government against papal claims and contributed to the establishment of the modern political theory of the independence of the state from the church.

In his philosophical works, Ockham proclaimed the primacy of logical method in all disciplines. He rejected all attempts to evade reason but he restricted the range of reason. His epistemology destroyed any relation between knowledge of the universe and knowledge of God. He especially pronounced animosity against all those who claimed to know the psychology of God. He even maintained that monotheism can be derived only from the prime being and not from the prime efficient cause. He rejected Thomist ontology and Augustine's belief in eternal ideas which constitute the archetypes of the universe in the depth of divine essence, and he flatly denied the usefulness and truth of the speculations of all the great Doctors of the Church. He also held ethics to be independent of metaphysics.

In the struggle about universals, Ockham sided with those who held that universality can be attributed only to terms and propositions, not to things. But his interests did not center on this problem. To him, intuition of the singular is the basis of all concepts which

871

are signs of the real. Science has to verify the signs. All existing things depend on God's absolutely free will. All secondary causality is indemonstrable. It is only a fact which science has to interpret. While the will of God is absolutely free, Man has the freedom of alternative choice. Will is an essential attribute of any reasoning creature.

Ockham's diction is very precise but lacks charm. He influenced Wyclif and Erasmus. Luther borrowed some sentences from him, but would have repudiated his principal doctrines had he known them.

THE INDIVIDUAL AND THE UNIVERSAL

THE universals and second intentions are caused naturally by the knowledge of simple terms without any activity of the intellect and the will. They come about in this manner: first, I apprehend in particular some singular objects intuitively or abstractly. This is caused by the object or by a predisposition from a former act. This act consummated, presently, if there is no obstacle, another act follows naturally, distinct from the first and terminating in something of the same kind of logical reality as was seen before in the psychological reality. This second act produces the universals and second intentions. Something not there before is left behind in the imaginative faculty mediated by the intuitive cognition of particular sensation; yet this is not the object of the act, but some kind of a predisposition inclined to imagine the previously sensed object. I am certain that I perceive a stone in virtue of the sight of the stone and in virtue of primary vision. I am certain that I understand by experience because I see the image of the stone. The certainty of understanding the stone, however, comes by reasoning from effect to cause. I know fire by smoke when I see smoke alone, because I have on other occasions seen smoke caused by the presence of fire. In the same manner, I know the stone because on other occasions I have perceived intellectually the production of such an image in me.

Every universal is one singular thing and is universal only by the signification of many things. The universal is

872

one and a single intention of the soul meant to be predicated of many things; in so far, however, as it is a single form subsisting really in the intellect, it is called singular.

The universal is twofold: natural and conventional. The first is a natural sign predicable of many things, as smoke naturally signifies fire, and a groan the pain of the sick man, and laughter a certain interior joy. Such a universal is nothing else than such an intention of the soul that no substance outside of the soul, nor any accident outside of the soul, is a counterpart of it. The conventional universal is one by voluntary institution. Such is the spoken word, which is an actual quality, numerically one, and universal because of its being a voluntarily instituted sign for the signification of many things. Therefore as the word is called common, the same also may be called universal, adding that this is not by the nature of the thing but only by the agreement of users. Of a universal that is such by discretion, I do not speak, but I do speak of that one which has whatever is universal in it by its very nature.

I am inquiring, now, whether this universal and univocally common entity is something real from the part of the thing which is outside of the soul. All of whom I meet agree by saying that the entity which is somehow universal is really in the individual, although some say that it is distinguished really, others that it is distinguished only formally, and some that it is not distinguished at all according to the nature of the thing, but only according to reason or by the consideration of the intellect. All these opinions coincide in that the universals are allowed to exist somehow from the side of the thing, so that their universality is held to be really present in the singular objects themselves.

This latter opinion is simply false and absurd. Against it this is my case. There is no unitary, unvaried or simple thing in a multiplicity of singular things nor in any kind of created individuals, together and at the same time. If such a thing were allowed, it would be numerically one; therefore, it would not be in many singular objects nor would ıt be of their essence. But the singular and the universal thing are by themselves two things, really distinct and equally simple; therefore, if the singular thing is numerically one, the universal thing will be numerically one also, and one does not include a greater plurality intrinsic to things than does the other.

[270]

ORIGEN

ORIGEN (185-253). While Clement of Alexandria is considered the father of Christian apologetics, his pupil Origen has been called the creator of Christian theology. But Origen was not only Clement's disciple; he was also taught by the pagan philosopher Ammonius Saccas, Plotinus' teacher. Origen tried to integrate the Christian faith into a comprehensive explanation of the universe, such as was adopted by Platonism and Stoicism, but he also leaned toward Neo-Platonism which was nascent during his lifetime. He was one of the greatest scholars who ever lived, whose *Hexapla*, the juxtaposition of versions of the Bible in six columns, was of great consequence to the criticism and exegesis of the Bible. He wrote a defense of Christianity *Against Celsus* which, however, was condemned by later orthodox Catholics as containing inadmissible concessions to paganism, and *On Principles*, a treatise on systematic theology which has been preserved in a Latin translation by Rufinus. In the fourth century, the number of Origen's works was estimated at about six thousand.

Origen lived a life of complete asceticism, having castrated himself. While orthodox Catholics continued to suspect him of heresy, the condemnation of his views by the Bishop of Alexandria was more than once confirmed. Protestant theologians and secular historians have always been sympathetically attracted to him whose soul lived in harmony with the course of nature and in confidence in the divine Logos, firm in his unselfish love of God and of his fellow men, longing for the return to the heavenly world of spirit which he conceived, in accordance with Plato, as behind and superior to the temporal world.

Many problems stemming from the doctrine of emanation or the eschatology of the Orphics and various Gnostics have been introduced into Christian thinking by Origen. Some of them became the cause of schism and heresy, while others contributed to the definite formation of the dogma of the Trinity.

THE FIRE OF HELL

WE find in the prophet Isaiah, that the fire with which each one is punished is described as his own; for he says, "Walk in the light of your own fire, and in the flame which ye have kindled." By these words it seems to be indicated that every sinner kindles for himself the flame of his own fire, and is not plunged into some fire which has been already kindled by another, or was in existence before himself. Of this fire the fuel and food are our sins, which are called by the Apostle Paul wood, and hay, and stubble. And I think that, as abundance of food, and provisions of a contrary kind and amount, breed fevers in the body, and fevers, too, of different sorts and duration according to the proportion in which the collected poison supplies material and fuel for disease (the quality of this material, gathered together from different poisons, proving the causes either of a more acute or more lingering disease); so, when the soul has gathered together a multitude of evil works, and an abundance of sins against itself, at a suitable time all that assembly of evils boils up to punishment, and is set on fire to chastisements; when the mind itself, or conscience, receiving by divine power into the memory all those things of which it had stamped on itself certain signs and forms at the moment of sinning, will see a kind of history, as it were, of all the foul, and shameful, and unholy deeds which it has done, exposed before its eyes: then is the conscience itself harassed, and, pierced by its own goads, becomes an accuser and a witness against itself. And this, I think, was the opinion of the Apostle Paul himself, when he said, "Their thoughts mutually accusing or excusing them in the day when God will judge the secrets of men by Jesus Christ, according to my Gospel." From which it is understood that around the substance of the soul certain tortures are produced by the hurtful affections of sins themselves.

And that the understanding of this matter may not appear very difficult, we may draw some considerations from the evil effects of those passions which are wont to befall some souls, as when a soul is consumed by the fire of love, or wasted away by zeal or envy, or when the passion of anger is kindled, or one is consumed by the greatness of his madness or his sorrow; on which occasions some, finding the excess of these evils unbearable, have deemed it more tolerable to submit to death than to endure perpetually torture of such a kind. You will ask indeed whether, in the case of those who have been entangled in the evils arising from those vices above enumerated, and who, while existing in this life, have been unable to procure any amelioration for themselves, and have in this condition departed from the world, it be sufficient in the way of.punishment that they be tortured by the remaining in them of these hurtful affections, i.e., of the anger, or of the fury, or of the madness, or of the sorrow, whose fatal poison was in this life lessened by no healing medicine; or whether, these affections being changed, they will be subjected to the pains of a general punishment. Now I am of opinion that another species of punishment may be understood to exist; because, as we feel that when the limbs of the body are loosened and torn away from their mutual supports, there is produced pain of a most excruciating kind, so, when the soul shall be found to be beyond the order, and connection, and harmony in which it was created by God for the purposes of good and useful action and observation, and not to harmonize with itself in the connection of its rational movements, it must be deemed to bear the chastisement and torture of its own dissension, and to feel the punishments of its own disordered condition. And when this dissolution and rendering asunder of soul shall have been tested by the application of fire, a solidification undoubtedly into a firmer structure will take place, and a restoration be effected.

[271]

ORTEGA Y GASSET, JOSÉ

ORTEGA Y GASSET, JOSÉ (1883-). Although Ortega y Gasset disagrees with almost every important Spaniard of his time, he is generally acknowledged as the representative thinker of modern Spain. No wonder that he became an exile. He is strongly opposed to Franco's dictatorship; however, he had little sympathy with the government of the Spanish republic and its supporters. As the editor of the *Revista del Occidente*, he acquainted the Spanish public with the spiritual life of the Anglo-Saxon countries, of France and Germany, and he gave readers in foreign countries a striking presentation of the main features of Spanish thought and Spanish cultural tradition. But, above all, he has proved to be an original thinker who, rooted in Spanish civilization, universally cultivated, has developed personal ideas of great consequence.

Ortega y Gasset was educated by the Jesuits and studied at the Central University of Madrid, where he became a professor of metaphysics in 1910. Earlier, he had been a disciple of Hermann Cohen, but he became more interested in the philosophy of Husserl and Dilthey. The final result of his preoccupation with German thought was an opposition to idealism. He adopted Dilthey's concept of historical reason, but tried to avoid his shortcomings and went far beyond Dilthey's views.

He insists that human thinking is much less logical than it is generally supposed to be, that man is born at a definite date, formed by a definite tradition, and that his environment is equally determined by historical factors. Therefore, he concludes, whoever aspires to understand man, must throw overboard all immobile concepts and learn to think in ever-shifting terms. Because human life is radical reality that includes any other reality, history, and not physics, is the highest science.

Concerning the idealistic philosophy that starts from a concept of reality in which the subject, the ego, exists enclosed within itself, within its mental acts and states, he objects that such an existence is the opposite of living, whose meaning is to reach out of oneself, to be devoted to what is called the world. Consciousness is historical but the importance of history is not exhausted with the past. Historical knowledge is valued as a preparation for the future, and this conception involves a new appraisal of thinking. For, to Ortega, action without thought means chaos.

877

BOTH Bolshevism and Fascism are two false dawns; they do not bring the morning of a new day, but of some archaio day, spent over and over again: they are mere primitivism. And such will all movements be which fall into the stupidity of starting a boxing-match with some portion or other of the past, instead of proceeding to digest it. No doubt an advance must be made on the liberalism of the XIX century. But this is precisely what cannot be done by any movement such as Fascism, which declares itself anti-liberal. Because it was that fact—the being anti-liberal or non-liberal—which constituted man previous to liberalism. And as the latter triumphed over its opposite, it will either repeat its victory time and again, or else everything—liberalism and anti-liberalism—will be annihilated in the destruction of Europe. There is an inexorable chronology of life. In it liberalism is posterior to anti-liberalism, or what comes to the same, is more vital than it, just as the gun is more of a weapon than the lance.

At first sight, an attitude "anti-anything" seems posterior to this thing, inasmuch as it signifies a reaction against it and supposes its previous existence. But the innovation which the *anti* represents fades away into an empty negative attitude, leaving as its only positive content an "antique." When his attitude is translated into positive language, the man who declares himself anti-Peter does nothing more than declare himself the upholder of a world where Peter is non-existent. But that is exactly what happened to the world before Peter was born. The anti-Peterite, instead of placing himself after Peter, makes himself previous to him and reverses the whole film to the situation of the past, at the end of which the re-apparition of Peter is inevitable. The same thing happens to these *antis* as, according to the legend, happened to Confucius. He was born, naturally, after his father, but he was born at the age of eighty while his progenitor was only thirty! Every *anti* is nothing more than a simple, empty *No.*

This would be all very nice and fine if with a good, round *No* we could annihilate the past. But the past is of its essence a *revenant*. If put out, it comes back, inevitably. Hence, the only way to separate from it is not to put it out, but to accept its existence, and so to have in regard to it as to dodge it, to avoid it. In a word, to live "at the height of our time," with an exaggerated consciousness of the historical circumstances.

The past has reason on its side, its own reason. If that reason is not admitted, it will return to demand it. Liberalism had its reason, which will have to be admitted *per saecula saeculorum*. But it had not the whole of reason, and it is that part which was not reason that must be taken from it. Europe needs to preserve its essential liberalism. This is the condition for superseding it.

If I have spoken here of Fascism and Bolshevism it has been only indirectly, considering merely their aspect as anachronisms. This aspect is, to my mind, inseparable from all that is apparently triumphant to-day. For to-day it is the mass-man who triumphs, and consequently, only those designs inspired by him, saturated with his primitive style, can enjoy an apparent victory. But apart from this, I am not at present discussing the true inwardness of one or the other, just as I am not attempting to solve the eternal dilemma of revolution and evolution. The most that this essay dares to demand is that the revolution or the evolution be historical and not anachronistic.

The theme I am pursuing in these pages is politically neutral, because it breathes an air much ampler than that of politics and its dissensions. Conservative and Radical are none the less mass, and the difference between them—which at every period has been very superficial—does not in the least prevent them both being one and the same man—the common man in rebellion.

There is no hope for Europe unless its destiny is placed in the hands of men really "contemporaneous," men who feel palpitating beneath them the whole subsoil of history, who realize the present level of existence, and abhor every archaic and primitive attitude. We have need of history in its entirety, not to fall back into it, but to see if we can escape from it.

[272]

OWEN, ROBERT

OWEN, ROBERT (1771-1858). It is more by his activities than by his thoughts that Owen influenced the mind and practical life of later ages. He was a man of one idea which he called "socialism" but which rather means "cooperative settlements." He was obsessed by this idea, and not very capable of explaining and developing it in a scientific manner. But he devoted much of his time, energy and fortune to its realization, and influenced British social legislation by his restless insistence on the removal of the most flagrant abuses of the early industrial system.

After being a cotton-twist manufacturer in Manchester, Owen acquired, in 1797, a factory in New Lanfark which, under his direction, became a model factory and attracted the curiosity of many thousands of visitors from various countries. Employing 1,700 hands out of the 3,000 inhabitants of the village, Owen refused to employ children under the age of ten, or adults for more than ten and a half hours a day. He provided the families of his workers with schools, a cooperative store, the opportunity to hear music and to take physical exercises. Later he tried to organize cooperative settlements elsewhere in England and in the United States. But he was rather a despotic, though benevolent, ruler, and always a sworn foe of political democracy, educating his adherents to political indifference. In his book *New View of Society* (1813) and in numerous periodicals, he tried to propagate the idea that the existing evils were not due to lack of religion, against which Owen always proclaimed his animosity, but to a wrong distribution of wealth and to a deficient regulation of production which caused economic crises as a consequence of over-production. The rise of the factory system was defended by Owen, who, against Malthus, maintained that the increase of the productive capacity of the human race would be more rapid than the increase of the population. Owen's aim was revolutionary but not his method of realizing it.

INDIVIDUAL INTEREST AND UNIVERSAL GOOD

IT has been, and still is, a received opinion among theorists in political economy, that man can provide better for himself, and more advantageously for the public, when left to his own individual exertions, opposed to, and in competition with his fellows, than when aided by any social arrangements, which shall unite his interests individually and generally with society. This principle of individual interest, opposed, as it is perpetually, to the public good, is considered, by the most celebrated political economists, to be the cornerstone of the social system and without which, society could not subsist. Yet when they shall know themselves, and discover the wonderful effects, which combination and unity can produce, they will acknowledge that the present arrangement of society is the most antisocial, impolitic, and irrational, that can be devised; that under its influence, all the superior and valuable qualities of human nature are repressed from infancy, and that the most unnatural means are used to bring out the most injurious propensities; in short, that the utmost pains are taken to make that which by nature is the most delightful compound for producing excellence and happiness, absurd, imbecile, and wretched. Such is the conduct now pursued by those who are called the best and wisest of the present generation, although there is not one rational object to be gained by it. From this principle of individual interest have arisen all the divisions of mankind, the endless errors and mischiefs of class, sect, party, and of national antipathies, creating the angry and malevolent passions, and all the crimes and misery with which the human race has been hitherto afflicted. In short, if there be one closet doctrine more contrary to truth than another, it is the notion that individual interest, as the term is now understood, is a more advantageous principle on which to found the social system, for the benefit of all, or of any, than the principle of union and mutual cooperation. The former acts like an immense weight to repress the most valuable faculties and dispositions, and to give a wrong direction to all the human powers. It is one of those magnificent errors (if the expression may be allowed) that when enforced in practice, brings ten thousand evils in its train. The principle on which these economists proceed, instead of adding to the wealth of nations or of individuals, is itself the sole cause of poverty; and but for its operation, wealth would long ago have ceased to be a subject of contention in any part of the world. If, it may be asked, experience has proved that union, combination, and extensive arrangement among mankind, are a thousand times more powerful to *destroy*, than the efforts of an unconnected multitude, where each acts individually for himself,—would not a similar increased effect be produced by union, combination, and extensive arrangement, to *create and conserve?* Why should not the result be the same in the one case as in the other? But it is well known that a combination of men and of interests, can effect that which it would be futile to attempt, and impossible to accomplish, by individual exertions and separate interests. Then why, it may be inquired, have men so long acted individually, and in opposition to each other?

This is an important question, and merits the most serious attention.

Men have not yet been trained in principles that will permit them *to act in unison,* except to defend themselves or to destroy others. For self-preservation, they were early compelled to unite for these purposes in war. A necessity, however, equally powerful will now compel men to be trained to act together, to *create and conserve,* that in like manner they may preserve life in peace. Fortunately for mankind, the system of individual opposing interests, has now reached the extreme point of error and inconsistency;—in the midst of the most ample means to create wealth, all are in poverty, or in imminent danger, from the effects of poverty upon others.

The reflecting part of mankind, have admitted in theory, that the characters of men are formed chiefly by the circumstances in which they are placed; yet the science of the influence of circumstances, which is the most important of all the sciences, remains unknown for the great practical business of life. When it shall be fully developed, it will be discovered, that to unite the mental faculties of men, for the attainment of pacific and civil objects, will be a far more easy task than it has been to combine their physical powers to carry on extensive warlike operations.

The discovery of the distance and movements of the heavenly bodies; of the time-pieces; of a vessel to navigate the most distant parts of the ocean; of the steam engine, which performs, under the easy control of one man, the labor of many thousands; and of the press, by which knowledge and improvements may be speedily given to the most ignorant, in all parts of the earth;—these have, indeed, been discoveries of high import to mankind; but important as these and others have been in their effects, on the condition of human society, their combined benefits in practice, will fall far short of those which will be speedily attained by the new intellectual power, which men will acquire through the knowledge of "the science of the influence of circumstances over the whole conduct, character, and proceedings of the human race." By this latter discovery, more shall be accomplished in one year, for the well-being of human nature, including, without any exceptions, all ranks and descriptions of men, than has ever yet been effected in one or in many centuries. Strange as this language may seem to those whose minds have not yet had a glimpse of the real state in which society now is, it will prove to be not more strange than true.

Are not the mental energies of the world at this moment in a state of high effervescence. Is not society at a stand, incompetent to proceed in its present course, and do not all men cry out that "something must be done"? That "something," to produce the effect desired, must be a complete renovation of the whole social compact; one not forced on prematurely, by confusion and violence; not one to be brought about by the futile measures of the Radicals, Whigs, or Tories, of Britain,—the Liberals or Royalists of France, —the Illuminati of Germany, or the mere party proceedings of any little local portion of human beings, trained as they have hitherto been, in almost every kind of error, and without any true knowledge of themselves. No! The change sought for, must be preceded by the clear development of a great and universal principle which shall unite in one, all the petty jarring interests, by which, till now, nature has been made a most inveterate enemy to itself. No! extensive, nay, rather, universal as the rearrangement of society must be, to relieve it from the difficulties with which it is now overwhelmed, it will be effected in peace and quietness, with the good will and hearty concurrence of all parties, and of every people. It will necessarily commence by common consent, on account of its advantages, almost simultaneously among all civilized nations; and, once begun, will daily advance with an accelerating ratio, unopposed, and bearing down before it the existing systems of the world. The only astonishment then will be that such systems could so long have existed.

*   *   *

Under the present system, there is the most minute division of mental power and manual labor in the individuals of the working classes; private interests are placed perpetually at variance with the public good, and, in every nation, men are purposely trained from infancy to suppose that their well-being is incompatible with the progress and prosperity of other nations. Such are the means by which old society seeks to obtain the desired effects of life. The details now to be submitted, have been devised upon principles which will lead to an opposite practice; to the combination of extensive mental and manual powers in the individuals of the working classes; to a complete identity of private and public interest, and to the training of nations to comprehend that their power and happiness cannot attain their full and natural development, but through an equal increase of the power and happiness of all other states. These, therefore, are the real points at variance between that which *is*, and that which *ought to be*.

[273]

𝒫

PAINE, THOMAS

PAINE, THOMAS (1737-1809). Contemporaries used to speak of Paine only in superlatives either of enthusiasm or contempt. Jefferson and Hamilton, though differing on so many points, agreed that Paine was a man to be avoided or distrusted. England, his native country, outlawed him. Jacobin France, where Paine at first had been made an honorary citizen and had been elected a member of the National Convention although he did not speak French, imprisoned him because he had agitated against the execution of the king. When Paine died, he had been poor, sick and ostracized for many years. A century after his death, Theodore Roosevelt sneered at him as a "filthy little atheist."

But independent historians have recognized that Paine, by his pamphlet *Common Sense* (1776) and by untiring agitation, convinced influential but hesitating Americans that independence should be declared because it was the only way to save the colonies. It was also Paine who insisted on the gathering of the Continental Congress, for the purpose of framing a Continental charter. Furthermore, it was Paine who earlier than any other proclaimed America's mission to be the defense of freedom and democracy by presenting to the whole world the example of a republic of free men.

Without any doubt, America and humanity in general owe him a grateful memory, although he was not free from vanity and his education was incomplete. But Paine was not a man to serve only one country. He defended the French Revolution against Edmund Burke in his book *The Rights of Man* (1791) with the same ardor as he had defended the American Revolution, and he tried to revolutionize England, though without success. In his *Age of Reason* (1794-96) he tried to emancipate humanity from Christian traditions and to establish a religion of deism. He did not recognize that the Age of Reason had ended when his book was printed.

After and throughout many failures in business while he lived in England, Paine had educated himself by confining his spiritual interests strictly to the science of his time. He was an artless writer although he displayed extraordinary talents for aphoristic formulas and for striking expressions.

THE RIGHTS OF MAN

EVERY history of the creation, and every traditional account, however they may vary in their opinion or belief of certain particulars, all agree in establishing one point, *the unity of man;* by which I mean that men are all of *one degree,* and consequently that all men are born equal, and with equal natural right, in the same manner as if posterity had been continued by *creation* instead of *generation,* the latter being the only mode by which the former is carried forward; and consequently every child born into the world must be considered as deriving its existence from God. The world is as new to him as it was to the first man that existed, and his natural right in it is of the same kind.

The duty of man is not a wilderness of turnpike gates through which he is to pass by tickets from one to the other. It is plain and simple, and consists but of two points: his duty to God, which every man must feel; and with respect to his neighbor, to do as he would be done by. If those to whom power is delegated do well, they will be respected; if not, they will be despised; and with regard to those to whom no power is delegated, but who assume it, the rational world can know nothing of them.

Natural rights are those which appertain to man in right of his existence. Of this kind are all the intellectual rights, or rights of the mind, and also all those rights of acting as an individual for his own comfort and happiness which are not injurious to the natural rights of others. Civil rights are those which appertain to man in right of his being a member of society. Every civil right has for its foundation some natural right pre-existing in the individual, but to the enjoyment of which his individual power is not, in all cases, sufficiently competent. Of this kind are all those which relate to security and protection.

887

From these premises two or three certain conclusions follow:

First, that every civil right grows out of a natural right; or, in other words, is a natural right exchanged.

Secondly, that civil power properly considered as such is made up of the aggregate of that class of the natural rights of man which becomes defective in the individual in point of power, and answers not his purpose, but when collected to a focus, becomes competent to the purpose of every one.

Thirdly, that the power produced from the aggregate of natural rights, imperfect in power in the individual, cannot be applied to invade the natural rights which are retained in the individual, and in which the power to execute is as perfect as the right itself.

We have now, in a few words, traced man from a natural individual to a member of society, and shown the quality of the natural rights retained, and of those which are exchanged for civil rights. Let us now apply these principles to governments.

It has been thought a considerable advance towards establishing the principle of freedom to say that government is a compact between those who govern and those who are governed; but this cannot be true, because it is putting the effect before the cause; for as man must have existed before governments existed, there necessarily was a time when governments did not exist.

Governments arising out of society do so by establishing a *constitution*. A constitution is not a thing in name only, but in fact. It has not an ideal, but a real existence; and wherever it cannot be produced in a visible form, there is none. A constitution is a thing *antecedent* to a government, and a government is only the creature of a constitution. The constitution of a country is not the act of its government, but of the people constituting its government. It is the body of elements to which you can refer and quote article by article; and which contains the principles on which the government shall be established, the manner in which it shall be organized, the powers it shall have, the mode of elections, the duration of parliaments, or by what other name such bodies may be called; the powers which the executive part of the government shall have; and, in fine, everything that relates to the complete organization of a civil government, and the principles on which it shall act, and by which it shall be bound.

A constitution, therefore, is to a government what the laws made afterward by that government are to a court of judicature. The court of judicature does not make the laws, neither can it alter them; it only acts in conformity to the laws made: and the government is in like manner governed by the constitution.

[274]

PARACELSUS

PARACELSUS (1493-1541). Theophrastus Bombastus of Hohenheim, called Paracelsus, has been decried as a charlatan, even as a scoundrel, and exalted as a precursor of modern knowledge and a martyr of modern science. In fact, he was an honest man who did wrong only when he was too exasperated by the obstinacy and evil tricks of his adversaries and competitors. He was a self-denying, and certainly also a very efficient physician, who fought routine and prejudices in his special field. But by no means did he attack routine and prejudice with the weapons of modern science, although he anticipated modern views in many ways. He demanded that a physician be an astrologist, an alchemist and a "philosopher," conceiving philosophy as knowledge of the arcana, founded upon a mystical grasp of the forces which work in the Universe. He warned his colleagues against observing the sick patient instead of contemplating the whole of nature, especially the qualities and the degeneration of metals from which he tried to draw conclusions about the sufferings of the human beings. Anatomy meant to him the astrological structure of the patient. Thus Paracelsus' criticism of medical traditions accepted alchemy, astrology, magic and the Church. "I write as a pagan," he declared, "but I am a Christian." His principal source was the Cabala which he thought proved the truth of Christianity.

But in the midst of his alchemist disquisitions, Paracelsus produced the elements of modern pharmacology. While trying to heal his patients by means of magic spells and sympathetic cures, he proceeded to treatments similar to those of modern psychotherapy, and his philosophy of the Universe led him to the idea of organic life. Although he declined to observe the patient and built his hopes for healing him upon speculation on the mystery of becoming and existence, he arrived at a sound view on the activities of medicine and pharmacology. Disease was considered by him to be a conflict between nature and demonic forces. In this conflict, the physician is "but the helper who furnishes nature with weapons," and the apothecary "the smith" who forges the needed weapons.

WHY NYMPHS, SYLPHS, ETC., EXIST

GOD has set guardians over nature, for all things, and he left nothing unguarded. Thus gnomes, pygmies and *mani* guard the treasures of the earth, the metals and similar treasures. Where they are, there are tremendous treasures, in tremendous quantities. They are guarded by such people, are kept hidden and secret so that they may not be found until the time for it has come. When they are found, people say: in times of old there used to be mountain manikins, earth people here, but now they are gone. This means that now the time has come for the treasures to be revealed. The treasures of the earth are distributed in such a way that the metals, silver, gold, iron, etc., have been found from the beginning of the world on, and are being discovered by and by. They are guarded and protected by these people so that they may not be found all at once, but one after another, by and by, now in this country, now in another. Thus the mines are shifted in the course of time from country to country and are distributed from the first day to the last. The same applies also to the fire people. They too are guardians, of the fireplaces, in which they live. In these places the treasures, that others guard, are forged, prepared, made ready. When the fire is extinguished, it is the earth manikins' turn to be on guard. And after the earth manikins' guard, the treasures are revealed. It is the same with the air people. They guard the rocks that lie on the surface, that have been made by the fire people, and put at the place where they belong, from where they get into man's hands. They guard them so long, until the time has come. Wherever there are treasures, such people are on hand. These are hidden treasures that must not be revealed yet. Since they are guardians of such matters, we can well understand that such guardians are not endowed with a soul, yet similar to and like men. The nymphs in the water are guardians of the great water treasures that lie in the sea and other waters, that have also been melted and forged by the fire people. It is, therefore, commonly understood that where nymphs are, there are considerable treasures and minerals and similar matters which they guard. This is apparent in many ways.

The cause of the sirens, giants, dwarfs, also of the will-o'-the-wisps, who are monsters of the fire people, is that they predict and indicate something new. They are not on guard, but signify that misfortune is threatening people. Thus when lights are seen it means the impending downfall of that country, that is, it commonly signifies the destruction of the monarchy and similar things. Thus the giants also signify great impending destruction of that country and land or some other such great disaster. The dwarfs signify great poverty among the people, in many parts. The sirens signify the downfall of princes and lords, the rise of sects or factions. For God wants us all to be of one essence. What is against it, He drops. And when this is going to happen, signs occur. These beings are such signs, as has been said, but not they alone; there are many more. You must know that the signs change each time. They do not appear in one way, but are hidden to our eyes.

And, finally, the last cause is unknown to us. But when the end of the world will come close, then all things will be revealed, from the smallest to the largest, from the first to the last, what everything has been and is, why it stood there and left, from what causes, and what its meaning was. And everything that is in the world will be disclosed and come to light. Then the fake scholars will be exposed, those who are highly learned in name only but know nothing by experience. Then, the thorough scholars and those who are mere talkers will be recognized for what they are, those who wrote truthfully and those who traded in lies, the thorough and the shallow ones. And to each will be measured according to his diligence, earnest endeavor and truth. At that place, not everyone will be or remain a master, or even a doctor, because there the tares will be separated from the wheat and the straw from the grain. He who now cries, will be quieted, and he who now counts the pages, will have his quills taken away. And all things will be revealed before the Day of Judgment breaks, in order that it be found of all scholars, from the past to that very day, who had knowledge and who not, whose writings were right and whose wrong. Now, in my time, this is still unknown. Blessed will be the people, in those days, whose intelligence will be revealed, for what they produced will be revealed to all the people as if it were written on their foreheads. For that time I also recommend my writings for judgment, asking that nothing be withheld. Thus it will be, for God makes the light manifest, that is, everyone will see how it has shone.

[275]

PARETO, VILFREDO

PARETO, VILFREDO (1848-1923). At the end of his life, Pareto, a professor of political economy at the University of Lausanne, Switzerland, was honored by Mussolini who had come to power. However, he remained indifferent to all Fascist eulogizers and even hinted that the Fascists misunderstood his thoughts. For a time, Pareto's ideas reached a position of power and prestige in democratic America too. Misunderstanding of Pareto's doctrines is not a little due to the fact, deplored by his most faithful admirers, that he had the habit of mentioning his most important points just casually, or even only in notes. Furthermore, he presented not a close and complete system but, rather a series of studies. What attracted Fascism to Pareto's ideas was not his doctrine itself, but some passages—namely his great admiration of

Machiavelli's *The Prince*, his small respect for ethics, and his contempt of metaphysics and religion.

Pareto was born in Paris. He was the son of an Italian nobleman who was a political refugee, and a French mother. When, in 1858, an amnesty allowed return to Italy, Pareto prepared himself for an engineering career and became manager of the railroad in the valley of the Arno River. In 1876, he began to write on economics and established "Pareto's law" which tries to express the relation between the amount of income and the number of its recipients. His *Manual of Political Economics* (1906) was much disputed. Even more controversies were provoked by his *Sociologia Generale* (1916) which was translated into English under the title *The Mind and Society* in 1935.

Pareto claimed to have raised sociology to a logico-experimental science. He stressed and explained the nonlogical factors in human actions by showing the components of social life which he divided into two principal groups—namely, the "residues" or fundamental factors and the derivations which often are erroneous and create myths. By "residues," of which he never gave a sufficient definition, Pareto meant the unexpressed postulates, the things one considers so obvious that they need no explanation, or beliefs which are not formed by logical processes. Social evolution is determined by economic interests, psychic and ideological factors and the "circulation of the elite." Pareto was opposed to "atomistic individualism," and he declared collectively to be "if not a person, at least a unity," and emphasized the importance of social classes.

ON CAUSE AND EFFECT

IN nonmathematical language, the independent variable x in an algebraic equation corresponds to a *cause*. Sometimes that is an admissible translation, sometimes it is not. For *cause*, colloquially speaking, must necessarily come before its effect. Thus, you can consider the price of something as the *effect* and the cost of its production as the *cause*, or you can turn it about and consider the cost of production as *effect* and the selling price to be the *cause*. For in that case there are a series of actions and reactions which permit you to suppose either that the supply of the product precedes the demand or that the demand precedes the supply on the market. In fact, there is a mutual dependence between supply and demand, and this mutual dependence can theoretically be expressed by an equation. You could not, in collo-quial language, invert similarly the relation in which you call the freezing of water the cause and the breaking of a pipe its effect, and say that the break *caused* the water to freeze. But, leaving terminology aside, if you are concerned only with the experimental relation between these two facts, isolating them from all others, you could easily deduce the existence of a break in a pipe from the freezing of the water in it and *vice versa*. For, in fact, there is a mutual depend-ence between the change of temperature which turns the water into ice and the resistance of the pipe containing it. Thermodynamics, thanks to the language of mathematics, expresses this mutual dependence in a rigorous way; a collo-quial language expresses the same thing, but imperfectly.

Suppose we have two quantities, x and y, in a state of mutual dependence. In mathematical terms, we say that there is an equation between these two variables, and it is un-necessary to say more. But if we speak colloquially, we shall say that x is determined by y, which at once reacts on x, and so y finds itself depending on the new x. You can invert the terms and equally well say that y is determined by x, but that y reacts on x, and so x finds itself also dependent on y. Sometimes this method gives the same results as the mathema-tical equations; sometimes it does not. So we can substitute the colloquial method only with a good deal of circumspec-tion.

[276]

PARMENIDES

PARMENIDES (About 504-456 B.C.). Down to recent times, phil-osophy has accepted fundamental concepts from Parmenides, not-withstanding considerable criticisms, modifications and combinations with other ideas. It was Parmenides who initiated the distinction be-tween a sensible and an intelligible world. It was he who first as-sumed an indestructible *substance* and used it as the basis of his speculations, although he did not formulate its concept. It was he who began to distinguish between scientific truth and popular opinion. In this way, Parmenides influenced Empedocles, Leucippus and Democritus, the Sophists and Plato, while Hegel was not the last philosopher who followed Parmenides by founding metaphysics upon logic.

A principal characteristic of the Greek mind, which is significant not only of Greek philosophy but of Greek art and the Greek feeling of existence, was shaped by Parmenides, the founder of the Eleatic school. This is his preference for unity, composure, and the comprehension of limits and contours. This longing for unity made him suspicious of the senses; this want of composure made him deny change; this need of limits made him conceive the unchanging world as of spherical form and repudiate the idea of the infinite, or the empty space.

Little is known about Parmenides' life. He was born in Elea (Velia) in Southern Italy; probably he was a disciple of Xenophanes and Ameinias, a Pythagorean. In all probability, he resided for some years in Athens where, according to Plato, Socrates met him and learned much from the aged philosopher.

THE WAY OF TRUTH

COME now, I will tell thee—and do thou hearken to my saying and carry it away—the only two ways of search that can be thought of. The first, namely, that It is, and that it is impossible for anything not to be, is the way of conviction, for truth is its companion. The other, namely, that It is not, and that something must needs not be, that, I tell thee, is a wholly untrustworthy path. For you cannot know what is not—that is impossible—nor utter it; for it is the same thing that can be thought and that can be.

It needs must be that what can be thought and spoken of is; for it is possible for it to be, and it is not possible for what is nothing to be. This is what I bid thee ponder. I hold thee back from this first way of inquiry, and from this other also, upon which mortals knowing naught wander in two minds; for hesitation guides the wandering thought in their breasts, so that they are borne along stupefied like men deaf and blind. Undiscerning crowds, in whose eyes the same thing and not the same is and is not, and all things travel in opposite directions!

For this shall never be proved, that the things that are not are; and do thou restrain thy thought from this way of inquiry. Nor let habit force thee to cast a wandering eye upon this devious track, or to turn thither thy resounding ear or thy tongue; but do thou judge the subtle refutation of their discourse uttered by me. One path only is left for us to speak of, namely, that It is. In it are very many tokens that what is, is uncreated and indestructible, alone, complete, immovable and without end. Nor was it ever, nor will it be; for now it is, all at once, a continuous one. For what kind of origin for it will you look for? In what way and from what source could it have drawn its increase? I shall not let thee say nor think that it came from what is not; for it can neither be thought nor uttered that what is not is. And, if it came from nothing, what need could have made it arise later rather than sooner? Therefore must it either be altogether or be not at all. Nor will the force of truth suffer aught to arise besides itself from that which in any way is. Wherefore, Justice does not loose her fetters and let anything come into being or pass away, but holds it fast.

"Is it or is it not?" Surely it is adjudged, as it needs must be, that we are to set aside the one way as unthinkable and nameless (for it is no true way), and that the other path is real and true. How, then, can what is be going to be in the future? Or how could it come into being? If it came into being, it is not; nor is it if it is going to be in the future. Thus is becoming extinguished and passing away not to be heard of.

Nor is it divisible, since it is all alike, and there is no more of it in one place than in another, to hinder it from holding together, nor less of it, but everything is full of what is. Wherefore all holds together; for what is, is in contact with what is.

Moreover, it is immovable in the bonds of mighty chains, without beginning and without end; since coming into being and passing away have been driven afar, and true belief has cast them away. It is the same, and it rests in the self-same place; abiding in itself. And thus it remaineth constant in its place; for hard necessity keeps it in the bonds of the limit that holds it fast on every side. Wherefore it is not permitted to what is to be infinite; for it is in need of nothing; while, if it were infinite, it would stand in need of everything.

Look steadfastly with thy mind at things afar as if they were at hand. You cannot cut off what anywhere is from holding fast to what is anywhere; neither is it scattered abroad throughout the universe, nor does it come together.

It is the same thing that can be thought and for the sake of which the thought exists; for you cannot find thought without something that is, to which it is betrothed. And there is not, and never shall be, any time other than that which is present, since fate has chained it so as to be whole and immovable. Wherefore all these things are but the names which mortals have given, believing them to be true—coming into being and passing away, being and not being, change of place and alteration of bright color.

Where, then, it has its farthest boundary, it is complete on every side, equally poised from the centre in every direction, like the mass of a rounded sphere; for it cannot be greater or smaller in one place than in another. For there is nothing which is not that could keep it from reaching out equally, nor is it possible that there should be more of what is in this place and less in that, since it is all inviolable. For, since it is equal in all directions, it is equally confined within limits.

[277]

PASCAL, BLAISE

PASCAL, BLAISE (1623-1662). Scientists honor Pascal as one of the greatest mathematicians and physicists, as one of the founders of hydrodynamics and the mathematical theory of probability, and as a man who also made significant contributions by his investigations of vacuum, and gravity, and by his theory of conic sections. Men of all creeds revere Pascal's piety which was free from bigotry. Historians of literature admire Pascal's prose which contributed to the formation of modern French style. Philosophers highly esteem him as a profound psychologist and a thinker devoted to truth.

Success and fame meant nothing to Pascal. He sought peace of mind. Dissatisfied with abstract science, Pascal turned to the study of man and his spiritual problems. His conviction that self-complacency is the most dangerous obstacle in the way to true knowledge led him to a severe examination of his own inclinations and disinclinations. In his search of truth, Pascal was steadily tormented by his passions and inner conflicts, but he overcame all these obstacles by his honesty of thought. He was equally opposed to those who despise human reason and to those who are over-confident of it. According to him, God enabled man to know religious truth by means of reason, and to feel truth, due to His grace. He protested with energy and courage any attempt to convert men to any creed by force. But he fought religious and moral laxity with no less energy, as his *Lettres Provinciales*, masterworks of polemics, have shown. In his *Pensées* (Thoughts), Pascal dealt with the fundamental problems of human existence from the psychological and theological point of view. He regarded truth as the expression of God's will and as a means to know and to love Him.

THOUGHTS ON MIND AND ON STYLE

THE *difference between the mathematical and the intuitive mind.*—In the one the principles are palpable, but removed from ordinary use; so that for want of habit it is difficult to turn one's mind in that direction: but if one turns it thither ever so little, one sees the principles fully, and one must have a quite inaccurate mind who reasons wrongly from principles so plain that it is almost impossible they should escape notice.

But in the intuitive mind the principles are found in common use, and are before the eyes of everybody. One has only to look, and no effort is necessary; it is only a question of good eyesight, but it must be good, for the principles are so subtle and so numerous, that it is almost impossible but that some escape notice. Now the omission of one principle leads to error; thus one must have very clear sight to see all the principles, and in the next place an accurate mind not to draw false deductions from known principles.

All mathematicians would then be intuitive if they had clear sight, for they do not reason incorrectly from principles known to them; and intuitive minds would be mathematical if they could turn their eyes to the principles of mathematics to which they are unused.

The reason, therefore, that some intuitive minds are not mathematical is that they cannot at all turn their attention to the principles of mathematics. But the reason that mathematicians are not intuitive is that they do not see what is before them, and that, accustomed to the exact and plain principles of mathematics, and not reasoning till they have well inspected and arranged their principles, they are lost in matters of intuition where the principles do not allow of such arrangement. They are scarcely seen; they are felt rather than seen; there is the greatest difficulty in making them felt by those who do not of themselves perceive them. These principles are so fine and so numerous that a very delicate and very clear sense is needed to perceive them, and to judge rightly and justly when they are perceived, without for the most part being able to demonstrate them in order as in mathematics; because the principles are not known to us in the same way, and because it would be an endless matter to undertake it. We must see the matter at once, at one glance, and not by a process of reasoning, at least to a certain degree. And thus it is rare that mathematicians are intuitive, and that men of intuition are mathematicians, because mathematicians wish to treat matters of intuition mathematically, and make themselves ridiculous, wishing to begin with definitions and then with axioms, which is not the way to proceed in this kind of reasoning. Not that the mind does not do so, but it does it tacitly, naturally, and without technical rules; for the expression of it is beyond all men, and only a few can feel it.

Intuitive minds, on the contrary, being thus accustomed

to judge at a single glance, are so astonished when they are presented with propositions of which they understand nothing, and the way to which is through definitions and axioms so sterile, and which they are not accustomed to see thus in detail, that they are repelled and disheartened.

But dull minds are never either intuitive or mathematical.

Mathematicians who are only mathematicians have exact minds, provided all things are explained to them by means of definitions and axioms; otherwise they are inaccurate and insufferable, for they are only right when the principles are quite clear.

And men of intuition who are only intuitive cannot have the patience to reach to first principles of things speculative and conceptual, which they have never seen in the world, and which are altogether out of the common.

There are different kinds of right understanding; some have right understanding in a certain order of things, and not in others, where they go astray. Some draw conclusions well from a few premises, and this displays an acute judgment.

Others draw conclusions well where there are many premises.

For example, the former easily learn hydrostatics, where the premises are few, but the conclusions are so fine that only the greatest acuteness can reach them.

And in spite of that these persons would perhaps not be great mathematicians, because mathematics contains a great number of premises, and there is perhaps a kind of intellect that can search with ease a few premises to the bottom, and cannot in the least penetrate those matters in which there are many premises.

There are then two kinds of intellect: the one able to penetrate acutely and deeply into the conclusions of given premises, and this is the precise intellect; the other able to comprehend a great number of premises without confusing them, and this is the mathematical intellect. The one has force and exactness, the other comprehension. Now the one quality can exist without the other; the intellect can be strong and narrow, and can also be comprehensive and weak.

Those who are accustomed to judge by feeling do not understand the process of reasoning, for they would understand at first sight, and are not used to seek for principles. And others, on the contrary, who are accustomed to reason from principles, do not at all understand matters of feeling, seeking principles, and being unable to see at a glance.

Mathematics, intuition.— True eloquence makes light of eloquence, true morality makes light of morality; that is to say, the morality of the judgment, which has no rules, makes light of the morality of the intellect.

For it is to judgment that perception belongs, as science belongs to intellect. Intuition is the part of judgment, mathematics of intellect.

To make light of philosophy is to be a true philosopher.

Those who judge of a work by rule are in regard to others as those who have a watch are in regard to others. One says, "It is two hours ago"; the other says, "It is only three-quarters of an hour." I look at my watch, and say to the one, "You are weary," and to the other, "Time gallops with you"; for it is only an hour and a half ago, and I laugh at those who tell me that time goes slowly with me, and that I judge by imagination. They do not know that I judge by my watch.

Just as we harm the understanding, we harm the feelings also.

The understanding and the feelings are moulded by intercourse; the understanding and feelings are corrupted by intercourse. Thus good or bad society improves or corrupts them. It is, then, all-important to know how to choose in order to improve and not to corrupt them; and we cannot make this choice, if they be not already improved and not corrupted. Thus a circle is formed, and those are fortunate who escape it.

The greater intellect one has, the more originality one

finds in men. Ordinary persons find no difference between men.

PATER, WALTER HORATIO

PATER, WALTER HORATIO (1839-1894). Most of Pater's disciples who pursued his doctrine of thrice-refined hedonism to its extreme consequences finally took refuge in the Church of Rome, and many of those who revolted against Pater's philosophy of life or against his way of criticizing art, after becoming sure of their victory, admitted their personal love of the man whose thoughts and views they had attacked. Pater's belief that nothing which ever has interested mankind can wholly lose its vitality, may be confirmed by the vicissitudes of his literary fame.

Oscar Wilde called Pater's *Renaissance* (1873) his "golden book" and said in *De Profundis* that it had "such a strange influence over my life." George Moore took Pater's *Marius the Epicurean* (1885), which he called his "Bible," as model for his own book *Confessions of a Young Man.* William Butler Yeats and others who later became noted poets and critics founded *The Rhymers' Club* whose program was the cult of Pater's ideas.

Great scholars have praised Pater's principal work *Plato and Platonism* (1893) because of its author's congeniality with the great Greek thinker. But Pater was no Platonist. He called himself an Epicurean, and was perhaps even more influenced by Heraclitus. The essence of what he called his humanism is the conviction that only the sharp apex of the present moment between two hypothetical eternities is secure, and that the art of living consists in the ability of making such passing moments yield the utmost of enjoyment. He tried to show that devotion to enjoyment of beauty gives the soul a strength and austerity which cannot be surpassed even by moral ascetism, and that delicacy of feeling does not exclude purity of thinking. Pater's way or regarding all things and principles as inconsistent did not allow him to acquiesce in any orthodoxy and maintained his curiosity in testing new opinions. But his instincts, which were opposed to academic dullness, let him also recoil from revolutionary excesses.

THREE WAYS OF CRITICISM

THERE are three different ways in which the criticism of philosophic, of all speculative opinion whatever, may be

902

conducted. The doctrines of Plato's *Republic*, for instance, may be regarded as so much truth or falsehood, to be accepted or rejected as such by the student of today. That is the dogmatic method of criticism; judging every product of human thought, however alien or distant from one's self, by its congruity with the assumptions of Bacon or Spinoza, of Mill or Hegel, according to the mental preference of the particular critic. There is, secondly, the more generous, eclectic or syncretic method, which aims at a selection from contending schools of the various grains of truth dispersed among them. It is the method which has prevailed in periods of large reading but with little inceptive force of their own, like that of the Alexandrian Neo-Platonism in the third century, or the Neo-Platonism of Florence in the fifteenth. Its natural defect is in the tendency to misrepresent the true character of the doctrine it professes to explain, that it may harmonize thus the better with the other elements of a preconceived system.

Dogmatic and eclectic criticism alike have in our own century, under the influence of Hegel and his predominant theory of the ever-changing "Time-spirit" or *Zeit-geist*, given way to a third method of criticism, the historic method, which bids us replace the doctrine, or the system, we are busy with, or such an ancient monument of philosophic thought as *The Republic*, as far as possible in the group of conditions, intellectual, social, material, amid which it was actually produced if we would really understand it. That ages have their genius as well as the individual; that in every age there is a peculiar *ensemble* of conditions which determines a common character in every product of that age, in business and art, in fashion and speculation, in religion and manners, in men's very faces; that nothing man has projected from himself is really intelligible except at its own date, and from its proper point of view in the never-resting "secular process"; the solidarity of philosophy, of the intellectual life, with common or general history; that what it behooves the student of philosophic systems to cultivate is the "historic sense":

by force of these convictions many a normal, or at first sight abnormal, phase of speculation has found a reasonable meaning for us. As the strangely twisted pine tree, which would be a freak of nature on an English lawn, is seen, if we replace it, in thought, amid the contending forces of the Alpine torrent that actually shaped its growth, to have been the creature of necessity, of the logic of certain facts; so, beliefs the most fantastic, the "communism" of Plato, for instance, have their natural propriety when duly correlated with those facts, those conditions round about them, of which they are in truth a part.

[279]

PEANO, GIUSEPPE

PEANO, GIUSEPPE (1858-1932). Modest, simple, kind-hearted, benevolent, affable in his personal behavior, Peano impressed his audiences and readers with the strict precision of his thinking. He was principally a mathematical logician but was also devoted to the idea of the perfection of human relations, international communications, spiritual and technical advance and rapprochement. It was scientific and humanitarian interest that drove him to the problem of universal language or, as he called it "inter-language" and to the purpose of achieving what Leibniz had planned in his program of a universal characteristic.

After publishing, in 1884, *Differential Calculus and Principles of the Integral Calculus,* and, in 1888, *The Geometrical Calculus,* Peano introduced new concepts and methods into mathematics, whose vocabulary he reduced to three words. He became convinced that, in order to maintain the strict character of mathematics, it was necessary to renounce common language and to shape an instrument of language that renders to thought the same services as the microscope does in biology. The ideography created by Peano uses for logical operations symbols that are shaped differently from algebraic symbols. His system permits writing every proposition of logic in symbols exclusively, in order to emancipate the strictly logical part of reasoning from verbal language and its vagueness and ambiguity. In his *Formulary of Mathematics* (1894-1908) he reduced mathematics to symbolic notation. Besides his efforts to systematize logic as a mathematical science, Peano tried to make the idea of an international language popular and to develop its practical use. As the president of the *Academia pro Inter-lingua* he was a devoted apostle of this idea.

ON UNIVERSAL LANGUAGE

SINCE most people are in mutual contact for reasons of politics, science and commerce, a need for an international language has always been manifest.

Under the Roman Empire various peoples adopted popular Latin with simplifications. Saxon people, in contact with Angles, have formed the modern English language which has simplified cases, genders, and, in part, person and mood. The English language has a tendency to get rid of all inflection and to become monosyllabic.

Likewise in historical time, *Lingua Franca* was formed in Mediterranean ports, pidgin-English in China, Urdu in India.

Today, every man in Europe and America who has relations with foreign countries, wants an international language. For a national language is sufficient only for those who have relations only within their own country. Knowledge of three or four principal languages may be sufficient for reading books which either in their original version or in translations have already become famous. But today Russians, Poles, Roumanians, Japanese and others are publishing important works in their own language.

The adoption of a living language as international language is, for political reasons, not possible.

Many scholars recommend classical Latin.

Dr. Zamenhof published, in 1887, Esperanto which simplifies gender and person but does not continue simplification in case and number. Esperanto reduces the whole grammar to sixteen rules, none of which is necessary.

Artificial language is analytic. It decomposes the idea of a common language. If, in the future, analysis and synthesis meet one another, just as two sources of mining workers meet each another after driving a tunnel, rational language and Leibniz' universal characteristics will do the same.

[280]

PEIRCE, CHARLES SAUNDERS

PEIRCE, CHARLES SAUNDERS (1839-1914). Until William James turned to philosophy and made pragmatism popular, his life-long friend, Peirce, the initiator of this movement, had been almost unknown. Peirce had lectured at Harvard during the periods 1864-65 and 1869-70 and at Johns Hopkins during 1879-84. He had contributed to scientific and general reviews, but no University was induced by his publications to appoint him a professor. For thirty years he had been associated with the United States Coast and Geodetic Survey. He had had no time to complete a book, except his *Grand Logic* which, however, was published after his death, together with other works he had left.

Before men like James and Dewey made Peirce's name famous, he could state: "I am a man of whom critics never found anything good to say." But once he was rather happy to be blamed by a malicious critic who reproached him for not being sure of his own conclusions. Peirce regarded this reproof as a praise. For to him any truth is provisional. In any proposition there must be taken account of coefficient of probability. This theory, called by Peirce "fallibilism," is a substitute for scepticism, and a constituent of his philosophical system, of no lesser importance than pragmatism, which he substitutes for positivism.

Peirce was the son of the great mathematician, Benjamin Peirce, and himself a mathematician who pioneered in various fields. Before he concentrated upon philosophical studies, he had worked for ten years in chemical laboratories, and had been devoted to exact sciences. He was, by nature, a logician, and it was his interest in logic that made him a philosopher. His conception of pragmatism was not a metaphysical but a logical theory. After studying German and English philosophies, Peirce declared that the Germans acquainted him with "a rich mine of suggestions," which were "of little argumentative weight," while the results of the British were "meager but more accurate."

Peirce's pragmatism, though a logical theory, interprets thought in terms of operation and control. Its striking feature is the inseparable connection between rational cognition and rational purpose. The whole function of thinking, says Peirce, is but one step in the production of habits of action. His statement of the close relation between thought and human conduct has often been misunderstood as though Peirce had proclaimed subordination of reason to action, or even to profit and particular interests. In fact, Peirce defined the meaning of a concept or proposition as that form which is most directly applicable to self-control in any situation and to any purpose. To him, the rational meaning of every proposition lies in the future which is regarded as the ultimate test of what truth means.

DIVISIONS OF SCIENCE

I RECOGNIZE two branches of science: theoretical, whose purpose is simply and solely knowledge of God's truth; and practical, for the uses of life. In branch 1, I recognize two subbranches, of which, at present, I consider only the first, [the sciences of discovery]. Among the theoretical sciences [of discovery], I distinguish three classes, all resting upon observation, but being observational in very different senses.

The first is mathematics, which does not undertake to ascertain any matter of fact whatever, but merely posits hypotheses, and traces out their consequences. It is observational, in so far as it makes constructions in the imagination according to abstract precepts, and then observes these imaginary objects, finding in them relations of parts not specified in the precept of construction. This is truly observation, yet certainly in a very peculiar sense; and no other kind of observation would at all answer the purpose of mathematics.

Class II is philosophy, which deals with positive truth, indeed, yet contents itself with observations such as come within the range of every man's normal experience, and for the most part in every waking hour of his life. Hence Bentham calls this class, *coenoscopic*. These observations escape the untrained eye precisely because they permeate our whole lives, just as a man who never takes off his blue spectacles soon ceases to see the blue tinge. Evidently, therefore, no microscope or sensitive film would be of the least use in this class. The observation is observation in a peculiar, yet perfectly legitimate, sense. If philosophy glances now and then at the results of special sciences, it is only as a sort of condiment to excite its own proper observation.

Class III is Bentham's *idioscopic;* that is, the special sciences, depending upon special observation, which travel or other exploration, or some assistance to the senses, either instrumental or given by training, together with unusual diligence, has put within the power of its students. This class manifestly divides itself into two subclasses, the physical and the psychical sciences; or, as I will call them, physiognosy and psychognosy. Under the former is to be included physics, chemistry, biology, astronomy, geognosy, and whatever may be like these sciences; under the latter, psychology, linguistics, ethnology, sociology, history, etc. Physiognosy sets forth the workings of efficient causation, psychognosy of final causation. But the two things call for different eyes. A man will be no whit the worse physiognosist for being utterly blind to facts of mind; and if we sometimes find observation in a psychognosist, it will, unless by exception, be found not to be of a purely physical fact. Thus, a philologist may have a fine ear for language-sounds; but it is by no means pure physical resemblance which determines whether a given sound is or is not "the" Italian close *o*, for example, as it is naively called: it is psychical habit. In any simple physical sense the sounds not distinguished from that differ much more from one another than almost any of them do from sounds which would not be tolerated for "the" close *o*. So, this fine phonetic observation of the linguist is a knack of understanding a virtual convention. The two kinds of observation are different; but they do not seem to be quite so different as both alike are from the observation of the philosopher and the mathematician; and this is why, though I, at first, was inclined to give each of them equal rank with those classes, it has at length appeared certain that they should be placed a little lower.

I still persist in leaving unnoticed a certain sub-branch of theoretical science [the sciences of review]; and as for the practical sciences, I shall merely mention a few of them, just to give an idea of what I refer to under that name. I mean, then, all such well-recognized sciences now *in actu,* as pedagogics, gold-beating, etiquette, pigeon-fancying, vulgar arithmetic, horology, surveying, navigation, telegraphy, printing, bookbinding, paper-making, deciphering, ink-making, librarian's work, engraving, etc. In short, this is by far the more various of the two branches of science. I must confess to being utterly bewildered by its motley crowd, but fortunately the natural classification of this branch will not concern us in logic—at least, will not do so as far as I can perceive.

Now let us consider the relations of the classes of science to one another. We have already remarked that relations of generation must always be of the highest concern to natural classification, which is, in fact, no more nor less than an account of the existential, or *natural,* birth concerning relations of things; meaning by birth the relations of a thing to its originating final causes.

Beginning with Class I, mathematics meddles with every other science without exception. There is no science whatever to which is not attached an application of mathematics. This is not true of any other science, since pure mathematics has not, as a part of it, any application of any other science, inasmuch as every other science is limited to finding out what is positively true, either as an individual fact, as a class, or as a law; while pure mathematics has no interest in whether a proposition is existentially true or not. In particular, mathematics has such a close intimacy with one of the classes of philosophy, that is, with logic, that no small acumen is required to find the joint between them.

Next, passing to Class II, philosophy, whose business it is to find out all that can be found out from those universal experiences which confront every man in every waking hour of his life, must necessarily have its application in every other science. For be this science of philosophy that is founded on those universal phenomena as small as you please, as long as it amounts to anything at all, it is evident that every special science ought to take that little into account before it begins work with its microscope, or telescope, or whatever special means of ascertaining truth it may be provided with.

It might, indeed, very easily be supposed that even pure mathematics itself would have need of one department of philosophy; that is to say, of logic. Yet a little reflection would show, what the history of science confirms, that that is not true. Logic will, indeed, like every other science, have its mathematical parts. There will be a mathematical logic just as there is a mathematical physics and a mathematical economics. If there is any part of logic of which mathematics stands in need—logic being a science of fact and mathematics only a science of the consequences of hypotheses—it can only be that very part of logic which consists merely in an application of mathematics so that the appeal will be, not of mathematics to a prior science of logic, but of mathematics to mathematics. Let us look at the rationale of this a little more closely. Mathematics is engaged solely in tracing out the consequences of hypotheses. As such, she never at all considers whether or not anything be existentially true, or not. But now suppose that mathematics strikes upon a snag; and that one mathematician says that it is evident that a consequence follows from a hypothesis, while another mathematician says it evidently does not. Here, then, the mathematicians find themselves suddenly abutting against brute fact; for certainly a dispute is not a rational consequence of anything. True, this fact, this dispute, is no part of mathematics. Yet it would seem to give occasion for an appeal to logic, which is generally a science of fact, being a science of truth; and whether or not there be any such thing as truth is a question of fact. However, because this dispute relates merely to the consequence of a hypothesis, the mere careful study of the hypothesis, which is pure mathematics, resolves it; and after all, it turns out that there was no occasion for the intervention of a science of reasoning.

It is often said that the truths of mathematics are infallible. So they are, if you mean practical infallibility,

infallibility such as that of conscience. They appear even as theoretically infallible, if they are viewed through spectacles that cut off the rays of blunder. I never yet met with boy or man whose addition of a long column, of fifty to a hundred lines, was absolutely infallible, so that adding it a second time could in no degree increase one's confidence in the result, nor ought to do so. The addition of that column is, however, merely a repetition of $1+1=2$; so that, however improbable it may be, there is a certain finite probability that everybody who has ever performed this addition of 1 and 1 has blundered, except on those very occasions on which we are accustomed to suppose (on grounds of probability merely) that they *did* blunder. Looked at in this light, every mathematical inference is merely a matter of probability. At any rate, in the sense in which anything in mathematics is certain, it is most certain that the whole mathematical world has often fallen into error, and that, in some cases, such errors have stood undetected for a couple of millennia. But no case is adducible in which the science of logic has availed to set mathematicians right or to save them from tripping. On the contrary, attention once having been called to a supposed inferential blunder in mathematics, short time has ever elapsed before the whole mathematical world has been in accord, either that the step was correct, or else that it was fallacious; and this without appeal to logic, but merely by the careful review of the mathematics as such. Thus, historically mathematics does not, as *a priori* it cannot, stand in need of any separate science of reasoning.

But mathematics is the only science which can be said to stand in no need of philosophy, excepting, of course, some branches of philosophy itself. It so happens that at this very moment the dependence of physics upon philosophy is illustrated by several questions now on the *tapis*. The question of non-Euclidean geometry may be said to be closed. It is apparent now that geometry, while in its main outlines, it must ever remain within the borders of philosophy, since it depends and must depend upon the scrutinizing of every-day experience, yet at certain special points it stretches over into the domain of physics. Thus, space, as far as we can see, has three dimensions; but are we quite sure that the corpuscles into which atoms are now minced have not room enough to wiggle a little in a fourth? Is physical space hyperbolic, that is, infinite and limited, or is it elliptic, that is, finite and unlimited? Only the exactest measurements upon the stars can decide. Yet even with them the question cannot be answered without recourse to philosophy. But a question at this moment under consideration by physicists is whether matter consists ultimately of minute solids, or whether it consists merely of vortices of an ultimate fluid. The third possibility, which there seems to be reason to suspect is the true one, that it may consist of vortices in a fluid which itself consists of far minuter solids, these, however, being themselves vortices of a fluid, itself consisting of ultimate solids, and so on in endless alternation, has hardly been broached. The question as it stands must evidently depend upon what we ought to conclude from every-day, unspecialized observations, and particularly upon a question of logic. Another still warmer controversy is whether or not it is proper to endeavor to find a mechanical explanation of electricity, or whether it is proper, on the contrary, to leave the differential equations of electrodynamics as the last word of science. This is manifestly only to be decided by a scientific philosophy very different from the amateurish, superficial stuff in which the contestants are now entangling themselves. A third pretty well defended opinion, by the way, is that instead of explaining electricity by molar dynamics, molar dynamics ought to be explained as a special consequence of the laws of electricity. Another appeal to philosophy was not long ago virtually made by the eminent electrician, the lamented Hertz, who wished to explain force, in general, as a consequence of unseen constraints. Philosophy alone can pronounce for or against such a theory. I will not undertake to anticipate questions which have not yet emerged; otherwise, I might suggest that chemists must ere long be making appeal to philosophy to decide whether compounds are held together by force or by some other agency. In biology, besides the old logico-metaphysical dispute about the reality of classifications, the momentous question of evolution has unmistakable dependence on philosophy. Then again, caryocinesis has emboldened some naturalists, having certain philosophical leanings, to rebel against the empire of experimental physiology. The origin of life is another topic where philosophy asserts itself; and with this I close my list, not at all because I have mentioned all the points at which just now the physical sciences are influenced by a philosophy, such as it is, but simply because I have mentioned enough of them for my present purpose.

The dependence of the psychical sciences upon philosophy is no less manifest. A few years ago, indeed, regenerate psychology, in the flush of her first success, not very wisely proposed to do without metaphysics; but I think that today psychologists generally perceive the impossibility of such a thing. It is true that the psychical sciences are not quite so dependent upon metaphysics as are the physical sciences; but, by way of compensation, they must lean more upon logic. The mind works by final causation, and final causation is logical causation. Note, for example, the intimate bearing of logic upon grammatical syntax. Moreover, everything in the psychical sciences is inferential. Not the smallest fact about the mind can be directly perceived as psychical. An emotion is directly felt as a bodily state, or else it is only known inferentially. That a thing is agreeable appears to direct observation as a character of an object, and it is only by inference that it is referred to the mind. If this statement be disputed (and some will dispute it), all the more need is there for the intervention of logic. Very difficult problems of inference are continually emerging in the psychical sciences. In psychology, there are such questions as free-will and innate ideas; in linguistics, there is the question of the origin of language, which must be settled before linquistics takes its final form. The whole business of deriving ancient history from documents that are always insufficient and, even when not conflicting, frequently pretty obviously false, must be carried on under the supervision of logic, or else be badly done.

The influence of philosophy upon the practical sciences is less direct. It is only here and there that it can be detected; and ethics is the division of philosophy which most concerns these sciences. Ethics is courteously invited to make a suggestion now and then in law, jurisprudence, and sociology. Its sedulous exclusion from diplomacy and economics is immense folly. We are unhappily debarred from calling this folly stupendous or egregious, because it is merely the ordinary blindness of those who profoundly believe that lies are the most wholesome of diet, who, as Edgar Poe sagaciously said, when they get home, have once locked themselves in their several chambers, have undressed, knelt down by the bedside and said their prayers, got into bed, and blown out the candle, then, at length, and not till then, indulge in one veracious wink—the only veracious act of the day—and lull themselves to sleep with an inward ditty that Right is a silly thing without wealth or vigor in this work-a-day world. One day man shall start up out of his slumber to see by broad daylight that that despised idea has all along been the one irresistible power. Then may begin an era when it is counted within the practical sciences, one and all—when, in a word, a man will not design a stove nor order a coat without stopping first and sifting out his real desire—and it is prophecy as simple as *Barbara,* that, when that comes to pass, those sciences will answer even their lower and nearest purposes far more perfectly than at present they do. So, at any rate, the student of minute logic will be forced to think.

[281]

PENN, WILLIAM

PENN, WILLIAM (1644-1718). The part that William Penn played in making freedom of conscience prevail in America is of primary importance, even granted that many other men and groups of people have struggled for the same cause. As soon as he had been converted to Quakerism, he gave powerful expression to his longing for freedom of worship and his opposition to religious intolerance. He was ready to sacrifice his own liberty for his faith, and while in prison, he told his jailer that he "scorned that religion which is not worth suffering for, and able to sustain those that are afflicted for it." But when he himself became the ruler over a territory that now is a state of the Union, second in its population, he provided that no one should be obliged "to frequent or maintain any religious worship, place or ministry contrary" to his conscience. Many of his provisions became basic to corresponding articles in the Constitution of the United States.

A curious combination of circumstances enabled Penn to undertake what he called "a holy experiment" and to establish a "theocratic democracy," different from all the other great British colonies in America. The inheritance of a claim for money advanced to the Crown by his father, Admiral Sir William Penn, gave him the opportunity of acquiring the territory of Pennsylvania and of founding there a state in accordance with his religious and political ideas. Without this opportunity, Penn would have been no more than an agitator, however influential and self-denying, confined to an environment which did not promise great success, or else merely the author of a Utopian scheme. He could not secure permanent realization of his ideal, but he established and maintained his government "without ever drawing a sword." His treaties with the Indians aroused even the admiration of Voltaire, who praised them because they were "not ratified by an oath and were never infringed."

Penn was a religious perfectionist and a man of the world. He wrote with great clarity of his religious experiences, but his interests were not limited to religion and theology. Many of his works reveal great erudition. Religious tolerance was the cornerstone of his political system, in which fundamental and circumstantial laws are distinguished. He repeatedly emphasized that "the political union of loyal citizens does not depend upon unity of belief."

THE world is the stage in which all men do act for eternity, and every venture of this brings its true weight of eternal life or death.

By revelation we understand the discovery and illumination of the light and spirit of God relating to those things that properly and immediately concern the daily information and satisfaction of our souls in the way of our duty to Him and our neighbors.

As there is this natural and intelligent spirit by which man is daily informed of the concerns of mortal life, so is a divine principle communicated to him, which we call the Light and that does illuminate and discover to his understanding the condition of his soul, and gives him a true knowledge of what is good, what he himself is, and what is regarded at his hands, either in obeying or suffering.

I know no religion that destroys courtesy, civility and kindness.

All men have reason, but all men are not reasonable. Is it the fault of the grain in the granary that it yields no increase, or of the talent in the napkin that it is not improved?

Conscience, truly speaking, is no other than the sense a man has, or judgment he makes of his duty to God, according to the understanding God gives him of his will.

Justice is the means of peace betwixt the government and the people and one man and company and another.

Liberty without obedience is confusion, and obedience without liberty is slavery.

Liberty of conscience is every man's natural right, and he who is deprived of it is a slave in the midst of the greatest liberty.

[282]

PERICLES

PER·ICLES (495-429 B.C.). Pericles' name is inseparably connected with a period that is generally considered the height of ancient Greek civilization. During the time he ruled Athens, the Parthenon was built, sculptors like Phidias, Myron, Polycletus, painters like Zeuxis, Parrhasius and Polygnotus, dramatists like Aeschylus, Sophocles and Euripides, created their immortal works, and Socrates began to meditate about the value of life. Pericles himself was taught philosophy by Anaxagoras. He entrusted to Protagoras an important mission. He developed what in Athens' democracy became of lasting political and humanitarian value, though he could not remove its shortcomings. As a statesman, Pericles has been judged differently. While Thucydides exalts him, Aristoteles and Isocrates think that Pericles' policy was not in Athens' best interest. Modern historians hold that his foreign policy was a failure but that he later learned to calculate the forces of Athens' adversaries more rightly. Even his enemies have recognized that Pericles never resorted to the tricks of a demagogue. As a speaker he was regarded by his contemporaries as the most powerful they knew or could even imagine. He was not a frequent orator but when he delivered a speech, his political success was almost certain. Despite all rivalries, he was elected commander-in-chief for fifteen terms. Until his last years his authority in matters of state was supreme.

In 430, at the close of the first year of the Peloponnesian War, which ended with Sparta's victory over Athens, Pericles, in an address celebrating the memory of the citizen-soldiers who were killed in action, defended Athens' democratic way of life.

THE DEMOCRATIC WAY OF LIFE

I WILL speak first of our ancestors, for it is right and becoming that now, when we are lamenting the dead, a tribute should be paid to their memory. There has never been a time when they did not inhabit this land, which by their valor they have handed down from generation to generation, and we have received from them a free state. But if they were worthy of praise, still more were our fathers, who added to their inheritance, and after many a struggle transmitted to us, their sons, this great empire. And we ourselves, assembled here today, who are still most of us in the vigor of life, have chiefly done the work of improvement, and have richly endowed our city with all things, so that she is sufficient for herself both in peace and war. Of the military exploits by which our various possessions were acquired, or of the energy with which we or our fathers drove back the tide of war, Hellenic or Barbarian, I will not speak, for the tale would be long and is familiar to you. But before I praise the dead, I should like to point out by what principles of action we rose to power, and under what institutions and through what manner of life our empire became great. For I conceive that such thoughts are not unsuited to the occasion, and that this numerous assembly of citizens and strangers may profitably listen to them.

Our form of government does not enter into rivalry with the institutions of others. We do not copy our neighbors, but are an example to them. It is true that we are called a democracy, for the administration is in the hands of the many and not of the few. But while the law secures equal justice to all alike in their private disputes, the claim of excellence is also recognized; and when a citizen is in any way distinguished, he is preferred to the public service, not as a matter of privilege but as the reward of merit. Neither is poverty a bar, but a man may benefit his country whatever be the obscurity of his condition. There is no exclusiveness in our public life, and in our private intercourse we are not suspicious of one another, nor angry with our neighbor if he does what he likes; we do not put on sour looks at him which, though harmless, are not pleasant. While we are thus unconstrained in our private intercourse, a spirit of reverence pervades our public acts; we are prevented from doing wrong by respect for authority and for the laws, having an especial regard to those which are ordained for the protection of the injured as well as to those unwritten laws which bring upon the transgressor of them the reprobation of the general sentiment.

And we have not forgotten to provide for our weary

spirits many relaxations from toil; we have regular games and sacrifices throughout the year; at home the style of our life is refined; and the delight which we daily feel in all these things helps to banish melancholy. Because of the greatness of our city the fruits of the whole earth flow in upon us; so that we enjoy the goods of other countries as freely as of our own.

We are lovers of the beautiful, yet simple in our tastes, and we cultivate the mind without loss of manliness. Wealth we employ, not for talk and ostentation, but when there is a real use for it. To avow poverty with us is no disgrace; the true disgrace is in doing nothing to avoid it. An Athenian citizen does not neglect the state because he takes care of his own household; and even those of us who are engaged in business have a very fair idea of politics. We alone regard a man who takes no interest in public affairs, not as a harmless, but as a useless character; and if few of us are originators, we are all sound judges of a policy. The great impediment to action is, in our opinion, not discussion, but the want of that knowledge which is gained by discussion preparatory to action. For we have a peculiar power of thinking before we act and of acting too, whereas other men are courageous from ignorance, but hesitate upon reflection. And they are surely to be esteemed the bravest spirits who, having the clearest sense both of the pains and pleasures of life, do not on that account shrink from danger. In doing good, again, we are unlike others— we make our friends by conferring, not by receiving, favors.

To sum up: I say that Athens is the school of Hellas, and that the individual Athenian in his own person seems to have the power of adapting himself to the most varied forms of action with the utmost versatility and grace. This is no passing and idle word, but truth and fact; and the assertion is verified by the position to which these qualities have raised the state. For in the hour of trial, Athens alone among her contemporaries is superior to the report of her. No enemy who comes against her is indignant at the reverses which he sustains at the hands of such a city; no subject complains that his masters are unworthy of him. And we shall assuredly not be without witnesses; there are mighty monuments of our power which will make us the wonder of all ages.

We have compelled every land and every sea to open a path for our valor, and have everywhere planted eternal memorials of our friendship and of our enmity. Such is the city for whose sake these men fought and died; they could not bear to think that she might be taken from them; and every one of us who survive should gladly toil on her behalf.

[283]

PERRY, RALPH BARTON

PERRY, RALPH BARTON (1876-   ). From his study of Kant, Perry, the author of the classic biography of William James, proceeded to a revision of the critical approach to natural knowledge. He was one of the most active members of the group of American philosophers who, about 1910, elaborated the program of the "New Realism." However, soon thereafter he dissented from its majority and, banishing "moral and spiritual ontology" of any kind, arrived at a point which, based upon a philosophy of disillusionment, allowed him to take a stand on the "hazard of faith."

In his booklet *The Hope for Immortality* (1935), Perry confesses to be empty-handed as far as theoretical evidence or even arguments for the probability of immortality are concerned. But he holds that, even in default of knowledge, belief is sometimes justified by the insistence or depth of the need which it satisfies. Assuming a less extremist attitude, Perry later explained his belief in freedom, which he defines as the exercise of enlightened choice. Freedom constitutes the dignity of Man but is also his generic attribute. Cultivation of freedom therefore does not set a man apart from his fellows but implies a sense of universal kinship. Consequently freedom and humanitarian consciousness, far from excluding one another, are inseparable. Philosophy, the social sciences and history are justified only as far as they contribute to the growth of freedom and humanitarian solidarity. The natural sciences can be regarded as part of humanitarian culture in so far as

920

they reveal the real world as a condition or source of human life. Neither does utility as such constitute the humanitarian character of a science, nor is science as such inescapably human. The philosopher of disillusionment maintains that humanity is always escapable. But, for that reason, Perry is an ardent advocate of a militant democracy which must be "total but not totalitarian."

LOVE

LOVE means . . . a favorable interest in the satisfaction of a second interest. In the present context it is assumed that the second interest is the interest of a second person. Love begins and ends abroad. That "charity begins at home" is one of those many proverbs which have been coined by the devil to flatter human weakness. Love is, in the next place, essentially *indulgent;* it coincides with, and supports, the interest which is its object. The success or defeat of the loving interest will be a function of what is judged to be the success or defeat of the loved interest. Other-love, in this sense, may be directed to any one, or to the whole system, of the second person's interest. Where love is directed to the whole person it may oppose one of that person's particular interests, in so far as the person is imperfectly integrated. Where a person suffers from internal conflict, another's love may side with the integral self against the insubordinate element; but if love is to be indulgent, there must already be such an integral self in some form or stage of development. Love, in other words, is an interested support of another's preexisting and independently existing interest.

There are several common meanings of love which this definition excludes. In the first place, love is neither approving nor censorious. It does not prescribe the object of the loved interest, but desires that that interest shall have its object *whatever* that object. Suppose a son to desire fame; then the father's desire for the son's fame, if founded on the father's admiration of fame, is not love; nor is it love if the father desires that the son shall substitute for fame some other object, such as knowledge, which he, the father, prefers. Action towards another dictated by the agent's belief that he knows better what is good for the other than does the other himself, may be praiseworthy, but it is not love. The true quality of love is to be found in that sensitive imagination which can find its way into the secret sources of a man's joy and sorrow. Similarly, censoriousness, though it may be just, is not love. Love does not rebuke the sinner, or rejoice in his merited punishment; but grieves for him, and seeks to *bring him in,* as the shepherd seeks his lost sheep. Love, like Thomson's "Hound of Heaven," follows its object relentlessly into every corner of the universe and refuses to be offended or repelled.

The support of another's interest that springs from a sense of plenitude and power, or that looks to bind the other in gratitude, is not love. Nor is it love when an appetite feeds upon another individual, even though the other be of the same species. So-called sex-love may be as unloving as cannibalism. Finally, love must have an object other than itself. To love another's love of oneself, supposing oneself to consist only in love of the other, would be meaningless, even though it occurs in poetry and fiction. The circle must be broken at some point by an interest directed to an object, in order that there may be something for love to indulge. What seems to be circular love is the gratification afforded to each of two individuals by the presence of the other. Other-love finds itself most purely embodied in parental love, for the very reason that it is commonly one-sided or unreciprocated. Reciprocity adds to the intensity of love, but tends to impair its purity through introducing an element of sensuous gratification or of self-reference.

Love in the present sense consists essentially, then, in an activity which supports the interested activity of another person; seeking to promote that other person's achievement of what he desires, or enjoyment of what he likes. Universal love would be such a disposition on the part of one person towards all persons. If it is psychologically possible (in the sense of the general capacity of human nature) towards one, it is psychologically possible towards two or more; or towards all members of a class, such as the family, the nation, mankind, or sentient creatures. This attitude of general kindly interest, or of amiability, has its negative form, as in Lincoln's maxim, "with malice toward none, with charity for all"; and its positive form, as in good Samaritanism and humanity. A personal integration dominated by such a purpose is known in the tradition of moral philosophy as 'good will.' [284]

PESTALOZZI, JOHANN HEINRICH

PESTALOZZI, JOHANN HEINRICH (1746-1827). Pestalozzi is generally regarded as the father of modern European pedagogics. Born in Switzerland, an ardent Swiss patriot, he not only influenced the educational system of his own country and of Germany, but also inspired French and Scandinavian educators, and men like Horace Mann and Henry Barnard in the United States.

It is true, Pestalozzi could never heed to order in his own house or in his enterprises, and neglected his appearance to a degree no progressive educator could approve if one of his pupils did so. But he was an extraordinarily gifted leader of young people. He thoroughly knew and loved children, and also knew and loved humanity. His educational ideas are embedded in a totality of ideas on the perfection of Man. Indignant of individual wickedness and terrified by events of contemporary history, Pestalozzi never lost confidence in what he considered true human nature. His pedagogical skill was founded upon a large experience. He had been not only a teacher of children and a teacher of teachers, but also a trustee of orphans, and it was from the observation of abandoned children that he learned the most.

Educational ardor made Pestalozzi write philosophical treatises, as it also caused him to write novels, the best known of which is *Lienhard and Gertrude,* which was widely read. By no means did he claim to be a philosopher. He was neither a rationalist nor an intellectual, and he declared that his whole work was a work of the heart, not of understanding. He even felt uneasy while writing on philosophical problems. But he thought it necessary in order to explain his aims and methods which are conditional on broad views on the destiny of humanity. He considered man as an animal, a member of society and an ethical power. After

923

trying to outline the course of nature in the development of humanity, he proceeded to the establishment of an ethical humanism which has to dominate the education of children and the conduct of adults—their economic, political and spiritual life. Development of the mind, the heart and manual work were the principal points of Pestalozzi's education. He did not ignore the fact that any political community is threatened by inner contradictions; but he hoped to overcome many difficulties by pedagogical care.

WHAT I AM AS THE WORK OF MYSELF

Is it true that state of nature is to civilization, and civilization is to morality as childhood is to years of apprenticeship and these to mature age?

Is it true that I could never obtain a disposition to morality without the error of my sensual enjoyment and without the wrong of my social claims?

Is it true that truth and Justice are the exclusive property of that disposition?

Is it true that this disposition is exclusively the matter of the individual? That morality in relation to two people, as a matter of these two, cannot subsist? That the natural state does not know that disposition, and society does not rely on it?

Is it true that animal proximity or distance of moral objects is the definite natural turn to true morality?

Is it true that my civil duty as such does not make me moral?

Is it true that everything I owe to my community or as a member of the masses incites me to immorality?

All that is true!

In the individual, morality is closely connected with its animal nature and its social relations. But essentially it is entirely founded upon the freedom of my will—that means upon that quality of myself through which I feel myself independent of my animal greeds.

As a moral being I walk in the way to perfection of myself, and thus I become capable of overcoming the contradictions that seem to lie in my nature.

[285]

PHILO JUDAEUS

PHILO JUDAEUS (About 25 B.C.—Before 50 A.D.). The importance of Philo to the history of philosophy is incomparably greater than the power of his personality or the relevance of his personal thinking. For about seventeen centuries his example was, consciously and unconsciously, followed by all European thinkers, notwithstanding their differences, no matter whether they were nominalists or realists, idealists or naturalists, orthodox or heretics, and today Catholic Neo-Scholasticism is still following him, not to mention his influence on Islamic and Jewish philosophy.

Philo was the first thinker to introduce into epistemology, metaphysics, physics and ethics the problem of reconciling speculative thought with the data of Biblical revelation; or, rather, he established these data, especially their characteristics of God, Man and Nature as the perfect truth with which the philosopher had to harmonize the results of his thinking. In this way, Philo created a spiritual situation, completely unknown in pagan Greek philosophy which had not to regard Sacred Scripture as the standard and source of truth. The impact of the belief in the pagan gods on philosophical thoughts had only occasionally caused conflicts and had become negligible. As a positive support of thinking, as a source of knowledge, the belief in the pagan gods was of no account even when some philosophers used the gods as symbols of forces which were comprehended by speculative methods. Philo initiated a new era in the history of philosophy, the earliest documents of which can be noted in the Gospel of St. John. Its great development begins with the Fathers of the Church, comprises the whole Middle Ages and part of modern times, Descartes included. It was Spinoza, a Jew like Philo, who removed Biblical revelation from the realm of philosophy.

But, unlike Spinoza, Philo, a contemporary of Jesus Christ and St. Paul, remained a faithful, professing Jew. He devoted the main part of his life to the interpretation of the Pentateuch and to the defense of the Jewish faith against attacks on the part of gentile critics by explaining the essence of Judaism from the historical, philosophical, ethical and juridical points of view. When he was elected leader of a Jewish embassy to Rome in 40 A.D., he tried also to defend his co-religionists against the arbitrary power of Emperor Caligula.

Although Philo borrowed much from Greek philosophers, his

system deviates widely from purely Greek lines. It is the doctrine of monotheistic mysticism, teaching that human mind is capable, by intuition, not by reasoning, to apprehend God's existence but not His nature. In this way, Philo was the first to outline a psychology of faith.

ALLEGORICAL MEANING
OF THE DOWNFALL OF MANKIND

ITS juggleries and deceits pleasure does not venture to bring directly to the man, but first offers them to the woman, and by her means to the man; acting in a very natural and sagacious manner. For in human beings the mind occupies the rank of the man, and the sensations that of the woman. And pleasure joins itself to and associates itself with the sensations first of all, and then by their means cajoles also the mind, which is the dominant part. For, after each of the senses has been subjected to the charms of pleasure, and has learnt to delight in what is offered to it, the sight being fascinated by varieties of colors and shapes, the hearing by harmonious sounds, the taste by the sweetness of flowers, and the smell by the delicious fragrance of the odors which are brought before it, these all having received these offerings, like handmaids, bring them to the mind as their master, leading with them persuasion as an advocate, to warn it against rejecting any of them whatever. And the mind being immediately caught by the bait, becomes a subject instead of a ruler, and a slave instead of a master, and an exile instead of a citizen, and a mortal instead of an immortal. For we must altogether not be ignorant that pleasure, being like a courtesan or mistress, is eager to meet with a lover, and seeks for panders in order by their means to catch a lover. And the sensations are her panders, and conciliate love to her, and she employing them as baits, easily brings the mind into subjection to her. And the sensations conveying within the mind the things which have been seen externally, explain and display the forms of each of them setting their seal upon a similar affection. For the mind is like wax, and receives the impressions of appearances through the sensations, by means of which it makes itself master of the body, which of itself it would not be able to do, as I have already said.

And those who have previously become the slaves of pleasure immediately receive the wages of this miserable and incurable passion. For the woman having received vehement pains, partly in her travail, and partly such as are a rapid succession of agonies during the other portions of her life, and especially with reference to the bringing forth and bringing up of her children, to their diseases and their health, to their good or evil fortune, to an extent that utterly deprives her of her freedom and subjects her to the dominion of the man who is her companion, finds it unavoidable to obey all his commands. And the man in his turn endures toils and labors, and continual sweats, in order to the providing of himself with necessaries, and he also bears the deprivation of all those spontaneous good things which the earth was originally taught to produce without requiring the skill of the farmer, and he is subjected to a state in which he lives in incessant labor, for the purpose of seeking for food and means of subsistence, in order to avoid perishing by hunger.

[286]

PICO DELLA MIRANDOLA, GIOVANNI

PICO DELLA MIRANDOLA, GIOVANNI (1463-1494). Popular legends and scholarly tradition used to represent Pico as a resuscitated Greek god who had taught, by means of Platonic ideas, a new religion of worldly individualism. But, in fact, Pico, who charmed his greatest contemporaries and was admired by Reuchlin and Erasmus, by Lorenzo of Medici and Savonarola, was no pagan thinker, no heretic, no pantheist. His great aim was to reconcile all philosophies which, according to him, conflicted with one another only in appearance. He especially tried to synthesize Plato and Aristotle, and constantly refused to depreciate Aquinas or Scholasticism in general, although his aesthetic sense was captivated by Platonism.

But it was the Jewish Cabala that inspired him most. He held that Christian faith was not fundamentally different from the Cabala and expressed his strong conviction that every great philosophical or religious doctrine uses esoteric wisdom to veil secret teachings, which only the cabalist scholar is able to unveil.

At the age of 24, Pico planned to challenge all scholars of the known world by defending 900 conclusions or theses in a public disputation at Rome, but papal authorities prevented him from doing so and condemned thirteen of his conclusions.

Pico's metaphysics, despite its Platonic wrappings, depended largely on Aquinas as well as on the Cabala. His *Heptaplas* is a commentary on the Cabalist doctrine of Sefiroth, the ten creative powers. His last work *De Ente et Uno* (On Being and One) was inspired by his Hebrew teacher Eliah Del Medigo who had written a book *De Esse, Essentia et Uno*.

Pico was one of the most elegant stylists. He had an extraordinary talent for striking formulas. Thus he expressed his standpoint in the short sentence: "No philosophy turns us away from the trend to mysticism; philosophy seeks, theology finds, religion possesses truth." Of princely descent, related to almost all ruling dynasties in Italy, handsome, learned, an untiring worker, a reliable friend, Pico enchanted everyone he met, except the officers of papal jurisdiction.

THE ATTRIBUTES OF GOD
AND HUMAN CONDUCT OF LIFE

WE conceive God first of all as the perfect totality of act, the plenitude of being itself. It follows from this concept that He is one, that a term opposite to Him cannot be imagined. See then how much they err who fashion many first principles, many gods! At once it is clear that God is truth itself. For, what can He have which appears to be and is not, He who is being itself? It follows with certainty that He is truth itself. But He is likewise goodness itself. Three conditions are required for the good as Plato writes in his *Philebus*: perfection, sufficiency, and desirability. Now the good which we conceive will be perfect, since nothing can be lacking to that which is everything; it will be sufficient, since nothing can be lacking to those who possess that in which they will find all; it will be desirable, since from Him and in Him are all things which can possibly be desired. God is therefore the fullest plenitude of being, undivided unity, the most solid truth, the most perfect good. This, if I am not mistaken, is that quaternity, by which Pythagoras swore and which he called the principle of everflowing nature. Indeed, in this quarternity, which is One God, we have demonstrated the principle of all things. But we also swear by that which is holy, true, divine; now, what more true, more holy, more divine than these four characters? If we attribute them to God as the cause of things, the entire order is inverted. First He will be one, because He is conceived in Himself before He is conceived as cause. Then He will be good, true, and finally being (*ens*). For since the final cause has priority over the exemplary cause, and that over the efficient (we first desire to have something to protect us from the weather, then we conceive the idea of a house, and finally we construct one by making it materially), if the good pertains to the final cause, the true to the exemplary, being to the efficient, God as cause will have first of all the attribute of good, then of true, and finally of being. We shall here terminate these brief remarks on a subject teeming with many important problems.

Let us, lest we speak more of other things than of ourselves, take care that, while we scrutinize the heights, we do not live too basely, in a manner unworthy of beings to whom has been given the divine power of inquiring into things divine. We ought, then, to consider assiduously that our mind, with its divine privileges, cannot have a mortal origin nor can find happiness otherwise than in the possession of things divine, and that the more it elevates and inflames itself with the contemplation of the Divine by renouncing earthly preoccupations while yet a traveller on this pilgrimage here below, the more it will approach felicity. The best precept, then, which this discussion can give us, seems to be that, if we wish to be happy we ought to imitate the most happy and blessed of all beings, God, by establishing in ourselves unity, truth, and goodness.

What disturbs the peace of unity is ambition, the vice that steals away from itself the soul which abandons itself to it, tearing it, as it were, in pieces, and dispersing it. The resplendent light of truth, who will not lose it in the mud, in the darkness of lust? Avarice and cupidity steal from us goodness, for it is the peculiar property of goodness to communicate to others the goods which it possesses. Thus, when Plato asked himself why God had created the world, he answered: 'Because He was good.' These are the three vices: pride of life, concupiscence of the flesh, concupiscence of the eyes, which, as St. John says, are of the world and not of the Father who is unity, goodness, and truth indeed.

[287]

PLANCK, MAX

PLANCK, MAX (1858-1947). The first revolutionary novelty since Newton was introduced into the science of physics by Planck, the founder of the quantum theory. Before Planck, physical thinking rested on the assumption that all causal interactions are continuous. Planck, after studying entropy and radiation, showed that in a light or heat wave of frequency, the energy of the wave does not vary continuously, and established an "elementary quantum of action" of a definite numerical value as the unit of these variations. Quantum theory has made an inroad upon the concept of mass but it is most important in the regular occurrences of all atomic processes.

Planck's elementary quantum of action could not be welded in the framework of classical physics. All theoretical difficulties were removed by Einstein's special theory of relativity which was published in 1905, five years after Planck had established his quantum theory. Through the cooperation of Planck and Einstein a new picture of the world emerged. Its elements are no longer chemical atoms but electrons and protons whose mutual interactions are governed by the velocity of light and the elementary quantum of action.

Planck regarded the quanta as the building blocks of the universe and as proof of the existence in nature of something real and independent of every human measurement. He rejected positivism and believed in the possibility of reconciling natural science and religion.

A VAST volume of experiences reaches each one of us in the course of a year; such is the progress made in the various means of communication that new impressions from far and near rush upon us in a never-ending stream. It is true that many of them are forgotten as quickly as they arrive and that every trace of them is often effaced within a day; and it is as well that it should be so: if it were otherwise modern man would be fairly suffocated under the weight of different impressions. Yet every person who wishes to lead more than an ephemeral intellectual existence must be impelled by the very variety of these kaleidoscopic changes to seek for some element of permanence, for some lasting intellectual possession to afford him a *point d'appui* in the confusing claims of everyday life. In the younger generation this impulse manifests itself in a passionate desire for a comprehensive philosophy of the world; a desire which looks for satisfaction in groping attempts turning in every direction where peace and refreshment for a weary spirit is believed to reside.

It is the Church whose function it would be to meet such aspirations; but in these days its demands for an unquestioning belief serve rather to repel the doubters. The latter have recourse to more or less dubious substitutes, and hasten to throw themselves into the arms of one or other of the many prophets who appear preaching new gospels. It is surprising to find how many people even of the educated classes allow themselves to be fascinated by these new religions—beliefs which vary from the obscurest mysticism to the crudest superstition.

It would be easy to suggest that a philosophy of the world might be reached from a scientific basis; but such a suggestion is usually rejected by these seekers on the ground that the scientific view is bankrupt. There is an element of truth in this suggestion, and, indeed, it is entirely correct if the term science is taken in the traditional and still surviving sense where it implies a reliance on the understanding. Such a method, however, proves that those who adopt it have no sense of real science. The truth is very different. Anyone who has taken part in the building up of a branch of science is well aware from personal experience that every endeavor in this direction is guided by an unpretentious but essential principle. This principle is faith—a faith which looks ahead. It is said that science has no preconceived ideas: there is no saying that has been more thoroughly or more disastrously misunderstood. It is true that every branch of science must have an empirical foundation: but it is equally true that the essence of science does not consist in this raw material but in the manner in which it is used. The material always is incomplete: it consists of a number of parts which however numerous are discrete, and this is equally true of the tabulated figures of the natural sciences, and of the various documents of the intellectual sciences.

The material must therefore be completed, and this must be done by filling the gaps; and this in turn is done by means of associations of ideas. And associations of ideas are not the work of the understanding but the offspring of the investigator's imagination—an activity which may be described as faith, or, more cautiously, as a working hypothesis. The essential point is that its content in one way or another goes beyond the data of experience. The chaos of individual masses cannot be wrought into a cosmos without some harmonizing force and, similarly, the disjointed data of experience can never furnish a veritable science without the intelligent interference of a spirit actuated by faith. . . .
[288]

PLATO

PLATO (427-347 B.C.). For two thousand and three hundred years Plato's work has been a living force that has given to some the firmest certainty while causing creative unrest in the minds of others. Plato's ascendancy over the philosophers of ancient Greco-

Roman civilization was immense. It remained great in the Middle Ages, increased in the Renaissance as well as in the eras of Descartes, Berkeley and Hegel, and still today there are outstanding thinkers in America and Europe who adhere to his doctrine. The discussion about its real meaning has not come to an end, and entails re-examinations of the principal methods of modern science and philosophy.

The man whose influence was so deep and lasting is known to posterity by his nickname which means "the Broad." His real name was Aristocles. Belonging to one of the oldest and noblest families of Athens' aristocracy whose members used to take part in governing the state, Plato also felt a leaning toward statesmanship. However, his attempts to play a political role resulted in frustration and disappointment. To these painful experiences Plato reacted by founding and directing his "Academy" which was a University and a center of research as well as a training school for future political leaders. For Plato was convinced that any state must perish if its rulers were not philosophers, and philosophy meant to him the ability to perceive the world of Ideas, immaterial essences, Forms which contain the true and ultimate realities while the world of sensible things is only a vague, transitory and untrustworthy copy. Only the cognition of the Ideas enables man to act with wisdom. The rules of rightful conduct of human life were derived by Plato from the laws that rule the universe. Plato's criteria of human behavior were rooted in his metaphysical conceptions.

Although Plato constantly emphasized his conviction that true knowledge can be obtained only by cognition of the eternal and immutable Ideas or Forms, he by no means neglected the phenomena of change or the imperfect phases of knowledge which are given by sensations or expressed by mere opinions. He was a keen observer of daily life, acquainted with arts and crafts, versed in empirical sciences and literature. He was a tough warrior and sportsman. He even proved to be a clever traveling salesman who dealt in oil when he visited Egypt, and he succeeded well although he found the Egyptians to be extremely shrewd businessmen.

Every work published by Plato is written in the form of a dialogue. Most of them are full of dramatic life. Some are gay comedies. Speech has been given to both historical and fictitious persons but hardly ever to the author himself who attributed most of his own thoughts to his teacher Socrates. The discussions allow representation of various, even opposed, points of view. Their principal means of explanation is the dialectic whose function is to illustrate the logical consequences of a hypothesis. In order to explain ideas difficult to understand, or to elucidate a hypothesis impossible to be proved true, Plato often resorts to the use of a myth which elucidates a thought or truth by means of images.

Plato's doctrine contains the elements of a religion, of positive sciences, of a political system and of legislation. He recognized the complexity of the problems with which he dealt and was aware of the precariousness of the results of his thinking. Until his death he continued to develop his ideas.

GOVERNMENT BY PHILOSOPHERS

WE were inquiring into the nature of absolute justice and into the character of the perfectly just, and into injustice and the perfectly unjust, that we might have an ideal. We were to look at these in order that we might judge of our own happiness and unhappiness according to the standard which they exhibited and the degree in which we resembled them, but not with any view of showing that they could exist in fact.

True, he said.

Would a painter be any the worse because, after having delineated with consummate art an ideal of a perfectly beautiful man, he was unable to show that any such man could ever have existed?

He would be none the worse.

Well, and were we not creating an ideal of a perfect state?

To be sure.

And is our theory a worse theory because we are unable to prove the possibility of a city being ordered in the manner described?

Surely not, he replied.

That is the truth, I said. But if, at your request, I am to try and show how and under what conditions the possibility is highest, I must ask you, having this in view, to repeat your former admissions.

What admissions?

I want to know whether ideals are ever fully realized in

language? Does not the word express more than the fact, and must not the actual, whatever a man may think, always, in the nature of things, fall short of the truth? What do you say?

I agree.

Then you must not insist on my proving the actual state will in every respect coincide with the ideal: if we are only able to discover how a city may be governed nearly as we proposed, you will admit that we have discovered the possibility which you demand; and will be contented. I am sure that I should be contented—will not you?

Yes, I will.

Let me next endeavor to show what is that fault in states which is the cause of their present maladministration, and what is the least change which will enable a state to pass into the truer form; and let the change, if possible, be of one thing only, or, if not, of two; at any rate, let the changes be as few and slight as possible.

Certainly, he replied.

I think, I said, that there might be a reform of the state if only one change were made, which is not a slight or easy though still a possible one.

What is it? he said.

Now then, I said, I go to meet that which I liken to the greatest of the waves; yet shall the word be spoken, even though the wave break and drown me in laughter and dishonor; and do you mark my words.

Proceed.

I said: *Until philosophers are kings, or the kings and princes of this world have the spirit and power of philosophy, and political greatness and wisdom meet in one, and those commoner natures who pursue either to the exclusion of the other are compelled to stand aside, cities will never have rest from their evils,—no, nor the human race, as I believe, —and then only will this our state have a possibility of life and behold the light of day.* Such was the thought, my dear Glaucon, which I would fain have uttered if it had not seemed too extravagant; for to be convinced that in no other state can there be happiness private or public is indeed a hard thing.

*   *   *

And thus, Glaucon, after the argument has gone a weary way, the true and the false philosophers have at length appeared in view.

I do not think, he said, that the way could have been shortened.

I suppose not, I said; and yet I believe that we might have had a better view of both of them if the discussion could have been confined to this one subject and if there were not many other questions awaiting us, which he who desires to see in what respect the life of the just differs from that of the unjust must consider.

And what is the next question? he asked.

Surely, I said, the one which follows next in order. Inasmuch as philosophers only are able to grasp the eternal and unchangeable, and those who wander in the region of the many and variable are not philosophers, I must ask you which of the two classes should be the rulers of our state?

And how can we rightly answer that question?

Whichever of the two are best able to guard the laws and institutions of our state—let them be our guardians.

Very good.

Neither, I said, can there be any question that the guardian who is to keep anything should have eyes rather than no eyes?

There can be no question of that.

And are not those who are verily and indeed wanting in the knowledge of the true being of each thing, and who have in their souls no clear pattern, and are unable as with a painter's eye to look at the absolute truth and to that original to repair, and having perfect vision of the other world to order the laws about beauty, goodness, justice in this, if not already ordered, and to guard and preserve the order of them—are not such persons, I ask, simply blind?

Truly, he replied, they are much in that condition.

And shall they be our guardians when there are others who, besides being their equals in experience and falling short of them in no particular of virtue, also know the very truth of each thing?

There can be no reason, he said, for rejecting those who have this greatest of all great qualities; they must always have the first place unless they fail in some other respect.

Suppose then, I said, that we determine how far they can unite this and the other excellences.

By all means.

In the first place, as we began by observing, the nature of the philosopher has to be ascertained. We must come to an understanding about him, and, when we have done so, then, if I am not mistaken, we shall also acknowledge that such a union of qualities is possible and that those in whom they are united, and those only, should be rulers in the state.

What do you mean?

Let us suppose that philosophical minds always love knowledge of a sort which shows them the eternal nature not varying from generation and corruption.

Agreed.

And further, I said, let us agree that they are lovers of all true being; there is no part whether greater or less, or more or less honorable, which they are willing to renounce; as we said before of the lover and the man of ambition.

True.

And if they are to be what we were describing, is there not another quality which they should also possess?

What quality?

Truthfulness: they will never intentionally receive into their mind falsehood, which is their detestation, and they will love the truth.

Yes, that may be safely affirmed of them.

"May be," my friend, I replied, is not the word; say rather, "must be affirmed": for he whose nature is amorous of anything cannot help loving all that belongs or is akin to the object of his affections.

Right, he said.

And is there anything more akin to wisdom than truth?

How can there be?

Can the same nature be a lover of wisdom and a lover of falsehood?

Never.

The true lover of learning then must from his earliest youth, as far as in him lies, desire all truth?

Assuredly.

But then again, as we know by experience, he whose desires are strong in one direction will have them weaker in others; they will be like a stream which has been drawn off into another channel.

True.

He whose desires are drawn towards knowledge in every form will be absorbed in the pleasures of the soul, and will hardly feel bodily pleasure—I mean, if he be a true philosopher and not a sham one.

That is most certain.

Such a one is sure to be temperate and the reverse of covetous; for the motives which make another man desirous of having and spending, have no place in his character.

Very true.

Another criterion of the philosophical nature has also to be considered.

What is that?

There should be no secret corner of illiberality; nothing can be more antagonistic than meanness to a soul which is ever longing after the whole of things both divine and human.

Most true, he replied.

Then how can he who has magnificence of mind and is the spectator of all time and all existence, think much of human life?

He cannot.

Or can such a one account death fearful?

No indeed.

Then the cowardly and mean nature has no part in true philosophy?

Certainly not.

Or again: can he who is harmoniously constituted, who is not covetous or mean, or a boaster, or a coward—can he, I say, ever be unjust or hard in his dealings?

Impossible.

Then you will soon observe whether a man is just and gentle, or rude and unsociable; these are the signs which distinguish even in youth the philosophical nature from the unphilosophical.

True.

There is another point which should be remarked.

What point?

Whether he has or has not a pleasure in learning; for no one will love that which gives him pain, and in which after much toil he makes little progress.

Certainly not.

And again, if he is forgetful and retains nothing of what he learns, will he not be an empty vessel?

That is certain.

Laboring in vain, he must end in hating himself and his fruitless occupation?

Yes.

Then a soul which forgets cannot be ranked among genuine philosophic natures; we must insist that the philosopher should have a good memory?

Certainly.

And one more, the inharmonious and unseemly nature can only tend to disproportion?

Undoubtedly.

And do you consider truth to be akin to proportion or to disproportion?

To proportion.

Then, besides other qualities, we must try to find a

naturally well-proportioned and gracious mind, which will move spontaneously towards the true being of everything.

Certainly.

Well, and do not all these qualities, which we have been enumerating, go together, and are they not, in a manner, necessary to a soul, which is to have a full and perfect participation of being?

They are absolutely necessary, he replied.

And must not that be a blameless study which he only can pursue who has the gift of a good memory, and is quick to learn,—noble, gracious, the friend of truth, justice, courage, temperance, who are his kindred?

The god of jealousy himself, he said, could find no fault with such a study.

And to men like him, I said, when perfected by years and education, and to these only you will intrust the state.

Here Adeimantus interposed and said: To these statements, Socrates, no one can offer a reply; but when you talk in this way, a strange feeling passes over the minds of your hearers: They fancy that they are led astray a little at each step in the argument, owing to their own want of skill in asking and answering questions; these littles accumulate, and at the end of the discussion they are found to have sustained a mighty overthrow and all their former notions appear to be turned upside down. And as unskilful players of draughts are at last shut up by their more skilful adversaries and have no piece to move, so they too find themselves shut up at last; for they have nothing to say in this new game of which words are the counters; and yet all the time they are in the right. The observation is suggested to me by what is now occurring. For any one of us might say, that although in words he is not able to meet you at at each step of the argument, he sees as a fact that the votaries of philosophy, when they carry on the study, not only in youth as a part of education, but as the pursuit of their maturer years, most of them become strange monsters, not to say utter rogues, and that those who may be considered the best of them are made useless to the world by the very study which you extol.

Well, and do you think that those who say so are wrong?

I cannot tell, he replied; but I should like to know what is your opinion.

Hear my answer; I am of opinion that they are quite right.

Then how can you be justified in saying that cities will not cease from evil until philosophers rule in them, when philosophers are acknowledged by us to be of no use to them?

You ask a question, I said, to which a reply can only be given in a parable.

Yes, Socrates; and that is a way of speaking to which you are not at all accustomed, I suppose.

I perceive, I said, that you are vastly amused at having plunged me into such a hopeless discussion; but now hear the parable, and then you will be still more amused at the meagerness of my imagination: for the manner in which the best men are treated in their own states is so grievous that no single thing on earth is comparable to it; and therefore, if I am to plead their cause, I must have recourse to fiction, and put together a figure made up of many things, like the fabulous unions of goats and stags which are found in pictures. Imagine then a fleet or a ship in which there is a captain who is taller and stronger than any of the crew, but he is a little deaf and has a similar infirmity in sight, and his knowledge of navigation is not much better. The sailors are quarreling with one another about the steering—every one is of opinion that he has a right to steer, though he has never learned the art of navigation and cannot tell who taught him or when he learned, and will further assert that it cannot be taught, and they are ready to cut in pieces any one who says the contrary. They throng about the captain, begging and praying him to commit the helm to them; and if at any time they do not prevail, but others are preferred to them, they kill the others or throw them overboard, and having first chained up the noble captain's senses with drink or some narcotic drug, they mutiny and take possession of the ship and make free with the stores; thus, eating and drinking, they proceed on their voyage in such manner as might be expected of them. Him who is their partisan and cleverly aids them in their plot for getting the ship out of the captain's hands into their own whether by force or persuasion, they compliment with the name of sailor, pilot, able seaman, and abuse the other sort of man, whom they call a good-for-nothing; but that the true pilot must pay attention to the year and seasons and sky and stars and winds, and whatever else belongs to his art, if he intends to be really qualified for the command of a ship, and that he must and will be the steerer, whether other people like or not—the possibility of this union of authority with the steerer's art has never seriously entered into their thoughts or been made part of their calling. Now in vessels which are in a state of mutiny and by sailors who are mutineers, how will the true pilot be regarded? Will he not be called by them a prater, a star-gazer, a good-for-nothing?

Of course, said Adeimantus.

Then you will hardly need, I said, to hear the interpretation of the figure, which describes the true philosopher in his relation to the state; for you understand already.

Certainly.

Then suppose you now take this parable to the gentleman who is surprised at finding that philosophers have no honor in their cities; explain it to him and try to convince him that their having honor would be far more extraordinary.

I will.

Say to him, that, in deeming the best votaries of philosophy to be useless to the rest of the world, he is right; but also tell him to attribute their uselessness to the fault of those who will not use them, and not to themselves. The pilot should not humbly beg the sailors to be commanded by him—that is not the order of nature; neither are "the wise to go to the doors of the rich"—the ingenious author of this

942

saying told a lie—but the truth is, that, when a man is ill, whether he be rich or poor, to the physician he must go, and he who wants to be governed, to him who is able to govern. The ruler who is good for anything ought not to beg his subjects to be ruled by him; although the present governors of mankind are of a different stamp; they may be justly compared to the mutinous sailors, and the true helmsmen to those who are called by them good-for-nothings and stargazers.

Precisely so, he said.

For these reasons, and among men like these, philosophy, the noblest pursuit of all, is not likely to be much esteemed by those of the opposite faction; not that the greatest and most lasting injury is done to her by her opponents, but by her own professing followers, the same of whom you suppose the accuser to say, that the greater number of them are arrant rogues, and the best are useless; in which opinion I agreed.

Yes.

And the reason why the good are useless has now been explained?

True.

Then shall we proceed to show that the corruption of the majority is also unavoidable, and that this is not to be laid to the charge of philosophy any more than the other?

By all means.

And let us ask and answer in turn, first going back to the description of the gentle and noble nature. Truth, as you will remember, was his leader, whom he followed always and in all things; failing in this, he was an imposter, and had no part or lot in true philosophy.

Yes, that was said.

Well, and is not this one quality, to mention no others, greatly at variance with present notions of him?

Certainly, he said.

And have we not a right to say in his defense, that the true lover of knowledge is always striving after being—that is his nature; he will not rest in the multiplicity of individuals which is an appearance only, but will go on—the keen edge will not be blunted, nor the force of his desire abate until we have attained the knowledge of the true nature of every essence by a sympathetic and kindred power in the soul, and by that power drawing near and mingling and becoming incorporate with very being, having begotten mind and truth, he will have knowledge and will live and grow truly, and then, and not till then, will he cease from his travail.

Nothing, he said, can be more just than such a description of him.

And will the love of a lie be any part of a philosopher's nature? Will he not utterly hate a lie?

He will.

And when truth is the captain, we cannot suspect any evil of the band which he leads?

Impossible.

Justice and health of mind will be of the company, and temperance will follow after?

True, he replied.

*　　*　　*

I omitted the troublesome business of the possession of women, and the procreation of children, and the appointment of the rulers, because I knew that the perfect state would be eyed with jealousy and was difficult of attainment; but that piece of cleverness was not of much service to me, for I had to discuss them all the same. The women and children are now disposed of, but the other question of the rulers must be investigated from the very beginning. We were saying, as you will remember, that they were to be lovers of their country, tried by the test of pleasures and pains, and neither in hardships, nor in dangers, nor at any other critical moment were to lose their patriotism—he was to be rejected who failed, but he who always come forth pure, like gold tried in the refiner's fire, was to be made a ruler, and to receive honors and rewards in life and after death. This was the sort of thing which was being said, and then the argument turned aside and veiled her face; not liking to stir the question which has now arisen.

I perfectly remember, he said.

Yes, my friend, I said, and I then shrank from hazarding the bold word; but now let me dare to say—that the perfect guardian must be a philosopher.

Yes, he said, let that be affirmed.

And do not suppose that there will be many of them; for the gifts which were deemed by us to be essential rarely grow together; they are mostly found in shreds and patches.

What do you mean? he said.

You are aware, I replied, that quick intelligence, memory, sagacity, cleverness, and similar qualities, do not often grow together, and that persons who possess them and are at the same time high-spirited and magnanimous are not so constituted by nature as to live orderly and in a peaceful and settled manner; they are driven any way by their impulses, and all solid principle goes out of them.

Very true, he said.

On the other hand, those steadfast natures which can better be depended upon, which in a battle are impregnable to fear and immovable, are equally immovable when there is anything to be learned; they are always in a torpid state, and are apt to yawn and go to sleep over any intellectual toil.

Quite true.

And yet we were saying that both qualities were necessary in those to whom the higher education is to be imparted, and who are to share in any office or command.

Certainly, he said.

And will they be a class which is rarely found?

Yes, indeed.

Then the aspirant must not only be tested in those labors and dangers and pleasures which we mentioned before, but there is another kind of probation which we did not mention—he must be exercised also in many kinds of knowledge, to see whether the soul will be able to endure the highest of all, or will faint under them as in any other studies and exercises.

* * *

Observe, Glaucon, that there will be no injustice in compelling our philosophers to have a care and providence of others; we shall explain to them that in other states, men of their class are not obliged to share in the toils of politics: and this is reasonable, for they grow up at their own sweet will, and the government would rather not have them. Being self-taught, they cannot be expected to show any gratitude for a culture which they have never received. But we have brought you into the world to be rulers of the hive, kings of yourselves and of the other citizens, and have educated you far better and more perfectly than they have been educated, and you are better able to share in the double duty. Wherefore each of you, when his turn comes, must go down to the general underground abode, and get the habit of seeing in the dark. When you have acquired the habit, you will see ten thousand times better than the inhabitants of the den, and you will know what the several images are, and what they represent, because you have seen the beautiful and just and good in their truth. And thus our state, which is also yours, will be a reality, and not a dream only, and will be administered in a spirit unlike that of other states, in which men fight with one another about shadows only and are distracted in the struggle for power, which in their eyes is a great good. Whereas the truth is that the state in which the rulers are most reluctant to govern is always the best and most quietly governed, and the state in which they are most eager, the worst.

Quite true, he replied.

And will our pupils, when they hear this, refuse to take their turn at the toils of state, when they are allowed to spend the greater part of their time with one another in the heavenly light?

Impossible, he answered; for they are just men, and the commands which we impose upon them are just; there can be no doubt that every one of them will take office as a stern necessity, and not after the fashion of our present rulers of state.

Yes, my friend, I said; and there lies the point. You must contrive for your future rulers another and a better life than that of a ruler, and then you may have a well-ordered state; for only in the state which offers this, will they rule who are truly rich, not in silver and gold, but in virtue and wisdom, which are the true blessings of life. Whereas if they go to the administration of public affairs, poor and hungering after their own private advantage, thinking that hence they are to snatch the chief good, order there can never be; for they will be fighting about office, and the civil and domestic broils which thus arise will be the ruin of the rulers themselves and of the whole state.

Most true, he replied.

And the only life which looks down upon the life of political ambition is that of true philosophy. Do you know of any other?

Indeed, I do not, he said.

And those who govern ought not to be lovers of the task? For, if they are, there will be rival lovers, and they will fight.

No question.

Who then are those whom we shall compel to be guardians? Surely they will be the men who are wisest about affairs of state, and by whom the state is administered, and who at the same time have other honors and another and better life than that of politics?

They are the men, and I will choose them, he replied.

* * *

And now let me remind you that, although in our former selection we chose old men, we must not do so in this. Solon was under a delusion when he said that a man when he grows old may learn many things—for he can no more learn much than he can run much; youth is the time for any extraordinary toil.

Of course.

And, therefore, calculation and geometry and all the other elements of instruction, which are a preparation for dialectic, should be presented to the mind in childhood; not, however, under any notion of forcing our system of education.

Why not?

Because a freeman ought not to be a slave in the acquisition of knowledge of any kind. Bodily exercise, when compulsory, does no harm to the body; but knowledge which is acquired under compulsion obtains no hold on the mind.

Very true.

Then, my good friend, I said, do not use compulsion, but let early education be a sort of amusement; you will then be better able to find out the natural bent.

That is a very rational notion, he said.

Do you remember that the children, too, were to be taken to see the battle on horseback; and that if there were no danger they were to be brought close up and, like young hounds, have a taste of blood given them?

Yes, I remember.

The same practice may be followed, I said, in all these things—labors, lessons, dangers—and he who is most at home in all of them ought to be enrolled in a select number.

At what age?

At the age when the necessary gymnastics are over: the period whether of two or three years which passes in this sort of training is useless for any purpose; for sleep and exercise are unpropitious to learning; and the trial of who is first in gymnastic exercises is one of the most important tests to which our youth are subjected.

Certainly, he replied.

After that time those who are selected from the class of twenty years old will be promoted to higher honor, and the sciences which they learned without any order in their early education will now be brought together, and they will be able to see the natural relationship of them to one another and to true being.

Yes, he said, that is the only kind of knowledge which takes lasting root.

Yes, I said; and the capacity for such knowledge is the great criterion of dialectical talent: the comprehensive mind is always the dialectical.

I agree with you, he said.

These, I said, are the points which you must consider; and those who have most of this comprehension, and who are most steadfast in their learning, and in their military and other appointed duties, when they have arrived at the age of thirty will have to be chosen by you out of the select class, and elevated to higher honor; and you will have to prove them by the help of dialectic, in order to learn which of them is able to give up the use of sight and the other senses, and in company with truth to attain absolute being.

*   *   *

Suppose, I said, the study of philosophy to take the place of gymnastics and to be continued diligently and earnestly and exclusively for twice the number of years which were passed in bodily exercise—will that be enough?

Would you say six or four years? he asked.

Say five years, I replied; at the end of the time they must be sent down again into the den and compelled to hold any military or other office which young men are qualified to hold: in this way they will get their experience of life, and there will be an opportunity of trying whether, when they are drawn all manner of ways of temptation, they will stand firm or flinch.

And how long is this stage of their lives to last?

Fifteen years, I answered; and when they have reached fifty years of age, then let those who still survive and have distinguished themselves in every action of their lives and in every branch of knowledge come at last to their consummation: the time has now arrived at which they must raise the eye of the soul to the universal light which lightens all things, and behold the absolute good; for that is the pattern according to which they are to order the state and the lives of individuals, and the remainder of their own lives also; making philosophy their chief pursuit, but, when their turn comes, toiling also at politics and ruling for the public good, not as though they were performing some heroic action, but simply as a matter of duty; and when they have brought up in each generation others like themselves and left them in their place to be governors of the state, then they will depart to the Islands of the Blest and dwell there; and the city will give them public memorials and sacrifices and honor them, if the Pythian oracle consent, as demigods, but if not, as in any case blessed and divine.

You are a sculptor, Socrates, and have made statues of our governors faultless in beauty.

Yes, I said, Glaucon, and of our governesses too; for you must not suppose that what I have been saying applies to men only and not to women as far as their natures go.

There you are right, he said, since we have made them to share in all things like the men.

Well, I said, and you would agree (would you not?) that what has been said about the state and the government is not a mere dream, and although difficult not impossible, but only possible in the way which has been supposed; that is to say, when the true philosopher kings are born in a state, one or more of them, despising the honors of this present world which they deem mean and worthless, esteeming above all things right and the honor that springs from right, and regarding justice as the greatest and most necessary of all things, whose ministers they are, and whose principles will be exalted by them when they set in order their own city?

How will they proceed?

They will begin by sending out into the country all the

inhabitants of the city who are more than ten years old, and will take possession of their children, who will be unaffected by the habits of their parents; these they will train in their own habits and laws, I mean in the laws which we have given them: and in this way the state and constitution of which we were speaking will soonest and most easily attain happiness, and the nation which has such a constitution will gain most.

Yes, that will be the best way. And I think, Socrates, that you have very well described how, if ever, such a constitution might come into being.

Enough then of the perfect state and of the man who bears its image—there is no difficulty in seeing how we shall describe him.

There is no difficulty, he replied; and I agree with you in thinking that nothing more need be said.

[289]

PLEKHANOV, GEORGE

PLEKHANOV, GEORGE (1857-1918). Although for many years, from 1904 until his death, Plekhanov strongly opposed Lenin and the Bolshevists, and was arrested by them after their victory in 1917, Lenin did not deny his spiritual indebtedness to his adversary and the rulers of Soviet Russia acknowledged the value of Plekhanov's works and permitted them to be re-edited by the Marx-Engels-Institute.

Plekhanov was the founder of the Russian Social-Democratic party which was subsequently divided into the Menshevik and Bolshevik parties.

He was the son of a noble, but not wealthy, landowner who treated his serfs ruthlessly. When, after his father's death, his mother tried to cheat her peasants, the son prevented her from doing so by threatening to set fire to the paternal home.

As a student, Plekhanov joined the Narodniki (Friends of the People) who advocated immediate socialization of Russia. But in 1880 he was converted to Marxism, and, on the ground of his interpretation of this doctrine, he opposed the Narodniki by arguing that Russian economic conditions had to ripen before socialism could be introduced into that country. Because of his revolutionary

951

activities, Plekhanov was exiled in 1882. In the following year he founded the "Union for Emancipation of Labor," the germ-cell of the Social-Democratic Party of Russia, whose program was elaborated by him. At the request of the German Social Democrats, he wrote *Anarchism and Socialism* (1894); in the following year he wrote against the Narodniki in *On the Question of the Development of the Monist View in History*; and in 1896 his *Essay on the History of Materialism* was published, which, like his *Fundamental Problems of Marxism* (1908), was generally acknowledged to be an authoritative interpretation of Marxism. Plekhanov fought the socialist revisionists in Germany and France but sided, in 1904, with the Russian Mensheviks against Lenin. When Plekhanov returned to Russia after the overthrow of Tsarism, he was hopelessly suffering from tuberculosis but struggled against Bolshevism to his last gasp.

BOURGEOIS AND SOCIALISTIC ART

UNDER socialism, the theory of art for art's sake will be logically impossible, in so far as social morality will lose its vulgarity, a vulgarity that is at present the inevitable consequence of the desire of the ruling class to retain its privileges.

Flaubert said: "Art is the quest for the useless," and in this sentence the principal theme of Pushkin's *The Mob* is observable. The fondness for this theme is simply an indication of the artist's protest against the narrow utilitarianism of a given ruling class or caste. With the disappearance of social classes, this narrow utilitarianism, so closely linked with selfishness, will also disappear. Selfishness has nothing to do with aesthetics. Artistic judgment invariably presupposes an absence of desire for personal gain on the part of him who exercises that judgment. Desire for collective gain, however, is quite another matter. The desire to be useful to society, which was the basis of ancient morality, inspired a spirit of self-sacrifice; and self-sacrifice, as the history of art so eloquently proves, inspires artistic creation. It is sufficient to note the songs of primitive peoples; or, less remotely, the monument to Harmodius and Aristogiton at Athens.

The thinkers of antiquity, including Plato and Aristotle, already realized how man is degraded by having to expend all his energy in the struggle for existence. Contemporary bourgeois philosophers also realize this, and feel the necessity of relieving man of the staggering burden of constant economic anxiety. But the man they have in mind is the man of the upper classes, who lives by exploiting the workers. Their solution of the problem is the same as that of the philosophers of antiquity: enslavement of the producers by a select few individuals, who approach more or less the ideal of the "superman." This solution, conservative in the time of Plato and Aristotle, in our time is ultra-reactionary. While the conservative slave-owners of ancient Greece believed that they could maintain their dominant position by relying upon their own "valor," contemporary advocates of the enslavement of the masses of the people are sceptical of the "valor" of bourgeois exploiters. For this reason they like to dream of the coming of a great genius, an omniscient superman who, if placed at the head of the state, by sheer force of his iron will would bolster up the now tottering structure of class rule. That is why decadents who are not averse to politics are often found to be ardent admirers of Napoleon.

Like Renan, who desired a powerful government, one that would compel the "good peasant" to work for him while he spent his time in meditation, our contemporary aesthetes want a social order that will compel the proletariat to labor while they indulge in loftier pursuits—such as the painting and tinting of little cubes and other stereometric figures. Organically incapable of any constructive effort, they become genuinely indignant at the thought of a society without idlers.

"He who lives with wolves usually learns to howl." While combatting philistinism verbally, our contemporary bourgeois aesthetes worship the golden calf as much as any bourgeois philistine. "They imagine there is a movement in the sphere of art," says Mauclair, "while in reality the movement is only in the picture market, where speculation goes on also in undiscovered genius." I might add in passing that one reason for this speculation in "undiscovered genius" is the feverish quest for "something new" which occupies so many artists today. When people look for "something new" it is because the old fails to satisfy them. The question is why it fails to satisfy them. A great many contemporary artists are dissatisfied with the old for the sole reason that so long as the public continues to hold it in esteem their own genius remains undiscovered. Their rebellion against the old is motivated not by love of new ideas, but rather by love for that "sole reality," their precious ego. Such a love does not inspire an artist except in so far as it tends to make him judge everything, even the Apollo Belvedere, by the standard of utility.

"The subject of money is so closely bound up with that of art," Mauclair continues, "that art criticism feels as if it were crushed in a vise. The best critics are unable to say what they think; the others say only that which is expedient in any given instance, since as they aver, they make their living by writing. I do not say that we should become indignant over this, but it would not be amiss to bear in mind the complexity of the problem." Thus we see that *art for art's sake has become art for money's sake*. Mauclair wished to determine the cause of this phenomenon; and this we can easily trace.

There was a time, as in the Middle Ages, when only the superfluity, the excess of production over consumption, was exchanged.

There was again a time, when not only the superfluity, but all products, all industrial existence, had passed into commerce, when the whole of production depended on exchange. . . .

Finally, there came a time when everything that men had considered as inalienable became an object of exchange, of traffic and could be alienated. This is the time when the very things which till then had been communicated, but never exchanged; given, but never sold;

acquired, but never bought—virtue, love, conviction, knowledge, conscience, etc.—when everything in short, passed into commerce. It is the time of general corruption, of universal venality, or, to speak in terms of political economy, the time when everything, moral or physical, having become a marketable value, is brought to the market to be assessed at its truest value.

Is it any wonder that in this period of universal venality, art, too, has become a commodity?

Mauclair says that we should not become indignant about this phenomena, and neither do I wish to judge it from the standpoint of morality. As the saying goes, I wish neither to cry nor to laugh, but simply to understand. I do not say that contemporary artists *must* seek inspiration in the emancipatory movement of the proletariat. Not at all. Just as apple-trees must give forth apples and pear-trees pears, so must artists who share the bourgeois point of view struggle against this movement. The art of a decadent epoch *must* be decadent. This is inevitable and it would be futile to become indignant about it. *The Communist Manifesto* correctly states:

In times when the class struggle nears the decisive hour, the process of dissolution going on within the ruling class, in fact within the whole range of old society, assumes such a violent, glaring character, that a small section of the ruling class cuts itself adrift, and joins the revolutionary class, the class that holds the future in its hands. Just as, therefore, at an earlier period, a section of the nobility went over to the bourgeoisie, so now a portion of the bourgeoisie goes over to the proletariat, and in particular, a portion of the bourgeois ideologists, who have raised themselves to the level of comprehending theoretically the historical movement as a whole.

Among bourgeois ideologists going over to the side of the proletariat, we find very few artists. This is probably due to the fact that to comprehend theoretically the historical process as a whole it is necessary to think; and contemporary artists, unlike the great masters of the Renaissance, for instance, think very little. *At any rate, there is no doubt that any artist of proven talent will increase considerably the forcefulness of his work by steeping himself in the great emancipatory ideas of our time. For this, it is necessary that these ideas permeate his spirit and that he express them through his artist's temperament.* He must also know how to assess correctly the "modernist" art of contemporary bourgeois ideologists. The ruling class is now in such a position that to go forward can only mean to go downward, and this sad fate is shared by all their ideologists as well. The foremost among them are those who have sunk lower than all their predecessors.

[290]

PLINY THE YOUNGER

PLINY THE YOUNGER (62-113). Among the most famous reports ever written are two letters of Pliny the Younger, who, at the age of seventeen, eye-witnessed the eruption of Mount Vesuvius in 79 A.D. and described the destruction of the city of Herculaneum to Tacitus, the historian. He was the nephew and adopted son of Pliny the Elder, admiral of the Roman fleet and noted naturalist, who was a victim of that disaster.

Pliny the Younger had a brilliant career under Emperor Trajan. He was appointed consul and later governor of Bithynia. In his reports to the Emperor, Pliny also mentioned the Christians whose customs he had to investigate. He described their conduct of life as impeccable, but censured their disobedience to the Roman authorities in matters of religion. His letters, most of which are real essays, give valuable information about the political, social and literary life in the Roman Empire during his lifetime. Pliny studied philosophy with Musonius Rufus, who was also the teacher of Epictetus. But Pliny's ideal was Cicero, the orator, the philosopher and letter-writer, and his ambition was to imitate his model. He followed Cicero's example too by branding corruption, and accusing officials who abused their power.

ON GOVERNMENT

CONSIDER that you are sent to that noble province to regulate the condition of free cities; sent, that is, to a society of men who breathe the spirit of true manhood and liberty; who have maintained the rights they received from Nature, by courage, by virtue, by alliances; in a word, by civil and religious faith.

Revere the gods their founders; their ancient glory, and even that very antiquity itself, venerable in men, is sacred in states.

Honor them therefore for their deeds of old renown, nay, their very legendary traditions.

Grant to every one his full dignity, privileges, yes, and the indulgence of his very vanity.

Remember it was from this nation we derived our laws; that she did not receive ours by conquest, but gave us hers by favor.

Reflect what these cities once were; but so reflect as not to despise them for what they are now.

Far be pride and asperity from you my friend; nor fear, by a proper condescension, to lay yourself open to contempt.

Can he who is vested with the power and bears the ensigns of authority, can he fail of meeting with respect, unless by pursuing base and sordid measures, and first breaking through that reverence he owes to himself?

*　　　*　　　*

Ill, believe me, is power proved by insult; ill can terror command veneration, and far more effectual is affection in obtaining one's purpose than fear. For terror operates no longer than its object is present, but love produces its effects with its object at a distance: and as absence changes the former into hatred, it raises the latter into respect.

Therefore you ought (and I cannot but repeat it too often) you ought to well consider the nature of your office, and to represent to yourself how great and important the task is of governing a free state. For what can be better for society than such government, what can be more precious than freedom? How ignominious then must his conduct be who turns good government into anarchy, and liberty into slavery?

To these considerations let me add, that you have an established reputation to maintain; the fame you have acquired by good administration elsewhere, the good opinion of the Emperor, the credit you obtained in other offices, in a word, this very government, which may be looked upon as the reward of your former services, are all so many glorious weights which are incumbent upon you to support with suitable dignity.

The more strenuously therefore you ought to endeavor that it may not be said you showed greater urbanity, integrity and ability in a province remote from the capital, than in one which lies so much nearer the capital; in the midst of a nation of slaves, than among a free people; that it may not be remarked, that it was chance, and not judgment, appointed you to this office; that your character was unknown and inexperienced, not tried and approved.

*   *   *

It should be an invariable rule to refer to the Emperor in all matters where there is doubt, for the highest authority is alone capable of removing scruples or informing one's ignorance.

If you are unacquainted with the nature of a particular crime or the measure of punishment, it is not wholly proper for you to enter into an examination concerning these things.

Force of character, or whatever else you may call a fixed determination in obtaining what one has a mind for, rightly applied, can effect infinite good. The misfortune is that there is less of this quality about good people than about bad people, and as ignorance begets rashness, and thoughtfulness produces deliberation, so modesty is apt to cripple the action of virtue, while confidence will become the aid of vice.

For (and it is a maxim which your reading and conversation must have often suggested to you) it is a far greater disgrace losing the name one has once acquired than never to have attained it.

I again beg you to be persuaded that I did not write this with a design of instruction, but of reminder.

Indeed, however, if I had, it would have only been in consequence of the great affection I bear you. It is a sentiment I am in no fear of carrying beyond its just bounds, for there can be no danger of excess where one cannot love too well.

[291]

PLOTINUS

PLOTINUS (205-270). Despite careful inquiries and heated controversies, no satisfying answer has been given to the question as to whether or not Plotinus possessed a real knowledge of the religion and philosophy of India to which his own teachings bear surprising analogies. It is, however, certain that Plotinus was eager to study the wisdom of India. For that purpose he participated in Emperor Gordianus' campaign against Perisia.

At any rate, Plotinus seems to be nearer to the spirit of India than any other thinker of the Mediterranean civilization. His doctrine that the reality perceived by the senses is a dispersion and degradation of the true Reality, conceived by Plotinus as the Trinity of the One, the *Nous* (Spirit) and the Soul, seems as much of Hindu origin as his advice that asceticism and ecstasy lead to wisdom. But, on the other hand, Saint Augustine was not entirely wrong in saying that Plotinus, in order to become a Christian, would have to change "only a few words." In fact, Christian theology and philosophy of the Middle Ages adopted many of Plotinus' thoughts. So did European mysticism and romanticism up to the present day.

Plotinus, notwithstanding the resemblance to, or affinity with, India and Christianity, persisted in honoring the gods of pagan Greece. Born in Egypt, he was the disciple of Ammonius Saccas who

959

had been converted from Christianity to paganism, and, in all probability, also studied the works of the Jewish philosopher Philo. From 245 until his death, Plotinus taught philosophy in Rome. He was consulted more than once by Emperor Gallienus. His disciples followed him with a religious devotion. Plotinus is also highly esteemed as a keen psychologist and a refined aesthete.

THE ONE

ALL things that exist do so by virtue of "unity"—in so far as they exist in any ultimate sense and in so far as they may be said to be real. For what would anything be if it were not "one"? Without the unity of which we speak things do not exist. There can be no army which is not a unit, nor a chorus, nor herd, unless each is "one." Neither is there a household or ship without unity; for the house is a unit and the ship is a unit, and if one took away the unity the household would no longer be a household nor the ship a ship. Continuous magnitudes would not exist if there were no unity to them. When divided, in so far as they lose unity they lose existence. So also with the bodies of plants and animals, each of which is a unit, if unity is lost—being broken up into multiplicity—they lose the being which they had, and no longer continue as they were. And they become other things even then only in so far as these have unity. Similarly there is health when the body is harmonized into unity, and beauty when the essence of unity controls the parts, and virtue in the soul when it is unified and brought into a single harmonious whole.

There must be something prior to all, simple, and different from the things which are posterior to it, self-existent, unmingled with the things which come from it, and yet able in another way to be present with the others, being really one, not something else first then secondarily one, of which it is false even that it is one; but of this One no description nor scientific knowledge is possible. Indeed it must be said to be beyond "being"; for if it were not simple, without any composition and synthesis, and really one, it would not be a first principle. And it is wholly self-sufficient by virtue of its being simple and prior to all things. What is not first needs that which is prior to itself, and that which is not simple demands those simple elements which are within it, that it may be composed of them. Such a One must be unique, for if there were another such both together would constitute a larger unit. For we hold that they are not two bodies nor is the Primary One a body. For no body is simple, and a body is subject to generation; it is not an ultimate principle. The ultimate principle is unoriginated, and being incorporeal and really one it is able to stand first.

Since substances which have an origin are of some form (for no one could say anything else of what is generated from the One), and since it is not any particular form but all, without exception, the first principle must be formless. And being formless it is not substance; for substance must be particular; and a particular is determinate. But this can not be regarded as particular, for it would not be a principle, but merely that particular thing which you may have called it. If then all things are included among what are generated, which of them will you say is the first principle? Only what is none of them could be said to stand above the rest. But these constitute existing things and Being in general. The First Principle then is beyond Being. To say that it is beyond Being does not assert it to be any definite thing. It does not define it. Nor does it give it a name. It applies to it only the appellation "not-this." In doing so it nowhere sets limits to it. It would be absurd to seek to delimit such a boundless nature. He who wishes to do this prevents himself from getting upon its track in any wise, even little by little. But just as he who wishes to see the Intelligible must abandon all imagery of the perceptible in order to contemplate what is beyond the perceptible, so he who wishes to contemplate what is beyond the Intelligible will attain the contemplation of it by letting go everything intelligible, through this means learning *that* it is, abandoning the search for *what* it is. To tell what it is would involve a reference to what it is not, for there is no quality in what has no particular character. But we are in painful doubt as to what we should say of it; so we speak of the ineffable and give it a name, meaning to endow it with some significance to ourselves so far as we can. Perhaps this name "The One" implies merely opposition to plurality. . . . But if The One were given positive content, a name and signification, it would be less appropriately designated than when one does not give any name. It may be said that description of it is carried thus far in order that he who seeks it beginning with that which indicates the simplicity of all things may end by negating even this, on the ground that it was taken simply as the most adequate and the nearest description possible for him who used it, but not even this is adequate to the revelation of that nature, because it is inaudible, not to be understood through hearing, and if by any sense at all by vision alone. But if the eye that sees seeks to behold a form it will not descry even this.

[292]

PLUTARCH OF CHAERONEA

PLUTARCH OF CHAERONEA (50-120). In the ancient world, Plutarch was considered "the true philanthropist"; in America, Emerson called him the embodiment of the highest ideal of humanity. As a biographer of heroes, as a moralist, as an unorthodox Platonist, Plutarch has been the world's most popular author for many centuries.

His spiritual life was centered in Athens and Delphi, in the Academy, founded by Plato, and in the temple whose priest he was. Plutarch was a pious man, an advocate of general peace and reconciliation. He was a cautious adviser of his troubled fellow men, and an experienced observer of human characters and customs. Notwithstanding his devotion to the old gods, the Fathers of the Church sympathized with him. Among the reformers of the sixteenth century Zwingli and Melanchthon loved him, while Calvin remained cool, and Luther ignored him. Montaigne was called

Plutarch's best disciple, and Shakespeare could have been called so. It was only in the nineteenth century, when the historical importance of collective factors was stressed, that Plutarch's influence weakened. But as long as people are interested in individual life, he will be read and re-read, and those who think that history must be conceived as the development of group life, will find in Plutarch's writings highly important information. For he was also one of the greatest folklorists. He wrote on almost everything that could interest, educate or edify his contemporaries, and, in doing so, he amassed a treasury of knowledge, from which modern psychologists, sociologists, educators and students of comparative science of religion may profit as much as historians and philosophers.

WISDOM AND PRUDENCE

THERE are those who thought that all human actions depended upon mere casualty, and were not guided by wisdom. If this be so, justice and equity have no place at all in the world, and temperance and modesty can do nothing in the direction and managing of our affairs.

We may grant that many occurrences came by fortune, but it is true that the world has in it temperance, justice and fortitude. What reason is there to say that there is no prudence and wisdom therein? Now if it be yielded that the world is not void of prudence, how can it be maintained that there should not be in it sage counsel? For temperance is a kind of prudence, and most certain it is that justice should be assisted by prudence, or to say more truly, ought to have it present with her continually.

*   *   *

Certainly, sage counsel and wisdom in the good use of pleasures and delights, whereby we continue honest, we ordinarily do call continence and temperance; the same in dangers and travails, we term tolerance, patience and fortitude; in contracts and management of state affairs, we give the name of loyalty, equity and justice; whereby it comes to pass, that if we will attribute the effects of counsel and wisdom unto fortune, we must likewise ascribe unto her the works of justice and temperance.

Take away sage and discreet counsel; farewell then all consultation as touching affairs, away with deliberation, consideration and inquisition into that which is useful and expedient, for surely then Sophocles talked idly when he said:

> "Seek, and be sure to find with diligence,
> But lose what you forfeit by negligence."

Now would I gladly know, what is it that men may find and what can they learn, in case all things in the world be directed by fortune? What senate house would not be dissolved and abolished? What council chamber would not be overthrown and put down, if all were at the disposition of fortune? We do her wrong in reproaching her for blindness, when we run upon her as we do, blind, and debasing ourselves unto her; for how can we choose but stumble upon her indeed, if we pluck out our own eyes, to wit, our wisdom and dexterity of counsel, and take a blind guide to lead us by the hand in the course of this our life?

Nature has bestowed upon us sight, hearing, taste and smell, with all of the parts of the body endowed with the rest of their faculties and powers, as ministers of counsel and wisdom. For it is the soul that sees, it is the soul and understanding that hears, all the rest are deaf and blind: and like as if there were no sun at all we should live in perpetual blindness. Even so, if man had not reason and intelligence, notwithstanding all his other senses, he should not differ in the whole race of his life from brute and wild beasts; but now in that we excel and rule them all, it is not by chance and fortune, but the use and discourse of reason is the very cause that has given us this in recompense. By experience, memory, wisdom and artifice we go beyond all animals, and thereby we have the mastery and use of them. We take from them whatsoever they have.

* * *

Artificers use altogether in every piece of work their squares, their rules, their lines and levels; they go by measures and numbers, to the end that in all their works there should not be anything found done rashly or at adventure. These arts are petty kinds of prudence, sprinkled and dispersed among the necessities of this life. It is a wonderful thing how these arts and sciences should have no dealing with fortune nor need her help, to attain their proper ends.

Shall we say then that the greatest and most principal things that are, even those that be most material and necessary for man's felicity, use not wisdom, nor participate one whit with providence and the judgment of reason? There is no man so void of understanding, that after he has tempered clay and water together, lets it alone and goes his way, when he has done, expecting that by fortune there will be bricks and tiles made; nor is anyone such a fool as when he has bought wool and leather, sits him down and prays fortune that he may have garments and shoes; or, being possessed of divers fair and stately houses, with their rich and costly furniture, will he deem that these can make him live happily, without pain, without grief, secure of change and alteration, if he does not possess wisdom.

[293]

POINCARÉ, HENRI

POINCARÉ, HENRI (1854-1912). The name of Poincaré is mostly associated with the person of Raymond Poincaré who was President of the Third French Republic during the First World War. Henri was his first cousin, and outside France he was known in the scientific world only. Eight foreign Universities conferred honorary doctors' degrees upon him; twenty-one foreign academies made him their honorary member, not to mention the honors he enjoyed in his native country. Poincaré himself, however, was more satisfied with the great influence he exercised on succeeding generations through his writings and lectures.

Poincaré made great strides in the history of mathematics, especially by his disquisitions on differential equations and analytical functions. The development of mechanics and astronomy owes to him admirable results concerning the capillarity, the equilibrium of fluid masses and rotating liquids, and, above all, the form of the planets. He made also very important contributions to geography and geodesy. In the field of physics, Poincaré dealt with the problems of vibration and elasticity, electricity and radioactivity, electrodynamics and gravitation, and published his views on relativity some months before Albert Einstein made known his famous theory.

Poincaré's philosophical inquiries concerned especially the process of hypothesis making, the relations between the logical and empirical elements of knowledge. From the statement that for any consistent and verifiable hypothesis there is a host of other likewise consistent and verifiable hypotheses, he proceeded to the conclusion that the choice between them is not dictated by logic or observation but by what he called convention. According to Poincaré, the value of science lies not so much in its usefulness as in its intrinsic worth, in the elevation of the soul which the true scientist feels while working. Poincaré was a fighter for human ideals. He courageously and successfully participated in the struggle for Dreyfus by destroying the arguments of the experts who were hired by the French general staff.

THE CHOICE OF FACTS IN SCIENCE

TOLSTOY somewhere explains why 'science for its own sake' is in his eyes an absurd conception. We can not know *all* facts, since their number is practically infinite. It is necessary to choose; then we may let this choice depend on the pure caprice of our curiosity; would it not be better to let ourselves be guided by utility, by our practical and above all by our moral needs; have we nothing better to do than to count the number of ladybugs on our planet?

It is clear the word utility has not for him the sense men of affairs give it, and following them most of our contemporaries. Little cares he for industrial applications, for the marvels of electricity or of automobilism, which he regards rather as obstacles to moral progress; utility for him is solely what can make man better.

For my part, it need scarce be said, I could never be content with either the one or the other ideal; I want neither that plutocracy grasping and mean, nor that democracy goody and mediocre, occupied solely in turning the other cheek, where would dwell sages without curiosity, who, shunning excess, would not die of disease, but would surely die of ennui. But that is a matter of taste and is not what I wish to discuss.

The question nevertheless remains and should fix our attention; if our choice can only be determined by caprice or by immediate utility, there can be no science for its own sake, and consequently no science. But is that true? That a choice must be made is incontestable; whatever be our activity, facts go quicker than we, and we can not catch them; while the scientists discover one fact, there happen milliards of milliards in a cubic millimeter of his body. To wish to comprise nature in science would be to want to put the whole into the part.

But scientists believe there is a hierarchy of facts and that among them may be made a judicious choice. They are right, since otherwise there would be no science, yet science exists. *One need only open the eyes to see that the conquests of industry which have enriched so many practical men would never have seen the light, if these practical men alone had existed and if they had not been preceded by unselfish devotees who died poor, who never thought of utility, and yet had a guide far other than caprice.*

As Mach says, *these devotees have spared their successors the trouble of thinking.* Those who might have worked solely in view of an immediate application would have left nothing behind them, and, in face of a new need, all must have been begun over again. Now most men do not love to think, and this is perhaps fortunate when instinct guides them, for most often, when they pursue an aim which is immediate and ever the same, instinct guides them better than reason would guide a pure intelligence. But instinct is routine, and if thought did not fecundate it, it would no more progress in man than in the bee or ant. It is needful then to think for those who love not thinking, and, as they are numerous, it is needful that each of our thoughts be as often useful as possible, and this is why a law will be the more precious the more general it is.

This shows us how we should choose: the most interesting facts are those which may serve many times, these are the facts which have a chance of coming up again. We have been so fortunate as to be born in a world where there are such. Suppose that instead of 60 chemical elements there were 60 milliards of them, that they were not some common, the others rare, but that they were uniformly distributed. Then, every time we picked up a new pebble there would be great probability of its being formed of some unknown substance; all that we knew of other pebbles would be worthless for it; before each new object we should be as the new-born babe; like it we could only obey our caprices or our needs. Biologists would be just as much at a loss if there were only individuals and no species and if heredity did not make sons like their fathers.

In such a world there would be no science; perhaps thought and even life would be impossible, since evolution could not there develop the preservational instincts. Happily it is not so; like all good fortune to which we are accustomed, this is not appreciated at its true worth.

[294]

POMPONAZZI, PIETRO

POMPONAZZI, PIETRO (1462-1524). While the philosophy of the Renaissance is characterized by the overthrow of the authority of Aristotle and the revival of Platonism, Pomponazzi, one of the most acute thinkers who lived in that period, remained a staunch Aristotelian, for he was not affected by the religious and artistic currents of his time, and possessed neither a reactionary nor traditional but rather a progressive and independent mind. He was the philosophical teacher of Copernicus, and in the middle of the 19th century his example encouraged Roberto Ardigo, the leader of Italian positivism to abandon the Church and to devote himself to secular science.

Pomponazzi was by no means uncritical when he adopted Aristotle's views, and he was opposed to both Aquinas' and Averroës' interpretation of his master, although he had also learned much from Averroës. His principal work *On the Immortality of the Soul*

(1516), in which he denied immortality, aroused a storm of indignation, and Pope Leo X charged Agostino Nifo with refuting it. Pomponazzi was insistent that the conviction of mortality of the soul allows man to be good and virtuous.

Pomponazzi's general design was to defend and secure experience, which he conceived so broadly that it included magic and miracles which he explained as natural and not performed by angels or demons. What he considered outside the wide range of natural causes assumed by him, he combated as superstition. From his investigation of the relation between prayer and fulfilment of the wishes expressed by prayer, he proceeded to views on the history of religions. He stated that religions are subject to the law of change and necessary decline, and he did not except Christianity from these laws. But he distinguished simple faith from the spirit of inquiry, and declared that philosophical thoughts must not influence man's behavior as a faithful Christian and member of the Catholic Church. This version of the Averroist assumption of "double truth" allowed him to remain unmolested as a professor at the Universities of Padua, Ferrara and Bologna.

TRUTH

TRUTH is a certain adequacy or mensurableness of the thing to the intellect, or of the intellect to the thing. . . . If a thing corresponds to a practical intellect it is true as far as it corresponds to such an intellect. All things in their totality are true as far as they are corresponding to the Divine intellect. For as far as every thing is an effect of God, either on the ground of efficient cause or of finality, everything has its idea within the Divine mind. Furthermore, since things have a similitude to their ideas, they are true, and the more they become similar to their ideas, the more they will become true. . . .

But if the question is broached whether God himself is true, I declare that all modes of truth are in God. He is true in all His modes, because in God there is total adequacy of all things to the intellect, and of the intellect to all things. For His essence is equal to His intellect, and His intellect is equal to His essence, and in no way can He practice any deception upon Himself.

[295]

PORPHYRY

PORPHYRY (232-304). Porphyry, a Syrian whose original name was Malchos, was one of the last defenders of classical paganism against the Sceptics and Christians. He was a disciple and friend of Plotinus, whose writings he edited. He was also an excellent interpreter of Aristotle.

In his objections to Christianity, Porphyry tried to do justice to the views he fought by informing himself as fully as possible about the history and doctrines of his adversaries, and he took a great many pains to refrain from open hostility. His book *Against the Christians* was considered very dangerous by Christian apologists. Porphyry was convinced that truly religious men do not desire formulas, cults, sacrifices or incantations. But, he said, men of pure heart and wise conduct of life being very rare, people need the images of the gods for their moral discipline and spiritual satisfaction.

VEGETARIANISM

HE who says that the man who extends the just as far as to brutes, corrupts the just, is ignorant that he does not himself preserve justice, but increases pleasure, which is hostile to justice. By admitting, therefore, that pleasure is the end [of our actions], justice is evidently destroyed. For to whom is it not manifest that justice is increased through abstinence? For he who abstains from every thing animated, though he may abstain from such animals as do not contribute to the benefit of society, will be much more careful not to injure those of his own species. For he who loves the genus, will not hate any species of animals; and by how much the greater his love of the genus is, by so much the more will he preserve justice towards a part of the genus, and that to which he is allied. He, therefore, who admits that he is allied to all animals, will not injure any animal. But he who confines justice to man alone, is prepared, like one enclosed in a narrow space, to hurl from him the prohibition of injustice. So that the Pythagorean is more pleasing than the So-

cratic banquet. For Socrates said that hunger is the sauce
of food; but Pythagoras said that to injure no one, and to
be exhilarated with justice, is the sweetest sauce; as the
avoidance of animal food, will also be the avoidance of unjust conduct with respect to food. For God has not so constituted things that we cannot preserve ourselves without injuring others; since, if this were the case, he would have
connected us with a nature which is the principle of injustice. Do not they, however, appear to be ignorant of the
peculiarity of justice, who think that it was introduced from
the alliance of men to each other? For this will be nothing
more than a certain philanthropy; but justice consists in ab-
staining from injuring any thing which is not noxious. And
our conception of the just man must be formed according to
the latter, and not according to the former mode. Hence,
therefore, since justice consists in not injuring any thing, it
must be extended as far as to every animated nature. On
this account, also, the essence of justice consists in the rational ruling over the irrational, and in the irrational being
obedient to the rational part. For when reason governs, and
the irrational part is obedient to its mandates, it follows,
by the greatest necessity, that man will be innoxious towards
every thing. For the passions being restrained, and desire
and anger wasting away, but reason possessing its proper empire, a similitude to a more excellent nature [and to deity]
immediately follows. But the more excellent nature in the
universe is entirely innoxious, and, through possessing a
power which preserves and benefits all things, is itself not
in want of any thing. We, however, through justice [when
we exercise it], are innoxious towards all things, but, through
being connected with mortality, are indigent of things of a
necessary nature. But the assumption of what is necessary
does not injure even plants, when we take what they cast
off; nor fruits, when we use such of them as are dead; nor
sheep, when through shearing we rather benefit than injure
them, and by partaking of their milk, we in return afford

them every proper attention. Hence, the just man appears to be one who deprives himself of things pertaining to the body; yet he does not [in reality] injure himself. For, by this management of his body, and continence, he increases his inward good, *i.e.* his similitude to God.

[296]

POSIDONIUS

POSIDONIUS (About 135-51 B.C.). The remnants of the works of Posidonius consist of sentences which have been quoted by later authors. In his time and by many succeeding generations, he was esteemed as the most learned scholar who was able to present dry matter in a popular, even picturesque style. Posidonius was born in Syria but taught mostly on the island of Rhodes and at Rome. He traveled through North Africa, Spain, France and Italy and wrote on philosophy, history, geography, physics, and astronomy. Religion played an important part in his thinking. He revered the Greek, Roman, and Oriental gods and rites, and combined the beliefs in the gods and demons with the traditional Stoic pantheism. His picture of the Universe, though preserved in fragments only, influenced many thinkers of the Middle Ages and the Renaissance, and his sayings, which blend reason with mysticism, sober experience with daring conjectures, inspired Leibniz and the romanticists.

MAN AND THE GODS

EVERY creature is attracted by what is identical with its intrinsic property. Man is a reasonable being. He therefore is not attracted to himself as an animal but to himself as a reasonable being. Man loves himself in so far as he is really human.

Everything that is visible, including the divine and the human, is one. We are members of a great body. Nature has made us related because it has created all of us out of one and the same. This origin makes us love one another and be sociable.

The whole world is a state, comprising gods and men. We cannot deny our duties to revere the gods. Utility is not the father of the law but rather equality, which is taught by Nature.

A holy demon abides within us. He is watching our good and evil actions. Just as we treat him, he will treat us. He is not born together with our body, and will not perish together with it. Under no circumstance can the state be interested in committing a crime. No state is allowed to command a citizen to do ugly things, because the state is founded upon law.

[297]

PROCLUS

PROCLUS (411-485). Pagan Neo-Platonism reached its last peak in the philosophy of Proclus who was revered as the embodiment of the ideal of the Sage. In accordance with the ideas of late antiquity, Proclus was, at the same time, a refined rationalist, an irresistible logician and dialectician, and a mystic to whom no secret was hidden. His mind is pictured by his contemporaries as the triumph of human reason and the source of superhuman powers. He was the priest of the gods of Greece, Asia Minor and Arabia, and conducted their worship with scientific knowledge and artistic skill. Only Christianity and Judaism were despised and defied by him.

But so great was his fame and the charm of his writings that the Fathers of the Church relied on the commentaries on Plato written by the enemy of Christianity, and Proclus' *Elementa Theologica*, the defense and glorification of paganism, became of basic importance to Christian theology of the Middle Ages. His influence extended even to the thinkers of the Renaissance and Hegelianism.

HYMN TO THE CULTURAL MUSES

I

WITH hymns let us celebrate the educative light that shows us the path to Heaven,
The sonorous Nine Daughters of the Supreme, who redeem
The souls that have lost their way along the depths of life,
With the blameless, inspiring mysteries of books,

973

FROM unseen sorrows preserving the terrestrials,
Teaching them to hasten to follow the path that leads above
the depths of oblivion,
Aiding them to arrive still pure at their native star,
Whence they had come; when they rushed into the childbirth
bed,
While intoxicated with the fumes of material pleasure.

II

I PRAY you, Goddesses, calm my tumultuous impulses,
And sober me with the liberal intelligible words of the wise;
Nor let the race of superstitious men stray from the path
divine;
The Path of ample splendor, and luxurious fruits!
Ever from the tumult of the straying generations
Allure my wandering soul to your chaste light,
Weighted by, and sanctified from your prolific books,
And may my soul ever enjoy the alluring glory of fine
diction!

III

LISTEN, Divinities, you hold the reins of sacred wisdom.
Who set men's souls on fire with flames indomitable,
Drawing them, through the cloudy depths, far up to the
Immortals,
Purging us with mystic rites of indescribable hymns;
LISTEN great saviors! from divine books
Grant me the innocent, blameless light that dissipates the
clouds,
So I may discover the truth about Man, and the immortal
Divinity!
Neither let the Evil-working Spirit restrain me under the
Lethean waters of Oblivion,
Ever far from the Blessed; for my soul
Would no longer continue to stray,
Nor suffer the cruel pains of imprisonment in the bands of
life!

IV

NAY, Gods of high and illustrious wisdom,
Masters and leaders, hear me, the hastener
Along the Upward Way!—Initiate me into the orgiac
  mysteries
And reveal them by the ceremonies of sacred words!

[298]

PROTAGORAS

PROTAGORAS (About 480-410 B.C.). Professor F. C. Schiller, the
founder of the English branch of modern pragmatism, used to call
himself a disciple of Protagoras. Possibly he did so because Plato
reports a saying of Protagoras, that expressed his disbelief in absolute truth, and maintains that one opinion can be better than
another one though it is not true.

For around 2300 years, the Sophists of whom Protagoras is
the oldest known in history, have been despised as unscrupulous
distorters of facts. It was Friedrich Nietzsche who rehabilitated them,
and since then their contribution to philosophy can no longer be
disregarded. Plato, who initiated the unfavorable opinion about the
Sophists and induced posterity to condemn them without hearing,
however, exempted Protagoras from that sentence.

Protagoras was born in Abdera and studied philosophy, if
not as a personal disciple of Democritus, yet as a pupil of atomistic
materialism. He came to Athens where his conditions seem to have
changed more than once. Pericles highly esteemed him and entrusted
him with drawing up a constitution for the Attic colony of Thurii.
But his books were publicly burned in Athens, and he was persecuted because of blasphemy. In 416, Protagoras was sentenced to
death but escaped to his native town.

Several disciples of Socrates had been previously taught by
Protagoras. None of them seems to have regarded the change of
teachers as a conversion to a very different philosophy. Protagoras,
however, insisted on sensation as the only source of knowledge and
claimed that the art of the Sophist could modify the sensations of
his audience. Any sensation is true as long as it is perceived, and
only that is true which is actually sensed. Protagoras was one of
the creators of Greek rhetoric, the science of language, and scientific
prose. He wrote numerous books, of which only four small fragments are extant.

975

FRAGMENTS

I DO not know whether or not there are gods, or what they are like. There are many circumstances that prevent us from knowing. The subject is obscure, and the span of time that is given to mortals is short. Man is the measure of all things, of being things that they exist, and of nonentities that they do not exist.

What seems to be just to a man is just only for him. What seems to be just to a city is just for that city.

[299]

PROUDHON, PIERRE JOSEPH

PROUDHON, PIERRE JOSEPH (1809-1865). Of all socialist theorists of the 19th century, Proudhon was the most abounding in ideas but the least capable of mastering them. He was a vigorous but poorly trained thinker, often very original and independent, but sometimes haunted by prejudices and whims. To him philosophy was only a means of changing the thoughts of men. Karl Marx, who met Proudhon in Paris, and admired him greatly though he shortly thereafter vilified him, adopted Proudhon's view that the philosopher has not only to interpret the world but to alter it. Marx learned much more from Proudhon, and gave him information about Hegel that confused Proudhon rather than inspired him. Proudhon, as Marx did after him, criticized his socialist predecessors with no lesser severity than the classical economists. He rejected any Utopian system and also communism as forms of government. He was fundamentally not a revolutionary but a reformer who intended to improve the existing methods of production and distribution instead of overthrowing them. His often quoted saying *La propriété c'est le vol* ("Property is theft") is not meant as a definition of property but as a condemnation of what he considers an abuse of it—namely, the power to provide unearned income. Apart from the right of escheat and lending on interest, private property, the disposal of the results of labor and savings, was declared by Proudhon as the essence of liberty and a necessary stimulant to labor and energy.

Proudhon's philosophy maintains that solidarity is a natural and original characteristic of human beings, and egoism the re-

976

sult of a deviation from natural conditions. Man must be guided back from his present isolation to a community in which the equilibrium between the rights of the individual and "public" or "collective" reason must be established anew, and too great inequality of wealth must be prohibited. He was opposed to the assumption that ideas of justice and morality are dependent on economic or social conditions. In this regard he professed to be a Platonist.

Proudhon was the son of a poor cooper who had not the means to give his children a higher education, and who died in misery because he refused to earn more than the medieval theory of the "just price" allowed. Proudhon therefore had to earn his living as a printer, compositor and proofreader before he became a free-lance writer. The first studies he made as an economist concerned his father's fate. From it he drew the conclusion that the world must be altered although he maintained his father's belief that no one should be permitted to earn beyond the "just price."

THE COMPLEXITY OF HUMAN NATURE

HUMAN society is *complex* in its nature. Though this expression is inaccurate, the fact to which it refers is none the less true; namely, the classification of talents and capacities. But who does not see that these talents and capacities, owing to their infinite variety, give rise to an infinite variety of wills, and that the character, the inclinations, and—if I may venture to use the expression—the form of the *ego*, are necessarily changed; so that in the order of liberty, as in the order of intelligence, there are as many types of individuals, as many characters as heads, whose tastes, fancies, and propensities, being modified by dissimilar ideas, must necessarily conflict? Man, by his nature and his instinct, is predestined to society; but his personality, ever varying, is adverse to it.

In societies of animals, all the members do exactly the same things. The same genius directs them; the same will animates them. A society of beasts is a collection of atoms, round, hooked, cubical, or triangular, but always perfectly identical. These personalities do not vary, and we might say that a single *ego* governs them all. The labors which animals perform whether alone or in society, are exact reproductions of their character. Just as the swarm of bees is composed of individual bees, alike in nature and equal in value, so the honeycomb is formed of individual cells, constantly and invariably repeated.

But man's intelligence, fitted for his social destiny and his personal needs, is of a very different composition, and therefore gives rise to a wonderful variety of human wills. In the bee, the will is constant and uniform, because the instinct which guides it is invariable, and constitutes the animal's whole life and nature. In man, talent varies, and the mind wavers; consequently, his will is multiform and vague. He seeks society, but dislikes constraint and monotony; he is an imitator, but fond of his own ideas, and passionately in love with his works.

If, like the bees, every man were born possessed of talent, perfect knowledge of certain kinds, and, in a word, an innate acquaintance with the functions he has to perform, but destitute of reflective and reasoning faculties, society would organize itself. We should see one man plowing a field, another building houses; this one forging metals, that one cutting clothes; and still others storing the products and superintending their distribution. Each one, without inquiring as to the object of his labor, and without troubling himself about the extent of his task, would obey orders, bring his product, receive his salary, and would then rest for a time; keeping meanwhile no accounts, envious of nobody, and satisfied with the distributor, who never would be unjust to any one. Kings would govern, but would not reign; for to reign is to be a *proprietor à l'engrais*, as Bonaparte said: and having no commands to give, since all would be at their posts, they would serve rather as rallying centers than as authorities or counsellors. It would be a state of ordered communism, but not a society entered into deliberately and freely.

But man acquires skill only by observation and experiment. He reflects, then, since to observe and experiment is to reflect; he reasons, since he cannot help reasoning. In reflecting, he becomes deluded; in reasoning, he makes mistakes, and, thinking himself right, persists in them. He is wedded to his opinions; he esteems himself, and despises others. Consequently, he isolates himself; for he could not submit to the majority without renouncing his will and his reason,—that is, without disowning himself, which is impossible. And this isolation, this intellectual egotism, this individuality of opinion, lasts until the truth is demonstrated to him by observation and experience.

[300]

PYTHAGORAS

PYTHAGORAS (578?-510? B.C.). Already in the days of Xenophanes and Heraclitus of Ephesus, about 500 B.C., Pythagoras had become a legendary figure, and all the efforts of ancient and modern scholars, to distinguish between fiction and truth or between Pythagoras' own performances and those of his disciples, the Pythagoreans, have resulted only in more or less probable conjectures. But his historical existence cannot be doubted. Some ancient authorities assert that he was born in Syria, but most of them think that he was born on the island of Samos, and that he emigrated to Southern Italy after Polycrates had seized power over his native country in 538 B.C. In Italy, Pythagoras seems to have founded a school which was like a religious and political order, and to have tried to interfere with politics.

There is general agreement that Pythagoras is regarded as the initiator of mathematical demonstration and deduction. Whether he himself or one of his disciples discovered the proposition about right-angled triangles which is named after him, cannot be ascertained. Pythagoras also is credited with having discovered the importance of numbers in music and having laid the fundaments of the theory of that art.

There is also general agreement that Pythagoras combined rational science and religious mysticism, and endeavored to use mathematical concepts and axioms for otherworldly speculations. He influenced Plato and Plotinus, and, through them, many mystics and metaphysicians up to the present day.

979

Pay honor first to the Immortal Gods,
As Order hath established Their Choirs:
Reverence the Oath. The heroes great and good
Revere thou next, and earth's good geniuses,
Paying to them such honors as are due.
Honor thy parents and thy nearest kin;
Of others make the virtuous thy friend:
Yield to his gentle words, his timely acts;
Nor for a petty fault take back thy love.
Bear what thou canst: pow'r cometh at man's need.
Know this for truth, and learn to conquer these:
Thy belly first; sloth, luxury, and rage.
Do nothing base with others or alone,
And, above all things, thine own self respect.
Next practice justice in thy word and deed
And learn to act unreasonably in naught;
But know that all must die. Wealth comes and goes.
Of ills the Goddess Fortune gives to man
Bear meekly thou thy lot, nor grieve at it;
But cure it as thou canst. Remember this:
Fate gives the least of evil to the good.
Many the reasonings that on men's ears
Fall; good and bad. Admire not all of such
Nor shun them neither. If one speaketh false,
Be calm. And practice ever this that now
I say. Let no man's word or deed seduce thee
To do or say aught not to thy best good.
First think, then act; lest foolish be thy deed.
Unhappy he who thoughtless acts and speaks:
But that which after vexes not do thou.
Do naught thou dost not understand; but learn
That which is right, and sweet will be thy life.
Nor shouldest thou thy body's health neglect,
But give it food and drink and exercise
In measure; that is, to cause it no distress.

Decent, without vain show, thy way of life:
Look well to this, that none thou envious make
By unmeet expense, like one who lacks good taste.
Nor niggard be: in all the mean is best.
Do that which cannot harm thee. Think, then act.
When first thou dost from soothing sleep uprise,
Hasten about thy day's intended work;
Nor suffer sleep to fall on thy soft lids
Till thrice thou hast each act of the day recalled:
How have I sinned? What done? What duty missed?
Go through them first to last; and, if they seem
Evil, reproach thyself; if good, rejoice.
Toil at and practice this; this must thou love;
This to the Path of Heavenly Virtue leads.
By Him Who gave the Tetractys to our soul,
Fount of Eternal Nature, this I swear.
Begin thy work, first having prayed the Gods
To accomplish it. Thou, having mastered this,
That essence of Gods and mortal men shalt know,
Which all things permeate, which all obey.
And thou shalt know that Law hath stablished
The inner nature of all things alike;
So shalt thou hope not for what may not be,
Nor aught, that may, escape thee. Thou shalt know
Self-chosen are the woes that fall on men—
How wretched, for they see not good so near,
Nor hearken to its voice—few only know
The Pathway of Deliverance from ill.
Such fate doth blind mankind, who, up and down,
With countless woes are carried by its wheel.
For bitter inborn strife companions them
And does them secret harm. Provoke it not,
O men, but yield, and yielding, find escape.
O Father Zeus, 'twould free from countless ills
Didst Thou but show what Genius works in each!
But courage! Men are children of the Gods,
And Sacred Nature all things hid reveals.

And if the Mysteries have part in thee,
Thou shalt prevail in all I bade thee do,
And, thoroughly cured, shalt save thy soul from toil.
Eat not the foods proscribed, but use discretion
In lustral rites and the freeing of thy soul:
Ponder all things, and stablish high thy mind,
That best of charioteers. And if at length,
Leaving behind thy body, thou dost come
To the free Upper Air, then shalt thou be
Deathless, divine, a mortal man no more.

[301]

R

RAMSEY, FRANK PLUMPTON

RAMSEY, FRANK PLUMPTON (1903-1930). The premature death of Ramsey at the age of twenty-six has been felt as a heavy loss by leading thinkers in the field of philosophy, mathematical logic, and theory of economics.

Ramsey tried to tackle problems at the point where Bertrand Russell and Ludwig Wittgenstein had left them. He makes a fundamental distinction between *human logic*, which deals with useful mental habits and is applicable to the logic of probability, and *formal logic*, which is concerned with the rules of consistent thought. Against John Maynard Keynes he holds that probability is concerned not with objective relations between propositions but with degrees of belief. Keynes partly yielded to Ramsey without abandoning his efforts to make induction an application of mathematical probability.

MY OUTLOOK ON THE WORLD

IF I was to write a *Weltanschauung* I should call it not "What I believe" but "What I feel." This is connected with Wittgenstein's view that philosophy does not give us beliefs, but merely relieves feelings of intellectual discomfort. Also, if I were to quarrel with Russell, it would not be with what he believed but with the indications given as to what he felt. Not that one can really quarrel with a man's feelings; one can only have different feelings oneself, and perhaps also regard one's own as more admirable or more conducive to a happy life. From this point of view, that it is a matter not of fact but of feeling, I shall conclude by some remarks on things in general, or, as I would rather say, not things but *life* in general.

Where I seem to differ from some of my friends is in attaching little importance to physical size. I don't feel the least humble before the vastness of the heavens. The stars may be large, but they cannot think or love; and these are qualities which impress me far more than size does. I take no credit for weighing nearly seventeen stone.

My picture of the world is drawn in perspective, and not like a model to scale. The foreground is occupied by human beings and the stars are all as small as threepenny bits. I don't really believe in astronomy, except as a complicated description of part of the course of human and possibly animal sensation. I apply my perspective not merely to space but also to time. In time the world will cool and everything will die; but that is a long time off still, and its present value at compound discount is almost nothing. Nor is the present less valuable because the future will be blank. Humanity, which fills the foreground of my picture, I find interesting and on the whole admirable. I find, just now at least, the world a pleasant and exciting place. You may find it depressing; I am sorry for you, and you despise me. But I have reason and you have none; you would only have a reason for despising me if your feeling corresponded to the fact in a way mine didn't. But neither can correspond to the fact. The fact is not in itself good or bad; it is just that it thrills me but depresses you. On the other hand, I pity you with reason, because it is pleasanter to be thrilled than to be depressed, and not merely pleasanter but better for all one's activities.

[302]

REICHENBACH, HANS

REICHENBACH, HANS (1891-1953). Reichenbach belongs to a generation of scientists who began to study after most of their teachers had already abandoned the concepts of classical physics; thus they were able to start with ideas and modes of thought found by their predecessors after much hardship, trial and error. Reichenbach, however, has actively participated in the further advance of science and philosophy. His contributions have been discussed by the greatest contemporary scientists and philosophers with respect if not with general consent, and are recognized either as real contributions or at least as working hypotheses or useful suggestions.

At first, Reichenbach was preoccupied with the clarification of the concepts of space and time, their relations, and the way of assimilating one to another. As a theorist of knowledge, Reichenbach comes in his own way closer to the methods of the Vienna Circle, but he even more vigorously insists that all our knowledge is only probable. The doctrine of probability, advanced by R. von Mises and Reichenbach, is based on the concept of "frequency," a statistical concept. Every definition of induction is involved in this doctrine. Induction is described as a process of predicting future events with the aid of propositions of probability which serve as instruments of indication. Reichenbach objects to classical logic that it classifies propositions according to their truth or falsity instead of lower or higher degrees of probability. He holds that true logic is probability logic, and has presented his views in *Wahrscheinlichkeitslehre* (Doctrine of Probability, 1935) and *Experience and Prediction* (1938).

In his *Elements of Symbolic Logic* (1947), Reichenbach acknowledges classical logic as the "mother of all logics" and admits that it can be carried through in the sense of approximation, even if refined analysis demands probability logic.

LOGIC AND LANGUAGE

If it is true that to a certain extent we can improve our thinking by studying logic, the fact is to be explained as a conditioning of our thought operations in such a way that the relative number of right results is increased.

When we call logic *analysis of thought* the expression should be interpreted so as to leave no doubt that it is not actual thought which we pretend to analyze. It is rather a substitute for thinking processes, their *rational reconstruction*, which constitutes the basis of logical analysis. Once a result of thinking is obtained, we can reorder our thoughts in a cogent way, constructing a chain of thoughts between point of departure and point of arrival; it is this rational reconstruction of thinking that is controlled by logic, and whose analysis reveals those rules which we call logical laws.

The two realms of analysis to be distinguished may be called *context of discovery* and *context of justification*. The context of discovery is left to psychological analysis, whereas logic is concerned with the context of justification, i.e., with the analysis of ordered series of thought operations so constructed that they make the results of thought justifiable. We speak of a justification when we possess a proof which shows that we have good grounds to rely upon those results.

It has been questioned whether all thinking processes are accompanied by linguistic utterances, and behavioristic theories stating that thinking *consists* in linguistic utterances have been attacked by other psychologists. We need not enter into this controversy here for the very reason that we connect logical analysis, not with actual thinking, but with thinking in the form of its rational reconstruction. There can be no doubt that this reconstruction is bound to linguistic form; this is the reason that logic is so closely connected with language. Only after thinking processes have been cast into linguistic form do they attain the precision that makes them accessible to logical tests; logical validity is therefore a predicate of linguistic forms. Considerations of this kind have led to the contention that logic is *analysis of language*, and that the term "logical laws" should be replaced by the term "rules of language." Thus in the theory of deduction we study the rules leading from true linguistic utterances to other true linguistic utterances. This terminology appears admissible when it is made clear that the term "rules of language" is not synonymous with "arbitrary rules." Not all rules of language are arbitrary; for instance, the rules of deduction are not, but are determined by the postulate that they must lead from true sentences to true sentences.

It is the value of such an analysis of language· that it makes thought processes clear, that it distinguishes meanings and the relations between meanings from the blurred background of psychological motives and intentions. The student of logic will find that an essential instrument for such clarification is supplied by the method of symbolization, which has given its name to the modern form of logic. It is true that simple logical operations can be performed without the help of symbolic representation; but the structure of complicated relations cannot be seen without the aid of symbolism. The reason is that the symbolism eliminates the specific meanings of words and expresses the general structure which controls these words, allotting to them their places within comprehensive relations. The great advantage of modern logic over the older forms of the science results from the fact that this logic is able to analyze structures that traditional logic never has understood, and that it is able to solve problems of whose existence the older logic has never been aware.

We said that logic cannot claim to replace creative thought. This limitation includes symbolic logic; we do not wish to say that the methods of symbolic logic will make unnecessary the imaginative forms of thought used in all domains of life, and it certainly would be a misunderstanding to believe that symbolic logic represents a sort of slide-rule technique by which all problems can be solved. The practical value of a new scientific technique is always a secondary question. Logic is primarily a theoretical science; and it proceeds by giving a determinate form to notions that until then had been employed without a clear understanding of their nature. Whoever has had such an insight into the structure of thought, whoever has experienced in his own mind the great clarification process which logical analysis accomplishes, will know what logic can achieve.

[303]

RICARDO, DAVID

RICARDO, DAVID (1772-1823). One of Ricardo's basic convictions, namely, the belief that businessmen are always acting with a full knowledge of all possible consequences of their actions, has been proved to be wrong. Also, some of his other propositions have been definitely refuted. Nevertheless, Ricardo's authority as an acute and informed thinker remains unshattered, and many of his discoveries have become commonplace. Important concepts, formulated by him, have been adopted by economists who defend either private enterprise or socialism.

Ricardo, the son of a Jewish stockbroker who had come to England from Holland, was a financier and member of the London Stock Exchange. He lacked classical education, having attended only an elementary school, but he had learned, as an autodidact, natural sciences and political economics. From 1819 until his death, he was a member of Parliament, and was, despite his radical opinions, revered by both sides of the House as the highest authority in matters of finance and currency. Although Ricardo was a clever businessman, his political and economic demands took no regard of vested interests, not even his own private interests. In his *Principles of Political Economy and Taxation* (1817), Ricardo states an "iron law" in virtue of which rent is always rising while real wages remain stationary, and the profits of the manufacturer and the farmer, kept at the same level by the competition of capital, are constantly declining. In order to change this state of things, Ricardo attempted in vain to ally the rest of the nations against the great landowners. His statements are founded upon exact observations of the economic situation of his own time and the preceding fifty years of British history, but from this reliable knowledge, Ricardo proceeded to rash generalizations. A powerful advocate of free trade, Ricardo was by no means an optimist. He expressed grave apprehensions concerning class struggle. Marx borrowed this and some other formulas from Ricardo but drew different conclusions from them. Bulwer-Lytton's novel *Pelham* and many other literary documents of the second and third decades of the 19th century testify to Ricardo's popularity, although his own style was rather dry. His premature death was mourned by the entire British nation.

ON WAGES

LABOR, like all other things which are purchased and sold, and which may be increased or diminished in quantity, has its natural and its market price. The natural price of labor is that price which is necessary to enable the laborers, one with another, to subsist and to perpetuate their race, without either increase or diminution.

The power of the laborer to support himself, and the

family which may be necessary to keep up the number of laborers, does not depend on the quantity of money which he may receive for wages, but on the quantity of food, necessaries, and conveniences become essential to him from habit which that money will purchase. The natural price of labor, therefore, depends on the price of the food, necessaries, and conveniences required for the support of the laborer and his family. With a rise in the price of food and necessaries, the natural price of labor will rise; with the fall in their price, the natural price of labor will fall.

With the progress of society the natural price of labor has always a tendency to rise, because one of the principal commodities by which its natural price is regulated has a tendency to become dearer from the greater difficulty of producing it. As, however, the improvements in agriculture, the discovery of new markets, whence provisions may be imported, may for a time counteract the tendency to a rise in the price of necessaries, and may even occasion their natural price to fall, so will the same causes produce the correspondent effects on the natural price of labor.

The natural price of all commodities, excepting raw produce and labor, has a tendency to fall in the progress of wealth and population; for though, on one hand, they are enhanced in real value, from the rise in the natural price of the raw material of which they are made, this is more than counter-balanced by the improvements in machinery, by the better division and distribution of labor, and by the increasing skill, both in science and art, of the producers.

The market price of labor is the price which is really paid for it, from the natural operation of the proportion of the supply to the demand; labor is dear when it is scarce and cheap when it is plentiful. However much the market price of labor may deviate from its natural price, it has, like commodities, a tendency to conform to it.

It is when the market price of labor exceeds its natural price that the condition of the laborers is flourishing and happy, that he has it in his power to command a greater proportion of the necessaries and enjoyments of life, and therefore to rear a healthy and numerous family. When, however, by the encouragement which high wages give to the increase of population, the number of laborers is increased, wages again fall to their natural price, and indeed from a reaction sometimes fall below it.

When the market price of labor is below its natural price, the condition of the laborers is most wretched: then poverty deprives them of those comforts which custom renders absolute necessaries. It is only after their privations have reduced their number, or the demand for labor has increased, that the market price of labor will rise to its natural price, and that the laborer will have the moderate comforts which the natural rate of wages will afford.

Notwithstanding the tendency of wages to conform to their natural rate, their market rate may, in an improving society, for an indefinite period, be constantly above it; for no sooner may the impulse which an increased capital gives to a new demand for labor be obeyed, than another increase of capital may produce the same effect; and thus, if the increase of capital be gradual and constant, the demand for labor may give a continued stimulus to an increase of people.

Capital is that part of the wealth of a country which is employed in production, and consists of food, clothing, tools, raw materials, machinery, etc., necessary to give effect to labor.

Capital may increase in quantity at the same time that its value rises. An addition may be made to the food and clothing of a country at the same time that more labor may be required to produce the additional quantity than before; in that case not only the quantity but the value of capital will rise.

Or capital may increase without its value increasing, and even while its value is actually diminishing; not only may an addition be made to the food and clothing of a country, but the addition may be made by the aid of machinery, without any increase, and even with an absolute diminution in the proportional quantity of labor required to produce them. The quantity of capital may increase, while neither the whole together, nor any part of it singly, will have a greater value than before, but may actually have a less.

In the first case, the natural price of labor, which always depends on the price of food, clothing, and other necessaries, will rise; in the second, it will remain stationary or fall; but in both cases the market rate of wages will rise, for in proportion to the increase of capital will be the increase in the demand for labor; in proportion to the work to be done will be the demand for those who are to do it.

In both cases, too, the market price of labor will rise above its natural price; and in both cases it will have a tendency to conform to its natural price, but in the first case this agreement will be most speedily effected. The situation of the laborer will be improved, but not much more improved; for the increased price of food and necessaries will absorb a large portion of his increased wages; consequently a small supply of labor, or a trifling increase in the population, will soon reduce the market price to the then increased natural price of labor.

In the second case, the condition of the laborer will be very greatly improved; he will receive increased money wages without having to pay any increased price, and perhaps even a diminished price for the commodities which he and his family consume; and it will not be till after a great addition has been made to the population that the market price of labor will again sink to its then low and reduced natural price.

Thus, then, with every improvement of society, with every increase in its capital, the market wages of labor will rise; but the permanence of their rise will depend on the question whether the natural price of labor has also risen; and this again will depend on the rise in the natural price of those necessaries on which the wages of labor are expended.

[304]

RICKERT, HEINRICH

RICKERT, HEINRICH (1863-1936). Closely associated with Wilhelm Windelband and his successor as professor of philosophy at the University of Heidelberg, Rickert was also a leader of the "South-West-German school of philosophy" and fought, as Windelband did, against a concept of science that comprises natural sciences only. His early works were concerned with the demonstration of the limits of the formation of concepts which natural sciences cannot extend, or with the thesis that natural sciences envisage only part of nature, leaving it to other sciences, namely historical sciences, to deal with the neglected aspects of reality.

In his later years, Rickert, without abandoning the views he shared with Windelband, concentrated more and more upon the problem of values. While declaring that the values of civilization are the real object of philosophy, Rickert refuted the doctrines according to which life in itself is the supreme value. Contrary to philosophers like Nietzsche and Bergson, Rickert emphasized that values demand a distance from life, and that what Bergson, Dilthey or Simmel called "vital values" were not true values. For Rickert, the connection between value and life was secured by the realm of meaning. While reality is to be explained and values are to be understood, meanings are to be interpreted. According to Rickert, the meaning of life can be interpreted only by understanding the value of civilization, even if civilization might be recognized as of no value.

NATURAL AND CULTURAL SCIENCE

IF we conceive the notion of natural science broadly enough so that it coincides with the conception of a generalizing science, is then knowledge of the material world by any procedure other than that of the natural sciences possible at all? . . . There are sciences that do not tend toward the establishment of natural laws, not even toward the formulation of general conceptions, and these are the historical sciences in the widest sense of the word. They don't seek to make only "ready-made suits" which fit Paul as well as Peter—that means, they want to present reality being never general but always individual in its complete individuality and, as soon as this individuality is to be considered, the concept of the natural science must fail because it is the characteristic of this concept that it eliminates the individual as negligible.

With Goethe, the historians will think concerning the general: "We use it but we don't like it; we like only the individual," and they certainly want to present this individual scientifically just as far as the object that shall be investigated is concerned as a whole. Let us, for a moment, leave it undecided in what way historical science presents the peculiarity and individuality of reality. Since reality as such, on account of its immense diversity, cannot be comprised in one concept, and since the elements of all concepts are general, the idea of an individualizing formation of concepts must appear problematical. One cannot, however, dispute the fact that history sees its task in the presentation of the peculiar and individual, and from the viewpoint of this task one has to explain its formal essence. For all concepts of sciences are concepts of tasks, and to understand them logically is only possible if one proceeds from comprehending their purposes to penetrating into the logical structure of their method. This is the road that leads to the goal. History, as "History," does not want to generalize in the manner as natural sciences do. That is as the decisive point of logic.

Recently the contradistinction between the procedure of the natural sciences, that is, the generalizing procedure, and the historical procedure has been clarified, at least in this one, if only negative, regard. . . . Without dwelling upon other contributions to the clarification of this point, I refer only to the studies of Windelband. He places at the side of the "nomothetical" procedure of the natural sciences the "idiographical" procedure of history, namely, the procedure that tends toward the presentation of what happens only once and in a particular way.

In order to obtain two exclusively logical and therefore exclusively formal concepts of nature and history, signifying not two different realities but the same reality under different aspects, I have formulated the logical fundamental problem of a division of the sciences according to their methods, as follows: Reality becomes nature if we consider it with regard to the general. It becomes history if we consider it with regard to the special and individual and, accordingly, I want to oppose the individualizing procedure of history to the generalizing procedure of natural sciences.

[305]

RIDPATH, JOHN CLARK

RIDPATH, JOHN CLARK (1840-1900). Ridpath, the editor of some of America's most popular encyclopedias, was by nature an encyclopedist, surveying the whole range of knowledge of his time, always working hard, aided by an extraordinarily reliable memory, reading untiringly, learning constantly, and able to teach what he had read and learned. In fact, his great talents for teaching are also the conspicuous quality of his writings.

Ridpath was born and grew up on a farm in the frontier community of Putnam County, Indiana, remote from high schools. He owed it to his highly cultivated parents that he could attend Indiana Asbury University, where he later had a brilliant career as teacher, professor, and vice-president. He taught English literature, history and normal instruction. In 1885, he renounced his professorship in order to devote his full time to writing. His principal works are *Encyclopedia of Universal History* (1880-85), *The Great Races of Mankind* (1884-94), and *The Ridpath Library of Universal Literature*, comprising 25 volumes (1898).

LITERATURE

LITERATURE is the highest blossom of the human spirit. It is higher than art; for if art survives for ages, literature survives forever; it is immortal.

Such is the nature of literature that it is susceptible of being translated from language to language, from race to race, from century to century, and, it may be, from world to world. For thought, we doubt not, is in some measure common to the inhabitants of all the spheres. Is not thought indeed a part and essence of the eternities?

While the conditions of purely aesthetic production suffer change, and while the canons of artistic criticism are frequently amended and reversed, literature remains coeval with mankind; it cannot suffer save in the decadence of the race and in the collapse of civilization.

Literature is recorded in the book; the book is its receptacle. Literature is the soul of the book, and the book is the body of the soul. The book is multifarious in form and presence. It may be of papyrus, and its pictured symbols may be the hieratic images and fictions of old Egypt. The book may be the sacred scroll of Brahma. It may be the inaccessible wedges on the sculptured face of the rocks of Behistun. It may be the parchment roll of Herodotus, from which he reads to the assembled Greeks. It may be the bark of the *beech* (from which, indeed, is the name of the *book*) written in runes on its inner, sappy surface, as by the old Goths beyond the Danube. The book may be the parchment rolls of Roman poet or orator. It may be the crude sheets marked from the black-letter blocks of Gutenberg and Faust. It may be the primitive book of Wyclif or of the old printers of Venice. It may be the printed paper book (albeit "paper" is *papyrus*) of our modern age, born of revolving cylinders and clattering binderies going always, pouring forth their infinity of volumes into the lap of civilization. And in these books is embodied the literature of the world.

Literature is not of one race, but of all enlightened races. Even the barbarians, though they have it not, possess its rudiments. No sooner do they become self-conscious than they begin to essay the expression of that consciousness in some record of themselves and their deeds.

To gather and preserve in an acceptable form the literature of the world, or the best of that literature, is a work not to be overlooked in estimating the means by which the civilized life is preserved and promoted. Certainly not all literature can be brought within the reach of all intelligences. Only *some* can be preserved and offered as a treasure *to* some; and perhaps a portion to all.

[306]

ROMAINS, JULES

ROMAINS, JULES (1885-   ). At the height of his literary successes as one of the greatest French novelists of our time, Jules Romains has been faithful to the ideal of "unanimism" which has dominated the poetry of his youth, but he has modified it and changed the means of expression.

"Unanimism" originally meant an opposition to individualism, or at least to the exaltation of individual particularities, universal sympathy with life, existence, humanity. In later years, the end of literature has been defined by Romains as "representation of the world without judgment," and his social ideal seems to comprise as well the highest conception of solidarity as the defense of individual rights. In his immense series of novels, *Men of Good Will*, Romains has not limited his task to the invention of characters and events but has also tried to live the lives of his figures with extreme concreteness, to let them think about questions of the day and the universe, about the principal problems of civilization, to let them criticize one another, develop their judgment, and he has indeed succeeded in uniting intellectual force, artistic vision, colorful description, and narrative dynamics. The result is a picture of French cultural life in its stratification, with its fundamental conflicts and common tendencies, on a scale which can be compared only with Balzac and Zola, but surpassing its rivals in spirituality and psychological refinement.

Romains is no sceptic. He does not believe that human mind is capable of discovering absolute and definite truth. He holds that there will always be an aspect of reality which challenges the dominant one. Reality means change. When man becomes tired of broaching new questions and when he acquiesces in a creed or system, he will lose contact with reality. But he believes that in the course of history man will come closer and closer to truth, although new aspects will be opened which let him see new problems. His "men of good will" respect reason and give experience the last word, though they do not exclude the possibility that intuition, in exceptional cases, may also discover reality.

THE ADVENTURE OF HUMANITY

IT is in the human sphere that the problem takes on breadth and vital interest. The reader may know that I have devoted a great deal of attention to human groups. When *unanimism* is discussed it ordinarily designates a specialized study, largely a literary one, of the life of human groups, and the relationship between the individual and these groups.

I believe, in fact, that the adventure of humanity is essentially an adventure of groups. It is also an adventure of individuals in conflict with groups or with each other. This conflict is maintained under conditions which bring into constant play the aptitude for forming multiple ties, truly biological associations, as well as the aptitude for warding off the forces of "dispossession," both spiritual and physical, which groups or collectivities of various kinds may exercise over the individual.

Reduced to its simplest form, this statement contains very little originality. The life of society, at whatever level, has always been considered important as a key to the explanation of human action.

Experience, however, has proved that this bare statement takes on a special power of illumination when one endows the idea of the group with its full richness of content, its efficacy, one might almost say its virulence. Especially when one need not be afraid to look for the organic bond elsewhere than in mere metaphors and abstractions.

This patient and painstaking quest for the organic bond down to its weakest manifestation is in brief the essence of unanimism: a quest rather than a doctrine.

It will be noted that this quest profits by one very remarkable circumstance. Man forms part of the groups, the organizations which he seeks to understand. The situation is analogous to that in which he finds himself when he attempts to probe human consciousness. As he himself is "human consciousness," the facts he investigates occur within him, form a part of himself. He manages to grasp many of them, and to grasp them (without detriment to other methods) in a firm and essential way by the direct means of introspection, that is to say by consciousness carried to a high degree of acuteness and subtlety. There is a direct connection of the same kind between man and the groups or communities of which he is part. This connection cannot be questioned even by the most positivist, the most critical minds. They, for instance, admit that as part of society we can more readily than if we were not part of it, take account of the internal mechanisms of that society and understand the *raison d'être* of the varied behavior of social man, his customs and manners, the influence exerted on him by group emotions, public institutions, etc.—even if this internal awareness does not reveal everything. But I for one go further. I hold, on the basis of an experience of a special nature, that we are able, with the aid of certain refinements of attention, to grasp the interhuman organic bond, even in its most essential and invisible form, its most fugitive nascent stages. This is, if you will, the counterpart of introspection when it functions most profoundly and permits us to grasp the psychic reality within us.

Now it becomes a question of reaching a psychic reality which is not external to us but which envelops us. I am far from believing—even if I have appeared to say so at certain times—that this enveloping psychic reality does not exceed the bounds of human groups. But human groups elaborate and condense it in a fashion, raise it one degree higher, just as the human consciousness condenses and raises to a higher plane some psychic reality which exceeds the limitations of personal identity.

It is not astonishing—and I emphasize this—that I have attributed a prominent part in this investigation to literature in all its forms. Literature has, for the same reasons, played an important part in the investigation of the spirit.

I have been reproached for having "deified" the group. And it is true I have pronounced words on the subject dangerous to the extent that they might provoke a confusion between the order of fact and the order of right, between the real and desirable. That groups, having achieved a certain degree of organic reality, should be termed by the poet "gods" or, better, "divine animals"—this is merely to express on the lyric or mystic plane a real fact. That fact arises from the disproportion in dimension and power (physical and psychic) between groups and individuals. It implies the change of magnitude occurring when one rises from one plane to the other. But it would obviously be hazardous to draw from this the unqualified conclusion that the group as opposed to the individual is always right, and that the individual's only attitude should be submission and worship.

In any case, formerly no less than now, I have always insisted that the power of the group over the individual is justified only to the extent to which it finds expression in and by the spontaneity of the individual. I condemned the restrictions imposed upon the individual from without by society and its institutions. As forcibly as I could, I emphasized the contrast between "society," conceived as a system of restraints and conventions, and "the unanimous life," conceived as the "free respiration" of human groups and implying the voluntary surrender of the individual to their influence and attractions. I indicated the danger lying in the very idea of the state, with all its germs of juridical formalism and of oppression. I even declared that a certain infusion of "anarchy" is indispensable to avert the demoniacal mechanization of society and salvage "the unanimous life." On the other hand, I have always maintained the extreme importance—for good or evil—of the leader.

The political and social events of the last twenty years have but confirmed these opinions. It has been said, ironically —and hardly to make me feel happy—that the founders of totalitarian governments are to some extent my disciples. My reply was that these governments are merely a burlesque of unanimism, and that they err and err gravely in two important respects. First, they proceed by coercion and are as far as possible from fostering the "free respiration" of the masses. Second, they have a shockingly over-simplified idea of unanimity. They interpret it as an inexorable uniformity of thought, an inflexible and sterile "union." Unanimism postulates the richest possible variety of individual states of consciousness, in a "harmony" made valuable by its richness and density. This harmony is necessary before any glimpse can be given of the birth of those states of consciousness that transcend the individual spirit.

[307]

ROMERO, FRANCISCO

ROMERO, FRANCISCO (1891-). As far as opposition to positivism prevails in Latin America, Romero is to be considered the present leader of the philosophic movement in these countries, especially in Argentina. Romero has become influential as a critic, as a translator from the German, and, even more so, as a stimulating teacher. He has not yet published systematic works but his treatises, *Old and New Concepts of Reality* (1932), *The Problems of Philosophy of Culture* (1938) and *Program of a Philosophy* (1940), attracted general attention and were much discussed. Inspired by Gestalt theory, Romero defends a structural conception of reality against Hume and rationalism, biological evolutionism and any atomistic conception. True being is identified by Romero with transcendence, and personality is its function.

THE MARCH OF PHILOSOPHY FOR CENTURIES

PHILOSOPHY has investigated with growing exactness and profoundness the problem of nature, the order and constitution of the physical world. The problem of cognition, namely, the question of how we obtain knowledge of this world, has been raised afterwards. And only much later has philosophy dealt with questions concerning the world of culture, meaning the world of the products of man and his manners of living. At first glance, it seems surprising that the object of research has been at first that which is farthest and most remote from us, the external world, and that only after-wards philosophical curiosity has spread to cognition itself and to culture, which is our most immediate environment, nearest to us not only as environment but also as our creation.

But this fact is strange only in appearance. That which concerns us most immediately is not generally the first to be noticed by us. In order to see things, a certain distance that permits perspective is indicated. If the distance does not exist, an effort must be made to adapt the sight in such a manner as to concentrate upon the object which, just by its immediacy and intimacy, is invisible for a spontaneous act of cognition. Of the whole field forming our natural scenery at any moment only a fraction is totally invisible: precisely what concerns us most closely, the square stones which support our feet. The piece of ground which sustains us is at any moment the one we cannot see.

This strange rule, according to which the cognition of that which is closest to us is the most difficult and the last, is fulfilled with relative, if not absolute, regularity. The movement of the stars was studied before the evolution of the insects. The child discovers above all the surrounding world and must wait until adolescence in order to realize with anxiety and astonishment the discovery of its intimate feelings. Philosophical thinking seems to follow the same path. The first philosophers of the Occident are called pre-Socratics, a designation which comprises the thinkers from Thales to the atomists, Leucippus and Democritus. Their problem is essentially the problem of being, of the things, the structure and the law of the world. The human spirit that thinks and knows the world, this center of all thought to be reality, this reality incomparable to any other, which is man, remains invisible to them. The pre-Socratics are the ancestors of western philosophy, but, at the same time, they are like children, absorbed by the magnificent spectacle of the exterior world, and ignoring that world which is their own personality. The adolescence of Greek thought, the discovery of the subject, of the problems man is confronted with occurs in the Attic stage with the much abused Sophists and with Socrates. When they formulated first questions concerning the essence of man, the problems of the things had already been examined from all sides.

[308]

ROSCELLIN

ROSCELLIN (About 1050-1120). The war waged by Roscellin against Platonism and every kind of realism is interesting because it induced him to adumbrate a criticism of language which impresses one as most modern. Proceeding from the statement that in nature only individuals exist and species are not things, Roscellin has inquired into the generalizing character of words and language. In 1092 he was accused of adhering to Tritheism, i.e., that he conceived of the Trinity as of three distinct deities. He denied such a doctrine but later returned to it. Roscellin taught at the schools of several French towns. Among his pupils was Abailard who later criticized him. Roscellin's thoughts are known to us only by quotations which his adversaries made. Of all his writings only a letter to Abailard is extant.

A TEACHER'S DEFENSE AGAINST HIS DISCIPLE

You assert, I be excluded from Christianity. I have been educated in the schools of the churches of Soissons and Rheims, as can be testified. Rome, the capital of the world, has friendlily received me, and listened to my words with great joy. In Tours where I was canon, you have been sitting at my feet as my humblest disciple as long as you have stayed in that town. . . .

I am very sad that you have called me the persecutor of good men. Maybe, I am not good: but I have always revered good men. . . . I will not justify myself, because, if I were seeking for my own glory, my glory would be nothing. . . .

If I have somewhat lapsed in my words and deviated from truth, I would not obstinately defend either words or

1002

assertion, but I am always more prepared to learn than to teach. . . . Words are only breaths of the voice.

[309]

ROSENZWEIG, FRANZ

ROSENZWEIG, FRANZ (1886-1929). Shortly before the outbreak of the First World War, a young German scholar of Jewish origin, who had become renowned because of his epoch-making discovery of the earliest outline of German idealism and his acute investigation of the relations between Schelling and Hegel, intended to embrace Christianity. But before making the decisive step he thought it would be appropriate to know what he intended to abandon. He therefore began to study Judaism, and subsequently became resolved not only to remain a Jew, but also to devote his life to the elaboration of a new conception of Judaism, based upon historical, linguistic, and philosophical research, and aimed at a moral and spiritual rejuvenation of his fellow Jews. The first fruit of these efforts was the book *Der Stern der Erloesung* (Star of Salvation), written during the war in the trenches and edited posthumously in 1930.

Rosenzweig's vindication of Judaism is anything but polemical toward Christianity. He is opposed to atheism and irreligion, but his historical consciousness prevents him from attacking, even from disputing, any religious tradition or any living faith. On the contrary, he has encouraged his closest friend and first cousin to embrace Christianity rather than to live apart from any religious community. Although opposed to Jewish nationalism, Rosenzweig thinks that Jewish religion concerns only born Jews, and, without any concession to racialism, founds his philosophy of history upon the fact that the Jews form a cultural unit with a common history and certain relatively constant characteristics. He even maintains that only the Jews, by virtue of being such a unit, can have a genuine philosophy of history in which their fate, regarded as a unit, is the decisive factor. The historical aspect is also of primary importance to Rosenzweig's philosophy of religion which, notwithstanding the tensions between religion and civilization, is at the same time a philosophy of culture.

THE NEW WAY OF THINKING

PEOPLE are still accustomed to thinking that philosophy must begin with epistemological considerations. In fact, however, philosophy might rather end with them. Kant's criticism, initiating the epistemological prejudice of our days, is nothing but the finishing accomplishment of a historical epoch that began with the natural sciences of the era of the Baroque. Kant's criticism proves to be correct only as far as the philosophy of that epoch is concerned. To the "Copernican revolution" of Copernicus that made man a particle of dust in the universe corresponds the "Copernican revolution" of Kant that, in order to compensate man, elevated him on the throne of the world. The two revolutions correspond one to another more precisely than Kant ever imagined. A dreadful humiliation of man at the expense of his humanity has been compensated, equally at the expense of his humanity, by a reckless correction. . . .

In truth, even in ultimate truth, there must be contained an "and." It must be, different from the philosopher's truth that knows only itself, truth for somebody. If it shall be the one truth, then it can be only truth for one. Our truth, therefore, necessarily becomes multifarious, and "the truth" will be transformed into "our truth." Truth ceases to be "what is true," and becomes what will stand the test of truth. The concept of standing the test becomes the fundamental concept of the new epistemology which replaces the old theory of consistency and objectivity by a dynamic one.
[310]

ROSHD, IBN. See AVERROËS.

ROSMINI-SERBATI, ANTONIO

ROSMINI-SERBATI, ANTONIO (1797-1855). Even to organize charity and enjoin poverty is not without grave consequences and above suspicion. That is what Rosmini-Serbati had to learn. This thinker who is classed as an ontologist in philosophy, is better known for the world-wide Institutes of Charity, the first of which he established in 1828 on Monte Calvario near Domodossola, Italy. Rosminians have to take vows of absolute poverty, which have been criticized at times as more affective than effective, and they must subscribe in their charitable work to two principles, that of passivity or not seeking out their cases and that of personal indifference or disinterestedness in the performance of their duty.

Rosmini was born at Rovereto in the Austrian Tyrol, studied at Trient and Padua, and in 1823 went to Rome with the avowed intention to resuscitate Catholic philosophy and fortify it against disbelief and doubt, in which purpose Pope Pius VII encouraged him. Deeply influenced by Cartesian thinking, he poured over the philosophy of St. Thomas, modifying it in the direction of an ideological psychologism.

Followers of the Society of Jesus opened a feud lasting for many years until silence was imposed by order of the Pope. Rosmini was devoted to Pius IX, even following him into exile. Still, even these circumstances did not prevent his books from being put on the *Index* at a later date, but, nothing detrimental to the Church being found in them, they were dismissed and thus given a semblance of papal approval. Rosmini lived just long enough to see himself thus partially justified.

THE FUNCTIONS OF THE HUMAN MIND
AND ITS METHODS

1. METHOD is a part of logic, and if taken in all its bearings, may be said to be itself logic, since the aim of the latter is throughout to establish the method of conducting our reasoning processes. . . .

2. The human mind has truth for its object, and, in relation to this most noble object, it exercises various functions. Some of these functions relate to truth already known; others, to truth which is still unknown, and the knowledge of which is sought for.

3. The functions of the mind, in relation to truths already known, may be reduced to three, namely, 1. The communication of it to others; 2. The defense of it; and, 3. The disentanglement of it from error.

4. The functions of the mind, in relation to truth as yet unknown, and which it seeks to know, may also be reduced to three, namely, 1. To find the demonstration of the truths known; 2. To find the consequences to be derived from them through their development and application; and, 3. and

lastly, to attain through the senses, by observation and experience, new data on which to base entirely new arguments.

5. Each of these functions of the human mind has its own method, which consists of an assemblage of rules for the guidance of the mind itself in the performance of its work: hence we may distinguish six kinds of method, as we have distinguished six functions of the mind in relation to truth.

6. These are, *the method of exposition*, which teaches how best to impart our knowledge to others; the *polemical method*, which teaches us how to defend truth and repel its assailants; the *critical method*, which teaches how to separate the true from the false. These are the three methods which must govern our mental processes in relation to truths already known. The remaining three are, the *demonstrative method*, which gives the rules for arriving at exact demonstrations; the *inductive*, which teaches how to reach the truths yet unknown, through inductions and conclusions from the known, developing from the knowledge we have ascertained in germ, as it were, the far larger body of that which we do not know; and, finally, the method we shall call the *perceptive-inductive*, which is not satisfied with arriving at new cognitions by inductions and conclusions from previously known data, but which leads us to the discovery of wholly new data through the perception of new phenomena, skilfully produced and made apparent to our senses. These are the three methods which govern the functions of the mind in relation to truths yet unknown. The last alone is the experimental method proper, the Baconian, to which is due the immense progress of physical science in modern times.

[311]

ROUSSEAU, JEAN JACQUES

ROUSSEAU, JEAN JACQUES (1712-1778). Rousseau was the first to diagnose, from secular aspects, the symptoms of the crisis of modern civilization. Both his approach and many of his conclusions have been exposed to criticism. Nevertheless, he gave us an early and powerful expression of a current of thoughts and sentiments that transformed cultural life and that has not yet come to an end in the age of two world wars.

Both modern civilization and the entire history that shaped its features were condemned by Rousseau as deviation from nature. Rousseau asserted that every man has a unique personality, and that all men are equal. But, in his eyes, state and society are the triumph of oppression, men have become unequal because of artificial conventions, and cultural life is degenerating more and more because vital needs of the human heart are neglected. He demanded a radical reform that does not mean return to primitive barbarism, but rather, a restitution of the natural order in which reason and sentiments become harmonized, and in which man meets his fellow man with neither artificial subordination nor any intention of subordinating him, both respecting the general will which is expressed by the majority of citizens.

Rousseau's criticism was determined to a large degree by his sense of justice and his aesthetic sentiments. In this way, he became the precursor of the French Revolution, and caused a literary revolution that started soon after the publication of his principal works. His call "back to nature" was echoed by the masses of oppressed peoples and by individuals who longed for a free development of their faculties. Since Rousseau, sincerity and intensity of feelings and expression, rather than formal perfection, have become the principal criteria of literary and artistic criticism. Rousseau enhanced the effects of his teachings by the charm and vigor of his style and, even more, by the unrestrained exhibition of his inner life, for he was by no means afraid of showing his flaws and vices to the public. His political doctrine emphasizes that the sovereignty belongs to the people. His religious creed is a deism that relies more on feelings than on reason, without excluding rational principles. Rousseau's literary influence remained strong from the times of Goethe and Byron to the days of R. L. Stevenson and D. H. Lawrence. Among the philosophers, his most important disciples, were Kant, Fichte and Hegel and, not the least among them, Karl Marx. In politics, Maximilian Robespierre was Rousseau's most devoted follower. Notwithstanding the excesses of the French Revolution, Rousseau continued to be regarded the apostle of democracy, although it was discovered that some of the aspects of his philosophy favor totalitarian dictatorship.

THE general will is always right and always tends to the public advantage; but it does not follow that the resolutions of the people have always the same rectitude. Men always desire their own good, but do not always discern it; the people are never corrupted, though often deceived, and it is only then that they seem to will what is evil.

There is often a great deal of difference between the will of all and the general will; the latter regards only the common interest, while the former has regard to private interests, and is merely a sum of particular wills; but take away from these same wills the pluses and minuses which cancel one another, and the general will remains as the sum of the differences.

If the people came to a resolution when adequately informed and without any communication among the citizens, the general will would always result from the great number of slight differences, and the resolution would always be good. But when factions, partial associations, are formed to the detriment of the whole society, the will of each of these associations becomes general with reference to its members, and particular with reference to the state; it may then be said that there are no longer as many voters as there are men, but only as many voters as there are associations. The differences become less numerous and yield a less general result. Lastly, when one of these associations becomes so great that it predominates over all the rest, you no longer have as the result a sum of small differences, but a single difference; there is then no longer a general will, and the opinion which prevails is only a particular opinion.

It is important, then, in order to have a clear declaration of the general will, that there should be no partial association in the state, and that every citizen should express his own opinion. Such was the unique and sublime institution of the great Lycurgus. But if there are partial associations, it is necessary to multiply their number and prevent inequality, as Solon, Numa, and Servius did. These are the only proper precautions for insuring that the general will may always be enlightened, and that the people may not be deceived.

*   *   *

If the state or city is nothing but a moral person, the life of which consists in the union of its members, and if the most important of its cares is that of self-preservation, it needs a universal and compulsive force to move and dispose of every part in the manner most expedient for the whole. As nature gives every man an absolute power over all his limbs, the social pact gives the body politic an absolute power over all its members; and it is this same power which when directed by the general will, bears the name of sovereignty.

But besides the public person, we have to consider the private persons who compose it, and whose life and liberty are naturally independent of it. The question, then, is to distinguish clearly between the respective rights of the citizens and of the sovereign, as well as between the duties which the former have to fulfill in their capacity as subjects and the natural rights which they ought to enjoy in their character as men.

It is admitted that whatever part of his power, property, and liberty each one alienates by the social compact is only that part of the whole of which the use is important to the community; but we must also admit that the sovereign alone is judge of what is important.

All the services that a citizen can render to the state he owes to it as soon as the sovereign demands them; but the sovereign, on its part, cannot impose on its subjects any burden which is useless to the community; it cannot even wish to do so, for, by the law of reason, just as by the law of nature, nothing is done without a cause.

The engagements which bind us to the social body are

obligatory only because they are mutual; and their nature is such that in fulfilling them we cannot work for others without also working for ourselves. Why is the general will always right, and why do all invariably desire the prosperity of each, unless it is because there is no one but appropriates to himself this word *each* and thinks of himself in voting on behalf of all? This proves that equality of rights and the notion of justice that it produces are derived from the preference which each gives to himself, and consequently from man's nature; that the general will, to be truly such, should be so in its object as well as in its essence; that it ought to proceed from all in order to be applicable to all; and that it loses its natural rectitude when it tends to some individual and determinate object, because in that case, judging of what is unknown to us, we have no true principle of equity to guide us.

Indeed so soon as a particular fact or right is in question with regard to a point which has not been regulated by an anterior general convention, the matter becomes contentious; it is a process in which the private persons interested are one of the parties and the public the other, but in which I perceive neither the law which must be followed, nor the judge who should decide. It would be ridiculous in such a case to wish to refer the matter for an express decision of the general will, which can be nothing but the decision of one of the parties, and which, consequently, is for the other party only a will that is foreign, partial, and inclined on such an occasion to injustice as well as liable to error. Therefore, just as a particular will cannot represent the general will, the general will in turn changes its nature when it has a particular end, and cannot, as general, decide about either a person or a fact. When the people of Athens, for instance, elected or deposed their chiefs, decreed honors to one, imposed penalties on another, and by multitudes of particular decrees exercised indiscriminately all the functions of government, the people no longer had any general will properly so called; they no longer acted as a sovereign power, but as magistrates. This will appear contrary to common ideas, but I must be allowed time to expound my own.

From this we must understand that what generalizes the will is not so much the number of voices as the common interest which unites them; for, under this system, each necessarily submits to the conditions which he imposes on others —an admirable union of interest and justice, which gives to the deliberations of the community a spirit of equity that seems to disappear in the discussion of any private affair, for want of a common interest to unite and identify the ruling principle of the judge with that of the party.

By whatever path we return to our principle we always arrive at the same conclusion, viz., that the social compact establishes among the citizens such an equality that they all pledge themselves under the same conditions and ought all to enjoy the same rights. Thus, by the nature of the compact, every act of sovereignty, that is, every authentic act of the general will, binds or favors equally all the citizens; so that the sovereign knows only the body of the nation, and distinguishes none of those that compose it.

What, then, is an act of sovereignty properly so called? It is not an agreement between a superior and an inferior, but an agreement of the body with each of its members; a lawful agreement, because it has the social contract as its foundation; equitable, because it is common to all; useful, because it can have no other object than the general welfare; and stable, because it has the public force and the supreme power as a guarantee. So long as the subjects submit only to such conventions, they obey no one, but simply their own will; and to ask how far the respective rights of the sovereign and citizens extend is to ask up to what point the latter can make engagements among themselves, each with all and all with each.

Thus we see that the sovereign power, wholly absolute, wholly sacred, and wholly inviolable as it is, does not, and cannot, pass the limits of general conventions, and that every man can fully dispose of what is left to him of his property and liberty by these conventions; so that the sovereign never has a right to burden one subject more than another, because then the matter becomes particular and his power is no longer competent.

These distinctions once admitted, so untrue is it that in the social contract there is on the part of individuals any real renunciation, that their situation, as a result of this contract, is in reality preferable to what it was before, and that, instead of an alienation, they have only made an advantageous exchange of an uncertain and precarious mode of existence for a better and more assured one, of natural independence for liberty, of the power to injure others for their own safety, and of their strength, which others might overcome, for a right which the social union renders inviolable. Their lives, also, which they have devoted to the state, are continually protected by it; and in exposing their lives for its defense, what do they do but restore what they have received from it? What do they do but what they would do more frequently and with more risk in the state of nature, when, engaging in inevitable struggles, they would defend at the peril of their lives their means of preservation? All have to fight for their country in case of need, it is true; but then no one ever has to fight for himself. Do we not gain, moreover, by incurring, for what insures our safety, a part of the risks that we should have to incur for ourselves individually, as soon as we were deprived of it?

*   *   *

By the social compact we have given existence and life to the body politic; the question now is to endow it with movement and will by legislation. For the original act by which this body is formed and consolidated determines nothing in addition as to what it must do for its own preservation.

What is right and conformable to order is such by the nature of things, and independently of human conventions. All justice comes from God, he alone is the source of it;

but could we receive it direct from so lofty a source, we should need neither government nor laws. Without doubt there is a universal justice emanating from reason alone; but this justice, in order to be admitted among us, should be reciprocal. Regarding things from a human standpoint, the laws of justice are inoperative among men for want of a natural sanction; they only bring good to the wicked and evil to the just when the latter observe them with every one, and no one observes them in return. Conventions and laws, then, are necessary to couple rights with duties and apply justice to its object. In the state of nature, where everything is in common, I owe nothing to those to whom I have promised nothing; I recognize as belonging to others only what is useless to me. This is not the case in the civil state, in which all rights are determined by law.

But then, finally, what is law? So long as men are content to attach to this word only metaphysical ideas, they will continue to argue without being understood; and when they have stated what a law of nature is, they will know no better what a law of the state is.

I have already said that there is no general will with reference to a particular object. In fact, this particular object is either in the state or outside of it. If it is outside the state, a will which is foreign to it is not general in relation to it; and if it is within the state, it forms part of it; then there is formed between the whole and its part a relation which makes of it two separate beings, of which the part is one, and the whole, less this same part, is the other. But the whole less one part is not the whole, and so long as the relation subsists, there is no longer any whole, but two unequal parts; whence it follows that the will of the one is no longer general in relation to the other.

But when the whole people decree concerning the whole people, they consider themselves alone; and if a relation is then constituted, it is between the whole object under one point of view and the whole object under another point of view, without any division at all. Then the matter respecting which they decree is general like the will that decrees. It is this act that I call law.

When I say that the object of the laws is always general, I mean that the law considers collectively, and actions as abstract, never a man as an individual nor a particular action. Thus the law may indeed decree that there shall be privileges, but cannot confer them on any person by name; the law can create several classes of citizens, and even assign the qualifications which shall entitle them to rank in these classes, but it cannot nominate such and such persons to be admitted to them; it can establish a royal government and a hereditary succession, but cannot elect a king or appoint a royal family; in a word, no function which has reference to an individual object appertains to the legislative power.

From this standpoint we see immediately that it is no longer necessary to ask whose office it is to make laws, since they are acts of the general will; nor whether the prince is above the laws, since he is a member of the state; nor whether the law can be unjust, since no one is unjust to himself; nor how we are free and yet subject to the laws, since the laws are only registers of our wills.

We see, further, that since the law combines the universality of the will with the universality of the object, whatever any man prescribes on his own authority is not a law; and whatever the sovereign itself prescribes respecting a particular object is not a law, but a decree, not an act of sovereignty, but of magistracy.

I therefore call any state a republic which is governed by laws, under whatever form of administration it may be; for then only does the public interest predominate and the commonwealth count for something. Every legitimate government is republican; I will explain hereafter what government is.

Laws are properly only the conditions of civil association. The people, being subjected to the laws, should be the authors of them; it concerns only the associates to determine the conditions of association. But how will they be determined? Will it be by a common agreement, by a sudden inspiration? Has a body politic an organ for expressing its will? Who will give it the foresight necessary to frame its acts and publish them at the outset? Or shall it declare them in the hour of need? How would a blind multitude, which often knows not what it wishes because it rarely knows what is good for it, execute of itself an enterprise so great, so difficult, as a system of legislation? Of themselves, the people always desire what is good, but do not always discern it. The general will is always right, but the judgment which guides it is not always enlightened. It must be made to see objects as they are, sometimes as they ought to appear; it must be shown the good path that it is seeking, and guarded from the seduction of private interests; it must be made to observe closely times and places, and to balance the attraction of immediate and palpable advantages against the danger of remote and concealed evils. Individuals see the good which they reject; the public desire the good which they do not see. All alike have need of guides. The former must be compelled to conform their wills to their reason; the people must be taught to know what they require. Then from the public enlightenment results the union of the understanding and the will in the social body; and from that the close cooperation of the parts, and, lastly, the maximum power of the whole. Hence arises the need of a legislator.

[312]

ROYCE, JOSIAH

ROYCE, JOSIAH (1855-1916). Royce was born in Grass Valley, Nevada County, California, a mining town which was about five years older than himself. Living among rough-handed pioneer people, the sensitive, timid boy who lacked physical strength and skill very early became aware of the value of an established social order because his environment was devoid of it. When his sixtieth birthday was celebrated, Royce, reviewing his mental development, expressed his strong feeling that his deepest motives and problems had centered about the idea of a community, although this idea had come only gradually to his clear consciousness. A Platonist vein in his mind caused him to base the idea of human community upon a theory of life and upon a conception of the nature of truth and reality. Idealistic metaphysics was to him the guarantee not only for absolute certainty, but also for a rule over the whole life by right judgment, directed by the sense of absolute truth. Royce's theoretical thinking, however, was always connected with and supported by his experience of religious life. His mother had been his first teacher in philosophy and the Bible his first textbook. Although he could claim to be born nonconformist and to be without connection with "any visible religious body," it was religious problems that drove him to philosophy, and it was religious faith that was regarded by him as the foundation of human solidarity and social loyalty, as the binding element of a community.

While in Royce's *Religious Aspect of Philosophy* (1885) the influence of Hegel is prevalent, Royce later, in *The World and the Individual* (1900-01) came closer to Fichte and Schopenhauer, and shifted his emphasis from thought, which in the earlier work designates the processus of the Absolute, to will, calling himself "a voluntarist and empiricist who yet believes in the Absolute." To Royce, will, as the manifestation of the Absolute, seems fit to reconcile idealist metaphysics and human experience; to corroborate in man the cardinal virtues of courage, industry, loyalty, and solidarity; and above all to unite the religious conception of God with the philosophical idea of the Absolute. While the Absolute had been conceived at first as the universal knower, as the unity of infinite thought, in Royce's later development the God of the idealist is presented as "no merely indifferent onlooker upon this our temporal world of warfare and dust and blood and sin and glory." Absolute reason is not abandoned by Royce but, according to him, does not exclude but rather implies absolute choice, and the divine unity of reason and will implies freedom of the individual which, in accordance with Kant, belongs not to the phenomenal and temporal world but to a higher order of which man is a part.

In his last years, Royce studied the works of Charles Peirce and, in *The Problem of Christianity* (1913), exposed a triple logic of perception, conception, and interpretation. Voluntarism became an integral factor in Royce's theory of knowledge. Knowing is characterized as an act. An idea, to become cognitive, must be part of a judgment or itself a judgment. This change, however, confirms Royce's early conviction that all reality is reality because true judgments can be made about it. The decision as to which judgments are true and which are false is up to the infinite thought of the Absolute, Supreme Being.

For about thirty years, Royce and William James were intimate friends and staunch adversaries. James secured Royce's appointment as professor at Harvard. While criticizing one another, they inevitably also influenced one another, be it by provoking contrasting ideas or by agreeing on certain views. Royce sometimes expressed his sadness about being forced to attack the philosophy of James to whom he felt himself obliged for practically everything he had written. James, whose criticism of Royce's books sometimes could be devastating, once exclaimed, "Two hundred and fifty years from now, Harvard will be known as the place where Josiah Royce once taught."

IMMORTALITY

So far as we live and strive at all, our lives are various, are needed for the whole, and are unique. No one of these lives can be substituted for another. No one of us finite beings can take another's place. And all this is true just because the Universe is one significant whole.

That follows from our general doctrine concerning our unique relation, as various finite expressions taking place within the single whole of the divine life. But now, with this result in mind, let us return again to the finite realms, and descend from our glimpse of the divine life to the dim shadows and to the wilderness of this world, and ask afresh: But *what* is the unique meaning of my life just now? What place do I fill in God's world that nobody else either fills or can fill?

How disheartening in one sense is still the inevitable answer. I state that answer again in all its negative harshness. I reply simply: For myself, I do not now know in any concrete human terms wherein my individuality consists. In my present human form of consciousness I simply cannot tell. If I look to see what I ever did that, for all I now know, some other man might not have done, I am utterly unable to discover the certainly unique deed. When I was a child I learned by imitation as the rest did. I have gone on copying models in my poor way ever since. I never felt a feeling that I knew or could know to be unlike the feelings of other people. I never consciously thought, except after patterns that the world or my fellows set for me. Of myself, I seem in this life to be nothing but a mere meeting-place in this stream of time where a mass of the driftwood from the ages has collected. I only know that I have always tried to be myself and nobody else. This mere aim I indeed have observed, but that is all. As for you, my beloved friend, I loyally believe in your uniqueness; but whenever I try to tell to you wherein it consists, I helplessly describe only a type. That type may be uncommon. But it is not you. For as soon as described, it might have other examples. But you are alone. Yet I never tell what you are. And if your face lights up my world as no other can—well, this feeling too, when viewed as the mere psychologist has to view it, appears to be simply what all the other friends report about their friends. It is an old story, this life of ours. There is nothing new under our sun. Nothing new, that is, for us, as we now feel and think. When we imagine that we have seen or defined uniqueness and novelty, we soon feel a little later the illusion. We live thus, in one sense, so lonesomely here. For we love individuals; we trust in them; we honor and pursue them; we glorify them and hope to know them. But after we have once become keenly critical and worldly wise, we know, if we are sufficiently thoughtful, that we men can never either find them with our eyes, or define them in our minds; and that hopelessness of finding what we most love makes some of us cynical, and turns others of us into lovers of barren abstractions, and renders still others of us slaves to monotonous affairs that have lost for us the true individual meaning and novelty that we had hoped to find in them. Ah, one of the deepest tragedies of this human existence of ours lies in this very loneliness of the awakened critics of life. We seek true individuality and the true individuals. But we find them not. For lo, we mortals see what our poor eyes can see; and they, the true individuals,—they belong not to this world of our merely human sense and thought.

They belong not to this world, in so far as our sense and our thought now show us this world! Ah, therein,—just therein lies the very proof that they even now belong to a higher and to a richer realm than ours. Herein lies the very sign of their true immortality. For they are indeed real, these individuals. We know this, first, because we mean them and seek them. We know this, secondly, because, in this very longing of ours, God too longs; and because the Absolute Life itself, which dwells in our life, and inspires these very longings, possesses the true world, and *is* that world. For the Absolute, as we now know, all life is individual, but is individual as expressing a meaning. Precisely what is unexpressed here, then, in our world of mortal glimpses of truth, precisely what is sought and longed for, but never won in this our human form of consciousness, just that is interpreted, is developed into its true wholeness, is won in its fitting form, and is expressed, in all the rich variety of individual meaning that love here seeks, but cannot find, and is expressed too as a portion, unique, conscious, and individual, of an Absolute Life that even now pulsates in every one of our desires for the ideal and for the individual. We all even now really dwell in this realm of a reality that is not visible to human eyes. We dwell there as individuals. The oneness of the Absolute Will lives in and through all this variety of life and love and longing that now is ours, but cannot live in and through all without working out to the full precisely that individuality of purpose, that will to choose and to love the unique, which is in all of us the deepest expression of the ideal. Just because, then, God is One, all our lives have various and unique places in the harmony of the divine life. And just because God attains and wins and finds this uniqueness, all our lives win in our union with him the individuality which is essential to their true meaning. And just because individuals whose lives have uniqueness of meaning are here only objects of pursuit, the attainment of this very individuality, since it is indeed real, occurs not in our present form of consciousness, but in a life that now we see not, yet in a life whose genuine meaning is continuous with our own human life, however far from our present flickering form of disappointed human consciousness that life of the final individuality may be. Of this our true individual life, our present life is a glimpse, a fragment, a hint, and in its best moments a visible beginning. That this individual life of all of us is not something limited in its temporal expression to the life that now we experience, follows from the very fact that here nothing final or individual is found expressed.

[313]

RUSH, BENJAMIN

RUSH, BENJAMIN (1745-1813). Rush Medical College, now affiliated with the University of Chicago, was so named in honor of Benjamin Rush, one of the most successful physicians of 18th century America, surgeon general in the Revolutionary Army, a signer of the Declaration of Independence, author of the first textbook on chemistry in America, treasurer of the United States Mint, social reformer, and a prolific writer on medicine, social problems, natural sciences and philosophy.

His approach to philosophy was determined by his medical profession, especially his experiences in psychiatry. He was mainly interested in investigating the effects of physical causes on the mind and the effects of psychic changes on the body. His *Inquiry Upon Physical Causes Upon the Moral Faculty* (1786) and *Medical Inquiries and Observations Upon the Diseases of the Mind* (1812) were for a long time considered standard works on psychiatry. Rush energetically advocated human understanding of mentally ill people, and he also advocated human treatment of criminals. He demanded abolition of capital punishment and slavery. However, his philanthropy did not imply any laxity in moral principles. Rush was firmly convinced that science and religion are in harmony, that ethics is founded upon the Christian faith, and he untiringly protested against any materialistic interpretation of the results of his psychological research. It was on religious grounds that Rush became an ardent American patriot, a revolutionary fighter, and a defender of popular government. He was an intimate friend of Thomas Paine who owed the title of his pamphlet *Common Sense* to Rush's suggestion. Rush was no deist but a Christian who was politically closely allied with Paine, together with whom he even challenged the authority of George Washington. His religious and political ideas made Rush a supporter of the advancement of learning and the improvement of public education. He actively participated in the foundation of colleges and elementary schools, always confident that the increase of knowledge would strengthen democracy and religious belief.

ATTRACTION, COMPOSITION AND DECOMPOSITION

ATTRACTION, composition, and decomposition belong to the passions as well as to the matter. Vices of the same species attract each other with the most force—hence the bad consequences of crowding young men (whose propensities are generally the same) under one roof, in our modern plans of education. The effects of composition and decomposition upon vices appear in the meanness of the school boy, being often cured by the prodigality of a military life, and by the precipitation of avarice, which is often produced by ambition and love.

If physical causes influence morals, may they not also influence religious principles and opinions?—I answer in the affirmative; and I have authority, from the records of physic, as well as from my own observations, to declare, that religious melancholy and madness, in all their variety of species, yield with more facility to medicine, than simply to polemical discourses, or to casuistical advice. But this subject is foreign to the business of the present inquiry.

We are led to contemplate with admiration, the curious structure of the human mind. How distinct are the number, and yet how united! How subordinate and yet how coequal are all its faculties! How wonderful is the action of the mind upon the body! Of the body upon the mind!—And of the divine spirit upon both! What a mystery is the mind of man to itself!—O! nature!—Or to speak more properly, —O! thou God of Nature!—In vain do we attempt to scan thy immensity, or to comprehend thy various modes of existence, when a single particle of light issued from thyself, and kindled into intelligence in the bosom of man, thus dazzles and confounds our understandings!

[314]

RUSKIN, JOHN

RUSKIN, JOHN (1819-1900). No understatement can be found in Ruskin's writing which is, as he himself said, as vacillating as his temper, changing from delight into horror, from indignation into enthusiasm. Ruskin was a critic and historian of art, bitterly opposed to the conception of art for art's sake, always considering the artist's work as the test of his moral disposition, acknowledging only those as artists who are recognized as men of a pure heart, and using "sincerity" as the standard of his aesthetic judgment. He limited sincerity to the Gothic style only and upheld it as much on moral as on aesthetical grounds, while he branded the Renaissance, and even the "flamboyant style" of the end of the Gothic period, as moral and artistic decay.

Ruskin was by nature a zealot, even an eccentric. His dislike of modern technics, railroads included, induced him to expensive efforts to become independent of modern means of transportation. Criticism of art was for him a solemn duty, but his moralist aesthetics did not allow him to confine his views to the realm of the arts. He was sensitive to injustice and misery. When, in Venice, he read in the newspaper that a seamstress in London had died of starvation, he became incapable of enjoying his beloved pictures. Ruskin, therefore, by 1860, turned to political economy, and proceeded to regard economic justice, moral and artistic sincerity as one and inseparable. He complained of the substitution of factory work for handicraft, and protested violently against reckless competition. Above all, Ruskin indignantly fought any evaluation of the human individual which identified wealth with worth. Ruskin was one of the first to deny the "economic man."

"In the height of black anger," as Ruskin said, he wrote the first volume of his *Modern Painters* (1842-60) in which he excepted modern landscape painting from his general condemnation of his own time. Another deviation from his general attitude was his defense of British colonial expansion. As a professor at Oxford, he used his lectures on art for converting his audience to imperialism. Among the undergraduates who listened to Ruskin were Cecil Rhodes and Alfred Milner, bound to enlarge the British empire.

TRUE BOOKS

THE good book of the hour, then,—I do not speak of the bad ones,—is simply the useful or pleasant talk of some person whom you cannot otherwise converse with, printed for you. Very useful often, telling you what you need to know; very pleasant often, as a sensible friend's present talk would be. These bright accounts of travels; good-humoured and witty discussions of question; lively or pathetic story-telling in the form of novel; firm fact-telling, by the real agents concerned in the events of passing history;—all these books of the hour, multiplying among us as education becomes more general, are a peculiar possession of the present age; we ought to be entirely thankful for them, and entirely ashamed of ourselves if we make no good use of them. But we make the worst possible use if we allow them to usurp the place of true books; for, strictly speaking, they are not books at all, but merely letters or newspapers in good print. Our friend's letter may be delightful, or necessary, to-day; whether worth keeping or not, is to be considered. The newspaper may be entirely proper at breakfast time, but assuredly it is not reading for all day. So, though bound up in a volume, the long letter which gives you so pleasant an account of the inns, and roads, and weather, last year at such a place, or which tells you that amusing story, or gives you the real circumstances of such and such events, however valuable for occasional reference, may not be, in the real sense of the word, a 'book' at all, nor, in the real sense, to be read. A book is essentially not a talking thing, but a written thing; and written, not with a view of mere communication, but of permanence. The book of talk is printed only because its author cannot speak to thousands of people at once; if he could, he would—the volume is mere multiplication of his voice. You cannot talk to your friend in India; if you could, you would; you write instead; that is mere conveyance of voice. But a book is written, not to multiply the voice merely, not to carry it merely, but to perpetuate it. The author has something to say which he perceives to be true and useful, or helpfully beautiful. So far as he knows, no one has yet said it; so far as he knows, no one else can say it. He is bound to say it, clearly and melodiously if he may; clearly at all events. In the sum of his life he finds this to be the thing, or group of things, manifest to him;— this, the piece of true knowledge, or sight which his share of sunshine and earth has permitted him to seize. He would fain set it down forever; engrave it on rock, if he could; saying, "This is the best of me; for the rest, I ate, and drank, and slept, loved, and hated, like another; my life was as the vapor, and is not; but this I saw and knew; this, if anything of mine, is worth your memory." That is his "writing"; it is, in his small human way, and with whatever degree of true inspiration is in him, his inscription, or scripture. That is a "Book."

MAN'S BEST WISDOM

VERY ready we are to say of a book, "How good this is— that's exactly what I think!" But the right feeling is, "How strange that is! I never thought of that before, and yet I see it is true; or if I do not now, I hope I shall some day." But whether thus submissively or not, at least be sure that you go to the author to get at his meaning, not to find yours. Judge it afterwards if you think yourself qualified to do so; but ascertain it first. And be sure, also, if the author is worth anything, that you will not get at his meaning all at once;—nay, that at his whole meaning you will not for a long time arrive in any wise. Not that he does not say what he means, and in strong words too; but he cannot say it all;

and what is more strange, will not, but in a hidden way and in parables, in order that he may be sure you want it. I cannot quite see the reason of this, nor analyze that cruel reticence in the breasts of wise men which makes them always hide their deeper thought. They do not give it you by way of help, but of reward; and will make themselves sure that you deserve it before they allow you to reach it. But it is the same with the physical type of wisdom, gold. There seems, to you and me, no reason why the electric forces of the earth should not carry whatever there is of gold within it at once to the mountain tops, so that kings and people might know that all the gold they could get was there; and without any trouble of digging, or anxiety, or chance, or waste of time, cut it away, and coin as much as they needed. But Nature does not manage it so. She puts it in little fissures in the earth, nobody knows where; you may dig long and find none; you must dig painfully to find any.

And it is just the same with men's best wisdom. When you come to a good book, you must ask yourself, "Am I inclined to work as an Australian miner would? Are my pickaxes and shovels in good order, and am I in good trim myself, my sleeves well up to the elbow, and my breath good, and my temper?" And, keeping the figure a little longer, even at cost of tiresomeness, for it is a thoroughly useful one, the metal you are in search of being the author's mind or meaning, his words are as the rock which you have to crush and smelt in order to get at it. And your pickaxes are your own care, wit, and learning; your smelting furnace is your own thoughtful soul. Do not hope to get at any good author's meaning without those tools and that fire; often you will need sharpest, finest chiselling, and patientest fusing, before you can gather one grain of the metal.

[315]

1025

RUSSELL, BERTRAND

RUSSELL, BERTRAND (1872-   ). As late as in 1940, the appointment of Bertrand Russell as professor of philosophy at the College
of the City of New York has roused the fury of bigots of all de-
nominations. It was denounced as "the establishment of a chair of
indecency" and withdrawn by the Board of Education after a trial
had ended with Russell's condemnation as "immoral" and a danger
for the youth of the city.

The victim of this persecution has been accustomed to making
sacrifices for his convictions. During World War I he had been
imprisoned because of his radical pacifism. He had also been accustomed to having his opinions explained by radical leftists as
being determined by his connection with the British aristocracy.
His grandfather, Lord John Russell, who had been Prime Minister
and Foreign Secretary, had tried to defend European solidarity
against Bismarck's national egoism, and had brought about the
repeal of the Test and Corporation Act which barred from public
office anyone not belonging to the established Church of England.

Russell is regarded as the most controversial figure of modern
Anglo-Saxon philosophy, even by those who recognize him as one
of the greatest thinkers of the twentieth century and who agree
with Albert Einstein who has confessed that he owes "innumerable
happiness to the reading of Russell's works." Russell's mind is
uncompromising, not afraid of running risks, yet always ready to
change and to admit errors. He always has maintained the independence of his thought and judgment although he underwent many
influences. Russell is a prolific writer who attributes the clarity and
fluency of his style to his absence from the influence of public
school education. Conspicuous qualities of his books are the firm
direction of the course of ideas, his ability to continue or check
a discussion according to his principal intention, and particularly
his easy humor and his devastating irony.

Russell has taken an outstanding part in the foundation of
modern mathematical logic. Together with Alfred North Whitehead he has written *Principia Mathematica* (1910-13), one of the
most comprehensive systems of mathematics. At first, Russell regarded mathematics as the ideal of philosophy. Then, abandoning
Platonism, he thought of mathematics as an instrument of science,
and finally declared that logic is not a part of philosophy but of
a general theory of science.

To Russell, philosophy is a conception of life and the world which is the product of two factors. The one consists of inherited religious and ethical concepts, the other of investigations which may be called scientific. Philosophy is regarded as something intermediate between theology and science. Like theology it is concerned with speculations on matters concerning which knowledge has been unascertainable. Like science it appeals to human reason rather than to authority. Russell holds that all human knowledge remains uncertain, inexact and partial, and that scepticism, while logically faultless, is psychologically impossible. To obtain some results which may be useful for humanity, philosophy should take its problems from natural sciences, not from theology or ethics.

At least in its broad outline, scientific knowledge is to be accepted. But, against traditional concepts, Russell maintains that knowledge is an intimate, almost mystical contact between subject and object by perception. Although perception is far more complicated than is generally supposed, common-sense realism comes closer to truth than idealism. Subjectivism is justified to ask how knowledge of the world is obtained but not to say what sort of world exists in which we live. Kant's claim to have effected a "Copernican revolution" is refuted by Russell who declares that Kant rather achieved a "Ptolemaic counter-revolution." Knowledge is characterized as a subclass of true belief, but not every true belief is to be recognized as knowledge. In *Human Knowledge* (1948) Russell deals with the problem of the relation between individual experience and the general body of scientific knowledge, and arrives at the result that science cannot be wholly interpreted in terms of experience. He demands that the description of the world be kept free from influences derived from the nature of human knowledge, and declares that "cosmically and causally, knowledge is an unimportant feature of the universe." Like Whitehead, he holds that the distinction between mind and body is a dubious one. It will be better to speak of organism, leaving the division of its activities between the mind and the body undetermined. What is true or false is a state of organism. But it is true or false in general, in virtue of occurrences outside the organism.

THE LIMITS OF PHILOSOPHICAL KNOWLEDGE

MOST philosophers—or, at any rate, very many—profess to be able to prove, by *a priori* metaphysical reasoning, such things as the fundamental dogmas of religion, the essential rationality of the universe, the illusoriness of matter, the unreality of all evil, and so on. There can be no doubt that the hope of finding reason to believe such theses as these has been the chief inspiration of many life-long students of philosophy. This hope, I believe, is vain. It would seem that knowledge concerning the universe as a whole is not to be obtained by metaphysics, and that the proposed proofs that, in virtue of the laws of logic, such and such things *must* exist and such and such others cannot, are not capable of surviving a critical scrutiny. . . . We shall briefly consider the kind of way in which such reasoning is attempted, with a view to discovering whether we can hope that it may be valid.

The great representative, in modern times, of the kind of view which we wish to examine, was Hegel (1770-1831). Hegel's philosophy is very difficult, and commentators differ as to the true interpretation of it. According to the interpretation I shall adopt, which is that of many, if not most, of the commentators, and has the merit of giving an interesting and important type of philosophy, his main thesis is that everything short of the Whole is obviously fragmentary, and obviously incapable of existing without the complement supplied by the rest of the world. Just as a comparative anatomist, from a single bone, sees what kind of animal the whole must have been, so the metaphysician, according to Hegel, sees from any one piece of reality, what the whole of reality must be—at least in its large outlines. Every apparently separate piece of reality has, as it were, hooks which grapple it to the next piece; the next piece, in turn, has fresh hooks, and so on, until the whole universe is reconstructed. This essential incompleteness appears, according to Hegel, equally in the world of thought and in the world of things. In the world of thought, if we take any idea which is abstract or incomplete, we find, on examination, that if we forget its incompleteness, we become involved in contradictions; these contradictions turn the idea in question into its opposite, or antithesis; and in order to escape, we have to find a new, less incomplete idea, which is the synthesis of our original idea and its antithesis. This new idea we started with, will be found, nevertheless, to be still not wholly complete, but to pass into its antithesis, with which it must be combined in a new synthesis. In this way Hegel advances until he reaches the "Absolute Idea," which, according to him, has no incompleteness, no opposite, and no need of further development. The Absolute Idea, therefore, is adequate to describe Absolute Reality; but all lower ideas only describe reality as it appears to a partial view, not as it is to one who simultaneously surveys the Whole. Thus Hegel reaches the conclusion that Absolute Reality forms one single harmonious system, not in space or time, not in any degree evil, wholly rational, and wholly spiritual. Any appearance to the contrary, in the world we know, can be proved logically—so he believes—to be entirely due to our fragmentary piecemeal view of the universe. If we saw the universe whole, as we may suppose God sees it, space and time and matter and evil and all striving and struggling would disappear, and we should see instead an eternal perfect unchanging spiritual unity.

In this conception, there is undeniably something sublime, something to which we could wish to yield assent. Nevertheless, when the arguments in support of it are carefully examined, they appear to involve much confusion and many unwarrantable assumptions. The fundamental tenet upon which the system is built up is that what is incomplete must be not self-subsistent, but must need the support of other things before it can exist. It is held that whatever has relations to things outside itself must contain some reference to those outside things in its own *nature,* and could not, therefore, be what it is if those outside things did not exist. A man's nature, for example, is constituted by his memories and the rest of his knowledge, by his loves and hatreds, and so on; thus, but for the objects which he knows or loves or hates, he could not be what he is. He is essentially and obviously a fragment: taken as the sum-total of reality he would be self-contradictory.

This whole point of view, however, turns upon the notion of the "nature" of a thing, which seems to mean "all the truths about the thing." It is of course the case that a truth which connects one thing with another thing could not subsist if the other thing did not subsist. But a truth about a thing is not part of the thing itself, although it must, according to the above usage, be part of the "nature" of the thing. If we mean by a thing's "nature" all the truths about the thing, then plainly we cannot know a thing's "nature" unless we know all the thing's relations to all the other things in the universe. But if the word "nature" is used in this sense, we shall have to hold that the thing may be known when its "nature" is not known, or at any rate is not known completely. There is a confusion, when this use of the word "nature" is employed, between knowledge of things and knowledge of truths. We may have knowledge of a thing by acquaintance even if we know very few propositions about it—theoretically we need not know any propositions about it. Thus, acquaintance with a thing does not involve knowledge of its "nature" in the above sense. And although acquaintance with a thing is involved in our knowing any one proposition about a thing, knowledge of its "nature," in the above sense, is not involved. Hence, (1) acquaintance with a thing does not logically involve a knowledge of its relations, and (2) a knowledge of some of its relations does not involve a knowledge of all of its relations nor a knowledge of its "nature" in the above sense. I may be acquainted, for example, with my toothache, and this knowledge may be as complete as knowledge by acquaintance ever can be, without knowing all that the dentist (who is not acquainted with it) can tell me about its cause, and without therefore knowing its "nature" in the above sense. Thus the fact that a thing has relations does not prove that its relations are logically necessary. That is to say, from the mere fact that it is the thing it is we cannot deduce that it must have the various relations which in fact it has. This only *seems* to follow because we know it already.

It follows that we cannot prove that the universe as a

whole forms a single harmonious system such as Hegel believes that it forms. And if we cannot prove this, we also cannot prove the unreality of space and time and matter and evil, for this is deduced by Hegel from the fragmentary and relational character of these things. Thus we are left to the piecemeal investigation of the world, and are unable to know the characters of those parts of the universe that are remote from our experience. This result, disappointing as it is to those whose hopes have been raised by the systems of philosophers, is in harmony with the inductive and scientific temper of our age, and is borne out by the whole examination of human knowledge which has occupied our previous chapters.

Most of the great ambitious attempts of metaphysicians have proceeded by the attempt to prove that such and such apparent features of the actual world were self-contradictory, and therefore could not be real. The whole tendency of modern thought, however, is more and more in the direction of showing that the supposed contradictions were illusory, and that very little can be proved *a priori* from considerations of what *must* be. A good illustration of this is afforded by space and time. Space and time appear to be infinite in extent, and infinitely divisible. If we travel along a straight line in either direction, it is difficult to believe that we shall finally reach a last point, beyond which there is nothing, not even empty space. Similarly, if in imagination we travel backwards or forwards in time, it is difficult to believe that we shall reach a first or last time, with not even empty time beyond it. Thus space and time appear to be infinite in extent.

Again, if we take any two points on a line, it seems evident that there must be other points between them, however small the distance between them may be: every distance can be halved, and the halves can be halved again, and so on *ad infinitum*. In time, similarly, however little time may elapse between two moments, it seems evident that there will be other moments between them. Thus space and time appear to be infinitely divisible. But as against these apparent facts—infinite extent and infinite divisibility—philosophers have advanced arguments tending to show that there could be no infinite collections of things, and that therefore the number of points in space, or of instants in time, must be finite. Thus a contradiction emerged between the apparent nature of space and time and the supposed impossibility of infinite collections.

Kant, who first emphasized this contradiction, deduced the impossibility of space and time, which he declared to be merely subjective; and since his time very many philosophers have believed that space and time are mere appearance, not characteristic of the world as it really is. Now, however, owing to the labors of the mathematicians, notably Georg Cantor, it has appeared that the impossibility of infinite collections was a mistake. They are not in fact self-contradictory, but only contradictory of certain rather obstinate mental prejudices. Hence the reasons for regarding space and time as unreal have become inoperative, and one of the great sources of metaphysical constructions is dried up.

The mathematicians, however, have not been content with showing that space as it is commonly supposed to be is possible; they have shown also that many other forms of space are equally possible, so far as logic can show. Some of Euclid's axioms, which appear to common sense to be necessary, and were formerly supposed to be necessary by philosophers, are now known to derive their appearance of necessity from our mere familiarity with actual space, and not from any *a priori* logical foundation. By imagining worlds in which these axioms are false, the mathematicians have used logic to loosen the prejudices of common sense, and to show the possibility of spaces differing—some more, some less— from that in which we live. And some of these spaces differ so little from Euclidean space, where distances such as we can measure are concerned, that it is impossible to discover by observation whether our actual space is strictly

Euclidean or of one of these other kinds. Thus the position is completely reversed. Formerly it appeared that experience left only one kind of space to logic, and logic showed this one kind to be impossible. Now, logic presents many kinds of space as possible apart from experience, and experience only partially decides between them. Thus, while our knowledge of what is has become less than it was formerly supposed to be, our knowledge of what may be is enormously increased. Instead of being shut in within narrow walls, of which every nook and cranny could be explored, we find ourselves in an open world of free possibilities, where much remains unknown because there is so much to know.

What has happened in the case of space and time has happened, to some extent, in other directions as well. The attempt to prescribe to the universe by means of *a priori* principles has broken down; logic, instead of being, as formerly, the bar to possibilities, has become the great liberator of the imagination, presenting innumerable alternatives which are closed to unreflective common sense, and leaving to experience the task of deciding, where decision is possible, between the many worlds which logic offers for our choice. Thus knowledge as to what exists becomes limited to what we can learn from experience—not to what we can actually experience, for, as we have seen, there is much knowledge by description concerning things of which we have no direct experience. But in all cases of knowledge by description, we need some connection of universals, enabling us, from such and such a datum, to infer an object of a certain sort as implied by our datum. Thus in regard to physical objects, for example, the principle that sense data are signs of physical objects is itself a connection of universals; and it is only in virtue of this principle that experience enables us to acquire knowledge concerning physical objects. The same applies to the law of causality, or, to descend to what is less general, to such principles as the law of gravitation.

Principles such as the law of gravitation are proved, or rather are rendered highly probable, by a combination of experience with some wholly *a priori* principle, such as the principle of induction. Thus our intuitive knowledge, which is the source of all our other knowledge of truths, is of two sorts: pure empirical knowledge, which tells us of the existence and some of the properties of particular things with which we are acquainted, and pure *a priori* knowledge, which gives us connections between universals, and enables us to draw inferences from the particular facts given in empirical knowledge. Our derivative knowledge always depends upon some pure *a priori* knowledge and usually also depends upon some pure empirical knowledge.

Philosophical knowledge, if what has been said above is true, does not differ essentially from scientific knowledge; there is no special source of wisdom which is open to philosophy but not to science, and the results obtained by philosophy are not radically different from those obtained from science. The essential characteristic of philosophy, which makes it a study distinct from science, is *criticism*. It examines critically the principles employed in science and in daily life; it searches out any inconsistencies there may be in these principles, and it only accepts them when, as the result of a critical inquiry, no reason for rejecting them has appeared. If, as many philosophers have believed, the principles underlying the sciences were capable, when disengaged from irrelevant detail, of giving us knowledge concerning the universe as a whole, such knowledge would have the same claim on our belief as scientific knowledge has; but our inquiry has not revealed any such knowledge, and therefore, as regards the special doctrines of the bolder metaphysicians, has had a mainly negative result. But as regards what would be commonly accepted as knowledge, our result is in the main positive: we have seldom found reason to reject such knowledge as the result of our criticism, and we have seen no reason to suppose man incapable of the kind of knowledge which he is generally believed to possess.

When, however, we speak of philosophy as a *criticism* of knowledge, it is necessary to impose a certain limitation.

If we adopt the attitude of the complete sceptic, placing ourselves wholly outside all knowledge, and asking, from this outside position, to be compelled to return within the circle of knowledge, we are demanding what is impossible, and our scepticism can never be refuted. For all refutation must begin with some piece of knowledge which the disputants share; from blank doubt, no argument can begin. Hence the criticism of knowledge which philosophy employs must not be of this destructive kind, if any result is to be achieved. Against this absolute scepticism, no *logical* argument can be advanced. But it is not difficult to see that scepticism of this kind is unreasonable. Descartes' "methodical doubt," with which modern philosophy began, is not of this kind, but is rather the kind of criticism which we are asserting to be the essence of philosophy. His "methodical doubt" consisted in doubting whatever seemed doubtful; in pausing, with each apparent piece of knowledge, to ask himself whether, on reflection, he could feel certain that he really knew it. This is the kind of criticism which constitutes philosophy. Some knowledge, such as knowledge of the existence of our sense data, appears quite indubitable, however calmly and thoroughly we reflect upon it. In regard to such knowledge, philosophical criticism does not require that we should abstain from belief. But there are beliefs— such, for example, as the belief that physical objects exactly resemble our sense data—which are entertained until we begin to reflect, but are found to melt away when subjected to a close inquiry. Such beliefs philosophy will bid us reject, unless some new line of argument is found to support them. But to reject the beliefs which do not appear open to any objections, however closely we examine them, is not reasonable, and is not what philosophy advocates.

The criticism aimed at, in a word, is not that which, without reason, determines to reject, but that which considers each piece of apparent knowledge on its merits, and retains whatever still appears to be knowledge when this consideration is completed. That some risk of error remains must be admitted, since human beings are fallible. Philosophy may claim justly that it diminishes the risk of error, and that in some cases it renders the risk so small as to be practically negligible. To do more than this is not possible in a world where mistakes must occur; and more than this no prudent advocate of philosophy would claim to have performed.

[316]

S

S A A D I A

SAADIA (892-942). Until Saadia began to formulate his ideas, the spiritual atmosphere of his times had been, as one of his contemporaries complained, as follows:

> Muslims, Jews, Christians and Magicians, they all are walking in error and darkness. There are two kinds of people left in the world: the one group is intelligent but lacking in faith, the other has faith but is lacking in intelligence.

And so it became Saadia's purpose to teach not only his Jewish co-religionists but also Islamic and Christian thinkers that faith is not opposed to reason but only to pseudo-reason.

Born in Egypt, and educated as well in all branches of Arabian culture as in Biblical and Talmudic scholarship, Saadia went to Palestine, and then to Babylonia. There he accomplished his great work which became the foundation of Jewish philosophy and science. Acquainted with Greek philosophy, the various formulations of the Christian dogma, the doctrines of the Manicheans, of Zoroaster and even with the philosophy of India, Saadia developed the idea that Judaism is compatible with all truth, whatever its source. In his explanation of the nature of religion, the character of man and the way of conceiving God, Saadia criticized Plato's cosmology and refuted gnostic doctrines. He tried to reconcile the idea of freedom of man with that of the all-embracing foreknowledge of God.

Saadia was also a learned mathematician and a trained philologist, and he composed the first Hebrew dictionary as well as the first Jewish prayer-book.

ON ABEL'S DEATH AND ON THE PUNISHMENT OF THE WICKED ONES

WHEN his sons brought offerings God favored the younger, because he brought of the best of his fatlings to the ruling

King: what was vile and refuse, that the elder brought to the sanctuary. So He let him know that he was despised; but he did not repent, he hated.

He struck his brother, and God inquired of him so that he might confess, but in his reply he feigned [innocence] with cunning and craft. Therefore hath God wreaked His vengeance on him with a ruling anger; for He avengeth the blood of His servants and redeemeth their soul.

I shall reply to thy question with a strong reply. Thou sayest: "Why hath He not guarded him [Abel] so that his posterity should not have been destroyed?" Thus shouldst thou have said if there were but one world and one habitation, but since there is a second world, He chose everything with a view for reproof.

Let them not rejoice who exercise oppression here [in this world], for at the time when their foot shall slide there [in the next world] He will choose to pay with vengeance; and let him not mourn who is oppressed and crushed and circumvented, for God can change it into good, and he shall not return empty.

Because the oppressor will not cease from putting forth his hand, and the one who suffereth violence will not always rescue his possessions, therefore there is a day when every-one will be measured by His law, both he that serveth God and he that serveth Him not.

Thou hast asked further concerning the kinds of suffering; hunger and sickness, fear and desolation and destruction, and heat and cold, why they are not kept from men. All these are but one question and thou hast multiplied words.

Know thou and understand, that God chastiseth His creatures for their good, that they may know the pain of chastisement and the bitterness thereof; He delivereth them to it that they may forbear to do wrong. For they would not know [what punishment was] if He had withheld [suffering] from them.

Thou hast expressed wonder and amazement and hast

asked a difficult question, "Why doth man not live forever so that he shall not go down to Sheol?" Would that from the beginning he were created to be in the world that is to come for redemption, but thou desirest him to remain in siege and under a curse.

Though He doth all these things, there are many who yet rebel, and though He frighteneth them with calamities, there are [many] who are yet faithless to His decree. How much more if they had no cause to fear. They would then all with one accord not serve Him.

It is wise to make thy image live forever, or to save it from distress and anguish and trembling? What knowledge, dost thou judge, will save thee from falling [into ruin] that thou hast spoken rebellion against Him who dwelleth forever?

For the scorners judgments and stripes are prepared, Topheth is of old prepared for them in wrath. He preserved it against the time of trouble, against the day of battle and war. Thou also like one of them wilt share the anger of the God of vengeance.

[317]

SAINT-SIMON, CLAUDE HENRI, COMTE DE

SAINT-SIMON, CLAUDE HENRI, COMTE DE (1760-1825). In Saint-Simon's personality, the mind of a true philosopher was coupled with that of a smart businessman, that of a sincere philanthropist with that of an adventurous schemer. He fought at Yorktown for American independence. He was the first to advocate the building of the canals of Suez and Panama. More than a hundred years before the Young Plan, he demanded the foundation of an international bank, and his most faithful disciples became founders of joint-stock societies and constructors of canals and railroads, which, as Saint-Simon taught them, are necessary for the organization of human welfare and the realization of the ideals of human solidarity. Saint-Simon was the first to denounce "exploitation of men by their fellow men," and to prognosticate the increasing concentration of capital and industry. But he was also one of those "wicked speculators" who were branded by Robes-

1039

pierre, and he narrowly escaped execution. During the French Revolution he amassed a large fortune, but he died in poverty.

Saint-Simon's dominant idea was that the social system must be an application of the philosophical system, and that the function of philosophy is a prevalently social one. After ten years of studies devoted to physics, astronomy and chemistry, he turned to the study of human society and pronounced as its result that philosophical changes cause social changes, and that philosophy, as he conceived of it, must found a new society, a new religion, and a new evaluation of men. He especially emphasized that in modern times the industrial worker had become of far greater importance than the nobleman, the soldier and the priest, and, consequently, that he must occupy a higher social position than the former dignitaries. To industrial workers, scholars, and bankers he entrusted the organization of his new social system, which may be characterized as a kind of technocratic socialism. But the form of government was, in Saint-Simon's opinion, of lesser importance than the problem of administration. Therefore, he was not radically opposed to monarchism. After the publication of his works on the *Reorganization of Europe* (1814), *The Industrial System* and *Catechism of Industrials* (1821-1824), he wrote *The New Christianity* in the year of his death, 1825, by which he intended to substitute a secular religion of pantheistic and sensualistic color for the Christian faith. A small circle of enthusiastic disciples revered Saint-Simon who lived in obscurity and poverty as the founder of the religion of the future. After his death he became famous the world over, due to the propagandistic ardor of his pupils. He particularly influenced Goethe, Carlyle, Auguste Comte and Karl Marx.

APPEAL TO THE PRINCES TO BRING ABOUT SOCIAL JUSTICE

PRINCES, What is, in the eyes of God and Christians, the nature and character of the power which you exercise? What is the basis of the system of social organization which you seek to establish? What measures have you taken to ameliorate the moral and physical existence of the poor classes? You call yourselves Christians and still you found your power upon physical force. You are still only the successors of Caesar, and you forget that the true Christians set as the ultimate end of their work the complete annihilation of the power of the sword, the power of Caesar, which by its nature is essentially provisional. And this is the power which you have undertaken to form as the basis of social organization! According to you, the initiative to perform all the general reforms which the progress of enlightenment has been calling for is left to this power exclusively. In order to support this monstrous system you keep two million people under arms. All the tribunals had to adopt your principle and you have made the Catholic, Protestant and Greek clergy profess loudly the heresy that Caesar's power is the regulating power of the Christian society.

While reminding the nations of the Christian religion by the symbol of your union, while making them enjoy a peace which, for them, is the first of all goods, you have nevertheless not aroused their gratitude toward yourselves. Your personal interest dominates too much in the combinations which you present as being of a general interest. The supreme European power which lies in your hands is far from being a Christian power, as it should have become. Ever since you have acted, you have displayed the character and the insignia of physical force, of anti-Christian force.

All the measures of whatever importance which you have taken since you united one with another in the Holy Alliance, all these measures tend toward worsening the lot of the poor classes, not only for this actual generation, but even for the generations to come. You have raised the taxes, you raise them every year in order to cover the increase of expenses brought about by your armies of soldiers and by the luxury of your courts. The class of your subjects to which you grant a special protection is the aristocracy, a class which, like you, founds its rights upon the sword. However, your blamable conduct seems excusable from several angles: that which has led you into error is the approval received by your efforts to smash the power of the modern Caesar. While fighting him, you have acted in a very Christian manner, but so it was only because in his hands the authority of Caesar, which Napoleon has conquered, had much more force than in yours where it has come only by heritage. Your conduct has also another excuse: It should have been the task of the clergymen to stop you at the edge of the abyss; instead they precipitated themselves into it, together with you.

[318]

SANTAYANA, GEORGE

SANTAYANA, GEORGE (1863-1952). Santayana was the son of a Spanish father and an American mother. He hints at his own Spanish strain when he describes the southern mind as long-indoctrinated, disillusioned, distinct, sceptical, malicious, yet in its reflective phase detached and contemplative, able to despise all entanglements, to dominate will and to look truth in the eye without blinking. He thinks of the American mind as being more ingenuous than wise. American is the texture, Spanish is the structure of Santayana's mind. America impressed his spiritual outlook. But, successful as he was as an influential professor at Harvard, he never felt himself at ease there. The Spanish tradition corresponded more by far to his inclinations, and, although he did not care about authorities, he highly esteemed the soil of history, tradition or human institutions without which thought and imagination became trivial.

When Santayana resolved to spend the rest of his life in an Italian convent as guest, he did not give up his philosophical conviction, one of whose striking features was unrelenting materialism. He was "attached to Catholicism" but "entirely divorced from faith," and protested that his scepticism had rather confirmed than dispelled this attachment. He continued to hold that "most conventional ideals, the religious ones included, are not adequate to the actual nature and capacities of men who accept them." He did not acknowledge any Christian dogma but liked the Christian religion for aesthetic and historical reasons. Nevertheless he was far from holding romanticist predilections, and even farther from having any adoration of the tragic sense of living.

What was true for Santayana's attachment to Catholicism was also true for his relation to Platonism. Santayana thought in terms of two realms of being, that of existence and that of essences.

Concerning existence, he professed materialism. His realm of essences was of Platonist origin. But Santayana declined to regard essences as truer realities than existent things, or to found the realm of essences upon divine activity or to oppose essence to accident and modification.

According to Santayana, essences neither necessitate nor explain thoughts, nor do they determine the ground of concrete existence. The seat and principle of genesis is matter, not essence, which, for its part, is explanatory of intuition, assures the form of apperception, elucidates existence, and helps the mind to grasp and to retain the character and identity of the changing existences. However, while the evolution of existing things changes their character at every moment, the essences, representing every moment of this change, remain in their logical identity. An essence is anything definite capable of appearing and being thought of: it is senseless to believe in it because belief involves the assumption of real existence. Intuition of essence is no knowledge at all because illusion and error are also intuitions. Knowledge is a compound of instinctive conviction and expectation, animal faith and intuition of essence. It is essence by means of which the pursuit, attention and feelings which contribute to knowledge are transcribed in aesthetic, moral or verbal terms into consciousness. Matter is in flux; mind, conceived by Santayana as "simply sensibility in bodies," is existentially carried along the movement of that flux but is capable of arresting some datum, different from what the stimulated sensibility can articulate. This datum is essence in whose language alone mind can express its experiences.

Disillusioned, Santayana, although convinced of the truth of his work, did not except his philosophy from his general judgment of philosophical systems. To him they were all personal, temperamental, even premature. They were human heresies. The orthodoxy around which these heresies play, is no private or closed body of doctrine. It is "the current imagination and good sense of mankind," a body of beliefs and evaluations far too chaotic, subject to errors and too conventional to satisfy a reflective mind, but capable of correcting its errors. Hence the need for personal philosophical thought, hence the impossibility to attain the goal to shape a philosophy satisfying mankind. As for Santayana he acquiesced in this insight, and was fond of stating divergencies between his mind and that of his critics.

ART IN INSTINCT AND EXPERIENCE

Man Affects His Environment, Sometimes to Good Purpose.

MAN exists amid a universal ferment of being, and not only needs plasticity in his habits and pursuits but finds plasticity also in the surrounding world. Life is an equilibrium which is maintained now by accepting modification and now by imposing it. Since the organ for all activity is a body in mechanical relation to other material objects, objects which the creature's instincts often compel him to appropriate or transform, changes in his habits and pursuits leave their mark on whatever he touches. His habitat must needs bear many a trace of his presence, from which intelligent observers might infer something about his life and action. These vestiges of action are for the most part imprinted unconsciously and aimlessly on the world. They are in themselves generally useless, like footprints; and yet almost any sign of man's passage might, under certain conditions, interest a man. A footprint could fill Robinson Crusoe with emotion, the devastation wrought by an army's march might prove many things to a historian, and even the disorder in which a room is casually left may express very vividly the owner's ways and character.

Sometimes, however, man's traces are traces of useful action which has so changed natural objects as to make them congenial to his mind. Instead of a footprint we might find an arrow; instead of a disordered room, a well-planted orchard—things which would not only have betrayed the agent's habits, but would have served and expressed his intent. Such propitious forms given by man to matter are no less instrumental in the life of reason than are propitious forms assumed by man's own habit or fancy. Any operation which thus humanizes and rationalizes objects is called art.

Art Is Plastic Instinct Conscious of Its Aim.

All art has an instinctive source and a material embodiment. If the birds in building nests felt the utility of what

1044

they do, they would be practicing an art; and for the instinct to be called rational it would even suffice that their traditional purpose and method should became conscious occasionally. Thus weaving is an art, although the weaver may not be at every moment conscious of its purpose, but may be carried along, like any other workman, by the routine of his art; and language is a rational product, not because it always has a use or meaning, but because it is sometimes felt to have one. Arts are no less automatic than instincts, and usually, as Aristotle observed, less thoroughly purposive; for instincts, being transmitted by inheritance and imbedded in congenital structure, have to be economically and deeply organized. If they go far wrong they constitute a burden impossible to throw off and impossible to bear. The man harassed by inordinate instincts perishes through want, vice, disease, or madness. Arts, on the contrary, being transmitted only by imitation and teaching, hover more lightly over life. If ill-adjusted they make less havoc and cause less drain. The more superficial they are and the more detached from practical habits, the more extravagant and meaningless they can dare to become so that the higher products of life are the most often gratuitous. No instinct or institution was ever so absurd as is a large part of human poetry and philosophy, while the margin of ineptitude is much broader in religious myth than in religious ethics.

It Is Automatic.

Arts are instincts bred and reared in the open, creative habits acquired in the light of reason. Consciousness accompanies their formation; a certain uneasiness or desire and a more or less definite conception of what is wanted often precedes their full organization. That the need should be felt before the means for satisfying it have been found has led the unreflecting to imagine that in art the need produces the discovery and the idea the work. Causes at best are lightly assigned by mortals, and this particular superstition is no worse than any other. The data—the plan and its execution—as conjoined empirically in the few interesting cases which show successful achievement, are made into a law, in oblivion of the fact that in more numerous cases such conjunction fails wholly or in part, and that even in the successful cases other natural conditions are present, and must be present, to secure the result. In a matter where custom is so ingrained and supported by a constant apperceptive illusion, there is little hope of making thought suddenly exact, or exact language not paradoxical. We must observe, however, that only by virtue of a false perspective do ideas seem to govern action, or is a felt necessity the mother of invention. In truth invention is the child of abundance, and the genius or vital premonition and groping which achieve art simultaneously achieve the ideas which that art embodies; or, rather, ideas are themselves products of an inner movement which has an automatic extension outwards; and this extension manifests the ideas. Mere craving has no lights of its own to prophesy by, no prescience of what the world may contain that would satisfy, no power of imagining what would allay its unrest. Images and satisfactions have to come of themselves; then the blind craving, as it turns into an incipient pleasure, first recognizes its object. The pure will's impotence is absolute, and it would writhe for ever and consume itself in darkness if perception gave it no light and experience no premonition.

So Are the Ideas It Expresses.

Now, a man cannot draw bodily from external perception the ideas he is supposed to create or invent; and as his will or uneasiness, before he creates the satisfying ideas, is by hypothesis without them, it follows that creation or invention is automatic. The ideas come of themselves, being new and unthought-of figments, similar, no doubt, to old perceptions and compacted of familiar materials, but reproduced in a novel fashion and dropping in their sudden form from the blue. However instantly they may be welcomed, they were not already known and never could have been summoned. In the stock example, for instance, of groping for a forgotten name, we know the context in which that name should lie; we feel the environment of our local void; but what finally pops into that place, reinstated there by the surrounding tensions, is itself unforeseen, for it was just this that was forgotten. Could we have invoked the name we should not have needed to do so, having it already at our disposal. It is in fact a palpable impossibility that any idea should call itself into being, or that any act or any preference should be its own ground. The responsibility assumed for these things is not a determination to conceive them before they are conceived (which is a contradiction in terms) but an embrace and appropriation of them once they have appeared. It is thus that ebullitions in parts of our nature become touchstones for the whole; and the incidents within us seem hardly our own work till they are accepted and incorporated into the main current of our being. All invention is tentative, all art experimental, and to be sought, like salvation, with fear and trembling. There is a painful pregnancy in genius, a long incubation and waiting for the spirit, a thousand rejections and futile birthpangs, before the wonderful child appears, a gift of the gods, utterly undeserved and inexplicably perfect. Even this unaccountable success comes only in rare and fortunate instances. What is ordinarily produced is so base a hybrid, so lame and ridiculous a changeling, that we reconcile ourselves with difficulty to our offspring and blush to be represented by our fated works.

We Are Said to Control Whatever Obeys Us.

The propensity to attribute happy events to our own agency, little as we understand what we mean by it, and to attribute only untoward results to external forces, has its ground in the primitive nexus of experience. What we call ourselves is a certain cycle of vegetative processes, bringing a round of familiar impulses and ideas; this stream has a general direction, a conscious vital inertia, in harmony with which it moves. Many of the developments within it are dialectical; that is, they go forward by inner necessity, like an egg hatching within its shell, warmed but undisturbed by an environment of which they are wholly oblivious; and this sort of growth, when there is adequate consciousness of it, is felt to be both absolutely obvious and absolutely free. The emotion that accompanies it is pleasurable, but is too active and proud to call itself a pleasure; it has rather the quality of assurance and right. This part of life, however, is only its courageous core; about it play all sorts of incidental processes, allying themselves to it in more or less congruous movement. Whatever peripheral events fall in with the central impulse are accordingly lost in its energy and felt to be not so much peripheral and accidental as inwardly grounded, being, like the stages of a prosperous dialectic, spontaneously demanded and instantly justified when they come.

The sphere of the self's power is accordingly, for primitive consciousness, simply the sphere of what happens well; it is the entire unoffending and obedient part of the world. A man who has good luck at dice prides himself upon it, and believes that to have it is his destiny and desert. If his luck were absolutely constant, he would say he had the *power* to throw high; and as the event would, by hypothesis, sustain his boast, there would be no practical error in that assumption. A will that never found anything to thwart it would think itself omnipotent; and as the psychological essence of omniscience is not to suspect there is anything which you do not know, so the psychological essence of omnipotence is not to suspect that anything can happen which you do not desire. Such claims would undoubtedly be made if experience lent them the least color; but would even the most comfortable and innocent assurances of this sort cease to be precarious? Might not any moment of eternity bring the unimagined contradiction, and shake the dreaming god?

Utility Is a Result.

Utility like significance, is an eventual harmony in the arts and by no means their ground. All useful things have been discovered as ancient China discovered roast pig; and the casual feat has furthermore to be supported by a situation favorable to maintaining the art. The most useful act will never be repeated unless its secret remains embodied in structure. Practice and endeavor will not help an artist to remain long at his best; and many a performance is applauded which cannot be imitated. To create the requisite structure two preformed structures are needed: one in the agent, to give him skill and perseverance, and another in the material, to give it the right plasticity. Human progress would long ago have reached its goal if every man who recognized a good could at once appropriate it, and possess wisdom for ever by virtue of one moment's insight. Insight, unfortunately, is in itself perfectly useless and inconsequential; it can neither have produced its own occasion nor now insure its own recurrence. Nevertheless, being proof positive that whatever basis it needs is actual, insight is also an indication that the extant structure, if circumstances maintain it, may continue to operate with the same moral results, maintaining the vision which it has once supported.

The Useful Naturally Stable.

When men find that by chance they have started a useful change in the world, they congratulate themselves upon it and call their persistence in that practice a free activity. And the activity is indeed rational, since it subserves an end. The happy organization which enables us to continue in that rational course is the very organization which enabled us to initiate it. If this new process was formed under external influences, the same influences, when they operate again, will reconstitute the process each time more easily; while if it was formed quite spontaneously, its own inertia will maintain it quietly in the brain and bring it to the surface whenever circumstances permit. This is what is called learning by experiences. Such lessons are far from indelible and are not always at command. Yet what has once been done may be repeated; repetition reinforces itself and becomes habit; and a clear memory of the benefit once attained by fortunate action representing as it does the trace left by that action in the system, and its harmony with the man's usual impulses (for the action is felt to be *beneficial*), constitutes a strong presumption that the act will be repeated automatically on occasion; i.e., that it has really been learned. Consciousness, which willingly attends to results only, will judge either the memory or the benefit, or both confusedly, to be the ground of this readiness to act; and only if some hitch occurs in the machinery, so that rational behavior fails to take place, will a surprised appeal be made to material accidents, or to a guilty forgetfulness or indocility in the soul.

Intelligence Is Docility.

The idiot cannot learn from experience at all, because a new process, in his liquid brain, does not modify structure; while the fool uses what he has learned only inaptly and in frivolous fragments, because his stretches of linked experience are short and their connections insecure. But when the cerebral plasm is fresh and well disposed and when the paths are clear, attention is consecutive and learning easy; a multitude of details can be gathered into a single cycle of memory or of potential regard. Under such circumstances action is the unimpeded expression of healthy instinct in an environment squarely faced. Conduct from the first then issues in progress, and, by reinforcing its own organization at each rehearsal, makes progress continual. For there will subsist not only a readiness to act and a great precision in action, but if any significant circumstance has varied in the conditions or in the interests at stake, this change will make itself felt; it will check the process and prevent precipitate action. Deliberation or well-founded scruple has the same source as facility—a plastic and quick organization. To be sensitive to difficulties and dangers goes with being sensitive to opportunities.

Art Is Reason Propagating Itself.

Of all reason's embodiments art is therefore the most splendid and complete. Merely to attain categories by which inner experience may be articulated, or to feign analogies by which a universe may be conceived, would be but a visionary triumph if it remained ineffectual and went with no actual remodelling of the outer world, to render man's dwelling more appropriate and his mind better fed and more largely transmissible. Mind grows self-perpetuating only by its expression in matter. What makes progress possible is that rational action may leave traces in nature, such that nature in consequence furnishes a better basis for the life of reason; in other words progress is art bettering the conditions of existence. Until art arises, all achievement is internal to the brain, dies with the individual, and even in him spends itself without recovery, like music heard in a dream. Art, in establishing instruments for human life beyond the human body, and moulding outer things into sympathy with inner values, establishes a ground whence values may continually spring up; the thatch that protects from to-day's rain will last and keep out tomorrow's rain also; the sign that once expresses an idea will serve to recall it in future.

Not only does the work of art thus perpetuate its own function and produce a better experience, but the process of art also perpetuates itself, because it is teachable. Every animal learns something by living; but if his offspring inherit only what he possessed at birth, they have to learn life's lessons over again from the beginning, with at best some vague help given by their parent's example. But when the fruits of experience exist in the common environment, when new instruments, unknown to nature, are offered to each individual for his better equipment, although he must still learn for himself how to live, he may learn in a humaner school, where artificial occasions are constantly open to him for expanding his powers. It is no longer merely hidden inner processes that he must reproduce to attain his predecessors' wisdom; he may acquire much of it more expeditiously by imitating their outward habit—an imitation which, furthermore, they have some means of exacting from him. Wherever there is art there is a possibility of training. A father who calls his idle sons from the jungle to help him hold the plough not only inures them to labor but compels them to observe the earth upturned and refreshed, and to watch the germination there; their wandering thought, their incipient rebellions, will be met by the hope of harvest; and it will not be impossible for them, when their father is dead, to follow the plough of their own initiative and for their own children's sake. So great is the sustained advance in rationality made possible by art which, being embodied in matter, is teachable and transmissible by training; for in art the values secured are recognized the more easily for having been first enjoyed when other people furnished the means to them; while the maintenance of these values is facilitated by an external tradition imposing itself contagiously or by force on each new generation.

Beauty an Incident in Rational Art.

Art is action which transcending the body makes the world a more congenial stimulus to the soul. All art is therefore useful and practical, and the notable æsthetic value which some works of art possess, for reasons flowing for the most part out of their moral significance, is itself one of the satisfactions which art offers to human nature as a whole. Between sensation and abstract discourse lies a region of deployed sensibility or synthetic representation, a region where more is seen at arm's length than in any one moment could be felt at close quarters, and yet where the remote parts of experience, which discourse reaches only through symbols, are recovered and recomposed in something like their native colors and experienced relations. This region, called imagination, has pleasures more airy and luminous than those of sense. moie massive and rapturous than those of intelligence. The values inherent in imagination, in instant intuition, in sense endowed with form, are called æsthetic values; they are found mainly in nature and living beings, but often also in man's artificial works, in images evoked by language, and in the realm of sound.

Inseparable from the Others.

Productions in which an æsthetic value is or is supposed to be prominent take the name of fine art; but the work of fine art so defined is almost always an abstraction from the actual object, which has many non-æsthetic functions and values. To separate the æsthetic element, abstract and de-dependent as it often is, is an artifice which is more mislead-ing than helpful; for neither in the history of art nor in a rational estimate of its value can the æsthetic function of things be divorced from the practical and moral. What had to be done was, by imaginative races, done imaginatively; what had to be spoken or made, was spoken or made fitly, lovingly, beautifully. Or to take the matter up on its psy-chological side, the ceaseless experimentation and ferment of ideas, in breeding what it had a propensity to breed, came sometimes on figments that gave it delightful pause; these beauties were the first knowledges and these arrests the first hints of real and useful things. The rose's grace could more easily be plucked from its petals than the beauty of art from its subject, occasion, and use. An æsthetic fragrance, indeed, all things may have, if in soliciting man's senses or reason they can awaken his imagination as well; but this middle zone is so mixed and nebulous and its limits are so vague, that it cannot well be treated in theory otherwise than as it exists in fact—as a phase of man's sympathy with the world he moves in. If art is that element in the life of reason which consists in modifying its environment the better to attain its end, art may be expected to subserve all parts of the human ideal, to increase man's comfort, knowledge, and de-light. And as nature, in her measure, is wont to satisfy these interests together, so art, in seeking to increase that satis-faction, will work simultaneously in every ideal direction. Nor will any of these directions be on the whole good, or tempt a well-trained will, if it leads to estrangement from all other interests. The æsthetic good will be accordingly hatched in the same nest with the others, and incapable of flying far in a different air.

[319]

SARTRE, JEAN PAUL

SARTRE, JEAN PAUL (1905-   ). Evidently and avowedly, Sartre, of all younger French authors the one whose works are most eagerly read in America, has not yet come to a final formulation of his philosophical thoughts. In his *Baudelaire* (1947) and in his critical essays *Situations* (1947), he expresses ideas and sentiments which indicate some changes of viewpoint and standard of evaluation when compared with his principal philosophical works *Being and Nothingness* (1943) and *Existentialism is a Humanism* (1946). Also his drama *The Flies* (1943) leads to conclusions concerning human destiny which are not yet theoretically expressed by Sartre.

Sartre, always a man of delicate health, and an orphan at an early age, was a professor of philosophy at one of Paris' greatest colleges, after having studied at the Sorbonne and at the German University of Göttingen where he was a student of Husserl. In World War II he was made a prisoner but was released from the German prisoners' camp because of his sickness. When he returned to Paris, he became a leader of the resistance.

Sartre's philosophy as far as it has so far developed is deeply influenced by Heidegger. But Sartre's existentialism departs from that of Heidegger's by establishing an anti-theological morale, a phenomenology of the body, and principles of existential psycho-analysis. While anguish is Heidegger's fundamental experience, Sartre's is that which he calls nausea, disgust, revulsion against being, duration, repetition and continuance of life, as well as against the unending mobility of human existence. Sartre tried to banish all vagueness while confronting personal existence with general life but he also tried to find a way to vindicate freedom and the value of the individual.

REASONS AND WRITING

EACH one has his reasons: for one, art is a flight; for another, a means of conquering. But one can flee into a hermitage, into madness, into death. One can conquer by arms. Why does it have to be *writing*, why does one have to manage his escapes and conquests by *writing?* Because, behind the various aims of authors, there is a deeper and more immediate choice which is common to all of us. We shall try to elucidate this choice, and we shall see whether it is not in the name of this very choice of writing that the engagement of writers must be required.

Each of our perceptions is accompanied by the consciousness that human reality is a "revealer," that is, it is through human reality that "there is" being, or, to put it differently, that man is the means by which things are manifested. It is our presence in the world which multiplies relations. It is we who set up a relationship between this tree and that bit of sky. Thanks to us, that star which has been dead for millennia, that quarter moon, and that dark river are disclosed in the unity of landscape. It is the speed of our auto and our airplane which organizes the great masses of the earth. With each of our acts, the world reveals to us a new face. But, if we know that we are directors of being, we also know that we are not its producers. If we turn away from this landscape, it will sink back into its dark permanence. At least, it will sink back; there is no one mad enough to think that it is going to be annihilated. It is we who shall be annihilated, and the earth will remain in its lethargy until another consciousness comes along to awaken it. Thus, to our inner certainty of being "revealers" is added that of being inessential in relation to the thing revealed.

One of the chief motives of artistic creation is certainly the need of feeling that we are essential in relationship to the world. If I fix on canvas or in writing a certain aspect of the fields or the sea or a look on someone's face which I have disclosed, I am conscious of having produced them by condensing relationship, by introducing order where there was none, by imposing the unity of mind on the diversity of things. That is, I feel myself essential in relation to my creation. But this time it is the created object which escapes me;

I can not reveal and produce at the same time. The creation becomes inessential in relation to the creative activity. First of all, even if it appears to others as definitive, the created object always seems to us in a state of suspension; we can always change this line, that shade, that word. Thus, it never *forces itself.* A novice painter asked his teacher, "When should I consider my painting finished?" And the teacher answered, "When you can look at it in amazement and say to yourself '*I'm* the one who did *that!*' "

[320]

SCHELLING, FRIEDRICH WILHELM JOSEPH VON

SCHELLING, FRIEDRICH WILHELM JOSEPH VON (1775-1854). Schelling has been called the Proteus among philosophers. His mind was as changeable as it was impressible. In his early years, Schelling fascinated everyone he met. He was overflowing with ideas, versatile, and apt in understanding men and problems. Goethe considered him the most congenial philosopher he knew, and it was Schelling who inspired Hegel, although the latter would not admit it.

Schelling created the philosophy of identity by asserting that nature is not essentially different from mind; his way of representing the various forms of existence as the work of an unconsciously creating activity which is the same in shaping nature and mind, influenced not only his German contemporaries but English and French thinkers as well, and not the least among them—Bergson.

The aged Schelling was rigid in his attitude toward man and the universe. He recanted his earlier pantheistic belief in the identity of nature and mind and repudiated transcendental idealism, even idealism and judgments *a priori* at all. The "positive philosophy" of Schelling's last years considered empiricism the lesser evil compared with any kind of rational deduction. Originally an admirer of Epicurus and Spinoza, he had become the defender of Protestant and Catholic orthodoxy and the champion of political reaction. But he could not prevent liberals from referring to his words, spoken in earlier days, which extolled eternal change.

1056

ALL knowledge is based upon the agreement of an objective with a subjective. For we *know* only the true, and the truth is universally held to be the agreement of representations with their objects.

The sum of all that is purely objective in our knowledge we may call Nature; whereas the sum of everything subjective may be termed the *Ego,* or Intelligence. These two concepts are mutually opposed. Intelligence is originally conceived as that which solely represents, and nature as that which is merely capable of representation; the former as the conscious—the latter as the unconscious. But in all knowledge there is necessary a mutual agreement of the two—the conscious and the unconscious *per se.* The problem is to explain this agreement.

In knowledge itself, in that I know, the objective and subjective are so united that one cannot say which of the two has priority. There is here no first and no second—the two are contemporaneous and one. In any attempt to explain this identity, I must already have resolved it. In order to explain it, inasmuch as there is nothing else given me as a principle of explanation except these two factors of knowledge, I must of necessity place the one before the other, that is to say, must set out from the one in order to arrive at the other. From which of the two I shall set out is not determined by the problem.

There are, consequently, only two cases possible:

I. *Either the objective is made first, and the question arises how a subjective agreeing with it is superinduced.*

The idea of the subjective is not contained in the idea of the objective; on the contrary they mutually exclude each other. The subjective must therefore be *superinduced* upon the objective. It forms no part of the conception of nature that there must be likewise an intelligence to represent it.

1057

Nature, to all appearance, would exist even if there were nothing to represent it. The problem may therefore likewise be expressed thus: How is the intelligent superinduced upon nature? or, How does nature come to be represented?

The problem assumes nature, or the objective, as the first. It is, therefore, undoubtedly the task of natural science, which does the same. That natural science actually, and without knowing it, approximates, at least, to the solution of this problem can here be only briefly shown.

If all knowledge has, as it were, two poles, which mutually presuppose and demand each other, then they must seek each other in all sciences. There must, therefore, of necessity, exist two fundamental sciences; and it must be impossible to set out from one pole without being driven to the other. The necessary tendency of all natural science, therefore, is to proceed from nature to the intelligent. This, and this alone, lies at the foundation of the effort to bring theory into natural phenomena. The final perfection of natural science would be the complete intellectualization of all the laws of nature into laws of intuition and of thought. The phenomena, that is, the material, must completely vanish, and leave only the laws,—that is, the formal. Hence it happens that the more the conformity to law is manifested in nature so much the more the wrapping disappears—the phenomena themselves become more intellectualized, and at length entirely cease. Optical phenomena are nothing more than a geometry whose lines are drawn by aid of the light; and even this light itself is already of doubtful materiality. In the phenomena of magnetism every trace of matter has already vanished; and of the phenomena of gravitation, which even the natural philosopher believed could be attributed only to direct spiritual influence, there remains nothing but their law, whose performance on a large scale is the mechanism of the heavenly motions. The complete theory of nature would be that by virtue of which the whole of nature should be resolved into an intelligence. The dead and unconscious products of nature are only unsuccessful attempts of nature to reflect itself, but the so-called dead nature is merely an unripe intelligence; hence in its phenomena the intelligent character appears, though still unconscious. Its highest aim, that is of becoming wholly self-objective, nature does not attain, except in its highest and last reflection, which is none other than man, or more generally what we call reason. By its means nature first turns completely back upon itself, and thereby it is manifest that nature is originally identical with what in us is known as intelligent and conscious.

This may suffice to prove that natural science has a necessary tendency to render nature intelligent. By this very tendency it becomes natural philosophy, which is one of the two necessary fundamental sciences of philosophy.

II. *Or the subjective is made first, and the problem is, how an objective is superinduced agreeing with it.*

If all knowledge is based upon the agreement of these two, then the problem to explain this agreement is undoubtedly the highest for all knowledge; and if, as is generally admitted, philosophy is the highest and loftiest of all sciences, it becomes certainly the chief task of philosophy.

But the problem demands only the explanation of that agreement generally, and leaves it entirely undetermined where the explanation shall begin, what it shall make its first, and what its second. Since also the two opposites are mutually necessary, the result of the operation is the same, from whichever point one sets out. To make the objective the first, and to derive the subjective from it, is, as has just been shown, the task of natural philosophy.

If, therefore, there is a transcendental philosophy, the only direction remaining for it is the opposite, that is: to proceed from the subjective as the first and the absolute, and to deduce the origin of the objective from it. Natural and transcendental philosophy have divided between themselves these two possible directions of philosophy. And if all philosophy must have for an aim to make either an intelligence out of nature or a nature out of intelligence, then transcendental philosophy, to which this latter problem belongs, is the other necessary fundamental science of philosophy.

[321]

SCHILLER, FERDINAND CANNING SCOTT

SCHILLER, FERDINAND CANNING SCOTT (1864-1917). In strong opposition to the Hegelianism prevailing at Oxford University since T. H. Green and strengthened by F. H. Bradley, another professor of that same University, though a namesake of the German idealistic poet Schiller, combated any idealism of German provenience. F. C. S. Schiller called his philosophy *Humanism,* while calling himself a disciple of the sophist Protagoras, who said that man is the measure of all things. Schiller proceeds from the statement that all mental life is purposive to the establishment of a concept of truth whose criteria are given by the consequences of a proposition. This does not mean that truth corresponds to the organic or sentimental needs of the knower. As Schiller says, his humanism is merely the perception that the philosophic problem concerns human beings striving to comprehend a world of human experience by the resources of the human mind. He distinguishes humanism from pragmatism, to which it is in fact akin, by the claim that humanism is of larger range and is able to be applied not only to logic but to ethics, aesthetics, metaphysic and theology, and furthermore by his readiness to acknowledge as many metaphysics as there are tempers, while rejecting any absolute metaphysic. Schiller's principal works about humanism are *Humanism* (1903) and *Studies in Humanism* (1907). He wrote also about the problems of the day. In one of his pamphlets he declared that a government of the world administered by international bankers would by no means be the worst possible.

HOW IS "EXACTNESS" POSSIBLE?

IT is amazing what a spell the ideal of exactness has cast upon the philosophic mind. For hundreds, nay thousands, of years philosophers seem to have been yearning for exactness, and hoping that, if only they could attain it, all their troubles would be over. All the pitfalls in the way of philosophic progress would be circumvented, and every philosophic science, from psychology and logic to the remotest heights of metaphysics, would become accessible to the meanest understanding.

Yet what a gap there is between these professions and the practice of philosophers! Despite of their zeal for exactness, what body of learned men is more careless in their terminology and more contemptuous of all the devices which seem conducive to exactness?

Experience shows that it is quite impossible to pin any philosophic term down to any single meaning, even for a little while, or even to keep its meaning stable enough to avoid gross misunderstanding. Even the most express and solemn definitions are set at naught by the very writers who propounded them. The most famed philosophers are the very ones who have been the worst offenders. For example, Kant's fame rests in no small measure on the tricks he played with words like *"a priori,"* "category," "object," and his systematic confusion of "transcendental" and "transcendent." There is hardly a philosophy which does not juggle thus with ambiguous terms. If the theories of philosophers may be interpreted in the light of their practice, they should be the last persons in the world to laud "exactness."

On the other hand, they might fairly be expected to inform us what "exactness" means, or at least what they wish it to mean. I do not find, however, that they are at all eager to do this. Apparently they are content to refer to mathematics as an "exact" science, and to admonish philosophy to respect and aspire to the mathematical ideal.

To understand exactness, therefore, we must go to mathematics and inquire whether and in what senses mathematics are "exact." Now it is clear that mathematics are not exact in the sense that mathematical objects exactly reproduce physical realities; nor do physical realities exactly exemplify mathematical ideals. There are no straight lines nor circles to be found in nature, while all the physical constants, like the year, month, and day, are inexact. Plato knew this, but yet thought of God as a mathematician; he should have added that if God geometrizes, He does so very inexactly.

Hence, if the relation between realities and mathematical ideals is conceived as a *copying* or *reproduction*, it cannot possibly be "exact." Which is the archetype, and which the copy, does not matter: alike whether the real copies the mathematical ideal, or the latter is moulded upon the former, no exactness can be found.

There is, however, a sense in which exactness depends on definition; and mathematicians take great pride in the exactness of their definitions. A definition can be exact, because it is a *command* addressed to nature, and it sounds quite uncompromising. If the real will not come up to the definition, so much the worse for the real! In so far therefore as exactness depends on definitions, mathematics can be exact. It can be as exact as anything defined exactly.

But there appear to be limits to the exactness thus attainable. The exactness of a definition is limited by two difficulties. (a) In the first place things must be found to which the definition, when made, does actually apply. And secondly, (b) the definition has to be maintained against the growth of knowledge. Both these difficulties may easily prove fatal to exactness.

As to (a), it is clear that we cannot arbitrarily "define" the creatures of our fancy, without limits. Definitions which apply to nothing have no real meaning. The only sure way, therefore, of securing that a definition will be operative and will have application to the real, is to allow the real, idealized if necessary, to suggest the definition to the mathematician. The mathematician was sensible enough to adopt this procedure. He allowed a ray of sunlight to suggest the definition of a straight line, and this assured to Euclidean geometry a profitable field of application.

But it did *not* render the definition immutable, and im-

mune to the growth of knowledge. The mathematical definition remains dependent on the behavior of the real. If,
therefore, rays of light are found to curve in a gravitational
field, a far-reaching doubt is cast on the use of Euclidean
geometry for cosmic calculations.

As to (b), the definer retains the right to revise his
definitions. So the very framing of his definition may suggest to the mathematician the idea of developing it in some
promising and interesting direction. But this procedure may
entail a further definition, or redefinition, which destroys
the exactness of the first formula. Thus when he has accomplished the "exact" definition of a circle and an ellipse,
it may occur to a mathematician that after all a circle may
be taken as a special case of an ellipse, and that it would be
interesting to see what happens if he followed out this line
of thought. He does so, and arrives at "the points at infinity," with their paradoxical properties. Again the development of non-Euclidean geometries has rendered ambiguous
and inexact the Euclidean conceptions, e.g. of "triangle."
Even so elementary and apparently stable a conception as
that of the unit of common arithmetic undergoes subtle transformations of meaning as others beyond the original operation of addition are admitted.

In mathematics then, as in the other sciences, it is
inevitable that the conceptions used should *grow*. It is impossible to prohibit their growth, and to restrict them to the
definitions as they were conceived at first. Indeed the process of stretching old definitions so as to permit of new
operations is even particularly evident in mathematics.

The method by which it is justified is that of *analogy*.
If an analogy can be found which promises to bridge a gap
between one notion and another, their identity is experi-
mentally assumed. And if the experiment works for the
purposes of those who made it, the differences between them
are slurred over and ignored. If it were not possible to take
the infinitesimal, now as something, now as nothing, what

would be left of the logic of the calculus? But the logician at least should remind himself that analogy is not an exact and valid form of argument.

Can exactness be said to inhere in the symbols used by mathematicians? Hardly. $+$ and $-$, and even $=$, have many uses, and therefore senses, even in the exactest mathematics.

The truth is that mathematical definitions cannot be more exact than our knowledge of the realities to which, sooner or later, directly or indirectly, they refer. Nor can mathematical symbols be more exact than *words*. It is sheer delusion to think otherwise.

And what about words? Whence do they get their meanings, and how are they stabilized and modified?

Words get their meaning by being used successfully by those who have meanings to convey. *Verbal* meaning, therefore, is derivative from *personal* meaning. Once a verbal meaning is established and can be presumed to be familiar, personal meaning can employ a word for the purpose of transmitting a new meaning judged appropriate to a situation in which a transfer of meaning to others is judged necessary or desirable. Thus a transfer of meaning is always experimental, and generally problematic and inexact.

Moreover the situation which calls for it is always more or less *new*. Hence a successful transfer, that is the understanding of a meaning, always involves an *extension* of an old meaning; and in the course of time this may result in a complete reversal of the initial definition. For example, when the "atom" was first imported into physics, it was defined as the ultimate and indivisible particle of matter. Now, notoriously, it has been subdivided so often that there seems to be room in it for an unending multitude of parts; and its exploration is the most progressive part of physics. The word remains, but its definition has been radically changed. For the scientist always has an option when he finds that his old words are no longer adequate: he can either change his terms, or else his definitions. But there is, and can be, no fixity and no exactness about either.

There is a further difficulty about definitions. All words cannot be defined. Wherever the definer begins, or ends, he makes use of terms not yet defined, or has recourse to definitions revolving in a circle. So, if he hankers after exactness, he declares that some terms are indefinable and need no definition. This subterfuge is utterly unworthy of an exact logician. For if he holds that these indefinables are yet intuitively understood or apprehended, he enslaves his "logic" to psychology. If he admits that he cannot guarantee that any two reasoners will understand the indefinables alike, he explodes the basis of all exactness. Thus even the exactest definitions are left to float in a sea of inexactitude.

The situation grows still more desperate if the logician realizes that, to achieve exactness, he must eradicate and overcome the potential ambiguity of words. He must devise words which exactly fit the particular situation in which the words are used. For otherwise the same word will be permitted to mean one thing in one context, another in another. It will be what logicians have been wont to call "ambiguous." In this, however, they may have been mistaking for a flaw the most convenient property of words, namely their plasticity and capacity for repeated use as vehicles of *many* meanings.

For the alternative of demanding a one-one correspondence between words and meanings, seems incomparably worse. I remember this was tried once by Earl Bertrand Russell, in a sportive mood. It was not long after the war, and he had just emerged from the dungeon to which he had been consigned for an ill-timed jest, that he came to Oxford to read a paper to a society of undergraduate philosophers, on what he called "vagueness." I was requested to "open the discussion" on this paper, and so obtained what in Hollywood is called a "preview" of it. What was my amazement when I found that Russell's cure for "vagueness," that is, the applicability of the same word to different situations, was that there should be distinctive words enough for every situation! Certainly that would be a radical cure; but in what a state would it leave language! A language freed from "vagueness" would be composed entirely of *nonce words*, "hapax legomena," and almost wholly unintelligible. When I pointed out this consequence, Russell cheerfully accepted it, and I retired from the fray.

Russell had rightly diagnosed what was the condition of exactness. But he had ignored the fact that his cure was impracticable, and far worse than the alleged disease. Nor had he considered the alternative, the inference that *therefore* the capacity of words to convey a multitude of meanings must not be regarded as a flaw, but that a distinction must be made between plurality of meanings and actual ambiguity.

It is vital to logic that the part words play in transmitting meaning from one person to another should be rightly understood; but does not such understanding reduce the demand for "exactness" to a false ideal?

What finally is the bearing of these results on the pretensions of logistics?

It seems to reduce itself to a game with fictions and verbal meanings. (1) It is clear that it is a fiction that meanings can be fixed, and embodied in unvarying symbols. (2) It is clear that the verbal meanings to be fixed are never the personal meanings to be conveyed in actual knowing. The assumption that they can be identified is just a fiction too. (3) There appears to be no point of contact between the conventions of this game and the real problems of scientific knowing. This is the essential difference between logistics and mathematics. Pure mathematics is a game too, but it has application to reality. But logistics seems to be a game more remote from science than chess is from strategy. For in a science the meanings concerned are those of the investigators, that is, are *personal*. They are also experimental. They respond to every advance in knowledge, and are modified accordingly. Their fixity would mean stagnation, and the death of science. Words need have only enough stability of meaning, when they are used, for the old senses (which determine their selection) to yield a sufficient clue to the new senses to be conveyed, to render the latter intelligible. In their context, not in the abstract. In the abstract they may remain infinitely "ambiguous," that is, *potentially useful.* This does no harm, so long as it does not mislead in actual use. And when an experimenter ventures on too audacious innovations upon the conventional meanings of his words, the right rebuke to him is not "You contradict the meaning of the words you use," but "I do not understand; what do you mean?"

I am driven then to the conclusion that logistics is an intellectual game. It is a game of make-believe, which mathematically trained pedants love to play, but which does not on this account become incumbent on every one. It may have the advantage that it keeps logisticians out of other mischief. But I fail to see that it has either any serious significance for understanding scientific knowing or any educational importance for sharpening wits!

[322]

SCHLEGEL, FRIEDRICH VON

SCHLEGEL, FRIEDRICH VON (1772-1829). Friedrich Schlegel is one of the most characteristic representatives of German romanticism whose principal trait is the longing for a reality different from that which is determined by natural laws and historical circumstances. Dissatisfied with the civilization of his own time, Schlegel at first exalted the French Revolution, then the Middle Ages, and finally, considering the Roman Catholic Church as the keeper of the medieval mind, he was converted to it, and became a champion of political and cultural reaction. He began as an admirer and pupil of Kant, Fichte and Goethe, and later turned to Metternich and Joseph de Maistre who asserted the superiority of tradition over reason, and proclaimed papacy as the one legitimate ruler over humanity.

Schlegel was a poor poet. His novel *Lucinde*, although it scandalized middle-class morals, proved to be unreadable. His tragedy *Alarcos*, produced by Goethe in Weimar, fell flat. But in his early aphorisms and essays, Schlegel refined the understanding of poetry and evoked the sense of personality in every kind of spiritual activity, be it poetic, scientific, philosophical or religious. In his later works, Schlegel stiffened his opposition to Enlightenment, natural law, democracy and liberalism, but, despite his turn to traditionalism, he preserved a revolutionary strain of which he was conscious. He defined it as his faculty to perceive historical changes without sympathizing with them, and to combat the revolution with what he called "revolutionary spirit in a valid sense but different from the common conception." He therefore was as distrusted by Catholics as he was blamed by Protestants.

For many years, Schlegel led a destitute life for he was rather indolent. He would have perished without the help of his wife Dorothea, Moses Mendelssohn's daughter with whom he had eloped from the house of her husband Simon Veit. Dorothea, the "child of enlightenment," nine years older than Schlegel, followed him from folly to folly and, at the same time, provided him with money by writing novels and articles with untiring energy.

PHILOSOPHY OF LIFE

"THERE are," says a poet as ingenious as profound, "more things in heaven and earth, than are dreamt of in our philosophy." This sentiment, which Genius accidentally let drop, is in the main applicable also to the philosophy of our own day; and, with a slight modification, I shall be ready to adopt it as my own. The only change that is requisite to make it available for my purpose would be the addition— "and also between heaven and earth are there many things which are not dreamt of in our philosophy." And exactly because philosophy, for the most part, does nothing but dream —scientifically dream, it may be—therefore is it ignorant, ay, has no inkling even of much which nevertheless, in all propriety it ought to know. It loses sight of its true object, it quits the firm ground where, standing secure, it might pursue its own avocations without let or hindrance, whenever, abandoning its own proper region, it either soars up to heaven to weave there its fine-spun webs of dialectics, and to build its metaphysical castles in the air, or else, losing itself on the earth, it violently interferes with external reality, and determines to shape the world according to its own fancy, and to reform it at will. Half-way between these two devious courses lies the true road; and the proper region of philosophy is even that spiritual inner life between heaven and earth.

On both sides, many and manifold errors were committed, even in the earlier and better days of enlightened antiquity. Plato himself, the greatest of the great thinkers of Greece, set up in his Republic the model of an ideal polity, which, in this respect, cannot bear the test of examination. His design indeed finds, in some measure, its apology in the disorders and corruption which even in his day, had infected all the free states of Greece, whether great or small. His work too, by the highly finished style of the whole, the vivid perspicuity of its narrative, its rich profusion of pregnant ideas and noble sentiments, stands out in dignified contrast to the crude and ill-designed schemes of legislation so hastily propounded in our own day. Still, it will ever remain the weak point of this great man. One needs not to be a Plato to see how absolutely unfeasible, not to say practically absurd, are many of the propositions of this Platonic ideal. Accordingly it has ever been the fruitful occasion, not only among contemporaries, but also with posterity, of ridicule to the ignorant and of censure to the wise. In this respect it cannot but excite our regret that such great and noble powers of mind should have been wasted in following a false direction, and in pursuit of an unattainable end. The oldest philosophers of Greece, on the other hand—those first bold adventurers on the wide ocean of thought, combined together the elements of things, water, or air, or fire, or atoms, or lastly the all-ruling Intellect itself, into as many different systems of the universe. If, however, each in his own way thus set forth a peculiar creed of nature, we must ever bear in mind that the popular religion, with its poetical imagery, and the fabulous mythology of antiquity, as affording not only no sufficient, but absolutely no answer to the inquiring mind, as to the essence of things, and the first cause of all, could not possibly satisfy these earlier thinkers. Consequently they might well feel tempted to find, each for himself, a way to honor nature, and to contemplate the supreme Being. Since then, however, the world has grown older by nearly twenty-five centuries, and much in the meanwhile has been accomplished by, or fallen to the share of, the human race. But when philosophy would pretend to regard this long succession of ages, and all its fruits, as suddenly erased from the records of existence, and for the sake of change would start afresh, so perilous an experiment can scarcely lead to any good result, but in all probability, and to judge from past experience, will only give rise to numberless and interminable disputes. Such an open space in thought—cleared from all the traces of an earlier existence (a smoothly polished marble tablet, as it were, like the *tabula rasa* of a recent ephemeral philosophy)—would only serve as an arena for the useless though daring ventures of unprofitable speculation, and could never form a safe basis for solid thought, or for any permanent manifestation of intellectual life.

In itself it is nothing surprising if young and inexperienced minds, occupying themselves prematurely, or in a perverted sense, with the grand ideas of God and nature, liberty and the march of thought, should be wholly overmastered and carried away with them. It has often happened before now, and it is no new thing if youthful and ardent temperaments should either yield to the seductive temptation to make, not to say create, a new religion of their own; or else feel a deceitful impulse to censure and to change all that is already in existence, and, if possible, to reform the whole world by their newly acquired ideas.

That this twofold aberration and misuse of philosophical thought must prove universally injurious, and prejudicial both to education and the whole world, is so evident that it can scarcely be necessary to dwell upon it. Its effect has been to cause men, especially those whose minds have been formed in the great and comprehensive duties of practical life, to view the thing altogether in an evil light, although it must be confessed there is much injustice in this sweeping condemnation. In several of the great statesmen of Rome we may observe a similar contempt for Grecian philosophy as useless and unprofitable. And yet, as is happily indicated by its Greek name, this whole effort was assuredly based upon a noble conception, and, when duly regulated, a salutary principle. For in this beautiful word, according to its original acceptation, science is not regarded as already finished and mature, but is rather set forth as an object of search—of a noble curiosity and of a pure enthusiasm for great and sublime truths, while at the same time it implies the wise use of such knowledge. Merely, however, to check and to hinder the aberrations of a false philosophy, is not by itself sufficient. It is only by laying down and levelling the right road of a philosophy of life, that a thorough remedy for the evil is to be found. True philosophy, therefore, honoring that which has been given from above and that which is existent from without, must neither raise itself in hostility to the one, nor attempt to interfere violently with the other. For it is exactly when, keeping modestly within its proper limits of the inner spiritual life, it makes itself the handmaid neither of theology nor of politics, that it best asserts its true dignity and maintains its independence in its own peculiar domain. And thus, even while it abstains most scrupulously from intermeddling with the positive and actual, will it operate most powerfully on alien and remote branches of inquiry, and by teaching them to consider objects in a freer and more general light, indirectly it will exercise on them a salutary influence. Thus while it proceeds along its appointed path, it will, as it were, without effort disperse many a mist which spreads its dangerous delusion over the whole of human existence, or remove perhaps many a stone of stumbling, which offends the age and divides the minds of men in strife and discord. In this manner consequently will it most beautifully attest its healing virtue, and at the same time best fulfil its proper destination.

The object therefore of philosophy is the inner mental life (*geistige Leben*), not merely this or that individual faculty in any partial direction, but man's spiritual life with all its rich and manifold energies. With respect to form and method: the philosophy of life sets out from a single assumption—that of life, or in other words, of a consciousness to a certain degree awakened and manifoldly developed by experience—since it has for its object, and purposes to make known the entire consciousness and not merely a single phase of it. Now, such an end would be hindered rather than promoted by a highly elaborate or minutely exhaustive form and a painfully artificial method; and it is herein that the difference lies between a philosophy of life and the philosophy of the school. If philosophy be regarded merely as one part of a general scientific education, then is the instruction in method (whether under the old traditionary name of logic or any other) the chief point to be regarded. For such a mere elementary course, passing over, or at least postponing for a while the consideration of the matter, as possessing as yet but a very remote interest for the student, and, in the default of an adequate internal experience of his own, incapable of being understood by him, concerns itself rather with the practice of methodical thought, both as necessary for the future, and as applicable to all matters. But the preliminary exercise in philosophical thinking is only the introduction to philosophy, and not philosophy itself. This school-teaching of philosophy might perhaps be rendered productive of the most excellent consequences, if only it were directed to the history of the human intellect. What could be more interesting than a history which should enter into the spirit, and distinctly embody the various systems which the inventive subtlety of the Greeks gave birth to, or which, taking a still wider range, should embrace the science of the Egyptians, and some Asiatic nations, and illustrate the no less wonderful nor less manifold systems of the

1072

Hindoos—those Greeks of the primeval world! But this, perhaps, would be to encroach upon the peculiar domain of erudition, and might, moreover, fail to furnish equal interest for all; and at any rate the history of philosophy is not philosophy itself.

Now, the distinction between the philosophy of life and the philosophy of the school will appear in very different lights according to the peculiarity of view which predominates in the several philosophical systems. That species of philosophy which revolves in the dialectical orbit of abstract ideas, according to its peculiar character presupposes and requires a well-practiced talent of abstraction, perpetually ascending through higher grades to the very highest, and even then boldly venturing a step beyond. In short, as may be easily shown in the instance of modern German science, the being unintelligible is set up as a kind of essential characteristic of a true and truly scientific philosophy. I, for my part, must confess, that I feel a great distrust of that philosophy which dwells in inaccessible light, where the inventor indeed asserts of himself, that he finds himself in an unattainable certainty and clearness of insight, giving us all the while to understand thereby, that he does see well enough how of all other mortals scarcely any, or perhaps, strictly speaking, no one, understands or is capable of understanding him. In all such cases it is only the false light of some internal *ignis fatuus* that produces this illusion of the unintelligible, or rather of nonsense. In this pursuit of wholly abstract and unintelligible thought, the philosophy of the school is naturally enough esteemed above every other, and regarded as pre-eminently the true science—i.e., the unintelligible.

In such a system a philosophy of life means nothing more than a kind of translation of its abstruser mysteries into a more popular form, and an adaptation of them to the capacity of ordinary minds. But even such popular adaptations, though evincing no common powers of language and illustration, in spite of their apparent clearness, when closer examined, are found as unintelligible as the recondite originals. For inasmuch as the subject matter of these abstract speculations was, from the very first, confused and unintelligible, it was consequently incapable of being made clear even by the most perspicuous of styles. But the true living philosophy has no relation or sympathy with this continuous advance up to the unintelligible heights of empty abstraction. Since the objects it treats of are none other than those which every man of a cultivated mind and in any degree accustomed to observe his own consciousness, both has and recognizes within himself, there is nothing to prevent its exposition being throughout clear, easy, and forcible. Here the relation is reversed. In such a system the philosophy of life is the chief and paramount object of interest; while the philosophy of the school, or the scientific teaching of it in the schools, however necessary and valuable in its place, is still, as compared with the whole thing itself, only secondary and subordinate. In the philosophy of life, moreover, the method adopted must also be a living one. Consequently it is not, by any means, a thing to be neglected. But still it need not to be applied with equal rigor throughout, or to appear prominently in every part, but on all occasions must be governed in these respects by what the particular end in view may demand.

A few illustrations, drawn from daily experience, will perhaps serve to explain my meaning. Generally speaking, the most important arts and pursuits of life are ultimately based on mathematics. This science furnishes them, as it were, with the method they observe; but it is not practicable, nor indeed has man the leisure, to revert on every occasion, with methodical exactness, to these elements, but, assuming the principles to be well known and admitted, he attends rather to the results essential to the end he has in view. The economical management of the smallest as well as of the largest household, rests in the end on the elementary principles of arithmetic; but what would come of it, if, on every occasion, we were to go back to the simple "one-times-one" of the multiplication table, and reflected upon and sought for the proofs that the principle is really valid and can confidently be relied on in practice? In the same way the art of war is founded on geometry, but when the general arranges his troops for battle does he consult his Euclid to satisfy himself of the correctness and advantages of his position? Lastly, even the astronomer, whose vocation is preeminently dependent on accurate calculation, when he would make us acquainted with the phenomena of the sidereal heavens, confines himself almost entirely to them, without wearying those whom he wishes to interest, with the complicated reckonings which, however, in all probability, he was obliged himself to go through. With all these arts and pursuits of practical life, the intellectual business of thinking—of such thinking at least as is common to most men—and of communicating thought, has a sort of affinity and resemblance. For, unquestionably, it is one among the many problems of philosophy to establish a wise economy and prudent stewardship of that ever-shifting mass of incoming and outgoing thoughts which make up our intellectual estate and property. And this is the more necessary, the greater are the treasures of thought possessed by our age. For, in the highly rapid interchange of, and traffic in ideas, which is carrying on, the receipts and disbursements are not always duly balanced. There is much cause, therefore, to fear lest a thoughtless and lavish dissipation of the noblest mental endowments should become prevalent, or a false and baseless credit system in thought spring up amidst an absolute deficiency of a solid and permanent capital safely invested in fundamental ideas and lasting truths. As for the second simile: I should, by all means, wish to gain a victory, not indeed for you, but with you, over some of the many errors and many semblances of thought, which are, however, but cheats and counterfeits which distract the minds of the present generation, disturb the harmony of life, and banish peace even from the intellectual world. And as respects the third illustration: I should indeed rejoice as having, in a great measure, attained my object, if only I shall succeed in directing your attention to some star in the higher region of intellect, which hitherto was either totally unknown, or, at least, never before fully observed.

But above all, I think it necessary to observe further, that in the same way as philosophy loses sight of its true object and appropriate matter, when either it passes into and merges in theology, or meddles with external politics, so also does it mar its proper form when it attempts to mimic the rigorous method of mathematics. In the middle of the last century scarcely was there to be found a German manual for any of the sciences that did not ape the mathematical style, and where every single position in the long array of interminable paragraphs did not conclude with the solemn act of demonstrative phraseology. But it is also well known that the philosophy which was propounded in this inappropriate form and method was crammed full of, nay, rather, was hardly anything more than a tissue of arbitrary, now forgotten, hypotheses, which have not brought the world at all nearer to the truth,—not at least to that truth which philosophy is in search of, and which is something higher than a mere example of accurate computation.

[323]

SCHLEIERMACHER, FRIEDRICH DANIEL

SCHLEIERMACHER, FRIEDRICH DANIEL (1768-1834). The life, theology and philosophy of Schleiermacher may be characterized as a steady concordance of contraries. He was a minister of the Reformed Church, devoted to the spiritual welfare of his community and an influential professor of theology, but he shocked faithful Christians by his close association with Friedrich Schlegel when this romanticist author was an avowed libertine and defied Christian morality with his lascivious novel *Lucinde*, which Schleiermacher defended against general indignation. He offended not only the members of his congregation by his intimate friendship with the Jewess, Henriette Herz, but, even more so, by his love of a married woman, which was the talk of the town. Wilhelm Dilthey, his biographer, destroyed much of Schleiermacher's correspondence in order to remove, as he said, "ugly spots" from his memory. Yet all this could not, and cannot, cause us to question the sincerity of Schleiermacher's religious feelings, his spiritual dignity and the originality of his thinking.

Schleiermacher became known by his book *On Religion* (1799), in which he defended religion "against its educated scorners." He intended to found an eternal covenant between the Christian faith and independent science. He professed firm confidence that no rational criticism could destroy Christian religion, which he conceived as the "feeling of absolute dependence," indispensable to human life but not closely connected with thought, knowledge and will. Personally convinced of the truth of Christianity, Schleiermacher nevertheless denied its claim "to be universal and to rule alone over mankind as the sole religion." He was strongly opposed to uniformity, and, above all, to uniformity in religion. He was an ardent defender of the rights of each person to have a religion of his own that corresponds to the uniqueness of his individuality. But Schleiermacher, who, in theology and philosophy, vindicated the cause of the individual, regarded him always as a link in the chain of history. As a historically minded thinker and as a philosopher of religion he refused to identify the infinite value of the individual, whom he acknowledged, with his independence from historical tradition and present society, and regarded this standpoint as justification of his activities as a churchman. Theology was to him no rational science but a compound of knowledge and rules which are needed for the maintenance and direction of the Christian community, and individual faith, valuable as it remains, requires emotional response and moral support on the part of a community of voluntary and devoted members. In the history of the Church, Schleiermacher achieved a notable success by effecting the union between Lutheranism and Calvinism in Prussia.

In his philosophical writings, Schleiermacher also insisted on the value of the individual, whom he regarded in his connection with nature and history. Fichte sneered at him and Hegel hated him, but Schleiermacher retaliated shrewdly. In his frequent quarrels with his fellow professors he did not rely on the teachings of the Sermon on the Mount.

ON THE GORGIAS

THE intuition of the true and perfectly existent, in other words, of the eternal and unalterable, with which, as we have seen, every exposition of Plato's philosophy commenced, has its opposite pole in the equally general, and, to common thought and being, no less original and underived, intuition of the imperfectly existent, ever flowing and mutable, which yet holds bound under its form all action and thought as they can be apprehended in actual, tangible reality. Therefore the highest and most general problem of philosophy is exclusively this—to apprehend and fix the *essential* in that fleeting chaos, to display it as the essential and good therein, and so, drawing forth to the full light of consciousness the apparent contradiction between those two intuitions, to reconcile it at the same time. This harmonizing process necessarily resolves itself into two factors, upon whose different relation to each other rests the difference of the methods. Setting out from the intuition of the perfectly existent to advance in the exposition up to the semblance, and thus, simultaneously with its solution, for the first time to awaken and explain the consciousness of this contradiction; this is, in relation to philosophy, the immediate way of proceeding. On the other hand, starting from the consciousness of the contradiction as a thing given to advance to the primary intuition as the means of its solution, and to lead up by force of the very necessity of such a mean toward it, this is the method which we have named the indirect or mediate, and which, being for many reasons especially suited to one who commences on ethical ground, is here placed by Plato in the center, as the true mean of connection and progressive formation from the original intuition, his elementary starting post, to the constructive exposition, the goal of his systematic conclusion.

Now the relation which, in the sphere of nature, being and semblance or sensation bear to one another in this antithesis, is the same as that which in ethics exists between good and pleasure or feeling. Therefore the principal object for the second part of Plato's works, and their common problem, will be to show, that science and art cannot be discovered, but only a deceitful semblance of both must be ever predominant, so long as these two are exchanged with each other—being with appearance, and good with pleasure. And advances are made to the solution of this problem naturally in a two-fold way, yet without holding each course entirely apart in different writings: on the one hand, namely, that which hitherto had passed for science and art is laid bare in its utter worthlessness; on the other, attempts are made, from the very position of knowing and acknowledging that antithesis to develop rightly the essence of science and art and their fundamental outlines. The Gorgias stands at the head of this class, because it rather limits itself as preparatory to the former task, then ventures upon the latter; and starting entirely from the ethical side, attacks at both ends the confusion existing herein, fixing on its inmost spirit, as the root, and it is openly displayed, as the fruits. The remaining dialogues observe this general distinction: they partly go farther back in the observation of the scientific in mere seeming, partly farther forward in the idea of true science, and partly contain other later consequences of what is here first advanced in preparation.

From this point, then, we observe a natural connection between the two main positions demonstrated to the interlocutors with Socrates in this dialogue. The first, that their pretensions to this possession of an art properly so called in their art of speaking are entirely unfounded; and the second, that they are involved in a profound mistake in their confusion of the good with the pleasant. And, from the same point likewise, the particular manner in which each is proved, and the arrangement of the whole, may be explained. For when it is the good that is under consideration, and the ethical object is predominant, truth must be considered more in reference to art than science, if, that is, unity is to be preserved in the work generally. And, moreover, it is art in its most general and comprehensive form that is here discussed, for the dialogue embraces everything connected with it, from its greatest object, the state, to its

1079

least, the embellishment of sensuous existence. Only, as his custom is, Plato is most fond of using the greater form as the scheme and representation of the general, and the less, on the other hand, as an example and illustration of the greater; that no one may lose himself, contrary to Plato's purpose, in the object of the latter, which can never be anything but a particular.

[324]

SCHLICK, MORITZ

SCHLICK, MORITZ (1882-1936). When, in 1936 a lunatic murdered Professor Schlick, many of the numerous admirers of the assassinated scholar considered it a particularly tragic irony that this nonsensical misdeed put an end to a life that was devoted to the inquiry into the meaning of life.

Schlick's aim was not the construction of a system of ideas or thoughts but the investigation of the way of philosophizing that satisfies the demands of the most scrupulous scientific conscience. This task involved skill in seeing through wrongly set problems and in surveying the consequences of wrong approaches to them, and Schlick himself was never afraid of abandoning previously elaborated views when, in the course of his development, he recognized their falsehood.

The principal results of Schlick's thinking are: a distinct demarcation between experience which is immediate and knowledge which is no vision but rather calculation and organization by means of concepts and symbols, and, furthermore, a new foundation of empiricism, which leans upon Berkeley and Hume but profits from modern logic. Reality is defined as happening in time. Every Real has a definite place in time. The task of science is to obtain knowledge of reality, and the true achievements of science can neither be destroyed nor altered by philosophy. But the aim of philosophy is to interpret these achievements correctly and to expound their deepest meaning.

Schlick was fundamentally a man who preferred aesthetic contemplation to exact science. But as a thinker he was convinced of the unique philosophical significance of natural science, and he branded it as a grave mistake to believe that the arts and cultural sciences are in any way equivalent to natural science.

THE CONSTRUCTION OF THEORIES

THEORETICAL science, as is obvious from its name, consists of theories—that is, of systems of propositions. Propositions constitute a system when they are related to one another through being concerned with the same objects; or even when they can be deduced from one another. The process of formulating a law of nature is, fundamentally, always the same. It consists, in the first place, of recording the observations of a natural process in a table which always contains the relevant measured values of those variable magnitudes which characterize the process. The next step is to discover a function which will represent in a single formula the distribution of values in this table. This formula is then considered to be the law describing the process as long as all new observations are in agreement with it. Inasmuch as the formula always contains more than what is actually observed, and also because it must hold for all processes of a similar kind, the formulation of any law involves a generalization, or a so-called induction. There is no such thing as a logically valid deduction going from the particular to the general: the latter can only be conjectured, but never logically inferred. Thus, the universal validity, or truth, of laws must always remain hypothetical. All laws of nature have the character of hypotheses: their truth is never absolutely certain. Hence, natural science consists of a combination of brilliant guesses and exact measurements. . . .

In the same way as a special law is the result of a series of single observations, a general law is the consequence of the inductive combination of several individual laws, until finally a relatively small number of general propositions which include the totality of natural laws is obtained. Thus today, for instance, all chemical laws can, in principle, be reduced to physical laws; and the dividing line between the different domains of physics which used to be externally related to one another (mechanics, acoustics, optics, theory of heat, etc.) has long since completely disappeared. At the present time, only mechanics and electrodynamics are left; and these are nowise independent of each other, but interpenetrate everywhere. Whether biology will continue to remain a special province, or whether it also will become incorporated in the domain of physics, is a question that will be discussed in due course.

In order to obtain a concrete description of nature (i.e., of nature as it really is), it is not sufficient to formulate laws: the abstract laws must, as it were, be given content. And in addition to these abstract laws, the constellation of reality (at the time of consideration), to which the formulas can be applied, must be stated. Such constellations are called by physicists boundary or initial conditions; and mathematically, they are expressed by the introduction of constants.

Here, we are considering the system of laws in itself, independently of all applications—that is to say, we are only studying general, and not particular, propositions. We can thus select out of this system, a group of the most general propositions from which all the others are derivable. This derivation is a purely logical deduction which can be undertaken without knowledge of the meaning of the symbols which occur in the laws. Hence, we will disregard, not only all application to individual cases, but also the meaning of all words and symbols—until the system is reduced to a purely formal structure, or empty framework which does not consist of actual propositions, but only of their forms (in logic, these are known as propositional functions). A system of this kind, which does not represent nature in actuality, but *all the possibilities in nature,* or in other words, its most general form—is known as a hypothetico-deductive system (Pieri). The propositions forming a group at the apex of this system, are called axioms; and the choice as to which propositions shall be taken as axioms is, to a certain extent, arbitrary. We may regard any proposition as an axiom, so long as we fulfil one condition, which is that all the other propositions in the system be derivable from the chosen group of axioms. Thus, the quality of being an axiom is not only in any sense a natural, intrinsic attribute or characteristic of a law; the only reason for choosing certain propositions as axioms, are those of their expediency or convenience. In the propositions derived from these axioms, further symbols, other than those used in the axioms, are introduced *by definition*. A definition consists of the introduction of new symbols, or signs, for the purpose of abbreviation. The choice as to which of these signs shall be regarded as fundamental symbols and which as derived from the latter by definition, is likewise arbitrary.

Examples:

$$E = \tfrac{1}{2}mv^2 \qquad\qquad M = mv$$

Definition of Energy   *Definition of Momentum*

But instead of mass and velocity, we can also write:

$$\frac{\text{Energy}}{\text{Momentum}} \quad : \quad v = \frac{2E}{M}$$

Thus, it is immaterial which magnitudes or quantities occur in the axioms.

Hence, the structure of a theory consists of: 1) axioms; 2) derived propositions and 3) definitions. In the symbolic representation of natural science, whether by means of words or of mathematical symbols, the three structural elements cannot be outwardly distinguished from one another.

The symbolic representation of a theory consists of sentences which in their turn are constituted of certain series of spoken or written signs: the theory itself consists primarily of "propositions." The question as to whether a sentence represents a true proposition or only a definition for example depends on the interpretations which explain it and give it its meaning. These do not form part of the symbolic representation itself, but are added to it—that is, they are added to a hypothetico-deductive system—from outside as it were, for example, in the form of ostensive definitions. They constitute the rules of the application of the sentences and are conclusive for the philosophical interpretation of the latter. It is, after all, necessary to refer to a reality which is described by the system of signs or symbols since, at some time or another, we must break out from their system. Only those sentences which, by virtue of their interpretation, represent genuine propositions, can communicate something about nature; the others are merely internal rules for signs and consequently are definitions.

[325]

SCHOPENHAUER, ARTHUR

SCHOPENHAUER, ARTHUR (1788-1860). Schopenhauer almost became an Englishman when his father, a citizen of Danzig, then in Poland, fearing the annexation of his native town by Prussia (which in fact was imminent), intended to take his wife, who was expecting a baby, to England, so that his son would not be a subject of the hated Prussian monarchy. However, the son was born before the parents could reach the land of their hope.

Arthur Schopenhauer did not share his father's predilection for England or his opposition to Prussian despotism. But he nevertheless adopted some English habits, read the *London Times* regularly, and remained aloof from any political movement in Germany, indifferent to nationalism, yet hating democracy, Judaism and Christianity. He preferred animals to his fellow men, and particularly he disliked women. British empiricism did not satisfy him, and his German contemporaries, Fichte, Schelling and Hegel, were branded by him as humbugs. He respected Kant from whose criticism he proceeded to his own philosophy. The wisdom and religion of India, the Vedas, Upanishads and Buddhism, aroused his enthusiasm, and he untiringly proclaimed the superiority of Indian thought to the European mind.

Although to his father's satisfaction, Schopenhauer had forgotten the German language during his stay in Paris and London, and had had to learn it again, when, at the age of seventeen, he returned to Germany, he became one of the greatest masters of German prose style. His clear and well-organized sentences proved able to captivate readers who recoil from the language of most of the German philosophers. Goethe, whom Schopenhauer knew personally and highly esteemed both as a poet and thinker, wrote in

Schopenhauer's album an epigram, saying: "If you will enjoy the value of your own personality you must enjoy the value of the world." Nothing could be more contrary to Schopenhauer's doctrine, for, according to it, the world is fundamentally evil. Its reality cannot be grasped by reason which is only capable of perceiving delusive appearances of the real things. The only real, metaphysical, cosmic being is the will which comprises both mental acts of the human individual and the drive, urge or instinctive force of the entire organic world. Even the crystallization of the diamond, or the turning of the magnet to the pole, or chemical affinities are regarded by Schopenhauer as utterances of the will which is essentially one. The fact that man takes cognizance of his body as much by way of reason as by immediate feeling, enables him to become aware of the will that works within his organism, and thus of the cosmic will which is identical with the former. To Schopenhauer this procedure offers the key to the understanding of the real world.

But, while the world of appearances or ideas is delusive, the world of the will is fundamentally evil. Will is the source of crime and suffering. The only salvation available to mankind is mortification of the will, complete resignation, extinction of the self.

Schopenhauer's pessimism had many followers. Of even greater influence was his doctrine of the superiority of instinct, the will, the unconscious drive to reason and knowledge, after Nietzsche had dissolved its connection with pessimism.

WILL AND IDEA

"THE world is my idea:"—this is a truth which holds good for everything that lives and knows, though man alone can bring it into reflective and abstract consciousness: If he really does this, he has attained to philosophical wisdom. It then becomes clear and certain to him that what he knows is not a sun and an earth, but only an eye that sees a sun, a hand that feels the earth; that the world which surrounds him is there only as idea, i.e., only in relation to something else, the consciousness, which is himself. If any truth can be asserted *a priori*, it is this: for it is the expression of the most general form of all possible and thinkable experience: a form which is more general than time, or space, or causality, for they all presuppose it; and each of these, which we have seen to be just so many modes of the principle of sufficient reason, is valid only for a particular class of ideas; whereas the antithesis of object and subject is the common form of all these classes, is that form under which alone any idea of whatever kind it may be, abstract or intuitive, pure or empirical, is possible and thinkable. No truth therefore is more certain, more independent of all others, and less in need of proof than this, that all that exists for knowledge and therefore this whole world, is only object in relation to subject, perception of a perceiver, in a word, idea. This is obviously true of the past and the future, as well as of the present, of what is furthest off, as of what is near; for it is true of time and space themselves, in which alone these distinctions arise. All that in any way belongs or can belong to the world is inevitably thus conditioned through the subject, and exists only for the subject. The world is idea.

*　　　*　　　*

This world in which we live and have our being is in its whole nature through and through *will*, and at the same time through and through *idea;* that this idea, as such, already presupposes a form, object and subject, is therefore relative; and if we ask what remains if we take away this form and all those forms which are subordinate to it, and which express the principle of sufficient reason, the answer must be that as something *toto genere* different from idea, this can be nothing but *will*, which is thus properly the *thing-in-itself*. Every one finds that he himself is this will, in which the real nature of the world consists, and he also finds that he is the knowing subject, whose idea the whole world is, the world which exists only in relation to his consciousness, as its necessary supporter. Every one is thus himself in a double aspect the whole world, the microcosm; finds both sides whole and complete in himself. And what he thus recognizes as his own real being also exhausts the being of the whole world—the macrocosm; thus the world, like man, is through and through *will,* and through and through *idea,* and nothing more than this. So we see the philosophy of Thales, which concerned the macrocosm, unite at this point with the philosophy of Socrates, which dealt with the micro-cosm, for the object of both is found to be the same.

One question may be more particularly considered, for it can only properly arise so long as one has not fully penetrated the meaning of the foregoing exposition, and may so far serve as an illustration of it. It is this: Every will is a will towards something, has an object, and end of its willing; what then is the final end, or towards what is that will striving that is exhibited to us as the being-in-itself of the world? This question rests, like so many others, upon the confusion of the thing-in-itself with the manifestation. The principle of sufficient reason, of which the law of moti-vation is also a form, extends only to the latter, not to the former. It is only of phenomena, of individual things, that a ground can be given, never of the will itself, nor of the idea in which it adequately objectifies itself. So then of every particular movement or change of any kind in nature, a cause is to be sought, that is, a condition that of necessity produced it, but never of the natural force itself which is revealed in this and innumerable similar phenomena; and it is therefore simple misunderstanding, arising from want of consideration, to ask for a cause of gravity, electricity, and so on. Only if one had somehow shown that gravity and electricity were not original special forces of nature, but only the manifestations of a more general force already known, would it be allowable to ask for the cause which made this force produce the phenomena of gravity or of electricity here. All this has been explained at length above. In the same way every particular act of will of a knowing individual (which is itself only a manifestation of will as the thing-in-itself) has necessarily a motive without which that act would never have occurred; but just as material causes contain merely the determination that at this time, in this place, and in this manner, a manifestation of this or that natural force must take place, so the motive determines only the act of will of a knowing being, at this time, in this place, and under these circumstances, as a particular act, but by no means determines that that being wills in general or wills in this manner; this is the expression of his intelligible character, which, as will itself, the thing-in-itself, is without ground, for it lies outside the province of the principle of sufficient reason. Therefore every man has permanent aims and motives by which he guides his conduct, and he can always give an account of his particular actions; but if he were asked why he wills at all, or why in general he wills to exist, he would have no answer, and the question would indeed seem to him meaningless; and this would be just the expression of his consciousness that he himself is nothing but will, whose willing stands by itself and requires more particular determination by motives only in its individual acts at each point of time.

In fact, freedom from all aim, from all limits, belongs to the nature of the will, which is an endless striving. This was already touched on above in the reference to centrifugal force. It also discloses itself in its simplest form in the lowest grade of the objectification of will, in gravitation, which we see constantly exerting itself, though a final goal is obviously impossible for it. For if, according to its will, all existing matter were collected in one mass, yet within this mass gravity, ever striving towards the center, would still wage war with impenetrability as rigidity or elasticity. The tendency of matter can therefore only be confined, never completed or appeased. But this is precisely the case with all tendencies of all phenomena of will. Every attained end is also the beginning of a new course, and so on *ad infinitum.* The plant raises its manifestation from the seed through the stem and the leaf to the blossom and the fruit, which again is the beginning of a new seed, a new individual, that runs through the old course, and so on through endless time. Such also is the life of the animal; procreation is its highest point, and after attaining to it, the life of the first individual quickly or slowly sinks, while a new life insures to nature the endurance of the species, and repeats the same phenomena. Indeed, the constant renewal of the matter of every organism is also to be regarded as merely the manifestation of this continual pressure and change, and physiologists are now ceasing to hold that it is the necessary reparation of the matter wasted in motion for the possible wearing out of the machine can by no means be equivalent to the support it is constantly receiving through nourishment. Eternal becoming, endless flux, characterizes the revelation of the inner nature of will. Finally, the same thing shows itself in human endeavors and desires, which always delude us by presenting their satisfaction as the final end of will. As soon as we attain to them they no longer appear the same, and therefore they soon grow stale, are forgotten, and though not openly disowned, are yet always thrown aside as vanished illusions. We are fortunate enough if there still remains something to wish for and to strive after, that the game may be kept up of constant transition from desire to satisfaction, and from satisfaction to a new desire, the rapid course of which is called happiness, and the slow course sorrow, and does not sink into that stagnation that shows itself in fearful *ennui* that paralyzes life, vain yearning without a definite object, deadening languor. According to all this, when the will is enlightened by knowledge, it always knows what it wills now and here, never what it wills in general; every particular act of will has its end, the whole will has none; just as every particular phenomenon of nature is determined by a sufficient cause so far as concerns its appearance in this place at this time, but the force which manifests itself in it has no general cause, for it belongs to the thing-in-itself, to the groundless will. The single example of self-knowledge of the will as a whole is the idea as a whole, the whole world of perception. It is the objectification, the revelation, the mirror of the will.

[326]

1089

SCHWEITZER, ALBERT

SCHWEITZER, ALBERT (1875-   ). The greatest and most famous Universities of the world have offered to Albert Schweitzer a professorship endowed with all possible advantages. As the historian of *The Quest of the Historical Jesus* (Geschichte der Leben Jesu Forschung, 1906; English edition, 1910), of *Paul and his Interpreters* (1912), and *The Mysticism of Paul the Apostle* (1931); as the authoritative biographer of *Johann Sebastian Bach* (1904); as the author of *Civilization and Ethics* (1929) and *The Philosophy of Civilization* (1932), Schweitzer could have made his own choice whether to become a professor of theology or of philosophy, of musicology or of history, in America, England, France or Germany. But he declined the most promising offers. Sacrificing a brilliant academic career in order to study medicine, he became a missionary-physician in Lambarene, French West Africa. Since 1913, Schweitzer has lived in that plague-stricken area, devoting himself to the medical treatment and spiritual education of the Negroes. He travelled to Europe and, in 1949, to America to deliver lectures, to do research for his books, and to gather funds for the maintenance of his activities in Africa.

In the wilderness, Schweitzer remained a man of widest interests and original views on life, science, philosophy and religion. He interprets the teachings of Jesus as determined by the expectation of the imminent end of the world. Although far from Europe, he warned against Hitler's savageness, but was not heeded. The fundamental idea of Schweitzer's ethics and philosophy is "reverence for life," which involves sympathy with and respect for all creatures, as well as human solidarity and devotion to spiritual progress. While most other philosophers of life are somewhat inclined to exalt egoism, will to power or sensualism, to Schweitzer the cult of life means altruism, love of mankind without regard to origin, creed or color. Further, altruism does not mean resignation but rather enhanced activity on behalf of humanity.

INDIVIDUAL AND SOCIETY

ETHICAL conflicts between society and the individual continue to exist because the individual has not only a personal but also a supra-personal sense of responsibility. Where my own person only is in question I can always be patient, always forgive, always be sympathetic, always be compassionate. But we all have the experience of being placed in positions where we are responsible not only for ourselves but also for some affair or business, and are then forced to make decisions which run counter to personal morality. The manufacturer who directs a business, be it ever such a small one; the musician who conducts performances; these can no longer remain human beings merely, however much they would prefer to do so. The one must dismiss an inefficient or drunken workman, in spite of all the sympathy which he may feel with him and his family; the other must prevent a singer whose voice has given way from taking any further part, however much pain this may cause to her.

The more comprehensive is a man's activity the more he comes into the position of being obliged to surrender some portion of his humanity to his supra-personal responsibility. Current thought usually tries to escape from this dilemma by laying down as a dogma that personal responsibility is covered and superseded by that of society in general. In this way the community tries to console the individual. For the comfort of those to whom this dogma seems too categorical it may perhaps add certain other principles which undertake to determine in a universally valid manner to what extent personal morality has ever a right to interfere.

Current ethics cannot possibly avoid subscription to this surrender. It has not the means for defending the stronghold of personal morality, since it has no absolute notions of good and evil at its disposal. Not so the ethic of reverence for life. It is in actual possession of what the other lacks. Therefore it never surrenders the fortress, even when this is in a state of constant siege. It feels itself capable of holding it permanently, and of keeping the besiegers in a breathless condition by making repeated sallies.

Only that entirely universal and absolute purposiveness with regard to the maintenance and enhancement of life, which is the aim of reverence for life, is really ethical. All other necessity or purposiveness is not ethical, but more or less urgent necessity or more or less purposive purposiveness. In the conflict which goes on between the maintenance of my own existence and the destruction and injury of other existence, I can never unite the ethical and the necessary in a relatively ethical, but must always make my own decision between what is ethical and what is necessary, and, if I choose the latter, must shoulder the guilt of having injured life. Similarly, I may never imagine that in the struggle between personal and supra-personal responsibility it is possible to make a compromise between the ethical and the purposive in the shape of a relative ethic, or to let the ethical be superseded by the purposive. On the contrary, it is my duty to make my own decision as between the two. If, under the pressure of supra-personal responsibility, I surrender to the purposive, I am guilty to some extent through my failure to uphold the principle of reverence for life.

The attempt to combine in a relative ethic the purposive, dictated by supra-personal responsibility, and the really ethical, is particularly blatant, because it logically follows that the man who obeys the commands of suprapersonal responsibility is acting unegoistically.

[327]

SENECA, LUCIUS ANNAEUS

SENECA, LUCIUS ANNAEUS (4 B.C.-65 A.D.). Before Seneca fell into disgrace with Emperor Nero and was forced to commit suicide, he was generally considered, as Elder Pliny said, "the leader in letters and in government;" he was Nero's prime minister. The tragedies he wrote inspired dramatic authors until the days of Queen Elizabeth of England, Louis XIV of France and Napoleon I. Calling himself a Stoic, Seneca wrote treatises on the natural sciences, psychology and moral questions. He was a prominent jurist, and was acknowledged by his contemporaries to be an authority on geology, meteorology and marine zoology. The rise of Christianity was by no means detrimental to Seneca's fame and influence. He was said to have exchanged letters with Paul the Apostle; but these letters, often quoted, were evidently forged. Although the fathers of the Church knew that Seneca was no Christian, they highly appreciated his moral doctrines. So did later Christian philosophers and theologians until Thomas à Kempis. However, it was the age of the Renaissance that enhanced Seneca's importance to Western civilization. His Stoicism penetrated into the minds of Montaigne, Rabelais, Bacon, Shakespeare, Ben Jonson, Corneille and Racine, Milton and Dryden. Even in the 19th century it attracted poets like Wordsworth and thinkers like Emerson.

ON THE HAPPY LIFE

ALL men wish to live happily, but are dull at perceiving exactly what it is that makes life happy: and so far is it from being easy to attain to happiness that the more eagerly a man struggles to reach it the further he departs from it, if he takes the wrong road.

Let us not therefore decide whither we must tend, and by what path, without the advice of some experienced person who has explored the region which we are about to enter, because this journey is not subject to the same conditions as others.

True happiness consists in not departing from nature and in molding our conduct according to her laws and model. A happy life is one which is in accordance with its own nature, and cannot be brought about unless in the first place the mind be sound and vigorous, enduring all things with most admirable courage suited to the times in which it lives, and must be able to enjoy the bounty of Fortune without becoming her slave.

*   *   *

A happy life consists in a mind which is free, upright, undaunted and steadfast beyond the influence of fear or desire. A man must be accompanied by a continual cheerfulness, a high happiness, which comes indeed from on high because he delights in what he has. If we attain to this, then there will dawn upon us those invaluable blessings, the repose of a mind that is at rest in a safe haven, its lofty imaginings, its great and steady delight at casting out errors and learning to know the truth, its courtesy and its cheerfulness, in all of which we shall take delight.

Virtue is a lofty quality, sublime, royal, unconquerable, untiring. You will meet virtue in the temple, the market-place, the senate-house, manning the walls, covered with dust, sunburnt, horny-handed; you will find pleasure sulking out of sight, seeking for shady nooks.

The highest good is immortal. It knows no ending, and does not admit of either satiety or regret; for a right-thinking mind never alters or becomes hateful to itself, nor do the best things ever undergo any change. But pleasure dies at the very moment when it charms us most. It has no great scope, and therefore it soon cloys and wearies us, and fades away as soon as its first impulse is over. Indeed, we cannot depend upon anything whose nature is to change.

A man should be unbiased and ought not to be conquered by external things. He ought to feel confidence in his own spirit, and so order his life as to be ready alike for good or bad fortune. But let not his confidence be without knowledge, nor his knowledge without steadfastness. Let him abide by what he has determined, and let there be no erasure in his doctrine.

* * *

Let reason be encouraged by the senses to seek for the truth, and draw its first principles from thence. Indeed, it has no other base of operations or place from which to start in pursuit of truth: it must fall back upon itself. Even the all-embracing universe and God who is its guide extends Himself forth into outward things, and yet altogether returns from all sides back to Himself. Let our mind do the same thing.

By this means we shall obtain a strength and an ability which are united; we shall derive from it that reason which never halts between two opinions, nor is dull in forming its perceptions, beliefs or convictions. Such a mind, when it has ranged itself in order, made its various parts agree together, and, if I may so express myself, harmonized them, has attained to the highest good. For it has nothing evil or hazardous remaining, nothing to shake it or make it stumble. It will do everything under the guidance of its own will, and nothing unexpected will befall it, but whatever may be done by it will turn out well, and that, too, readily and easily, without the doer having recourse to any underhand devices.

You may, then, boldly declare that the highest good is singleness of mind, for where agreement and unity are, there must the virtues be. It is the vices that are at war with one another.

[328]

SEXTUS EMPIRICUS

SEXTUS EMPIRICUS (About 200 A.D.). The writings of Sextus Empiricus are an arsenal of scepticism which has furnished pagan thinkers with weapons to combat Christianity, Christian apologists with arguments to refute paganism, and, in later centuries, philosophers like Montaigne with reasons in defense of the independence of their minds on dogmatism of any kind.

Sextus, a physician by profession, was not so much an original thinker as an informed popularizer, a skilful and vigorous writer, who was able to summarize his thoughts by striking formulas. He attacked not only dogmatic philosophers and theologians but any expert, whether of mathematics or grammar, who claimed infallibility. In this way he has also given highly valuable information about the history of various sciences such as they had developed in his time.

TEN MODES OF THOUGHT

THEY are these: The first is based upon the differences in animals; the second upon the differences in men; the third upon the difference in the constitution of the organs of sense; the fourth upon circumstances; the fifth upon position, distance, and place; the sixth upon mixtures; the seventh upon the quantity and constitution of objects; the eighth upon relation; the ninth upon frequency or rarity of occurrences; the tenth upon systems, customs, laws, mythical beliefs, and dogmatic opinions. We make this order ourselves. These tropes come under three general heads: the standpoint of the judge, the standpoint of the thing judged, and the standpoint of both together. . . .

It is probable therefore, that the inequalities and differences in origin cause great antipathies, in the animals, and the result is incompatibility, discord, and conflict between the sensations of the different animals. Again, the differences in the principal parts of the body, especially in those fitted by nature to judge and to perceive, may cause the greatest differences in their ideas of objects, according to the differences in the animals themselves. As for example, those who have the jaundice call that yellow which appears to us white, and those who have bloodshot eyes call it blood-red. Accordingly, as some animals have yellow eyes, and others blood-shot ones, and still others whitish ones, and others eyes of other colors, it is probable, I think, that they have a different perception of colors. Furthermore, when we look steadily at the sun for a long time, and then look down at a book, the letters seem to us gold colored, and dance around. Now some animals have by nature a luster in their eyes, and these emit a fine and sparkling light so that they see at night, and we may reasonably suppose that external things do not appear the same to them as to us. Jugglers by lightly rubbing the wick of the lamp with metal rust, or with the dark yellow fluid of the sepia, make those who are present appear now copper colored and now black, according to the amount of the mixture used; if this be so, it is much more reasonable to suppose that because of the mixture of different fluids in the eyes of animals, their ideas of objects would be different. Furthermore, when we press the eye on the side, the figures, forms and sizes of things seen appear elongated and narrow. It is, therefore, probable that such animals as have the pupil oblique and long, as goats, cats, and similar animals, have ideas different from those of the animals which have a round pupil. Mirrors according to their different construction, sometimes show the external object smaller than reality, as concave ones, and sometimes long and narrow, as the convex ones do; others show the head of the one looking into it down, and the feet up. As some of the vessels around the eye fall entirely outside the eye, on account of their protuberance, while others are more sunken, and still others are placed in an even surface, it is probable that for this reason also the ideas vary, and dogs, fishes, lions, men and grasshoppers do not see the same things, either of the same size, or of similar form, but according to the impression on the organ of sight of each animal respectively. The same thing is true in regard to the other senses; for how can it be said that shellfish, birds of prey, animals covered with spines, those with feathers and those with scales would be affected in the same way by the sense of touch? And how can the sense of hearing perceive alike in animals which have the narrowest auditory passages, and in those that are furnished with the widest, or in those with hairy ears and those with smooth ones? For we, even, hear differently when we partially stop up the ears, from what we do when we use them naturally. The sense of smell also varies according to differences in animals, since even our sense of smell is affected when we have taken cold and the phlegm is too abundant, and also parts around our head are flooded with too much blood, for we then avoid odors that seem agreeable to others, and feel as if we were injured by them. Since also some of the animals are moist by nature and full of secretions, and still others have either yellow or black bile prevalent and abundant, it is reasonable because of this to think that odorous things appear different to each one of them. And it is the same in regard to things of taste, as some animals have the tongue rough and dry and others very moist. We too, when we have a dry tongue in fever, think that whatever we take is gritty, bad tasting, or bitter; and this we experience because of the varying degrees of the humors that are said to be in us. Since, then, different animals have different organs for taste, and a greater or less amount of the various humors, it can well be that they form different ideas of the same objects as regards their taste. For just as the same food on being absorbed becomes in some places veins, in other places arteries, and in other places bones, nerves, or other tissues, showing different power according to the difference of the parts receiving it; just as the same water absorbed by the trees becomes in some places bark, in other places branches, and in other places fruit, perhaps a fig or a pomegranate, or something else; just as the breath of the musician, one and the same when blown into the flute, becomes sometimes a high tone and sometimes a low one, and the same pressure of the hand upon the lyre sometimes causes a deep tone and sometimes a high tone, so it is natural to suppose that external objects are regarded differently according to the different constitution of the animals which perceive them. We may see this more clearly in the things that are sought for and avoided by animals. For example, myrrh appears very agreeable to men and intolerable to beetles and bees. Oil also, which is useful to men, destroys wasps and bees if sprinkled on them; and sea-water, while it is unpleasant and poisonous to men if they drink it, is most agreeable and sweet to fishes. Swine also prefer to wash in vile filth rather than in pure clean water. Furthermore, some animals eat grass and some eat herbs; some live in the woods, others eat seeds; some are carnivorous, and others lactivorous; some enjoy putrefied food, and others fresh food; some raw food, and others that which is prepared by cooking; and in general that which is agreeable to some is disagreeable and fatal to others, and should be avoided by them. Thus hemlock makes the quail fat, and henbane the hogs, and these, as it is known, enjoy eating lizards; deer also eat poisonous animals, and swallows, the cantharidae. Moreover, ants and flying ants, when swallowed by men, cause discomfort and colic; but the bear, on the contrary, whatever sickness he may have, becomes stronger by devouring them. The viper is benumbed if one twig of the oak touches it, as is also the bat by a leaf of the plane tree. The elephant flees before the ram, and the lion before the cock, and seals from the rattling of beans that are being pounded, and the tiger from the sound of the drum. Many other examples could be given, but that we may not seem to dwell longer than is necessary on this subject, we conclude by saying that since the same things are pleasant to some and unpleasant to others, and the pleasure and displeasure depend on the ideas, it must be that different animals have different ideas of objects. And since the same things appear different according to the difference in the animals, it will be possible for us to say how the external object appears to us, but as to how it is in reality we shall suspend our judgment. For we cannot ourselves judge between our own ideas and those of other animals, being ourselves involved in the difference, and therefore much more in need of being judged than being ourselves able to judge. And furthermore, we cannot give the preference to our own mental representations over those of other animals, either without evidence or with evidence, for besides the fact that perhaps there is no evidence, as we shall show, the evidence so called will be either manifest to us or not. If it is not manifest to us, then we cannot accept it with conviction; if it is manifest to us, since the question is in regard to what is manifest to animals, and we use as evidence that which is manifest to us who are animals, then it is to be questioned if it is true as it is manifest to us. It is absurd, however, to try to base the questionable on the questionable, because the same thing is to be believed and not to be believed, which is certainly impossible. The evidence is to be believed in so far as it will furnish a proof, and disbelieved in so far as it is itself to be proved. We shall therefore have no evidence according to which we can give preference to our own ideas over those so-called irrational animals. Since, therefore, ideas differ according to the difference in animals, and it is impossible to judge them, it is necessary to suspend the judgment in regard to external objects.

[329]

SHANKARA

SHANKARA (9th century A.D.). The reports on the life of Shankara, who is considered by some authorities the greatest commentator, even the greatest philosopher of the Hindus, are adorned with myths and legends that ascribe to him superhuman powers and the performance of many miracles. He was revered as a saint and as a scholar whose theoretical and practical teachings became of great consequence. He systematized the philosophy of the Upanishads, and, in his commentaries, elucidated many passages of the Vedanta. He is characterized as a gentle and tolerant reformer and also as an everready controversialist who was eager to refute any doctrine that differed from his own. He denied the relevance of caste and lineage, and denounced the desire for personal separateness as the cause of bondage to conditional existence, birth and death. Devotion is an instrument of emancipation from ignorance and enslavement. Devotion is not to be distinguished from contemplation. Truth is to be understood intellectually, but the highest spiritual intuition leads to the union of the knower, the known and knowledge. Shankara often described the way to that goal as the denial of selfness in thought, feeling and action.

THE KNOWLEDGE OF SOUL

KNOWLEDGE alone effects emancipation.
As fire is indispensable to cooking,
So knowledge is essential to deliverance.
Knowledge alone disperses ignorance,
As sunlight scatters darkness—not so acts;
For ignorance originates in works.
The world and all the course of mundane things
Are like the vain creation of a dream,
In which Ambition, Hatred, Pride and Passion
Appear like phantoms mixing in confusion.
While the dream lasts the universe seems real,
But when 'tis past the world exists no longer.

Like the deceptive silver of a shell,
So at first sight the world deludes the man
Who takes mere semblance for reality.
As golden bracelets are in substance one
With gold, so are all visible appearances
And each distinct existence one with Brahma.
By action of the fivefold elements
Through acts performed in former states of being,
Are formed corporeal bodies, which become
The dwelling-place of pleasure and of pain.
The soul inwrapped in five investing sheaths
Seems formed of these, and all its purity
Darkened, like crystal laid on colored cloth.
As winnowed rice is purified from husk
So is the soul disburdened of its sheaths
By force of meditation, as by threshing.
The soul is like a king whose ministers
Are body, senses, mind and understanding.
The soul is wholly separate from these,
Yet witnesses and overlooks their actions.
The foolish think the spirit acts, whereas
The senses are the actors; so the moon
Is thought to move when clouds are passing o'er it.
When intellect and mind are present, then
Afflictions, inclinations, pleasures, pains
Are active; in profound and dreamless sleep
When intellect is non-existent, these
Exist not; therefore they belong to mind.
As brightness is inherent in the sun,
Coolness in water, warmness in the fire,
E'en so existence, knowledge, perfect bliss,
And perfect purity inhere in soul.
The understanding cannot recognize
The soul, nor does the soul need other knowledge
To know itself, e'en as a shining light
Requires no light to make itself perceived.
The soul declares its own condition thus:

"I am distinct from body, I am free
From birth, old age, infirmity and death.
I have no senses; I have no connection
With sound or sight or objects of sensation.
I am distinct from mind, and so exempt
From passion, pride, aversion, fear and pain.
I have no qualities, I am without
Activity and destitute of option,
Changeless, eternal, formless, without taint,
Forever free, forever without stain.
I, like the boundless ether, permeate
The universe within, without, abiding
Always, forever similar in all,
Perfect, immovable, without affection,
Existence, knowledge, undivided bliss,
Without a second, One, Supreme am I."

*   *   *

That which is through, above, below, complete,
Existence, wisdom, bliss, without a second,
Endless, eternal, one—know that as Brahma.
That which is neither coarse nor yet minute,
That which is neither short nor long, unborn,
Imperishable, without form, unbound
By qualities, without distinctive marks,
Without a name—know that indeed as Brahma.
Nothing exists but Brahma, when aught else
Appears to be, 'tis, like the mirage, false.

[330]

SIDGWICK, HENRY

SIDGWICK, HENRY (1838-1900). Sidgwick, one of the founders
of the Society for Psychical Research and the Ethical Society in
Cambridge, England, where he was a professor, gave a number of
suggestions which have been of consequence for the latest development of philosophical thinking in England and America. A follower

of John Stuart Mill in ethics, politics and economics, Sidgwick endeavored, especially in his *Methods of Ethics* (1874) to found utilitarianism anew by resorting to Thomas Reid's "natural realism" and sweeping away all hedonistic theories. His efforts to combine utilitarian ethics with intuitionist theory of knowledge did not entirely satisfy Sidgwick, who was aware of the difficulty of his task and constantly tried to improve or correct his arguments without abandoning his fundamental position. He recognized that philosophical empiricism was based upon conceptions that cannot be traced back to experience but declined Kant's theory of experience. Sidgwick has studied "with reverent care and patience" what is called the morality of common sense. For he was convinced that, despite all historical changes and diversities of thoughts and actions, there is a large region of broad agreement in the details of morality, without any attempt to penetrate into the ultimate grounds upon which principles of moral action may be constructed. Sidgwick did not only regard this common-sense morality as the proper starting point for philosophical inquiries into ethical problems, but he thought that the work of the philosopher has to be aided, and, in a way, controlled by the moral judgment of "persons with less philosophy but more special experience."

MORALITY OF COMMON SENSE

THE philosopher's practical judgment on particular problems of duty is liable to be untrustworthy, unless it is aided and controlled by the practical judgment of others who are not philosophers. This may seem to some a paradox. It may be thought that so far as a philosopher has a sound general theory of right, he must be able to apply it to determine the duties of any particular station in life, if he has taken due pains to inform himself as to that station and its circumstances. And this would doubtless be true if his information could be made complete; but this it cannot be. He can only learn from others the facts which they have consciously observed and remembered; but there is an important element in the experience of themselves and their predecessors—the continuous experience of social generations—which finds no place in any statement of facts or reasoned forecast of consequences that they could furnish; it is only represented in their judgments as to what ought to be done and aimed at. Hence it is a common observation that the judgments of practical men as to what ought to be done in particular circumstances are often far sounder than the reasons they give for them; the judgments represent the result of experience unconsciously as well as consciously imbibed; the reasons have to be drawn from that more limited part of experience which has been the subject of conscious observation, information, and memory. This is why a moral philosopher, in my opinion, should always study with reverent care and patience what I am accustomed to call the morality of common sense. By this I do not mean the morality of "the world"—*i.e.*, the moral notions and judgments of persons who are not seriously concerned about their moral duty—who are always perhaps in a majority. Such persons, indeed, have a morality, and it is better than their actions; they approve rules which they do not carry out, and admire virtues which they do not imitate. Still, taking the morality of the worldly at its best, it would be wasted labor to try to construct it into a consistent system of thought; what there is in it of wisdom and truth is too much intermixed with a baser element, resulting from want of singleness of heart and aim in those whose thoughts it represents. What the worldly really want—if I may speak plainly—is not simply to realize the good life in virtue of its supreme worth to humanity, but to realize it as much as they can while keeping terms with all their appetites and passions, their sordid interests and vulgar ambitions. The morality that the world works out in different ages and countries and different sections of society, under the influence of the spirit of compromise, is not without interest for the historian and the sociologist; but it was not to this mixed stuff that I just now referred when I said that the moral philosopher should study with reverent and patient care the morality of common sense. I referred to the moral judgments—and especially the spontaneous unreflected judgments on particular cases, which are sometimes called moral intuitions—of those persons, to be found in all walks and

stations of life, whose earnest and predominant aim is to do their duty; of whom it may be said that
> "though they slip and fall,
> They do not blind their souls with clay,"

but after each lapse and failure recover and renew their rectitude of purpose and their sense of the supreme value of goodness. Such persons are to be found, not alone or chiefly in hermitages and retreats—if there are still any hermitages and retreats—but in the thick and heat of the struggle of active life, in all stations and ranks, in the Churches and outside the Churches. It is to their judgments on the duties of their station, in whatever station they may be found, that the moral philosopher should, as I have said, give reverent attention, in order that he may be aided and controlled by them in his theoretical construction of the science of right.

[331]

SIMMEL, GEORG

SIMMEL, GEORG (1858-1918). From about 1900 to the outbreak of the First World War, Simmel was considered one of the greatest contemporary philosophers. Not favored by the Prussian government, Simmel was a lecturer, then an associate professor at the University of Berlin, and only a few years before his death he was appointed full professor at the University of Strasbourg. As long as he lectured in Berlin, his audience was composed mostly of students from Russia and Central and Southern Europe where his fame was even greater than in Germany. Nevertheless, he did not form a school. Many of his former pupils died on the battlefield, others, uprooted by the events of war and revolution, were forced to renounce philosophy altogether, or turned to radical Marxism or nationalism, both of which were contrary to Simmel's mind which, despite all changes, maintained a relativist attitude.

Simmel's talents for psychological analysis are unsurpassed, and he always succeeded in elucidating psychological insight by philosophical aspects, no matter whether he dealt with Platonic ideas or fashions, Schopenhauer's pessimism or the flirt, the effects of money lending or the question of theistic faith. He interpreted Kant's *a priori*, which he himself adopted, psychologically and as

1105

supporting relativism. Later he developed, independently of American thinkers, a kind of pragmatism. Likewise, he was independent of Bergson when he tried to overcome his relativism by a belief in the self-transcendence of life. From a purely descriptive ethics he proceeded to one of valid values. He always remained an unorthodox Kantian, stressing the antagonism between immediate experience and the elaboration of this experience by the creative human spirit, insisting that the natural sciences as well as history offer only an image of reality that is transformed by the theoretical or historical *a priori*. According to Simmel, sociology does not belong to philosophy. Sociology and philosophy offer two different aspects of the situation of man in the world. They are two autonomous interpretations of mental life. Simmel started with studies *On Social Differentiation* (1890), then published his *Philosophy of Money* (1900) and *Sociology* (1908). A thorough student of Marx, he admitted the influence of economic facts on intellectual attitudes but insisted that the effects of intellectual patterns on economics act likewise. He maintained that the decisive factor of human attitudes is antecedent to changes of social or economic institutions. Sociology is conceived by Simmel as the doctrine of the forms of the relations between individuals, independent of spiritual contents which are subject to historical change. It is the "geometry of social life."

Religion and the arts represent to Simmel autonomous worlds which are independent of science but accessible to the philosopher, provided he does not disregard their autonomous foundations. In his monographies on *Goethe* (1913) and *Rembrandt* (1916), Simmel tried to show that the poet and artist while forming his own image of life, although determined by the historical situation of his lifetime, transcends historical conditions and testifies that life always hints beyond itself. The principal problem of culture is formulated by Simmel as the difficulty to seize life without violating it.

SOCIETY

SOCIETY, in its broadest sense, is found wherever several individuals enter into reciprocal relations. From a purely ephemeral association for the purpose of a casual promenade to the complete unity of a family, or a guild of the Middle Ages, one must recognize socialization of the most varying kind and degree. The particular causes and aims, without which socialization never takes place, comprise, to a certain extent, the body, the *material* of the social process. That the result of these causes, and the pursuance of these aims call forth, among the persons concerned, a reciprocal relationship, or a socialization, this is the *form* in which the content of social organization clothes itself. The entire existence of a special science of society rests upon the isolation of this form by means of scientific abstraction. For it is evident that the same form and the same kind of socialization can arise in connection with the most varied elements and take place for the most diverse ends. Socialization in general takes place as well in a religious congregation as in a band of conspirators, in a trust as well as in a school of art, in a public gathering as well as in a family; and we find also certain formal similarities in the special characteristics and development of all such unions. We find, for example, the same forms of authority and subordination, of competition, imitation, opposition, division of labor in social groups which are the most different possible in their aims and in their moral character. We find the formation of a hierarchy the embodiment of the group-forming principles in symbols, the division in parties, all stages of freedom or restriction of the individual in relation to the group, interaction and stratification of groups themselves, and definite forms of reaction against external influence. This similarity of form and its development, in the case of groups with the most complete heterogeneity of material conditions, reveals forces lying back of these immediate conditions, and suggests the possibility of constituting, by abstraction, a legitimate realm of investigation, namely that of socialization as such and the study of its forms. These forms are evolved through contact of the individuals, but relatively independent of the basis of such contact, and their sum makes up that concrete thing which we designate by the abstraction—society. [332]

SIRACH, JESUS

SIRACH, JESUS, son of (About 200 B.C.). Ever since the book written by Jesus, son of Sirach, has become known it has edified readers of all succeeding generations up to the present day. It has confirmed pious people in their faith. It has impressed sceptical-minded readers by its vigorous conviction. It has inspired poets, philosophers, statesmen and plain people. Above all, it has been valued as a rich fountain of proverbial wisdom and the personal confession of a man of large experience. Although it has not been accepted into the Protestant canon and was placed among the books of Apocrypha, it has generally been as highly appreciated as the books of the Bible itself.

The author was a contemporary of the high priest Simon II who died in 199 B.C., and he certainly was no longer alive when the Jewish people were afflicted by the persecutions which preceded the rise of the Maccabees. In his youth, Jesus ben Sirach had studied the Bible and books of popular wisdom. Then a calumniator endangered his life and forced him to flee from his native town, but after a while he was vindicated and lived for the rest of his life in Jerusalem. During his exile, he meditated on his misfortune, and observed the vicissitudes of life which others had to endure. These experiences, and not so much his previous readings, are the substance of his book. He was neither a priest nor a *Sofer* (skilled interpreter of the law), but a layman who used to deliver popular speeches. His book was translated into Greek by his grandson under the title *Wisdom of Jesus the Son of Sirach*. Its Latin title is *Ecclesiasticus*. It also was translated into many other languages. The Hebrew original was lost. In 1896, some parts of it were found in a cellar of the Ezra Synagogue in Cain. Later these were augmented so that now about three fifths of the original are extant.

WISE MEN AND FOOLS

THERE is a reproof that is not comely: again, some man holdeth his tongue, and he is wise.

It is much better to reprove, than to be angry secretly: and he that confesseth his fault shall be preserved from hurt.

How good is it, when thou art reproved, to shew repentance! for so shalt thou escape wilful sin.

As is the lust of a eunuch to deflower a virgin; so is he that executeth judgment with violence.

There is one that keepeth silence, and is found wise: and another by much babbling becometh hateful.

Some man holdeth his tongue, because he hath not to answer: and some keepeth silence, knowing his time.

A wise man will hold his tongue till he see opportunity: but a babbler and a fool will regard no time.

He that useth many words shall be abhorred; and he that taketh to himself authority therein shall be hated.

There is a sinner that hath good success in evil things; and there is a gain that turneth to loss.

There is a gift that shall not profit thee; and there is a gift whose recompense is double.

There is an abasement because of glory; and there is that lifteth up his head from a low estate.

There is that buyeth much for a little, and repayeth it sevenfold.

A wise man by his words maketh himself beloved: but the graces of fools shall be poured out.

The gift of a fool shall do thee no good when thou hast it; neither yet of the envious for his necessity: for he looketh to receive many things for one.

He giveth little, and upbraideth much; he openeth his mouth like a crier; to-day he lendeth, and to-morrow will he ask it again: such a one is to be hated of God and man.

The fool saith, I have no friends, I have no thanks for all my good deeds, and they that eat my bread speak evil of me.

How oft, and of how many shall he be laughed to scorn! for he knoweth not aright what it is to have; and it is all one unto him as if he had it not.

To slip upon a pavement is better than to slip with the tongue: so the fall of the wicked shall come speedily.

An unseasonable tale will always be in the mouth of the unwise.

A wise sentence shall be rejected when it cometh out of a fool's mouth; for he will not speak it in due season.

There is that is hindered from sinning through want: and when he taketh rest, he shall not be troubled.

There is that destroyeth his own soul through bashfulness, and by accepting of persons overthroweth himself.

There is that for bashfulness promiseth to his friend, and maketh him his enemy for nothing.

A lie is a foul blot in a man, yet it is continually in the mouth of the untaught.

A thief is better than a man that is accustomed to lie: but they both shall have destruction to heritage.

The disposition of a liar is dishonorable, and his shame is ever with him.

A wise man shall promote himself to *honor* with his words: and he that hath understanding will please great men.

He that tilleth his land shall increase his heap: and he that pleaseth great men shall get pardon for iniquity.

Presents and gifts blind the eyes of the wise, and stop up his mouth that he cannot reprove.

Wisdom that is hid, and treasure that is hoarded up, what profit is in them both?

Better is he that hideth his folly than a man that hideth his wisdom.

Necessary patience in seeking the Lord is better than he that leadeth his life without a guide.

[333]

SOCRATES

SOCRATES (470-399 B.C.). The Delphic Oracle, regarded as omniscient by great and small and old and young in ancient Greece, used to communicate its knowledge in obscure and equivocal phrases. However, when asked whether there was any man wiser than Socrates, it replied simply and clearly: No one is wiser.

Hearing of this pronouncement, Socrates himself was rather disturbed. For he had steadily disclaimed that he was wise or that he possessed any knowledge. Rather, it was his manner to proceed from the statement that he was an ignorant person, and the only merit he claimed was to be aware of his ignorance. So he went among pretentious people of various professions, particularly rhetoricians and sophists, questioning their knowledge, until he became convinced that they were quite as ignorant as he, but that they did not admit, nor were they even aware of, their ignorance.

Socrates was the son of a stone-cutter and a midwife, and he liked to draw a parallel between his method of making people think and his mother's calling. Before he began to teach, Socrates had served in the army of Athens, his native city, had distinguished himself on the battlefield, and had held offices in the Athenian administration. He owned a house in the city and a modest capital sum, which he was wise enough to entrust for investment to his friend and pupil Crito, an experienced businessman. Socrates, therefore, could afford to teach without demanding fees. While doing so, he embittered other teachers, and aroused suspicion in the minds of influential fellow citizens. His rather eccentric manners, his fondness of jesting, and, above all, his repeated refusal to subordinate his judgment to political party purposes aggravated his situation. Accused of corrupting the youth of Athens by his teaching, Socrates was sentenced to death. On several occasions he could have escaped from jail, but he insisted on his obligation to respect the sentence even though it be wrong. His preparedness to die and his serene fortitude during the last hours of his life gained the admiration of both his contemporaries and posterity.

Socrates did not put his doctrines into writing; he taught orally. His pupils adored him despite his ugliness and slovenliness. Many of them belonged to Athens' aristocracy, while others were humble people. Some of them became outstanding philosophers, like Euclid, Phaedo, Antisthenes, Aristippus, and Plato, the greatest of all of them. All these pupils agree that Socrates insisted on the belief on moral values, on an austere conduct of life, and on the unity of wisdom, knowledge and virtue. While Plato made him the mouthpiece of the doctrine of ideas, all other philosophers who were close to Socrates were opposed to that doctrine. It is therefore quite probable that Plato went far beyond the philosophical position of his master.

I AM A PHILOSOPHICAL MIDWIFE

Theaetetus. I can assure you, Socrates, that I have tried very often, when the report of questions asked by you was brought to me; but I can neither persuade myself that I have a satisfactory answer to give, nor hear of any one who answers as you would have him; and I cannot shake off a feeling of anxiety.

Socrates. These are the pangs of labor, my dear Theaetetus; you have something within you which you are bringing to the birth.

Theaetetus. I do not know, Socrates; I only say what I feel.

Socrates. And have you never heard, simpleton, that I am the son of a midwife, brave and burly, whose name was Phaenarete?

Theaetetus. Yes, I have.

Socrates. And that I myself practice midwifery?

Theaetetus. No, never.

Socrates. Well, my art of midwifery is in most respects like theirs; but differs, in that I attend men and not women, and I look after their souls when they are in labor, and not after their bodies: and the triumph of my art is in thoroughly examining whether the thought which the mind of the young man brings forth is a false idol or a noble and true birth. And like the midwives, I am barren, and the reproach which is óften made against me, that I ask questions of others and have not the wit to answer them myself, is very just—the reason is, that the god compels me to be a midwife, but does not allow me to bring forth. And therefore I am not myself at all wise, nor have I anything to show which is the invention or birth of my own soul, but those who converse with me profit. Some of them appear dull enough at first, but afterwards, as our acquaintance ripens, if the god is gracious to them, they all make astonishing progress; and this is in the opinion of others as well as in their own. It is quite clear that they never learned anything from me; the many fine discoveries to which they cling are of their own making. But to me and the god they owe their delivery. And the proof of my words, is that many of them in their ignorance, either in their self-conceit despising me, or falling under the influence of others, have gone away too soon; and have not only lost the children of whom I had previously delivered them by an ill bringing up, but have stifled whatever else they had in them by evil communications, being fonder of lies and shams than of the truth; and they have at last ended by seeing themselves, as others see them, to be great fools. Aristides, the son of Lysimachus, is one of them, and there are many others. The truants often return to me, and beg that I would consort with them again—they are ready to go to me on their knees—and then, if my familiar allows, which is not always the case, I receive them. My art is able to arouse and to allay in those who consort with me, just like the pangs of women in childbirth; night and day they are full of perplexity and travail which is even worse than that of the women. So much for them. And there are others, Theaetetus, who come to me apparently having nothing in them; and as I know that they have no need of my art, I coax them into marrying some one, and by the grace of God I can generally tell who is likely to do them good. Many of them I have given away to Prodicus, and many to other inspired sages. I tell you this long story, friend Theaetetus, because I suspect, as indeed you seem to think yourself, that you are in labor—great with some conception. Come then to me,—who am a midwife's son and myself a midwife, and do your best to answer the questions which I will ask you. And if I abstract and expose your first-born, because I discover upon inspection that the conception which you have formed is a vain shadow, do not quarrel with me on that account, as the manner of women is when their first children are taken from them. For I have actually known some who were ready to bite me when I deprived them of a darling folly; they did not perceive that I acted from goodwill, not knowing that no god is the enemy of man—that was not within the range of their ideas; neither am I their enemy in all this, but it would be wrong for me to admit falsehood, or to stifle the truth. Once more, then, Theaetetus, I repeat my old question, "What is knowledge?"—and do not say that you cannot tell; but quit yourself like a man, and by the help of God you will be able to tell.

Theaetetus. At any rate, Socrates, after such an exhortation I should be ashamed of not trying to do my best.

[334]

SOLOVIEV, VLADIMIR

SOLOVIEV, VLADIMIR (1853-1900). Soloviev has been called "the Russian Newman" or "the Russian Carlyle," and he could easily be called "the Russian Kierkegaard" with equal, or even more justice. For the struggle against the established Church, against the alliance between Church and State, which, in his opinion, meant domination of the Church by the State, and the effort to take the doctrine of Christ seriously was Soloviev's great purpose just as it was Kierkegaard's. Soloviev protested against the division of mankind into a Church which claimed to possess divine truth and to represent the will of God, and all the rest. This division, as it has been developed in the history of Christianity, was deplored by Soloviev and regarded by him as seducing the Church to abuse its lust of power. Deeply convinced of the truth of Christianity, Soloviev asserted the idea of "Godmanhood," bequeathed to humanity, and the ideal of universal theocracy, which he conceived as absolutely incompatible with the claims of the Orthodox Church.

Soloviev was the son of the noted Russian historian Sergius Soloviev, who was devoted to Tsarism, the Orthodox Church and Slavophile ideas. His career promised to become brilliant, but he renounced it, in 1881, after the assassination of Tsar Alexander II, when he publicly asked for mercy for the assassins. He always was a strong adversary of capital punishment. Then retired to private life, Soloviev became one of the greatest Russian philosophers of religion.

It is not so much the originality of Soloviev's ideas that makes his works important as rather their connection with fundamental trends of Russian thought, and his view of the crisis of European civilization. Soloviev's hostility against nationalism, especially Russian nationalism, is no less ardent than his opposition to the claims of the Orthodox Church. At the end of his life, he recognized Rome as the center of Christianity, without, however, converting to the Roman Church. His positive doctrine culminated in the "justification of the good," founded upon a psychology of human conscience and upon his strong belief that man cannot be entirely wicked. He was a man who lived in accordance with his

1114

ideas, and was revered as a saint by people of all classes. His tombstone became a place of pilgrimage.

HUMANITY BEFORE NATIONALITY

THE good embraces all the details of life, but in itself it is *indivisible*. Patriotism as a virtue is part of the right attitude to everything, and in the moral order this part cannot be separated from the whole and opposed to it. In the moral organization not a single nation can prosper *at the expense of* others; it cannot positively affirm itself to the detriment or the disadvantage of others. Just as the positive moral dignity of a private person is known from the fact that his prosperity is truly useful to all others, so the prosperity of a nation true to the moral principle is necessarily connected with the universal good. This logical and moral axiom is crudely distorted in the popular sophism that we must think of our own nation only, because it is good, and therefore its prosperity is a benefit to every one. It either thoughtlessly overlooks or impudently rejects the obvious truth that this very alienation of one's own nation from others, this *exclusive* recognition of it as pre-eminently good, is in itself evil, and that nothing but evil can spring from this evil root. It must be one or the other. Either we must renounce Christianity and monotheism in general, according to which "there is none but one, that is, God," and recognize our nation *as such* to be the highest good—that is, put it in the place of God—or we must admit that a people becomes good not in virtue of the simple fact of its particular nationality, but only in so far as it conforms to and participates in the absolute good. And it can only do so if it has a right attitude to everything, and, in the first place, to other nations. A nation cannot be really good so long as it feels malice or hostility against other nations, and fails to recognize them as its neighbors and to love them as itself.

The moral duty of a true patriot is then to serve the nation in the good, or to serve the true good of a nation, inseparable from the good of all, or, what is the same thing,

1115

to serve the nation in humanity, and humanity in the nation.
Such a patriot will discover a positive aspect in every foreign race and people, and by means of it will seek to relate
this race or people with his own for the benefit of both.

When we hear of a *rapprochement* between nations, of
inter-national agreements, friendships, and alliances, we
must, before rejoicing or being grieved about it, know *in
what* it is that the nations are being united, in good or
in evil. The fact of union as such decides nothing. If two
private people or two nations are united by the hatred of
a third, their union is an evil and a source of fresh evil.
If they are united by mutual interest or by common gain,
the question still remains open. The interest may be unworthy, the gain may be fictitious, and in that case the
union of nations, as well as of individuals, even if it is
not a direct evil, can certainly not be a good desirable
for its own sake. The union of men and nations can be
positively approved only in so far as it furthers the moral
organization of humanity, or the organization of the absolute good in it. We have seen that the ultimate *subject* of
this organization, the real bearer of the *moral order*, is the
collective man or humanity, successively differentiated into
its organs and elements—nations, families, persons.

[335]

SOREL, GEORGES

SOREL, GEORGES (1847-1922). The name of Georges Sorel has
been connected with the history of both bolshevism and fascism.
Jean Jaurès called him "the metaphysician of syndicalism." But, in
fact, Sorel was a metaphysician of industrial production, and tried
to utilize the working class and its ideologies as the instrument for
attaining his aims.

By vocation an engineer and always very bourgeois in his
conduct of life, Sorel turned to social and economic studies only
after his fortieth year. From 1893 to 1897, he adopted Marx's
ideas; thereafter, he professed animosity not only toward Marx but
also toward democracy, rationalism and intellectualism, expressing

his views in his principal books, *The Decomposition of Marxism, Reflections on Violence* (both 1908) and *Illusions of Progress* (1911). Inspired by Henri Bergson, whom he respected despite his constant animosity toward the Jews, Sorel heralded the "Myth of the General Strike," and took great care to distinguish between the Utopia and the myth. The latter term was used by Sorel as the image of a fictitious, even unrealizable future that expresses the sentiments of the revolutionary masses and incites them to revolutionary action. "Violence" was proclaimed by Sorel as the way to power. But this "Violence," Sorel protested, is not meant as "Jacobinic" action but as "psychic warfare" whose means are sabotage, strike and the boycott of workers who decline to participate in that warfare.

For a time, Sorel succeeded in winning over the French syndicalists. But very soon, the militant workers turned against him who, with his pupil Georges Valois as intermediary, negotiated with the royalist Charles Maurras, the leader of the "Action Française." The outbreak of the war, in 1914, prevented their alliance. After the war, Sorel built his hopes upon bolshevism, but Lenin rebuked him in his polemics against empiriocriticism. Only Mussolini acknowledged Sorel and frequently proclaimed his indebtedness to him.

Sorel was not interested in socialism, communism or any other politico-economic system but in the increase of industrial production to the highest possible degree. His experiences as an engineer had convinced him that capitalists or industrial entrepreneurs would be incapable of attaining this goal. He therefore entrusted the employees and workers with the fulfillment of the task. This idea of Sorel's might have impressed Thorstein Veblen, who expressed similar views on the incompetency of capitalists.

OPTIMISM AND PESSIMISM
IN SOCIAL DEVELOPMENT

THE immense successes obtained by industrial civilization have created the belief that, in the near future, happiness will be produced automatically for everybody. "The present century," writes Hartmann, "has for the last forty years only entered the third period of illusion. In the enthusiasm and enchantment of its hopes, it rushes towards the realization of the promise of a new age of gold. Providence takes care that the anticipations of the isolated thinker do not disarrange the course of history by prematurely gaining too many adherents." He thinks that for this reason his readers will have some difficulty in accepting his criticism of the illusion of future happiness. The leaders of the contemporary world are pushed towards optimism by economic forces.

So little are we prepared to understand pessimism, that we generally employ the word quite incorrectly: we call pessimists people who are in reality only disillusioned optimists. When we meet a man who, having been unfortunate in his enterprises, deceived in his most legitimate ambitions, humiliated in his affections, expresses his grief in the form of a violent revolt against the duplicity of his associates, the stupidity of society, or the blindness of destiny, we are disposed to look upon him as a pessimist; whereas we ought nearly always to regard him as a disheartened optimist who has not had the courage to start afresh, and who is unable to understand why so many misfortunes have befallen him, contrary to what he supposes to be the general law governing the production of happiness.

The optimist in politics is an inconstant and even dangerous man, because he takes no account of the great difficulties presented by his projects; these projects seem to him to possess a force of their own, which tends to bring about their realization all the more easily as they are, in his opinion, destined to produce the happiest results. He frequently thinks that small reforms in the political constitution, and, above all, in the personnel of the government, will be sufficient to direct social development in such a way as to mitigate those evils of the contemporary world which seem so harsh to the sensitive mind. As soon as his friends come into power, he declares that it is necessary to let things alone for a little, not to hurry too much, and to learn how to be content with whatever their own benevolent intentions prompt them to do. It is not always self-interest that suggests these expressions of satisfaction, as people have often believed; self-interest is strongly aided by vanity and by the illusions of philosophy. The optimist passes with remarkable facility from revolutionary anger to the most ridiculous social pacificism.

If he possesses an exalted temperament, and if unhappily he finds himself armed with great power, permitting him to realize the ideal he has fashioned, the optimist may lead his country into the worst disasters. He is not long in finding out that social transformations are not brought about with the ease that he had counted on; he then supposes that this is the fault of his contemporaries, instead of explaining what actually happens by historical necessities; he is tempted to get rid of people whose obstinacy seems to him to be so dangerous to the happiness of all. During the Terror, the men who spilt most blood were precisely those who had the greatest desire to let their equals enjoy the golden age they had dreamt of, and who had the most sympathy with human wretchedness: optimists, idealists, and sensitive men, the greater desire they had for universal happiness the more inexorable they showed themselves.

Pessimism is quite a different thing from the caricatures of it which are usually presented to us; it is a philosophy of conduct rather than a theory of the world; it considers the *march towards deliverance* as narrowly conditioned, on the one hand, by the experimental knowledge that we have acquired from the obstacles which oppose themselves to the satisfaction of our imaginations (or, if we like, by the feeling of social determinism), and, on the other, by a profound conviction of our natural weakness. These two aspects of pessimism should never be separated although, as a rule, scarcely any attention is paid to their close connection.

The conception of pessimism springs from the fact that literary historians have been very much struck with the complaints made by the great poets of antiquity on the subject of the griefs which constantly threaten mankind. There are few people who have not, at one time or another, experienced a piece of good fortune; but we are surrounded by malevolent forces always ready to spring out on us from

1119

some ambuscade and overwhelm us. Hence the very real sufferings which arouse the sympathy of nearly all men, even of those who have been more favorably treated by fortune; so that the literature of grief has always had a certain success throughout the whole course of history. But a study of this kind of literature would give us a very imperfect idea of pessimism. It may be laid down as a general rule, that in order to understand a doctrine it is not sufficient to study it in an abstract manner, nor even as it occurs in isolated people: it is necessary to find out how it has been manifested in historical groups.

The pessimist regards social conditions as forming a system bound together by an iron law which cannot be evaded, so that the system is given, as it were, in one block, and cannot disappear except in a catastrophe which involves the whole. If this theory is admitted, it then becomes absurd to make certain wicked men responsible for the evils from which society suffers; the pessimist is not subject to the sanguinary follies of the optimist, infatuated by the unexpected obstacles that his projects meet with; he does not dream of bringing about the happiness of future generations by slaughtering existing egoists.

[336]

SPENCER, HERBERT

SPENCER, HERBERT (1820-1903). An engineer by training, Spencer tried to survey the whole range of human thought with the intention of interpreting "the phenomena of life, mind and society in terms of matter, motion and force." Defining philosophy as "knowledge of the highest degree of generality," he established the formula of evolution as the general law which enabled him to explain all phenomena in the above mentioned terms. Under its simplest and most general aspect, evolution is characterized by Spencer as "the integration of matter and concomitant dissipation of movement: while dissolution is the absorption of motion and concomitant disintegration of matter." To Spencer, evolution was universal and one, dominating the realms of biology, psychology, ethics and sociology. He was the first philosopher to maintain the genetic

1120

principle, according to which the more developed thing must be interpreted by the less developed one. He was also the first to use a biological standard for human ethics. He complained that "men do not even know that their sensations are their natural guides and (when not rendered morbid by long-continued disobedience) their most trustworthy guides," because he thought that the senses of man were molded in accordance with the all-embracing law of evolution from a less perfect to a more perfect state. In this way, Spencer identified evolution with progress.

Spencer's notion of evolution has a curious history. At first he borrowed it from Coleridge, and adopted at the same time the latter's idea of social organism, both of which have been conceived of as in opposition to utilitarianism. Later, he came closer to the utilitarian point of view, espoused the cause of rugged individualism, strictly opposed any encroachment upon private enterprise by the state, and became a grim adversary of socialism. He was deeply disappointed when Beatrice Potter, his favorite pupil, married Sidney Webb, the theorist of British labor, and he then cancelled her appointment as his literary executor. At the end of his life, Spencer expressed very pessimistic views about the future of humanity.

PHILOSOPHY DEFINED

AFTER concluding that we cannot know the ultimate nature of that which is manifested to us, there arise the questions —What is it that we know? In what sense do we know it? And in what consists our highest knowledge of it? Having repudiated as impossible the philosophy which professes to formulate being as distinguished from appearance, it becomes needful to say what philosophy truly is—not simply to specify its limits, but to specify its character within those limits. Given a certain sphere as the sphere to which human intelligence is restricted, there remains to define the peculiar product of human intelligence which may still be called philosophy.

In doing this, we may advantageously avail ourselves of the method followed at the outset, of separating from conceptions that are partially or mainly erroneous, the element of truth they contain. It was previously inferred that religious beliefs, wrong as they might individually be in their particular forms, nevertheless probably each contained an essential verity, and that this was most likely common to them all; so in this place it is to be inferred that past and present beliefs respecting the nature of philosophy, are none of them wholly false, and that that in which they are true is that in which they agree. We have here, then, to do what was done there—"to compare all opinions of the same genus; to set aside as more or less discrediting one another those various special and concrete elements in which such opinions disagree; to observe what remains after the discordant constituents have been eliminated; and to find for this remaining constituent that abstract expression which holds true throughout its divergent modifications."

Earlier speculations being passed over, we see that among the Greeks, before there had arisen any notion of philosophy in general, apart from particular forms of philosophy, the particular forms of it from which the general notion was to arise, were hypotheses respecting some universal principle that constituted the essence of all concrete kinds of being. To the question—"What is that *invariable existence* of which these are *variable states?*" there were sundry answers—water, air, fire. A class of hypotheses of this all-embracing character having been propounded, it became possible for Pythagoras to conceive of philosophy in the abstract, as knowledge the most remote from practical ends; and to define it as "knowledge of immaterial and eternal things:" "the cause of the material existence of things," being, in his view, number. Thereafter, we find continued a pursuit of philosophy as some ultimate interpretation of the universe, assumed to be possible, whether actually reached in any case or not. And in the course of this pursuit, various such ultimate interpretations were given us as that "One is the beginning of all things;" that "the One is God;" that "the One is Finite;" that "the One is Infinite;" that "Intelligence is the governing principle of things;" and so on. From all which it is plain that the knowledge supposed to constitute philosophy, differed from other knowledge in its transcendent, exhaustive character. In the subsequent course of speculation, after the sceptics had shaken men's faith in their powers of reaching such transcendent knowledge, there grew up a much-restricted conception of philosophy. Under Socrates, and still more under the Stoics, philosophy became little else than the doctrine of right living. Its subject matter was practically cut down to the proper ruling of conduct, public and private. Not indeed that the proper ruling of conduct, as conceived by sundry of the later Greek thinkers to constitute subject matter of philosophy, answered to what was popularly understood by the proper ruling of conduct. The injunctions of Zeno were not of the same class as those which guided men from early times downwards, in their daily observances, sacrifices, customs, all having more or less of religious sanction; but they were principles of action enunciated without reference to times, or persons, or special cases. What, then, was the constant element in these unlike ideas of philosophy held by the ancient? Clearly the character in which this last idea agrees with the first is that within its sphere of inquiry, philosophy seeks for wide and deep truths, as distinguished from the multitudinous detailed truths which the surfaces of things and actions present.

By comparing the conceptions of philosophy that have been current in modern times, we get a like result. The disciples of Schelling, Fichte, and their kindred, join the Hegelian in ridiculing the so-called philosophy which has usurped the title in England. Not without reason, they laugh on reading of "philosophical instruments;" and would deny that any one of the papers in the *Philosophical Transactions* has the least claim to come under such a title. Retaliating on their critics, the English may, and most of them do, reject as absurd the imagined philosophy of the German schools. As consciousness cannot be transcended, they hold that whether consciousness does or does not vouch for the existence of something beyond itself, it at any rate cannot comprehend that something; and that hence, in so far as any philosophy professes to be an ontology, it is false. These two views cancel one another over large parts of their areas. The English criticism of the German cuts off from philosophy all that is regarded as absolute knowledge. The German criticism of the English tacitly implies that if philosophy is limited to the relative, it is at any rate not concerned with those aspects of the relative which are embodied in mathematical formulas, in accounts of physical researches, in chemical analyses, or in descriptions of species and reports of physiological experiments. Now what has the too-wide German conception in common with the conception general among the English men of science; which, narrow and crude as it is, is not so narrow and crude as their misuse of the word philosophical indicates? The two have this in common, that neither Germans nor English apply the word to unsystematized knowledge—to knowledge quite uncoordinated with other knowledge. Even the most limited specialist would not describe as philosophical, an essay which, dealing wholly with details, manifested no perception of the bearings of those details on wider truths.

The vague idea thus raised of that in which the various conceptions of philosophy agree, may be rendered more definite by comparing what has been known in England as natural philosophy with that development of it called positive philosophy. Though, as M. Comte admits, the two consist of knowledge essentially the same in kind; yet, by having put this kind of knowledge into a more coherent form, he has given it more of that character to which the term philosophical is applied. Without expressing any opinion respecting the truth of his co-ordination, it must be conceded that by the fact of its co-ordination, the body of knowledge organized by him has a better claim to the title philosophy, than has the comparatively unorganized body of knowledge named natural philosophy.

If subdivisions of philosophy, or more special forms of it, be contrasted with one another, or with the whole, the same implication comes out. Moral philosophy and political philosophy agree with philosophy at large in the comprehensiveness of their reasonings and conclusions. Though under the head of moral philosophy, we treat of human actions as right or wrong, we do not include special directions for behavior in the nursery, at table, or on the exchange; and though political philosophy has for its topic the conduct of men in their public relations, it does not concern itself with modes of voting or details of administration. Both of these sections of philosophy contemplate particular instances, only as illustrating truths of wide application.

Thus every one of these conceptions implies the belief in a possible way of knowing things more completely than they are known through simple experiences, mechanically accumulated in memory or heaped up in cyclopedias. Though in the extent of the sphere which they have supposed philosophy to fill, men have differed and still differ very widely; yet there is a real if unavowed agreement among them in signifying by this title a knowledge which transcends ordinary knowledge. That which remains as the common element in these conceptions of philosophy, after the elimination of their discordant elements, is—*knowledge of the highest degree of generality*. We see this tacitly asserted by the simultaneous inclusion of God, nature, and man, within its scope; or still more distinctly by the division of philosophy as a whole into theological, physical, ethical, etc. For that which characterizes the genus of which these are species, must be something more general than that which distinguishes any one species.

What must be the specific shape here given to this conception? The range of intelligence we find to be limited to the relative. Though persistently conscious of a power manifested to us, we have abandoned as futile the attempt to learn anything respecting the nature of that power; and so have shut out philosophy from much of the domain supposed to belong to it. The domain left is that occupied by science. Science concerns itself with the coexistences and sequences among phenomena; grouping these at first into generalizations of a simple or low order, and rising gradually to higher and more extended generalizations. But if so, where remains any subject matter for philosophy?

The reply is—philosophy may still properly be the title retained for knowledge of the highest generality. Science means merely the family of the sciences—stands for nothing more than the sum of knowledge formed of their contributions; and ignores the knowledge constituted by the *fusion* of all these contributions into a whole. As usage has defined it, science consists of truths existing more or less separated; and does not recognize these truths as entirely integrated. An illustration will make the difference clear.

If we ascribe the flow of a river to the same force which causes the fall of a stone, we make a statement, true as far as it goes, that belongs to a certain division of science. If, in further explanation of a movement produced by gravitation in a direction almost horizontal, we cite the law that fluids subject to mechanical forces exert reactive forces which are equal in all directions, we formulate a wider fact, containing the scientific interpretation of many other phenomena; as those presented by the fountain, the hydraulic press, the steamengine, the airpump. And when this proposition, extending only to the dynamics of fluids, is merged in a proposition of general dynamics, comprehending the laws of movement of solids as well as of fluids, there is reached a yet higher truth; but still a truth that comes wholly within the realm of science. Again, looking around at birds and mammals, suppose we say that airbreathing animals are hot-blooded; and that then, remembering how reptiles, which also breathe air, are not much warmer than their media, we say, more truly, that animals (bulks being equal) have temperatures proportionate to the quantities of air they breathe; and that then, calling to mind certain large fish which maintain a heat considerably above that of the water they swim in, we further correct the generalization by saying that the temperature varies as the rate of oxygenation of the blood; and that then, modifying the statement to meet other criticisms, we finally assert the relation to be between the amount of heat and the amount of molecular change— supposing we do all this, we state scientific truths that are successively wider and more complete, but truths which, to the last, remain purely scientific. Once more if, guided by mercantile experiences, we reach the conclusion that prices rise when the demand exceeds the supply; and that commodities flow from places where they are abundant to places where they are scarce; and that the industries of different localities are determined in their kinds mainly by the facilities which the localities afford them; and if, studying these generalizations of political economy, we trace them all to the truth that each man seeks satisfaction for his desires in ways costing the smallest efforts—such social phenomena being *resultants* of individual actions so guided; we are still dealing with the propositions of science only.

And now how is philosophy constituted? It is constituted by carrying a stage further the process indicated. So long as these truths are known only apart and regarded as independent, even the most general of them cannot without laxity of speech be called philosophical. But when, having been severally reduced to a simple mechanical axiom, a principle of molecular physics, and a law of social action, they are contemplated together as corollaries of some ultimate truth, then we rise to the kind of knowledge that constitutes philosophy proper.

The truths of philosophy thus bear the same relation to the highest scientific truths, that each of these bears to lower scientific truths. As each widest generalization of science comprehends and consolidates the narrower generalizations of its own division; so the generalizations of philosophy comprehend and consolidate the widest generalizations of science. It is therefore a knowledge the extreme opposite in

1127

kind to that which experience first accumulates. It is the final product of that process which begins with a mere colligation of crude observations, goes on establishing propositions that are broader and more separated from particular cases, and ends in universal propositions. Or to bring the definition to its simplest and clearest form:—knowledge of the lowest kind is *un-unified* knowledge; science is *partially unified* knowledge; philosophy is *completely unified* knowledge.

Such, at least, is the meaning we must here give to the word philosophy, if we employ it at all. In so defining it, we accept that which is common to the various conceptions of it current among both ancients and moderns—rejecting those elements in which these conceptions disagree, or exceed the possible range of intelligence. In short, we are simply giving precision to that application of the word which is gradually establishing itself.

Two forms of philosophy, as thus understood, may be distinguished. On the one hand, the things contemplated may be the universal truths: all particular truths referred to being used simply for proof or elucidation of these universal truths. On the other hand, setting out with the universal truths as granted, the things contemplated may be the particular truths as interpreted by them. In both cases we deal with the universal truths; but in the one case they are passive and in the other case active—in the one case they form the products of exploration and in the other case the instruments of exploration. These divisions we may appropriately call general philosophy and special philosophy respectively.

[337]

SPINOZA, BENEDICTUS DE
(Baruch de Spinoza)

SPINOZA, BENEDICTUS DE (BARUCH DE SPINOZA) (1632-1677). For more than a century after Spinoza's works were published, their author was objurgated with embitterment by Catholics, Protestants, Jews and freethinkers alike. Even David Hume, in general a man of kindly disposition, branded him as "infame," and Moses Mendelssohn, the affable advocate of tolerance, was horrified and disbelieving when he heard that his friend Lessing had adopted Spinoza's doctrine. A great change was inaugurated by Herder and Goethe who became Spinozists, and revered Spinoza as a saint. So did Heinrich Heine. Post-Kantian philosophers and Romantic poets in Germany were deeply influenced by Spinoza's conception of nature. In modern times, Spinoza is universally recognized as a philosopher of unsurpassed sublimity and profundity. Even his critics agree that Spinoza had a most lovable personality, one of the purest characters in the history of mankind. Despite his delicate feelings and the subtlety of his definitions, Spinoza's mind was unsophisticated, and regardless of the boldness of his thoughts and the sternness of his will to draw his conclusions logically and without any regard to personal inclinations, Spinoza was calm, benevolent, fond of plain people. He earned his living by grinding optical lenses and declined an appointment as professor at the University of Heidelberg because he preferred independence to honor.

Spinoza belonged to a Jewish family which had been exiled from Spain and Portugal, and had finally settled in Holland. Before studying Latin, the natural sciences, and the philosophy of Hobbes and Descartes, he had studied the Hebrew Bible, the Talmud, medieval Jewish literature, and probably cabala. In 1656, he was put under the ban by the Jewish community of Amsterdam because of his opposition to traditional doctrines of Judaism, including those that were also sacred tenets of Christianity. Detached from the Jewish community, Spinoza manifested indifference to Jews and Judaism. With his investigation of the sacred Scriptures he gave an impetus to modern Biblical criticism. But the elements of his Jewish education, especially his acquaintance with medieval Jewish philosophy, remain visible in his conception of the oneness of God and in his personal piety.

Spinoza's chief work is entitled *Ethics*. It could have been named "Metaphysics" with equal justice, for Spinoza was thoroughly convinced that the knowledge of the ultimate reality involves the norm of human action and implies the measure of personal perfection. Philosophical thinking was, to Spinoza, self-education and improvement of the mind of the thinker. His aim was to obtain, by means of reason and science, the same trust in rules of human behavior that religious traditions claimed to grant their believers. Contrary to Descartes, he denied the possibility of harmonizing reason with Biblical revelation, and, in that way, Spinoza, not Descartes, became the symbol of the end of medieval philosophy. The scientific method offered to Spinoza not only the measure of moral evaluation but a means of gaining eternal bliss. To win supreme happiness or "unceasing joy," Spinoza said, man has to attain knowledge of his union with the whole of nature.

All individual beings, whatever is popularly supposed to be a real thing, are regarded by Spinoza as mere modifications of but one infinite substance which has an infinite number of attributes, of which, however, only two, namely thought and extension, are perceptible by man. This one substance which is in itself and conceived through itself alone, is the only object of true knowledge, and is identical with God whose will is identical with the laws of nature. He who knows nature knows God. Increasing knowledge of nature means increasing love of God. From this proposition of the oneness and universality of God, Spinoza has deduced *more geometrico,* in a manner following the example of geometrical demonstrations, his definitions of all particular objects in the realms of extension and thought. He finally arrived at his much admired description of the intellectual love of God which is characterized as an absolutely disinterested feeling, the humble cognizance of all-governing necessity and at the same time the complete liberation of the soul from disturbing passions. Neither to laud nor to blame but to understand is the principle of Spinoza's attitude toward life.

ON THE IMPROVEMENT OF THE MIND

AFTER experience had taught me that all things which are ordinarily encountered in common life are vain and futile, and when I saw that all things which occasioned me any anxiety or fear had in themselves nothing of good or evil, except in so far as the mind was moved by them; I at length determined to inquire if there were anything which was a true good capable of imparting itself, by which the mind could be solely affected to the exclusion of all else; whether, indeed, anything existed by whose discovery and acquisition I might be put in possession of a joy continuous and supreme to all eternity. I say that *I at length deter-*

mined; for at the first glance it appeared to me to be foolish to be willing to part with something certain for something then uncertain. I saw, forsooth, the advantages which accrue from honor and riches, and that I should be forced to abstain from seeking these if I wished to apply myself seriously to another and new undertaking; and if, by chance, perfect happiness should lie in those things, I perceived that I must go without it; but if, on the other hand, it did not lie in them, and I applied myself only to them, I must then also go without the highest happiness. I turned it over, therefore, in my mind whether it might not perchance be possible to carry out my new purpose or, at least, to arrive at some certainty with regard to it, without changing the order and ordinary plan of my life, a thing I had often attempted in vain. Now, the things which generally present themselves in life, and are considered by men as the highest good, so far as can be gathered from their actions, are included in these three, riches, honor, and sensual indulgence. By these three the mind is so distracted, that it is scarcely possible for it to think of any other good thing. For example, as regards sensual indulgence, the mind is engrossed by it to such a degree as to rest in it as in some good, and is thereby entirely prevented from thinking of anything else, but, after it has been satisfied, there follows a very great melancholy, which, if it does not check the action of the mind, nevertheless disturbs and blunts it. Through the pursuit of honor and riches also the mind is not a little distracted, especially if the latter are sought for their own sake, because in that case they are supposed to be the highest good. By honor the mind is even more distracted; for it is always regarded as a good in itself, and, as it were, the ultimate end to which everything is directed. Again, in the case of honor and riches there is no repentance, as in the case of sensual indulgence, but the more we have of them, the more our joy is increased; and consequently we are more and more incited to increase them; nevertheless, if by any chance our expectations are deceived, then very great sorrow arises.

Finally, honor is a great hindrance to us, because it is necessary, if we would attain it, to direct our lives according to the notions of men—that is to say, by avoiding what they commonly avoid, and seeking what they commonly seek.

Since, therefore, I saw that all these things stood in the way of my devoting myself to any new purpose; that, in fact, they were so opposed to it, that either they or it must be relinquished, I was compelled to inquire what was most useful to me, for as I have said, it seemed as if I were willing to lose a certain good for that which was uncertain. But after I had reflected a little on the subject, I discovered, in the first place, that if forsaking riches and honor and sensual indulgence, I should address myself to my new purpose, I should be giving up a good uncertain in its very nature, as may clearly be seen from what has already been said, for one uncertain not in its very nature (for I sought a good which was stable), but only so far as its attainment was concerned, and after careful reflection, I came to see that, if only I could apply myself wholly to thought, I should then be giving up certain evils for a certain good. For I saw that I was situated in the greatest danger, and I forced myself to seek with all my strength a remedy, even although it might be uncertain, just as a sick man suffering from a mortal disease, who foresees certain death unless a remedy be applied, is forced to seek it with all his strength, even though it be uncertain, for therein lies the whole of his hope. All those things, however, which the majority of persons pursue, not only contribute no means whereby to preserve our being, but even are a hindrance to its preservation. They frequently cause the destruction of those who possess them, and always cause the destruction of those who are possessed by them.

For there are very many examples of men who have suffered persecution even to death for the sake of their riches, and also of men, who, in order that they might obtain wealth, have exposed themselves to so many dangers that at length they have paid with their lives the penalty of their folly. Nor are there fewer examples of men, who, in order that they might obtain honor, or guard it, have endured most miserable calamities; and, lastly, innumerable are the examples of those who, through excess of sensual indulgence, have hastened their death. The cause of these evils appeared to be that all happiness or unhappiness solely depends upon the quality of the object to which we are attached by love. For on account of that which is not loved no strife will arise, there will be no sorrow if it perishes, no jealousy if it is appropriated by another, no fear, no hatred, and, in a word, no agitations of the mind. All these, however, arise from the love of that which is perishable, as all those things are of which we have just spoken. But love for an object eternal and infinite feeds the mind with joy alone, and a joy which is free from all sorrow. This is something greatly to be desired and to be sought with all our strength.

But not without reason did I use the words *if I could but apply myself wholly to thought.* For although I saw all this so clearly in my mind, I could not therefore put aside all avarice, sensual desire, and love of honor. This one thing I saw, that so long as my mind was occupied with these thoughts, so long it was turned away from the things mentioned above, and seriously reflected on the new purpose. This confronted me greatly. For I saw that those evils were not of such a kind that they would not yield to remedies. And although in the beginning these intervals were rare and lasted but for a very short time, nevertheless, when the true good was by degrees better known to me, they became more frequent and longer, especially when I came to see that the acquisition of wealth, or sensual desire and love of honor, are injurious so long as they are sought for their own sake and not as means for other things; but if they are sought as means they will be enjoyed in moderation and will not be injurious: on the contrary, they will be very conducive to the end for which they are sought, as we shall show in the proper place.

Here I will explain, but only briefly, what I under-stand by a true good, and at the same time what is the highest good. In order that this may be rightly understood, it is to be observed that the words "good" and "evil" are only used relatively, so that one and the same thing may be called good and evil according to its different relations, just as from different points of view it may be called perfect or imperfect. For nothing considered in its own nature can be called perfect or imperfect, especially after we have discerned that everything comes to pass according to an eternal order and according to fixed laws of nature. But since human weakness cannot reach that order by its own thought, and meanwhile man can imagine a human nature much stronger than his own, and sees no obstacle to prevent his acquiring such a nature, he is urged to seek the means which may lead him to such perfection. Everything, therefore, which may be a means by which to arrive thereat, he calls a true good, but the highest good is to obtain, with as many other individuals as possible, the enjoyment of that nature. But what that nature is we shall show in the proper place—that it is a knowledge of the union between the mind and the whole of nature. This, therefore, is the end towards which 1 strive—to acquire this nature and to endeavor that others may acquire it with me—that is to say, it is essential to my happiness to try to make many others understand what I understand, so that their intellect and desire may entirely agree with my intellect and desire. In order to achieve this end, it is necessary to understand so much of nature as may be sufficient for acquiring the desired nature; then to form a society such as is desirable for enabling as many people as possible with the greatest ease and security to acquire it. Furthermore, we must pay attention to moral philosophy as well as to the science of the education of children, and be-cause health is by no means an insignificant means to the attainment of this end, the whole of medicine is to be studied. Because also many things which are difficult are rendered easier by art and we can thereby gain much time and comfort in life, mechanics are by no means to be despised. But above everything a means of healing the mind must be sought out, and of purifying it as much as possible at the outset so that it may happily understand things without error and as completely as possible. Hence everybody can now see that I wish to direct all the sciences to a single end and purpose, namely, that we may reach the highest human perfection of which we have spoken. Therefore everything in the sciences which in no way advances us towards our end will be rejected as useless, that is to say, in one word, all our actions as well as our thoughts are to be directed to this end. Since, however, while we are seeking to attain it and are endeavoring to constrain our intellect into the right way, it is necessary to live, we must first of all assume certain rules of life to be good. They are these:—

I. To speak and act in accordance with the notions of the majority, provided no hindrance thereby arises to the attainment of our purpose. For we can obtain not a little profit from them, if we conform as much as possible to their notions, and, besides, in this way they will lend friendly ears to listen to the truth.

II. To indulge in pleasures only so far as is consistent with the preservation of health.

III. To seek only so much of wealth or of anything else as is sufficient to preserve life and health, and to conform to such customs of the state as are not opposed to our purpose.

Having laid down these rules, I will attempt that which stands first, and is to be achieved before anything, that is to say, to improve the intellect and make it fit to understand things in the way which is necessary in order to obtain our end. To do this, natural order requires that I should here review all the kinds of knowledge which I have hitherto possessed whereby to affirm or deny positively, in order that I may choose the best of them all, and at the same time may begin to know my powers and that nature which I wish to perfect.

If I consider accurately, they may all be reduced generally to four.

I. There is the knowledge which we derive from hearing or from some arbitrary sign.

II. There is the knowledge which we derive from vague experience, that is to say, from experience which is independent of the intellect and which is so called only because it presents itself casually and we have no experimental proof to the contrary. Therefore it abides with us undisturbed.

III. There is the knowledge which arises when the essence of a thing is deduced from another thing, but not adequately. This happens when we either infer the cause from some effect, or when we make an inference from some universal which is always accompanied by some property.

IV. Finally there is the knowledge which arises when a thing is perceived through its essence alone, or through the knowledge of its proximate cause.

All this I will illustrate by examples. From mere *hearing* I know my birthday, and that I had certain parents, and other things of the same kind which I have never doubted. Through *vague experience* I know that I shall die, for I affirm it because I have seen other people die of the same nature as myself, although they have not all lived equally long, nor have they died of the same disease. Again through vague experience I also know that oil is the proper food for feeding flame, and that water is fit for extinguishing it; I know also that a dog is a barking animal and man is a rational animal, and in this way I have learned nearly everything which appertains to the service of life. We deduce *from some other thing* in this way: when we clearly perceive that we are sensible of a particular body and no other, then we clearly deduce, I say, from that perception that our mind is united to that body, and that this union is the cause of that sensation but we cannot understand directly from it the nature of that union and of sensation. Again, after I have come to know the nature of sight, and at the same time that it has this property, that at a great distance we see one and the same thing to be less than when we see it near at hand, I deduce that the sun is greater than he appears to be, and other conclusions of the same kind.

Finally, a thing is perceived through *its essence alone,* when from the fact that I have known something, I understand what it is to have known something; as, for instance, from the fact that I have known the essence of the soul I understand it to be united to the body. By this kind of knowledge we know that two and three are five, and that if there be two lines parallel to a third, they are parallel to one another. But the things which I can as yet understand by this kind of knowledge are very few.

In order that all these things may be better understood I will give only one example as follows. Three numbers are given: a fourth is required which shall be to the third as the second is to the first. In such a case merchants generally say that they know what is to be done in order to find the fourth, because they have not as yet forgotten the rule which they heard nakedly, without any demonstration, from their teachers. Others from their experience of particular cases construct a universal axiom. When, for example, the fourth number is self-evident, as in the series 2, 4, 3, 6, they see that if the second be multiplied by the third and the product divided by the first the quotient is 6. Since they observe that the quotient is the same number which, without this rule, they knew to be the proportional, they conclude that the rule is always valid for the discovery of a fourth proportional number. Mathematicians, however, by the help of the demonstration of Euclid, Prop. 19, bk. vii, know what numbers are proportional to one another—that is to say, that from the nature and property of proportion a number which is the product of the first and fourth is equal to a number which is the product of the second and third, but they do not see the adequate proportionality of the given numbers, or if they do see it, it is not by the help of this proposition, but intuitively and without any calculation.

In order to select the best of these kinds of knowledge it is necessary that we should briefly enumerate what are the necessary means to the attainment of our end. They are these:—

1. To know exactly our own nature which we desire to perfect, and at the same time so much of the nature of things as is necessary.

2. To form correct inductions with regard to the differences, agreements, and oppositions of things.

3. To understand properly how far they can and how far they cannot be acted upon.

4. To compare the result with the nature and power of man. It will then clearly appear what is the highest perfection to which man can attain. Having thus considered these matters, let us see what kind of knowledge we ought to choose.

As to the first, without taking into account that it is something altogether uncertain, it is self-evident that from hearing, as appears from our example, no essence of a thing can be perceived, and since, as will afterwards be seen, the particular existence of a thing is not known unless its essence be known, we clearly infer that all the certainty which we derive from hearing must be distinguished from science. For no one can be affected by simple hearing unless his own intellect has first acted.

As to the second, no one can say that he obtains thereby the idea of that proportion which he seeks. Not only is it something altogether uncertain, not only is no definite object in view, but by means of it nothing of natural objects is ever perceived save accidents, which are never clearly understood unless the essences of the things be previously known. Therefore also this method is to be set aside.

By the third it may in some measure be said that we have an idea of the thing, and that thence we can conclude without danger of error, but, nevertheless, this by itself will not be the means whereby we may obtain our perfection.

The fourth mode alone grasps the adequate essence of the thing without danger of error, and therefore is the one of which we are to avail ourselves above all others. We will take care to explain in what manner it is to be applied, so that by this kind of knowledge unknown things may be understood by us, and how this may be achieved as succinctly as possible.

[338]

SPIR, AFRICAN

SPIR, AFRICAN (1837-1890). During the siege of Sevastopol in the Crimean War, two young Russian officers distinguished themselves while defending the same bastion. Both of them were decorated with the high order of St. George's Cross. But, although they fought next to each other, they never became acquainted one with another. The one was Count Leo Tolstoy, then an artillery officer, who soon thereafter became world-famous as a great novelist and religious thinker. The other was African Spir, a lieutenant in the Russian navy who, in 1856, renounced his military career and emigrated from Russia in 1867, and whose philosophical writings remained relatively unknown. One of the few who were vitally interested in Spir's philosophy was Friedrich Nietzsche. With his friend, the theologian Franz Overbeck, he discussed Spir's ideas and adopted some of Spir's views.

Only six years after Spir's death, Tolstoy read the books written by his former companion in arms, whose existence he had ignored until then. He was deeply and sympathetically impressed, and succeeded in gaining permission from the Russian censorship for the publication of a Russian version of Spir's works, which had been written in German.

Spir's intention, especially in his principal work *Thought and Reality* (1873), was to establish philosophy as the science of first principles, and he held that its task was to investigate immediate knowledge, to demonstrate the delusion of the empirical world and the true nature of things by strict statements of facts and logically controlled inference. This method led him to proclaim the principle of identity as the fundamental law of knowledge which is opposed to the changing appearance of the empirical world, and the superiority of the moral over the physical elements. Spir was a profoundly religious thinker, but he regarded God as not responsible for the crimes committed by mankind because God has nothing to do with external causality. Spir therefore felt that the old religions are of merely historical importance. He demanded just distribution of material goods but disapproved collectivism.

ON INDIVIDUAL IMMORTALITY

WHAT I intend to consider here is not so much the question of whether individual immortality is probable, but rather the question of whether it is desirable or whether the desire for it is justified. These two questions, however, cannot be entirely separated one from another. For the same reasons which prove that individual immortality is not desirable also prove that it is not probable, and, inversely, men are inclined to regard their very desires as a guarantee for the fulfilment of that which they desire.

There are principally four reasons for desiring, and believing in, individual immortality. One of them is theoretical; the second is, so to speak, animal; the others are moral or ethical. . . . The theoretical reason lies in the fact that everyone recognizes, and must recognize, himself in his consciousness as an absolute entity, a substance. A substance, however, is by virtue of its concept imperishable. It is, therefore, inconceivable and incredible to us that our ego or self could be destroyed. As it is generally known, the spiritualists have asserted that this reason that our ego or self is a substance and therefore imperishable, is a scientifically valid proof of immortality. But Kant and others have shown that this argument is untenable. . . .

A substance is nothing but an object which has an essence proper to itself, not borrowed from outside and not determined by external conditions. A substance therefore is something in itself, independent of other things.

If we inspect ourselves closely, it undoubtedly becomes

evident that we are no substance, and that we do not possess a truly proper essence that is independent of other things. What we find in ourselves are only feelings, desires, ideas and the like, which are only various ways and manners of our reacting to effects from without, but which show nothing in themselves, nothing that exists independently of these effects. A closer inquiry demonstrates that we are a compound and a mere product of conditions, and that all our essence is constantly floating and changing. Even the apparently persistent ego or self is in fact created anew at every moment. For that reason, this ego or self can be destroyed or suspended at any moment. A mere pressure on the brain is sufficient to suppress all our psychic life.

Just because we are not real substances, and do not possess a real self or a content really proper to us, our individuality could not subsist without the natural delusion by virtue of which we appear as substances in our self-consciousness and by which we apparently have a proper, persistent and independent essence, without this delusion we would not be ourselves, and there would be no question of our ego. Our existence is therefore inseparable from our self-consciousness, or rather our existence consists of it. We only exist because we are understanding ourselves.

[339]

STEINER, RUDOLF

STEINER, RUDOLF (1861-1925). By 1900, Rudolf Steiner, then at the age of forty, surprised his friends by a complete change of personality. He had been a faithful disciple of Ernst Haeckel and a devoted adherent of evolutionist materialism, when he suddenly became a mystic. He had been a Bohemian, and suddenly became a saint. He had been nonchalant, and suddenly proved to be a fanatic. Only his admiration of Goethe did not change; but now Steiner interpreted his works in a new way, claiming that his understanding of Goethe was the only correct and congenial one, and that it was, at the same time, a justification of his new creed. Dissatisfied with natural sciences, Steiner became devoted to theosophy which he regarded as the legitimate and consequent continuance of biology and psychology. For a time he adopted the doctrine of Annie Besant, and was its enthusiastic propagator in Germany, winning influential adherents among the industrialists, army officers, even clergymen and poets. But when he tried to graft European ideas upon the "ancient wisdom," he and his followers were excluded from the Theosophical Society. Thereupon Steiner founded the "Anthroposophical Society" whose center was in Dornach, Switzerland. Steiner, who regarded himself an occult scientist rather than a mystic, taught that moral purification, emancipation from egoistic drives, and training in meditation developed spiritual qualities which enabled him and his followers to know realms of human and cosmic existence which otherwise remain hidden to the profane mind. Steiner was also interested in rhythmics, dancing, social questions and medicine. In 1917 he advanced a program for general peace. He exposed his doctrine in *Vom Menschenraetsel* (On the Riddle of Man, 1916) and *Von Seelenraetseln* (On the Riddles of the Soul, 1917).

INTUITION

INTUITION. In the language of occult science this word expresses, in many respects, the exact opposite of that to which it is often applied in ordinary life. People talk of intuition as if they mean some notion, dimly felt to be true, but lacking any clear and exact knowledge. They imagine it to be a preliminary step towards cognition rather than as cognition itself. Such a fancy as this may illuminate a great truth as by a flash of lightning, but it can only be counted as cognition when confirmed by accurate judgment. Further, by intuition is generally denoted something which is "felt" as truth, and of which a person is quite convinced, but which he will not burden with intellectual judgment. People who are approaching a knowledge of occult science often say that this or that was always clear to them "intuitively." But we must put all this entirely aside and fix our attention on the true meaning which the term intuition here implies. It is, from this point of view, a method of cognition in no way inferior in clearness to intellectual knowledge, and far surpassing it.

1142

Through inspiration the experiences of the higher worlds speak out what they mean. The observer lives in the qualities and deeds of beings of those higher worlds. When he follows with his ego, as described above, the direction of a line or the shape of a form, he knows that he is not within the being itself but within its qualities and deeds. In imaginative cognition he has already experienced the feeling of being no longer outside but inside the color-pictures, and now he understands just as clearly that these color-pictures are not in themselves independent beings but only the *qualities* of those beings. In inspiration he is conscious of becoming one with the *deeds* of such beings and with the manifestations of their will. In intuition he first melts his own personality with beings which are in themselves complete. This can only happen in the right way when the melting together takes place, not through the obliteration of his own being but with its perfect maintenance. To "lose oneself" in another being is wrong. Therefore it is only an ego fortified within itself to a very high degree that can be submerged in the being of another with impunity.

[340]

STERN, WILLIAM

STERN, WILLIAM (1871-1938). When William Stern, in 1927, wrote his autobiography, he summarized his external life in two lines by naming three cities: Berlin where he was born and had studied philosophy, and Breslau and Hamburg where he had been, and was then, a professor. He had no idea that six years later Hitler would oust him, notwithstanding all his merits, and that he would thus come to teach at Duke University and Harvard.

Stern became famous as a pioneer in applied psychology. His contributions to the psychology of deposition created a sensation among jurists, and his investigations of the psychology of childhood attracted the attention of educators. Of equal importance were Stern's concept of the intelligence quotient and other studies on intelligence testing.

This successful psychologist also became a highly respected and influential philosopher. According to Stern, psychology and

1143

philosophy must follow the strategic principle of "marching separately and battling commonly."

Stern was strongly opposed to what he called "scientification of psychology" because its result was "mechanization of spiritual life." His philosophy of critical personalism tries to overcome the antagonism between common sense, which believes in separate persons, gods, or vital forces, and impersonal science, which regards the whole world as a system of elementary units and all individuals as physico-chemical aggregates. Stern declared that the person is the primordial and most pervasive unity in the range of the experimental world. Any attempt to dissect it, to typify or to reduce it to notions or principles he rejected as distortion of facts. Stern's concept of person is larger that that of the human individual. It comprises also groups. The person is to be distinguished from the thing. The person is a whole, individuality, quality, while the thing is an aggregate, quantity, comparable with other things. Personal development is no mechanical interchange between the person and his environment. It involves a constant, though not necessarily conscious, readiness to realize values which are suggested by environment. Stern's concept of history denies both biological evolution and the dialectical process, and also Rickert's reference to general values. Stern's personalism begins as ontology and proceeds to "axiosophy."

PLAY

IF we compare the play of children and adults a common principle is revealed; *make-believe* is produced in the midst of the world of reality. Like the playing of soldiers by youngsters, the billiard playing of grownups is a sham battle between people who in reality bear no enmity toward each other; an actor's role is as fictitious as the role of mother assumed by a girl playing with dolls. In both instances all the meaning of the play lies in the *present;* unlike work or artistic creation, play does not incline toward some systematic objective; it has no sequels, and it is not serious, however seriously the player may take it during its course.

The differences between the play of young and old become clear when certain *lines of development* are disclosed. In early childhood, play is definitely central to the child's behavior (wherefore this period is also called the "playing age"). Here there is no sharp separation of the world of play and the world of real earnest; all environmental objects and all the child's actions, including the realistic ones like eating, dressing, etc., become entangled in play and charged with playfulness; even when things are frankly "taken seriously" there is no clear-cut distinction between make-believe and reality. In terms of inner experience there is scarcely any difference between a girl's helping her mother dress the baby by handing her the garments, and dressing her own doll. The school age brings about fundamental changes, inasmuch as the child experiences *side by side* the two spheres of work and play, which are now clearly separate; at this point serious activity begins to develop with increasing strength, along with restraint of playfulness. In adolescence the intermediate and mixed forms appear; intermediate forms are athletics, which, by the principle of constant increase of prowess, no longer yields gratification purely in the present but imposes future goals, collecting, and other hobbies directed upon the promotion of lasting concerns. A mixed form is "serious play" (*Ernstspiel*), a behavior which, while subjectively of serious import, retains objectively the freedom and lack of consequence of play.

In adulthood play, sports, and hobbies become more and more definitely a mere adjunct to life, supplementing and completing it while affording a contrast to the severity of occupational routine and to the momentous responsibilities of domestic and public concerns.

The changing place of *imagination* also correlates with development. In early childhood imagination is very free and spontaneous, wanton, unorganized and bubbling. In play everything is grist for the mill; both player and objects played with can assume any sort of "part" without rules or restrictions; the child is sole ruler of his world of play.

When socialized play becomes more prominent, the individual's imagination must be curbed in certain respects; the game, its setting, and its rules impose limitations and directions which, without eliminating imagination, discipline and organize it. In athletics the principle of organization attains great strictness; each action is prescribed and established, and there is little room for free imagination, which receives new impulsion in the "serious play" of adolescence where instincts, desires, and anxieties are elaborated in an highly imaginative manner.

The play of adults, however, is well-nigh devoid of imagination; forms of solitary amusement like collecting have their course laid out for them in greater or less strictness by the objective and the material. Social games (cards, table games, sporting games) are hedged by such a mass of fixed rules that very limited freedom of action remains to creative imagination.

[341]

STIRNER, MAX

STIRNER, MAX (1806-1856). In the daytime, Herr Kaspar Schmidt was a teacher at a young ladies' school, a respectable citizen of Berlin and a loyal subject of his king, Frederick William IV of Prussia. In the evening, he drank wine in a restaurant where he met some writers of left-wing Hegelianism and discussed with them philosophical problems. More often than not, these debates and the wine fired the imagination of the speakers who competed one with another in exalting, both earnestly and parodistically, their personal mission as radical revolutionaries. Some members of that company later became notorious as political adventurers, others became more or less prominent socialists. Kaspar Schmidt, after coming home, worked, late in the night, at a manuscript which he published under the title *Der Einzige und sein Eigentum* (The Ego and his Own, 1845). The author of this book, calling himself Max Stirner is generally considered as the founder of theoretical anarchism and the most radical individualist in the history of philosophy. While most of his contemporaries conceived the individual as determined by collective factors of various kinds, Stirner proclaimed the uniqueness and absolute independence of his ego. For even the notion of the individual is in Stirner's opinion a useless concession to collectivism. He leaves it to other egos to claim the same uniqueness for themselves. While establishing the ego as the

1146

sole reality and the sole value, Stirner emphasizes his opposition against society, against the state, against reactionary and revolutionary parties, against liberalism and socialism, against any legislation and social conventions. For Stirner, the negation of all values except the ego means the only guarantee of personal freedom and the sole way of constructing a philosophical system by independent thinking. His motto is, "I am dependent on nothing," and his cardinal principle is, "For me there is nothing like myself." Whatever other people regard as value, ideas, notions, tenets or laws, are dealt with by Stirner as spectres which haunt unenlightened men. While trying to exorcise these spectres by exposing their unreality, Stirner becomes a mythologist on his own. He was severely attacked by Marx and Engels; however, his book remained practically ignored during his lifetime. Stirner gave his adventurous spirit a free course only in his inward life. What later became known as political anarchism would have terrified him, and he would have opposed it as contrary to his cult of the ego.

THE POSSESSED

MAN, your head is haunted; you have wheels in your head! You imagine great things, and depict to yourself a whole world of gods that has an existence for you, a spirit-realm to which you suppose yourself to be called, an ideal that beckons to you. You have a fixed idea!

Do not think that I am jesting or speaking figuratively when I regard those persons who cling to the Higher, and (because the vast majority belongs under this head) almost the whole world of men, as veritable fools, fools in a madhouse. What is it, then, that is called a "fixed idea"? An idea that has subjected the man to itself. When you recognize, with regard to such a fixed idea, that it is a folly, you shut its slave up in an asylum. And is the truth of the faith, say, which we are not to doubt; the majesty of (e.g.) the people, which we are not to strike at (he who does is guilty of lesemajesty); virtue, against which the censor is not to let a word pass, that morality may be kept pure; etc.,—are these not "fixed ideas"? Is not all the stupid chatter of (e.g.) most of our newspapers the babble of fools who suffer from the fixed idea of morality, legality, Christianity, etc., and only seem to go about free because the madhouse in which they walk takes in so broad a space? Touch the fixed idea of such a fool, and you will at once have to guard your back against the lunatic's stealthy malice. For these great lunatics are like the little so-called lunatics in this point too, that they assail by stealth him who touches their fixed idea. They first steal his weapon, steal free speech from him, and then they fall upon him with their nails. Every day now lays bare the cowardice and vindictiveness of these maniacs, and the stupid populace hurrahs for their crazy measures. One must read the journals of this period, and must hear the Philistines talk, to get the horrible conviction that one is shut up in a house with fools. "Thou shalt not call thy brother a fool; if thou dost—etc." But I do not fear the curse, and I say, my brothers are arch-fools. Whether a poor fool of the insane asylum is possessed by the fancy that he is God the Father, Emperor of Japan, the Holy Spirit, etc., or whether a citizen in comfortable circumstances conceives that it is his mission to be a good Christian, a faithful Protestant, a loyal citizen, a virtuous man, etc.,—both these are one and the same "fixed idea." He who has never tried and dared not to be a good Christian, a faithful Protestant, a virtuous man, etc., is *possessed* and prepossessed by faith, virtuousness, etc. Just as the schoolmen philosophized only *inside* the belief of the church; as Pope Benedict XIV wrote fat books *inside* the papist superstition, without ever throwing a doubt upon this belief; as authors fill whole folios on the State without calling in question the fixed idea of the State itself; as our newspapers are crammed with politics because they are conjured into the fancy that man was created to be a *zoon politicon*,—so also subjects vegetate in subjection, virtuous people in virtue, liberals in humanity, etc., without ever putting to these fixed ideas of theirs the searching knife of criticism. Undislodgeable, like a madman's delusion, those thoughts stand on a firm footing, and he who doubts them lays hands on the *sacred!* Yes, the "fixed idea," that is the truly sacred!

1148

Is it perchance only people possessed by the devil that meet us, or do we as often come upon people *possessed* in the contrary way,—possessed by "the good," by virtue, morality, the law, or some "principle" or other? Possessions of the devil are not the only ones. God works on us, and the devil does; the former "workings of grace," the latter "workings of the devil." Possessed people are *set* in their opinions.

If the word "possession" displeases you, then call it prepossession; yes, since the spirit possesses you, and all "inspirations" come from it, call it inspiration and enthusiasm. I add that complete enthusiasm—for we cannot stop with the sluggish, half-way kind—is called fanaticism.

It is precisely among cultured people that *fanaticism* is at home; for man is cultured so far as he takes an interest in spiritual things, and interest in spiritual things, when it is alive, is and must be *fanaticism*; it is a fanatical interest in the sacred (*fanum*). Observe our liberals, look into the *Saechsischen Vaterlandsblaetter*, hear what Schlosser says: "Holbach's company constituted a regular plot against the traditional doctrine and the existing system, and its members were as fanatical on behalf of their unbelief as monks and priests, Jesuits and Pietists, Methodists, missionary and Bible societies, commonly are for mechanical worship and orthodoxy."

Take notice how a "moral man" behaves, who today often thinks he is through with God and throws off Christianity as a bygone thing. If you ask him whether he has ever doubted that the copulation of brother and sister is incest, that monogamy is the truth of marriage, that filial piety is a sacred duty, etc., then a moral shudder will come over him at the conception of one's being allowed to touch his sister as wife also, etc. And whence this shudder? Because he *believes* in those moral commandments. This moral *faith* is deeply rooted in his breast. Much as he rages against the *pious* Christians, he himself has nevertheless as thoroughly remained a Christian,—to wit, a *moral* Christian. In the form of morality Christianity holds him a prisoner, and a prisoner under *faith*. Monogamy is to be something sacred, and he who may live in bigamy is punished as a *criminal;* he who commits incest suffers as a *criminal.* Those who are always crying that religion is not to be regarded in the state, and the Jew is to be a citizen equally with the Christian, show themselves in accord with this. Is not this of incest and monogamy a *dogma of faith?* Touch it, and you will learn by experience how this moral man is a *hero of faith* too, not less than Krummacher, not less than Philip II. These fight for the faith of the Church, he for the faith of the State, or the moral laws of the State; for articles of faith, both condemn him who acts otherwise than *their faith* will allow. The brand of "crime" is stamped upon him, and he may languish in reformatories, in jails. Moral faith is as fanatical as religious faith! They call that "liberty of faith" then, when brother and sister, on account of a relation that they should have settled with their "conscience," are thrown into prison. "But they set a pernicious example." Yes, indeed: others might have taken the notion that the State had no business to meddle with their relation, and thereupon "purity of morals" would go to ruin. So then the religious heroes of faith are zealous for the "sacred God," the moral ones for the "sacred good."

Those who are zealous for something sacred often look very little like each other. How the strictly orthodox or old-style believers differ from the fighters for "truth, light, and justice," from the Philalethes, the Friends of Light, the Rationalists, etc. And yet, how utterly unessential is this difference! If one buffets single traditional truths (*e.g.* miracles, unlimited power of princes, etc.), then the rationalists buffet them too, and only the old-style believers wail. But, if one buffets truth itself, he immediately has both, as *believers*, for opponents. So with moralities; the strict believers are relentless, the clearer heads are more tolerant. But he who attacks morality itself gets both to deal with. "Truth, morality, justice, light, etc.," are to be and remain "sacred." What any one finds to censure in Christianity is simply supposed to be "unchristian" according to the view of these rationalists; but Christianity must remain a "fixture," to buffet it is outrageous, "an outrage." To be sure, the heretic against pure faith no longer exposes himself to the earlier fury of persecution, but so much more does it now fall upon the heretic against pure morals.

[342]

STRAUSS, DAVID FRIEDRICH

STRAUSS, DAVID FRIEDRICH (1808-1874). Before Strauss published his *Life of Jesus* (1835), it seemed that the authority of the Christian faith was defended in Germany far more efficiently than it had been during the preceding century. Hegel and Schleiermacher, bitterly opposed one to another, had produced a synthesis of Christian religion and modern thought that was supposed to satisfy all spiritual needs of German intellectuals, not to mention that pressure was exercised by more orthodox theologians who used to denounce really or allegedly un-Christian opinions, and by the governments which were always ready to punish the expression of such opinions. The appearance of Strauss' book had the effect of a bombshell and changed the situation completely. It made Germany the arena of a religious struggle whose violence was unheard of since the end of the Thirty Years War.

Strauss, without denying the historical existence of Jesus, inexorably criticized the sources of the New Testament, proved their inner contradictions in principal and minor points, and demonstrated that many reports on the life of Jesus, narrated in the Gospels, were entirely unreliable, products of, as he said, "mythical" literature which, to a large extent, was patterned on tales and sayings of the Old Testament. The synthesis of theology and science was destroyed, and could not be saved either by orthodox theologians who called for the police or by rightist Hegelians who protested that Strauss had misunderstood their master.

The book that made Strauss famous, destroyed his happiness. He was not a fighter, and the permanent hostilities which culminated in an open revolt of the people of Zurich, where he had been appointed professor, undermined his health. But his sense of truth remained unshattered. In his *Doctrine of the Christian Faith* (1840), Strauss definitely broke with Christian theology and Christianity completely. His frankness surpassed that of the most daring thinkers

1151

in Germany previous to him. He maintained his standpoint in his later works, especially in his *The Old Faith and the New* (1872), while flatly answering "No" to the question "Can we still be Christians?," and trying to harmonize the doctrine of Ludwig Feuerbach with Darwinism. Certainly, this last work of a tired, constantly persecuted and physically suffering man has many weak points. But it did not deserve the violent attack made by Friedrich Nietzsche who ignored that Strauss, at least in his early writings, had accomplished that which Nietzsche himself demanded from a valiant thinker.

POLYTHEISM AND MONOTHEISM

POLYTHEISM was the original, and in some respects the natural form of religion. A multiplicity of phenomena presented themselves to man, a multiplicity of forces pressed in upon him, from which he either wished himself protected, or of whose favor he desired to be assured; then also a variety of relations which he craved to have sanctified and securely established; thus naturally arose, also, a multiplicity of divinities. This conclusion is confirmed by the observation, that all those tribes of the earth which are still to a certain extent in a state of nature, continue now, as formerly, to be polytheists. Monotheism appears everywhere in history, the Jewish not excepted, as something secondary, as something educed in the lapse of time out of a more primitive polytheism. How was this transition effected?

It is said, certainly, that a more exact observation of Nature must have led man to perceive the connection of all her phenomena, the unity of design in which all her laws converge. And in like manner the development of man's powers of reflection must have rendered it evident that a plurality of deities must mutually limit each other, and in consequence deprive each other of the very attributes of divinity, so that the deity, in the true and complete sense of that word, could only be a unit. Insight of this kind, it is argued, came to a few highly gifted individuals of antiquity, and these became in consequence the founders of monotheism.

We know full well the highly gifted individuals who acquired insight in this manner: they were the Greek philosophers; but they became founders, not of religion, but of philosophical systems and schools. Of a like nature is the oscillating monotheism of the Indian religion: it is an esoteric, mystical doctrine, the presentiment of a few, developed from the popular polytheism.

Monotheism first occurs among the Jews in the firm serried form of a popular religion. And here also we can clearly apprehend its origin. Hebrew monotheism was certainly not produced by a deeper observation of nature; the Hebrews for a long while caring only for nature in its relation to their own wants. Neither did it arise from philosophical speculation; for before the impulse communicated to them by the Greeks, the Jews did not speculate, at least not in the philosophical sense. Monotheism (the fact becomes evident in that of the Jews, and is further confirmed by Islamism) is originally and essentially the religion of a wandering clan. The requirements of such a nomadic band are very simple, as are also its social arrangements; and although at first (as may also here be assumed to have been the primitive idea) these may have been presided over by distinct fetishes, dæmons, or deities, nevertheless this distinction disappeared in proportion as the horde concentrated itself (as did, for example, the Israelites in their invasion of Canaan) and receded more and more, as in course of warfare with hordes like themselves, or with tribes and nations of different institutions, the contrast to these latter gained prominence. As it was but a single enthusiasm which inspired the clan, which strengthened it in its conflict with others, gave it hope in victory, and even in defeat the trust in future triumph; even thus it was only one god whom it served, from whom it expected all things; or, rather even this god was, in fact, only its deified popular spirit. True, at first the gods of other tribes and nations were conceived as antagonistic to the one god of the clan—the gods of the Canaanites

to the god of Israel; but as the weaker, the inferior, destined
to be overcome by the god of the clan—vain gods, who at
last must actually vanish into nothing, leaving the one true
God alone.

[343]

SWEDENBORG, EMANUEL

SWEDENBORG, EMANUEL (1688-1772). Emerson once remarked
that it would require "a colony of men" to do justice to Swedenborg's work. Goethe adopted several of Swedenborg's ideas. Balzac
founded essential views on human and cosmic nature on Swedenborg's doctrine. So have many modern authors. And today there are
thousands of faithful Swedenborgians in Europe and America.

Until his fifty-third year, Swedenborg had been known as a
great engineer, a scholar and a scientist. He had written important
books on mathematics, mechanics, physiology and astronomy. Then
he experienced a grave crisis. As a lad, he had already yearned to
know God and had eagerly discussed theological questions with
clergymen. In his advanced age he became more and more anxious
about his spiritual conditions. He was deeply impressed by dreams
in which he had visions. In 1757 he became convinced of having
witnessed in one of his visions the Last Judgment. In his *Arcana
Coelestia* (in 12 volumes, 1749-56) he offered a mystical interpretation of the first books of the Old Testament which, according
to him, was purposely written to prevent profanation, and by exposing their true meaning, he developed his own religious and
philosophical system.

Of fundamental importance to Swedenborg's system is his
doctrine of correspondence, which, as he asserts, was known to the
ancient peoples in Canaan, Chaldea, Syria and Egypt and since
had been forgotten. Greek travelers who visited these countries
misunderstood the doctrine and changed it into fabulous stories
which, however, allow a reconstruction of the true sense. According to this doctrine, everything in our visible, natural or material
world corresponds to something in the invisible, spiritual astral
world. The total natural world corresponds to the spiritual world
not only in general but in particular. Thus, everything in the natural world represents an idea.

Swedenborg distinguishes four styles in the world. The first,
the style of the most ancient mankind which extends until Noah and
the Flood, has been transcribed by Moses but has an offspring in

1154

the third style, the prophetic, while the second, the historic, extends from Abraham to the time of the kings of Judah and Israel. The fourth style, that of David's psalms, is mixed with the prophetic style and common speech. The restitution of the most ancient religion is Swedenborg's purpose. He claims to be sent by God to announce the end of the Christian and the beginning of the New Jerusalem dispensation. He recognizes Jesus Christ as Saviour but rejects the Christian doctrine of Trinity and excludes the Epistles of Paul from the Biblical Canon. God is one, both in essence and person. He is uncreated, eternal, infinite, omnipotent, the union of love and wisdom.

Related with the doctrine of correspondence is Swedenborg's doctrine of degrees. Man is a recipient of three degrees, and capable of thinking analytically and rationally of things within the sphere of nature, and of spiritual and celestial things above the natural sphere. At the highest degree, man may see God.

Swedenborg's behavior showed nothing eccentric. Apart from his visions, he was very practical and free from emotion. He was a strict vegetarian and admonished his disciples to refrain from eating meat. His modesty and simplicity won him many friends and admirers even among those who did not share his opinions.

ON HUMAN MIND

EVERY created thing is finite; and the Infinite is in finite things as in its receptacles, and is in men as in its images. Every created thing is finite because all things are from Jehovah God through the sun of the spiritual world, which most nearly encompasses Him; and that sun is composed of the substance that has gone forth from Him, the essence of which is love. From the sun, by means of its heat and light, the universe has been created from its firsts to its lasts. But this is not the proper place to set forth in order the process of creation. . . . All that is important now is to know that one thing was formed from another, and thus degrees were constituted, three in the spiritual world and three corresponding to them in the natural world, and the same number in the passive materials of which the terraqueous globe is composed. The origin and nature of these degrees has been fully explained in the *Angelic Wisdom concerning the Divine Love and the Divine Wisdom* (published at Amsterdam in 1763), and a small work on *The Intercourse of the Soul and the Body* (published at London in 1769). Through these degrees all things posterior are made receptacles of things prior, and these again of things still prior, and so on in succession receptacles of the primitive elements which constitute the sun of the angelic heaven; and thus have things finite been made receptacles of the infinite. This is in agreement with the wisdom of the ancients, according to which each thing and all things are divisible to infinity. It is a common idea that, because the finite cannot grasp the infinite, things finite cannot be receptacles of the infinite; but in what has been set forth in my works respecting creation it has been shown that God first rendered His infinity finite by means of substances emitted from Himself, from which His nearest surrounding sphere, which constitutes the sun of the spiritual world, came into existence; and that then through that sun He perfected the other surrounding spheres, even to the outmost, which consists of passive materials; and in this manner, by means of degrees, He rendered the world more and more finite. This much has been said to satisfy human reason, which never rests until it perceives a cause.

That the infinite Divine is in men as in its images is evident from the Word, where we read:—

And God said, Let us make man in Our image, after Our likeness. So God created man to His own image, into the image of God created He him (*Gen.* i. 26, 27).

From this it follows that man is an organic form recipient of God, and is an organic form that is in accordance with the kind of reception. The human mind, which makes man to be man, and in accordance with which man is man, is formed into three regions in accordance with the three degrees; in the first degree, in which also are the angels of the highest heaven, the mind is celestial; in the second degree, in which are the angels of the middle heaven, it is spiritual; and in the third degree, in which are the angels of the lowest heaven, it is natural. The human mind, organized in accordance with these three degrees, is a receptacle of Divine influx; nevertheless, the Divine flows into it no further than man prepares the way or opens the door. If man does this as far as to the highest or celestial degree he becomes truly an image of God, and after death an angel of the highest heaven; but if he prepares the way or opens the door only to the middle or spiritual degree, he becomes an image of God, but not in the same perfection; and after death he becomes an angel of the middle heaven. But if man prepares the way or opens the door only to the lowest or natural degree, in case he acknowledges God and worships Him with actual piety he becomes an image of God in the lowest degree, and after death an angel of the lowest heaven. But if man does not acknowledge God and does not worship Him with actual piety he puts off the image of God and becomes like some animal, except that he enjoys the faculty of understanding, and consequently of speech; and if he then closes up the highest natural degree, which corresponds to the highest celestial, he becomes as to his loves like a beast of the earth; and if he closes up the middle natural degree, which corresponds to the middle spiritual degree, he becomes in his love like a fox, and in his intellectual vision like a bird of night; while if he also closes up the lowest natural degree in its relation to his spiritual he becomes in his love like a wild beast, and in his understanding of truth like a fish.

[344]

1157

T

TAGORE, RABINDRANATH

TAGORE, RABINDRANATH (1861-1941). Rabindranath Tagore, the greatest lyrical poet of modern India, also a successful dramatist and novelist, and a highly respected author of philosophical treatises, was the descendant of an old Brahman family. The great aim of his life was to revive the ideals of ancient India and at the same time to obtain a better understanding between East and West. His attitude was opposed to that of Gandhi, whose methods he held in contempt.

After studying law in England, Tagore managed his family's estate for seventeen years. In 1901 he founded his school, *Abode of Peace*, where pupils were educated in accordance with his principles. When he came to England in 1911, where his poems *Gitanjali* (Song of Offerings) were published in an English version prepared by the author, he was enthusiastically received, and his fame spread over Europe and America. He was the first Asian to receive, in 1913, the Nobel Prize. In 1915, he was knighted. After the massacre of Amritsar he intended to renounce his knightship in order to protest against the British administration of India but instead consented to a compromise.

Tagore's poems have been translated into many languages, and the music of his diction remained charming and strong in most of the versions. The harmonious balance of his personality, which found expression in his writings, never failed to impress everyone he met. His ethics did not tolerate morals of expediency or sanction of means according to their ends. Always ready to protest against injustice and persecution, he was a staunch adversary of German nationalism and Hitler's regime. His philosophy is based on the belief in the progressive realization of the divine in man, and it shows little interest in celestial destiny. He insists that man's perfection shall come in the world in which he is living.

1158

LOVE AS THE FULFILLMENT OF LIFE

ONE DAY I was out in a boat on the Ganges. It was a beautiful evening in autumn. The sun had just set; the silence of the sky was full to the brim with ineffable peace and beauty. The vast expanse of water was without a ripple, mirroring all the changing shades of the sunset glow. Miles and miles of a desolate sandbank lay like a huge amphibious reptile of some antediluvian age, with its scales glistening in shining colours. As our boat was silently gliding by the precipitous river-bank, riddled with the nest-holes of a colony of birds, suddenly a big fish leapt up to the surface of the water and then disappeared, displaying on its vanishing figure all the colours of the evening sky. It drew aside for a moment the many-coloured screen behind which there was a silent world full of the joy of life. It came up from the depths of its mysterious dwelling with a beautiful dancing motion and added its own music to the silent symphony of the dying day. I felt as if I had a friendly greeting from an alien world in its own language, and it touched my heart with a flash of gladness. Then suddenly the man at the helm exclaimed with a distinct note of regret, "Ah, what a big fish!" It at once brought before his vision the picture of the fish caught and made ready for his supper. He could only look at the fish through his desire, and thus missed the whole truth of its existence. But man is not entirely an animal. He aspires to a spiritual vision, which is the vision of the whole truth. This gives him the highest delight, because it reveals to him the deepest harmony that exists between him and his surroundings. It is our desires that limit the scope of our self-realisation, hinder our extension of consciousness, and give rise to sin, which is the innermost barrier that keeps us apart from our God, setting up disunion and the arrogance of exclusiveness. For sin is not one mere action, but it is an attitude of life which takes for granted that our goal is finite, that our self is the ultimate truth, and that we are not all essentially one but exist each for his own separate individual existence.

So I repeat we never can have a true view of man unless we have a love for him. Civilisation must be judged and prized, not by the amount of power it has developed, but by how much it has evolved and given expression to, by its laws and institutions, the love of humanity. The first question and the last which it has to answer is, Whether and how far it recognises man more as a spirit than as a machine? Whenever some ancient civilisation fell into decay and died, it was owing to causes which produced callousness of heart and led to the cheapening of man's worth; when either the state or some powerful group of men began to look upon the people as a mere instrument of their power; when, by compelling weaker races to slavery and trying to keep them down by every means, man struck at the foundation of his greatness, his own love of freedom and fairplay. Civilisation can never sustain itself upon cannibalism of any form. For that by which alone man is true can only be nourished by love and justice.

As with man, so with this universe. When we look at the world through the veil of our desires we make it small and narrow, and fail to perceive its full truth. Of course it is obvious that the world serves us and fulfills our needs, but our relation to it does not end there. We are bound to it with a deeper and truer bond than that of necessity. Our soul is drawn to it.   [345]

TELESIO, BERNARDINO

TELESIO, BERNARDINO (1508-1588). By his refusal to be nominated Archbishop by Pope Paul IV, Telesio renounced a brilliant ecclesiastical career in order to devote his life to independent thought and the study of the sciences. He did not break with the Church, but became one of the initiators of the scientific movement which, though not identical with it, resulted from the spirit of the Renaissance.

Telesio accepted the traditional division of psychic life into vegetative, sensitive and intellectual spheres, and he followed the tradition by insisting upon the fundamental difference between the human soul, created by and endowed with the divine spirit, and the animal soul, which is considered a natural formation. But these traditional views allowed him to state numerous physiological and psychical qualities which are common to both man and animals, and to observe that man's psychic life is not sufficiently characterized by the divine origin of his soul but that its description must be completed by a purely empirical study which shows the part played by the animal character in him.

Knowledge is founded, according to Telesio, upon sensation and memory. Essential as sensual perception is considered, an at least equal importance is attributed to the memory of perceiving. Without memory, Telesio said, no formation of thought is possible. While adumbrating a doctrine of psychic atomism, Telesio anticipated both the sensualism and the associationism of later centuries. He also tried to establish the compatibility of psychic and physical motions, as well as relations between time and motion. Physical facts were reduced to contraction and expansion, which are caused by heat and cold.

In his later years, Telesio founded and directed his own academy, the *Academia Telesiana* at Naples, which became instrumental to the propagation and growth of the scientific spirit in Galileo's epoch.

MAN HAS A DIVINE SOUL

BE it permitted to mention that even though the spirit in animals drawn from the sperms shall be considered the substance of the soul, it does not follow that one shall also take this spirit as the substance of the soul of man, because not only the Holy Script but even human reasons convince us that in man dwells another entirely divine substance placed here by God himself. We recognize in man, namely, actions, sufferings and strivings quite distinct from animals, which must be ascribed to a higher substance than the spirit drawn from the sperms; for man is not satisfied, as the rest of the animals are, with sensation, cognitions and enjoyments of the things that feed, conserve and please him, but he also investigates with greatest zeal the substance and effects of such things as are of no use to him and cannot even be conceived by any sense, especially those concerning the divine essence and divinity. Nay, he even forgets, disdains and neglects, while persistently and blissfully contemplating them, even that which pertains to the well-being and enjoyment of his body. Entirely in opposition to the other animals, which are satisfied with the goods that maintain them and make them sufficiently happy and neither desire nor ask for anything beyond that man alone finds no satisfaction in the present goods, whatever they might be, but shows by his outlook on the future, his longing for the remote and the prediction of a still happier life that there is a substance, a spirit in him that tends anxiously toward his Creator and Father (God) as toward his highest and proper good, and, being deprived of the intuition of it, he cannot be enticed by anything to such a degree that he could forget it or would not crave it. Finally, the intellect of man considers evil men, even if he sees them in highest abundance and happiness, as contemptible and pitiful, but he likes, honors and considers happy the good ones. This proves too that here is in man a divine sense that is a divine substance and nature.

[346]

TEMPLE, WILLIAM

TEMPLE, WILLIAM (1881-1944). When William Temple, who had been Archbishop of York since 1929, became in 1942, Archbishop of Canterbury and in this way succeeded his father, Frederick Temple, the event was considered unheard of in the history of the English Church. But even greater astonishment was caused by the fact that the new Archbishop, the highest ecclesiastical dignitary of the British kingdom, was an avowed student of Karl Marx. Temple had had a thorough classical education, combined with training in logic, ethics, metaphysics and the history of philosophy. His tutor, Edward Caird, had initiated him in the philosophy of Plato and Hegel, but he also read with admiration Aristotle and Aquinas, and finally two such different thinkers as Bergson and Marx induced him to break with traditional idealism and to adopt a kind of dialectical realism. He adopted Marxian dialectics and subscribed to many points of the socialist program, especially those concerning public ownership; but the most radical realization of socialist ideas seemed to him insufficient for the thorough reform of human conditions. He remained convinced that only Christian faith can fulfil this task and that Christianity is necessary for the completion of human thought and life, as well as for the cultural progress in which he firmly believed.

While in philosophy Temple turned from idealism to realism, in theology he turned from liberalism to orthodoxy. But just as he could say that, while being a liberal, he never for a moment had doubted the divinity of Christ, Temple, while an orthodox theologian, retained a liberal and tolerant attitude in questions of religious convictions. He defended discussion and believed in democracy, vital need for which is discussion. Temple never faced doubt as a personal problem. He was as happy as he was pious, and as simple and good-humored as he was dignified. The energetic manner in which he insisted on the close connection between faith and life revealed his judgment on mystical religion. Temple would not deny that the mystical experience might be the purest and intensest of all religious experiences. But just for the reason that it claims to be the most detached from nonreligious interests, he held that it is the least representative and least important of all religious forms. He declared that any philosophy that arrives at theism arrives at the study of the real world which is created and explained by God.

THE PROBLEM OF EVIL

THE problem of evil is always a problem in terms of purpose. No one is much interested in finding out how it came here, as a matter of historical fact; that does not much matter. The problem is, what is it doing here? What is it for? Why does God permit it? Or, if God is omnipotent, in which case permission and creation are the same, why did God create it? While we are sitting at our ease it generally seems to us that the world would be very much better if all evil were abolished, and indeed had never existed. But would it? Which are our own best days,—the days when we have nothing to perplex us, or trouble us? or the days when, at considerable cost to ourselves, we have made some real effort against the evil which afflicted either ourselves or other people? Surely the latter. Surely we know that one of the best of the good things in life is victory and particularly moral victory. But to demand victory without an antagonist is to demand something with no meaning. If, then, goodness is to exist up to the limit of what even we can understand, there must at least be an antagonist to be overcome. If you take all the evil out of the world you will remove the possibility of the best thing in life. That does not mean that evil is good. What one means by calling a thing good is that the spirit rests permanently content with it for its own sake. Evil is precisely that with which no spirit can rest content; and yet it is the condition, not the accidental but the essential condition, of what is in and for itself the best thing in life, namely moral victory.

[347]

TERTULLIAN

TERTULLIAN (About 165-220). At the age of forty, Tertullian, the son of a Roman army officer, was converted to Christianity and became its most ardent apologist. Living during the reigns of emperors Septimius Severus and Caracalla, he courageously protested against the cruelties committed by the magistrates and against the excesses of the mob against Christians, but he was equally prepared to recommend violence against any adversary of his new co-religionists in case persuasion did not help. His works, of which, besides the *Apology*, thirty-three are extant, exhibit fervor, zealotism, knowledge of his times and of past history, and an extremely aggressive spirit. Tertullian was untiring in expressing his contempt of pagan philosophers. To him faith was above reason, and logical contradiction a means to refutation of creed. His saying *Credo quia absurdum est*, however, is often quoted in a sense which its author did not mean. For twenty years, Tertullian intervened in every controversy concerning Christian doctrine. He introduced, in his book *Adversus Praxean*, the term *Trinitas* into the Latin language in order to signify the one God in three persons, although he did not live to see the dogma of the Trinity firmly established. With uncompromising rigor he fought aggressively against Jews, pagans, heretics and secular authorities. He eagerly objected to second marriages and branded Christians who held offices in the imperial administration or did military service. Further, he could not tolerate Christian artists. However in his last years, Tertullian, with ascetic leanings adhering to the sect of Montanists, became himself a heretic.

THE PARTS OF THE SOUL

THAT position of Plato's is quite in keeping with the faith, in which he divides the soul into two parts—the rational and the irrational. To this definition we take no exception, except that we would not ascribe this twofold distinction to the nature (of the soul). It is the rational element which we must believe to be its natural condition, impressed upon it from its very first creation by its Author, who is Himself essentially rational. For how should that be other than rational, which God produced on His own prompting; nay more, which He expressly sent forth by His own *afflatus* or breath? The irrational element, however, we must understand to have accrued later, as having proceeded from the instigation of the serpent—the very achievement of (the first) transgression—which thenceforward became inherent in the soul, and grew with its growth, assuming the manner by this time of a natural development, happening as it did immediately at the beginning of nature. But, inasmuch as the same Plato speaks of the rational element only as existing in the soul of God Himself, if we were to ascribe the irrational element likewise to the nature which our soul has received from God, then the irrational element will be equally derived from God, as being a natural production, because God is the author of nature. Now from the devil proceeds the incentive to sin. All sin, however, is irrational: therefore the irrational proceeds from the devil, from whom sin proceeds; and it is extraneous to God, to whom also the irrational is an alien principle. The diversity, then, between these two elements arises from the difference of their authors. When, therefore, Plato reserves the rational element (of the soul) to God alone, and subdivides it into two departments the *irascible*, which they call *tymikon*, and the *concupiscible*, which they designate by the term *epitymetikon* (in such a way

1165

as to make the first common to us and lions, and the second shared between ourselves and flies, whilst the rational element is confined to us and God)—I see that this point will have to be treated by us, owing to the facts which we find operating also in Christ. For you may behold this triad of qualities in the Lord. There was the *rational* element, by which He taught, by which He discoursed, by which He prepared the way of salvation; there was moreover *indignation* in Him, by which He inveighed against the scribes and the Pharisees; and there was the principle of *desire*, by which He so earnestly desired to eat the passover with His disciples. In our own cases, accordingly, the irascible and the concupiscible elements of our soul must not invariably be put to the account of the irrational (nature), since we are sure that in our Lord these elements operated in entire accordance with reason. God will be angry, with perfect reason, with all who deserve His wrath; and with reason, too, will God desire whatever objects and claims are worthy of Himself. For He will show indignation against the evil man, and for the good man will He desire salvation. To ourselves even does the apostle allow the concupiscible quality. "If any man," says he, "desireth the office of a bishop, he desireth a good work." Now, by saying "a good work," he shows us that the desire is a reasonable one. He permits us likewise to feel indignation. How should he not, when he himself experiences the same? "I would," says he, "that they were even cut off which trouble you." In perfect agreement with reason was that indignation which resulted from his desire to maintain discipline and order. When, however, he says, "We were formerly the children of wrath," he censures an irrational irascibility, such as proceeds not from that nature which is the production of God, but from that which the devil brought in, who is himself styled the lord or "master" of his own class, "Ye cannot serve *two masters*," and has the actual designation of "father:" "Ye are of your *father* the devil." So that you need not be afraid to ascribe to him the mastery and dominion over that second, later, and deteriorated nature (of which we have been speaking), when you read of him as "the sower of tares," and the nocturnal spoiler of the crop of corn.

[348]

THALES

THALES (About 625-545 B.C.). The earliest philosophical school in the history of Western civilization was founded by Thales, a citizen of Miletus in Asia Minor. Although he is unanimously recognized as the initiator of Greek philosophy, he was not of Greek origin but descended from a Semitic (Carian) family, and he owed much of his scientific and technical knowledge to Babylonian and Egyptian influences.

Thales took the initiative in Greek philosophical thinking with his conception of the existing world as the transformation of a single cosmic matter, declaring that water was the fundamental substance and source of all living beings. Although this special hypothesis did not satisfy his successors, his way of distinguishing between the apparent nature and a reality which becomes comprehensible through the unifying and relating functions of reason was of lasting consequence and continued to inspire Greek thinkers.

The whole Græco-Roman antiquity revered Thales as one of the "Seven Sages." He became famous because of his many important inventions and discoveries in the fields of astronomy, geometry, meteorology and navigation, and above all because he predicted the solar eclipse which took place on May 28, 585 B.C., while a great battle was raging between the Lydian and Median armies. He was also a clever businessman who made a fortune by monopolizing the olive trade in years of shortage, which he had foreseen. Thales taught in the Greek language but wrote no books.

FRAGMENTS

THALES was the first person who affirmed that the souls of men were immortal; and he was the first person, too, who discovered the path of the sun from one end of the ecliptic to the other; and who, as one account tells us, defined the magnitude of the sun as being seven hundred and twenty times as great as that of the moon. He was also the first person who called the last day of the month the thirtieth.

And likewise the first to converse about natural philosophy, as some say. But Aristotle and Hippias say that he attributed souls also to lifeless things, forming his conjecture from the nature of the magnet, and of amber.

He asserted water to be the principle of all things, and that the world had life, and was full of demons; they say, too, that he was the original definer of the seasons of the year, and that it was he who divided the year into three hundred and sixty-five days. And he never had any teacher except during the time that he went to Egypt, and associated with the priests. Hieronymus also says that he measured the Pyramids: watching their shadow, and calculating when they were of the same size as that was. He lived with Thrasybulus the tyrant of Miletus, as we are informed by Minyas.

These are quoted as some of his lines:

It is not many words that real wisdom proves;
Breathe rather one wise thought,
Select one worthy object,
So shall you best the endless prate of silly men reprove.

And the following are quoted as sayings of his:—"God is the most ancient of all things, for he had no birth: the world is the most beautiful of things, for it is the work of God; place is the greatest of things, for it contains all things: intellect is the swiftest of things, for it runs through everything, necessity is the strongest of things, for it rules everything: time is the wisest of things, for it finds out everything."

He said also that there was no difference between life and death. "Why, then," said some one to him, "do not you die?" "Because," said he, "it does make no difference." A man asked him which was made first, night or day, and he replied, "Night was made first by one day." Another man asked him whether a man who did wrong, could escape the notice of the gods. "No, not even if he thinks wrong," said he. An adulterer inquired of him whether he should swear that he had not committed adultery. "Perjury," said he, "is no worse than adultery." When he was asked what was very difficult, he said, "To know one's self." And what was easy,

"To advise another." What was most pleasant? "To be successful." To the question, "What is the divinity?" he replied, "That which has neither beginning nor end." When asked what hard thing he had seen, he said, "An old man a tyrant." When the question was put to him how a man might most easily endure misfortune, he said, "If he saw his enemies more unfortunate still." When asked how men might live most virtuously and most justly, he said, "If we never do ourselves what we blame in others." To the question, "Who was happy?" he made answer, "He who is healthy in his body, easy in his circumstances, and well-instructed as to his mind." He said that men ought to remember those friends who were absent as well as those who were present, and not to care about adorning their faces, but to be beautified by their studies. "Do not," said he, "get rich by evil actions, and let not any one ever be able to reproach you with speaking against those who partake of your friendship. All the assistance you give to your parents, the same you have a right to expect from your children." He said that the reason of the Nile overflowing was that its streams were beaten back by the Etesian winds blowing in a contrary direction.
[349]

THOREAU, HENRY DAVID

THOREAU, HENRY DAVID (1817-1862). Thoreau was not satisfied merely to entertain an opinion and to enjoy it; he was resolved to live it. For himself and for any individual he claimed the right of revolution against bad government, and he regarded the authority of good government still an impure one, defended civil disobedience, and refused to pay taxes after facing and suffering imprisonment. "Under a government," Thoreau wrote, "which imprisons any unjustly, the true place for a just man is also a prison." The spirit of revolt, the impulse to isolation, the ideal to live alone with thought, nature and God, as well as practical considerations, caused him to retreat to Walden Pond (1845-46) where he contemplated nature and meditated upon it.

Thoreau was a scholar and poet, an eccentric and a shrewd

realist. His *Walden* (1854), the work of a great naturalist and an even greater poet of nature, has been translated into many languages.

"To be a philosopher," says Thoreau, "is not merely to have subtle thought, or even to found a school but so to love wisdom as to live, according to its dictates, a life of simplicity, independence, magnanimity and trust." No serene sage, Thoreau's ferocity often disturbed his most faithful friends, and estranged from him Emerson with whom he had been, for a time, closely associated. His temperament committed him to action, his faith to contemplation. Until 1850, Thoreau was an enthusiast of community life. Thereafter he became a staunch opponent of popular movements.

The essential life meant to him life in nature. To him, the burden of the civilization of his age was not caused by mere defects in industrial organization and distribution, but rather by the domination of industry itself over human interests. Against a cultural evolution which he condemned as resulting in the neglect of human values, Thoreau was resolved to live his own time by his own terms.

HIGHER LAWS

OUR whole life is startlingly moral. There is never an instant's truce between virtue and vice. Goodness is the only investment that never fails. In the music of the harp which trembles round the world it is the insisting on this which thrills us. The harp is the traveling patterer for the Universe's Insurance Company, recommending its laws, and our little goodness is all the assessment that we can pay. Though the youth at last grows indifferent, the laws of the universe are not indifferent, but are forever on the side of the most sensitive. Listen to every zephyr for some reproof, for it is surely there, and he is unfortunate who does not hear it. We cannot touch a string or move a stop but the charming moral transfixes us. Many an irksome noise, go a long way off, is heard as music, a proud sweet satire on the meanness of our lives.

We are conscious of an animal in us, which awakens in proportion as our higher nature slumbers. It is reptile and sensual, and perhaps cannot be wholly expelled; like the worms which, even in life and health, occupy our bodies. Possibly we may withdraw from it, but never change its nature. I fear that it may enjoy a certain health of its own; that we may be well, yet not pure. The other day I picked up the lower jaw of a hog, with white and sound teeth and tusks, which suggested that there was an animal health and vigor distinct from the spiritual. This creature succeeded by other means than temperance and purity. "That in which men differ from brute beasts," says Mencius, "is a thing very inconsiderable; the common herd lose it very soon; superior men preserve it carefully." Who knows what sort of life would result if we had attained to purity? If I knew so wise a man as could teach me purity I would go to seek him forthwith. "A command over our passions, and over the external senses of the body, and good acts, are declared by the Veda to be indispensable in the mind's approximation to God." Yet the spirit can for a time pervade and control every member and function of the body, and transmute what in form is the grossest sensuality into purity and devotion. The generative energy, which, when we are loose, dissipates and makes us unclean, when we are continent invigorates and inspires us. Chastity is the flowering of man; and what are called genius, heroism, holiness, and the like, are but various fruits which succeed it. Man flows at once to God when the channel of purity is open. By turns our purity inspires and our impurity casts us down. He is blessed who is assured that the animal is dying out in him day by day, and the divine being established. Perhaps there is none but has cause for shame on account of the inferior and brutish nature to which he is allied. I fear that we are such gods or demigods only as fauns and satyrs, the divine allied to beasts, the creatures of appetite, and that, to some extent, our very life is our disgrace—

"How happy's he who hath due place assigned
To his beasts and disafforested his mind! . . .
Can use his horse, goat, wolf, and ev'ry beast,
And is not ass himself to all the rest!

1171

Else man not only is the herd of swine,
But he's those devils too which did incline
Them to headlong rage and made them worse."

All sensuality is one, though it takes many forms; all purity is one. It is the same whether a man eat, or drink, or cohabit, or sleep sensually. They are but one appetite, and we only need to see a person do any one of these things to know how great a sensualist he is. The impure can neither stand nor sit with purity. When the reptile is attacked at one mouth of his burrow, he shows himself at another. If you would be chaste, you must be temperate. What is chastity? How shall a man know if he is chaste? He shall not know it. We have heard of this virtue, but we know not what it is. We speak conformably to the rumor which we have heard. From exertion come wisdom and purity; from sloth ignorance and sensuality. In the student sensuality is a sluggish habit of mind. An unclean person is universally a slothful one, one who sits by a stove, whom the sun shines on prostrate, who reposes without being fatigued. If you would avoid uncleanness, and all the sins, work earnestly, though it be at cleaning a stable. Nature is hard to be overcome, but she must be overcome. What avails that you are Christian, if you are not purer than the heathen, if you deny yourself no more, if you are not more religious? I know of many systems of religion esteemed heathenish whose precepts fill the reader with shame, and provoke him to new endeavors, though it be to the performance of rites merely.

I hesitate to say these things, but it is not because of the subject,—I care not how obscene my *words* are,—but because I cannot speak of them without betraying my impurity. We discourse freely without shame of one form of sensuality, and are silent about another. We are so degraded that we cannot speak simply of the necessary functions of human nature. In earlier ages, in some countries, every function was reverently spoken of and regulated by law. Nothing was too trivial for the Hindoo lawgiver, however offensive it may be to modern taste. He teaches how to eat, drink,

cohabit, void excrement and urine, and the like, elevating
what is mean and does not falsely excuse himself by calling
these things trifles.

Every man is the builder of a temple, called his body,
to the god he worships, after a style purely his own, nor
can he get off by hammering marble instead. We are all
sculptors and painters, and our material is our own flesh
and blood and bones. Any nobleness begins at once to refine
a man's features, any meanness or sensuality to imbrute
them.

[350]

TOLSTOY, LEO

TOLSTOY, LEO (1828-1910). In *Resurrection* (1899), the third
of Tolstoy's great novels, the author summarized the experiences
of his life by asserting his conviction that in every human being a
spiritual and altruistic principle is working against an animal and
egoistic one "which is ready to sacrifice the well-being of the whole
world to one's own comfort." The defeat of the animal in man by
the spirit, which was identified by Tolstoy with conscience, is the
underlying principle in all Tolstoy's works, as well as the aim of
his life. The antagonism between spirit and animal is the standard
of valuing which Tolstoy applied to modern humanity and civilization, and he has not concealed that he himself could not stand
its test. Tolstoy was a rigorous moralist but he far from simplified the things his moral judgment condemned. His art penetrated
into the inner secrets of a society and of persons despised by him.
He knew what was important to an officer of the imperial bodyguard, what troubled the nerves of a lady of fashion, what lured
the ambition of an official, and he showed the vanity of their hopes
and apprehensions with such a power that the outstanding critics
of all civilized nations agree with William Dean Howells who said
that "Tolstoy's imagination leaves all tricks of fancy, all effects
of art immeasurably behind."

Yet it was Tolstoy's moralism that turned against his own art.
Though in his youth he had been very fond of the power of literary
imagination, in his later years he rejected every kind of power, not
the least of which being the power of art. He had conquered the
world with his novel *War and Peace* (1869), and he seemed to have
secured this conquest by his novel *Anna Karenina* (1877). But in

1173

My Confession (1882) he declared: "When I had ended *Anna Ka-renina* my despair reached such a height that I could do nothing but think of the horrible condition in which I found myself. I saw only one thing, Death. Everything else was a lie."

Tolstoy saw only one way out of his crisis, namely the strict obeyance to the Sermon on the Mount which, according to him, involves social repentance, religious purification, radical opposition to the interests and institutions of the world, rejection of property, power, war, oath and political statutes. He fought the Church because, while ruling the world, it was dominated by the world. He revered Christ but did not look back to the events narrated in the New Testament. He was looking forward, expecting the coming kingdom of God and the end of the rule of earthly power.

Every philosophy was to Tolstoy an evil in so far as it tried to form a system, an artificial order of thoughts. But he was interested in the efforts of some philosophers—especially Descartes, Leibniz, Rousseau, Kant, Schopenhauer and African Spir—to deal with the power of evil or to know God, although he protested that no philosopher had given more than a vague idea of God. Tolstoy himself conceived of God not as a person in the proper sense of the word but rather through man's relations to God as comparable with personal loyalty, and the feeling of God as the source of love and moral law. He regarded the uneducated, poor, enslaved Russian peasant as the most reliable guide to the way to God and as the true representative of humanity.

CHURCH AND HERESY

IN the Gospels the word "Church" is used twice. Once in the sense of an assembly of men to settle a dispute, and again in connection with the obscure utterance about the rock, Peter and the gates of hell. From these two mentions of the word "Church" (means merely an assembly) what is now meant by the word "Church," has been deduced.

But Christ could certainly not have established the Church, that is, the institution we now call by that name, for nothing resembling our present conception of the Church—with its sacraments, its hierarchy, and especially its claim to infallibility—is to be found either in Christ's words or in the conception of the men of his time.

The fact that people called an institution established

1174

later by a name Christ has used to designate something quite different, in no way gives them the right to assert that Jesus founded "the one true Church." Besides, had Christ really founded such an institution as the Church for the basis of our entire faith and doctrine, he would probably have announced this institution clearly and definitely . . . and would have given this one true Church unmistakable tokens of genuineness. . . . The conception of one holy Church only arose from the quarrels and strife of two parties, each of which, denouncing the other as a heresy, claimed to be the one infallible Church. . . .

Heresy is the obverse side of the Church. Wherever the Church exists, there must be the conception of heresy. A Church is a body of men who assert that they are the possessors of infallible truth. Heresy is the opinion of people who do not admit the indubitability of the Church's truth. . . .

Whatever stage of comprehension and perfection a follower of Christ may reach, he always feels the inadequacy of his conception and of his fulfilment of Christ's teaching, and always strives towards an increase of both. Therefore a claim by any individual or society to be in possession of a perfect understanding and a complete fulfilment of Christ's teaching is to renounce the spirit of Christ's teaching.

[351]

TUFTS, JAMES HAYDEN

TUFTS, JAMES HAYDEN (1862-1942). After having hesitated between mathematics and philosophy, Tufts concentrated upon studies in the history of philosophy but turned to ethics because he considered changes in moral values and concepts to be of even more significance than changes in science and knowledge. However, his ethical research was not limited to the reading of books. As a professor at the then newly founded Chicago University, Tufts was also a member of the Board of Arbitration, and the chairman of a committee of the social agencies of Chicago; through these affiliations he acquired insight into economic and social struggles which inspired his thinking about the questions of justice, responsibility, rights of the underdog, conflicts of relatively justified claims and other moral problems quite as much as through his studies in the history of ethical principles. In *Ethics* (in collaboration with John Dewey, 1917), Tufts grouped the various factors of moral changes under the captions of "psychological" and "sociological" agencies. According to him, moral ideas are shaped under the influence of religious, social and economic forces but that they do not remain objects of pure contemplation; they themselves become patterns of action, and thereby modify the state of mind of men involved in social, political and economic struggles. This conception of mutual influences is opposed to both Marxism and idealism. The most urgent task of ethical analysis in the present time was defined by Tufts as the endeavor not to conceive an image of a perfect state of society but to watch the forces which are at work and challenge the habitual concepts of political democracy, capitalism, religious and social institutions. From this point of view Tufts dealt with *America's Social Morality* (1933).

DEMOCRACY AT TRIAL

WHETHER democracies in Europe and the Americas are to be permitted to retain any of the progress gained in freedom, welfare, equality, and peace seems likely to be decided, not by reason but by arms. But in the faith that right makes might we may at least consider what internal policies and course of action will tend to safeguard from destruction not only our way of life but also what we have come to hold as right and good.

As regards our institutions and organizations, how can we be safe from the rise of despotic power? The outstanding lessons from Communism and National Socialism would seem to be the danger of concentration of all power in a single organization as contrasted with such pluralism, or division of power, as is found, for instance, in Scandinavian countries and the United States. Power is a necessary instrument of civilization. The preservation and advancement of moral ideals need the support of collective agencies as do trade, industry, and the administration of justice. But power, either over natural forces or over actions and minds

1176

of men is now seen to be, if possible, more dangerous than ever, to freedom and to life itself. History has seen various attempts to resist oppressive power, but effective restraint of power wielded by collective organization has usually been secured only by the collective strength of some other organization. Both Communism and National Socialism are totalitarian states. They are systems of absolute power. They permit no counter-balancing or restraining agency. No opposition may organize. Secret police are vigilant to prevent even the beginnings of questioning. Neither organized wealth nor organized labor is allowed to influence. No opposition party appears at the polls.

In the free democracies, on the contrary, are numerous collective agencies, not only for manifold educational, philanthropic, recreational, and social purposes, but for representing interests or groups of those who wish to influence or even to oppose government. In the United States there are a chamber of commerce, a manufacturers' association, two labor unions, a farm group, various religious groups, scientific and educational associations. All these inform or shape public opinion, secure or oppose legislation, influence national policies. At times, indeed, it has been charged that organized wealth was writing tariffs or controlling the press, or that organized labor was carrying elections. And at times government has seemed to be unable to act promptly in emergencies because of the numerous checks and balances provided by the cautious founders. Yet, on the whole, we have both kept our freedom and advanced justice. In the light of what totalitarian governments are doing we may well think that we have built better than we knew in encouraging such a variety of organized groups. Pluralism seems safer than totalitarianism.

Yet pluralism is no sure reliance for maintenance of rights or for ensuring advance in moral ideals or moral standards. It affords agencies through which the spirit may act, but if the spirit is dead or lacking, the agencies are dead likewise. The spirit which must preserve moral gains is the same spirit which has won them; it lives only as it grows. Life for institutional as for individual morality must combine stability with change. Reverence for what we hold right, just, and good, must be matched with open-minded sensitiveness to new claims by or for those who hitherto have had small share in the vast increase in goods provided by science, invention, and mass production. Moral dilemmas are experienced when older morals and institutions fail as yet to meet new situations. Hard resistance to just changes provokes either violence or despair or apathy. Certain forces of the day, notably the power of mass—in industry, in business, in social and political pressure groups, in subtler forms of propaganda—make for disintegration of older moral structures. Family and religious influence has suffered. On the other hand, in the present century we have made fairly steady progress in protection against disease, ignorance, hunger, industrial accidents, excessive hours of labor in factories, waste of natural resources. We have made provision for old age, have given legal standing to collective bargaining, and have recognized the plight of the farmer caught between low prices for his products and high prices for what he must buy. We have not yet learned how to prevent business depressions, but we have at least come to see that the moral injury of prolonged unemployment for workmen and of closed opportunity for youth is a more serious and difficult problem than that of bodily hunger. It is hard to believe that the enormous advances in means of communication through transport, electricity, and radio will not ultimately lower older barriers between peoples and make for better international understanding.

But there is no prospect of Utopia, either for individuals or for peoples. Moral life will continue to need alertness, courage, faith in the good cause, and at times sacrifice. A new invention like the airplane may place at the disposal of ruthless force a terrible weapon; a new idea like that of *Lebensraum* may touch off with explosive violence a new train; an economics of force may change the problem of just distribution. What we may hope for, if the present threat to all our rights and values can be met, is the opportunity to work out further the promise of free American life.

[352]

TYNDALL, JOHN

TYNDALL, JOHN (1820-1893). There are scientists who occupy themselves with the facts of their research without ever asking what implications they may be effecting. There are other scientists who keep science and religion separate and remain untroubled by any incongruity between them. Tyndall did not belong to either of these groups. Always he was conscious that every scientific inquiry, pursued to the end, must leave him face to face with metaphysics or religion. Always he felt himself obliged to become aware of the consequences of his scientific work, and to express them publicly, all the more so since he liked to combine daring research work in unknown fields and pioneering in many branches of science with the dissemination of knowledge by popular writings and lectures. As a result, he was brilliantly successful in popularizing science. Tyndall made highly important contributions to molecular physics, to the knowledge of magnetism, electricity, theory of heat, optics and acoustics, and he promoted bacteriology by his method of sterilizing liquids. His achievements were greatly respected by Pasteur, Maxwell, Lister, Kelvin and his intimate friend Thomas Henry Huxley; and Herbert Spencer especially praised him because of his "scientific use of imagination." It is the combination of enthusiasm and reason, rightly characterized by Spencer, that is significant of Tyndall's mind. To him, man is not mere intellect; he cannot be satisfied with the products of understanding alone. Tyndall held that the scientist, too, is a man. He protested: "Believing in continuity of nature, I cannot stop abruptly where our miscroscope ceases to be of use." But he spoke of himself when he defined the calling of a scientist as a continued exercise of realization and self-correction. His endeavor was to draw a sharp line to mark the boundary where, in his view, science ends and speculation begins. Although he refuted the claims of theologians, Tyndall was not at war with religion. But he was devoted to humanitarian ideals, and strongly opposed to any kind of injustice and oppression.

THE doctrine of evolution derives man, in his totality, from the interaction of organism and environment through countless ages past. The human understanding, for example—that faculty which Mr. Spencer has turned so skilfully round upon its own antecedents—is itself a result of the play between organism and environment through cosmic ranges of time. Never, surely, did prescription plead so irresistible a claim. But then it comes to pass that, over and above his understanding, there are many other things appertaining to man whose prescriptive rights are quite as strong as those of the understanding itself. It is a result, for example, of the play of organism and environment that sugar is sweet, and that aloes are bitter; that the smell of henbane differs from the perfume of a rose. Such facts of consciousness (for which, by the way, no adequate reason has ever been rendered) are quite as old as the understanding; and many other things can boast an equally ancient origin. Mr. Spencer at one place refers to that most powerful of passions—the amatory passion—as one which, when it first occurs, is antecedent to all relative experience whatever; and we may press its claim as being at least as ancient, and as valid, as that of the understanding itself. Then there are such things woven into the texture of man as the feeling of awe, reverence, wonder—and not alone the sexual love just referred to, but the love of the beautiful, physical, and moral, in nature, poetry, and art. There is also that deep-set feeling, which, since the earliest dawn of history, and probably for ages prior to all history, incorporated itself in the religions of the world. You, who have escaped from these religions into the high-and-dry light of the intellect, may deride them; but in so doing you deride accidents of form merely, and fail to touch the immovable basis of the religious sentiment in the nature of man. To yield this sentiment reasonable satisfaction is the problem of problems at the present hour.

And grotesque in relation to scientific culture as many of the religions of the world have been and are—dangerous, nay, destructive, to the dearest privileges of freemen as some of them undoubtedly have been, and would, if they could, be again—it will be wise to recognize them as the forms of a force, mischievous if permitted to intrude on the region of objective *knowledge,* over which it holds no command, but capable of adding, in the region of *poetry* and *emotion,* inward completeness and dignity to man.

Feeling, I say again, dates from as old an origin and as high a source as intelligence, and it equally demands its range of play. The wise teacher of humanity will recognize the necessity of meeting this demand, rather than of resisting it on account of errors and absurdities of form. What we should resist, at all hazards, is the attempt made in the past, and now repeated, to found upon this elemental bias of man's nature a system which should exercise despotic sway over his intellect. I have no fear of such a consummation. Science has already to some extent leavened the world; it will leaven it more and more. I should look upon the mild light of science breaking in upon the minds of the youth of Ireland, and strengthening gradually to the perfect day, as a surer check to any intellectual or spiritual tyranny which may threaten this island than the laws of princes or the swords of emperors. We fought and won our battle even in the Middle Ages: should we doubt the issue of another conflict with our broken foe?

The impregnable position of science may be described in a few words. We claim, and we shall wrest from theology, the entire domain of cosmological theory. All schemes and systems which thus infringe upon the domain of science must, in so far as they do this, submit to its control, and relinquish all thought of controlling it. Acting otherwise proved always disastrous in the past, and it is simply fatuous to-day. Every system which would escape the fate of an organism too rigid to adjust itself to its environment must be plastic to the extent that the growth of knowledge demands. When this truth has been thoroughly taken in, rigidity will be relaxed, exclusiveness diminished, things now deemed essential will be dropped, and elements now rejected will be assimilated. The lifting of the life is the essential point, and as long as dogmatism, fanaticism, and intolerance are kept out, various modes of leverage may be employed to raise life to a higher level.

[353]

TZU SSU

TZU SSU (About 335-288 B.C.). Tzu Ssu was a grandson of Confucius. Often he evoked his ancestor's authority; but he also expressed thoughts of his own. Confucius had begun to distinguish between true and supposed knowledge, while Tzu Ssu proceeded to meditations on the relativity of human knowledge of the Universe. He tried to analyze as many types of action as possible, and believed that the reality of the universe can be copied in the character of any wise man who is conscious of his moral and intellectual duties.

THE WAY OF THE MEAN

CHUNG-NI [Confucius] said, "The man of true breeding is the mean in action. The man of no breeding is the reverse. The relation of the man of true breeding to the mean in action is that, being a man of true breeding, he consistently holds to the Mean. The reverse relationship of the man of no breeding is that, being what he is, he has no sense of moral caution."

The Master said, "Perfect is the mean in action, and for a long time now very few people have had the capacity for it."

The Master said, "I know why the Way is not pursued. (It is because) the learned run to excess and the ignorant fall short. I know why the Way is not understood. The good run to excess and the bad fall short. . . ."

The Master said, "Alas, this failure to pursue the Way!"

The Master said, "Consider Shun, the man of great wisdom. He loved to ask advice and to examine plain speech. He never referred to what was evil, and publicly praised what was good. By grasping these two extremes he put into effect the Mean among his people. In this way he was Shun [i.e. a sage-emperor], was he not?"

The Master said. "All men say 'I know,' but they are driven into nets, caught in traps, fall into pitfalls, and not one knows how to avoid this. All men say 'I know,' but, should they choose the mean in action, they could not persist in it for a round month."

The Master said, "Hui, a real man! He chose the mean in action, and, if he succeeded in one element of good, he grasped it firmly cherished it in his bosom, and never let it go."

The Master said, "The states and families of the Great Society might have equal divisions of land: men might refuse noble station and the wealth that goes with it: they might trample the naked sword under foot; but the mean in action, it is impossible for them to achieve that."

Tzu Lu inquired about strong men, and the Master said, "It is strong men of the southern kind, or strong men of the northern kind, or, maybe, making yourself strong (that you have in mind)? The (typical) strong man of the south is magnanimous and gentle in instructing people, and he takes no revenge for being treated vilely: it is the habit of a man of true breeding to be like this. The (typical) strong man of the north lives under arms and dies without a murmur: it is the habit of a man of true force to be like this. Hence the man of true breeding, how steadfast he is in his strength, having a spirit of concord and not giving way to pressure. He takes up a central position, and does not waver one way or another. How steadfast his strength, for, when there is good government, he does not change his original principles, and, when there is vile government, he does not change, even though his life be at stake."

The Way of the enlightened man is widely apparent and yet hidden. Thus the ordinary man and woman, ignorant though they are, can yet have some knowledge of it; and yet in its perfection even a sage finds that there is something there which he does not know. Take the vast size of heaven and earth; men can still find room for criticism of it. Hence, when the enlightened man speaks of supreme bigness, it cannot be contained within the world of our experience; nor, when he speaks of supreme smallness, can it be split up in the world of our experience into nothing. As is said in the *Odes*: "The hawk beats its way up to the height of heaven, the fish dives down into the abyss." That refers to things being examined from above and from below. Thus the Way of the enlightened man, its early shoots coming into existence in the ordinary man and woman, but in its ultimate extent to be examined in the light of heaven and earth.

The master said, "The Way is not far removed from men. If a man pursues a way which removes him from men, he cannot be in the Way. In the *Odes* there is the word, 'When hewing an axe handle, hew an axe handle. The pattern of it is close at hand.' You grasp an axe handle to hew an axe handle, although, when you look from the one to the other [i.e. from the axe in your hand to the block of wood], they are very different." Therefore the right kind of ruler uses men to control men and attempts nothing beyond their correction; and fidelity and mutual service (these two human qualities) cannot be outside the scope of the Way. The treatment which you do not like for yourself you must not hand out to others. . . .

The acts of the enlightened man agree with the station in life in which he finds himself, and he is not concerned with matters outside that station. If he is a man of wealth and high position, he acts as such. If he is a poor man and low in the social scale, he acts accordingly. So also if he is among barbarians, or if he meets trouble. In fact, there is no situation into which he comes in which he is not himself.

In a high station he does not disdain those beneath him. In a low station he does not cling round those above him. He puts himself in the right and seeks no favors. Thus he is free from ill will, having no resentment against either Heaven or men. He preserves an easy mind, as he awaits the will of Heaven: (in contrast to) the man who is not true, who walks in perilous paths and hopes for good luck.

The Way of the enlightened man is like a long journey, since it must begin with the near at hand. It is like the ascent of a high mountain, since it must begin with the low ground. As is said in the *Odes*:

The happy union with wife and child
Is like the music of lutes and harps.
When concord grows between brother and brother,
The harmony is sweet and intimate.
The ordering of your household!
Your joy in wife and child!

The Master said, "How greatly parents are served in this!" He also said, "How irrepressible is the spiritual power in the spirits of the great dead! Look for them, and they are not to be seen. Listen for them, and they are not to be heard. They are in things, and there is nothing without them. They stir all the people in the Great Society to fast and purify themselves and wear their ritual robes, in order that they may sacrifice to them. They fill the air, as if above, as if on the left, as if on the right. The *Odes* has it, 'The coming of the Spirits! Incalculable! And yet they cannot be disregarded.' " Even so is the manifestation of the imperceptible and the impossibility of hiding the real.

[354]

1185

U

UNAMUNO Y JUGO, MIGUEL DE

UNAMUNO Y JUGO, MIGUEL DE (1864-1936). Any appraisal of
Unamuno's philosophy is incomplete without taking into account
his poetry. Unamuno the thinker and Unamuno the poet are one
and inseparable. He accepted the word of a French critic, according to which Unamuno, the poet, had written only commentaries,
perpetual analyses of his ego, the Spanish people, their dreams and
ideals, but he maintained that Homer and Dante equally had
written only commentaries. His greatest commentary was devoted
to the figure of Don Quixote whom he presents as a fighter for
glory, life and survival. The mortal Quixote is a comic character.
The immortal, realizing his own comicalness, superimposes himself upon it and triumphs over it without renouncing it. The longing for immortality is the ever-recurring theme of Unamuno's philosophy and poetry. It finds no consolation in reason, which is regarded as a dissolving force, or in the intellect, which means
identity and which, on its part, means death. Rather, it relies on
faith. But faith is a matter of will, and will needs reason and intellect. Thus faith and reason, or philosophy and religion, are
enemies which nevertheless need one another. Neither a purely
religious nor a purely rationalistic tradition is possible. This insight leads not to compromise but creates instead the tragic sentiment. The tragic history of human thought is the history of the
struggle between veracity and sincerity, between the truth that is
thought and the truth that is felt, and no harmony between the two
adversaries is possible, although they never cease to need each
other.

Unamuno called himself "an incorrigible Spaniard." But his
erudition was universal. In a conversation he was able to explain
the particular Scotticism in a verse of Robert Burns, or the difference between two German mystics of whom only German specialists
had ever heard. He combined a utilitarian mind with the search
for God. But he confessed that his idea of God was different each

time that he conceived it. Proud of his Basque origin, Unamuno, like Loyola, another Basque, was imbued with stern earnestness and a tragic sense of life. He felt himself as the descendant of saints and mystics. But he loved fools and regarded even Jesus as a divine fool. To him, dreaming meant the essence of life, and systematic thinking the destruction of that essence. He declined any philosophic system, but contemplation of the way of philosophizing was to him a source of profound wisdom. He was indeed the knight errant of the searching spirit.

LANGUAGE AND PHILOSOPHERS

OUR language itself, like every cultured language, contains within itself an implicit philosophy.

A language, in effect, is a potential philosophy. Platonism is the Greek language which discourses in Plato, unfolding its secular metaphors; scholasticism is the philosophy of the dead Latin of the Middle Ages wrestling with the popular tongues; the French language discourses in Descartes, the German in Kant and in Hegel, and the English in Hume and in Stuart Mill. For the truth is that the logical starting point of all philosophical speculation is not the I, neither is it representation (*Vorstellung*), nor the world as it presents itself immediately to the senses; but it is mediate or historical representation, humanly elaborated and such as it is given to us principally in the language by means of which we know the world; it is not psychical but spiritual representation. When we think, we are obliged to set out, whether we know it not and whether we will or not, from what has been thought by others who came before us and who environ us. Thought is an inheritance. Kant thought in German, and into German he translated Hume and Rousseau, who thought in English and French respectively. And did not Spinoza think in Judeo-Portuguese, obstructed by and contending with Dutch?

Thought rests upon prejudgments, and prejudgments pass into language. To language Bacon rightly ascribed not a few of the errors of the *idola fori*. But is it possible to philosophize in pure algebra or even in Esperanto? In order to see the result of such an attempt one has only to read the work of Avenarius on the criticism of pure experience (*reine Erfahrung*), of this prehuman or inhuman experience. And even Avenarius, who was obliged to invent a language, invented one that was based upon the Latin tradition, with roots which carry in their metaphorical implications a content of impure experience, of human social experience.

All philosophy is, therefore, at bottom philology. And philology, with its great and fruitful law of analogical formations, opens wide the door to chance, to the irrational, to the absolutely incommensurable. History is not mathematics, neither is philosophy. And how many philosophical ideas are not strictly owing to something akin to rhyme, to the necessity of rightly placing a consonant! In Kant himself there is a great deal of this, of esthetic symmetry, rhyme.

Representation is, therefore, like language, like reason itself—which is simply internal language—a social and racial product, and race, the blood of the spirit, is language, as Oliver Wendell Holmes has said, and as I have often repeated.

It was in Athens and with Socrates that our Western philosophy first became mature, conscious of itself, and it arrived at this consciousness by means of the dialogue, of social conversation. And it is profoundly significant that the doctrine of innate ideas, of the objective and normative value of ideas, of what scholasticism afterwards knew as realism, should have formulated itself in dialogues. And these ideas, which constitute reality, are names, as nominalism showed. Not that they may not be more than names (*flatus vocis*), but that they are nothing less than names. Language is that which gives us reality, and not as a mere vehicle of reality, but as its true flesh, of which all the rest, dumb or inarticulate representation, is merely the skeleton. And thus logic operates upon aesthetics, the concept upon the expression, upon the word, and not upon the brute perception.

[355]

V

VEBLEN, THORSTEIN

VEBLEN, THORSTEIN (1857-1929). Before Veblen turned to the study of social and economic facts and theories, he had concentrated upon philosophy, especially the works of Kant, Comte and Spencer, and, in his later years, the problems of economics remained closely connected in Veblen's mind with fundamental problems of life, civilization and the general theory of science. Intending to integrate political economy into the general movement of science, Veblen discussed the evolution of the scientific point of view, the place of science within the framework of civilization, and the function of evolution within political economy. Although Veblen was strongly impressed by the doctrine of evolution, he was opposed to the simple application of the evolutionary principles to the study of social phenomena. He was also strongly opposed to positivism, and relied more upon German idealism and romanticism. He sometimes flirted with theorists of racialism like Gobineau and H. S. Chamberlain, and, if not influenced by Georges Sorel, he came in his own way very close to the latter's standpoint. Both Sorel and Veblen were inspired by Marx and criticized him by similar arguments. Both were enthusiasts of the idea of promoting industrial production by social and political changes. Also, both considered the capitalist unfit to achieve technical progress and they advocated recruitment of industrial leaders from the classes of salaried technicians and workers.

Veblen's violent attacks on the business class and its ideology have caused violent controversies in America. In Europe Veblen remained nearly unknown. Brought up in a clannish community of immigrants from Norway, Veblen never became completely at ease with the American way of living. He had no talent for teaching, and his academic career was hampered by the troubles of his private life. But his writing, especially his first and principal book *Theory of the Leisure Class* (1899), had a fermenting effect on economic and social thinking in America.

THE PLACE OF WOMEN AND PETS
IN THE ECONOMIC SYSTEM

BARNYARD fowl, hogs, cattle, sheep, goats, draught horses are of the productive nature of goods, and serve a useful, often a lucrative end; therefore beauty is not readily imputed to them. The case is different with those domestic animals which ordinarily serve no industrial end; such as pigeons, parrots and other cage birds, cats, dogs, and fast horses. These commonly are items of conspicuous consumption, and are therefore honorific in their nature and may be accounted beautiful. This class of animals is conventionally admired by the body of the upper classes, while the pecuniarily lower classes—and that select minority of the leisure class among which the rigorous canon that abjures thrift is in a measure obsolescent—find beauty in one class of animals as in another, without drawing a hard and fast line of pecuniary demarcation between the beautiful and the ugly.

In the case of those domestic animals which are honorific and are reputed beautiful, there is a subsidiary basis of merit that should be spoken of. Apart from the birds which belong in the honorific class of domestic animals, and which owe their place in this class to their nonlucrative character alone, the animals which merit particular attention are cats, dogs, and fast horses. The cat is less reputable than the other two just named, because she is less wasteful; she may even serve a useful end. At the same time the cat's temperament does not fit her for the honorific purpose. She lives with man on terms of equality, knows nothing of what is the ancient basis of all distinctions of worth, honor, and repute, and she does not lend herself with facility to an invidious comparison between her owner and his neighbors. The exception to this last rule occurs in the case of such scarce and fanciful products as the Angora cat, which have some slight honorific value on the ground of expensiveness, and have, therefore, some special claim to beauty on pecuniary grounds.

The dog has advantages in the way of usefulness as well as in special gifts of temperament. He is often spoken of, in an eminent sense, as the friend of man, and his intelligence and fidelity are praised. The meaning of this is that the dog is man's servant and that he has the gift of an unquestioning subservience and a slave's quickness in guessing his master's mood. Coupled with these traits, which fit him well for the relation of status—and which must for the present purpose be set down as serviceable traits—the dog has some characteristics which are of a more equivocal aesthetic value. He is the filthiest of the domestic animals in his person and the nastiest in his habits. For this he makes up in a servile, fawning attitude towards his master, and a readiness to inflict damage and discomfort on all else. The dog, then, commends himself to our favor by affording play to our propensity for mastery, and as he is also an item of expense, and commonly serves no industrial purpose, he holds a well-assured place in men's regards as a thing of good repute. The dog is at the same time associated in our imagination with the chase—a meritorious employment.

Even those varieties of the dog which have been bred into grotesque deformity by the dog-fancier are in good faith accounted beautiful by many. These varieties of dogs—and the like is true of other fancy-bred animals—are rated and graded in aesthetic value somewhat in proportion to the degree of grotesqueness and instability of the particular fashion which the deformity takes in the given case. For the purpose in hand, this differential utility on the ground of grotesqueness and instability of structure is reducible to terms of a greater scarcity and consequent expense. The commercial value of canine monstrosities, such as the prevailing styles of pet dogs both for men's and women's use, rests on their high costs of production, and their value to their owners lies chiefly in their utility as items of conspicuous consumption. Indirectly, through reflection upon their honorific expensiveness, a social worth is imputed to them; and so, by an easy substitution of words and ideas, they come to be admired and reputed beautiful.

The case of the fast horse is much like that of the dog. He is on the whole expensive, or wasteful and useless—for the industrial purpose. What productive use he may possess, in the way of enhancing the well-being of the community or making the way of life easier for men, takes the form of exhibitions of force and facility of motion that gratify the popular aesthetic sense. This is of course a substantial serviceability. The horse is not endowed with the same spiritual aptitude for servile dependence in the same measure as the dog; but he ministers effectually to his master's impulse to convert the "animate" forces of environment to his own use and discretion and so express his own dominating individuality through them. The fast horse is at least potentially a race horse, of high or low degree; and it is as such that he is peculiarly serviceable to his owner. The utility of the fast horse lies largely in his efficiency as a means of emulation; it gratifies the owner's sense of aggression and dominance to have his own horse outstrip his neighbor's. This use not being lucrative, but on the whole pretty consistently wasteful, and quite conspicuously so, it is honorific, and therefore gives the fast horse a strong presumptive position of reputability. Beyond this, the race horse proper has also a similarly non-industrial but honorific use as a gambling instrument.

It is only with respect to consumable goods—including domestic animals—that the canons of taste have been colored by the canons of pecuniary reputation. Something to the like effect is to be said for beauty in persons. In order to avoid whatever may be matter of controversy, no weight will be given in this connection to such popular predilection as there may be for the dignified (leisurely) bearing and portly presence that are by vulgar tradition associated with opulence in mature men. These traits are in some measure accepted as elements of personal beauty. But there are certain elements of feminine beauty, on the other hand, which come under this head, and which are of so concrete and

1192

specific a character as to admit of itemized appreciation. It is more or less a rule that in communities at which women are valued by the upper class for their service, the ideal of female beauty is a robust, large-limbed woman. The ground of appreciation is the physique, while the conformation of the face is of secondary weight only. A well-known instance of this ideal of the early predatory culture is that of the maidens of the Homeric poems.

This ideal suffers a change in the succeeding development, when, in the conventional scheme, the office of the high-class wife comes to be a vicarious leisure simply. This ideal then includes the characteristics which are supposed to result from or go with a life of leisure consistently enforced. The ideal accepted under these circumstances may be gathered from descriptions of beautiful women by poets and writers of the chivalric times. In the conventional scheme of those days ladies of high degree were conceived to be in perpetual tutelage, and to be scrupulously exempt from all useful work. The resulting chivalric or romantic ideal of beauty takes cognizance chiefly of the face, and dwells on its delicacy, and on the delicacy of the hands and feet, the slender figure, and especially the slender waist. In the pictured representations of the women of that time, and in modern romantic imitators of the chivalric thought and feeling, the waist is attenuated to a degree that implies extreme debility. The same ideal is still extant among a considerable portion of the population of modern industrial communities; but it is said that it has retained its hold most tenaciously in those modern communities which are least advanced in point of economic and civil development, and which show the most considerable survivals of status and predatory institutions. That is to say, the chivalric ideal is best preserved in those existing communities which are substantially least modern. Survivals of this lackadaisical or romantic ideal occur freely in the tastes of the well-to-do classes of Continental countries.

In modern communities which have reached the higher

levels of industrial development, the upper leisure class has accumulated so great a mass of wealth as to place its women above all imputation of vulgarly productive labor. Here the status of women as vicarious consumers is beginning to lose its place in the affections of the body of the people, and as a consequence the ideal of feminine beauty is beginning to change back again from the infirmly delicate, translucent, and hazardously slender, to a woman of the archaic type that does not disown her hands and feet, nor, indeed, the other gross material facts of her person. In the course of economic development the ideal of beauty among the peoples of Western culture has shifted from the woman of physical presence to the lady, and it is beginning to shift back again to the woman; and all in obedience to the changing conditions of pecuniary emulation. The exigencies of emulation at one time required lusty slaves; at another time they required a conspicuous performance of vicarious leisure and consequently an obvious disability; but the situation is now beginning to outgrow this last requirement, since, under the higher efficiency of modern industry, leisure in women is possible so far down the scale of reputability that it will no longer serve as a definitive mark of the highest pecuniary grade.

It has already been noticed that at the stages of economic evolution at which conspicuous leisure is much regarded as a means of good repute, the ideal requires delicate and diminutive hands and feet and a slender waist. These features, together with the other, related faults of structure that commonly go with them, go to show that the person so affected is incapable of useful effort and must therefore be supported in idleness by her owner. She is useless and expensive, and she is consequently valuable as evidence of pecuniary strength. It results that at this cultural stage women take thought to alter their persons, so as to conform more nearly to the requirements of the instructed taste of the time; and under the guidance of the canon of pecuniary decency, the men find the resulting artificially induced pathological features attractive. So, for instance, the constricted waist which has had so wide and persistent a vogue in the communities of the Western culture, and so also the deformed foot of the Chinese. Both of these are mutilations of unquestioned repulsiveness to the untrained sense. Yet there is no room to question their attractiveness to men into whose scheme of life they fit as honorific items sanctioned by the requirements of pecuniary reputability. They are items of pecuniary and cultural beauty which have come to do duty as elements of the ideal of womanliness.

In the so-called "New Woman" movement there are at least two elements discernible, both of which are of an economic character. These two elements or motives are expressed by the double watchword, "emancipation" and "work." Each of these words is recognized to stand for something in the way of a widespread sense of grievance. The prevalence of the sentiment is recognized even by people who do not see that there is any real ground for a grievance in the situation as it stands today. It is among the women of the well-to-do classes, in the communities which are farthest advanced in industrial development, that this sense of grievance to be redressed is most alive and finds most frequent expression. The demand comes from that portion of womankind which is excluded by the canons of good repute from all effectual work, and which is closely reserved for a life of leisure and conspicuous consumption.

More than one critic of this new-woman movement has misapprehended its motive. The case of the average American "new woman" has lately been summed up with some warmth by a popular observer of social phenomena: "She is petted by her husband, the most devoted and hard-working of husbands in the world. . . . She is the superior of her husband in education, and in almost every respect. She is surrounded by the most numerous and delicate attentions. Yet she is not satisfied. . . . The Anglo-Saxon 'new woman' is the most ridiculous production of modern times, and destined to be the most ghastly failure of the century." Apart from the deprecation—perhaps well placed—which is contained in this presentment, it adds nothing but obscurity to the woman question. The grievance of the new woman is made up of those things which this typical characterization of the movement urges as reasons why she should be content. She is petted, and she is permitted, or even required, to consume largely and conspicuously—vicariously for her husband or other natural guardian. She is exempted, or debarred, from vulgarly useful employment—in order to perform leisure vicariously for the good repute of her natural (pecuniary) guardian. These offices are the conventional marks of the un-free, at the same time that they are incompatible with the human impulse to purposeful activity. But the woman is endowed with her share—which there is reason to believe is more than an even share—of the instinct of workmanship, to which futility of life or of expenditure is obnoxious. She must unfold her life activity in response to the direct, unmediated stimuli of the economic environment with which she is in contact. The impulse is perhaps stronger upon the woman than upon the man to live her own life in her own way and to enter the industrial process of the community at something nearer than the second remove.

So long as woman's place is consistently that of a drudge, she is, in the average of cases, fairly contented with her lot. She not only has something tangible and purposeful to do, but she has also no time or thought to spare for a rebellious assertion of such human propensity to self-direction as she has inherited.

[356]

VINCI, LEONARDO DA

VINCI, LEONARDO DA (1452-1519). For nearly four centuries after Leonardo's death, humanity remained uninformed about the scientific and philosophical performances of one of the greatest painters of the Italian Renaissance. Leonardo himself published only his *Treatise on Painting* in which the author combined the display of his artistic skill and experiences with epistemological and mathematical disquisitions. But the immense range of Leonardo's studies, researches and knowledge remained hidden in his diaries, notebooks and sketchbooks, which were printed late in the nineteenth century. They make manifest that Leonardo anticipated many important discoveries. He knew that the earth is a star which turns around the sun, and that moonlight is a result of reflection. He invented a submarine and an airplane, a parachute, poison gas and shrapnel. But, as one of his notes clearly indicates, he kept his inventions secret because he did not wish these instruments of destruction to be used.

To Leonardo, sensual experience is the interpreter between man and nature. But the visible form is regarded by him as the symbol of a spiritual reality. The artist's eye is a perfect instrument of experience but mathematical thought has to control it, and every practice must be founded upon sound theory. Leonardo was of a religious mind though independent of traditional faith. No other artist of the Renaissance but Leonardo could have dared to portray St. John the Baptist and Bacchus, the pagan god, as resembling one another like brothers. And none of that age could combine the character of an altar piece with that of a psychological study, as Leonardo did in his "Last Supper."

ON PAINTING

How painting surpasses all human works by reason of the subtle possibilities which it contains:

The eye, which is called the window of the soul, is the chief means whereby the understanding may most fully and abundantly appreciate the infinite works of Nature; and the ear is the second, inasmuch as it acquires its importance from the fact that it hears the things which the eye has seen. If you historians, or poets, or mathematicians had never seen things with your eyes, you would be ill able to describe them in your writings. And if you, O poet, represent a story by depicting it with your pen, the painter with his brush will so render it as to be more easily satisfying and less tedious to understand. If you call painting "dumb poetry," then the painter may say of the poet that his art is "blind painting." Consider then which is the more grievous

1197

affliction, to be blind or to be dumb! Although the poet has as wide a choice of subjects as the painter, his creations fail to afford as much satisfaction to mankind as do paintings, for while poetry attempts to represent forms, actions, and scenes with words, the painter employs the exact images of these forms in order to reproduce them. Consider, then, which is more fundamental to man, the name of man or his image? The name changes with change of country; the form is unchanged except by death.

And if the poet serves the understanding by way of the ear, the painter does so by the eye, which is the nobler sense.

I will only cite as an instance of this how, if a good painter represents the fury of a battle and a poet also describes one, and the two descriptions are shown together to the public, you will soon see which will draw most of the spectators, and where there will be most discussion, to which most praise will be given and which will satisfy the more. There is no doubt that the painting, which is by far the more useful and beautiful, will give the greater pleasure. Inscribe in any place the name of God and set opposite to it His image, you will see which will be held in greater reverence!

Since painting embraces within itself all the forms of Nature, you have omitted nothing except the names, and these are not universal like the forms. If you have the results of her processes we have the processes of her results.

Take the case of a poet describing the beauties of a lady to her lover and that of a painter who makes a portrait of her; you will see whither nature will the more incline the enamoured judge. Surely the proof of the matter ought to rest upon the verdict of experience!

In art we may be said to be grandsons unto God. If poetry treats of moral philosophy, painting has to do with natural philosophy; if the one describes the workings of the mind, the other considers what the mind effects by movements of the body; if the one dismays folk by hellish fictions, the other does the like by showing the same things in action. Suppose the poet sets himself to represent some image of beauty or terror, something vile and foul, or some monstrous thing, in contest with the painter, and suppose in his own way he makes a change of forms at his pleasure, will not the painter still satisfy the more? Have we not seen pictures which bear so close a resemblance to the actual thing that they have deceived both men and beasts?

If you know how to describe and write down the appearance of the forms, the painter can make them so that they appear enlivened with lights and shadows which create the very expression of the faces; herein you cannot attain with the pen where he attains with the brush.

That sculpture is less intellectual than painting, and lacks many of its natural parts:

As practicing myself the art of sculpture no less than that of painting, and doing both the one and the other in the same degree, it seems to me that without suspicion of unfairness I may venture to give an opinion as to which of the two is the more intellectual, and of the greater difficulty and perfection.

In the first place, sculpture is dependent on certain lights, namely, those from above, while a picture carries everywhere with its own light and shade; light and shade, therefore, are essential to sculpture. In this respect, the sculptor is aided by the nature of the relief, which produces these of its own accord, but the painter artificially creates them by his art in places where Nature would normally do the like. The sculptor cannot render the difference in the varying natures of the colors of objects; painting does not fail to do so in any particular. The lines of perspective of sculptors do not seem in any way true; those of painters may appear to extend a hundred miles beyond the work itself. The effects of aerial perspective are outside the scope of sculptors' work: they can neither represent transparent bodies nor luminous bodies nor angles of reflection nor shining bodies, such as mirrors and like things of glittering surface, nor mists, nor dull weather, nor an infinite number of things which I forbear to mention lest they should prove wearisome.

The one advantage which sculpture has is that of offering greater resistance to time; yet painting offers a like resistance if it is done upon thick copper covered with white enamel and then painted upon with enamel colors and placed in a fire and fused. In degree of permanence it then surpasses even sculpture.

*　　　*　　　*

Show first the smoke of the artillery mingled in the air with the dust stirred up by the movement of the horses and of the combatants. This process you should express as follows: the dust, since it is made up of earth and has weight, although by reason of its fineness it may easily rise and mingle with the air, will nevertheless readily fall down again, and the greatest height will be attained by such part of it as is the finest, and this will in consequence be the least visible and will seem almost the color of the air itself.

The smoke which is mingled with the dust-laden air will as it rises to a certain height have more and more the appearance of a dark cloud, at the summit of which the smoke will be more distinctly visible than the dust. The smoke will assume a bluish tinge, and the dust will keep its natural color. From the side whence the light comes this mixture of air and smoke and dust will seem far brighter than on the opposite side.

As for the combatants, the more they are in the midst of this turmoil, the less they will be visible, and the less will be the contrast between their lights and shadows.

You should give a ruddy glow to the faces and the figures and the air around them, and to the gunners and those near to them, and this glow should grow fainter as it is farther away from its cause. The figures which are between you and the light, if far away, will appear dark

1200

against a light background, and the nearer their limbs are to the ground, the less will they be visible, for there the dust is greater and thicker. And if you make horses galloping away from the throng, make little clouds of dust as far distant one from another as is the space between the strides made by the horse, and that cloud which is farthest away from the horse should be the least visible, for it should be high and spread out and thin, while that which is nearest should be most conspicuous and smallest and most compact.

Let the air be full of arrows going in various directions, some mounting upwards, others falling, others flying horizontally; and let the balls shot from the guns have a train of smoke following their course. Show the figures in the foreground covered with dust on their hair and eyebrows and such other level parts as afford the dust a space to lodge.

Make the conquerors running, with their hair and other light things streaming in the wind, and with brows bent down; and they should be thrusting forward opposite limbs; that is, if a man advances the right foot, the left arm should also come forward. If you represent anyone fallen, you should also show the mark where he has been dragged through the dust which has become changed to blood-stained mire, and roundabout in the half-liquid earth you should show the marks of the trampling of men and horses who have passed over it.

Make a horse dragging the dead body of his master, and leaving behind him in the dust and mud the track of where the body was dragged along.

Make the beaten and conquered pallid, with brows raised and knit together, and let the skin above the brows be all full of lines of pain; at the sides of the nose show the furrows going in an arch from the nostrils and ending where the eye begins, and show the dilatation of the nostrils which is the cause of these lines; and let the lips be arched displaying the upper row of teeth, and let the teeth be parted after the manner of such as cry in lamentation. Show someone using his hand as a shield for his terrified eyes, turning the palm of it towards the enemy, and having the other resting on the ground to support the weight of his body; let others be crying out with their mouths wide open, and fleeing away. Put all sorts of armour lying between the feet of the combatants, such as broken shields, lances, swords, and other things like these. Make the dead, some half-buried in dust, others with the dust all mingled with the oozing blood and changing into crimson mud; and let the line of the blood be discerned by its color, flowing in a sinuous stream from the corpse to the dust. Show others in the death agony grinding their teeth and rolling their eyes, with clenched fists grinding against their bodies and with legs distorted. Then you might show one, disarmed and struck down by the enemy, turning on him with teeth and nails to take fierce and inhuman vengeance; and let a riderless horse be seen galloping with mane streaming in the wind, charging among the enemy and doing them great mischief with his hoofs.

You may see there one of the combatants, maimed and fallen on the ground, protecting himself with his shield, and the enemy bending down over him and striving to give him the fatal stroke; there might also be seen many men fallen in a heap on top of a dead horse; and you should show some of the victors leaving the combat and retiring apart from the crowd, and with both hands wiping away from eyes and cheeks the thick layer of mud caused by the smarting of their eyes from the dust.

And the squadrons of the reserves should be seen standing full of hope but cautious, with eyebrows raised, and shading their eyes with their hands, peering into the thick, heavy mist in readiness for the commands of their captain; and so, too, the captain with his staff raised, hurrying to the reserves and pointing out to them the quarter of the field where they are needed; and you should show a river, within which horses are galloping, stirring the water all around with a heaving mass of waves and foam and broken water, leaping high into the air and over the legs and bodies of the horses; but see that you make no level spot of ground that is not trampled over with blood.

[357]

VIVEKANANDA, SWAMI

VIVEKANANDA, SWAMI (1862-1902). Educated abroad, Swami Vivekananda was an agnostic, whose rationalistic doubts were dispersed by the teachings of Ramakrishna Paramahamsa. His simple belief in the philosophy of the monistic Vedanta of Sankara and the attempt to re-emphasize the unity of all religions made Vivekananda a disciple, who devoted the remainder of his life to the dissemination of his teacher's ideas. He founded the Ramakrishna Mission for humanitarian service, brought to Hinduism an enthusiastic missionary approach, and emphasized the positive aspect of Vedanta: "that all is Brahma, and, therefore, that service of man as God is better than quiescent meditation." His influence has been seen in the works of such philosophers as Radhakrishnan and Aurobindo, in the social service and spread of Hindu ideas throughout the world, and it is even apparent in the political attitude of Mahatma Gandhi.

SWAMI VIVEKANANDA'S WORKS

SIDE BY SIDE with the modern theory of evolution, there is another thing: atavism. There is a tendency in us to revert to old ideas, in religion. Let us think something new, even if it be wrong. It is better to do that. Why should you not try to hit the mark? We become wiser through failures. Time is infinite. Look at the wall. Did the wall ever tell a lie? It is always the wall. Man tells a lie,—and becomes a god, too. It is better to do something; never mind even if it proves to be wrong; it is better than doing nothing. The cow never tells a lie, but she remains a cow, all the time. Do something! Think some thought; it doesn't matter whether you are right or wrong. But think something! Because my forefathers did not think this way, shall I sit down quietly and gradually lose my sense of feeling, and my own thinking faculties? 1 may as well be dead! And what is life worth if we have no living ideas, no convictions of our own about religion? There is some hope for the Atheists because though they differ from others, they think for themselves. The people who never think anything for themselves, are not yet born into the world of religion; they have a mere jelly-fish existence. They will not think; they do not care for religion. But the disbeliever, the atheist, cares, and he is struggling. So think something! Struggle Godward! Never mind if you fail, never mind if you get hold of a queer theory. If you are afraid to be called queer, keep it in your own mind;— you need not go and preach it to others. But do something! Struggle Godward! Light must come. If a man feeds me every day of my life, in the long run I shall lose the use of my hands. Spiritual death is the result of following each other like a flock of sheep. Death is the result of inaction. Be active; and wherever there is activity, there must be difference. Difference is the sauce of life; it is the beauty, it is the art of everything: difference makes all beautiful here. It is variety that is the source of life, the sign of life. Why should we be afraid of it?   [357A]

VOLTAIRE, FRANÇOIS MARIE AROUET DE

VOLTAIRE, FRANÇOIS MARIE AROUET DE (1694-1778). W. Somerset Maugham, the well-known novelist and playwright, has declared: "Before I start writing a novel, I read *Candide* over again so that I may have in the back of my mind the touchstone of that lucidity, grace and wit."

Voltaire's *Candide* is, however, not only a literary masterwork that defies the change of time and taste; it is also an attack on Leibniz' *Theodicy*. With mordant irony it castigates the belief that the existing world is the best of all possible ones. Life and studies confirmed Voltaire in his bitter criticism of man and human institutions. Three times imprisoned in the *Bastille* in Paris, Voltaire was then banished from France. As an exile in England, he studied Locke and Newton, and adopted Bolingbroke's deism. The result of these studies, Voltaire's *Lettres philosophiques* (1734), was publicly burned by the hangman in Paris. Dissatisfied with his own time, Voltaire, one of the initiators of modern history of civilization, saw that in the past the triumph of error and injustice had been even more outrageous. But he persisted in teaching that man is capable of shaping the future of humanity in accordance with true morality by making prevail the results of secular science and by resisting arbitrary power and intolerance. Until the last day of his life, Voltaire struggled for liberty of thought and conscience. He, a single man, defeated the organized power of fanaticism by rehabilitating Jean Calas, the victim of a judicial murder, and by saving his relatives from imprisonment. Voltaire passed the watchword of resistance to fanaticism. It became a battle cry that is heard and echoed in the present time.

ON TOLERANCE

ONE does not need great art and skilful eloquence to prove that Christians ought to tolerate each other—nay, even to regard all men as brothers. Why, you say, is the Turk, the Chinese, or the Jew my brother? Assuredly; are we not all children of the same father, creatures of the same God?

But these people despise us and treat us as idolaters. Very well; I will tell them that they are quite wrong. It seems to me that I might astonish, at least, the stubborn pride of a Mohammedan or a Buddhist priest if I spoke to them somewhat as follows:

This little globe, which is but a point, travels in space like many other globes; we are lost in the immensity. Man, about five feet high, is certainly a small thing in the universe. One of these imperceptible beings says to some of his neighbors, in Arabia or South Africa: "Listen to me, for the God of all these worlds has enlightened me. There are nine hundred million little ants like us on the earth, but my ant-hole alone is dear to God. All the others are eternally reprobated by him. Mine alone will be happy."

They would then interrupt me, and ask who was the fool that talked all this nonsense. I should be obliged to tell them that it was themselves. I would then try to appease them, which would be difficult.

I would next address myself to the Christians, and would venture to say to, for instance, a Dominican friar—an inquisitor of the faith: "Brother, you are aware that each province in Italy has its own dialect, and that people do not speak at Venice and Bergamo as they do at Florence. The Academy of La Crusca has fixed the language. Its dictionary is a rule that has to be followed, and the grammar of Matei is an infallible guide. But do you think that the consul of the Academy; or Matei in his absence, could in conscience cut out the tongues of all the Venetians and the Bergamese who persisted in speaking their own dialect?"

The inquisitor replies: "The two cases are very different. In our case it is a question of your eternal salvation. It is for your good that the heads of the inquisition direct that you shall be seized on the information of any one person, however infamous or criminal; that you shall have no advocate to defend you; that the name of your accuser shall not be made known to you; that the inquisitor shall promise you pardon and then condemn you; and that you shall then be subjected to five kinds of torture, and afterwards either flogged or sent to the galleys or ceremoniously burned. On this Father Ivonet, Doctor Chucalon, Zanchinus, Campegius, Royas, Telinus, Gomarus, Diabarus, and Gemelinus are explicit, and this pious practice admits of no exception."

I would take the liberty of replying: "Brother, possibly you are right. I am convinced that you wish to do me good. But could I not be saved without all that?"

It is true that these absurd horrors do not stain the face of the earth every day; but they have often done so, and the record of them would make up a volume much larger than the gospels which condemn them. Not only is it cruel to persecute, in this brief life, those who differ from us, but I am not sure if it is not too bold to declare that they are damned eternally. It seems to me that it is not the place of the atoms of a moment, such as we are, thus to anticipate the decrees of the Creator. Far be it from me to question the principle, "Out of the Church there is no salvation." I respect it, and all that it teaches; but do we really know all the ways of God, and the full range of his mercies? May we not hope in him as much as fear him? Is it not enough to be loyal to the Church? Must each individual usurp the rights of the Deity, and decide, before he does, the eternal lot of all men?

When we wear mourning for a king of Sweden, Denmark, England, or Prussia, do we say that we wear mourning for one who burns eternally in hell? There are in Europe forty million people who are not of the Church of Rome. Shall we say to each of them: "Sir, seeing that you are infallibly damned, I will neither eat, nor deal, nor speak with you"?

What ambassador of France, presented in audience to the Sultan, would say in the depths of his heart: "His Highness will undoubtedly burn for all eternity because he has been circumcised"? If he really believed that the Sultan is the mortal enemy of God, the object of his vengeance, could he speak to him? Ought he to be sent to him? With whom could we have intercourse? What duty of civil life could we ever fulfil if we were really convinced that we were dealing with damned souls?

Followers of a merciful God, if you were cruel of heart; if, in worshipping him whose whole law consisted in loving one's neighbor as oneself, you had burdened this pure and holy law with sophistry and unintelligible disputes; if you had lit the fires of discord for the sake of a new word or a single letter of the alphabet; if you had attached eternal torment to the omission of a few words or ceremonies that other peoples could not know, I should say to you:

"Transport yourselves with me to the day on which all men will be judged, when God will deal with each according to his works. I see all the dead of former ages and of our own stand in his presence. Are you sure that our Creator and Father will say to the wise and virtuous Confucius, to the lawgiver Solon, to Pythagoras, to Zaleucus, to Socrates, to

Plato, to the divine Antonines, to the good Trajan, to Titus, the delight of the human race, to Epictetus, and to so many other model men: 'Go, monsters, go and submit to a chastisement infinite in its intensity and duration; your torment shall be eternal as I. And you, my beloved, Jean Chatel, Ravaillac, Damiens, Cartouche, etc. [assassins in the cause of the Church], who have died with the prescribed formulæ, come and share my empire and felicity for ever.' "

You shrink with horror from such sentiments; and, now that they have escaped me, I have no more to say to you.

[358]

VON BAADER, FRANCIS XAVIER. See BAADER, FRANCIS XAVIER VON.

W

WAHLE, RICHARD

WAHLE, RICHARD (1857-1935). Proceeding from extreme positivism, Wahle, once a professor of philosophy at the Universities of Czernovitz and Vienna, pronounced in his *Tragicomedy of Wisdom* (2nd edition, 1925) his death sentence on philosophy. He acknowledged only "definite, agnostic, absolute critique of knowledge" and psychology as surviving, or rather he maintained that critiques of knowledge, logic and psychology have nothing to do with philosophy. As a consequence of his fundamental attitude, Wahle did not recognize the ego as a nucleus of forces but only as a changing whirl or as some stitches in the texture of the universe. But in his *Formation of Character* (2nd edition, 1928) he made important contributions to modern characterology. Wahle's devastating criticism of philosophers has spared only very few such as Spinoza, Hume and Herbart, whose works he praised as useful.

TIME

TIME—it is embarrassing for philosophy still to have to talk about such things—is not as Kant wanted it an *a priori* conception; it has no real being, no special content of consciousness, no quality, but it is an afterwards reflected abstraction concerning changes altogether. To consider time, a continuously flowing, developing thing or an ever-existing, everlasting thing, as a substance, is as absurd as if somebody wanted to believe that the stupidity which becomes manifest in some person is a stupidity substance that is permeating the whole world. Time can only be thought of and measured by increases, decreases and changes. Duration and rest can only be thought about through the possibility of changes which, however, do not occur. Time is not the stuff out of which everything is made, nor is it the place in which everything would become. As little as the concept of youth or age designates an undivided objective real thing an entity, but rather, as we understand it, only an abstract comprehension of all processes occurring in young or old individuals—so time too does not refer to an entity existing for itself but it, instead, is nothing but a completely dependent reflected abstraction of a possibility on the basis of real increases or decreases, of growth or reduction. Each being noticing an increment—for instance, a beginning increase—in a thing could build the abstraction "time" immediately, the content of which would be just the idea of such changes together with the thought that if there are changes there are also possibilities for mutations, developments and innovations. The possibility of the continuous accumulation of changes is "time."

Since time is an abstraction of the possibilities of changes, it could be conceived as an abstraction of the possibility of increases; it could also be an abstraction from numbers, but only by counting them through the successive intentional increase of the series of numbers. The ideal series of numbers, therefore, does not need to have any relation to time, for the series of numbers can be imagined as stationary. Also in another sense it is rather unfortunate to symbolize time by means of the number, for the series of numbers is not absolutely continuous but rather the unities and even their smallest differences are separated from each other.

[359]

WEBER, MAX

WEBER, MAX (1864-1920). Very few scholars have been so severely tormented by the conflict between their scientific convictions and their vital instincts as was Max Weber, and hardly any other one has, in his writings and teachings, so sternly disciplined himself as did he. His penetrating analysis of social formations, of the economic factor in history, of the relations between religion and economics and the general trends of human civilization, proceeds from and results in the statement that the victory of rational impersonality over irrational impulses is inevitable and historically justified. But Weber himself, a man of impulsive vehemence, afflicted by psychic tensions and disturbances, bitterly resented any loss of irrational privacy which was imposed on him by the development of depersonalizing tendencies, although his insight forced him to accept it. His constant endeavor was not to betray personal feelings in his teachings and to keep his statements and characteristics of the objects of his science free from intrinsic value judgments. According to him, science has to give only technical knowledge which may be useful for the domination of things and human beings. Social science is defined by him as a method of interpreting social action and of explaining its course and its effects by the quest for its intention and the means of its accomplishment, without any regard to its desirability.

Only on the occasion of literary feuds and political debates did Weber allow eruptions of his feelings. He was a formidable controversialist, capable of knocking down his adversaries with ice-cold irony or with truculent impetuosity. He was an ardent German nationalist but, for the greater part of his life, believed that democracy was more efficient than any authoritarian regime, and therefore he advocated Germany's democratization. Still opposed to the Treaty of Versailles, Weber, at the end of his life, came closer to nationalist extremists whom he had energetically combated during the war.

THE FATE OF SCIENCE

IN science, each of us knows that what he has accomplished will be antiquated in ten, twenty, fifty years. That is the fate to which science is subjected; it is the very *meaning* of scientific work, to which it is devoted in a quite specific sense, as compared with other spheres of culture for which in general the same holds. Every scientific "fulfilment" raises new "questions"; it *asks* to be "surpassed" and outdated. Whoever wishes to serve science has to resign himself to this fact. Scientific works certainly can last as "gratifications" because of their artistic quality, or they may remain important as a means of training. Yet they will be surpassed scientifically—let that be repeated—for it is our common fate and, more, our common goal. We cannot work without hoping that others will advance further than we have. In principle, this progress goes on *ad infinitum*. And with this we come to inquire into the *meaning* of science. For, after all, it is not self-evident that something subordinate to such a law is sensible and meaningful in itself. Why does one engage in doing something that in reality never comes, and never can come, to an end?

One does it, first, for purely practical, in the broader sense of the word, for technical, purposes: in order to be able to orient our practical activities to the expectations that scientific experience places at our disposal. Good. Yet this has meaning only to practitioners. What is the attitude of the academic man towards his vocation—that is, if he is at all in quest of such a personal attitude? He maintains that he engages in "science for science's sake" and not merely because others, by exploiting science, bring about commercial or technical success and can better feed, dress, illuminate, and govern. But what does he who allows himself to be integrated into this specialized organization, running on *ad infinitum*, hope to accomplish that is significant in these productions that are always destined to be outdated? This question requires a few general considerations.

Scientific progress is a fraction, the most important fraction, of the process of intellectualization which we have been undergoing for thousands of years and which nowadays is usually judged in such an extremely negative way. Let us first clarify what this intellectualist rationalization, created by science and by scientifically oriented technology, means practically.

Does it mean that we, today, for instance, have a greater knowledge of the conditions of life under which we exist than has an American Indian or a Hottentot? Hardly. Unless he is a physicist, one who rides on the streetcar has no idea how the car happened to get into motion. And he does not need to know. He is satisfied that he may "count" on the behavior of the streetcar, and he orients his conduct according to this expectation; but he knows nothing about what it takes to produce such a car so that it can move. The savage knows incomparably more about his tools. When we spend money today I bet that almost every one will hold a different answer in readiness to the question: How does it happen that one can buy something for money—sometimes more and sometimes less? The savage knows what he does in order to get his daily food and which institutions serve him in this pursuit. The increasing intellectualization and rationalization do *not*, therefore, indicate an increased and general knowledge of the conditions under which one lives.

It means something else, namely, the knowledge or belief that if one but wished one *could* learn it at any time. Hence, it means that principally there are no mysterious incalculable forces that come into play, but rather that one can, in principle, master all things by calculation. This means that the world is disenchanted. One need no longer have recourse to magical means in order to master or implore the spirits, as did the savage, for whom such mysterious powers existed. Technical means and calculations perform the service. This above all is what intellectualization means.

[360]

WERTHEIMER, MAX

WERTHEIMER, MAX (1880-1943). Wertheimer's article *Experimental Studies on the Vision of Movement*, published in *Zeitschrift für Psychologie* (1912), led to the development of *Gestalt* theory which has been formulated at first psychologically, and then enlarged into a philosophical conception of physical, biological and social facts. Wertheimer broke away from the purely summative theory of sensory experience. Instead he held that the phenomena must be considered autonomous unities, coherent wholes, that the existence of each element of such an unity is dependent on the latter's structure, and that the knowledge of the whole cannot be derived from that of its elements. Neither psychologically nor physiologically is the element anterior to the whole.

In his *Productive Thinking*, published posthumously in 1945, Wertheimer defined thinking as "envisaging, realizing structural features, structural requirements, proceeding in accordance with, and determined by, these requirements; thereby changing the situation in the direction of structural improvement." He claimed that *Gestalt* theory had started scientific study of the problems of thinking, clarified them theoretically, and that it tried to form appropriate tools for dealing with the facts and laws involved in them in a scientific manner.

GESTALT THEORY

GESTALT theory does *not* attempt to patch up or evade, nor does it endeavor to settle the problem by decreeing: this is science, life is different; other factors are at work in the spiritual realm than in the material. Gestalt theory does not seek a solution in a separation of the subject matter of knowledge. It endeavors at a crucial point to probe the innermost core of the problem, by asking: at this precise point is there not something in the approach, the basic thesis, the fundamental preconceptions, that used to be considered indispensable to the realm of science but in actuality is not so at all?

For a long time it seemed self-evident, and very characteristic of European epistemology and science, that the scientist could only proceed in the following way: if I have before me a phenomenon to be investigated and understood, I must view it first as an aggregate, as something to be dissected into piecemeal elements; then I must study the laws governing such elements. Only by compounding the elementary data and by establishing the relations between the separate pieces can the problem be solved. All this is not new; during recent decades it has raised problems in the minds of most scientists. Briefly characterized, one might say that the paramount presupposition was to go back to particles, to revert to piecemeal single relations existing between such individual particles or elements, to analyze and synthesize by combining the elements and particles into larger complexes.

Gestalt theory believes it has discovered a decisive aspect in recognizing the existence of phenomena and contexts of a different—of a formally different—nature. And this not merely in the humanities. The basic thesis of gestalt theory might be formulated thus: there are contexts in which what is happening in the world cannot be deduced from the characteristics of the separate pieces, but conversely; what happens to a part of the whole is, in clear-cut cases, determined by the laws of the inner structure of its whole. . . .

If I view the situation from the standpoint of set theory, and ask, how would a world look in which there was no science, no understanding, no penetration or grasp of inner relationships, the answer is very simple. Such a world would consist of a mere agglomeration of disparate elements. The next question would be: what would a world be like, how must a plurality be conceived, if science should be able to proceed in a piecemeal way? This can also be quite simply characterized. The only requirements would be the recurrence of couplings of a senseless, piecemeal nature; then everything needed to operate traditional logic, piecemeal mathematics and science would be at hand. There is a third kind of formation of set theory which, up to now, has not been sufficiently studied—that is, those sets where a manifold is not built up of separate elements but the whole conditions of a set determine the character and place of any particular part of this set.

Figuratively speaking, then, what is the situation we are in? Everyone sees one particular sector of this world and this sector in itself is small indeed. Imagine the world consisting of a large plateau on which musicians are seated, each playing. As I walk around I hear and see. Here there are various possibilities, which are different in principle. Firstly, the world could be a senseless plurality. Everyone acts arbitrarily—everyone for himself. The combination I would gain if I could hear ten of them or all of them at the same time, would be an accidental effect of what each of them does individually. This would correspond to a radically piecemeal theory such as the kinetic theory of gases. A second possibility would be that whenever one musician played C, another would play F so and so many seconds later; I would establish some blind piecemeal relationship linking the acts of the individual musicians which would again result in something totally meaningless. That is the conception most people have of physics. However, correctly regarded, physics interprets the world differently. Our third possibility would for instance be a Beethoven symphony where from a part of the whole we could grasp something of the inner structure of the whole itself. The fundamental laws, then, would not be piecemeal laws but structural characteristics of the whole. And with this I will conclude.

[361]

WHITEHEAD, ALFRED NORTH

WHITEHEAD, ALFRED NORTH (1861-1947). Whitehead had become famous as a scientist, as one of the founders of modern mathematical logic, before he concentrated upon philosophy. He was sixty-three years old when he renounced his professorship of mathematics at the Imperial College of Science and Technology, London, in order to become professor of philosophy at Harvard. However, his mathematical investigations remained relevant to his metaphysics, and even Whitehead, the metaphysician who protested that "the final outlook of philosophical thought cannot be based upon the exact statements which form the basis of special sciences," retained his grand vision of the possibilities of abstract theory.

Whitehead never hesitated to confess his indebtedness to William James, Samuel Alexander and Henri Bergson for the development of his own philosophical thoughts, or that Minkowski's assimilation of space and time and Einstein's theory of relativity had stimulated his thought. But this indebtedness meant not so much an actual influence as rather the creation of a new situation which allowed Whitehead to proceed in his own way.

The decisive feature of this new situation was shaped by James' denial that the subject-object relation is fundamental to knowledge. By denying that in the occurrence of knowing one entity, regarded as the knower, as a mind or soul, standing in front of an object, be it externally existent or the self-consciousness of the knower himself, James also removed the habitual distinction of mind and matter. Whitehead, while constantly contending that the "bifurcation of nature," the sharp division between nature and mind, established by Descartes, had "poisoned all subsequent philosophy" and jeopardized the very meaning of life, restored the subject-object relation as a fundamental structural pattern of experience, "but not in the sense in which subject-object is identified with knower-known." To Whitehead, "the living organ or experience is the living body as a whole." Human experience has its origin in the physical activities of the whole organism which tends to readjustment when any part of it becomes unstable. Although such experience seems to be more particularly related to the brain, Whitehead held that "we cannot determine with what molecules the brain begins and the rest of the body ends." Human experience therefore is defined as "an act of self-origination, including the whole of nature, limited to the perspective of a focal region, located within the body, but not necessarily persisting in any fixed coordination within a definite part of the brain."

Upon this concept of human experience, Whitehead founded his new philosophy of the organism, his cosmology, his defense of speculative reason, his ideas on the process of nature, his rational approach to God. The aim of his speculative philosophy was "to frame a coherent, logical, necessary system of general ideas in terms of which every item of our experience can be interpreted." Whitehead thought that philosophy, speculative metaphysics included, was not, or should not be, a ferocious debate between irritable professors but "a survey of possibilities and their comparison with actualities," balancing the fact, the theory, the alternatives and the ideal. In this way the fundamental beliefs which determine human character, will be clarified.

The first period of Whitehead's activities was devoted to mathematics and logic. It began with *Universal Algebra* published in 1898 after seven years of work, continued with *Mathematical Concepts of the Material World* (1905) and culminated in the monumental *Principia Mathematica* (1910-1913) written in collaboration with Bertrand Russell. Characteristic of Whitehead's second period, in which he was preoccupied with a philosophy of natural science without metaphysical exposition, are *An Enquiry Concerning the Principles of Natural Knowledge* (1919), *The Concept of Nature* (1920), *The Principle of Relativity* (1922) and *Science and the Modern World* (1925), which already mentions but not yet attempts a metaphysical synthesis of existence.

Most significant of Whitehead's metaphysical views are *Process and Reality* (1929), *Adventures of Ideas* (1933) and *Modes of Thought* (1938).

1217

THE proper satisfaction to be derived from speculative thought is elucidation. It is for this reason that fact is supreme over thought. This supremacy is the basis of authority. We scan the world to find evidence for this elucidatory power.

Thus the supreme verification of the speculative flight is that it issues in the establishment of a practical technique for well-attested ends, and that the speculative system maintains itself as the elucidation of that technique. In this way there is the progress from thought to practice, and regress from practice to the same thought. This interplay of thought and practice is the supreme authority. It is the test by which the charlatanism of speculation is restrained.

In human history, a practical technique embodies itself in established institutions—professional associations, scientific associations, business associations, universities, churches, governments. Thus the study of the ideas which underlie the sociological structure is an appeal to the supreme authority. It is the Stoic appeal to the "voice of nature."

But even this supreme authority fails to be final, and this for two reasons. In the first place the evidence is confused, ambiguous, and contradictory. In the second place, if at any period of human history it had been accepted as final, all progress would have been stopped. The horrid practices of the past, brutish and nasty, would have been fastened upon us for all ages. Nor can we accept the present age as our final standard. We can live, and we can live well. But we feel the urge of the trend upwards: we still look toward the better life.

We have to seek for a discipline of the speculative reason. It is of the essence of such speculation that it transcends immediate fact. Its business is to make thought creative of the future. It effects this by its vision of systems of ideas, including observation but generalized beyond it. The need of discipline arises because the history of speculation is analogous to the history of practice. If we survey mankind, their speculations have been foolish, brutish, and nasty. The true use of history is that we extract from it general principles as to the discipline of practice and the discipline of speculation.

The object of this discipline is not stability but progress. There is no true stability. What looks like stability is a relatively slow process of atrophied decay. The stable universe is slipping away from under us. Our aim is upwards.

The men who made speculation effective were the Greek thinkers. We owe to them the progressive European civilization. It is therefore common sense to observe the methods which they introduced into the conduct of thought.

In the first place, they were unboundedly curious. They probed into everything, questioned everything, and sought to understand everything. This is merely to say that they were speculative to a superlative degree. In the second place, they were rigidly systematic both in their aim at clear definition and at logical consistency. In fact, they invented logic in order to be consistent. Thirdly, they were omnivorous in their interests—natural science, ethics, mathematics, political philosophy, metaphysics, theology, esthetics, and all alike attracted their curiosity. Nor did they keep these subjects rigidly apart. They very deliberately strove to combine them into one coherent system of ideas. Fourthly, they sought truths of the highest generality. Also in seeking these truths, they paid attention to the whole body of their varied interests. Fifthly, they were men with active practical interests. Plato went to Sicily in order to assist in a political experiment, and throughout his life studied mathematics. In those days mathematics and its applications were not so separated as they can be today. No doubt, the sort of facts that he observed were the applications of mathematical theory. But no one had a keener appreciation than Plato of the divergence between the exactness of abstract thought and the vague margin of ambiguity which haunts all observation. Indeed in this respect Plato, the abstract thinker, far surpasses John Stuart Mill, the inductive philosopher. Mill in his account of the inductive methods of science never faces the difficulty that no observation ever does exactly verify the law which it is presumed to support. Plato's feeling for the inexactness of physical experience in contrast to the exactness of thought certainly suggests that he could look for himself. Mill's determinism is, according to his own theory, an induction respecting the exactness of conformation to the conditions set by antecedent circumstances. But no one has ever had any such experience of exact conformation. No observational basis whatsoever can be obtained for the support of Mill's doctrine. Plato knew this primary fact about experience, Mill did not. Determinism may be the true doctrine, but it can never be proved by the methods prescribed by English empiricism.

When we come to Aristotle the enumeration of his practical activities makes us wonder that he had any time for thought at all. He analyzed the constitutions of the leading Greek states, he dissected the great dramatic literature of his age, he dissected fishes, he dissected sentences and arguments, he taught the youthful Alexander. A man, who had done these things and others, might well have been excused if he had pleaded lack of time for mere abstract thought.

In considering the culmination of Greek speculation in Plato and Aristotle the characteristics which finally stand out are the universality of their interests, the systematic exactness at which they aimed, and the generality of their thoughts. It is no rash induction to conclude that these combined characteristics constitute one main preservative of speculation from folly.

The speculative reason works in two ways so as to submit itself to the authority of facts without loss of its mission to transcend the existing analysis of facts. In one way it accepts the limitations of a special topic, such as a science or a practical methodology. It then seeks speculatively to enlarge and recast the categorical ideas within the limits of that topic. This is speculative reason in its closest alliance with the methodological reason.

In the other way, it seeks to build a cosmology express-ing the general nature of the world as disclosed in human interests. In order to keep such a cosmology in contact with reality, account must be taken of the welter of established institutions constituting the structures of human society throughout the ages. It is only in this way that we can ap-peal to the widespread effective elements in the experience of mankind. What those institutions stood for in the exper-ience of their contemporaries represents the massive facts of ultimate authority.

The discordance at once disclosed among the beliefs and purposes of men is commonplace. But in a way, the task is simplified. The superficial details at once disclose them-selves by the discordance which they disclose. The concord-ance in general notions stands out. The very fact of institu-tions to effect purposes witnesses to unquestioned belief that foresight and purpose can shape the attainment of ends. The discordance over moral codes witnesses to the fact of moral experience. You cannot quarrel about unknown ele-ments. The basis of every discord is some common exper-ience, discordantly realized.

A cosmology should above all things be adequate. It should not confine itself to the categorical notions of one science, and explain away everything which will not fit in. Its business is not to refuse experience but to find the most general interpretive system. Also it is not a mere juxtaposi-tion of the various categorical notions of the various sci-ences. It generalizes beyond any special science, and thus provides the interpretive system which expresses their inter-connection. Cosmology, since it is the outcome of the highest generality of speculation, is the critic of all speculation in-ferior to itself in generality.

But cosmology shares the imperfections of all the ef-forts of finite intelligence. The special sciences fall short of their aim, and cosmology equally fails. Thus when the novel speculation is produced a threefold problem is set. Some special science, the cosmological scheme, and the novel concept will have points of agreement and points of variance. Reason intervenes in the capacity of arbiter and yet with a further exercise of speculation. The science is modified, the cosmological outlook is modified, and the novel concept is modified. The joint discipline has eliminated elements of folly, or of mere omission, from all three. The purposes of mankind receive the consequential modification, and the shock is transmitted through the whole sociological structure of technical methods and of institutions.

Every construction of human intelligence is more special, more limited than was its original aim. Cosmology sets out to be the general system of general ideas applicable to this epoch of the universe. Abstraction is to be made from all subordinate details. Thus there should be one cosmology presiding over many sciences. Unfortunately this ideal has not been realized. The cosmological outlooks of different schools of philosophy differ. They do more than differ, they are largely inconsistent with each other. The discredit of philosophy has largely arisen from this warring of the schools.

So long as the dogmatic fallacy infests the world, this discordance will continue to be misinterpreted. If philosophy be erected upon clear and distinct ideas, then the discord of philosophers, competent and sincere men, implies that they are pursuing a will-o'-the-wisp. But as soon as the true function of rationalism is understood, that it is a gradual approach to ideas of clarity and generality, the discord is what may be expected.

The various cosmologies have in various degrees failed to achieve the generality and the clarity at which they aim. They are inadequate, vague, and push special notions beyond the proper limits of their application. For example, Descartes is obviously right, in some sense or other, when he says that we have bodies and that we have minds, and that they can be studied in some disconnection. It is what we do daily in practical life. This philosophy makes a large generalization which obviously has some important validity. But if you turn it into a final cosmology, errors will creep in. The same is true of other schools of philosophy. They all say something which is importantly true. Some types of philosophy have produced more penetrating cosmologies than other schools. At certain epochs a cosmology may be produced which includes its predecessors and assigns to them their scope of validity. But at length, that cosmology will be found out. Rivals will appear correcting it, and perhaps failing to include some of its general truths.

In this way mankind stumbles on in its task of understanding the world.

[362]

WHITMAN, WALT

WHITMAN, WALT (1819-1892). Not only in America but also in England, France, Germany and other countries, Whitman has been celebrated as the prophet of the age of democracy, a title which the poet himself relished. The new technique of lyrical expression and description which he initiated has been adopted by outstanding French poets and by many minor poets in several languages.

The function of poetry was conceived by Whitman as not only enjoying but leading and teaching mankind, and in many of his poems he attempted to answer philosophical questions. Whitman also dealt with philosophical problems in his notebooks. In 1847 he did not believe himself to have become a great philosopher, and in 1860 he wrote, in a similar mood, that he had not founded a philosophical school. In a way, he even repudiated philosophy as a bond of thinking, and exclaimed: "I leave all free, I charge you to leave all free." But he also claimed that the poet of the cosmos "advances through all interpositions, coverings and turmoils and stratagems to first principles." In *Passage to India* he declared that the poet fuses nature and man who were diffused before. In fact, Whitman was devoted to a philosophy which combined pantheism with a strong belief in human action, which unites the human soul with cosmic life but stresses the uniqueness of human personality and human relations. His civil, democratic, human consciousness was rooted in an all-embracing feeling of cosmic solidarity, and he was anxious to avoid any attenuation, and not to be deterred by psychic transmigration to the remotest objects. There is a tension between Whitman's firmness of conviction and his universal receptivity for impressions, sensations, ideas and phenomena, between his feelings of being a missionary of democracy and his mythical imagination. But this same tension strengthened his poetical power and did not endanger the unity of his character. From cosmic vagaries he always found the way back to simple truth and common sense.

LITERATURE'S SERVICE

THE chief trait of any given poet is always the spirit he brings to the observation of humanity and nature—the mood out of which he contemplates his subjects. What kind of temper and what amount of faith report these things? Up to how recent a date is the song carried? What the equipment, and special raciness of the singer—what his tinge of coloring? The last value of artistic expressers, past and present —Greek aesthetes, Shakespeare—or in our own day Tennyson, Victor Hugo, Carlyle, Emerson—is certainly involv'd in such questions. I say the profoundest service that poems or any other writings can do for their reader is not merely to satisfy the intellect, or supply something polish'd or interesting, nor even to depict great passions, or persons or events, but to fill him with vigorous and clean manliness, religiousness, and give him *good heart* as a radical possession and habit. The educated world seems to have been growing more and more ennuied for ages, leaving to our time the inheritance of it all. Fortunately there is the original inexhaustible fund of buoyancy, normally resident in the race, forever eligible to be appeal'd to and relied on.

Democracy's Need

I SAY that democracy can never prove itself beyond cavil, until it founds and luxuriantly grows its own forms of art, poems, schools, theology, displacing all that exists, or that has been produced anywhere in the past, under opposite influences. It is curious to me that while so many voices, pens, minds, in the press, lecture rooms, in our Congress, etc., are discussing intellectual topics, pecuniary dangers, legislative problems, the suffrage, tariff and labor questions, and the various business and benevolent needs of America, with propositions, remedies, often worth deep attention, there is one need, a hiatus the profoundest, that no eye seems to perceive, no voice to state. Our fundamental want today in the United States, with closest, amplest reference to present conditions, and to the future, is of a class, and the clear idea of a class, of native authors, literatures, far different, far higher in grade, than any yet known, sacerdotal, modern, fit to cope with our occasions, lands, permeating the whole mass of American mentality, taste, belief, breathing into it a new breath of life, giving it decision, affecting politics far more than the popular superficial suffrage, with results inside and underneath the elections of Presidents or Congresses—radiating, begetting appropriate teachers, schools, manners, and as its grandest result, accomplishing (what neither the schools nor the churches and their clergy have hitherto accomplished, and without which this nation will no more stand, permanently, soundly, than a house will stand without a substratum), a religious and moral character beneath the political and productive and intellectual bases of the States. For know you not, dear, earnest reader, that the people of our land may all read and write, and may all possess the right to vote—and yet the main things may be entirely lacking?— (and this to suggest them).

Viewed, today, from a point of view sufficiently overarching, the problem of humanity all over the civilized world is social and religious, and is to be finally met and treated by literature. The priest departs, the divine literatus comes. . . .

Few are aware how the great literature penetrates all, gives hue to all, shapes aggregates and individuals, and, after subtle ways, with irresistible power, constructs, sustains, demolishes at will. Why tower, in reminiscence, above all the nations of the earth, two special lands, petty in themselves, yet inexpressibly gigantic, beautiful, columnar? Immortal Judah lives, and Greece immortal lives, in a couple of poems.

[363]

WILSON, WOODROW

WILSON, WOODROW (1856-1924). Most of Wilson's admirers hold that his idealism enhanced his statesmanship while most of his adversaries assert that it was his idealism that led him astray. But neither his sound nor his erroneous judgments and measures can be explained by his philosophical or religious attitude alone. At times, Wilson, the idealist, was rightly considered "America's most practical president," and sometimes Wilson became the victim of his illusions when he tried to act as a shrewd politician. His power to exercise sound judgment increased and deteriorated independently of his idealism that always was a constant element of his personality. The mystical faith in his mission must be distinguished from his religious belief and his philosophical conviction, both of which nourished his missionary zeal but were not identical with it. He was not the man to create original ideas but rather to make the adopted ideas into living forces which had to serve his mission, and the efforts to accomplish this mission made evident the conflicting tendencies of his personality which finally caused his personal failure without refuting the principal ideas supported by him.

Wilson was moved by strong emotional impulses though always on guard against his own emotions. He was a deeply convinced Christian but humility was not the significant trait of his nature. He struggled for the rights of the individual but confessed that he was "not fond of thinking of Christianity as the means of saving individual souls." Service and sacrifice of selfish interests was preached by him, and he earnestly endeavored to live and act in accordance with his teaching, but he was intolerant of any dissent. No President of the United States had studied so intensely the lives, achievements and failures of his predecessors in office as Wilson had done. The result of these studies was his firm belief that he, the President, by virtue of his election, "can speak what no man else knows, the common meaning of the common voice." But in

1226

case of disagreement with the majority of the people, Wilson believed in his higher judgment. It was this mystical belief in his faculty to express the innermost thoughts of the nations that led him on a dangerous way when he tried to impose on the world a peace treaty which should be, as ex-President Taft remarked, "his and nobody's else's peace" because he claimed to know better than anyone else the meaning of justice. It was not vanity that let him make such assumptions. If Wilson did not distrust his convictions he at least steadily distrusted his emotions. His motives have been best expressed in Rudyard Kipling's poem *If*, which Wilson regarded as his personal credo, and which he carried in his pocket and later had framed to hang beside him when he died, a hero in defeat. It was Wilson's motto "to keep your head when all about you are losing theirs and blaming it on you," to "trust yourself when all men doubt you," to "dream and not make dream your master" and to "talk with crowds and keep your virtue."

CONDITIONS OF SOCIAL LIFE

Co-operation is the vital principle of social life, not organization merely. I think I know something about organization. I can make an organization, but it is one thing to have an organization and another thing to fill it with life. And then it is a very important matter what sort of life you fill it with. If the object of the organization is what the object of some business organizations is, to absorb the life of the community for its own benefit, then there is nothing beneficial in it. But if the object of the organization is to afford a mechanism by which the whole community can cooperatively use its life, then there is a great deal in it. An organization without the spirit of cooperation is dead and may be dangerous. . . .

Legislation cannot save society. Legislation cannot even rectify society. The law that will work is merely the summing up in legislative form of the moral judgment that the community has already reached. Law records how far society has got; there have got to be instrumentalities preceding the law that get society up to that point where it will be ready to record. . . . Law is a record of achievement. It is not a process of regeneration. Our wills have to be regenerated, and our purposes rectified before we are in a position to enact laws that record those moral achievements. And that is the business, primarily, it seems to me, of the Christian. . . .

All the transforming influences in the world are unselfish. There is not a single selfish force in the world that is not touched with sinister power, and the church is the only embodiment of the things that are entirely unselfish, the principles of self-sacrifice and devotion. . . . America is great in the world, not as she is a successful government merely, but as she is the successful embodiment of a great ideal of unselfish citizenship.

[364]

WINDELBAND, WILHELM

WINDELBAND, WILHELM (1848-1915). As a historian of philosophy and as the founder of the "South-West-German school of philosophy," Windelband exercised considerable influence. In both activities, he emphasized that philosophy must reflect on civilization and its historical evolution. Windelband belongs to those German philosophers who proceed from Kant's criticism, but he protested against other neo-Kantians who mainly confined their thinking to a renewal of Kant's epistemology, and he stressed the importance of his inquiries into ethics, aesthetics, and philosophy of law and religion. Windelband's program, however, maintained that "to understand Kant rightly means to go beyond him." While Kant considered only mathematics and natural sciences, founded upon mathematics, as real sciences, Windelband held that history in the broadest sense of the word, comprising views on all kinds of human activities, must be acknowledged as a true science. He distinguished between the natural sciences, which are concerned with the establishment of laws, and the historical sciences, which try to grasp, to describe and explain individual facts. The methods of the natural sciences are characterized as being of a generalizing, nomothetic character, those of the historical sciences as "idiographic." From this distinction, Windelband proceeded to a sharp opposition to epistemological naturalism, and broached the question, of whether the nomothetic or the idiographic sciences are of more essential importance to philosophy. He decided in favor of the historical sciences, because, according to him philosophy must interpret spiritual life and explain values, and the sense of values is rooted in the sense of the individual.

In his efforts to "go beyond Kant," Windelband relied on Hegel, Herbart and Lotze. Closely associated with Windelband was Heinrich Rickert. Among Windelband's disciples were not only noted philosophers but sociologists like Max Weber and theologians like Ernst Troeltsch.

PHILOSOPHY

THE man who wishes to make a serious study of philosophy must be prepared to find that in its light the world and life will present a different aspect from that which he saw previously; to sacrifice, if it prove necessary, the preconceived ideas with which he approached it.

It is quite possible, perhaps inevitable, that the results of philosophy will diverge considerably from the conclusions that one had in advance, but the things which philosophy discusses are not remote and obscure objects that need some skill to discover them. On the contrary, they are precisely the things which life itself and the work of the various sciences force upon a man's attention. It is the very essence of philosophy to examine thoroughly what lies at hand and all round us. In the whole of our intellectual life there are uncritized assumptions and ideas lightly borrowed from life and science. The practical life of man is pervaded and dominated by the pre-scientific ideas, naively developed, which usage has incorporated in our speech. These ideas, it is true, are modified and clarified in the special sciences as far as it is necessary for their particular purpose of arranging and controlling their material; but they still demand consideration in connection with the problems and inquiries of philosophy. Just as life affords material to the scientific worker in its pre-scientific ideas, so life and the sciences together provide, in their pre-scientific and *pre-philosophic* ideas, material for the operations of the philosopher. Hence it is that the frontier between the special sciences and philosophy is not a definite line, but depends in each age on the state of knowledge. In common life we conceive a body as a thing that occupies space and is endowed with all sorts of properties. Out of this pre-scientific notion physics and chemistry form their ideas of atoms, molecules, and elements. They were first formed in the general impulse to acquire knowledge which the Greeks called "philosophy." To-day these scientific ideas are pre-philosophic concepts, and they suggest to us so many problems of philosophy.

These assumptions which have not been thoroughly examined have a legitimate use in the field for which they are intended. Practical life manages very well with its pre-scientific ideas of bodies; and the pre-philosophical ideas of atoms, etc., are just as satisfactory for the special needs of physics and chemistry. While, however, they are thus suited to the demands of empirical theory it may be that they will present serious problems in the more general aspects in which philosophy has to consider them. The idea of natural law is an indispensable requirement both for practical life and for scientific research, which has to discover the several laws of nature. But what a natural law is, and what is the nature of the dependence of our various concrete experiences upon this general idea, are difficult problems which must be approached, not by empirical investigation, but by philosophical reflection.

In the special sciences and in common life, therefore, these fundamental assumptions are justified by success; but the moment they are considered more deeply, the moment a man asks himself whether these things which are naively taken for granted are really sound, philosophy is born. It is, as Aristotle says, the *taumagein*, the hour in which the mind is puzzled and turns upon itself. It is the *esetagein*, the demand of proof, with which Socrates disturbed the illusory self-complacency of himself and his fellow-citizens. It is complete honesty of the intellect with itself. We can never reflect on things without assumptions which must be taken for granted; but we must not leave them indefinitely without investigation, and we must be prepared to abandon them if they are found to be wrong. This testing of one's assumptions is philosophy.

Every great philosopher has passed through this phase of examining what had been taken for granted, and it is the same impulse which directs a man to the study of philosophy. In the life of every thoughtful man there comes a time when everything that had been assumed, and on which we had confidently built, collapses like a house of cards, and, as during an earthquake, even the most solid-looking structure totters. Descartes has very vividly described this, with the most exquisite simplicity and fineness, in his first *Meditation*. He experiences, as Socrates did, the real mission of scepticism; which is, both in history and in the very nature of human thought, to lead us onward to a final security through the dissolution of our unreflecting assumptions.

[365]

WITTGENSTEIN, LUDWIG

WITTGENSTEIN, LUDWIG (1889-1951). For a time, Wittgenstein was preoccupied with architecture and only intermittently interested in philosophy. But his *Tractatus Logico-Philosophicus* (1922) became of great consequence to the development of logical positivism or scientific empiricism, while its author, then about thirty years old, inspired older thinkers like Moritz Schlick, Bertrand Russell and Alfred Whitehead.

In this treatise, Wittgenstein offers a general way of removing philosophical difficulties by investigating the logical structure of language. Incapability of seeing through the logic of language, or at least neglect of its importance, is the cause of apparently or really insoluble philosophical problems. Wittgenstein insists that whatever can be said, can be said clearly. Philosophy is not a doctrine but, rather, an activity. Its result is not new propositions but clarification of propositions. Philosophy will mean the inexpressible by presenting the expressible as clearly as possible.

Some years after the publication of his treatise, Wittgenstein concentrated upon his philosophical studies, and was called to Cambridge, England, where later he was appointed successor to G. E. Moore.

1231

BEGINNING OF THE TRACTATUS
LOGICO-PHILOSOPHICUS

1   The world is everything that is the case.*

1.1   The world is the totality of facts, not of things.

1.11   The world is determined by the facts, and by these being *all* the facts.

1.12   For the totality of facts determines both what is the case, and also all that is not the case.

1.13   The facts in logical space are the world.

1.2   The world divides into facts.

1.21   Any one can either be the case or not be the case, and everything else remain the same.

2   What is the case, the fact, is the existence of atomic facts.

2.01   An atomic fact is a combination of objects (entities, things).

2.011   It is essential to a thing that it can be a constituent part of an atomic fact.

2.012   In logic nothing is accidental: if a thing *can* occur in an atomic fact the possibility of that atomic fact must already be prejudged in the thing.

2.0121   It would, so to speak, appear as an accident, when to a thing that could exist alone on its own account, subsequently a state of affairs could be made to fit.

If things can occur in atomic facts, this possibility must already lie in them.

(A logical entity cannot be merely possible. Logic treats of every possibility, and all possibilities are its facts.)

Just as we cannot think of spatial objects at all apart from space, or temporal objects apart from

---

* The decimal figures as numbers of the separate propositions indicate the logical importance of the propositions, the emphasis laid upon them in my exposition. The propositions *n*.1, *n*.2, *n*.3, etc., are comments on proposition No. *n*; the propositions *n.m*1, *n.m*2, etc., are comments on the proposition No. *n.m*; and so on.

time, so we cannot think of *any* object apart from the possibility of its connection with other things.

If I can think of an object in the context of an atomic fact, I cannot think of it apart from the *possibility* of this context.

2.0122   The thing is independent, in so far as it can occur in all *possible* circumstances, but this form of independence is a form of connection with the atomic fact, a form of dependence. (It is impossible for words to occur in two different ways, alone and in the proposition.)

2.0123   If I know an object, then I also know all the possibilities of its occurrence in atomic facts.

(Every such possibility must lie in the nature of the object.)

A new possibility cannot subsequently be found.

2.01231   In order to know an object, I must know not its external but all its internal qualities.

2.0124   If all objects are given, then thereby are all *possible* atomic facts also given.

2.013   Every thing is, as it were, in a space of possible atomic facts. I can think of this space as empty, but not of the thing without the space.

2.0131   A spatial object must lie in infinite space. (A point in space is a place for an argument.)

[366]

WOLFF, CHRISTIAN

WOLFF, CHRISTIAN (1679-1754). Frederick William I, the "soldier king" of Prussia, dismissed Wolff, in 1723, from his post as professor at the University of Halle, forced him to leave the kingdom within forty-eight hours, and, some years later, decreed that everyone who used a book of Wolff's should be sentenced to wheelbarrow labor. What incited the fury of the king was an address given by Wolff in which he had praised the ethical teachings of Confucius, and had added that a man could be happy and good without the Divine grace or revelation. Furthermore, the king was impressed by the apprehension, expressed by some of his generals, that Wolff, as an adherent of determinism, might endanger the discipline of the Prussian army.

Wolff's international fame was enhanced by the King's measures. Other governments offered him a professorship. Learned societies in France and England awarded him degrees and honors. However, the University of Halle suffered from the consequences of Wolff's expulsion, so that the King, reluctantly, invited Wolff to come back. Before the negotiations were completed, Frederick William I died, and his successor Frederick II used Wolff's final reappointment to exhibit himself as a tolerant ruler.

Wolff was a disciple of Leibniz, but he completed the latter's system, or, as Leibniz saw it, deformed it, by concessions to Aquinas, Descartes, and even to Locke. Despite different opinions, Leibniz remained friendly to Wolff, and continued to recommend and advise him. For Leibniz was aware that Wolff had a faculty of clear expression and systematization which he himself lacked. Wolff's authority and influence with the German Enlightenment were immense until Kant shook the fundamentals of Wolff's system. But even Kant revered him as "the most powerful representative of dogmatic rationalism, of the standpoint of pure, unshaken confidence in the strength of reason."

DUTIES TOWARD OTHERS

SINCE Man shall not only perfect himself and his status and make himself safe from imperfection, but since he shall contribute, as far as possible and without failing in his duties toward himself, to the perfection of others and their status whenever they need his help, and since he shall also refrain from everything which would make them and their status more imperfect, it follows that each man owes to his fellow men the same things he owes to himself in the same measure as far as the other person has these things not in his powers and he himself can do them for this other person without neglecting his duty toward himself. Consequently, the duties of a person toward others are the same as his duties toward himself. Therefore these duties be incumbent on others.

Every man, therefore, shall, as far as it is in his power, help any other person who needs his help; he shall improve the goods of the soul, of the body and of fortune and consequently take precautions lest the others would be overtaken by the diseases of the soul or of the body and ill fortune. Since natural law does not restrict help to certain goods we shall not refuse our help to others so that they may enjoy better welfare than we enjoy ourselves. That could not be so if we envied another person for his happiness. One shall never envy anyone for a joy he lacks. Envy is opposed to the very nature of Man.

Natural obligation is absolutely unchangeable. If another person does not fulfil this obligation, this fact does not allow you not to fulfil it either. Consequently it is not permissible to transgress natural law by referring to the examples of others, and our duties toward others do not cease because they fail in their duties toward us. This being understood also concerning the things the natural law prohibits, it follows too that we owe the duties of humanity to those who harm us.

The duties of Man toward others being the same as those toward himself, everybody shall have a constant and perpetual will to advance the perfection and happiness of any other person. Consequently, because love or our fellow man is the essence of this will, and love the essence of the disposition of the soul to feel pleasure through the happiness of another person, everybody should have sympathy and love for his fellow man as well as for himself, and should not hate him

Since men shall be friends to each other, each shall strive not to make others his enemies but to obtain and to keep their friendship. However, one cannot be exempted from natural obligation. One shall, therefore, not do anything out of friendship which would be contrary to natural law

Perfection of the soul consists in the intellectual and moral virtues. We have therefore to be careful to extend them and, by our example, we have to teach them to others and make them love those virtues. Consequently we shall give them good examples—that means examples that teach those virtues—and inspire them to like them and not to give them bad ones—that means examples by which one teaches them vices and which inspire them to vices. One shall not mislead anybody to vices. Since we shall omit actions by which another or his status is made more imperfect, and since we shall contribute to the perfection of other people as much as we can, it follows that nobody shall prevent another from obtaining any perfection nor shall he prevent a third person from helping him in it. This concerns any good of the soul, the body of the fortune. It seems also that nobody shall prevent anyone from eliminating another person's sickness of the soul or of the body or ill fortune, or from delivering him from these evils. Even less shall one deprive him from any good, either by acting himself or through others.

[367]

WOODBRIDGE, FREDERICK JAMES EUGENE

WOODBRIDGE, FREDERICK JAMES EUGENE (1867-1940). Woodbridge, one of the most attractive and stimulating teachers in the history of American universities, called himself a naive realist. In his later years he was deeply impressed by Santayana's writings which he highly praised and acknowledged as illuminating and enhancing his own understanding of philosophical and cultural problems. But the basis of his philosophy, such as it is presented in his books *The Purpose of History* (1916) and *The Realm of Mind* (1926), was laid before he became acquainted with Santayana's thoughts.

The originality of Woodbridge's realism is veiled by his own characterization of his philosophy as "a synthesis of Aristotle and Spinoza, tempered by Locke's empiricism." Woodbridge avowed his indebtedness to Aristotle's naturalism and the conception of productivity, and to Spinoza's "rigid insistence on structure," while it was Locke who he said had taught him "fundamentally sound thinking." "Far less acute than Descartes, and far less subtle than Kant, he was far more solid than any of them."

But it is taken for granted that Woodbridge, by historically deriving his own thoughts from Aristotle, Spinoza and Locke, had wronged himself. The three philosophers were more influential

1236

to him as examples of philosophizing than as transmitters of ideas, and Spinoza and Locke particularly impressed him more as human personalities than as shapers of doctrines. Woodbridge's inquiry into the nature of structure and activity and their relations is the work of an independent thinker. To him, structure determines what is possible, and activity determines what exists. These concepts were elaborated by cautious and flexible analysis of reality as Woodbridge himself saw it.

WHAT IS PERSONALITY

WHAT is personality? If by the question we mean to ask, What is the nature of personality as a given conscious fact to be analyzed?, we get the answer from psychology. As such a fact personality is found to be, not a cause of consciousness, not something back of it and distinct from it, but is itself a content, an arrangement of element. But if we mean by the question what an individual with such a conduct of life, what is he a factor in society, what is he revealed in the fullness of human experience, we get the answer from history—to be a person is to use the material and machinery of life in the service of ideals. Let us think of ourselves as masses of sensations if we must; but let us never be so absurd as to forget that such masses of sensations have made human history what it is, and can, if they will, make the history of the future immeasurably more glorious. Let us not quarrel with psychology or the results of science, but let the wonder of it all possess us; that there should appear in the natural history of the world creatures whose lot in life should be constantly to reach beyond themselves in order to live at all, whose whole existence should be a world-transformation and a self-tranformation in the interest of what they would have prevail, who, while they must draw the materials of their work from what they could discover of nature's constitution and their own, must none the less draw life's inspiration and motives, must get the mainspring of the activity and progress, not from what they are, but from what they might be; creatures who, under this necessity and this compulsion, should find no permanent peace until they would commit themselves, freely and wholly, in complete self-surrender, to what their ideals reveal them to be—let us wonder at it. And we should be wondering, not at some theory of things, but at one of the plainest facts we know. No psychology can destroy that fact, and no metaphysics enhance the wonder of it. It is the truth of experience, and in that truth our personality is disclosed.

[368]

WUNDT, WILHELM

WUNDT, WILHELM (1832-1920). The first psychological laboratory was founded in 1879 at Leipzig by Wundt who was a professor at that University from 1875 until his death, and who attracted to his lectures and demonstrations not only young students but scholars who had distinguished themselves, from almost all countries. Wundt developed physiological psychology by experimental methods, measuring reactions to physical and physiological changes, effects, stimulations. But, to him, physiological psychology covers only part of psychology. It is to be completed by introspective analysis of "internal experience," founded upon a philosophical system and integrated into the general doctrine of science. Wundt's introspective psychology is characterized by his conviction that will, together with the emotional states closely connected with it, is the constituent of psychological experience, and is far more important than sensations and ideas; all the other psychical processes must be conceived of by analogy to the experience of will. To him, the soul is a subject but no substance. It is event, activity, evolution.

Wundt's philosophical system is described by himself as a synthesis of Hegelianism and positivism, though he intended to avoid the one-sidedness of each. The fundamental principle of his metaphysics maintained that all material and mechanical things are but the outer shell behind which spiritual activities and strivings are hidden. According to Wundt, the world is the purposive evolution of the spirit. To this extent, Wundt agreed with Hegel. However, he tried to found his philosophy upon a thorough study of the empirical sciences.

GENERAL LAWS OF PSYCHICAL DEVELOPMENTS

THE *law of mental growth* is as little applicable to all con-

1238

tents of psychical experience as is any other law of psychical development. It holds only under the limiting condition which applies to the principle of resultants, the application of which is, namely, the condition of the *continuity of the processes*. But since the circumstances that tend to prevent the realization of this condition, are, of course, much more frequent when the mental developments concerned include a greater number of psychical syntheses, than in the case of the simple syntheses themselves, it follows that the law of mental growth can be demonstrated only for certain developments taking place under normal conditions, and even here only within certain limits. Within these limits, however, the more comprehensive developments, as for example the mental development of the normal individual and the development of mental communities, are obviously the best exemplifications of the fundamental principle of resultants, which principle lies at the basis of this development.

The *law of heterogony of ends* is most closely connected with the principle of relations, but it is also based on the principle of resultants, which latter is always to be taken into consideration when dealing with the larger interconnections of psychical development. In fact, we may regard this law of heterogony of ends as a principle of development which controls the changes arising as results of successive creative syntheses, in the relations between the single partial contents of psychical compounds. The resultants arising from united psychical processes include contents which were not present in the components, and these new contents may in turn enter into relation with the old components, thus changing again the relations between these old components and consequently changing the new resultants which arise. This principle of continually changing relations is most strikingly illustrated when an *idea of ends* is formed on the basis of the given relations. In such cases the relation of the single factors to one another is regarded as an interconnection of means, which interconnection has for its end the product arising from the interconnection. The relation in such a case between the actual *effects* and the ideated ends, is such that secondary effects always arise which were not thought of in the first ideas of end. These new effects enter into new series of motives, and thus modify the earlier ends or add new ends to those which existed at first.

The law of heterogony of ends in its broadest sense dominates all psychical processes. In the special teleological coloring which has given it its name, however, it is to be found primarily in the sphere of *volitional processes*, for here the ideas of end together with their affective motives are of the chief importance. Of the various spheres of applied psychology, it is especially *ethics* for which this law is of great importance.

The *law of development towards opposites* is an application of the principle of intensification through contrast, to more comprehensive interconnections which form in themselves series of developments. In such series of developments there is a constant play of contrasting feelings in accordance with the fundamental principle of contrasts. First, certain feelings and impulses of small intensity begin to arise. Through contrast with the predominating feelings this rising group increases in intensity until finally it gains the complete ascendency. This ascendency is retained for a time and then from this point on the same alteration may be, once, or even several times, repeated. But generally the laws of mental growth and heterogony of ends operate in the case of such an oscillation, so that succeeding phases, though they are like corresponding antecedent phases in their general affective direction, yet differ essentially in their special components.

The law of development towards opposites shows itself in the mental development of the individual, partly in a purely individual way within shorter periods of time, and partly in certain universal regularities in the relation of various periods of life. It has long been recognized that the predominating temperaments of different periods of life

1240

present certain contrasts. Thus, the light, sanguine excitability of childhood, which is seldom more than superficial, is followed by the slower but more retentive temperament of youth with its frequent touch of melancholy. Then comes manhood with the mature character, generally quick and active in decision and execution, and last of all, old age with its leaning towards contemplative quiet. Even more than in the individual does the principle of development toward opposites find expression in the alternation of mental tendencies which appear in social and historical life, and in the reaction of those mental tendencies on civilization and customs and on social and political development.

As the law of heterogony of ends applies chiefly to the domain of *moral* life, so the law of development towards opposites finds its chief significance in the more general sphere of *historical* life.

[369]

X

XENOPHANES

XENOPHANES (About 580-485 B.C.). Xenophanes was born in Colophon in Asia Minor. He was the first thinker of Greek culture to present the idea of the one, true, eternal, supreme God in opposition to the ideas of the gods of the poets and the popular cults which, as Xenophanes vigorously declared, were shaped after human images. God, as conceived by Xenophanes, defies all human ways of comprehending. In his ideas on physics, Xenophanes, a contemporary of Pythagoras, relied principally on the Milesian school. Possibly it was because of his religious rigorism that Xenophanes led a migratory life, wandering restlessly after he had left his native country for Italy.

FRAGMENTS

THERE is one god, supreme among gods and men; resembling mortals neither in form nor in mind.

The whole of him sees, the whole of him thinks, the whole of him hears.

Without toil he rules all things by the power of his mind.

And he stays always in the same place, nor moves at all, for it is not seemly that he wander about now here, now there.

But mortals fancy gods are born, and wear clothes, and have voice and form like themselves.

Yet if oxen and lions had hands, and could paint with their hands, and fashion images, as men do, they would make the pictures and images of their gods in their own likeness; horses would make them like horses, oxen like oxen.

Ethiopians make their gods black and snub-nosed;
Thracians give theirs blue eyes and red hair.

Homer and Hesiod have ascribed to the gods all deeds
that are a shame and a disgrace among men: thieving, adultery, fraud.

The gods did not reveal all things to men at the start;
but, as time goes on, by searching, they discover more and
more.

There never was, nor ever will be, any man who knows
with certainty the things about the gods and about all things
which I tell of. For even if he does happen to get most things
right, still he himself does not know it. But mere opinions all
may have.

[370]

XIRAU PALAU, JOAQUIN

XIRAU PALAU, JOAQUIN (1895-   ). After a brilliant academic
career in Spain, his native country, Xirau became a refugee from
the Franco dictatorship, and went to Mexico. Next to Ortega y Gasset, with whom he studied philosophy, Xirau is considered the most
profound thinker of modern Spain. Firmly rooted in the spiritual
tradition of his country and well-acquainted with French, German
and Anglo-Saxon philosophy, Xirau was particularly inspired by
Bergson, Husserl and Heidegger, though he by no means adopted
their views uncritically. His main objection to modern existentialism
is that in it all ideas of transcendence disappear. He holds that
fundamental existence is a preconscious experience of pure tempor-
ality, and that reality is revealed by prerational intuition. Reality
is conceived by Xirau as destiny which remains unfulfilled, and the
task of philosophy is to explore the ways to advance fulfilment, although it cannot be reached. After historical and critical studies on
Descartes, Leibniz and Rousseau, Xirau affirmed his principal
views in *Amor y Mundo* (Love and World, 1940).

THE METAPHYSICAL BACKGROUND
OF THE CRISIS OF CIVILIZATION

THE social and political crisis through which the world is
passing has a metaphysical background that has been little

1243

noticed or is wholly unknown to the great majority of men. It persists in the very air that we breathe, its presence is so familiar as to be imperceptible. Only by withdrawing can we contemplate it "en masse." Hence our surprise in the face of unprecedented events which in reality were foreseeable and natural. The lightning flames from the heights and fire from the depth of the volcano, and since both spring from invisible sources they seem instantaneous. For a long time man lived heedless, caring not for the disasters that the gods were forging in his midst. Men continued to speak of progress, of liberty, of civilization, failing to see that even the strains of their voices were dying in the echo. Every alarming symptom was summarily dispatched with a solemn declaration that in "these days" certain things were no longer possible. Whence dismay and terror when it was realized that in these times "Things" were possible such as no century has ever suspected. . . .

Modern life is chaos, not Cosmos. As such it lacks a center, is meaningless, aimless. The ancient world was an organism. And, as in every organism, each part served the whole, and the whole gave service to the parts. Life was lived centered between the material which constituted the telluric root and the luminous crown of the ideal. The living body of reality had its foundation in the contents of the material and its culmination in the splendor of the spirit. Both were functions of a central organism that gave them meaning and form. Descartes stripped away the living flesh of the world. The organism splits and disappears. We are left only the base and the apex, matter and spirit, the real and the ideal. The pomp and glory of the world is reduced to one or the other. Thus transformed into a thin thread of ideas or an endless flux of causes and effects, the world becomes an illusion, and through idealism and materialization, mathematical calculus or atomic movement, tends to dissolve into nothingness.

[371]

1244

Y

YAJNAVALKYA

YAJNAVALKYA (About 600 B.C.). There is no agreement among scholars whether Yajnavalkya was a historical person or the fictitious name for a group of thinkers and teachers. At any rate, this name is connected with the *Brhadaranyaka Upanishad* which does not only belong to the thirteen oldest Upanishads but is considered the most coherent and illuminating of all of them. It is representative of the earliest philosophical development of the Vedic religion, previous to the earliest beginnings of Greek philosophy.

The Upanishads teach the belief in Brahma, the one great reality, as the ground of existence, the belief in transmigration and *karma*, which originally meant sacrificial acts, but later the influence of human action, as the explanation of apparently unjust or incomprehensible distribution of good and evil and the home of liberation of the soul through union of the individual with Brahma. The *Brhadaranyaka Upanishad* presents these tenets in a relatively concentrated form.

THE SELF

IN sooth, a husband is dear,—not because you love the husband; but a husband is dear because you love the Self. In sooth, a wife is dear,—not because you love the wife; but a wife is dear because you love the Self. . . . In sooth, the gods are dear,—not because you love the gods; but gods are dear because you love the Self. In sooth, beings are dear,—not because you love beings; but beings are dear because you love the Self. In sooth, the whole world is dear, —not because you love the whole world; but the whole world is dear because you love the Self.

In very truth, it is the Self that should be seen, heard, thought and meditated. . . . Indeed, when the Self is seen, heard, thought and understood, everything is comprehended. . . .

It is as when a drum is beaten: You cannot lay hold of the sound at large, but by laying hold of the drum or the beater of the drum, the sound is seized. . . .

It is as with a lump of salt: Thrown into water, it dissolves [making] it impossible to retrieve it; but wherever you may dip, it is salty throughout. In the same manner it is, truly, with this great, infinite, boundless Being which consists of intelligence: Emerging from the elements, it becomes immersed in them again. After death there is no consciousness. . . . For, where there is, as it were, a duality, there you see one another, smell one another, hear one another, talk to one another, understand one another, recognize one another. But where everything has become one's self,—how could you smell anything, see anything, hear anything, talk to anyone, think anything, discern anything? How could you discern that by which all is discerned? How could you discern the discerner? . . .

. . . It is your self which is in all things. . . . You could not see the seer in seeing, you could not hear the hearer in hearing, you could not think the thinker in thinking, you could not discern the discerner in discerning. It is your self that is in everything. Anything else [means] woe. . . .

. . . That which [though] dwelling in all being, beings do not know, whose body all beings are, governs all beings from within,—that is your Self, the inner controller, the immortal one. . . . It is the seer that is not seen, the hearer that is not heard, the thinker that is not thought, the discerner that is not discerned. There is nothing apart from it that sees, nothing apart from it that hears, nothing apart from it that thinks, nothing apart from it that discerns. It is your Self, the inner controller, the immortal. . . .

. . . That which is above the heavens, that which is below the earth, that which is between both heaven and earth, is what is called the past, present and future. It is woven, warp and woof, in space. . That [which space is woven in] Brahmans call the Imperishable: It is not coarse, not fine, not short, not long, not glowing, not clinging, not shadowy, not dark; it is windless, etherless, unattached, tasteless, odorless, eyeless, earless, speechless, nonenergetic, breathless, mouthless, descentless, endless, without inside or outside; it does not consume anything, nor is it consumed by anything. .

Verily, . . he who does not know this Imperishable and [yet] sacrifices, worships and practices penance in this world for thousands of years on end,—to him it is of limited [avail]. Indeed, . . . who departs from this world and does not know this Imperishable, he is to be pitied. But he . . . who departs from this world and knows that Imperishable, he is a Brahman.

. The Self is not this, it is not that. It is inconceivable, for it cannot be conceived. It is indestructible, for it cannot be destroyed. It is unattached, for it does not attach itself. It is unbound. It does not come to naught. It does not fail. . . .

[372]

YU-LAN FUNG

YU-LAN FUNG (1895-). Professor Yu-Lan Fung, the author of the standard *History of Chinese Philosophy* (1930-33) and *The New Rational Philosophy* (1939), is not only a historian of philosophy but a systematic philosopher whose way of thinking and conceiving reality shows striking analogies to George Santayana's views, though he is firmly rooted in the traditions of Confucianism. He has revived the rational philosophy of the brothers Ch'eng Ming-tao and Ch'eng I Ch'uan (1032-1086 and 1033-1107, respectively) in order to "continue" but not to "follow" them. He distinguishes two realms, that of truth and that of actuality. Reason, according to him, belongs to the realm of truth. It is not in or above the world but rather it is a regulating principle of everything that appears in the actual world. The realm of actuality is not created by reason; it is self-existent. Since reason cannot create, it

1247

is a principle which is neither in reason nor in the actual world that brings things into real existence. This principle is called "the Vital Principle of the True Prime Unit." The essences of the realm of truth which are not the causes but the models of the real things can be known only by the objective and systematic studies, by means of inductive method and experimental logic. In this way, Fung has purified Neo-Confucianism from the Buddhist elements which had pervaded it in previous times.

PHILOSOPHY OF CONTEMPORARY CHINA

CHINA is now at a present that is not the natural growth of her past, but something forced upon her against her will. In the completely new situation that she has to face, she has been much bewildered. In order to make the situation more intelligible and to adapt to it more intelligently, she has to interpret sometimes the present in terms of the past and sometimes the past in terms of the present. In other words, she has to connect the new civilization that she has to face with the old that she already has and to make them not alien but intelligible to each other. Besides interpretation, there is also criticism. In interpreting the new civilization in terms of the old, or the old in terms of the new, she cannot help but to criticize sometimes the new in the light of the old, and sometimes the old in the light of the new. Thus the interpretation and criticism of civilizations is the natural product in China of the meeting of the West and the East and is what has interested the Chinese mind and has constituted the main current of Chinese thought during the last fifty years.

It may be noticed that the interpretation and criticism of the civilizations new and old, within the last fifty years, differ in different periods according to the degree of the knowledge or of the ignorance of the time regarding the new civilization that comes from outside. Generally speaking there have been three periods. The first period is marked with the ill-fated political reformation with the leadership of Kan Yu-wei under the Emperor Kuang-su in 1898. Kan Yu-wei was a scholar of one of the Confucianist schools, known as the Kung Yang school. According to this school,

Confucius was a teacher with divine personality. He devised a scheme that would cover all stages of human progress. There are mainly three stages. The first is the stage of disorder; the second, the stage of progressive peace; and the third, the stage of great peace. In the stage of disorder, every one is for one's own country. In the stage of progressive peace, all the civilized countries are united in one. In the stage of great peace, all men are civilized and humanity is united in one harmonious whole. Confucius knew beforehand all these that are to come. He devised accordingly three systems of social organization. According to Kan Yu-wei, the communication between the East and the West and the political and social reformations in Europe and America show that men are progressing from the stage of disorder to the higher stage, the stage of progressive peace. Most, if not all, of the political and social institutions of the West are already implied in the teaching of Confucius. Kan Yu-wei was the leader of the New Movement at his time. But in his opinion, what he was doing was not the adoption of the new civilization of the West, but rather the realization of the old teaching of Confucius. He wrote many Commentaries to the Confucian classics, reading into them his new ideas. Besides these he also wrote a book entitled *The Book on The Great Unity*, in which he gave a concrete picture of the utopia that will become a fact in the third stage of human progress according to the Confucianist scheme. Although the nature of this book is so bold and revolutionary that it will startle even most of the utopian writers, Kan Yu-wei himself was not an utopian. He insisted that the programme he set forth in his book cannot be put into practice except in the highest stage of human civilization, the last stage of human progress. In his practical political programme he insisted to have a constitutional monarchy.

One of the colleagues of Kan Yu-wei in the New Movement of that time was Tan Tse-tung, who was a more philosophical thinker. He wrote a book entitled *On Benevolence* in which he also taught the Confucianist teaching of the three stages of human progress. According to him although Confucius set forth the general scheme of the three stages, most of the teaching of Confucius was for the stage of disorder. It is the reason why Confucius was often misunderstood as the champion of traditional institutions and conventional morality. The Christian teaching of universal love and the equality of men before God is quite near the Confucian teaching for the stage of progressive peace. The teaching that is near the Confucian teaching for the last stage of human progress is Buddhism which goes beyond all human distinctions and conventional morality.

The main spirit of this time is that the leaders were not antagonistic to the new civilization that came from the West, nor did they lack appreciation of its value. But they appreciated its value only in so far as it fits in the imaginary Confucian scheme. They interpreted the new in terms of, and criticized it in the light of, the old. It is to be noticed that the philosophical justification of the Revolution of 1911 with the result of the establishment of the Republic was mainly taken from Chinese philosophy. The saying of Mencius that "the people is first important, the country the second, the sovereign unimportant" was much quoted and interpreted. The teaching of the European revolutionary writers such as Rousseau also played its role, but people often thought that they are right because they agree with Mencius.

The second period is marked with the New Culture Movement which reached its climax in 1919. In this period the spirit of the time is the criticism of the old in the light of the new. Chen Tu-siu and Hui Shih were the leaders of the criticism. The latter philosopher wrote *An Outline of the History of Chinese Philosophy*, of which only the first part was published. It is in fact a criticism of Chinese philosophy rather than a history of it. The two most influential schools of Chinese philosophy, Confucianism and Taoism, were much criticized and questioned from a utilitarian and pragmatic point of view. He is for individual liberty and development and therefore he found that Confucianism is wrong in the teaching of the subordination of the individual to his sovereign and his father, to his state and his family. He is for the spirit of struggle and conquering nature and therefore he found that Taoism is wrong in the teaching of enjoying nature. In reading his book one cannot but feel that in his opinion the whole Chinese civilization is entirely on the wrong track.

In reaction there was a defender of the old civilization. Soon after the publication of Hui Shih's *History*, another philosopher, Lu Wang, published another book entitled *The Civilizations of the East and the West and their Philosophies*. In this book Liang Shu-ming maintained that every civilization represents a way of living. There are mainly three ways of living: the way of aiming at the satisfaction of desires, that at the limitation of desires and that at the negation of desires. If we choose the first way of living, we have the European civilization; if the second, the Chinese civilization; if the third, the Indian civilization. These three civilizations should represent three stages of human progress. Men should at first try their best to know and to conquer nature, After having secured sufficient ground for their place in nature, they should limit their desires and know how to be content. But there are certain inner contradictions in life that can not be settled within life. Therefore the last resort of humanity is the way of negating desires, negating life. The Chinese and the Indians are wrong not in the fact that they produced civilizations that seem to be useless. Their civilizations are of the first order and in them there are some things that humanity is bound to adopt. The Chinese and the Indians are wrong in the fact that they adopted the second and the third ways of living without living through the first. They are on the right track but at the wrong time. Thus the defender of the East also thought there must be something wrong in it. His book therefore is also an expression of the spirit of his time.

The third period is marked with the Nationalist Movement of 1926 with the result of the establishment of the National Government. This movement was originally undertaken with the combined force of the Nationalists and the Communists. Sun Yat-sen, the leader of the Revolution of 1911 and of this movement, held the communistic society as the highest social ideal. But he was not a communist in that he was against the theory of class struggle and the dictatorship of the proletariat. He thought that the ideal society should be the product of love, not that of hatred. The Nationalists and the Communists soon split. With this movement the attitude of the Chinese towards the new civilization of the West takes a new turn. The new civilization of the West as represented in its political and economical organizations, once considered as the very perfection of human institutions, is now to be considered as but one stage of human progress. History is not closed; it is in the making. And what is now considered as the final goal that history is achieving, the peace of the world and the unity of man, looks more congenial to the old East than to the modern West. In fact, if we take the Marxian theory of human progress without its economical explanation of it, we see that between it and the teaching of the Kung Yang school as represented by Kan Yu-wei there is some similarity. Indeed Tan Tse-tung, in his book *On Benevolence*, knowing nothing about either Hegel or Marx, also pointed out what the Marxists may call the dialectical nature of human progress. He pointed out that there is some similarity between the future ideal society and the original primitive ones. But when we attain to the ideal, we are not returning to the primitive, we advance.

Is the spirit of this third period the same as that of the first? No, while the intellectual leaders of the first period were interested primarily in interpreting the new in terms of the old, we are now also interested in interpreting the old in terms of the new. While the intellectual leaders of the second period were interested in pointing out the difference between the East and the West, we are now interested in seeing what is common to them. We hold that if there is any difference between the East and the West, it is the product of different circumstances. In different circumstances men have different responses. If we see the response with the circumstances that produce it, we may probably say with Hegel that what is actual is also reasonable. Thus we are not interested now in criticizing one civilization in the light of the other, as the intellectual leaders of the first and the second periods did, but in illustrating the one with the other so that they may both be better understood. We are now interested in the mutual interpretation of the East and the West rather than their mutual criticism. They are seen to be the illustrations of the same tendency of human progress and the expressions of the same principle of human nature. Thus the East and the West are not only connected, they are united.

The same spirit is also seen in the work in technical philosophy. The Chinese and European philosophical ideas are compared and studied not with any intention of judging which is necessarily right and which is necessarily wrong, but simply with the interest of finding what the one is in terms of the other. It is expected that before long we will see that the European philosophical ideas will be supplemented with the Chinese intuition and experience, and the Chinese philosophical ideas will be clarified by the European logic and clear thinking.

These are what I consider to be the characteristics of the spirit of time in the three periods within the last fifty years in Chinese history. If we are to apply the Hegelian dialectic, we may say that the first period is the thesis, the second the antithesis, and the third the synthesis.

[373]

1253

Z

ZENO of ELEA

ZENO of ELEA (About 490-430 B.C.). The subtleties of Zeno of Elea have been endlessly discussed by philosophers and mathematicians, including those of the twentieth century.

Zeno was a scholar and a politician. According to tradition, he combated tyranny and, when a Sicilian tyrant tortured him in order to make him betray his political associates, Zeno cut his own tongue with his teeth, and threw it in the face of the torturer.

Zeno shared his teacher Parmenides' ideas on unity and the impossibility of change. He denied the Pythagorean identification of arithmetical units with geometrical points. His paradoxical arguments against the concept of motion, of which those of Achilles and the tortoise and the flying arrow became famous, were advanced in order to defend the doctrine of Parmenides; they are the crude precursors of the mathematical concepts of continuity and infinity.

Like Parmenides, Zeno resided for some years in Athens. He is said to have invented the art of dialectics which Socrates learned from him.

FRAGMENTS

IF things are a many, they must be just as many as they are, and neither more nor less. Now, if they are as many as they are, they will be finite in number.

But again, if things are a many, they will be infinite in number; for there will always be other things between them, and others again between them.

*   *   *

If things are a many, they are both great and small; so great as to be of an infinite magnitude, and so small as to have no magnitude at all.

That which has neither magnitude nor thickness nor bulk, will not even be. For, moreover, if it be added to any other thing it will not make it any larger; for nothing can gain in magnitude by the addition of what has no magnitude, and thus it follows at once that what was added was nothing. . . . But if, when this is taken away from another thing, that thing is no less; and again, if, when it is added to another thing, that does not increase, it is plain that what was added was nothing, and what was taken away was nothing.

But, if we assume that the unit is something, each one must have a certain magnitude and a certain thickness. One part of it must be at a certain distance from another, and the same may be said of what surpasses it in smallness; for it, too, will have magnitude, and something will surpass it in smallness. It is all the same to say this once and to say it always; for no such part of it will be the last, nor will one thing be nonexistent compared with another. So, if things are a many, they must be both small and great, so small as not to have any magnitude at all, and so great as to be infinite.

If there is space, it will be in something; for all that is is in something, and to be in something is to be in space. This goes on ad infinitum, therefore there is no space.

You cannot traverse an infinite number of points in a finite time. You must traverse the half of any given distance before you traverse the whole, and the half of that again before you can traverse it. This goes on ad infinitum, so that (if space is made up of points) there are an infinite number in any given space, and it cannot be traversed in a finite time.

And then is the famous puzzle of Achilles and the tortoise. Achilles must first reach the place from which the tortoise started. By that time the tortoise will have got on a little way. Achilles must then traverse that, and still the tortoise will be ahead. He is always coming nearer, but he never makes up to it.

The third argument against the possibility of motion through a space made up of points is that, on this hypothesis, an arrow in any given moment of its flight must be at rest in some particular point. Aristotle observes quite rightly that this argument depends upon the assumption that time is made up of "nows," that is, of indivisible instants. This, no doubt, was the Pythagorean view.

[374]

ZENO the STOIC

ZENO the STOIC (About 340-265 B.C.). Stoicism has a long history. It was initiated by Zeno of Citium who was of Phoenician descent, and almost all of its early representatives were not Greeks but Asians. For a time Stoicism was regarded as the last bulwark of Greek paganism. Then it was harmonized with the spirit of Christianity by some Fathers of the Church. Although Stoicism was by no means dormant in the thought of the Middle Ages, the great period of its revival began with the Renaissance and lasted until the beginning of the nineteenth century. Stoic morality inspired Shakespeare, Corneille and Schiller, Spinoza, Immanuel Kant and many leaders of the French Revolution.

Stoicism takes its name from a portico (*stoa*) in Athens, where Zeno, the founder of the school, taught his disciples. He had come to that city from his native town, situated on the island of Cyprus, after having made a fortune as a clever businessman. Fragments of twenty-six books written by him are extant. But more of his works have been lost. His successors often changed the Stoic doctrine and deviated from many original views, or enlarged them, or assumed a considerably more austere attitude toward life. But all of them adhered to the ideal of the sage who endeavors to act in accordance with his self and with nature, indifferent to the vicissitudes of life, and most of them proclaimed the equality of all men, as Zeno did.

FRAGMENTS

NOTHING incorporeal feels with body, nor does body feel

with the incorporeal, but body with body. Now the soul feels with the body in sickness or under the knife, and the body feels with the soul turning red when the soul is ashamed, and pale when the soul is afraid. Therefore the soul is body.

Death is separation of soul from the body. But nothing incorporeal is separated from the body, as, on the other hand, there is no contact between the incorporeal and the body. But the soul is in contact with body, and is separated from body. Therefore the soul is body.

No evil is glorious. But there are cases of a glorious death. Death therefore is no evil.

*　　　*　　　.

Time is the extension of motion

*　　　*　　　*

The parts of the world are sensing. The world does not lack feeling.

*　　　*　　　*

To live in accordance with nature is to live in accordance with virtue. In doing so, the wise man secures a happy and peaceful course to his own life

[375]

References

ughts on Religion, London, 1819.
dies on the Foundations of the Sciences of the Mind.
urwissenschaft und Philosophie (Records of the Eighth International gress of Philosophy.)
Value of Life.
ctions from Medieval Philosophers, from Oxford Commentary on the r Books of the Master of the Sentences, Richard McKeon; Charles bner's Sons, New York, 1929.
Rules of Sociological Method. Emile Durkheim, tr. S. A. Solovay and Mueller, ed. G. E. G. Catlin; copyright University of Chicago, 1938.
ter Eckhart's Writings and Sermons.
dom of Will; New York, 1840.
World as I See It; Philosophical Library, New York.
ys, George Eliot.
Reliance, R. W. Emerson.
y Greek Thinkers, edited and translated by John Burnet; A. & C. k, Ltd., London, 1930.
lution in Science, tr. Emile Burns; New York, 1931.
itations, tr. George Long, Cassell & Co., Ltd., London.
urus, the Extant Remains, tr. Sir Cyril Bailey; Clarendon Press, Ox- 1926.
Whole Familiar Colloquies of Erasmus; London, 1877.
inted from Selections from Medieval Philosophers ed. and tr. by rd McKeon; Charles Scribner's Sons, New York, 1929. Used by ission of the publisher.
Life of the Spirit. tr. F. L. Pogson; New York, 1909.
Twelve Books of Euclid's Elements, tr. Sir Thomas L. Heath; Cam- e University Press, New York, 1926.
After Death, tr. Mary C. Wadsworth; Pantheon Books, New York,

esen des Christentums. tr. Marian Evans, 1840.
llage der Gesammten Wissenschaftslehre, tr. A. F. Kroeger, 1794.
Richard's" Editorials. Courtesy Think Magazine.
ings of Mahatma Gandhi. Indian Printing Works. Lahore, 1949.
ary of Gassendi's Philosophy, ed. F. Bernier, vol. 7; Lyon, 1864.
heory of Mind as Pure Act. Giovanni Gentile, tr. H. Wildon Carr; illan & Co., Ltd., London, & St. Martin's Press, New York, 1922.
ess and Poverty, Henry George.
mot ha-Shem, tr. by Benzion Halper, in Post-Biblical Hebrew Litera- Jewish Publication Society of America, Philadelphia.

Inity of Philosophical Experience, Etienne Gilson; Charles Scrib- Sons, New York, 1937.
ed Essays by Ahad Ha-'Am, tr. Leon Simon; Jewish Publication y of America, Philadelphia, 1944.
uction to the Study of Philosophy; Brussels, 1844.
equality of Human Races, tr. Adrian Collins; New York, 1915.
nsistence of the Continuum Hypothesis, Kurt Goedel.
m Meister's Apprenticeship.
le.
omena to Ethics.
e Belli ac Pacis, tr. Whewell; 1853.
bject of Psychology, Berlin, 1921.
ok of the Chazars, tr. H. Hirschfeld.
ritings, ed. Otto Mann; Leipzig, 1937.
deralist, ed. G. Smith.

REFERENCES

1. The Ethics, Abailard, tr. J. Ramsay McCallum; Basil Blackwell & Mott, Ltd., Oxford.
2. In Time and Eternity, ed. Nahum Glatzer; Schocken Books, Inc., New York, 1946.
2A. Dialoghi di Amore.
3. Die Schriften des Uriel Da Costa.
4. The Works of John Adams, John Adams, 1851.
5. The Science of Living, Alfred Adler; Greenberg, Publisher, New York, 1929.
6. Creed and Deed, Felix Adler, 1878.
7. Analogy Between God and Man, Albertus Magnus.
8. Sefer Ha-Ikkarim, Joseph Albo, tr. Isaac Husik; Jewish Publication Society of America, Philadelphia, 1929.
9. Orphic Sayings and Table Talk, Amos Bronson Alcott.
10. Dialogue on the Virtues, Flaccus Albinus Alcuin, tr. Slee.
11. Elements of Intellectual Philosophy, Joseph Alden, 1866.
12. Philosophical & Literary Pieces, Samuel Alexander; St. Martin's Press, Inc., New York, 1939.
13. The Main Problems of Abu Nasr Al-Farabi.
14. The Renovation of the Science of Religion, Abu Hamid Mohammed Ibn Ghazzali Alghazzali, tr. Syed Nawab Ali.
15. The Book of Alkindi on the Subject of Intellect, Albino Nagy edition.
16. Reason the Only Oracle of Man, Ethan Allen, 1784.
17 Classifications of Science in Medieval Jewish Philosophy, David Ibn Mer- wan Al-Mukammas, ed. H. A. Wolfson, 1925.
18. Early Greek Philosophy, ed. and tr. John Burnet, A & C. Black Ltd., London, 1930
19. Early Greek Philosophy, ed. and tr. John Burnet; A. & C. Black Ltd., London, 1930.
20 Early Greek Philosophy, ed and tr. John Burnet; A. & C. Black Ltd., London, 1930.
21 Prologium, Anselm, tr Sidney N. Deane, Open Court Publ. Co., LaSalle, Illinois.
22. Diogenes Laertius.
23 Summa Theologica, Thomas Aquinas, tr. Dominican Fathers, Burns, Oates & Washbourne Ltd., London, 1912
24. Source Book, Bakewell.
25. La Revue Internationale de Sociologie, 1898
26. Diogenes Laertius.
27. Metaphysics, Aristotle.
28 Enchiridon, Augustine, tr J E. Shaw, Charles Scribner's Sons, New York; 1917
28A. Meditations, tr. George Long, Cassell.
28B. The Indian Philosophical Congress Silver Jubilee Commemoration Volume -1950.
29 Attributed to Thomas à Kempis.
30. Critique of Pure Experience.
31 Regime of the Solitary Man, Avenpace, tr. Moses Narboni

32. *The Metaphysics of Averroes*, Fourth Treatise.
33. *A Compendium on the Soul*, tr. Edward A. van Dyck.
34. *Die Russische Revolution.*
35. *Die Weltalter*, ed. Franz Hoffmann, 1868.
36. *In Time and Eternity*, ed. Nahum Glatzer; Schocken Books, Inc., New York, 1946.
37. *Novum Organum*, tr. James Spedding from *The Philosophical Works of Francis Bacon.*
38. *Opus Majus*, tr. Robert B. Burke; Univ. of Pennsylvania Press, Philadelphia, 1928.
39. *Hobot ha-Lebabot*, tr. Benzion Halper in *Post-Biblical Hebrew Literature*; Jewish Publication Society of America, Philadelphia.
40. *God and the State*, tr. Benjamin R. Tucker, 1885.
41. *Dogmatics in Outline*; Philosophical Library, New York, 1949.
42. *Talks About Farming*, 1842; *Star Papers*, 1851; *The Overture of Angels*, 1870; *Yale Lectures on Preaching*, 1873; *A Summer Parish*, 1875; *Sermons on Evolution and Religion*, 1885.
43. *The Treason of the Intellectuals*, Julien Benda, tr. Richard Aldington; William Morrow & Co., Inc., New York, 1928.
44. *Adam Smith to Karl Marx*, edited by A. Castell & M. Shaw; Webb Publishing Company, St. Paul, 1946.
45. *Wisdom of the Hebrews*, ed. Brian Brown, tr. H. Gollanez; Brentano Publ. Co., New York, 1925.
46. *The End of Our Time*, Nicolas Berdyaev, tr. Donald Atwater; Geoffrey Bles, Ltd., London, 1933.
47. *Creative Evolution*, Henri Bergson, tr. Arthur Mitchell; Henry Holt & Co., Inc., New York, 1911.
48. *A Treatise Concerning the Principles of Human Knowledge*; Dublin, 1710.
49. *Meditations of Saint Bernard*; tr. Stanhope.
50. *The Three Principles of Divine Essence*, Jacob Boehme.
51. *De Consolatione Philosophiae*, Boethius.
52. *Wissenschaftslehre.*
53. *The Life of St. Francis of Assisi*, tr. Lockhart; New York, 1898.
54. *Laws of Thought*, Boole.
55. *The Philosophical Theory of the State*, London, 1899.
56. *The Contingency of the Laws of Nature*, tr. Fred Rothwell; Chicago, 1916.
57. *The Principles of Ethics*, 1892.
58. *Appearance and Reality*, Francis H. Bradley, 1893.
59. *The Brandeis Guide to the Modern World*, ed. Alfred Lief; Little Brown & Co., Boston, 1941.
60. *Von der Klassifikation der Psychischen Phänomene.*
61. *Reflections of a Physicist*, Bridgman; Philosophical Library, New York.
62. *A Philosophy of the Infinite Universe*, Bruno, tr. John Toland.
63. *Religion et Philosophie*, Brunschwicg.
64. *Hasidism*, Buber; Philosophical Library, New York, 1948.
65. *Nyayasutras.*
66. *Reflections on History*, Jakob Burckhardt; George Allen & Unwin Ltd., London, 1943.
67. *Thoughts on the Cause of the Present Discontents*; *Letters on a Regicide Peace*; Burke.
68. *Under the Apple-Trees*; Houghton Mifflin Co., Boston, 1916.
69. *The Note-Book of Samuel Butler*, ed. Henry F. Jones; New York, 1913.
70. *The Good Man and the Good*; New York, 1918.
71. *The City of the Sun in Total Commonwealths*, tr. Thomas Halliday, London, 1901.
72. *Paradoxes of Legal Science*, Benjamin N Press, 1928.
73. *On Heroes, Hero Worship and the Heroi*
74. *The Fallacy of the Criterion of Truth.*
75. *The Point of View*, ed. Catherine Cook; (
76. *An Essay on Man*, Ernst Cassirer; Yale 1944.
77. *La Possession du Sol.*
78. *The Common Nature and Its Reason.*
79. From the book *Chinese Philosophy in* (R. Hughes, Everyman's Library, publish New York.
80. *On Friendship.*
80A. *On Justice*, from the *De Officiis.*
81. *Hymn to Zeus*, tr. Edward Beecher.
82. *In the Evening of My Thought*, George son & John Heard, Jr.; Houghton Miffl
83. *Clement of Alexandria*, tr. G. W. Butter
84. *Kant as the Founder of the Philosophy*
85. *Conception of Philosophy in Recent Di*
86. a. *Lectures on Shakespeare*
    b. *Notebooks.*
    c. *Anima Poetae.*
    d. *The Friend*, Essay VII.
    e. *Preface to Aids to Reflection.*
87. *The Confession*, Comenius.
88. *Cours de Philosophie Positive*, tr. Pau
89. *Treatise on Sensations*, tr. Geraldine Los Angeles, 1930.
90. *The Doctrine of the Mean.*
90A. *The Great Learning.*
91. *Biology*, Cook, 1877.
92. *Researches into the Mathematical P* A. A. Cournot; trans. by Nathaniel York, 1927.
93. *Philosophical Essays*, tr. George Ripl
93A. *Cours de l'Histoire de la Philosophie.*
94. *Studies in Speculative Philosophy*; N
95. *Or Adonai, Crescas' Critique of Arist* Univ. Press, Cambridge, 1929.
96. *History, Its Theory and Practice*, tr.
97. *A Treatise Concerning Eternal and*
98. *The Vision of God*, Nicolaus de Cu Dutton & Co., Inc., New York, 1928.
99. *Anecdotes of Bossuet*, tr. John Aikir
100. *Charles Darwin*, Francis Darwin, Ne
101. *L'Essor de la Physique en France.*
102. *Essays on the Theory of Numbers*, t
103. *Elim* (Psalms).
104. *Die Fragments der Vorsokratiker* (*Philosophy*, Bakewell.
105. *Formal Logic*, London, 1847.
106. *History of Italian Literature*, Frar Harcourt Brace & Co., Inc., New Yc
107. *Meditationes de prima philosophia*,
108. *Problems of Men*, Dewey; Philosop

151 From the book *Chinese Philosophy in Classical Times* edited by E. H. Hughes, Everyman's Library, published by E. P. Dutton & Co., Inc., New York.

152. *The Last Judgment*, W. T. Harris.

153. *Philosophie des Unbewussten*, tr. W. C. Coupland.

154. *Das Wertproblem in der Philosophie der Gegenwart* (Actes du Huitième Congres Internationale de Philosophie, 1934.)

155. *Lectures on the Philosophy of History*, tr. J. Sibree, 1902.

156 *Sefer Hasidim*, tr. by Benzion Halper, in *Post-Biblical Hebrew Literature*; Jewish Publication Society of America, Philadelphia.

157 *Was ist Metaphysik?*; Bonn, 1930.

158. *Popular Lectures on Scientific Subjects*, tr. E. Atkinson

159. *De l'Esprit, or, Essays on the Mind*; London, 1809.

160 *Early Greek Philosophy*, edited and translated by John Burnet; A. & C. Black Ltd., London, 1930.

161 *Letters and Lectures on Education*, tr. Henry M. and E. Felkin; London, 1898.

162. *Outlines of a Philosophy of Humanity*, tr. T. Churchill.

163. *Moses Hess et la Gauche Hegelienne*; in *Vorwaerts*, Dec. 12, 1844.

164. *Hegyon he-Nefesh*, from *Studies in Pre-Tibbonian Terminology*. Jewish Quarterly Review, New Series, vol. 17

165. *Leviathan.*

166 *Human Nature and Its Remaking*, William E. Hocking; Yale University Press, New Haven, 1929.

167. *The Metaphysic of Experience.*

168. *A Philosophical Confession*, in *Journal of Philosophy, Psychology and Scientific Methods*; February 16, 1905

169 *The System of Nature*, London, 1797

170 *Pages from An Old Volume of Life.*

171. *The Mind and Faith of Justice Holmes*, Max Lerner; Little Brown & Co., 1943.

172 From the book *Chinese Philosophy in Classical Times*, edited by E. H. Hughes. Everyman's Library, published by E. P. Dutton & Co., Inc., New York.

173 From the book *Chinese Philosophy in Classical Times*, edited by E. H. Hughes. Everyman's Library, published by E. P Dutton & Co., Inc., New York.

174. Reprinted from *In the Shadow of Tomorrow* by Jacob Huizinga, tr. J. F. Huizinga, copyright 1936 by W W Norton & Co., Inc. By permission of the publisher.

175. *The Sphere and Duties of Government*, tr Joseph Coulthard

176. *A Treatise of Human Nature*, 1739

177. *The Sayings of the Philosophers.*

177A. *Ideas*, Edmund Husserl, tr. by W R. B. Gibson; Macmillan Co., New York.

178. *The Evolution of Theology.*

179 *Seek Wisdom*, tr. by Benzion Halper, in *Post-Biblical Hebrew Literature*, Jewish Publication Society of America, Philadelphia.

180 *The Improvement of Human Reason, (Hai Ebn Yokdhan)* tr. Simon Ockley.

181. *God and the Astronomers*, Dean Inge; Longmans Green & Co., London

182. *The Works of Robert G. Ingersoll*, New York, 1900

183. *Panegyric of Athens*, tr. Gillies.

184 *Das Buch ueber die Elemente*, Salomon Fried, Leipzig, 1885

185 *Samkya Karika.*

186 *Christianity and Paganism*, tr F H. Hedge

187. *Jamblicus' Exhortations*, tr. Thomas H. Johnson; Osceola, Mo., 1917.
188. *Substance and Shadow*, 1863.
189. *Pragmatism*; Longmans Green & Co., New York, 1907.
190. *The Perennial Scope of Philosophy*, Karl Jaspers; Philosophical Library, New York.
191. *Physics and Philosophy*, James H. Jeans; Cambridge University Press, New York, 1942.
192. *Letter to Dr. Walter Jones;* and *Notes on Virginia.*
193. *Decadence*, C. E. M. Joad; Philosophical Library, New York.
194. *Frivolities of Courtiers and Footprints of Philosophers*, Joseph P. Pike; University of Minnesota Press, Minneapolis, 1938.
195. *The Idler.*
196. *Relaxation of Studies;* and *Discoveries.*
197. *The Use of Words*, tr. Matthew Arnold.
198. *Psychology and Religion*, C. G. Jung; Yale University Press, New Haven.
199. *The Apologies of Martyr Justin*, tr. William Reeves.
200. *The Liberal Spirit*, H. M. Kallen; Cornell University Press, Ithaca, 1948.
201. *Kritik der reinen Vernunft*, tr. John Watson; Riga, 1787.
202. *Sören Kierkegaard's Papirer*, tr. Alexander Dru.
203. *The Science of Character*, Ludwig Klages, tr. Johnston; George Allen & Unwin Ltd., London, 1929
204. *Revolutionary Pamphlets*, edited by Roger Baldwin; Vanguard Press, Inc., New York, 1927.
205. *Theism and Cosmology*, John Laird; Philosophical Library, New York.
206. *On the Mission of Philosophy in Our time* (Actes du Huitième Congres Internationale de Philosophie, 1943.)
207. *Recherches sur les Causes des Principaux Faits Physiques*, Paris, 1794.
208. *Essays of Elia.*
209. *Words of a Believer.*
210. *Man a Machine*, tr. Marquis d'Argens.
211. *History of Materialism*, tr. Ernest C. Thomas; London, 1881.
212. From the book *Chinese Philosophy in Classical Times*, edited by E. H. Hughes. Everyman's Library, published by E. P. Dutton & Co., Inc., New York.
213. *Reflections.*
214. *What is Capital?*, tr. F. Keddez; New York, 1900.
215. *Aphorisms on Man.*
216. *Discours de la metaphysique*, tr. George R. Montgomery; 1686.
217. *Karl Marx, Selected Works*, ed. V. Adoratsky and C. P. Dutt.
218. *The Education of the Human Race*, tr. John Dearling Haney; New York, 1913.
219. *Early Greek Philosophy*, edited and translated by John Burnet; A. &. C. Black Ltd., London, 1930.
220. *Primitive Mentality*, tr. Lilian A. Clare; New York, 1923.
221. *A Biographical History of Philosophy.*
222. *An Analysis of Knowledge and Valuation*, Clarence Irving Lewis; Open Court Publishing Company, La Salle, 1947.
223. *Selected Writings of George C. Lichtenberg*, ed. Adolf Wilbrandt; Stuttgart, 1893.
224. *The First Inaugural; The Emancipation Proclamation; The Gettysburg Address.*
225. *The Study of Nature*, tr. Sir James Edward Smith.
226. *Aesthetics;* Hamburg and Leipzig, 1903.
227. *An Essay Concerning Human Understanding.*
228. Reprinted from *Selections from Medieval Philosophers* by Richard McKeon; used by permission of the publishers, Charles Scribner's Sons.
229. *On the Sublime.*

230 *Microcosmus*, tr Elizabeth Hamilton and E. E. Constance Jones, Edinburgh, 1888.

231 *The Great Chain of Being*. Arthur O. Lovejoy; Harvard University Press, Cambridge, 1942.

232. *On the Nature of Things*, tr. H. A. J Munro; G. Bell & Sons Ltd., London, 1914.

233 *The Book of the Lover and the Beloved*, tr. E. A. Peers; New York, 1923.

234. *Lu Shian-Shan—A Dissertation in Philosophy* by Siu-Chi Huang, taken from *Lu Hsiang-Shan—A Twelfth Century Chinese Idealist Philosopher*, American Oriental Series, Volume 27, publ. by American Oriental Society, New Haven, Conn., 1944.

235 *Mesillat Yesharim*, tr. by Benzion Halper, in *Post-Biblical Hebrew Literature*; Jewish Publication Society of America, Philadelphia.

236. *Analysis of the Sensations*; Open Court Publishing Co., 1897

237. *Il Principe*, tr. Henry Morley

238. *Think Magazine*.

239. *Salomon Maimon, An Autobiography*, tr. S. Clark Murray; London, 1888.

240. *Code, Hilkot De'ot*, tr. by Benzion Halper, in *Post-Biblical Hebrew Literature*; Jewish Publication Society of America, Philadelphia.

241. *The Influence of Habit on the Faculty of Thinking*, Psychology Classics, Vol. III, tr. Margaret Donaldson Boehm; Williams & Wilkins Co., Baltimore, 1929

243. *Dialogues on Metaphysics and on Religion*, tr. Morris Ginsberg. The Macmillan Company, New York, 1923.

244. *Existence and the Existent*, Jacques Maritain, tr. Galantiere and Phelan; Pantheon Books, Inc., New York.

245. *Capital*.

246. *The Ideals of Humanity*, Thomas G Masaryk; tr. W P Warren; George Allen & Unwin Ltd., London, 1938.

247 *The Duties of Man and Other Essays*; London, 1907

248. *The Group Mind*; New York, 1920.

249. *Mind, Self, and Society*, H. Mead; University of Chicago Press, 1924.

250. *Proof of the General Law of Causality*.

251. *Early Greek Philosophy*, edited and translated by John Burnet; A. & C. Black Ltd., London, 1930.

252. *The Conciliator*, tr. E. H. Lindo; London, 1842

253. *Four Books*; from *Think Magazine*.

254. *Jerusalem: A Treatise on Ecclesiastical Authority and Judaism*, tr. M. Samuels, in *Wisdom of the Hebrews*, ed Brian Brown, Brentano Publ. Co., New York, 1925

255. *On Liberty*.

256. *The Koran*.

257 Reprinted by permission from *The Ways of Things*, by William P. Montague (copyright, 1940, by Prentice-Hall, Inc., New York), pp. 526-529.

258. *Essays*, Montaigne; tr. Jacob Zeitlin; Alfred A. Knopf, Inc., New York, 1934.

259. *L'Esprit des Lois*, tr. Thomas Nugent; London, 1878.

260. *Principia Ethica*, Moore; Cambridge University Press, New York, 1929.

261. *Hellenistic Philosophies*, P. E. More; Princeton University Press.

262. *Emergent Evolution*, C. Lloyd Morgan; Williams & Norgate Ltd., London, 1933.

263 From the book *Chinese Philosophy in Classical Times*, edited by E. H. Hughes. Everyman's Library, published by E. P. Dutton & Co., Inc., New York.

264 *By The River of Babylon*, Kaj Munk; Lutheran Publishing House, Blair, Nebraska, 1945.

265. *The External Values;* Boston, 1909.
266. *Philosophy, its Problem and its Problems.* Gottingen, 1911.
267. *About My Scholarly Upbringing,* Leipzig, 1934.
268. *Also Spake Zarathustra,* tr. Thomas Common.
269. *Human Destiny,* Lecomte de Noüy; Longmans Green & Co., Inc., New York.
270. *Ockham: Studies and Selections,* ed. Stephen Tornay; Open Court Publishing Co., La Salle, 1938
271. *De Principiis,* Origen, tr. Frederick Crombie; Charles Scribner's Sons, New York, 1925.
272. *The Revolt of the Masses,* José Ortega y Gasset; W. W. Norton & Co., Inc., New York, 1932.
273. *Adam Smith to Karl Marx,* edited by A. Castell & Mary Shaw; Webb Publishing Company, St. Paul, 1946.
274. *The Rights of Man.*
275. *Four Treatises on Theophrastus from Hohenheim,* ed. and tr. Henry E. Sigerist, Johns Hopkins Press, Baltimore, 1941.
276. *The Mind and Society,* Harcourt, Brale & Co., Inc., New York.
277. *Early Greek Philosophy,* edited and translated by John Burnet; A. & C. Black, Ltd., London, 1930.
278. *Pensées,* tr. by William F. Trotter, appearing in *Harvard Classics,* Volume 48; P. F. Collier & Son, Publisher, New York.
279. *Plato and Platonism;* London, 1893.
280. *Revista Matematica.* Vol. 8; 1902.
281. *Collected Papers,* ed. Charles Hartshorne and Paul Weiss.
282. *Fruits of An Active Life,* ed. William Wistar Comfort; Friends Central Bureau, Philadelphia, Pa., 1943.
283. *Funeral Oration,* delivered in Athens in 430 B.C., Courtesy Think Magazine.
284. *General Theory of Value,* Ralph B. Perry; Longmans Green & Co., New York, 1926.
285. *Meine Nachforschungen ueber den Gang der Natur in der Entwicklung des Menschengeschlechts,* 1797.
286. *The Works of Philo;* tr. C. D. Jonge; London, 1854.
287. *On Being and One.*
288. *The Philosophy of Physics.*
289. *The Republic,* tr. Benjamin Jowett.
290. *Art and Society,* tr. Paul S. Leitner, Alfred Goldstein, L. H. Crout; Critics Group, New York, 1936.
291. *Letters.* Courtesy Think Magazine.
292. *Enneads,* tr. Albert Edwin Avey.
293. *Morals,* Courtesy Think Magazine.
294. *The Foundations of Science,* Henri Poincaré, tr. Halsted; The Science Press, Lancaster, 1913.
295. *Commentarii in Libros Aristotelis De Anima,* ed. L. Ferri; Rome, 1871.
296. *Selected Works,* tr. N. Taylor; London, 1823.
297. *Poseidonios' Metaphysische Schriften,* I. Heinemann; Breslau, 1921.
298. *Life, Hymns & Works,* ed. K. S. Guthrie, tr. Johnson; Platonist Press, New York, 1925.
299. *Fragments.*
300. *What is Property?* tr. Benj. R. Tucker; Princeton, Mass., 1876.
301. *The Golden Verses,* in *Shrines of Wisdom.*
302. *The Foundations of Mathematics and Other Logical Essays,* Ramsay, ed. Braithwaite; Routledge & Kegan Paul, Ltd., London, 1931; distributed in U. S. by Humanities Press, New York.

303 *Symbolic Logic*, Hans Reichenbach; Macmillan Co., New York, 1947 **By** permission of the publishers.
304 *Adam Smith to Karl Marx*, edited by A Castell & Mary Shaw, Webb Publishing Company, St. Paul, 1946
305. *Cultural and Natural Sciences*.
306. *The Ridpath Library of Universal Literature*.
307 *I Believe: The Personal Philosophies of 23 Eminent Men and Women*, copyright Simon & Schuster, Inc., 1939.
308. *The Problems of the Philosophy of Culture*.
309 *Roscellin's Letter to Abailard*, ed. Johan Andreas Schmeller, Munich, 1849.
310. *Kleinere Schriften*; Berlin, 1937.
311 *The Ruling Principle of Method Applied to Education*, tr. Mrs. William Grey; Boston, 1893.
312 *Social Contract*, tr. Henry J. Tozer.
313. *The Conception of Immortality*, Houghton Mifflin Co., Boston, 1900.
314. *The Influence of Physical Causes Upon the Moral Faculty*
315. *Sesame and Lilies*.
316 *The Problems of Philosophy*, Oxford Univ. Press, London.
317 *Polemic Against Hiwi al-Balkhi*, ed. and tr Israel Davidson, New York, 1915.
318. *The Work of St. Simon*
319 Reprinted from *Reason in Art* by George Santayana, copyright 1905, 1933, by the author; used by permission of the publisher, Charles Scribner's Sons, New York.
320. *What is Literature?*, Jean-Paul Sartre, Philosophical Library, New York.
321 *System des transcendentalen Idealismus*, tr Benjamin Rand; Tubingen, 1800.
322. Actes du Huitième Congres Internationale de Philosophie, 1934
323 *Philosophie des Lebens*, tr. A. J. W. Morrison.
324. *Introduction to the Dialogues of Plato*, tr. William Dobson.
325 *Philosophy of Nature*, Moritz Schlick, Philosophical Library, New York.
326. *Die Welt als Wille und Vorstellung*, tr. R. B. Haldane and J. Kemp.
327 *The Philosophy of Civilization* by Albert Schweitzer, tr C. T Campion, Macmillan Company, New York, 1949
328 *Essays*
329 *Pyrrhonic Sketches*, tr Mary M Patrick, Courtesy Think Magazine
330 *Atma-Bodha*.
331. *Ethics and Religion*, ed. Society of Ethical Propa., London, 1900
332. *The Problem of Sociology*; Philadelphia, 1895.
333 *A Bible for the Liberal*; ed. D D. Runes, Philosophical Library, New York.
334. *Theatetus*, tr. Benjamin Jowett.
335. *The Justification of the Good*, tr Nathalie A Duddington, New York, 1918.
336. *Reflections on Violence*, tr. T. E. Holme, New York, 1912
337 *First Principles*.
338. *De Intellectus Emendatione*, tr. Amelia Hutchison Stirling.
339. *Collected Works*; Leipzig, 1885.
340 *Stages of Higher Knowledge*, G. P Putnam's Sons, New York, 1922
341. *Play*.
342. *The Ego and His Own*, tr. Steven T. Byington.
343. *The Old Faith and the New*, tr. Mathilde Blind; New York, 1873.
344 *The True Christian Religion*· The Swedenborg Foundation, New York, 1925.
345 *Sadhana*, Rabindranath Tagore; Macmillan Company, New York, 1914

1269

346. *Life and Scientific Opinions of Famous Physicists.*
347. *The Faith and Modern Thought;* London, 1910.
348. *The Ante-Nicene Fathers,* ed. Rev. Alex Robert and James Donaldson, tr. Peter Holmes.
349. *Early Greek Philosophy,* edited and translated by John Burnet; A. & C. Black Ltd., London, 1930.
350. *Walden.*
351. *The Kingdom of God is Within You,* Tolstoy, tr. Louise and Aylmer Maude; Oxford University Press, London, 1941.
352. *Twentieth Century Philosophy,* ed. D. D. Runes; Philosophical Library, New York.
353. The Belfast Address, Lectures and Essays.
354. From the book *Chinese Philosophy in Classical Times,* edited by E. H. Hughes. Everyman's Library, published by E. P. Dutton & Co., Inc., New York.
355. *The Tragic Sense of Life,* tr. E. Crawford Flitch; St. Martin's Press, London and New York, 1921.
356. *The Theory of the Leisure Class.*
357. *On Cause and Effect.*
357A. *The Complete Works of the Swami Vivekananada.*
358. *Selected Works,* tr. Joseph McCabe; Watts & Co., London, 1921.
359. *The Tragicomedy of Wisdom.*
360. From Max Weber: *Essays in Sociology,* translated, edited and with introduction by H. H. Gerth and C. Wright Mills, copyright 1946 by Oxford University Press, Inc., New York.
361. *Gestalt Theory,* Max Wertheimer, tr. N. Nairn-Allison; Social Research for February, 1944. New School for Social Research, New York.
362. *The Function of Reason,* Alfred North Whitehead; Princeton University Press, 1929.
363. *A Backward Glance; Democratic Vistas.*
364. *Memorial Day Address,* Arlington, Virginia, May 31, 1915.
365. *An Introduction to Philosophy,* tr. Joseph McCabe; Heidelberg, 1914.
366. *Tractatus Logico-Philosophicus,* Ludwig Wittgenstein, tr. C. K. Ogden; Routledge & Kegan Paul, Ltd., London, 1922, distributed in U. S. by Humanities Press, New York.
367. *Institutions of the Natural Right and the Right of Men.*
368. *Nature and Mind. Selected Essays,* F. J. E. Woodbridge; Columbia University Press, 1937.
369. *Outlines of Psychology.*
370. *Die Fragmente der Vorsokratiker* (Diels) and *Source Book in Ancient Philosophy,* Bakewell.
371. "Crisis", *The Personalist,* Summer, 1946; by Joaquin Xirau.
372. *Brhadaranyaka Upanishad.*
373. *Actes du Huitième Congres Internationale de Philosophie,* 1934.
374. *Early Greek Philosophy,* tr. by John Burnet; A. & C. Black, Ltd., London, 1930.
375. *Hellenistic Philosophies,* tr. Paul Elmer More; *Fragments from Cicero and Seneca.*

INDEX

REFERENCES

1. *The Ethics*, Abailard, tr. J. Ramsay McCallum; Basil Blackwell & Mott, Ltd., Oxford.
2. *In Time and Eternity*, ed. Nahum Glatzer; Schocken Books, Inc., New York, 1946.
2A. *Dialoghi di Amore.*
3. *Die Schriften des Uriel Da Costa.*
4. *The Works of John Adams*, John Adams, 1851.
5. *The Science of Living*, Alfred Adler; Greenberg, Publisher, New York, 1929.
6. *Creed and Deed*, Felix Adler, 1878.
7. *Analogy Between God and Man*, Albertus Magnus.
8. *Sefer Ha-Ikkarim*, Joseph Albo, tr. Isaac Husik; Jewish Publication Society of America, Philadelphia, 1929.
9. *Orphic Sayings* and *Table Talk*, Amos Bronson Alcott.
10. *Dialogue on the Virtues*, Flaccus Albinus Alcuin, tr. Slee.
11. *Elements of Intellectual Philosophy*, Joseph Alden, 1866.
12. *Philosophical & Literary Pieces*, Samuel Alexander; St. Martin's Press, Inc., New York, 1939.
13. *The Main Problems of Abu Nasr Al-Farabi.*
14. *The Renovation of the Science of Religion*, Abu Hamid Mohammed Ibn Ghazzali Alghazzali, tr. Syed Nawab Ali.
15. *The Book of Alkindi on the Subject of Intellect*, Albino Nagy edition.
16. *Reason the Only Oracle of Man*, Ethan Allen, 1784.
17. *Classifications of Science in Medieval Jewish Philosophy*, David Ibn Merwan Al-Mukammas, ed. H. A. Wolfson, 1925.
18. *Early Greek Philosophy*, ed. and tr. John Burnet, A & C. Black Ltd., London, 1930
19. *Early Greek Philosophy*, ed. and tr. John Burnet; A. & C. Black Ltd., London, 1930.
20. *Early Greek Philosophy*, ed and tr. John Burnet; A. & C. Black Ltd., London, 1930.
21. *Prologium*, Anselm, tr Sidney N. Deane, Open Court Publ. Co., LaSalle, Illinois.
22. *Diogenes Laertius.*
23. *Summa Theologica*, Thomas Aquinas, tr. Dominican Fathers, Burns, Oates & Washbourne Ltd., London, 1912
24. *Source Book*, Bakewell.
25. *La Revue Internationale de Sociologie*, 1898
26. *Diogenes Laertius.*
27. *Metaphysics*, Aristotle.
28. *Enchiridon*, Augustine, tr J. E. Shaw, Charles Scribner's Sons, New York; 1917
28A. *Meditations*, tr. George Long, Cassell.
28B. The Indian Philosophical Congress *Silver Jubilee Commemoration Volume* -1950.
29. Attributed to Thomas à Kempis.
30. *Critique of Pure Experience.*
31. *Regime of the Solitary Man*, Avenpace, tr. Moses Narboni

32. *The Metaphysics of Averroes*, Fourth Treatise.
33. *A Compendium on the Soul*, tr. Edward A. van Dyck.
34. *Die Russische Revolution.*
35. *Die Weltalter*, ed. Franz Hoffmann, 1868.
36. *In Time and Eternity*, ed. Nahum Glatzer; Schocken Books, Inc., New York, 1946.
37. *Novum Organum*, tr. James Spedding from *The Philosophical Works of Francis Bacon.*
38. *Opus Majus*, tr. Robert B. Burke; Univ. of Pennsylvania Press, Philadelphia, 1928.
39. *Hobot ha-Lebabot*, tr. Benzion Halper in *Post-Biblical Hebrew Literature*; Jewish Publication Society of America, Philadelphia.
40. *God and the State*, tr. Benjamin R. Tucker, 1885.
41. *Dogmatics in Outline*; Philosophical Library, New York, 1949.
42. *Talks About Farming*, 1842; *Star Papers*, 1851; *The Overture of Angels*, 1870; *Yale Lectures on Preaching*, 1873; *A Summer Parish*, 1875; *Sermons on Evolution and Religion*, 1885.
43. *The Treason of the Intellectuals*, Julien Benda, tr. Richard Aldington; William Morrow & Co., Inc., New York, 1928.
44. *Adam Smith to Karl Marx*, edited by A. Castell & M. Shaw; Webb Publishing Company, St. Paul, 1946.
45. *Wisdom of the Hebrews*, ed. Brian Brown, tr. H. Gollanez; Brentano Publ. Co., New York, 1925.
46. *The End of Our Time*, Nicolas Berdyaev, tr. Donald Atwater; Geoffrey Bles, Ltd., London, 1933.
47. *Creative Evolution*. Henri Bergson, tr. Arthur Mitchell; Henry Holt & Co., Inc., New York, 1911.
48. *A Treatise Concerning the Principles of Human Knowledge*; Dublin, 1710.
49. *Meditations of Saint Bernard*; tr. Stanhope.
50. *The Three Principles of Divine Essence*, Jacob Boehme.
51. *De Consolatione Philosophiae*, Boethius.
52. *Wissenschaftslehre.*
53. *The Life of St. Francis of Assisi*, tr. Lockhart; New York, 1898.
54. *Laws of Thought*, Boole.
55. *The Philosophical Theory of the State*, London, 1899.
56. *The Contingency of the Laws of Nature*, tr. Fred Rothwell; Chicago, 1916.
57. *The Principles of Ethics*, 1892.
58. *Appearance and Reality*, Francis H. Bradley, 1893.
59. *The Brandeis Guide to the Modern World*, ed. Alfred Lief; Little Brown & Co., Boston, 1941.
60. *Von der Klassifikation der Psychischen Phänomene.*
61. *Reflections of a Physicist*, Bridgman; Philosophical Library, New York.
62. *A Philosophy of the Infinite Universe*, Bruno, tr. John Toland.
63. *Religion et Philosophie*, Brunschwicg.
64. *Hasidism*, Buber; Philosophical Library, New York, 1948.
65. *Nyayasutras.*
66. *Reflections on History*, Jakob Burckhardt; George Allen & Unwin Ltd., London, 1943.
67. *Thoughts on the Cause of the Present Discontents; Letters on a Regicide Peace*; Burke.
68. *Under the Apple-Trees*; Houghton Mifflin Co., Boston, 1916.
69. *The Note-Book of Samuel Butler*, ed. Henry F. Jones; New York, 1913.
70. *The Good Man and the Good*; New York, 1918.
71. *The City of the Sun in Total Commonwealths*, tr. Thomas Halliday, London, 1901.

1262

72. *Paradoxes of Legal Science*, Benjamin N. Cardozo; Columbia University Press, 1928.
73. *On Heroes, Hero Worship and the Heroic in History*, New York, 1893.
74. *The Fallacy of the Criterion of Truth.*
75. *The Point of View*, ed. Catherine Cook; Chicago, 1927.
76. *An Essay on Man*, Ernst Cassirer; Yale University Press, New Haven, 1944.
77. *La Possession du Sol.*
78. *The Common Nature and Its Reason.*
79. From the book *Chinese Philosophy in Classical Times*, edited by E. H. R. Hughes, Everyman's Library, published by E. P. Dutton & Co., Inc., New York.
80. *On Friendship.*
80A. *On Justice*, from the *De Officiis.*
81. *Hymn to Zeus*, tr. Edward Beecher.
82. *In the Evening of My Thought*, Georges Clemenceau, tr. C. M. Thompson & John Heard, Jr.; Houghton Mifflin Co., Boston, 1929.
83. *Clement of Alexandria*, tr. G. W. Butterworth.
84. *Kant as the Founder of the Philosophy of Science*, Hermann Cohen.
85. *Conception of Philosophy in Recent Discussion*, 1910.
86. a. *Lectures on Shakespeare*
    b. *Notebooks.*
    c. *Anima Poetae.*
    d. *The Friend, Essay VII.*
    e. *Preface to Aids to Reflection.*
87. *The Confession*, Comenius.
88. *Cours de Philosophie Positive*, tr. Paul Descours and H. G. Jones.
89. *Treatise on Sensations*, tr. Geraldine Carr; Univ. Southern California, Los Angeles, 1930.
90. *The Doctrine of the Mean.*
90A. *The Great Learning.*
91. *Biology*, Cook, 1877.
92. *Researches into the Mathematical Principles of the Theory of Wealth*, A. A. Cournot; trans. by Nathaniel Bacon; Macmillan Company, New York, 1927.
93. *Philosophical Essays*, tr. George Ripley, Edinburgh, 1839.
93A. *Cours de l'Histoire de la Philosophie.*
94. *Studies in Speculative Philosophy*; New York, 1925.
95. *Or Adonai, Crescas' Critique of Aristotle*, tr. Harry A Wolfson; Harvard Univ. Press, Cambridge, 1929.
96. *History, Its Theory and Practice*, tr. Douglas Ainstre; New York, 1921.
97. *A Treatise Concerning Eternal and Immutable Morality*, London, 1731.
98. *The Vision of God*, Nicolaus de Cusa, tr. Emma Gurney Salter; E. P Dutton & Co., Inc., New York, 1928.
99. *Anecdotes of Bossuet*, tr. John Aikin.
100. *Charles Darwin*, Francis Darwin, New York, 1893.
101. *L'Essor de la Physique en France.*
102. *Essays on the Theory of Numbers*, tr. Wooster W Beman; Chicago, 1909
103. *Elim* (Psalms).
104. *Die Fragments der Vorsokratiker* (Diels) and *Source Book in Ancient Philosophy*, Bakewell.
105. *Formal Logic*, London, 1847.
106. *History of Italian Literature*, Francesco De Sanctis, tr. Joan Redfern, Harcourt Brace & Co., Inc., New York, 1931.
107. *Meditationes de prima philosophia*, tr. John Veitch; Paris, 1641.
108. *Problems of Men*, Dewey; Philosophical Library, New York.

109. *Thoughts on Religion*, London, 1819.
110. *Studies on the Foundations of the Sciences of the Mind.*
111. *Naturwissenschaft und Philosophie* (Records of the Eighth International Congress of Philosophy.)
112. *The Value of Life.*
113. *Selections from Medieval Philosophers*, from *Oxford Commentary on the Four Books of the Master of the Sentences*, Richard McKeon; Charles Scribner's Sons, New York, 1929.
114. *The Rules of Sociological Method.* Emile Durkheim, tr. S. A. Solovay and J. Mueller, ed. G. E. G. Catlin; copyright University of Chicago, 1938.
115. *Master Eckhart's Writings and Sermons.*
116. *Freedom of Will;* New York, 1840.
117. *The World as I See It;* Philosophical Library, New York.
118. *Essays*, George Eliot.
119. *Self-Reliance*, R. W. Emerson.
120. *Early Greek Thinkers*, edited and translated by John Burnet; A. & C. Black, Ltd., London, 1930.
121. *Revolution in Science*, tr. Emile Burns; New York, 1931.
122. *Meditations*, tr. George Long, Cassell & Co., Ltd., London.
123. *Epicurus, the Extant Remains*, tr. Sir Cyril Bailey; Clarendon Press, Oxford, 1926.
124. *The Whole Familiar Colloquies of Erasmus;* London, 1877.
125. Reprinted from *Selections from Medieval Philosophers* ed. and tr. by Richard McKeon; Charles Scribner's Sons, New York, 1929. Used by permission of the publisher.
126. *The Life of the Spirit*, tr. F. L. Pogson; New York, 1909.
127. *The Twelve Books of Euclid's Elements*, tr. Sir Thomas L. Heath; Cambridge University Press, New York, 1926.
128. *Life After Death*, tr. Mary C. Wadsworth; Pantheon Books, New York, 1944.
129. *Das Wesen des Christentums*, tr. Marian Evans, 1840.
130. *Grundlage der Gesammten Wissenschaftslehre*, tr. A. F. Kroeger, 1794.
131. "Poor Richard's" Editorials. Courtesy Think Magazine.
133. *Teachings of Mahatma Gandhi.* Indian Printing Works. Lahore, 1949.
134. *Summary of Gassendi's Philosophy*, ed. F. Bernier, vol. 7; Lyon, 1864.
135. *The Theory of Mind as Pure Act*, Giovanni Gentile, tr. H. Wildon Carr; Macmillan & Co., Ltd., London, & St. Martin's Press, New York, 1922.
136. *Progress and Poverty*, Henry George.
137. *Milhamot ha-Shem*, tr. by Benzion Halper, in *Post-Biblical Hebrew Literature;* Jewish Publication Society of America, Philadelphia.
138. *Ethica.*
139. *The Unity of Philosophical Experience*, Etienne Gilson; Charles Scribner's Sons, New York, 1937.
140. *Selected Essays by Ahad Ha-'Am*, tr. Leon Simon; Jewish Publication Society of America, Philadelphia, 1944.
141. *Introduction to the Study of Philosophy;* Brussels, 1844.
142. *The Inequality of Human Races*, tr. Adrian Collins; New York, 1915.
142A. *The Consistence of the Continuum Hypothesis*, Kurt Goedel.
143. *Wilhelm Meister's Apprenticeship.*
144. *Aristotle.*
145. *Prolegomena to Ethics.*
146. *De Jure Belli ac Pacis*, tr. Whewell; 1853.
147. *The Object of Psychology*, Berlin, 1921.
148. *The Book of the Chazars*, tr. H. Hirschfeld.
149. *Main Writings*, ed. Otto Mann; Leipzig, 1937.
150. *The Federalist*, ed. G. Smith.

151 From the book *Chinese Philosophy in Classical Times* edited by E. H. Hughes, Everyman's Library, published by E. P. Dutton & Co., Inc., New York.
152. *The Last Judgment,* W. T. Harris.
153. *Philosophie des Unbewussten,* tr. W. C. Coupland.
154. *Das Wertproblem in der Philosophie der Gegenwart* (Actes du Huitième Congres Internationale de Philosophie, 1934.)
155. *Lectures on the Philosophy of History,* tr. J. Sibree, 1902.
156 *Sefer Hasidim,* tr. by Benzion Halper, in *Post-Biblical Hebrew Literature;* Jewish Publication Society of America, Philadelphia.
157 *Was ist Metaphysik?;* Bonn, 1930.
158. *Popular Lectures on Scientific Subjects,* tr. E. Atkinson
159. *De l'Esprit, or, Essays on the Mind;* London, 1809.
160 *Early Greek Philosophy,* edited and translated by John Burnet; A. & C. Black Ltd., London, 1930.
161 *Letters and Lectures on Education,* tr. Henry M. and E. Felkin; London, 1898.
162. *Outlines of a Philosophy of Humanity,* tr. T. Churchill.
163. *Moses Hess et la Gauche Hegelienne;* in *Vorwaerts,* Dec. 12, 1844.
164. *Hegyon he-Nefesh,* from *Studies in Pre-Tibbonian Terminology.* Jewish Quarterly Review, New Series, vol. 17
165. *Leviathan.*
166 *Human Nature and Its Remaking,* William E. Hocking; Yale University Press, New Haven, 1929.
167. *The Metaphysic of Experience.*
168. *A Philosophical Confession,* in *Journal of Philosophy, Psychology and Scientific Methods;* February 16, 1905
169 *The System of Nature,* London, 1797
170 *Pages from An Old Volume of Life.*
171. *The Mind and Faith of Justice Holmes,* Max Lerner; Little Brown & Co., 1943.
172 From the book *Chinese Philosophy in Classical Times,* edited by E. H. Hughes. Everyman's Library, published by E. P. Dutton & Co., Inc., New York.
173 From the book *Chinese Philosophy in Classical Times,* edited by E. H. Hughes. Everyman's Library, published by E. P Dutton & Co., Inc., New York.
174. Reprinted from *In the Shadow of Tomorrow* by Jacob Huizinga, tr. J. F. Huizinga, copyright 1936 by W W Norton & Co., Inc. By permission of the publisher.
175. *The Sphere and Duties of Government,* tr Joseph Coulthard
176. *A Treatise of Human Nature,* 1739
177. *The Sayings of the Philosophers.*
177A. *Ideas,* Edmund Husserl, tr. by W R. B. Gibson; Macmillan Co., New York.
178. *The Evolution of Theology.*
179 *Seek Wisdom,* tr. by Benzion Halper, in *Post-Biblical Hebrew Literature,* Jewish Publication Society of America, Philadelphia.
180 *The Improvement of Human Reason. (Hai Ebn Yokdhan)* tr. Simon Ockley.
181. *God and the Astronomers.* Dean Inge; Longmans Green & Co., London
182. *The Works of Robert G. Ingersoll,* New York, 1900
183. *Panegyric of Athens,* tr. Gillies.
184 *Das Buch ueber die Elemente.* Salomon Fried, Leipzig, 1885
185 *Samkya Karika.*
186 *Christianity and Paganism,* tr F H. Hedge

187. *Jamblicus' Exhortations*, tr. Thomas H. Johnson; Osceola, Mo., 1917.
188. *Substance and Shadow*, 1863.
189. *Pragmatism*; Longmans Green & Co., New York, 1907.
190. *The Perennial Scope of Philosophy*, Karl Jaspers; Philosophical Library, New York.
191. *Physics and Philosophy*, James H. Jeans; Cambridge University Press, New York, 1942.
192. *Letter to Dr. Walter Jones*; and *Notes on Virginia.*
193. *Decadence*, C. E. M. Joad; Philosophical Library, New York.
194. *Frivolities of Courtiers and Footprints of Philosophers*, Joseph P. Pike; University of Minnesota Press, Minneapolis, 1938.
195. *The Idler.*
196. *Relaxation of Studies;* and *Discoveries.*
197. *The Use of Words*, tr. Matthew Arnold.
198. *Psychology and Religion*, C. G. Jung; Yale University Press, New Haven.
199. *The Apologies of Martyr Justin*, tr. William Reeves.
200. *The Liberal Spirit*, H. M. Kallen; Cornell University Press, Ithaca, 1948.
201. *Kritik der reinen Vernunft*, tr. John Watson; Riga, 1787.
202. *Sören Kierkegaard's Papirer*, tr. Alexander Dru.
203. *The Science of Character*, Ludwig Klages, tr. Johnston; George Allen & Unwin Ltd., London, 1929
204. *Revolutionary Pamphlets*, edited by Roger Baldwin; Vanguard Press, Inc., New York, 1927.
205. *Theism and Cosmology*, John Laird; Philosophical Library, New York.
206. *On the Mission of Philosophy in Our time* (Actes du Huitième Congres Internationale de Philosophie, 1943.)
207. *Recherches sur les Causes des Principaux Faits Physiques*, Paris, 1794.
208. *Essays of Elia.*
209. *Words of a Believer.*
210. *Man a Machine*, tr. Marquis d'Argens.
211. *History of Materialism*, tr. Ernest C. Thomas; London, 1881.
212. From the book *Chinese Philosophy in Classical Times*, edited by E. H. Hughes. Everyman's Library, published by E. P. Dutton & Co., Inc., New York.
213. *Reflections.*
214. *What is Capital?*, tr. F. Keddez; New York, 1900.
215. *Aphorisms on Man.*
216. *Discours de la metaphysique*, tr. George R. Montgomery; 1686.
217. *Karl Marx, Selected Works*, ed. V. Adoratsky and C. P. Dutt.
218. *The Education of the Human Race*, tr. John Dearling Haney; New York, 1913.
219. *Early Greek Philosophy*, edited and translated by John Burnet; A. & C. Black Ltd., London, 1930.
220. *Primitive Mentality*, tr. Lilian A. Clare; New York, 1923.
221. *A Biographical History of Philosophy.*
222. *An Analysis of Knowledge and Valuation*, Clarence Irving Lewis; Open Court Publishing Company, La Salle, 1947.
223. *Selected Writings of George C. Lichtenberg*, ed. Adolf Wilbrandt; Stuttgart, 1893.
224. *The First Inaugural; The Emancipation Proclamation; The Gettysburg Address.*
225. *The Study of Nature*, tr. Sir James Edward Smith.
226. *Aesthetics;* Hamburg and Leipzig, 1903.
227. *An Essay Concerning Human Understanding.*
228. Reprinted from *Selections from Medieval Philosophers* by Richard McKeon; used by permission of the publishers, Charles Scribner's Sons.
229. *On the Sublime.*

230 *Microcosmus*, tr Elizabeth Hamilton and E. E. Constance Jones, Edinburgh, 1888.

231 *The Great Chain of Being*. Arthur O. Lovejoy; Harvard University Press, Cambridge, 1942.

232. *On the Nature of Things*, tr. H. A. J Munro; G. Bell & Sons Ltd., London, 1914.

233 *The Book of the Lover and the Beloved*, tr. E. A. Peers; New York, 1923.

234. *Lu Shian-Shan—A Dissertation in Philosophy* by Siu-Chi Huang, taken from *Lu Hsiang-Shan—A Twelfth Century Chinese Idealist Philosopher*, American Oriental Series, Volume 27, publ. by American Oriental Society, New Haven, Conn., 1944.

235 *Mesillat Yesharim*, tr. by Benzion Halper, in *Post-Biblical Hebrew Literature*; Jewish Publication Society of America, Philadelphia.

236. *Analysis of the Sensations*; Open Court Publishing Co., 1897

237. *Il Principe*, tr. Henry Morley

238. *Think Magazine*.

239. *Salomon Maimon, An Autobiography*, tr. S. Clark Murray; London, 1888.

240. *Code, Hilkot De'ot*, tr. by Benzion Halper, in *Post-Biblical Hebrew Literature*; Jewish Publication Society of America, Philadelphia.

241. *The Influence of Habit on the Faculty of Thinking*, Psychology Classics, Vol. III, tr. Margaret Donaldson Boehm; Williams & Wilkins Co., Baltimore, 1929

243. *Dialogues on Metaphysics and on Religion*, tr. Morris Ginsberg. The Macmillan Company, New York, 1923.

244. *Existence and the Existent*, Jacques Maritain, tr. Galantiere and Phelan; Pantheon Books, Inc., New York.

245. *Capital*.

246. *The Ideals of Humanity*, Thomas G Masaryk; tr. W P Warren; George Allen & Unwin Ltd., London, 1938.

247 *The Duties of Man and Other Essays*; London, 1907

248. *The Group Mind*; New York, 1920.

249. *Mind, Self, and Society*, H. Mead; University of Chicago Press, 1924.

250. *Proof of the General Law of Causality*.

251. *Early Greek Philosophy*, edited and translated by John Burnet; A. & C. Black Ltd., London, 1930.

252. *The Conciliator*, tr. E. H. Lindo; London, 1842

253. *Four Books*; from *Think Magazine*.

254. *Jerusalem: A Treatise on Ecclesiastical Authority and Judaism*, tr. M. Samuels, in *Wisdom of the Hebrews*, ed Brian Brown, Brentano Publ. Co., New York, 1925

255. *On Liberty*.

256. *The Koran*.

257 Reprinted by permission from *The Ways of Things*, by William P. Montague (copyright, 1940, by Prentice-Hall, Inc., New York), pp. 526-529.

258. *Essays*, Montaigne; tr. Jacob Zeitlin; Alfred A. Knopf, Inc., New York, 1934.

259. *L'Esprit des Lois*, tr. Thomas Nugent; London, 1878.

260. *Principia Ethica*, Moore; Cambridge University Press, New York, 1929.

261. *Hellenistic Philosophies*, P. E. More; Princeton University Press.

262. *Emergent Evolution*, C. Lloyd Morgan, Williams & Norgate Ltd., London, 1933.

263 From the book *Chinese Philosophy in Classical Times*, edited by E. H. Hughes. Everyman's Library, published by E. P. Dutton & Co., Inc., New York.

264 *By The River of Babylon*, Kaj Munk; Lutheran Publishing House, Blair, Nebraska, 1945.

265. *The External Values*; Boston, 1909.
266. *Philosophy, its Problem and its Problems*. Gottingen, 1911.
267. *About My Scholarly Upbringing*, Leipzig, 1934.
268. *Also Spake Zarathustra*, tr. Thomas Common.
269. *Human Destiny*, Lecomte de Noüy; Longmans Green & Co., Inc., New York.
270. *Ockham: Studies and Selections*, ed. Stephen Tornay; Open Court Publishing Co., La Salle, 1938
271. *De Principiis*, Origen, tr. Frederick Crombie; Charles Scribner's Sons, New York, 1925.
272. *The Revolt of the Masses*, José Ortega y Gasset; W. W. Norton & Co., Inc., New York, 1932.
273. *Adam Smith to Karl Marx*, edited by A. Castell & Mary Shaw; Webb Publishing Company, St. Paul, 1946.
274. *The Rights of Man*.
275. *Four Treatises on Theophrastus from Hohenheim*, ed. and tr. Henry E. Sigerist, Johns Hopkins Press, Baltimore, 1941.
276. *The Mind and Society*, Harcourt, Brale & Co., Inc., New York.
277. *Early Greek Philosophy*, edited and translated by John Burnet; A. & C. Black, Ltd., London, 1930.
278. *Pensées*, tr. by William F. Trotter, appearing in *Harvard Classics*, Volume 48; P. F. Collier & Son, Publisher, New York.
279. *Plato and Platonism*; London, 1893.
280. *Revista Matematica*. Vol. 8; 1902.
281. *Collected Papers*, ed. Charles Hartshorne and Paul Weiss.
282. *Fruits of An Active Life*, ed. William Wistar Comfort; Friends Central Bureau, Philadelphia, Pa., 1943.
283. *Funeral Oration*, delivered in Athens in 430 B.C., Courtesy Think Magazine.
284. *General Theory of Value*, Ralph B. Perry; Longmans Green & Co., New York, 1926.
285. *Meine Nachforschungen ueber den Gang der Natur in der Entwicklung des Menschengeschlechts*, 1797.
286. *The Works of Philo*; tr. C. D. Jonge; London, 1854.
287. *On Being and One*.
288. *The Philosophy of Physics*.
289. *The Republic*, tr. Benjamin Jowett.
290. *Art and Society*, tr. Paul S. Leitner, Alfred Goldstein, L. H. Crout; Critics Group, New York, 1936.
291. *Letters*. Courtesy Think Magazine.
292. *Enneads*, tr. Albert Edwin Avey.
293. *Morals*, Courtesy Think Magazine.
294. *The Foundations of Science*, Henri Poincaré, tr. Halsted; The Science Press, Lancaster, 1913.
295. *Commentarii in Libros Aristotelis De Anima*, ed. L. Ferri; Rome, 1871.
296. *Selected Works*, tr. N. Taylor; London, 1823.
297. *Poseidonios' Metaphysische Schriften*, I. Heinemann; Breslau, 1921.
298. *Life, Hymns & Works*, ed. K. S. Guthrie, tr. Johnson; Platonist Press, New York, 1925.
299. *Fragments*.
300. *What is Property?* tr. Benj. R. Tucker; Princeton, Mass., 1876.
301. *The Golden Verses*, in *Shrines of Wisdom*.
302. *The Foundations of Mathematics and Other Logical Essays*, Ramsay, ed. Braithwaite; Routledge & Kegan Paul, Ltd., London, 1931; distributed in U. S. by Humanities Press, New York.

303 *Symbolic Logic*, Hans Reichenbach; Macmillan Co., New York, 1947 By permission of the publishers.

304 *Adam Smith to Karl Marx*, edited by A Castell & Mary Shaw, Webb Publishing Company, St. Paul, 1946

305. *Cultural and Natural Sciences.*

306. *The Ridpath Library of Universal Literature.*

307 *I Believe: The Personal Philosophies of 23 Eminent Men and Women*, copyright Simon & Schuster, Inc., 1939.

308. *The Problems of the Philosophy of Culture.*

309 *Roscellin's Letter to Abailard*; ed. Johan Andreas Schmeller; Munich, 1849.

310. *Kleinere Schriften*; Berlin, 1937.

311 *The Ruling Principle of Method Applied to Education*, tr. Mrs. William Grey; Boston, 1893.

312 *Social Contract*, tr. Henry J. Tozer.

313. *The Conception of Immortality*, Houghton Mifflin Co., Boston, 1900.

314. *The Influence of Physical Causes Upon the Moral Faculty*

315. *Sesame and Lilies.*

316 *The Problems of Philosophy*, Oxford Univ. Press, London.

317 *Polemic Against Hiwi al-Balkhi*, ed. and tr Israel Davidson, New York, 1915.

318. *The Work of St. Simon*

319 Reprinted from *Reason in Art* by George Santayana, copyright 1905, 1933, by the author; used by permission of the publisher, Charles Scribner's Sons, New York.

320. *What is Literature?*, Jean-Paul Sartre, Philosophical Library, New York.

321 *System des transcendentalen Idealismus*, tr Benjamin Rand; Tubingen, 1800.

322. Actes du Huitième Congres Internationale de Philosophie, 1934

323 *Philosophie des Lebens*, tr. A. J. W. Morrison.

324. *Introduction to the Dialogues of Plato*, tr. William Dobson.

325 *Philosophy of Nature*, Moritz Schlick, Philosophical Library, New York.

326. *Die Welt als Wille und Vorstellung*, tr. R. B. Haldane and J. Kemp.

327 *The Philosophy of Civilization* by Albert Schweitzer, tr C. T Campion, Macmillan Company, New York, 1949

328 *Essays*

329 *Pyrrhonic Sketches*, tr Mary M Patrick, Courtesy Think Magazine

330 *Atma-Bodha.*

331. *Ethics and Religion*, ed. Society of Ethical Propa., London, 1900

332. *The Problem of Sociology*; Philadelphia, 1895.

333 *A Bible for the Liberal*; ed. D D. Runes, Philosophical Library, New York.

334. *Theatetus*, tr. Benjamin Jowett.

335. *The Justification of the Good*, tr Nathalie A Duddington, New York, 1918.

336. *Reflections on Violence*, tr. T. E. Holme, New York, 1912

337 *First Principles.*

338. *De Intellectus Emendatione*, tr. Amelia Hutchison Stirling.

339. *Collected Works*; Leipzig, 1885.

340 *Stages of Higher Knowledge*, G. P Putnam's Sons, New York, 1922

341. *Play.*

342. *The Ego and His Own*, tr. Steven T. Byington.

343. *The Old Faith and the New*, tr. Mathilde Blind; New York, 1873.

344 *The True Christian Religion·* The Swedenborg Foundation, New York, 1925.

345 *Sadhana*, Rabindranath Tagore; Macmillan Company, New York, 1914

346. *Life and Scientific Opinions of Famous Physicists.*
347. *The Faith and Modern Thought;* London, 1910.
348. *The Ante-Nicene Fathers,* ed. Rev. Alex Robert and James Donaldson, tr. Peter Holmes.
349. *Early Greek Philosophy,* edited and translated by John Burnet; A. & C. Black Ltd., London, 1930.
350. *Walden.*
351. *The Kingdom of God is Within You,* Tolstoy, tr. Louise and Aylmer Maude; Oxford University Press, London, 1941.
352. *Twentieth Century Philosophy,* ed. D. D. Runes; Philosophical Library, New York.
353. The Belfast Address, Lectures and Essays.
354. From the book *Chinese Philosophy in Classical Times,* edited by E. H. Hughes. Everyman's Library, published by E. P. Dutton & Co., Inc., New York.
355. *The Tragic Sense of Life,* tr. E. Crawford Flitch; St. Martin's Press, London and New York, 1921.
356. *The Theory of the Leisure Class.*
357. *On Cause and Effect.*
357A. *The Complete Works of the Swami Vivekananada.*
358. *Selected Works,* tr. Joseph McCabe; Watts & Co., London, 1921.
359. *The Tragicomedy of Wisdom.*
360. From Max Weber: *Essays in Sociology,* translated, edited and with introduction by H. H. Gerth and C. Wright Mills, copyright 1946 by Oxford University Press, Inc., New York.
361. *Gestalt Theory,* Max Wertheimer, tr. N. Nairn-Allison; Social Research for February, 1944. New School for Social Research, New York.
362. *The Function of Reason,* Alfred North Whitehead; Princeton University Press, 1929.
363. *A Backward Glance; Democratic Vistas.*
364. *Memorial Day Address,* Arlington, Virginia, May 31, 1915.
365. *An Introduction to Philosophy,* tr. Joseph McCabe; Heidelberg, 1914.
366. *Tractatus Logico-Philosophicus,* Ludwig Wittgenstein, tr. C. K. Ogden; Routledge & Kegan Paul, Ltd., London, 1922, distributed in U. S. by Humanities Press, New York.
367. *Institutions of the Natural Right and the Right of Men.*
368. *Nature and Mind. Selected Essays,* F. J. E. Woodbridge; Columbia University Press, 1937.
369. *Outlines of Psychology.*
370. *Die Fragmente der Vorsokratiker* (Diels) and *Source Book in Ancient Philosophy,* Bakewell.
371. *"Crisis", The Personalist,* Summer, 1946; by Joaquin Xirau.
372. *Brhadaranyaka Upanishad.*
373. Actes du Huitième Congres Internationale de Philosophie, 1934.
374. *Early Greek Philosophy,* tr. by John Burnet; A. & C. Black, Ltd., London, 1930.
375. *Hellenistic Philosophies,* tr. Paul Elmer More; *Fragments from Cicero and Seneca.*

INDEX